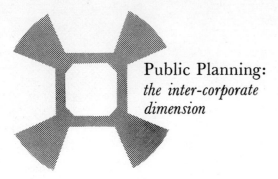

Public Planning:
*the inter-corporate
dimension*

Public Planning:
the inter-corporate dimension

J. K. Friend,
J. M. Power,
C. J. L. Yewlett

Tavistock Publications

First published in 1974
By Tavistock Publications Limited
11 New Fetter Lane, London E.C.4
Typeset in Great Britain by
Preface Ltd, Salisbury, Wilts
and printed in Great Britain by
Butler & Tanner, Frome and London
© *Tavistock Institute of Human Relations 1974*

This book was written under the auspices of
The Tavistock Institute of Human Relations
(the Institute for Operational Research)
56/60 Hallam Street, London W.1 and
4 Copthall House, Station Square, Coventry, Warwickshire

Maps and diagrams, other than those for which acknowledgements
have been made, were drawn by Michael Wyatt.

ISBN 0422 74450 6

c

C

6003573752

Contents

The Publishers wish to thank the following bodies for permission to reproduce maps:

The County Planning Officer of Worcestershire County Council for *Figure 30*, a simplified version of the Droitwich Town Map. Droitwich Development Committee for *Figure 31*, the Master Plan Proposals; for *Figure 50*, a map of Droitwich Industrial Estate; and for *Figure 54*, a map of the Central Area Proposals. The Central Office of Information for *Figure 49*, 'The Development Areas', which is reprinted from *Regional Development in Britain* (1967): 13. The Controller of Her Majesty's Stationery Office for *Figure 49*, 'The Assisted Areas', which is reprinted from *Industrial and Regional Development* (1972): 12; for *Figure 72*, which is reprinted from *Patterns of Growth Report* (1967): 35; and for *Figure 76*, which is adapted from *Social Trends* (1972): 136. The Director General, Ordnance Survey in connection with *Figures 58* and *61*, which are both based on an ordnance survey map of central Droitwich. The Town Clerk of Droitwich Borough Council for *Figure 61*, a map of a General Improvement Area plan for Newtown, Droitwich. The Town Clerk wishes it to be known that the proposals contained in this plan have since been substantially changed.

Introductory: Origins and acknowledgements

Background

This book results from a fusion of many different influences. For this reason, it seems fitting that any explanation of its origins should lead on to an expression of acknowledgement from the authors to all those who have contributed in one way or another towards the form and content of the finished product.

The history of this volume is closely interwoven with that of the Institute for Operational Research (IOR), which was founded in London in 1963 under the direction of the late Neil Jessop. From the outset, the mission of the Institute was conceived as one of carrying forward into new fields the practice of operational research — broadly defined as the application of scientific method to the making of complex decisions in industrial or other organizations. Above all, it was hoped to make practical contributions to the solution of important problems of social and governmental policy. The new Institute found its home within the administrative framework of the Tavistock Institute of Human Relations, an independent non-profit association concerned with the pursuit of research in a number of fields of social science, and associated teaching and advisory services. By 1973, IOR had grown to be the largest of the five units within Tavistock, working from offices in London, Coventry, and Edinburgh. In that year, a significant step was taken through the decision of members of IOR and one of the other established units, the Human Resources Centre, to come together to form a new centre within Tavistock, so providing a firmer inter-disciplinary foundation for further advances in the fields of organizational relations and applied policy sciences.

Looking back to the period when IOR was founded, operational research was then becoming increasingly widely accepted as an internal service within large industrial firms, and also, as a subject of post-graduate teaching in universities. However, these developments had been paralleled by a growing tendency for OR to become identified with a well-defined range of mathematical techniques, of most direct relevance to certain somewhat limited classes of industrial problem. Neil Jessop was one of several members of the Council of the Operational Research Society who were disturbed by this trend and who shared an interest in bringing OR into closer contact with the social sciences, in order to broaden its scope and increase its relevance to problems of wider significance to society. A series of discussions with members of the then staff of the Tavistock Institute revealed a complementary interest in broadening the Tavistock's disciplinary base, and laid the foundations upon which the growth of IOR was to be based.

On appointment as the first Director of IOR, Neil Jessop's first task was to attract funding for an initial set of projects that might provide the opportunity for the Institute to work towards its ambitious aims in a realistic practical setting, in association with colleagues in other parts of Tavistock. The result was the launching of one project on communications within the building industry, another on adaptation and change in hospital management, and a third on the processes of planning and policy-making in local government. All three of these projects were to have their influence on the subsequent research activities from which this book derives. However, it was the four-year project on 'Policy Research for Local Government', funded by the Nuffield Foundation and based on a study in depth of the decision processes of Coventry City Council, that can be regarded as the most direct progenitor.

The concern with inter-organizational problems

Towards the end of 1967, the Nuffield project was drawing to its close and the results were being prepared for publication under the title of *Local Government and Strategic Choice* (Friend and Jessop, 1969). During the same year, John Stringer — then Deputy Director and subsequently Director of IOR — published a paper in the

Operational Research Quarterly (Stringer, 1967) on the theme of 'Operational Research for Multi-Organizations'. This drew on accumulated IOR experience in building, hospital management, and local government, among other fields, to discuss the question of how the OR approach might have to be adapted in confronting decision problems where the scientist could no longer assume a clear-cut stance of 'advising the manager', as implied in much of the literature. On the contrary, he was liable to find himself attempting to play his role as adviser within a complex set of interests, to all of which he was in some degree accountable. Such a situation might often arise, for instance, in relation to a set of quasi-autonomous departments of a single organization, as in local government, or indeed within the industrial firm. It became even more difficult to avoid in the case of a public agency exercising only partial control over independent professional interests (as in hospital management), or in that of an *ad hoc* team drawn together from several independent organizations to collaborate in the performance of some agreed task (as in the building industry). Indeed, in important matters of public policy, the evidence was that the 'multi-organizational' context of decision-making would have to be regarded not so much the exception as the rule.

The problem of carrying out successful operational research in a situation of multiple accountability, and indeed of making mutually acceptable arrangements for the sponsorship of such work, appeared to open up a whole new dimension to be explored in the systematic development of the subject. For this reason, when IOR was invited during 1967 to submit proposals for a major research programme for the consideration of the then newly-formed Social Science Research Council, it was the theme of 'Operational Research Methods for Multi-Organizations' that appeared to offer the greatest scope.

There followed much discussion and re-formulation of proposals, leading to a suggestion from the Council that the Institute should submit a comparatively closely-defined application for work within this theme, concentrating its attention on a selected problem field as opposed to the original proposition of drawing on accumulated experience in working with a variety of different types of 'client system'. In the subsequent re-appraisal, one especially promising field of study was identified: that of the planning of new and expanding towns, where a high intensity of interaction between different governmental and other agencies was likely to be found. That this was so had become clear not only through IOR's experience in local government and hospital management, but also in shorter-term contract assignments concerned with the planning of electricity, gas, and transport undertakings, and with the provision of further education. Furthermore, a project concerned with the multi-organizational aspects of the planning of new communities appeared to provide much scope for carrying forward the analytical approach to the processes of public planning which had been gradually evolving within the Nuffield local government project.

Accordingly, in 1968, a submission was made to SSRC for a project of two and a half years' duration to pursue the general theme of multi-organizational planning in this more specific context. In the event, the Council was only prepared to commit itself to supporting one year's work in the first instance, to cover the initial exploratory phase that had been proposed by IOR together with the preparation of a report on its results. Despite the disappointment caused by this lack of assurance of continuity, the Institute was able to take two important steps forward during this period. First, a very promising site for intensive study was identified — the expanding town of Droitwich in the West Midlands — and relations were established with the local agencies concerned which subsequently proved to be of great value. Second, it became clear that in any subsequent research there would be a strong case for extending the focus beyond that of the application of OR methods to a broader concern with the design and adaptation of inter-organizational relationships. In this light, it seemed important also to extend the scope of the field-work outwards towards the general issue of regional development, of which the creation of new communities could be regarded as only one of the more prominent aspects.

A paper arising from the first-year's work was submitted for early publication (Friend and Hunter, 1970), and a submission was made to SSRC for continued support of the work for another two years, under the title 'Decision Networks in Regional Development', which reflected the change in orientation. Fortunately, this was accepted by the Council in time to secure continuity of the research effort. The opportunities were therefore now open for intensifying and extending the field-work at Droitwich, for gradually enlarging the focus to embrace the regional setting of the expansion scheme, and for more sustained effort to develop models and theories that might subsequently be tested through a series of visits to other new and expanding towns.

Some parallel activities

Meanwhile, the activities of IOR were extending in other directions also of relevance to the problem of multi-organizational planning, both within and outside the public sector. This general pattern of development is indicated in *Figure 1*. The Institute's work in hospital management had gathered a good deal of momentum, leading to a continuing programme of activities in the wider field of community health under the auspices of the Department of Health and Social Security (Luck, Luckman, Smith, and Stringer, 1971). A further long-term programme had also become established under the auspices of the Civil Service Department, concerned with problems of career planning and organization throughout central government, and leading in particular to IOR's close involvement in a large-scale project on the location of government offices. Apart from involving a study of the communication patterns of most of the major ministries, this work inevitably involved considering the regional implications of any possible dispersal decisions (Elton *et al,* 1970).

At the same time, there were encouraging signs that the approach to the analysis of public planning options presented in the book *Local Government and Strategic Choice* was seen to be both relevant and applicable in practice by local authority planners. This prompted IOR, in association with the Institute of Local Government Studies at Birmingham University (INLOGOV), to take the initiative in setting up an experiment to test the approach in parallel on a number of 'live' problems of local authority decision-making over an intensive six-month period. The Centre for Environmental Studies was approached for support and agreed to meet the main costs of the exercise.

Of the six problems tackled, one was concerned with a cathedral city congested with traffic, another with a strip of green-belt land with unexploited potential for recreational use, one with the planned expansion of a seaside commuter district, one with a multi-purpose central area property development, one with a town whose future growth depended on the outcome of a current regional planning exercise, and one with an ageing residential district, the future of which was threatened by industrial pollution and motorway planning proposals. The preliminary results of this experiment (code-named LOGIMP as an abbreviation of Local Government Implementation) were reported at a conference in November 1970 (CES, 1970). Since then, the approach has been further applied to other planning problems in several of the local authorities concerned (Bunker,1973).

The relevance of this experience to the work discussed in this book arises first from the fact that three of the eight members of IOR staff involved were involved at the same time in the SSRC 'Decision Networks' project, and second from the direct experience gained of working in problem-solving groups drawn from different

Figure 1   The research in its historical context

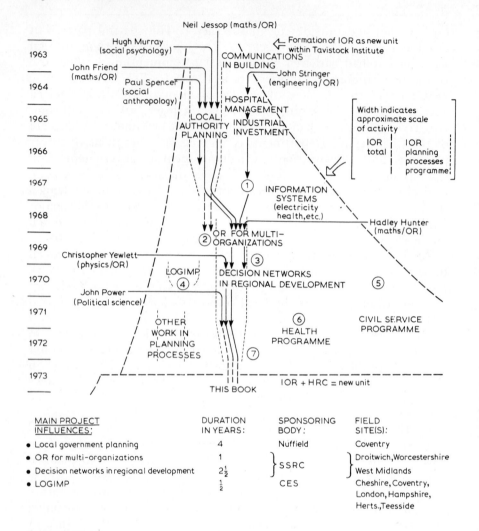

MAIN PROJECT INFLUENCES:	DURATION IN YEARS:	SPONSORING BODY:	FIELD SITE(S):
• Local government planning	4	Nuffield	Coventry
• OR for multi-organizations	1	} SSRC	} Droitwich,Worcestershire West Midlands
• Decision networks in regional development	2½		
• LOGIMP	½	CES	Cheshire, Coventry, London, Hampshire, Herts.,Teesside

Salient Publications:
(1) J. Stringer. Operational Research for Multi-Organisations. *OR Quarterly*, Dec 1967.
(2) J. K. Friend and W. N. Jessop. *Local Government and Strategic Choice*. Tavistock 1969.
(3) J. K. Friend and J. M. 'H. Hunter. Multi-Organizational Decision Processes in the Planned Expansion of Towns. *Environment and Planning*, Jan. 1970.
(4) The LOGIMP experiment. CES Information Paper IP25, 1970.
(5) M. C. J. Elton *et al. An Approach to the Location of Government*. Institute of Management Science, 1970.
(6) G. M. Luck, J. Luckman, B. W. Smith, J. Stringer. *Patients, Hospitals, and Operational Research*. Tavistock 1971.
(7) J. K. Friend, C. J. L. Yewlett, J. M. Power. *Beyond Local Government Reform*. IOR Conference Papers.

organizations on a variety of kinds of problem within the general
field of local and regional planning. Most of the six teams were
inter-professional, including local government officers drawn from
planning, finance, and surveyors' departments. Further, two of the
teams brought together representatives of counties and constituent
county districts, while another involved tripartite working between
officers of the Greater London Council and two contiguous London
Boroughs. In acting as advisers to such multi-organizational problem-
solving groups, the IOR staff concerned were accumulating experience that directly complemented the longer-term observational
studies then under way at Droitwich.

A number of other comparatively brief projects undertaken in
parallel with our research served to deepen the range of experience
on which we were able to draw. These ranged from a study of
problems of neighbourhood participation in housing improvement
policies in an inner area of Coventry, to a pilot study concerned with
systematic methods for forming interdepartmental long-range planning groups within the Federal German Government.

The collaboration of the authors

At this point, it becomes necessary for us to make more explicit
reference to the personal roles played by the three of us under whose
names the present publication appears. As *Figure 1* indicates, the
backgrounds of experience which we brought to our collaboration
differed quite considerably. In one case (Friend), the experience
contributed was of close collaboration with the late Neil Jessop in
the earlier local government research in Coventry, following some ten
years of more conventional operational research work in industrial
and other organizations. In another case (Yewlett), the background
was one of joining IOR directly after completing a post-graduate
course in operational research and management studies in 1969. In
the third case (Power), the background was one of several years of
teaching and research experience in political science in Australia and
the United States. The basis for his involvement in the project was
first laid in 1970, when Power initiated an exchange of ideas by
sending Friend a draft of a critique of *Local Government and
Strategic Choice* which was later to appear in the Australian journal,
Public Administration (Power, 1971a).

During 1971, Power was granted a year's sabbatical leave by the
University of Sydney and opted to spend this period with IOR in
Coventry. Consequently, the perspectives brought to the research
were suddenly broadened, at a time when much of the work on

empirical case studies at Droitwich had already been completed by
Friend and Yewlett. The interplay of operational research and
political science perspectives at a comparatively late stage of the
project was sometimes a mutually exacting process, but always a
highly stimulating one; and the influence of Power was felt mainly in
a gradual transformation of the theoretical framework, which before
his arrival had been evolving relatively cautiously from that of *Local
Government and Strategic Choice* in the direction of a rather more
explicit integration of influences from the fields of sociology and
political science.

In this developing process of collaboration, an important focus
was provided by a commitment to present papers on the research at a
half-day conference in London in December 1971, shortly before
Power was due to return to Australia. When first agreeing to support
the 'Decision Networks' project, the SSRC had put forward a
recommendation that IOR should hold such a conference towards
the end of the work, and it was decided to seize the opportunity this
provided to contribute to the debate on the then topical issue of
local government reform. A small supplementary grant was provided
by the Council for this purpose, and two papers were prepared, one
jointly by Friend and Yewlett (1971) and the other by Power
(1971b). Preparation of these papers served, in retrospect, as a very
valuable discipline. The audience at the meeting included representatives of several central and local government organizations, as well as
operational research and social scientists from academic and other
institutions. The challenge of presenting the emergent themes of the
research to a large and diverse public audience proved to be a
difficult one; however, it helped us to focus more clearly on those
aspects of the analytical framework that would have to be further
clarified in our final publication, and on the types of proposition
about inter-agency planning that would have to be more explicitly
tested and validated against the case material we had gathered from
our Droitwich study.

The return of Power to Australia shortly after the conference
presentation precipitated an abrupt change to a process of communication by correspondence, at a stage at which our thinking about the
form and content of the book was rapidly beginning to converge, and
ways of overcoming the residual gaps in concepts were beginning to
appear tantilizingly close. It became inevitable that most of the final
drafting and editing of the manuscript should fall to Friend and
Yewlett, with Power's function largely that of a constructive critic;
all the more constructive because of the firm basis of mutual
understanding and personal friendship which his work during his
sabbatical year had helped to establish.

A personal tribute

Turning to the role of others who helped to lay the foundation for the work presented here, the first tribute must be to Neil Jessop. His death from a long-standing illness, of the severity of which none of us had been fully aware, followed tragically soon after the publication of *Local Government and Strategic Choice* in 1969. Shortly before his death, he was able to play an active role in the formulation of the proposals to SSRC for the main 'Decision Networks' project, and in this way to contribute directly towards the further advancement of a style of operational research to which he had been strongly committed since the foundation of IOR in 1963. As a colleague, he was always stimulating and often inspiring, combining much warmth and wit with a clear perspective on research priorities, which was a crucial factor in charting the directions of the Institute's evolution. In the writing of this book, one of our foremost aims has been to maintain as far as possible the momentum that had been growing steadily under his leadership, in the kinds of direction that we believe he would have sought.

Acknowledgements

John Stringer, who succeeded to the Directorship of IOR in 1969, had also been actively involved in the formulation of the research proposal to SSRC, following his earlier work in identifying the problems of operational research in the multi-organizational setting (Stringer, 1967). The responsibilities of the Directorship were to prevent his becoming involved as directly in the 'Decision Netweorks' project as had been originally envisaged; but he and many other members of IOR staff have contributed constructively to discussion of the progress of the work at different stages. During much of 1969 and 1970 the development of the work was influenced in particular by the participation of Dr Hadley Hunter, who was an active member of the team during the initial phase of the work at Droitwich, but became more intermittently involved thereafter because of the pressure of other project commitments. His influence during the formative period was an incisive and important one. So also, looking back to the earlier Nuffield project, was the influence of two social scientists from other units of the Tavistock Institute — Dr Hugh Murray and Dr Paul Spencer — the first of whom opened up opportunities for the observation of group decision processes in Coventry City Council, while the latter was able to demonstrate how those opportunities could be most effectively exploited in practice. In this way, they were able to add a new dimension to the ccnventional range of operational research methods, and one that we have attempted to exploit as fully as possible in the further field-work at Droitwich.

We are much indebted to the Chairman of the Council of the Tavistock Institute, Lord Fulton of Falmer, for agreeing to take the Chair at the open conference held in London in 1971 to discuss the emerging themes of the research. We are further indebted to the three invited discussants on that occasion for their readiness to give up valuable time to take part in the proceedings: Dr Jeremy Bray, author of *Decision in Government* (1970) and former Parliamentary Secretary at the Ministry of Technology; Sir Arthur Peterson, then Director-General of the Greater London Council and now Permanent Under-Secretary at the Home Office; and Professor N. Lichfield of the School of Environmental Studies at University College, London. Also we have benefited much from the readiness of several fellow research workers in other institutions at home and abroad to enter into dialogue over our methods and offer constructive criticism of draft papers and chapters. Among these, mention must be made of Professor Andreas Faludi of Delft University of Technology, Mr R.G.S. Brown of the Department of Social Administration at the University of Hull, Professor John Stewart and Mr Felix Wedgewood-Oppenheim of the Institute of Local Government Studies at Birmingham University, and members of the Centre for Urban and Regional Studies at the same University, including especially Dr Brian Goodey, Mr Randall Smith, and Mrs Barbara Smith.

Because of our primary concern with problems of multi-organizational planning, our field-work in Droitwich was to bring us into contact with a very wide range of local authority officers, elected representatives, civil servants, and others, making it difficult for us to give adequate recognition of their individual contributions to our learning process. Among past and present civil servants, our main acknowledgement must be to Mr Bill Ogden, formerly Principal Planning Officer for the West Midlands Region, Department of the Environment and now in active retirement on the lecturing staff of Lanchester Polytechnic in Coventry. It was he who first suggested Droitwich as a prospective site for field work, since when he has continued to show a lively interest in the course of the work and to provide an invaluable point of reference on regional affairs.

Turning to Droitwich itself, the Chief Administrative Officer of the Development Group, Mr Eric Nicklin, proved receptive to the aims of our research from the start, and we are especially grateful to him for tolerating our presence with self-deprecating good humour through all the alternating tedium and drama involved in the

management of a town development operation. We are also grateful
to his fellow-officers — most notably the Chief Planner/Architect, Mr
Gwilym Rhys, and the Group's Senior Engineer, Mr Tony Hartshorne,
with whom we are fortunate to have been able to spend many hours
in stimulating discussion. Among the many officers from the two
original parent authorities of the Droitwich Development Committee
who gave us help, special acknowledgement must go to the Town
Clerk of Droitwich, Mr Wakefield Russell, to the Deputy Clerk of
Worcestershire County Council, Mr James Phelips, and to the County
Treasurer, Mr W.E. Prince. Among elected representatives, almost all
the sixteen members of the Droitwich Development Committee readily
agreed to meet us to talk about their varying perspectives on the
town expansion programme. Among these were the Chairman of the
County Council, Sir Michael Higgs, who had played a leading role in
the early history of the scheme; the Chairman of the Joint
Committee, Councillor S. B. Harris; and the Chairman of the
Droitwich Planning and General Purposes Committee, Colonel R. D.
N. Fabricius.

Turning to the financial sponsors of the research, our first
acknowledgement must of course be to the Social Science Research
Council for their direct support of the two successive stages of the
work reported here, and for their financial assistance in the
organization of the 1971 conference. Also, we must acknowledge the
role of the University of Sydney in supporting Dr Power's involvement during his sabbatical year. Looking further back, however, the
opportunity to write this type of book would not have arisen had it
not been for the willingness of the Nuffield Foundation to support
the earlier basic research in Coventry; and our subsequent experience
would have been considerably the poorer had it not been for the help
of the Centre for Environmental Studies in financing the LOGIMP
experiment which, by allowing IOR staff to collaborate actively in
implementing new concepts of planning in a range of different
organizational settings, directly complemented our observational
experiences in Droitwich.

The pursuit of innovation in the processes of public planning is
not a task that lends itself easily to the application of well-established research techniques; and, in long-term exploratory projects of
the kind here reported, it has been our experience that any initial
proposal that attempts to define successive stages of the research
process can serve as no more than a very approximate guide to the
exacting processes of observation, conceptualization, interpretation,
and re-interpretation which must follow. Accordingly, we found that
much of the final re-structuring and re-drafting of the manuscript

had to be completed after the SSRC grant had come to its end in the spring of 1972. By that time, it had already become the policy of IOR to deploy part of the modest reserves of working capital which it had accumulated over the years in support of activities of an internal developmental nature, and it was agreed that the work on the completion of this manuscript should take first priority in this respect. An important note of acknowledgement must therefore go to other colleagues for their sacrifice of alternative opportunities for drawing on these reserves in support of other research interests and initiatives; and also to the whole range of governmental and other clients for whom members of staff have been working over the years, for the various complementary insights they have helped us to form into the problems and processes of decision-making both at the organizational and the inter-agency levels.

Mercifully, this was not a project where there was much computational work to be done but, again mercifully, Mrs Pat Abel was at hand when the need arose. As in the case of *Local Government and Strategic Choice*, the burden of typing and re-typing this manuscript has fallen almost entirely on Mrs Betty Fox, whose unfailing resources of skill and good humour allowed her to combine this onerous task with all the other complex problems of running the Institute's Coventry office.

Introductory: Scope and structure

Scope

Corporate planning is not enough. That, distilled into as few words as possible, is the central thesis around which this book is built. Especially in the public sector — with which we shall be primarily but by no means exclusively concerned — the making of strategic decisions must be considered not merely as a corporate but also as an inter-organizational process. The point may be familiar enough to many of those most deeply involved, including politicians, political commentators, urban and regional planners, and senior administrators in both local and central governments. However, the increasing dominance of large corporate bodies in both public and private affairs has brought with it pressures to introduce more formal structures and techniques for the co-ordination of planning activities within the corporate setting; and this in turn has led many people towards an implicit assumption that planning at the corporate level somehow represents a clear pinnacle towards which all those engaged in other forms of planning within an organization should aspire.

To many managers and consultants there is considerable appeal in a view of planning as an activity that can be organized entirely in a given hierarchical framework, wherein objectives can be clearly formulated and then methodically pursued. All too often, however, the goal of purposive corporate planning is found to be an illusory

Figure 2 Structure of the book

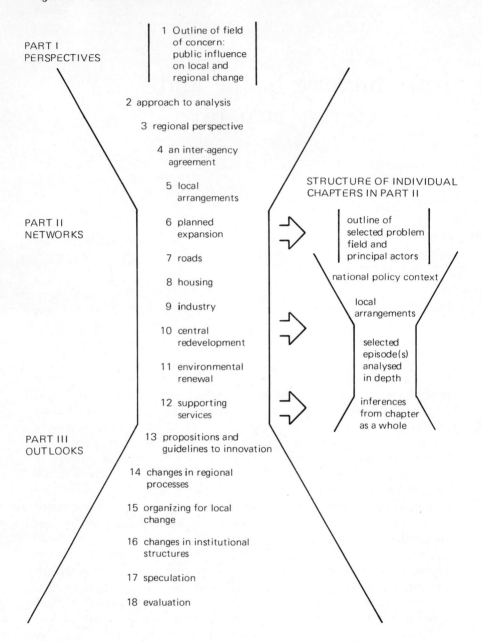

PART I
PERSPECTIVES

1 Outline of field
  of concern:
  public influence
  on local and
  regional change

2 approach to analysis

3 regional perspective

4 an inter-agency
  agreement

5 local
  arrangements

PART II
NETWORKS

6 planned
  expansion

7 roads

8 housing

9 industry

10 central
   redevelopment

11 environmental
   renewal

12 supporting
   services

PART III
OUTLOOKS

13 propositions and
   guidelines to innovation

14 changes in regional
   processes

15 organizing for local
   change

16 changes in institutional
   structures

17 speculation

18 evaluation

STRUCTURE OF INDIVIDUAL
CHAPTERS IN PART II

outline of
selected problem
field and
principal actors

national policy context

local
arrangements

selected
episode(s)
analysed
in depth

inferences
from chapter
as a whole

one. The more comprehensively those in large corporate organizations seek to plan, the more they find themselves dependent on the outcomes of other agencies, both public and private; also, the more aware they become of the many subtle relationships — economic, social, political, and ecological — that extend into other parts of their environment which may be less clearly structured in formal organizational terms. Demands for participation from the grass-roots become more vocal as the technical and organizational obstacles to such participation appear to proliferate; increasingly, therefore, questions of how to develop effective systems of democratic guidance over the course of local and national affairs seem to become uncomfortably intermeshed with issues of global survival.

In essence, our aim will be to move towards a richer understanding of the inter-organizational — or 'inter-corporate' — dimension of the planning process, and to contribute towards the development of practical working guidelines for use by those who must operate within this general field, including those concerned with the design or adaptation of relevant institutional forms. For reasons explained in the preceding section, we shall attempt to work towards this aim through a focus on problems arising in that broad field of public affairs that may be described as 'the management of local and regional change'; in other words, the whole range of possible actions by local authorities, by national or regional agencies of government, and by other public bodies whereby the richly interactive processes of change in local communities can be regulated, influenced, and planned.

Most of our case material will be drawn from observations of decision-making in relation to different aspects of the planned expansion of one small English town in order to accommodate population and industry from a nearby metropolitan centre, in accordance with regional policies for the relief of urban congestion. Our interpretation of the regional and local processes concerned will then be used as a basis for articulating some more general propositions relating to the processes of inter-organizational planning. These will provide a basis from which we can consider the opportunities for innovation that may be open to those concerned in the development of planning processes in any given institutional setting, taking as a specific illustration the challenges facing Britain as it enters a period of exceptionally sweeping reforms in established governmental institutions. To this end, the content of the book will be structured as indicated diagramatically in *Figure 2*.

Structure

The first of the three parts into which the book is divided will present a series of perspectives — institutional, theoretical, regional, and historical — which together converge to provide a background for the more detailed case material that follows. In the second part, the town development scheme at Droitwich will be used as a vantage point from which to explore networks of inter-agency planning activity in a variety of different yet related fields of public policy. The third part will be more outward-looking and forward-looking, beginning with the formulation of a set of general propositions and then proceeding to explore a range of questions relating to the future outlook for multi-organizational planning. This discussion will focus particularly on the opportunities created through a series of structural reforms in the institutions of local, regional, and central government in the United Kingdom; but the parallel implications for countries with different institutional structures will, wherever possible, be kept in view.

Synopsis of Part I

Part I begins with a short chapter outlining a broad field of policy concern, which will be referred to as 'the management of local and regional change', both in general terms and in the particular circumstances of Great Britain. The changing institutional structure of central and local government in Britain is briefly outlined, and a general institutional 'map' is introduced as a base for plotting patterns of organizational relationships. The second chapter introduces a more analytical perspective, by presenting a framework for analysis based on the theory of strategic choice as developed in the earlier work of IOR in Coventry. No prior knowledge of this approach is assumed; and, in order to increase its relevance to the inter-organizational aspects of planning, the chapter introduces a number of extensions and modifications to the basic framework. These changes are intended in particular to bring the approach into closer alignment with that of political sociology. Among the more important of the concepts to be introduced are those of the 'policy system', the 'decision network', and the network-forming or 'reticulist' judgement, through which different actors in a decision process select strategies for managing the uncertainties that they encounter and the variety of solutions that may be available. Because such concepts are most effectively demonstrated through practical example, they will be introduced fairly briefly in Chapter 2, and subsequent chapters will be written so as to reinforce the basic ideas without placing too much reliance on a prior understanding of their significance. The busy reader may therefore prefer to give Chapter 2 only a cursory reading in the first instance, before proceeding to the analysis of specific cases in later chapters.

The remaining three chapters of Part I introduce a series of progressively more localized perspectives for the subsequent analysis of issues arising in the course of the Droitwich development programme. Chapter 3 focuses on the regional planning problems of the West Midlands during the decade of the nineteen-fifties, which generated considerable conflict between local planning authorities and led ultimately to a set of urgent pressures for the expansion of Droitwich. Chapter 4 proceeds to analyse the processes of bargaining through which a local agreement was eventually reached to expand the town by means of a voluntary partnership between County and District Councils, while Chapter 5 describes the less formal patterns of relationships that subsequently evolved between the primary agencies and individual actors involved in the local decision-making process.

Synopsis of Part II

From this basis, Part II moves on to consider a variety of issues confronted during the course of the Droitwich expansion. Chapter 6 begins with a discussion of the fifteen-year capital programme for the expansion scheme as a whole, and its status at a point some five years after its initiation is analysed with the aid of information obtained from an experimental group exercise. In this, different professional officers of the local development group were asked independently to record their perceptions of the ranges of uncertainty over the timing of different development proposals, after which they were invited to come together to discuss the reasons for any divergences in their judgements. The following six chapters concern themselves in turn with issues of road construction, housing policy, industrial development, central area redevelopment, neighbourhood improvement, and various supporting services provided for the local community by more specialized agencies. In each case, the same broad sequence is adopted for the analysis; as illustrated in *Figure 2,* this sequence in effect reproduces within each chapter the same kind of structure used to organize the book as a whole. First, a particular problem area is selected, and the principal agencies and actors identified; then, the discussion converges on to the context of local decision-making in Droitwich, through a series of increasingly localized perspectives beginning with an outline of national policy influences and their evolution. The scene is thus set for a more detailed analysis of one or more specific episodes in the local decision-making process, from which certain more general inferences can be drawn. Those episodes are largely taken from the period 1969 to 1971, when we were best able to take advantage of opportunities for observing ongoing processes of decision-making in Droitwich.

It is in these chapters that the conceptual framework first outlined in Chapter 2 is introduced most explicitly as an aid to analysis. Each of Chapters 7 to 12 will introduce certain variations in the patterns of involvement of the principal actors in the Droitwich expansion, and in their patterns of relationship both to each other and also to other interests such as central departments, local community groups, and commercial organizations. An attempt will be made in each case to develop analytical representations both of the structure of linkages between problems, and also of the structure of human and organizational relations involved, moving as freely as possible between one framework and the other with a view to identifying any factors that assisted or inhibited the ability of those concerned to form problem-solving networks in an intelligently selective way. Chapters 10 to 12 in particular concern problems which, it will be argued, are characteristic not only of expanding communities but also of those where the dominant concerns are with the arrest of processes of physical, economic, or social decline. Indeed, it is suggested that many of the sources of difficulty, uncertainty, and conflict which had to be confronted at Droitwich are by no means peculiar either to the specific circumstances of a planned local expansion scheme, or to the particular choice of organizational configuration which happens to be adopted for the management of the local processes of change. We shall thus be following a method similar to Crozier (1964:4), who claimed that 'a clinical approach which bears upon particular cases, and generalizes only from an intimate understanding of these cases, can serve us better than a systematic approach that seeks immediately to establish rigorous laws and thus gives the appearance of being more scientific'.

Synopsis of Part III

Part III opens with a chapter that develops a series of general propositions about planning in complex organizational environments. These concern the inescapability of inter-agency processes; the strategies people adopt in responding to complexity; the influence on decisions of the interactive learning processes that take place; the inevitability, given limited resources, of adopting a selective approach to the formation and manipulation of decision networks; the dependence of such an approach on the exercise of local judgement wherever problem linkages do not follow foreseeable patterns; and the types of skill and organizational resource that are relevant to such network-forming or 'reticulist' judgements. It is argued that the degree to which planning processes exercise an effective influence on decision-making is very much dependent on the disposition of reticulist skills and resources among different publicly accountable agencies, local, regional, and central; and, from this standpoint, some practical guidelines are suggested for those who are concerned to bring about innovation in the ways in which public planning is done.

The stress is placed on an experimental approach to innovation, in which an attempt is first made to understand other forces of change currently acting on the planning process and to discover whatever opportunites for experimental intervention they may afford. In this light, Chapter 14 looks at some significant trends in regional planning in Britain since the early nineteen-sixties, with special reference to an evolving pattern of interacting regional processes in the West Midlands. This indicates something of the crucial catalytic roles played by key officials in the regional civil service, and the reticulist skills through which relevant connections were maintained between the agencies concerned. The following chapter reviews a range of differing patterns of organizational relations which evolved during this period at a more local level for managing processes of externally induced change. This review covers a selection of town expansion schemes other than at Droitwich, and also some major expansions of existing cities through the provisions of the New Town legislation. It also examines some recent local experiments in the mobilization of change in deprived urban neighbourhoods, and discusses some factors which have encouraged or inhibited the emergence of reticulist skills to help in maintaining access to relevant executive agencies.

In Chapter 16, the discussion turns to various institutional reforms introduced or pending in Britain during the early seventies, including especially the re-structuring of the local government system. It is argued that these changes are likely to bring the inter-corporate dimension of public planning into even greater prominence, and make it important to open up new opportunities for encouraging the more conscious development of reticulist skills. In particular, it is suggested that there are certain levels of community representation where investment in the experimental deployment of network-forming skills is especially likely to yield returns in the form of a more responsive planning process. These include the levels of the region and the parish or urban neighbourhood, at which concentrations of executive power are likely to remain restricted and the motivations to work through inter-agency channels are correspondingly increased.

Chapter 17 follows up these diagnoses in a speculative vein, by developing a hypothetical case example set in a fictitious region, where it is supposed that a number of difficulties have arisen in the relationships between public authorities representing different constituencies of local and regional interest. A situation is hypothesized in which initiatives by a few individuals lead to a broadly based experiment in which a number of 'community reticulists' are appointed in different localities to explore the practical opportunities and difficulties that arise in an attempt to engage systematically with representatives of other agencies in exploring the implications of locally significant policy problems.

Chapter 18 concludes the book by arguing that the process of evaluating any innovations in public planning, such as those advanced in the speculative case example, must inevitably be a continuous and widely diffused one, so that the question of evaluative method raises issues that are more social and political than narrowly technical in scope. If it proves possible to sustain the type of experimental approach which is advocated, and to advance it on a continually expanding front, then it is suggested that the long-term implications could be far-reaching. Possibly, new orientations and demarcations may begin to emerge within the various professional disciplines that service the processes of public policy formation; some of the more imaginative members of emergent generations may begin to find new and creative channels for employing their energies in the service of society; and a lasting enrichment may be within reach in the difficult political dialogue through which any democratic society must seek to regulate its affairs.

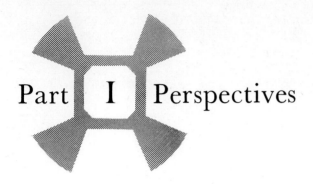

Part I Perspectives

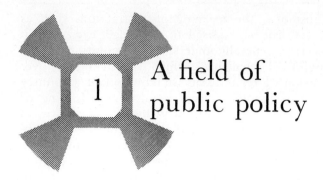

1　A field of public policy

An operational perspective

Interdependence between institutions is a pervasive feature of the structure of all societies. However, these interdependences become especially difficult to deal with in modern societies which must contend with accelerating processes of technical and economic change. Within any such society, there are many different operational perspectives from which the general topic of inter-organizational planning might be explored, including for instance that of advanced technology at one extreme or of alleviation of poverty at the other. The selection of one such perspective as a starting-point for analysis need not of course constrain the focus of subsequent exploration; no system of inter-organizational decision-making can be entirely self-contained, and any analyst of such processes must be prepared to work within an essentially open network, with a rich variety of connections between its component parts.

The perspective which we shall adopt here is that of the *management of local and regional change.* In this phrase, we mean to cover all powers of decision through which governmental agencies — central, local, or intermediate — can act to influence the distribution of people, wealth, and opportunities between or within some set of geographically defined areas in any national or supernational context. Of course, any working definition of this kind has its imperfections: for instance, the meaning of abstractions such as wealth and opportunity can be exposed to challenge, even though such terms do carry certain generally understood connotations in any society. Another point of challenge, which we shall pass over quickly, is the definition of region. Any sub-division of a country into a set of smaller geographical areas requires the drawing of boundaries which are to some extent arbitrary; and even nations with a federal system of government may find it important for certain purposes to define regional units that violate the administrative boundaries of their component states or provinces. Indeed, it is comparatively rarely that the word 'region' is used to describe an established unit of administration; to that extent, the word itself is an indicator of the difficulty of containing any problems of planning that have a spatial dimension within the territorial bounds of any single administrative agency.

One point at which our initial definition can be more specific is in regarding the *management* of local and regional change as being a matter of primary concern to public rather than private institutions. Although there may be many non-governmental decision-makers — ranging from the largest international corporation to the most impoverished migrant worker and his family — whose actions will have some influence over the territorial distribution of population, wealth, and opportunity, they are almost invariably motivated by considerations other than the generation of local and regional change as such. Certainly, their actions may combine to generate highly significant changes within and between regions, but any guidance of such changes in accordance with social policies will generally depend on the actions of governmental institutions, whether through the exercise of statutory powers of prohibition or control, through selective local investments or forms of regional incentive, or through periodic public commitments to plans, strategies, or other forms of statement of political intent.

Local and regional change in Great Britain

The case material which we shall use to develop our analysis will be drawn almost exclusively from the context of local and regional change in Great Britain during the nineteen-sixties and early seventies, looking back where necessary to earlier decades but at the same time looking ahead to the later seventies and beyond. In Britain, the processes of local and regional change over this whole period do reflect certain specific national circumstances: in particular, the problems arising in the aftermath of early industrialization and urbanization, and the inheritance of an institutional structure in which most powers of government have for long been divided between a central executive under the control of the national parliament in London, and a set of elected local authorities of differing types and sizes. However, it is hoped that much of what we shall have to say will have equal relevance to the circumstances of other countries, including those whose state of economic development or whose institutional structure may differ significantly from that of Britain.

In *Figure 3*, recent patterns of population change are indicated for each of the eight regional divisions of England for which advisory Economic Planning Councils were set up in 1964, and also for the separate national units of Scotland and Wales, each treated as a single regional entity. The actual geographical boundaries of these units are indicated on a map which also shows relative population densities in 1971, while the main population changes between censuses of 1951, 1961, and 1971 are set out on a simplified map in which the contiguity of regions has been preserved, but their areas have been distorted to make them proportional to their shares of the total national population.

Although it will be noticed that all population changes have been in an upward direction, the highest rates of increase were registered in the heavily populated South-East region (with London at its centre) and in the four adjoining regions, with much more modest rates of increase in Scotland, Wales, and the three Northern regions of England. By world standards, none of the rates of growth indicated on *Figure 3* are particularly high; nevertheless, they do pose some challenging social, political, and environmental problems in an island that combines a high population density with a high level of expectation of material standards of living.

So far as wealth and social opportunity are concerned, almost all available indicators reveal consistent imbalances between the comparatively prosperous South and East and the more economically deprived Northern and Western regions. In particular, levels of unemployment in the North and West have remained consistently higher than those in the South and East, despite attempts by successive governments to counteract these trends through increasingly discriminating policies of regional development. The resulting migrations in search of employment opportunities largely explain the divergences in regional population growth revealed in *Figure 3*.

However, the most striking redistributions of population in Great Britain have been not so much between regions as within them. By the end of the Second World War in 1945, living conditions in

Figure 3 Regional distribution of population in Great Britain, 1951-71

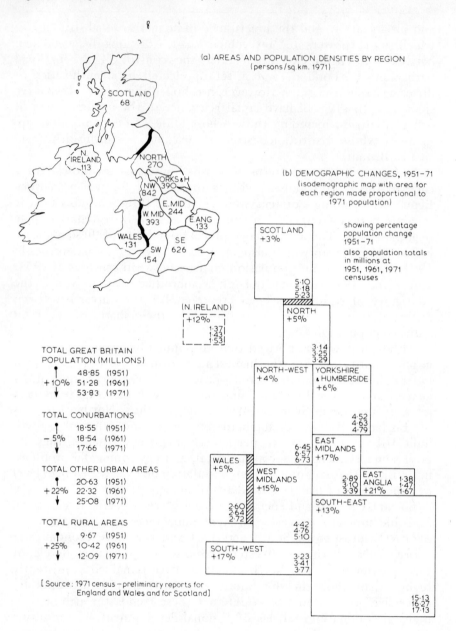

(a) AREAS AND POPULATION DENSITIES BY REGION
(persons/sq.km. 1971)

SCOTLAND 68

N IRELAND ~113

NORTH 270

YORKS&H 390

NW 842

E.MID 244

W.MID 393

E.ANG 133

WALES 131

SW 154

SE 626

(b) DEMOGRAPHIC CHANGES, 1951–71
(isodemographic map with area for
each region made proportional to
1971 population)

showing percentage
population change
1951–71

also population totals
in millions at
1951, 1961, 1971
censuses

SCOTLAND
+3%
5·10
5·18
5·23

(N.IRELAND)
+12%
1·37
1·43
1·53

NORTH
+5%
3·14
3·25
3·29

NORTH-WEST
+4%
6·45
6·57
6·73

YORKSHIRE
& HUMBERSIDE
+6%
4·52
4·63
4·79

EAST MIDLANDS
+17%
2·89
3·10
3·39

EAST ANGLIA
+21%
1·38
1·47
1·67

WALES
+5%
2·60
2·64
2·72

WEST MIDLANDS
+15%
4·42
4·76
5·10

SOUTH-EAST
+13%
15·13
16·27
17·13

SOUTH-WEST
+17%
3·23
3·41
3·77

TOTAL GREAT BRITAIN
POPULATION (MILLIONS)
48·85 (1951)
+10% 51·28 (1961)
53·83 (1971)

TOTAL CONURBATIONS
18·55 (1951)
–5% 18·54 (1961)
17·66 (1971)

TOTAL OTHER URBAN AREAS
20·63 (1951)
+22% 22·32 (1961)
25·08 (1971)

TOTAL RURAL AREAS
9·67 (1951)
+25% 10·42 (1961)
12·09 (1971)

[Source: 1971 census – preliminary reports for
England and Wales and for Scotland]

London and a number of other large cities had deteriorated, through population pressures, war damage, and lack of opportunity to replenish or maintain housing stock, to such a point that planned emigration or 'overspill' of population to less congested areas had become an extremely urgent political priority. To some extent, the resulting dispersal of population is reflected in the broad breakdown of population changes between conurbations, other urban areas, and rural areas as indicated at the foot of *Figure 3*.

However, the patterns of population change within regions can be illustrated more dramatically by analysing changes in the electorates of parliamentary constituencies between the general elections of 1955 and 1970 — a period over which direct comparisons can be made because no changes in constituency boundaries were introduced. Leaving aside the twelve constituencies of Northern Ireland, the electorates of which were made of abnormally large size for special constitutional reasons, the remaining 618 constituencies of the United Kingdom were defined in 1955 in such a way as to include roughly similar populations within their boundaries, with an average electorate of approximately 55,000, corresponding to a total population of some 80,000. The first frequency chart in *Figure 4* shows the distribution of size of electorate about this average in 1955, when the only deliberate inequalities were those introduced in favour of certain comparatively scattered constituencies in thinly populated areas of Scotland and Wales.

By 1970, however, variations in the size of constituencies had become much more marked through migration, as indicated by the much broader scatter of the second distribution in *Figure 4*. Largely as a result of slum clearance programmes, many of the least populous constituencies were now to be found in the inner areas of London and the four largest provincial cities: Birmingham in the West Midlands, Glasgow in Scotland, and Manchester and Liverpool in the North West. Each of these cities had a population in the range of 600,000 to 1,200,000, and formed the dominant metropolitan centre of a continuous conurbation including several associated urban areas. The third frequency diagram in *Figure 4* reveals that it was largely within the eighty-eight constituencies representing these older metropolitan centres that the most significant losses of population were registered over the fifteen years in question.

Figure 4 also shows that a total of thirteen constituencies registered a net gain of 40,000 electors or more. Significantly, six of these constituencies lay just beyond the boundaries of the London conurbation, and included within their areas the sites of New Towns specially designated by central government to receive 'overspill'

Figure 4   Local population changes as indicated by variations in electorates of British parliamentary constituencies, 1955–1970

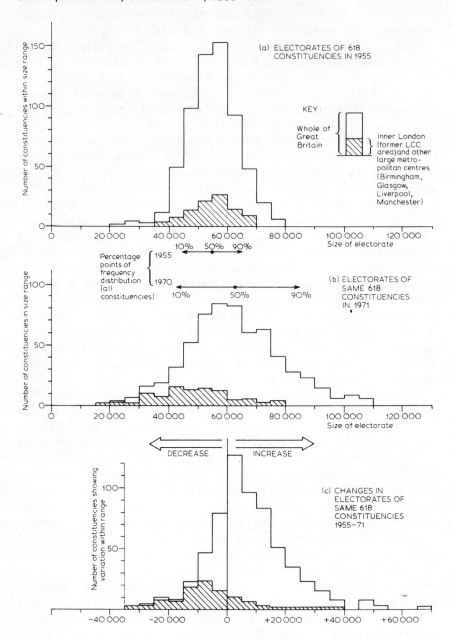

population from the metropolitan area, largely through provision of publicly rented housing. A further three of these thirteen constituencies lay at the peripheries of the Birmingham, Liverpool, and Manchester conurbations and included large-scale housing developments initiated by the respective city authorities. Such migrations of population from inner cities to areas of planned overspill of course also carried implications for the distribution of social and economic opportunity within regions, in so far as the migrant families became able to enjoy higher standards of housing and other physical amenities. On the other hand, these benefits were accompanied by widespread dislocations of established patterns of social relationships, the effects of which were much more difficult to evaluate.

Governmental influences on regional change

Looking into the future from the mid-seventies, there is a widespread expectation that the tendency towards dispersal from the conurbations is likely to continue, as also is the tendency for migration southwards in search of improved employment opportunities and living environments. However, some gradual yet significant changes have taken place since the fifties and sixties in the nature of the controls available to government to exert influence over these trends. On the one hand, there has been a gradual shift of emphasis from public towards private housing, as the immediate problems of post-war reconstruction have receded and the economics of the housing market have increasingly asserted themselves. These trends have left government with less direct power to channel the movement of population out of the more congested urban areas. On the other hand, the persistence of higher levels of unemployment in the North and West has forced governments in introduce a steadily increasing range of measures to influence the regional distribution of employment opportunity, a problem lately becoming subject to supranational policy influences through accession to the European Economic Community.

Meanwhile, the continuing spread of car ownership has increased the mobility of a large sector of the working population, making it a more difficult matter to integrate government controls over housing, employment, transportation, and other services. The result has been a search for increasingly sophisticated methods of local and regional planning, seeking to combine skills of physical, social, and economic analysis, while at the same time calling for an increased level of co-ordination between the relevant public authorities.

In Great Britain, most of the public controls over the processes of

Figure 5 History of changes in central government departments concerned with fields of policy relating to local and regional change within England*

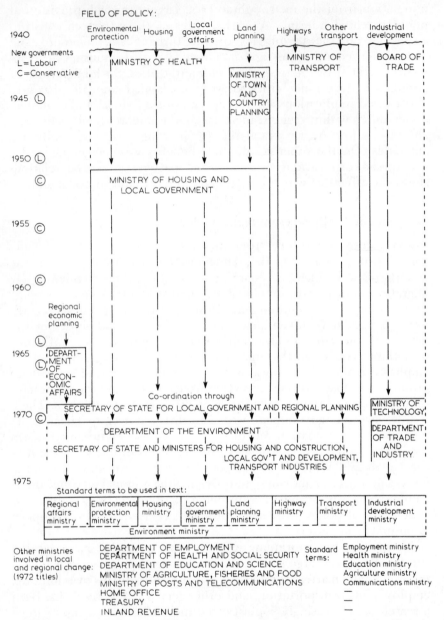

* *Some of these fields of policy are grouped under separate national offices in Scotland and in Wales*

local and regional change have evolved either within the structure of central departments controlled by the national parliament, or within that of local authorities controlled by independently elected councils. However, a growing awareness of the failures of these institutions to adapt to new and more complex processes has led, especially during the late sixties and early seventies, to a series of sweeping structural reforms. In introducing the various governmental and other institutions concerned with local and regional change in Britain, we shall therefore begin by outlining the more basic characteristics of the main central and local government agencies, mentioning briefly some of the ways in which these have been modified by recent reform proposals. A fuller analysis of some of the implications of these changes will follow in later chapters.

Departments of central government

The authority of central government in Great Britain derives from the parliamentary system, the conventions of which have evolved over several centuries without the support of a formal written constitution. The political party returned to power at each general election, for a maximum period of five years, expects to see its leader appointed as Prime Minister by the Sovereign, after which he in turn appoints a Cabinet including Ministers responsible for the main Departments of State. Continuity of administration is assured through a strictly non-party-political Civil Service, and the Permanent Secretaries and other senior officials of Departments can generally expect security of tenure in their appointments despite periodic changes of parliamentary control. Of the two dominant national parties, Labour held power from 1945 to 1951 and again from 1964 to 1970, with the Conservative party in control in the intervening years and also after the 1970 general election. These changes of control often led directly to certain changes in departmental organization, and an attempt is made in *Figure 5* to set out graphically the main changes introduced in those departments concerned with the functions most directly related to the processes of local and regional change.

Within England, the war-time years saw a Ministry of Town and Country Planning established for the first time, taking its place alongside the three other Departments that were then responsible for fields of policy related to regional development: the Ministry of Health (then carrying responsibility for housing and local government); the Ministry of Transport; and the Board of Trade, which was responsible for controls over industrial location among other aspects of commercial affairs. In 1951, responsibility for land-use planning was re-integrated with that for housing and local government affairs in a new Ministry of Housing and Local Government; and the next significant change came in 1964 with the creation of a new (but in the event short-lived) Department of Economic Affairs. Set up as a counterweight to the influence of the Treasury in the field of economic management, this Department had among its tasks a co-ordinating responsibility in the field of regional economic planning, to be exercised through a system of Regional Boards of civil servants representing different functional departments. These Boards in turn were to be advised by Regional Economic Planning Councils whose members were to be appointed to reflect broad regional interests. Thus, for the first time within England, an embryonic form of regional government was introduced, albeit with purely advisory powers.

On the disbandment of the DEA in 1969, its regional responsibilities were transferred to the Ministry of Housing and Local Government, which was by this time loosely federated with the Ministry of Transport under a Secretary of State for Local Government and Regional Planning. The process of integration was taken a step further in 1970 with the creation of a large new Department of the Environment. In this department, under the overall control of a Secretary of State, the main responsibilities were divided among Ministers concerned respectively with housing and construction, with local government and development (including regional planning and, until 1972, highways), and with all other transport affairs. Meanwhile, the industrial location powers of the Board of Trade, briefly transferred to an enlarged Ministry of Technology, were brought within another large new Department of State, the Department of Trade and Industry, within which a new senior post of Minister for Industrial Development was created in 1972.

These various changes in the machinery of government over the period we shall be analysing make it advisable for us to avoid confusion by adopting a consistent set of terms in the text, and the simplified designations near the foot of *Figure 5* are introduced with this in view. For example, where we refer in future chapters to the 'Land Planning Ministry'—following the usage adopted by Lady Sharp in her authoritative account of the work of the Ministry of Housing and Local Government (Sharp, 1969) — this should be taken to refer to whichever Department of State happened to have this field of policy within its terms of reference at the time. The term 'Environment Ministry' will be reserved for use where the more comprehensive aspects of the work of the new federated department are being discussed. In Scotland and Wales, it should be noted, several of the fields of policy mentioned in *Figure 5* are covered by separate national Departments of State. Also, there are a number of other government departments in Britain which have important fields of responsibility within the regions, and which will be referred to from time to time in the text. Their titles are mentioned at the foot of *Figure 5*, along with standard descriptions which may help the reader unfamiliar with the British system. The term 'Ministry' is used in place of the now more common term 'Department' to avoid confusion with local government and other institutions which are organized internally on departmental lines.

Local government in Great Britain

For most—though not all—of the fields of public policy with which we shall be primarily concerned, central departments can only act through the exercise of various controls over the activities of independently elected local authorities. The British system of local government has evolved slowly, building on long-established traditions of municipal self-government through Royal Charter and of separate County administration. However, the sixties saw a widespread acceptance of a case for more radical modernization of this structure, and a protracted debate took place over the form that this structural change should take. This debate culminated in the introduction of a new structure for England and Wales, becoming operational in 1974, with broadly similar changes scheduled for the following year in Scotland.

Figure 6 compares the structure of local government in England before and after the 1974 reform. No boundary changes were proposed within Greater London, where a new two-tier structure had already been introduced as recently as 1965, dividing the main responsibilities of local government between a new Greater London Council and thirty-two London Boroughs, with the Corporation of the small inner City of London retaining much of its unique historic role. Elsewhere, however, some sweeping changes were introduced. Under the established system, most provincial towns and cities of over about 80,000 population had acquired County Borough status, giving them responsibility for all local government functions within their areas, while elsewhere these functions were divided between County Councils and 'lower-tier' County Districts. These districts were of three different types, as indicated in the diagram. The distinction between Municipal Borough and Urban District was essentially one of formal civic status and electoral procedure rather

Figure 6 Structure of local government in England

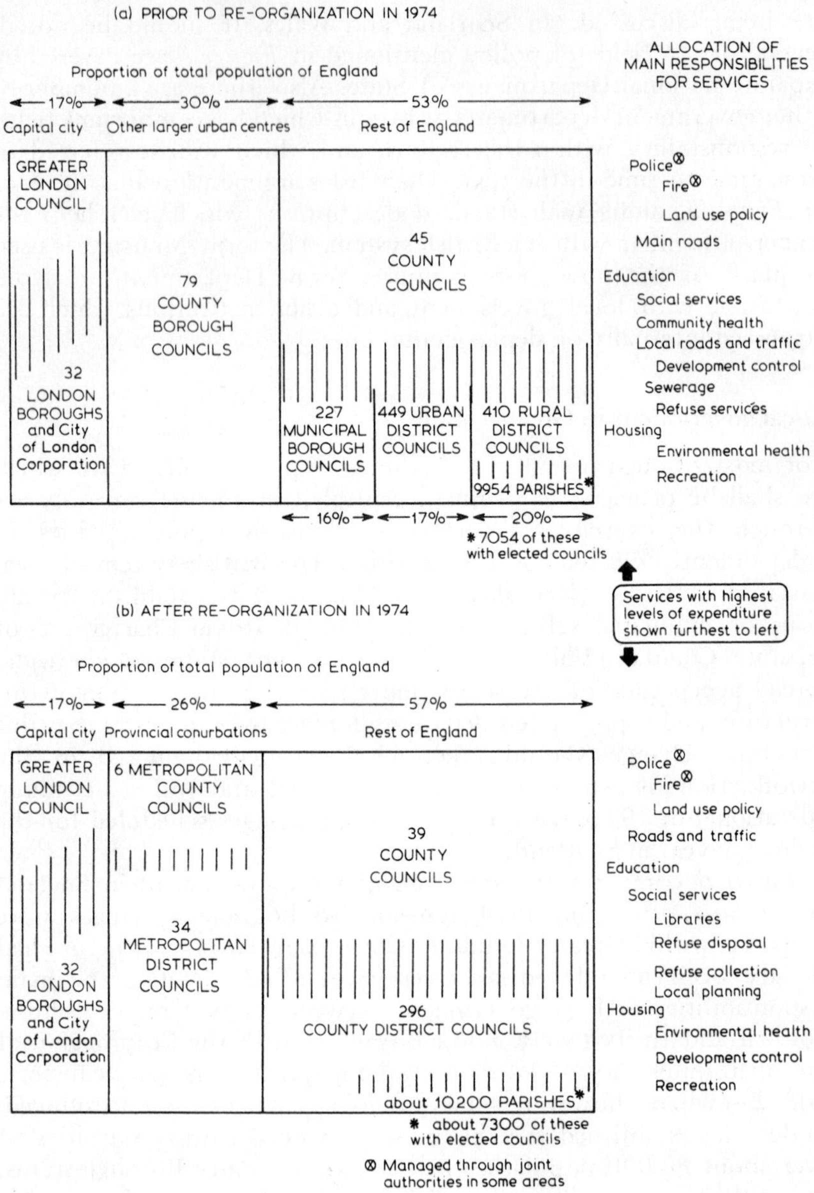

(a) PRIOR TO RE-ORGANIZATION IN 1974

ALLOCATION OF
MAIN RESPONSIBILITIES
FOR SERVICES

Proportion of total population of England

←17%→ ←——30%——→ ←———— 53% ————→

Capital city   Other larger urban centres   Rest of England

GREATER LONDON COUNCIL	79 COUNTY BOROUGH COUNCILS	45 COUNTY COUNCILS		
32 LONDON BOROUGHS and City of London Corporation		227 MUNICIPAL BOROUGH COUNCILS	449 URBAN DISTRICT COUNCILS	410 RURAL DISTRICT COUNCILS
				9954 PARISHES*

← 16% → ←—17%—→ ←— 20%—→

* 7054 of these with elected councils

Police⊗
Fire⊗
Land use policy
Main roads

Education
Social services
Community health
Local roads and traffic
Development control
Sewerage
Refuse services
Housing
Environmental health
Recreation

Services with highest
levels of expenditure
shown furthest to left

(b) AFTER RE-ORGANIZATION IN 1974

Proportion of total population of England

←17%→ ←— 26% —→ ←———— 57% ————→

Capital city Provincial conurbations   Rest of England

GREATER LONDON COUNCIL	6 METROPOLITAN COUNTY COUNCILS	39 COUNTY COUNCILS
32 LONDON BOROUGHS and City of London Corporation	34 METROPOLITAN DISTRICT COUNCILS	296 COUNTY DISTRICT COUNCILS
		about 10200 PARISHES*

* about 7300 of these with elected councils

⊗ Managed through joint authorities in some areas

Police⊗
Fire⊗
Land use policy
Roads and traffic

Education
Social services
Libraries
Refuse disposal
Refuse collection
Local planning
Housing
Environmental health
Development control
Recreation

than of function; but the Rural Districts differed in being themselves sub-divided into Rural Parishes, sometimes but not invariably represented by elected Parish Councils. While possessing only vestigial powers of local expenditure, many such Parish Councils were able to demonstrate an ability to play a significant role in reflecting the special local interests of scattered rural communities.

In the reformed system of local government in England, the most significant changes were the disappearance of the independent County Boroughs in a new two-tier pattern of Counties and Districts, and the amalgamation of many smaller County Districts into larger units at the District level. For six of the main provincial conurbations, the powers of the new Districts were made considerably more significant than in the remaining 'non-metropolitan' Counties, by the allocation of responsibility for the major functions of education and social services. This meant that the Metropolitan Districts became roughly similar in status to those twenty outer London Boroughs which had become independent education authorities after the creation of the Greater London Council in 1965. The distribution of functions between tiers under the old and new systems is indicated broadly to the right of *Figure 6*, with the shaded bands representing not only the approximate dividing line between functions, but also the approximate relationship between the total expenditure levels of the various different levels per head of population. In detail, the pattern is complicated by various local arrangements for dividing certain responsibilities between Counties and Districts both before and after reorganization, and by other special circumstances in the Greater London area.

The reformed system has a number of basic features in common with its predecessor. Local taxation is levied exclusively through a property tax known as the 'rate', with each authority acting independently in determining the level of its rate for the following year, although the rates for upper tier authorities are in practice collected through the agency of the second tier. This local revenue is extensively supplemented by a system of supporting grants met from national taxation. In terms of electoral procedure, each authority retains full independence, with a four-yearly cycle of elections in the new Counties and Districts replacing the previous combination of a triennial cycle in the Counties with annual elections in the Municipal and County Boroughs.

In most of the larger authorities, the electoral process has come to be dominated by the organizations of the two main national political parties, Conversative and Labour, but with the Liberal party and other groups gaining much strength in particular areas. Traditionally, there has always been a more rigid separation between elected representatives and paid officials than in some other countries, with the latter enjoying a good deal of security in the tenure of their appointments. In most larger towns and cities, the role of Mayor is divorced from that of political leadership and is treated as of primarily ceremonial significance.

Traditionally, decision-making within local authorities has been highly decentralized, with the heads of professionally oriented departments enjoying considerable autonomy, and usually reporting for most purposes through specialist committees of elected members. In the decade or so prior to local government reform, dissatisfaction with the obstacles to co-ordination which such a system presented led several authorities to experiment in the introduction of more centralized management structures; very often, the Clerk of the Council would be designated as Chief Executive and vested with increased formal authority, reporting to some form of central Policy Committee. Although the introduction of the new structure in 1974 was expected to give a further impetus to such changes, the relationships to be established between Chief Executive, specialist committees, and departmental hierarchies remained a source of some ambiguity and potential conflict. Fears were also widely expressed that the problems of internal co-ordination would be compounded by those of establishing new working relationships between tiers of local government and between neighbouring authorities.

Other sectors and their influence

Having now reviewed the structures of British central and local government, it is also necessary to refer briefly to a third, and increasingly significant, sector of governmental activity; that of specialist agencies controlled by Boards or Councils whose members are appointed by government, but which otherwise have a high degree of management autonomy. At a national scale, there are boards concerned with the operation of the rail system, of postal and telecommunication services, of energy supply, and of basic industries such as coal and steel; while at a regional level, there are other boards concerned for instance, with electricity distribution and, from 1974 onwards, with health service and water resource management. It is significant that control of many of these functions was transferred from local government at various times during the twentieth century because of changes in technology which created a demand for more centralization; between them, they now control a substantial sector of total public expenditure.

A very different type of appointed agency operating at the regional level was created in 1965 in the form of the Regional Economic Planning Councils, already mentioned, with equivalent bodies operating in Scotland and in Wales. The members of each Council were appointed to include as wide a spectrum of regional interests as possible, with the aim of providing a channel of communication with the regional officers of government departments. There has been much scepticism about the practical influence of the Regional Economic Planning Councils; however, the prospect of any immediate change in their role was deferred when a Royal Commission on the Constitution (1973) was announced in 1968, with a remit to look into the whole question of relationships between the constituent parts of the United Kingdom.

There is another, more localized, form of appointed agency with which we shall be directly concerned; this is the New Town Development Corporation, several of which have been appointed by the Land Planning Ministry since 1946, as agencies for executing large-scale local programmes of urban development planned in accordance with regional policies. By the early seventies seventeen such Corporations were operating in England, with five in Scotland and two in Wales. Although most of the earlier schemes involved the creation of almost entirely 'new' communities in rural areas, with a strong emphasis on the re-housing of overspill population from nearby cities, the task of some of the more recently appointed Corporations has been to expand existing urban centres, which have been designated as suitable for further large-scale population growth, in some form of partnership with existing local authorities. The structure of these agencies and their relationships with local government will be discussed more fully in Chapter 15.

Inevitably, the management of local and regional change introduces many interfaces with decision-makers operating outside the public sector. The patterns of regional change are often strongly influenced by the cumulative effects of decisions by both large and small private enterprises, particularly where questions arise of expansion or contraction of industries on their existing sites, or prospective moves to new locations. In both manufacturing and distributive industries, recent decades have seen steady trends towards concentration into larger management units, with the result that decisions with regional implications increasingly tend to be taken in the boardrooms of large-scale national or international enterprises.

The final sector of decision-making with which our analysis will be concerned includes the whole range of non-commercial private

Figure 7   An institutional base map

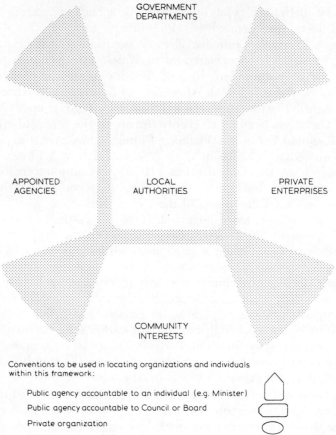

Conventions to be used in locating organizations and individuals
within this framework:

Public agency accountable to an individual (e.g. Minister)

Public agency accountable to Council or Board

Private organization

Individual

interests to which government must retain some degree of responsivness. At one extreme, there are individual citizens who, in their family groups, face decisions concerning whether or at what times to change their jobs, their places of residence, their methods of travel to and from work, or other aspects of their patterns of day-to-day activity. At the other extreme, there are voluntary associations, some of which—such as the churches or the trade unions—may have highly organized national structures of decision-making, but are bound together more by shared beliefs or interests than by involvement in commercial enterprises. In between these extremes can be located a wide range of other groupings, such as residents' or tenants' associations, and sports or social clubs, based on common interests which can only find expression at a more localized level.

The mapping of organizational relationships

In subsequent chapters, we shall be concerned with organizational relationships spanning all the various sectors described in this chapter, and it will be of value to relate these to a common frame of reference. Such a frame of reference is introduced in *Figure 7,* in the form of a 'base map' in which the local authority sector is located in a central position. Around it are grouped the other four sectors, defined respectively as departments of central government; appointed governmental agencies; private (commercial) enterprises; and (non-commercial) community interests. Additional conventions for plotting the positions of particular institutions, or of individual actors within those institutions, will be introduced within this framework as the book unfolds. Some of these conventions are sketched at the foot of the diagram. Because the boundaries between the five principal sectors may not always be clear-cut, the base map avoids showing clear lines of demarcation between them, so that certain agencies or actors can if necessary be plotted in the immediate shaded areas.

It must be stressed, however, that the frame of reference provided by *Figure 7* is intended as no more than a visual aid for the reader as he or she progresses through the book. There are no theoretical inferences to be drawn from the placing of one organization above or below, or to the right or left of another. The conventions which we shall use in placing an organization or actor are arbitrary; however, we do intend in our use of the base map to be consistent in our arbitrariness.

Thus, the local authority sector appears at the centre of the map, not because it is considered the most important in any absolute sense, but because most of the executive powers through which the processes of local and regional change can be subjected to public influence fall within the competence of elected local authorities. In locating different types of local authority within the central square, we shall adopt the convention of placing higher tier authorities near the top of the square, with the more urban type of unit appearing towards the left and the more rural authorities towards the right, in line with the layout already used in *Figure 6*. Within the top sector, government departments and their sub-divisions will be located towards the left or right in accordance with the spectrum of policy concerns as set out in *Figure 5*, with the activities of regional offices located towards the lower margin. For the other three sectors, institutions or individuals acting at a more local level will be located close to the central square, while those operating at a regional or a national level will be plotted in more peripheral locations.

These conventions reflect the general perspective of this book, in which local and sometimes regional vantage points are used to observe and interpret a wide variety of processes of inter-organizational planning and adjustment. If the layout of *Figure 7* is thought of as translated from a plane to the surface of a sphere, one can conceive of the four sectors of government departments, appointed agencies, private enterprises, and community interests as converging again on the obverse side, where a further set of inter-organizational processes can be observed from a national as opposed to a local or regional perspective—as, for instance, Anthony Sampson has done in his successive studies of the anatomy of Britain (Sampson, 1971).

This national perspective is one that we shall endeavour to keep in mind when drawing general inferences from the analysis of particular processes and events from our local and regional viewpoint. A further influence which we shall wish to distinguish at times is that of the supranational level of government—including, especially in the case of Great Britain, the European Economic Community, whose involvement in questions of regional policy may well be of growing significance in future.

Although the case material we shall present is drawn exclusively from the British context, we shall endeavour to interpret it sufficiently generally to make the conclusions we draw of wider relevance to other systems of government. Indeed, our collective experience of working in other countries suggests that there are some striking similarities in the inter-organizational problems arising in the management of local and regional change in different national contexts. In attempting to apply the framework of *Figure 7* more generally, there is, however, at least one important proviso to be made; in countries with a federal system of government, the sector of 'government departments' must be interpreted to include the separate influences of legislative assemblies and administrative departments at both Federal and State or Provincial levels.

However, the purpose of this chapter has been simply to introduce in general terms the meaning we attach to our chosen field of local and regional change, and also to introduce the principal types of agency concerned in the complex patterns of public influence whereby these processes are managed. But before we can develop our central theme of inter-agency planning in this context, we shall now have to pause to introduce a framework of analytical concepts which we shall find useful in interpreting the specific case material that follows.

2 An approach to analysis

The perspective of strategic choice

The approach to analysis which we shall introduce in this chapter begins by recognising that decision-makers involved in the management of local and regional change, as in many other fields of public policy, must work within a setting in which managerial and political responsibilities tend to be diffuse and ill-structured. Within such a setting, individuals must expect to encounter difficulties not merely in arriving at an appreciation of the problems they face, but also in weighing up the political pressures to which they must be responsive, and in anticipating the actions of other decision-makers. We shall argue that it is only realistic to expect such sources of difficulty to persist, no matter what attempts may be made to combat them by seeking consensus on long-term plans, strategies, or frameworks of objectives. Our approach will not therefore begin with any attempt to form a panoramic or synoptic view of a comprehensive planning system, as seen from some central vantage point. Rather, it will start with a much more localized perspective, which we shall seek to extend progressively as this chapter develops.

We shall begin by introducing some concepts relating to any current situation of choice in which some individual or group recognises the existence of a *decision problem* — or, in other terms, experiences a state of uncertainty in selecting a preferred course of action. This starting point will lead into a view of planning as a continuing *process of strategic choice,* in which it is sought to reduce the difficulties encountered in dealing with current decision problems by exploring them within a wider strategic context, embracing other related problems of present and future choice. This view of planning has already been presented in the book *Local Government and Strategic Choice* (Friend and Jessop, 1969), following extensive opportunities for observation of group decision processes in a large urban local authority. However, because of our present concern with processes at the inter-agency level, we shall in this chapter be concerned not only to introduce this basic approach, but to relate it in a more explicit way than hitherto to some relevant concepts from political science. This will help us, in subsequent chapters, to preserve a balance between methods of representing the structure of complex decision problems, and methods of representing equally complex patterns of human and organizational relations, treating these two frameworks as complementary and seeking ways in which to move as freely as possible from the one to the other.

The policy system as a vehicle for decision-making

Whether consciously or otherwise, every decision-maker behaves in accordance with a complex set of social and cultural influences, which may themselves be in a state of continuing flux. Such influences combine to shape both the relations between decision-makers and also the problems that concern them; further they will affect their perceptions of these relations and problems. In order to impose some order on the problematic situations in which they find themselves, decision-makers inevitably make all kinds of distinctions, classifications, and other judgements which relate to this social and cultural context. In particular, they must relate themselves in some way to a structure of authority, which will provide them with a map of the distribution of relevant spheres of responsibility and competence, and will provide at least some guidance towards accepted modes of procedure.

Most structures of authority evolve in such a way as to deal not with individual decision problems — which are by definition transient—but with *classes* of problem situation which are expected to recur over time. This applies in particular to the structure of governmental institutions, both central and local, the responsibilities of which are often defined with some degree of precision, both in territorial and in functional terms. For instance, a City Housing or Parks Department may be authorized to take decisions in relation to a well-understood class of decision problems concerned with the operation of specified public services or the regulation of private activities within prescribed territorial boundaries. We shall introduce the term *policy system* to refer to any set of organizational and inter-personal arrangements which has evolved to deal with some identifiable class of decision problems, however simple or complex this may be. Sometimes, the overall field of decision covered by a policy system may include many different types of problem, which may be interrelated in quite a subtle way. To reflect the possibility that there will be many dimensions to the total field of decision situations with which any particular policy system is directly concerned, we shall refer to this field as its *action space*. In the chapters that follow, we shall regard the description of the action space as a fundamental element in the definition of any policy system.

A policy system is by no means the only form of social system that may influence decision-making. It may however be distinguished from other social systems by the existence of some set of recognized rules, policies, objectives, or precedents which those playing roles within the system acknowledge as factors that should influence their search for preferred courses of action within the recognized action space. These we shall refer to collectively as the *policy guidelines* of the policy system. It does not follow that each of the individuals involved will be directly or exclusively motivated by these policy guidelines; however, especially in so far as they may be a matter of public record, he must pay them some recognition if only as constraints over his choice of preferred actions. In practice, it is often found difficult to articulate policy guidelines that match at all fully the complexity of the action space, because it is rarely feasible to use more than a limited set of simple parameters to discriminate between problem situations for which alternative forms of action are to be selected.

In consequence, the decision-makers may sometimes find themselves called upon to exercise a considerable degree of discretion in working within an agreed set of policy guidelines. However, in situations where the pressures for clear specification of policy guidlines are strongest — especially in areas of governmental decision where there is a demand for fairness in dealing with successive cases — the complexity of the problem situations which arise may be dealt with through the imposition of routines that allow little scope for discretion.

In such circumstances, an appearance of simplicity becomes imposed on even the most complex of problem situations. For instance, the decision-maker dealing with applications for benefit under a sickness insurance scheme, or for planning permission for the extension of private houses, may be highly constrained in his behaviour by formal procedures and policy guidelines. Officially, he may not acknowledge the existence of a new problem situation until he receives a duly completed application form; thereupon, he may briefly consider alternative solutions with reference to approved policy guidelines, before informing the applicant of a 'yes' or 'no' verdict, if necessary after endorsement by a higher source of authority. However, even an ostensibly simple process such as this may become modified by the existence of an appeal procedure, or by the creation of opportunities for preliminary discussion with the applicant before the formal application is submitted, thus implicitly acknowledging the difficulty of relating the full circumstances of the case to the approved policy guidelines. To the applicant, the situation may indeed be a very complex one; and the simplicity of the process may lie more in the way it is organized and its capacity for handling information than in the characteristics of the problem situations with which it must deal.

Nevertheless, even this limited degree of simplification may represent a considerable accomplishment in organizational design. We may begin our analysis of decision-making with well-structured processes of this kind, as it is here that we can distinguish most clearly, as consecutive phases, the three primary elements that are characteristic of any decision-making process: the perception of a decision problem, the exploration of possible solutions, and the commitment to certain selected lines of action. Such a distinction between the inputs, internal operations, and outputs of a decision-making process is essentially similar to that adopted by several other writers on decision-making, planning, and control. For instance, Faludi (1973) builds up his general approach to planning theory from a cybernetic model in which stimuli impinge on a 'receptor' and responses are made through an 'effector' with some form of 'selector' mechanism in between.

The attributes of a policy system

In *Figure 8*, the three basic elements of the decision-making process are related to the context of a policy system operating within a particular action space to which certain policy guidelines apply, and a set of further attributes is indicated through which that policy system can be more fully described. Such a description becomes most straightforward where the policy guidelines are most explicit and the

Figure 8 The policy system as a vehicle for decision

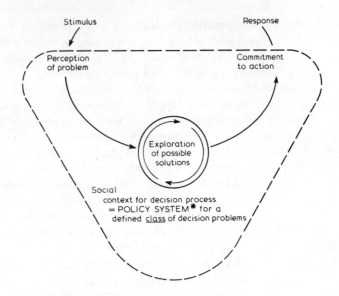

* To DESCRIBE a policy system it is necessary to say something about:

— CLASS OF DECISION PROBLEMS within its competence
                                                       `ACTION SPACE`

— SET OF PEOPLE playing roles in decision process for this
class of problems
                                                       `ACTORS`

— PATTERNS OF RELATIONS between actors
(mutual accountability, membership of groups, etc.)
                                                       `INTERNAL RELATIONS`

— Set of RULES, POLICIES, OBJECTIVES, or PRECEDENTS
acknowledged by actors as guidelines to choice within
action space
                                                       `POLICY GUIDELINES`

— Relations to actors and systems outside this policy system
(see Figure 9)
                                                       `EXTERNAL RELATIONS`

number of participants is most limited, as in routine processes of the type already discussed where a single decision-maker may sometimes be able to work through all three elements consecutively, one case at a time. In contrast, more complex processes, of the type with which we shall later be mainly concerned, typically stimulate correspondingly rich processes of interaction between individuals playing different specialized roles. In keeping with normal sociological usage, we shall call the set of people involved the *actors* in a policy system. In order to describe such a complex policy system at all adequately, we shall have to reach some understanding both of the *internal relations* between these actors and also of any *external relations* to those outside the boundaries of the system.

The relations between actors may include not only those based on hierarchical patterns of formal authority, but also others of a less formal nature. For instance, the actors may be interrelated through membership of various informal groups, and various opportunities or obstacles relating to different media of inter-personal communication. In general, the larger the number of actors in the policy system, the more it is to be expected that they will make specialized contributions to the three elements of problem identification, exploration of solutions, and commitment to action within the decision process. Within governmental organizations especially, it is usually regarded as important that actions which have significant external impacts should carry the formal authority of some publicly identifiable and accountable individual or group. Thus, a distinction can be drawn between the decision 'takers' who must ultimately endorse the outcomes of the decision process, and the wider group of decision 'makers' who may contribute to the selection of these outcomes. This distinction is an important one, for it helps to free us from an assumption, which is very easy to make implicitly, that the actors within a policy system must all owe allegiance to a single corporate organization. Indeed, we shall be much concerned with situations in which this condition does not apply, and where even those contributing to the formal endorsement of actions may act as representatives of two or more different corporate agencies.

The environment of a policy system

In *Figure 9,* we begin to explore further the external relations of the actors in a policy system, by introducing a differentiation between three main facets of its environment, which will later lead us into a classification of the basic sources of uncertainty in decision-making. The first facet, which we shall term the *operating environment,*

Figure 9   The policy system and its environment

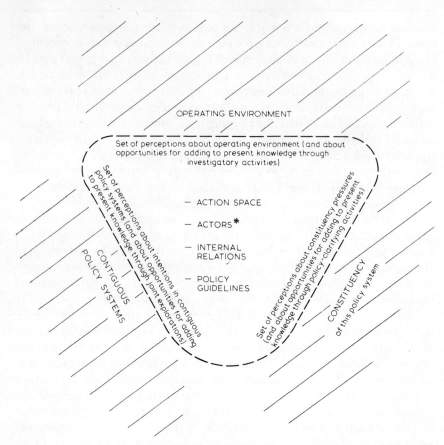

OPERATING ENVIRONMENT

Set of perceptions about operating environment (and about
opportunities for adding to present knowledge through
investigatory activities)

Set of perceptions about intentions in contiguous
policy systems (and about opportunities for adding
to present knowledge through joint explorations)

Set of perceptions about constituency pressures
(and about opportunities for adding to present
knowledge through policy-clarifying activities)

CONTIGUOUS
POLICY SYSTEMS

CONSTITUENCY
of this policy system

— ACTION SPACE

— ACTORS*

— INTERNAL
    RELATIONS

— POLICY
    GUIDELINES

*
Note that actors within a policy system do not necessarily all have the same
organizational allegiance. Indeed, they seldom do in public planning, where
many classes of problem impinge significantly on more than one type of
constituency interest

includes all those aspects of the environment of a policy system from which problems emerge that can be classified as falling within its recognized action space. The structure of the operating environment may itself be complex and dynamic, including both human and material elements; thus, for the traffic engineer the operating environment may consist of patterns of roads, sets of people who interact with each other in using these roads as pedestrians or in vehicles, mechanical systems of regulation over their movements such as traffic lights, and various relationships between these disparate elements.

Another facet of the environment which may be differentiated for our purposes — though it may be by no means unrelated to the operating environment — is what we may call the *constituency* of the policy system, comprised of that set of public or other interests to which the actors in the policy system consider themselves to be responsible for the actions which they may select. To describe such a constituency fully, it will often be necessary to go beyond an identification of the set of individuals involved — for instance, the set of citizens of a nation or a town — and to appreciate the manner and extent of their interest in the field of decision concerned. For instance, a multi-purpose local authority, viewed as a corporate policy system, may have to be responsive to the citizens of a town not only as electors but also as contributors to local taxation, as users of local roads, and as recipients of welfare services. While any two citizens may be equally weighted on the local electoral roll, their interests may be far from equally weighted as local taxpayers or users of different forms of service; and these are aspects of their local constituency of interests to which the actors within the policy system may well have to be sensitive. Further, problems at this local scale may sometimes raise questions of meeting expenditure through national as well as local taxation accounts, so the policy system may have to be responsive in some degree to a set of national as well as purely local constituency interests. As we shall see, such a situation often brings actors from departments of central government into direct interaction with local authority actors within a local policy system, so that the policy system begins to extend beyond its original corporate boundaries.

A further situation we shall encounter is that of the 'latent constituency' where certain actors — most typically professional planners — are drawn to assume the role of advocates for future generations or newcomers to an area, as a counterweight to those who are primarily accountable to shorter term interests. The notion of 'constituency' may therefore sometimes lead on to consideration of a complex system of overt and latent political forces — which may be termed a *constituency system*. The appreciation of its structure will exert some degree of influence on all the actors in the policy system in working within their recognized policy guidelines, but will often be most fully developed among elected representatives or others whose role exposes them most directly to conflicting constituency pressures.

The third facet, which we shall distinguish in the environment of any policy system, embraces any further policy systems concerned with other action spaces within which related decision problems may arise. While the boundaries of the action space for any one policy system are necessarily limited, both in functional and in territorial terms, it is a matter of common observation that decision problems are frequently interrelated in ways that transcend these system boundaries, and that induce those concerned to engage in communications or transactions across them, often on a reciprocal basis. Such interdependences between policy systems arise wherever the choices faced in either are seen to be sensitive to the assumptions made about future intentions within the other. Examples would include the now widely-recognised reciprocal relationships between land use and transportation decisions, or the relationships between decisions about the future development of some particular public service in adjacent geographical areas.

In *Figure 9*, we have therefore described the third facet of the environment of any policy system in terms of 'contiguous policy systems'. The concept of contiguity is here introduced with systems boundaries rather than geographical boundaries in view, and will be more fully explored as the chapter develops. At this point, it is sufficient to note that the membership of contiguous policy systems is not necessarily mutually exclusive; the same actors may often play roles in two or more such systems, as is frequently the case with politicians and senior officials who are responsible for co-ordinating the work of several different agencies or departments.

Information and uncertainty in the policy system

Each actor in a policy system will tend to develop, over the course of time, some set of perceptions relating to each of the three facets of the system's environment — the operating environment, the constituency system, and the contiguous policy systems. As *Figure 9* indicates, it is important to view these perceptions not only in terms of existing knowledge about each facet, but also in terms of perceived deficiencies in that knowledge. It is the perception of such deficiencies that will lead to a recognition of different forms of exploratory action which might be initiated by the actors in order to arrive at more confident decisions.

The importance of such perceptions became apparent through the observations of group decision processes reported in *Local Government and Strategic Choice*. In any situation of difficulty in choosing between alternative courses of action, it was observed that demands would be heard for various further forms of exploratory activity, and that these could be analysed according to three more or less distinct classes, related to the perception of different *sources of uncertainty*. These we shall define in such a way as to correspond to the three facets of environment already indentified in *Figure 9*.

The first type of demand which was observed to arise for reducing the level of uncertainty encountered in decision-making – or, in other words, for increasing the level of confidence with which a preference could be expressed – was for recourse to various kinds of investigatory activity into environmental factors considered as external to the decision-making group, calling for the use of a variety of survey or predictive techniques. Such demands would typically be expressed in terms of a need for further 'study' or 'research' into specified aspects of the operating environment. Second, there could be demands for clarification of the group's 'policies', of objectives', or of goals', relating implicitly to uncertainties about the relative values (or weightings) that ought to be attached to different types of consequence expected to follow from alternative courses of action. Often, the action called for would involve the initiation of wider political consultations with those held to be more directly representative of the interests concerned. In terms of the model of *Figure 9*, it would therefore involve a process of exploration in the direction of the interface with the constituency of the policy system concerned. Third, there could be demands for extending the context in which the problem was currently being explored, to embrace other fields of choice which were perceived to be related. Such demands implied that the choice of assumptions about future intentions in these other fields was seen to have a significant bearing on the group's preference in their current decision situation. Often, demands of this kind would be expressed in terms of advocacy of 'a more strategic view' or of 'more co-ordination' between those responsible for different aspects of decision-making, thus taking the process further towards – and perhaps across – the interfaces with contiguous policy systems.

In *Figure 10*, a view is presented of these three contrasting types of exploratory activity, each interpreted as a response to a different

Figure 10 Sources of uncertainty in decision-making

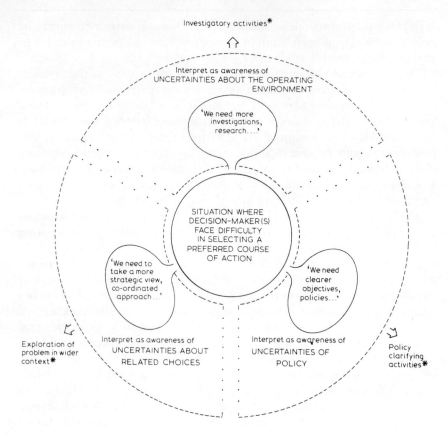

* Each of these three types of activity can be regarded as a different form of RESPONSE TO UNCERTAINTY in decision-making. Important choices may therefore be faced, in any difficult decision situation, as to which forms of response (if any) should be initiated

class of uncertainty perceived by those dealing with a particular decision-making situation. This model is essentially similar to that presented at the end of Chapter 4 in *Local Government and Strategic Choice*; however, it introduces a rearrangement of the relative positions of the three sectors, together with certain modifications in terminology, in order to relate it more clearly to our present line of argument. As indicated in *Figure 10*, we shall from now on refer to the three basic classes of uncertainty as *Uncertainties about the Operating Environment, Uncertainties of Policy,* and *Uncertainties about Related Choices* respectively. Of these, Uncertainties of Policy will correspond to what were referred to in *Local Government and Strategic Choice* as uncertainties about appropriate value judgements (referring specifically to the value judgements of the decision-makers in balancing any expected impacts of their choices within different sectors of constituency interest).

In practice, this tripartite classification has been found to provide a sufficient framework for the analysis of uncertainties in many different types of decision situation; to this extent, the corresponding differentiation of the environment of any policy system, as shown in *Figure 9*, may be held to give an exhaustive classification of relevant interfaces. However, ambiguities can sometimes arise in deciding how a particular source of uncertainty should be classified within the tripartite framework, both when it is being applied in an operational context and when it is being used to interpret observed processes (as will usually be the case in the chapters that follow). The possibility of such ambiguities is recognised in *Figure 10* by using broken lines to indicate the boundaries of the three sectors of uncertainty, and in *Figure 9* by the avoidance of firm demarcations between the corresponding facets of the environment.

The choice of response to uncertainty

Any ambiguities in the classification of uncertainties can be seen as a reflection of doubts or differences of opinion about appropriate forms of exploratory action. Sometimes, the actors in a policy system may hold different views about whether some perceived source of difficulty is of a kind to be confronted through investigatory, policy-clarifying, or co-ordinative activity. For instance, the town planners in a team involved in the choice of design for a town centre renewal scheme might disagree over how to respond to uncertainties about the future intentions of local shopkeepers. Whereas they might all agree that any uncertainty about the future intentions of consumers or road users would call for survey or predictive exercises, involving no direct interaction because of the numbers of independent actors involved, and whereas they might see any uncertainty about the future intentions of public utility organizations as calling for initiation of co-ordinative processes, the case of the local shopkeepers might be seen as something of an intermediate case. Although the shopkeepers might be loosely organized through a local Chamber of Trade, some planners in the team might argue that the Chamber could not be considered a cohesive decision-making body: in other words, there might be doubts as to the realism of treating the traders collectively as a contiguous policy system, rather than as a part of the operating environment to be explored through more impersonal methods. At some points in the planners' explorations, differences of opinion might also arise as to whether they should consider the local trading community as a distinct part of their local constituency. If so, the Chamber of Trade might be approached as a vehicle for policy clarification even in relation to problems where no processes of co-ordinative decision-making were envisaged.

Thus, the distinction between facets of the environment relates in a sense to the degree of *political differentiation* which it is felt necessary to accord to people outside the policy system, either as relevant sectors of interest in weighing up the impacts of the problem under review, or as actors in contiguous policy systems with whom processes of interactive decision-making may be initiated. We shall not pursue this question further at this stage; but it is important to recognise that the choice of response to uncertainty, and therefore the way in which the environment of a policy system is differentiated, may vary both according to the nature of the decision situation currently under review and also according to the perceptions of individual actors. This means that, in applying the classification of uncertainties introduced in *Figure 10*, we shall always have to be careful to relate it clearly to a specified problem situation, and also to the vantage point either of a single individual or of a group within which a high degree of consensus can be assumed.

Even given a consensus between actors as to exploratory actions that are relevant in dealing with different sources of uncertainty, they may differ in their appreciations of which sources of uncertainty are most salient and what resources — if any — it is worth devoting towards reducing them. Any initiative in the area of investigative, policy-clarifying, or co-ordinative activity must involve some level of cost to the decision-makers in terms of time, money, or — perhaps — damage to valued political relationships; and they may not consider these costs justified in relation to whatever (possibly marginal) gains of confidence they expect to achieve. Further, some actors may have personal or professional biases which provide an inbuilt preference towards investigative, policy-directed, or co-ordinative forms of exploratory activity.

Levels of policy system

As we shall see in later chapters, the very processes of selecting responses to uncertainty in confronting a succession of decision problems can lead to important exchanges of information between the actors in a policy system, and to processes of continuing adjustment between them in their perceptions of the various facets of the environment. *Figure 11* builds on our earlier models by representing the three types of strategy for reducing uncertainty as loops reaching outwards from an internal exploratory process. Although there will be some instances in which it may be sufficient for the actors concerned merely to extend their explorations to embrace other actors in the same policy system who are in closer contact with relevant facets of the environment, there will be other instances where the extensions to the exploratory process will reach further out, to penetrate directly the interfaces with the operating environment, with the constituency or with some contiguous policy system, as indicated by the way the three subsidiary loops have been drawn in *Figure 11*.

We shall be concerned here especially with the type of loop which translates the decision process into a broader exploratory context. In *Local Government and Strategic Choice*, it was postulated that the genesis of any planning activity could be found in a perception that certain current situations of choice could be faced more confidently if explored against a background of their relationships to other prospective areas of choice. It was argued that any simple decision process – of the type indicated in Figure 8 – could be said to become part of a wider *process of strategic choice* as soon as the context of exploration becomes broadened in such a way as to embrace fields of choice other than that which is of immediate concern to the decision-takers. The expected consequence will be a gain in the level of confidence with which the immediate decision can be reached – and possibly a choice of action different to that which would otherwise have been selected – even in situations where it may be considered both possible and advantageous for commitments to action in some or all of the related areas of choice to be deferred.

Sometimes, the related areas of choice may lie entirely within the

Figure 11   Levels of policy system

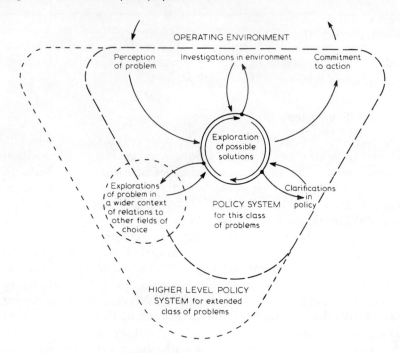

*
Exploration of a problem in a wider context sometimes takes the process into a
higher level of policy system, extending the bounds of both the operating environment
and the constituency, and opening up interfaces with further contiguous policy systems.
However, the higher level policy system may often be more 'open' in that policy
guidelines are likely to be less specific when relating to more complex levels of problem.

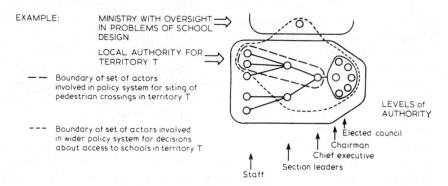

EXAMPLE: MINISTRY WITH OVERSIGHT⟶
                IN PROBLEMS OF SCHOOL
                DESIGN

                LOCAL AUTHORITY FOR⟶
                TERRITORY T

— —   Boundary of set of actors
       involved in policy system for siting of
       pedestrian crossings in territory T

- - -   Boundary of set of actors involved
         in wider policy system for decisions
         about access to schools in territory T

action space of the policy system dealing with the immediate decision situation; but even if this is not so, it is often possible to identify a higher level of policy system, concerned with a more broadly defined action space, within which the wider set of problems remains contained. This possibility is illustrated in *Figure 11*, so making the general point that the definition of a policy system is by no means an absolute matter; rather, it can be treated by the analyst as a matter of convenience in relation to any chosen focus of concern. In the kind of situation indicated in the diagram, the decision to extend the exploratory process across the boundary with another contiguous policy system can be regarded as translating it into the context of an extended policy system within which the original system can be regarded as a sub-system. The extended definition of the action space will mean corresponding extensions both to the operating environment and, possibly, to the constituency. At the foot of *Figure 11*, these concepts are illustrated by means of a simple example of a decision problem about the siting of a pedestrian crossing, perceived as within the action space of a departmental policy system concerned with local traffic issues, which becomes translated to the context of a wider inter-departmental policy system because of a perceived connection to a problem of extending a school in that neighbourhood. In such a case, it may be that the process is extended from a corporate to an inter-corporate context, because of the involvement of one or more actors from a controlling government department.

Higher levels of policy system are generally likely to be more 'open' in the sense that it becomes more difficult to agree policy guidelines that match the complexity of the action space. Uncertainties of our three basic classes may therefore arise once more at this higher level of the exploratory process, often in an accentuated form where it is much more difficult to agree on appropriate forms of response. This may lead towards still further extensions in the context of the process of strategic choice; and the higher the level of policy system to which the exploratory process is extended, the greater will be the tendency towards administrative separation between those levels of exploration which lead directly towards action commitments and those which are of a broader co-ordinative or *planning* form. The planning process now acquires its own internal momentum based on the anticipatory perception of problems, and is no longer so directly geared to the perception of problems where there are urgent pressures for commitment.

In a differentiated planning process of this kind, the same variations of style can become apparent as at a lower level of

Figure 12   Interaction between policy systems

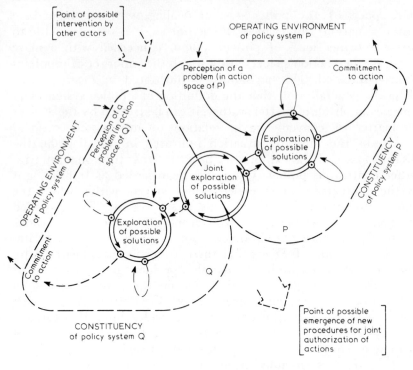

Point of possible intervention by other actors

OPERATING ENVIRONMENT of policy system P

Perception of a problem (in action space of P)

Commitment to action

OPERATING ENVIRONMENT of policy system Q

Perception of a problem (in action space of Q)

Exploration of possible solutions

Joint exploration of possible solutions

Exploration of possible solutions

CONSTITUENCY of policy system P

Commitment to action

P

Q

CONSTITUENCY of policy system Q

Point of possible emergence of new procedures for joint authorization of actions

⊸ = Points of discretion in 'switching' of the exploratory process into alternative channels within a DECISION NETWORK for a field embracing the concerns of both policy systems

A DECISION NETWORK can be described in terms of
— CLASS OF PROBLEMS   FIELD OF DECISION *

— Set of all ACTORS potentially contributing to decision-making for this class of problems (whether or not acting within a relevant policy system)   ACTORS

— PATTERNS OF RELATIONS among these actors (including relations within and between policy systems)   RELATIONS AMONG ACTORS

* Sometimes but not invariably corresponding to the action space of a policy system

decision-making. At this level, the relative prominence given to investigatory, policy-clarifying, and co-ordinative modes of behaviour may depend not only on personal or professional biases, but on broader institutional commitments. For instance, the management of a corporate agency may become committed to a programme-budgeting structure which places much stress on the reduction of uncertainties in policy through attempts to formulate clear hier-archies of objectives. Another organization might have invested in a computerized management information system through which to project forward trends in its operating environment, so that the 'planning style' of the organization becomes one of more systematic adaptation to those trends; while yet another may become dedicated to the pursuit of long-term strategies to which every conceivable type of decision must be related. Organizational commitments to the ideal of comprehensiveness in any one of these directions tend to lead towards commitments to comprehensiveness in other directions; and thus to mask the essential element of *selectivity* in deciding how far, and in what ways, the exploratory process should be extended when confronting different types of decision situations. Also, such commitments may lead towards an over-estimation of the extent to which planning can be contained within the corporate framework, or even within that of a recognisable policy system at the inter-agency level.

Inevitably, the problem must be confronted of co-ordinative or *connective* planning across the boundaries between contiguous policy systems which are virtually independent, in that each operates through a distinctive set of policy guidelines with little or no common ground between them. This style of planning has not been given much attention in the development of formal techniques and procedures, in contrast to the styles based on passive adaptation to predicted trends on the one hand or a more conscious search for corporate objectives on the other. However, it is a style that is frequently encountered in practice, and with which we shall be much concerned in the following chapters.

Interaction between policy systems

The situation of interaction between two distinct policy systems in exploring solutions to a set of related problems is illustrated in *Figure 12*, through a model in which the two systems appear as mirror images of each other. If it were possible to extend the model into three dimensions, then it could be used to demonstrate a situation involving any number of contiguous policy systems pivoting around the common axis. In the absence of consensually based policy guidelines, the situation veers towards the kind which Lindblom, in his book *The Intelligence of Democracy* (1965) has described as 'partisan mutual adjustment'. Lindblom is concerned in particular with the indentification of different modes of co-ordination in decision-making, and contrasts the situation of partisan mutual adjustment with that of 'central co-ordination', which is dependent on the existence of some decision-maker who is in a 'symmetric control relation' with every other member of the set of decision-makers concerned. 'Partisanship', on the other hand, is defined by Lindblom in terms of the absence of mutually acceptable criteria to govern adjustments between the decision-makers; it therefore compares with our situation of interaction between separate policy systems.

Lindblom's analysis proceeds to identify various sub-categories of partisan mutual adjustment, in which a key determinant is the level of reciprocity in the mutual adjustment process. Among the more symmetrical modes of adjustment, Lindblom identifies various forms of negotiation; this analysis has been recently adapted and extended by Power (1974a), who is especially interested in the distinction between those simple forms of negotiation or bargaining that are not embedded in ongoing social relationships, and those,where current concessions can be traded off against expected future obligations.

Within any process of interaction of the kind indicated in *Figure 12*, there may of course be variations in the extent to which the actors in each policy system gain mutual benefit, either in the short term or in the context of their ongoing relationships, by engaging in exploration of related problems across the interface between them. The pay-off in terms of gains in confidence in decision-making, or the political risks involved in any activation of communication channels between them, may be of a different order for the actors in one policy system than for those within the other. Furthermore, it is more likely to be the exception than the rule that the relationships between the respective sets of problems are identified simultaneously within each system, or that the same degree of urgency is attached to the selection of an appropriate response. The two decision processes shown in *Figure 12* will therefore typically be out of phase; and some difficult judgements may be faced on both sides in deciding at what times and in what ways the processes of mutual adjustment should be initiated.

In *Figure 12*, representing the simplest case of interaction between two contiguous policy systems, several different points are identified where judgements may be faced relating to the 'switching' of the decision process into alternative channels. At one level, judgements about how and when to initiate investigatory or policy-clarifying activities, or to enter into processes of mutual adjustment with other actors, are faced during the internal processes of exploration within each policy system. However, the same types of judgement may also be faced at a higher level, during the processes of joint exploration across the interface between the policy systems. Judgements must also be faced, at either level, about the points at which the exploratory process should be steered towards conclusive outcomes, enabling commitments to specific lines of action to be selected.

The more complex the set of problems under review, the more likely it will be — as we shall see in later chapters — that commitments to action will emerge *incrementally*, relating only to those problems where the pressures for decision are currently most insistent, while explorations continue into other related problem areas. In the case of *Figure 12*, it will be noted that — in the absence of any machinery for central authorization of actions selected within the two policy systems P and Q — any eventual commitments to action will be entered into separately and, in a situation of continuous bargaining, may not necessarily emerge in a synchronized manner.

Patterns of incremental commitment and of continuous exploration may of course also evolve within the setting of a single policy system, where those within it must contend with a complex set of related problems within their own action space. In such circumstances, we may still encounter several different levels of the exploratory process, involving different sets of actors, as in the case illustrated in *Figure 11* where the process is shown as translated from a lower level to a higher level of policy system. However, the more complex the action space becomes, the more difficult it may be to establish acknowledged policy guidelines to meet all contingencies; therefore, the more the reality of the situation may approximate to that of interaction between separate policy systems or — in the terms of Lindblom — to a process of co-ordination through partisan mutual adjustment.

Actors in a planning process

Processes of incremental commitment to action, coupled with continuing exploration of possible future actions, tend in their turn to lead towards patterns of problem perception in which the operating environment is actively scanned in order to identify future problems, as opposed to a more passive stance of reacting to specific stimuli as they arise. In this way, any planning activity, seen as part of a process of strategic choice which originates in a perception of difficulties in taking specific decisions, comes to be increasingly directed towards future problem situations the further its focus of concern extends. The value of such an activity, however, still remains ultimately dependent on the extent to which it is found to be helpful in reaching specific commitments to current action, which may appear of a highly incremental nature when seen from the wider planning perspective.

As *Figure 12* suggests, a process of anticipatory perception of problems through a scanning of the operating environment may create a role for actors who stand outside those policy systems directly concerned. Even though such actors may not be concerned directly in the selection of specific courses of action, they may nevertheless be able to intervene and play a catalytic role in the exploration of future patterns of alternatives, by suggesting problem linkages which might not otherwise be apparent. Such actors may include politicians as well as professional planners and other types of expert; and one of the most significant kinds of judgement which they face may concern at what time and in what manner to make an intervention in a process within which they may have no explicitly defined role to play.

In recognising the possibility of external inputs along the central axis of *Figure 12*, we must also consider the possibility of direct outputs of commitment to action along this same central axis. However, such a possibility can usually be expressed in another way because, wherever there exists some actor who is in a symmetric control relationship to actors in both policy systems, he can himself be regarded as an actor in both policy systems and therefore to be in a position to contribute directly to the decision outputs of each. One example would be the case of the representative of a central ministry who exercises direct financial or other sanctions over the actions of adjoining local authorities. However, a different type of decision output along the central axis, which cannot be treated in this way, arises where independent local authorities or other bodies come together to form joint agencies with prescribed powers to take actions in certain specified fields. This becomes a case of what Stringer has termed a *multi-organization*, defined as a union of parts of separate organizations formed by the interaction of individuals in pursuance of some common task (Stringer, 1967). More specifically, in so far as any mutually accepted policy guidelines may be agreed for the performance of this task, the resulting joint agency can be seen as a special case of a single policy system, which we shall call a *multi-organizational policy system.*

We shall encounter instances where such a multi-organizational policy framework is agreed upon because of a recognition of the difficulties of working entirely through processes of partisan mutual adjustment; this means in effect that a situation which begins like that in *Figure 12* becomes transformed into one more like that of *Figure 11* through a deliberate act of organizational design. However, such a joint policy system may not always be very effective, especially where the actors must remain responsive to conflicting constituency interests. As in the more structured type of conflict situation analysed by writers in coalition theory (Riker, 1962), rational but partisan decision-makers will only be concerned to maintain a sufficient level of coalition to maximize their expected gains. In future chapters, we shall encounter instances where a multi-organizational policy system becomes ineffective as a direct vehicle for decision-taking, because its nominal authority is over-ridden by more direct sectional pressures acting on its component parts.

Exploration through decision networks

Were it not for problems in terms of graphics, the basic model of *Figure 12* might well be elaborated to indicate multiple levels of problem exploration within any one policy system, as well as processes of joint exploration across the boundaries with other contiguous policy systems, each of which might itself be highly complex in terms of organizational structure. To cope with the complex patterns of communication which may arise between decision-makers in such circumstances, a further concept will now be introduced, which can be regarded as complementary to that of the policy system. This is the concept of the *decision network*, regarded as an open network of communications among people acting either within policy systems or across the interfaces between them, which may influence the commitments reached in any specified class of decision problems. A decision network is therefore a form of social network in the sense used by social anthropologists (Barnes, 1954, 1969; Bott, 1957), in that it is shaped by patterns of relations in which each individual has developed a communication linkage with at least one other member of the network, but is not necessarily fully connected to every other member. However, the characteristic of a decision network by which we shall distinguish it from other forms of social network is that the channels which connect it are identified as those along which communications can pass relating to choices between alternative actions within some specified field of decision. More generally, we can talk of an open 'planning network' which connects the actors concerned in many different fields of decision.

However, the term 'decision network' recognizes that the value of all planning activity ultimately rests on its influence upon commitments to action in more specific fields of choice. The concept of a planning network will remain a nebulous one unless a view of its overall texture can be formed by the mapping of a number of interconnected decision networks, built up by looking outwards from certain selected fields of decision.

For the analyst, the most practical approach is therefore to focus on one field of decision at a time, seeking to discover the ways in which choices of action become explored through processes of communication within a decision network. Given a focus of this kind, it will often be possible at an early stage to identify a central complex of role relationships which has most of the attributes of a distinctive policy system. Within such a central 'core', opportunities for internal communication are likely to be especially well developed; and the analyst is likely to discover one or more individuals, or perhaps a collegial group, who occupy nodal positions in the wider decision network. It is likely to be at such nodal points that judgements will be faced most frequently as to which further links in the network to activate in the course of exploring particular decision problems, and how much information should be transmitted through these links. Such judgements have been described by Power (1971b, 1974a) as *reticulists* (literally, networking) judgements, and we shall later be much concerned with the ways in which they are made in practice. Each of the points identified in *Figure 12* at which the course of a decision process can be 'switched' can now be regarded as a point where some form of reticulist judgement may be faced. In particular, judgements may be called for as to how far people outside the bounds of a policy system should be regarded not only passively as elements in the operating environment, but more actively as members of contiguous policy systems who can be consulted directly in the process of exploring solutions to the problem currently in hand, through the activation of existing links in a decision network or the forging of new ones. To make matters more complicated, there may well be people — with whom channels of communication are well established — who may be consulted directly as members of contiguous policy systems in relation to some types of problem, but not in relation to others where it may be deemed sufficient to predict their intentions in a more passive way.

Motives in the activation of decision networks

In later chapters, we shall develop the argument that the use of reticulist judgements in activating, fashioning, re-fashioning, and —

occasionally — creating decision networks provides one of the most important dynamic elements of the decision-making process, especially in complex fields of public policy such as the management of local and regional change. Such decision networks can best be described as *aformal*, in that they may embody both formal and informal elements, and it is important for the actor upon whom the more crucial reticulist judgements depend to appreciate how both types of element may be utilized.

It is important, however, to avoid slipping into the assumption that reticulist judgements will invariably be made in such a way as to exercise an entirely benign influence on decision-making (or for that matter an entirely malign one), whether such an assessment is made from a partisan viewpoint or from some more abstract conception of the public interest. Any actor will behave in accordance with some set of personal, professional, or institutional motives in deciding how to utilize the decision networks in which he operates, and in selecting what information to transmit through any channels that he may activate. Some people may be motivated, or may be constrained by personal attributes, to avoid the activation of extensive links outside their more formal lines of authority, so minimizing the risks that politically delicate information may ultimately reach destinations over which they have little or no control. Others may be more inclined to take risks in this direction, in the expectation of achieving commensurate gains.

The politician, the administrator and the professional expert may all be inclined towards different styles of reticulist activity, through temperament as well as through their differing roles in the decision process, and these styles may in turn be related to differences in their perception of relevant sources of uncertainty. For instance, the inclination of the specialist will often be to respond to uncertainty in decision-making through engaging in elegant forms of investigation into aspects of the operating environment that catch his professional interest or are likely to enhance his status. As pointed out by Crozier (1964), wherever a particular source of uncertainty is seen to be salient, the expert who is able to reduce that uncertainty possesses power over other decision-makers. In the course of his explorations, such an expert may wish to discuss his problem widely within a network of professional colleagues which extends far beyond the boundaries of the organization that employs him; and, in so doing, he may be regarded as posing threats to the influence of the politicians to whom he is accountable.

Partisan motivations may not only enter into choices as to whether or not some channel of communication should be activated, but also into the processes by which information about the range of possible solutions to a problem is transmitted through any such channel. Where the range of possible solutions is recognized to be wide and complex in structure, a decision-maker will often feel unable to present to other parties more than a limited set of alternatives; he may also be tempted to present these in such a way as to gain ready acceptance of one favoured solution, through a judicious selection of supporting evidence. The question of *transmission of variety* in the exploration of complex fields of decision has been explored by Scharpf (1972), who identifies the extremes of 'positive co-ordination' — in which people interact freely in the open discussion of alternative actions — and 'negative co-ordination', in which each actor merely puts forward a specific proposal for action and tests whether or not it arouses any adverse reactions. Although Scharpf recognizes that the more interactive mode of co-ordination is likely to be considerably more effective than the more negative or reactive mode, he argues that it can also be much more costly and may therefore have to be concentrated within selected 'clusters' of policy concern within a governmental system.

As we shall argue later, skills in selecting which channels of communication to activate at a given point in a decision-making process, and also how much information to transmit through them, must be regarded as crucial factors in the manipulation of decision networks. However, it must be recognized that such judgements are always likely to be made with some degree of partisanship wherever any set of actors is working within a political environment in which there exists a possibility of conflict between the motivations of individuals or between the constituency interests to which they must be responsive.

The analysis of problem structure

In order to apply the general approach that we have now developed to specific fields and instances of decision-making, we shall require to move between two complementary forms of analytical method. The first will concern the analysis of relationships between actors and agencies in the decision process. For this purpose, we shall rely on the two related concepts of the policy system and the decision network, applying these to specific sets of relations between local and regional agencies which we shall represent within the framework of the institutional base-map presented in *Figure 7*. The more specific graphical conventions which we shall use in this analysis will be introduced progressively in the course of the next few chapters.

The other form of analytical method which we shall use relates not to the structure of relations between actors and agencies, but to the structure of relationships between the decision problems with which they deal. We shall approach the analysis of problem structure through the method of *Analysis of Interconnected Decision Areas* − normally abbreviated to AIDA (pronounced in two syllables as opposed to the three of Verdi's opera). This method was originally developed within IOR as an aid to the management of design processes in architecture (Luckman, 1967) and engineering (Morgan, 1971). Its application in the field of public planning was first suggested by Friend and Jessop (1969), and it has since been used as a practical aid to decision in several local authorities (CES, 1970). In the chapters that follow, we shall be primarily concerned with using the method to describe and interpret observed processes of decision, rather than to suggest how those processes might be modified. Ultimately, however, we shall wish to speculate about the applicability of such methods as practical aids to communication within an inter-agency planning context.

The central concept of AIDA is that of a *decision area*, defined as a dimension of choice within which at least two alternative and mutually exclusive courses of action, or *options*, can be postulated. Where a decision problem has a complex structure, then it may be more realistically represented not as a single decision area, but as a set of several related decision areas. This can be set out diagrammatically as an arrangement of nodes on a 'decision graph', with links joining those pairs of decision areas that are believed to be structurally related.

An example of the simplest form of decision graph, known as the *strategy graph*, appears in *Figure 13*. The diagram goes no further than to link those pairs of decision areas between which some form of direct inter-dependence is believed to exist, without attempting to specify the nature of the interdependence more exactly. The inclusion of a link merely expresses a belief that preferences between choices in the two decision areas taken together may not necessarily correspond to preferences in each area considered independently, given the same set of assumptions about actions in all other decision areas. For instance, taking the practical examples of decision areas indicated at the foot of *Figure 13*, it might be thought to be less costly − or perhaps more convenient in terms of temporary disturbances to traffic flow − to build a new road on one or other of two alternative alignments if the scheduled start on a nearby redevelopment project were delayed; furthermore, perhaps such a delay might be thought to exclude certain options of alignment on technical design grounds.

Figure 13 Use of the strategy graph in analysis of problem structure

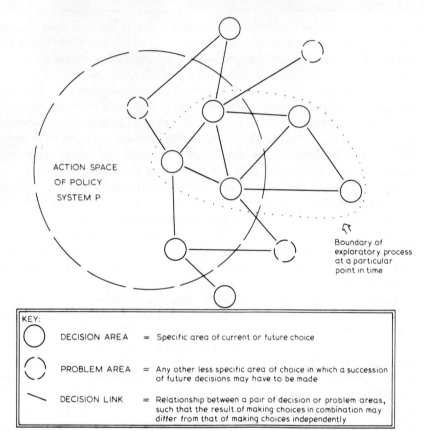

ACTION SPACE
OF POLICY
SYSTEM P

Boundary of
exploratory process
at a particular
point in time

KEY:

DECISION AREA = Specific area of current or future choice

PROBLEM AREA = Any other less specific area of choice in which a succession of future decisions may have to be made

DECISION LINK = Relationship between a pair of decision or problem areas, such that the result of making choices in combination may differ from that of making choices independently

SOME EXAMPLES OF DECISION AREAS:

— Choice of line for new road from X to Y
— Choice of use for vacant plot of land adjoining X
— Choice of whether or not to start redevelopment project Z in current financial year
— Choice of working for policy statement on car parking in town T

SOME EXAMPLES OF LESS SPECIFIC PROBLEM AREAS:

— Future choices of agency for housing construction in town T
— Future choices of response to applications for purchase of properties in prospective redevelopment area

As *Figure 13* indicates, not all the types of decision which are connected in the strategy graph may lend themselves to formulation as specific decision areas which can be considered to have been fully resolved once a specific option has been chosen. Some nodes in the graph may therefore be described more loosely as 'problem areas', or fields of future choice in which a succession of commitments may be required over the course of time. Any such problem area may of course form part of the action space of a recognised policy system, so that choices within it may be constrained by commitments to particular policy guidelines. Sometimes, however, when a public commitment is demanded to an explicit policy statement for some field at a specific point of time — for instance, the field of car parking in a particular town — then (as in the example quoted in *Figure 13*), the choice of wording for that policy statement may best be regarded as a specific decision area which is duly resolved once the statement is published.

In the chapters that follow, we shall be especially concerned with situations where interconnected decision areas or problem areas fall within the fields of responsibility of different organizations or policy systems. In such circumstances, a decision-maker acting within one system may see a linkage between decision problems as significant in terms of his own appreciation of the situation, or of impact on his own constituency interests, whereas another decision-maker might perceive this linkage to be either unimportant or non-existent. By exposing such differences in perception in a systematic way, the device of the strategy graph has been found to provide an aid to communication which helps to transcend the barriers between different professional frames of reference. For this reason, we shall make use of strategy graphs from time to time in the chapters which follow, in such a way as to relate the observed processes of communication within decision networks to the structural relationships of the problems with which the decision-makers are confronted.

Relationships between options

As an exploratory process moves through different channels of a decision network, so its focus is likely to change. In the example of *Figure 13*, it is supposed that the focus of exploration has temporarily closed in upon a set of five of the more specific decision areas within the strategy graph, as a result of judgements made about their relative levels of importance or urgency, about the degree of linkage between them, and about the costs and benefits associated

Figure 14   Use of the option graph in exploring possible solutions

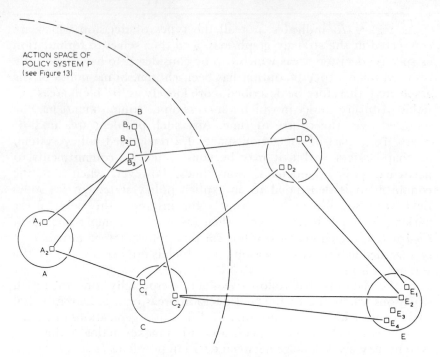

ACTION SPACE OF
POLICY SYSTEM P
(see Figure 13)

In the option graph, the linkages represent OPTION BARS indicating an assumption that certain combinations of options should be ruled out as incompatible, either on technical or policy grounds. Such assumptions can be challenged and modified in the course of the exploratory process with any decision to initiate communications with other actors in contiguous policy systems.

In such a situation, it will sometimes be useful to take the process of structural analysis one stage further. This can be done by expanding all or part of the strategy graph into the more detailed form of an *option graph*. In this, the alternatives believed to be available in each decision area are spelt out as a set of exclusive options; sometimes, these can be enumerated exhaustively, but in other cases it may only be practicable to define a set of options that is representative of a more continuous range of choice. Any pair of options from related decision areas which are believed to be mutually incompatible — or to have such disadvantageous effects when taken in combination as to be ruled out of further consideration — can then be indicated in the option graph through more specific forms of linkage known as *option bars*. As an illustration, *Figure 14* takes the set of five linked decision areas picked out in *Figure 13* and expands it to show two or more discrete options within each. These are supposed to be linked by a total of ten option bars, through which certain combinations of pairs are eliminated as unacceptable on either technical or policy grounds. Given such information, methods of logical analysis can be used to enumerate the total set of feasible solutions that is available. In this illustration, the effect of the option bars is to reduce the set of available combinations within the five decision areas from a theoretical total of ninety-six to a selection of only eleven in which none of the incompatibilities are violated.

In practice, it is often difficult to pursue the structural analysis of complex planning problems at this more detailed level without introducing a series of assumptions about which the analyst may be far from confident. The range of options available in some of the decision areas may not be easy to define as a discrete set; it may be found difficult to specify unambiguous constraints of the kind that can be expressed through option bars; and it may therefore become necessary to resort to more intuitive methods in reaching an appreciation of the variety of acceptable solutions. However, it will be helpful for us at this stage to pursue a little further the comparatively well-structured illustration of *Figure 14,* in order to demonstrate an important general point; that perceptions about the structural characteristics of problems can exercise a crucial influence on the dynamics of a decision process in which the interests of two or more different decision-makers may be involved.

Figure 15 Effect of decisions on flexibility of future choice

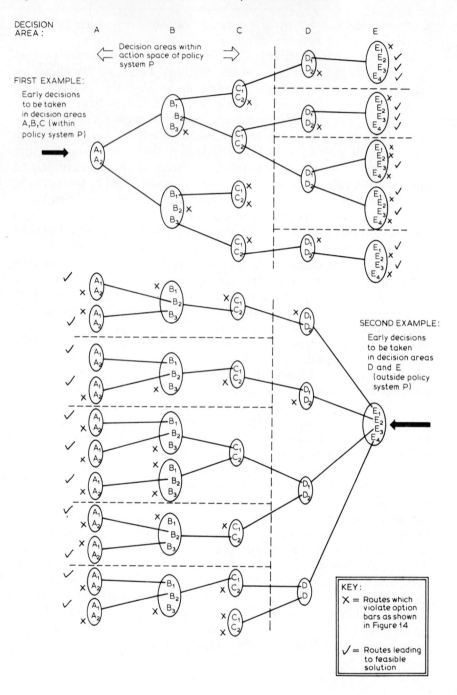

DECISION AREA: A   B   C   D   E

← Decision areas within action space of policy system P ⇒

FIRST EXAMPLE:
Early decisions to be taken in decision areas A,B,C (within policy system P)

SECOND EXAMPLE:
Early decisions to be taken in decision areas D and E (outside policy system P)

KEY:
X = Routes which violate option bars as shown in Figure 14

✓ = Routes leading to feasible solution

Problem structure and political relations

In *Figure 15*, the eleven feasible solutions to the problem defined by the option graph of *Figure 14* are set out in the form of what is sometimes called a 'decision tree', first on the supposition that early decisions are required only in the three decision areas *A, B,* and *C,* and second on the contrary assumption that it is decisions in areas *D* and *E* that must be taken first. Also, it will be supposed in both cases that the two decision areas *D* and *E,* which do not come within the action space of policy system *P,* both fall within the action space of the same contiguous policy system *Q*.

In the first situation, it will be noticed that any set of actions selected within *P* has the effect of pre-empting the future choice in decision area *D* for those within the other policy system, unless the particular combination $A_1 B_2 C_2$ is chosen. Also, certain choices within *P* are more restrictive than others in terms of the room for manoeuvre left within decision area *E*. In the situation where it falls to the actors within *Q* to make their choices first, there are similar effects on the freedom of manoeuvre of those in policy system *P*; indeed, constraints are imposed even within decision area *A* which is only indirectly linked to *D* and *E*. The two situations illustrated are only extreme examples of a whole range of possibilities that exist for taking incremental decisions within the two policy systems, either separately or jointly, with a corresponding range of implications for the future freedom of manoeuvre of each.

The importance that either set of decision-makers attaches to the preservation or restriction of freedom of manoeuvre, either for themselves or for the other party, will depend on an appreciation – often highly intuitive – of what consequences might arise from each line of action left open, and of how the advantages or disadvantages of such consequences should be balanced against each other. In such an appreciation, a crucial consideration may be the political costs or benefits which may be associated with any deliberate attempt either to constrain the options of the other decision-makers, or to leave them room to adapt to future contingencies.

In *Local Government and Strategic Choice*, the question of flexibility of future choice was approached mainly through the concept of 'robustness' as defined by Gupta and Rosenhead (1968). A 'robust action set' was defined as a set of immediate actions selected from a set of related decision areas, which scored highly in terms of a count of the number of future opportunities for choice remaining open in the longer term. For instance, applying this kind of criterion to a situation requiring incremental choice in decision area A in *Figure 15*, the more robust action would be a commitment to option A_1, because it leaves a range of nine total solutions open to those in policy systems P and Q, as opposed to the two solutions available under option A_2. However, our present concern with decision-making in the inter-agency context makes it important that we should seek to look somewhat beyond the concept of robustness as thus defined, so as to be able to consider questions of flexibility of future choice from the vantage points of several different actors or agencies.

This we shall seek to do by reference to a distinction between the action space and *opportunity space* of a policy system, with the latter embracing all decision or problem areas over which those acting in the policy system can range while participating in wider exploratory processes with others. Decision situations within both the action space and the opportunity space can be represented analytically through the device of the strategy graph and also, at least in the more well structured situations, through the more specific device of the option graph. However, in a continuing process of strategic choice, it must be expected that the form and boundaries of the opportunity space may be considerably more difficult to define than those of the action space; they may be continually expanding, contracting, or shifting ground in an amoeba-like fashion, as new opportunities for initiative in the mobilization of aformal decision networks are recognized and seized, or as new obstacles are encountered in terms of limited information capacity or potential damage to valued political relations.

Just as the action space of a policy system can be considered a part of a wider opportunity space, so the latter can be considered a part of a still wider 'indeterminacy space', embracing also those uncertainties in the operating environment that relate to the future actions of other parties with whom opportunities for direct communication have not been identified. Within this wider space, the boundaries of the 'opportunity space' can be enlarged as opportunities are recognized for bargaining with actors whose future intentions would otherwise have had to be treated as uncontrolled variables; in this way, uncertainties of the operating environment are converted into uncertainties in related choices. As we shall see, it is never easy for a decision-maker to appreciate clearly the boundaries of his future opportunity space; but we shall nevertheless find the concept a useful one when it comes to understanding decision problems of much greater complexity than that represented in *Figures 14* and *15*.

The approach and its application

The framework for analysis which we have now presented makes much use of the imagery of the network, on the one hand to indicate linkages between problems, and on the other hand to discuss linkages between decision-makers. However, the two types of network have to be recognized as relating to different forms of structural analysis, the one concerned with the structure of relations between situations of choice and the other to the structure of relations between people acting in roles. To avoid possible confusion, we have deliberately used the term 'graph', in its formal mathematical sense, when referring to networks of relations between problems rather than people. For a similar reason, we shall restrict our use of the term 'system' to systems of relationships between decision-makers, and have avoided its use in describing relationships between the problems with which they deal.

In dealing with questions of problem structure, we have tried to maintain some logical distinctions in our use of the terms 'area', 'field', and 'space'. Whereas the concepts of the decision area (and the less specific problem area) are used in mapping the structure of the problem situations which lie ahead at a specific point in time, the term 'field of decision' is used more generally to describe any class of problem situations without adopting any particular time perspective. Meanwhile, the terms 'action space' and 'opportunity space' are intended to describe the changing scope for manoeuvre of specific sets of decision-makers over the course of time.

In the chapters that follow, and especially in those of *Part II*, we shall wish to move as freely as possible between the two sets of convention᾽ which are used to give a spatial mapping of relations between people and between problems respectively, in order to understand the various practical situations of inter-agency planning which we shall encounter. The crucial link between our two forms of spatial representation will be the series of general schematic models with which we opened this chapter, starting with those which show a process of decision-making embedded within the social context of a policy system (*Figures 8* and *9*), and moving on to one that introduces three classes of uncertainty in relation to any specific current decision problem (*Figure 10*). This leads us on to some models of a process of strategic choice, which may either be contained within a single policy system – possibly extended as in *Figure 11* – or may reach across the interface between policy systems whose interaction is governed more by processes of partisan mutual adjustment than by acknowledgement of common policy guidelines, as in *Figure 12*. It is from this point on that our series of schematic diagrams becomes inadequate to describe the rich variety of alternative ways in which a planning process may evolve. Therefore, the concept of a decision network is introduced, seen as a form of social network which finds its driving force in pressures to arrive at more acceptable decisions within some particular field. This leads on to a discussion of the opportunities for manipulating decision networks, bringing in the concept of reticulist judgement. Finally, the concepts of the strategy graph and option graph are introduced as aids to the exploration of complex problem situations, and to the description of the ways in which their structure may change over time.

In the following chapters, our concern will be especially with processes of *connective planning* which transcend the boundaries of individual corporate agencies, viewed within our general conceptual framework of planning as a process of strategic choice. Indeed, we may bring together many of the definitions presented in this chapter in a formal statement which defines our field of interest as follows:

> Opportunities for *connective planning* arise when people acting in *policy systems* which operate in particular *action spaces* are stimulated by their perceptions of *decision problems* to activate and shape *networks of decision-makers* in order to *explore alternatives* and from among them select *commitments to action*.

We shall be especially concerned in later chapters, to identify more clearly the characteristics of a co-ordinative or connective style of planning — not because we believe that this style should be given absolute precedence over other styles of planning which can be more easily pursued within a single corporate framework, but because we believe it has not yet received the attention it deserves at the analytical and methodological level, especially in view of its widespread influence on public sector decision-making.

Although we may encounter many instances of inter-corporate planning even in the private sector of organized decision-making — where the ethos of free competition imposes limits on its social acceptability — we shall find inter-agency planning processes becoming much more pervasive in the public sector, where the ethos of co-operation is widely accepted (if not quite so widely practiced), and at the interfaces between public and private bodies. Indeed, we may now define the field of public planning a little more formally in the following terms:

> Public planning is the domain of all processes wherein people acting on behalf of publicly accountable agencies take part in the

exploration of patterns of related choices which are of recognized concern to more than one constituency of public or private interest.

Our emphasis on publicly accountable agencies directs attention in particular to governmental bodies. However, it may be noted that other organizations such as trade unions, chambers of commerce, or indeed individual commercial firms may also be regarded, in differing degrees, as publicly accountable to their respective constituencies of members or shareholders. The distinction between 'public' and 'private' decision-making may best be related not so much to organizational form as to Sir Geoffrey Vickers's distinction between 'political' and 'market' choice (1965); that is, the distinction between choices in which a decision-maker is acting on behalf of others and those where he is acting essentially on his own behalf.

It should be noted that the definition of public planning as presented above does not necessarily imply that all participants are acting on behalf of publicly accountable bodies, and are therefore primarily concerned with public choices in the sense indicated above. As we shall see, public planning often extends to include exploratory processes at the interfaces between public and private interests. However, we shall note in conclusion that our definition does serve to exclude any processes of bargaining in which only private interests are involved. Also, we shall note that some of the planning activities of public agencies may be regarded as purely of a private nature, where these do not impinge significantly on more than a single constituency. For instance, the process whereby a state enterprise plans the replacement of some specialized piece of technical equipment might, in some circumstances, be regarded as having no significant impact other than in terms of internal economy of operations, and therefore as being purely a matter of 'private planning' for the enterprise concerned.

Essentially, it is the need for adjustment between different constituencies of public interest, and between matters of public and private concern, that generates the demand for those activities that we have described as within the domain of public planning. Consequently, politics must be regarded as an inescapable, and indeed a potentially creative, element in the public planning process.

3 A regional perspective

The West Midlands region

Most of our analyses in the chapters that follow will be set in the land-locked West Midlands region of England. Among the ten regional sub-divisions of Great Britain identified earlier in *Figure 3*, the West Midlands is one of the least well defined in terms of natural boundaries; nor has it as strong an identity as some other regions in terms of distinctive cultural traditions. However, the region, as defined for economic planning purposes, does possess a certain cohesion in that much of it lies within the sphere of influence of the largest metropolitan centre of England outside London – the city of Birmingham, with a population of approximately one million. Together with a cluster of adjacent industrial towns known collectively as the Black Country, Birmingham forms part of a continuous conurbation within which roughly half the total regional population of some five million are concentrated. The economy of the conurbation is based on a variety of specialized metal-working and engineering activities which developed rapidly during the nineteenth century, with many mutual linkages between them. During the twentieth century, the motor industry has gradually become a dominant employer, though increasingly vulnerable to external market influences and recurrent industrial disputes.

The Birmingham overspill problem

The problem with which we shall be concerned in this chapter is one which has dominated the planning of the region's development for several decades; that of bringing about a controlled dispersal of population and employment away from the conurbation, and especially from the congested central areas of Birmingham, to selected locations within the adjoining counties. This problem has become generally known as that of Birmingham 'overspill', even though it has been increasingly argued that this should be considered as only one aspect of a wider problem concerned with the guidance of regional pressures of population growth and economic change.

In this chapter, we shall be concerned especially with a period of some fifteen years from the end of the Second World War in 1945, by which time the overspill problem had acquired a new note of urgency. The city's stock of housing was considerably depleted by war; much of what remained was in poor physical condition; and there was a long waiting list of families seeking low-rent municipal accommodation. Also, there was a national commitment to post-war reconstruction, with a particular emphasis on improving living conditions within the major cities.

Our focus on this historical period will serve two purposes. Ultimately, it will provide a background for the more forward-looking discussion in Chapter 14 of subsequent trends in the development of planning processes in the region, from which we shall be concerned to formulate some more general pointers for the future evolution of arrangements for inter-authority co-ordination. In a more immediate context, this chapter will explain the regional setting for the commitment in the early sixties to expand the small town of Droitwich, some thirty kilometres south-west of Birmingham, as one practical step towards coping with the Birmingham overspill problem. It is this particular scheme that will provide the focus for much of the analysis that follows of specific issues encountered in the management of local and regional change.

Agencies and interests

A simplified map of the administrative structure of the West Midlands region appears in *Figure 16*. This indicates only those upper tier local authorities with a strategic responsibility for guiding the physical disposition of population and other activities within the region; however, the picture is complicated by two sets of boundary changes during the period with which we shall be concerned in this

Figure 16   Main planning authorities in West Midland region

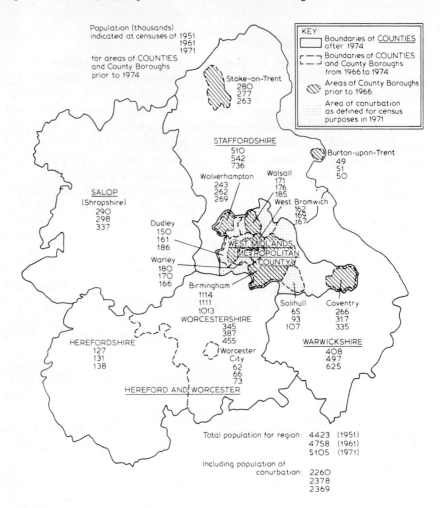

Population (thousands)
indicated at censuses of 1951
1961
1971

for areas of COUNTIES
and County Boroughs
prior to 1974

KEY:
Boundaries of <u>COUNTIES</u>
after 1974
Boundaries of COUNTIES
and County Boroughs
from 1966 to 1974
Areas of County Boroughs
prior to 1966
Area of conurbation
as defined for census
purposes in 1971

Stoke-on-Trent
280
277
263

STAFFORDSHIRE
510
542
736

Burton-upon-Trent
49
51
50

Wolverhampton
243
262
269

Walsall
171
176
185

West Bromwich
162
169
167

SALOP
(Shropshire)
290
298
337

Dudley
150
161
186

Warley
180
170
166

WEST MIDLANDS
METROPOLITAN
COUNTY

Birmingham
1114
1111
1013

Solihull
65
93
107

Coventry
266
317
335

WORCESTERSHIRE
345
387
455

WARWICKSHIRE
408
497
625

HEREFORDSHIRE
127
131
138

Worcester
City
62
66
73

HEREFORD AND WORCESTER

Total population for region: 4423   (1951)
4758   (1961)
5105   (1971)

Including population of
conurbation: 2260
2378
2369

and later chapters. First, in 1966, a review of boundaries throughout the region led to the merger of a number of adjoining towns in the Black Country area into five larger units. Along with the town of Solihull to the south-east of Birmingham, these were granted independent status as County Boroughs, involving marginal losses of territory on the part of the administrative Counties of Staffordshire, Warwickshire, and Worcestershire. Another more radical change followed in 1974 when — under the general reorganization of local government in England — a new Metropolitan County Council assumed strategic planning powers over the whole area of the conurbation, together with an adjoining area stretching eastwards to Coventry. Also, the County Boroughs in other parts of the region lost their independent status at this time, while the administrative Counties of Worcestershire and Herefordshire were amalgamated.

The focus of this chapter will be primarily on relations between the City Council of Birmingham and the three adjacent County Councils of Staffordshire, Warwickshire, and Worcestershire. Historically, it was these four units, as local planning authorities, which were to be most closely and continuously involved in the problems of regional overspill. As will be seen later, however, there were several other local authorities which were subsequently to play a role as either exporters or importers of population; and in any forward-looking perspective, the new West Midlands Metropolitan County must be expected to introduce a new and highly significant influence.

In *Figure 17*, the agencies most directly involved in the earlier attempts to cope with the Birmingham overspill problem are plotted within the format of the institutional base-map which was introduced at the end of Chapter 1. Apart from the four dominant local planning authorities, the public agency most directly involved was the Ministry of Town and Country Planning, which in 1951 became absorbed within the Ministry of Housing and Local Government, later in its turn to be absorbed within the Department of the Environment. In this chapter, we shall follow the conventions established in *Figure 5* and refer simply to the Land Planning Ministry. The role of this ministry will emerge as that of exercising a degree of central co-ordination over the planning activities of the various local authorities within the region. Sometimes, it was able to play such a role more actively or more effectively than at other times; at all times, its freedom of action was constrained by problems of adjustment at the interface with other government departments, including the Treasury as the channel for central control over all competing claims for expenditure from the national taxation accounts.

Figure 17   Main organizations concerned in planning of overspill in West Midlands, 1948-59

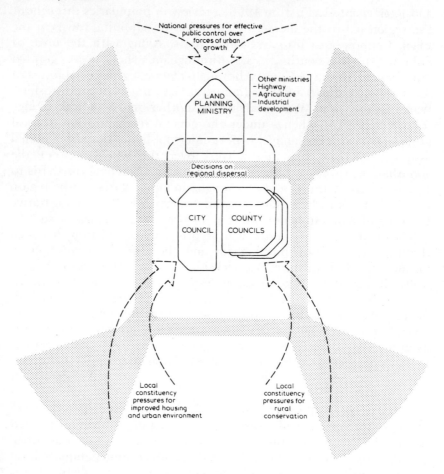

Each of the five main agencies identified in *Figure 17* carried a primary accountability to a different local or national constituency, making it subject to different forms of community pressure. Some of the pressures bearing most directly on the issue of Birmingham overspill are identified around the periphery of the diagram. In Birmingham's case, the dominant demands in the post-war years were for the provision of new housing to meet the needs of its expanding population, and for the clearance of unfit housing, with accompanying improvements to the more oppressive features of the urban environment which the citizens had inherited. In the case of the three County Councils — and especially in the case of Worcestershire — one salient demand was for the conservation of countryside and of historic county towns, underpinned by fears about the effects of disrupting established patterns of community life. The demands coming to bear on the Land Planning Ministry were especially related to the priorities of post-war reconstruction, and the dissatisfactions that had built up with the lack of central control over the forces of urban growth in the immediate pre-war years.

These various pressures were of course accompanied by continuing demands on each type of agency to economize in their use of financial and other scarce resources, while both the urban and rural local authorities were also required to be responsive to wider pressures to maintain the economic viability of the communities to which they were accountable.

Within each of the three Counties, there was a somewhat different range of constituency pressures and interests to be kept in mind. The most receptive to the accommodation of overspill population was Staffordshire, a comparatively industrialized County which included several urban communities where the injection of new population, employment opportunities, and public investment through the reception of overspill could be regarded with equanimity or in some cases enthusiasm; while the least receptive was Worcestershire, where there was a long history of resistance to successive proposals for the peripheral expansion of Birmingham.

In terms of party political control, the three County Councils tended to be dominated by Conservative and Independent members, with the Labour party a more significant force in Staffordshire than in either Warwickshire or Worcestershire. In Birmingham, control was to pass from Conservative to Labour in 1952, back to Conservative in 1966, and again to Labour in 1972 — in keeping with a well-documented tendency for voting at local elections to reflect reaction against the party in power nationally as much as any assessment of purely local performance. There is little evidence that these changes

in political control made much practical difference in relations with
the Counties over overspill. Indeed, some representatives of County
interests were to express to us the opinion that relationships were, if
anything, a little less difficult at times when the City was of different
political colour to the Counties, because the future actions of the
city authority then became more predictable. In terms of the
classification of uncertainties introduced in the previous chapter, this
opinion implied that in these circumstances the County actors
recognised at least a marginal reduction in the level of those
uncertainties concerning the city's intentions in related fields of
choice.

This observation supports the view that the interests of the various
public agencies involved in the Birmingham overspill problem
diverged not so much because of the known policies of their
controlling groups, but more because of the differing sets of
constituency interests with a bearing upon those policies. Of course,
the picture of constituency pressures presented in *Figure 17* involves
a degree of over-simplification, as indeed does any attempt to define
the 'interests' of any public authority as if it were a cohesive
purposive body. In reality, each such authority must be regarded as
an assembly of actors and departments concerned in the provision of
different public services, each influenced by its own internal set of
professional orientations and personal value commitments.

Resources and constraints

In pursuit of their respective interests, each of the agencies involved
in the Birmingham overspill problem had at its disposal certain
resources in the shape of legal powers, opportunities to mobilize
finance and professional skills, and means of influencing or obstructing the actions of other bodies. Such resources were by no means
immutable; indeed, any proposed solution to the overspill problem
could itself be expected to alter their distribution between the
major parties. Not only would any planned movement of population
and industry demand financial investments from the various parties
in proportions yet to be determined; also, it would have the effect of
modifying the taxable base of each of the local authorities
concerned.

The legal powers of the various local agencies to influence the
movement of population and industry in the post-war years rested
primarily on the comprehensive Town and Country Planning
legislation introduced in 1947. This piece of legislation designated all
County and County Borough Councils as Local Planning Authorities,

with powers to exercise detailed control over all changes of land use within their boundaries, subject to a requirement that they should prepare and publish comprehensive development plans to indicate their policies for land zoning and other related matters. Such plans would be open to objection from any interested party, and would only become operative upon the approval of the Land Planning Ministry, which was also to provide a source of appeal for any private interests refused permission to develop by the Local Planning Authority.

Thus, the Local Planning Authorities were equipped with significant powers of control over the actions of private developers, while themselves constrained to act within a context of approved policy guidelines requiring the endorsement of the central Land Planning Ministry. Meanwhile, a more positive means of intervention in the planned movement of population and industry had been provided by the New Towns legislation of 1946, empowering central government to initiate major programmes of urban development within specially designated local areas. These provisions were quickly invoked to designate a ring of New Towns some way outside the fringes of the London conurbation, where the most urgent problems of urban congestion were then to be found. In these initiatives, the accent was on construction of public housing for tenants nominated by the city, accompanied by balanced provision of employment and social opportunities.

Although the New Towns legislation provided an important practical means of influencing the dispersal of population and industry from the conurbations, it tended to make heavy demands on the national capacity for public investment and was therefore to be employed only sparingly outside London in the early post-war years. In other major cities, the local authorities were themselves faced with the onus of finding sites within or beyond their boundaries on which to build through their established powers for the provision of public rented housing.

The City Council of Birmingham, as the largest housing authority outside London, proceeded quickly in the post-war years to build up a large-scale programme of compulsory clearance of unfit housing, coupled with construction of new rented accommodation within the city boundaries. However, if the local authority's resources were to be deployed directly in the planned movement of population out of the city, it was necessary either for the City Council to apply for planning permission to undertake development of its own within the Counties, or for it to reach voluntary agreement with other local housing authorities by which they could themselves build dwellings to accommodate tenants nominated by the city.

Within the Counties, however, the main powers of housing development lay not with the County Councils themselves but with the local County District Councils. If they were to be given an incentive to provide overspill housing then it was clear that they would require the inducement of financial and possibly also technical assistance from other more powerful sources, whether central government, the exporting city, or the County Council for their area; and such provisions were not to become available until the introduction of the Town Development Act of 1952, a measure which will be discussed more fully later. However, for our purposes, it is necessary to start the story of inter-agency relationships in the West Midlands some years before this particular means of influencing planned movement of population became available.

The initiation of a planning process

The recognition of the Birmingham overspill problem as an important focus for regional planning can be traced back at least as far as the war-time activities of an informal study group known as the West Midlands Group on Post-War Reconstruction and Planning. However, the first major public initiative was the decision of the Land Planning Ministry shortly after the end of the war to commission a special study of the problem from two independent planning consultants: Sir Patrick Abercrombie, who had already been responsible for the Greater London Plan which had recommended a regional overspill strategy based on New Town developments, and a West Midlands expert by the name of Herbert Jackson.

The results of the consultants' exploratory study were submitted to the Ministry in the form of a draft edition of a *West Midlands Plan* covering the conurbation and the three adjoining Counties (Abercrombie and Jackson, 1948). Among the main conclusions was that a total of some 130,000 to 140,000 people from the conurbation should be accommodated in the surrounding counties over the next fifteen years. The consultants proposed that this growth should be located at some distance from the conurbation, in accordance with the principle of the 'Green Belt' which had already been adopted in the London area as a means of checking peripheral growth. In practice, this meant that a protective ring of predominantly rural land was to be maintained around the present boundaries of the conurbation by means of deliberately restrictive policies for development control.

Beyond this Green Belt, Abercrombie and Jackson suggested that the population surplus could be absorbed entirely through the

expansion of existing towns, without any need for designation of
New Towns as in the South-East. For all possible centres of
expansion in the region, studies were made of levels of unemployment, physical constraints on expansion, and other factors, and a list
of seventeen towns was produced where significant increases of
population might be considered, with or without accompanying
industrial development. One of the smaller of these was Droitwich in
Worcestershire, with a target increase from 5,850 to 10,000
inhabitants.

Although the consultants were explicit in expressing their preference for such a solution over the alternatives of higher density
redevelopment in the conurbation on the one hand and peripheral
growth on the other, their report expressed a sensitivity to the
limitations of planning technique and availability of information
under which they had been forced to work. Specifically, it was
acknowledged that 'unknown factors in the equation' might create
pressures for departures from their recommendations, either through
higher densities of urban housing or through limited peripheral
incursions into the Green Belt. That Abercrombie and Jackson
regarded their plan as by no means a definitive solution is suggested
by the opening words of their Introduction: 'Assuming this work to
be merely an incident in a continuing processs .... '. Thus, their
report was put forward as by no means the inflexible 'master plan'
which both the title and the planning philosophy of that period
might suggest.

The Land Planning Ministry had commissioned this study in order
to provide a policy background for the preparation of local authority
development plans, and so it remained for the Ministry to take
soundings among local planning authorities and other bodies in the
region before making any firm commitments to the promulgation of
official policy guidelines for land use within the region. When such
official guidelines were finally published in the form of a memorandum some two years later, the consultants' general recommendations
for a strategy of constraining peripheral growth and expanding
existing towns were accepted in principle. However, commitment to
the suggested scale of overspill movement from the conurbation was
deferred in the light of new uncertainties over projections of
population growth, and also a wish to examine further the
possibilities for increasing residential densities within the conurbation itself. Thus, important sources of uncertainty were identified,
concerning both the Ministry's operating environment and also
future intentions in related areas of choice.

In its recommendations for immediate action, the Ministry

proposed that initial development should be concentrated in some, but not all, of the proposed reception towns. The selected towns included four in Staffordshire which were then short of labour and thus might accommodate residential development without any need for supporting industry, together with a further five towns — including Redditch and Droitwich in Worcestershire — where a combination of housing and industrial development was envisaged.

As a means of following through their proposals, Abercrombie and Jackson had made a recommendation in their report for the establishment of 'a new kind of regional authority'. However, the Ministry in its memorandum found itself forced to concede that this proposal had attracted strong antipathy among the local planning authorities on whose powers any such authority could be expected to impinge. The local authorities had argued that they already had adequate machinery for co-ordination in the form of a joint regional conference which had been convened to debate reactions to the West Midlands Plan, and which had subsequently appointed a 'Technical Committee' for continuing liaison between the Chief Planning Officers (or equivalents) of Birmingham and the three surrounding Counties.

The Ministry was therefore forced to concede that the machinery for continuing co-ordination of dispersal within the region should be multi-organizational rather than institutional in form. The result was that each local planning authority remained able to reserve its position on land-use policy within its own boundaries, subject only to the minister's powers to demand amendment of development plan proposals prior to their formal endorsement. The machinery of the 'Technical Committee', with formal accountability to a 'joint conference' of local planning authorities, was in fact to prove durable over time, although sometimes of limited effectiveness; and some subsequent developments in its role and resources will be traced later, in Chapter 14.

Moves towards mutual adjustment

In giving a cautious official welcome to the proposal for continuing co-ordination through the Technical Committee, the Ministry urged that the authorities should 'proceed with all possible speed' in formulating their more detailed planning proposals. However, the evidence of the following decade was that the processes of mutual adjustment were cautious and often highly partisan, most notably in the case of relations between Birmingham and Worcestershire.

In formulating their own reactions to the West Midlands Plan,

Worcestershire County Council had cast doubt on the overall targets proposed for population overspill, commenting that 'the needs of agriculture and industry' would make it very difficult to provide space within the County for absorption of more than 20,000 people from the conurbation. When it came to the submission in 1952 of the County's first Development Plan, a population increase of 50,000 over the County as a whole was predicted, including allowances for natural growth and voluntary migration; and it was argued that such a target was generally consistent with Ministry policy on the overspill issue. However, at that time, agreement was still to be reached on the planned level of total overspill from the conurbation, on its distribution between the Counties, on the particular towns where it was to be received, and on the ways in which financial and other responsibilities might be divided under the recently published provisions of the Town Development legislation.

Some of these uncertainties began to diminish when it was agreed through the Technical Committee that the three Counties should adopt a joint working target of 2,000 overspill houses a year 'as a basis for further negotiation' with District Councils. Subsequent bargaining led to a proposal that this figure should be sub-divided between Staffordshire, Warwickshire, and Worcestershire in the proportions 625:975:400, after the Worcestershire representative had successfully argued that the County was the least well placed for the early initiation of town development schemes.

Within Worcestershire, the next step was for County officials to meet elected representatives of the District Councils for the two towns of Droitwich and Redditch where early overspill development had been proposed, in order to discuss the financial and administrative provisions of the Town Development Act. It was explained that the legislation provided for new forms of housing subsidy from the national exchequer and the exporting city, together with powers for the compulsory acquisition of land at values relating to its expected future use in the absence of the proposed development – an important factor in a land market where planning controls had led to sharp differentials in value between agricultural and urban areas. Further, there was provision for Ministry help towards any necessary water and sewerage investments, although no specific formula was as yet mentioned.

The Act allowed a considerable range of options so far as the choice of agency for development was concerned. It was possible for the main executive responsibility to be taken on either by the exporting city or by the receiving town. Alternatively, the County Council for the receiving area could take on this role; or various forms of 'joint venture' could be considered involving two or more of these parties. However, the field of mutual adjustment between Birmingham and Worcestershire was at this time to focus more closely on questions of finance than of agency, with the City Council maintaining a reluctance to make more than the minimum contribution towards the cost of overspill housing that was required of it under the Act. In response to this position, Worcestershire and the other two County Councils put forward the argument that such a level of contribution, amounting to £8 a year for each house in the receiving district occupied by an overspill tenant, was becoming increasingly inadequate at a time of rising construction costs and interest rates.

In the light of this financial impasse, the Treasurers of all three Counties joined forces to present arguments both to Birmingham and to the Ministry for further contributions towards the costs of overspill, speaking not only on behalf of their own Councils but also on behalf of their component districts. Meanwhile, in Worcestershire, the Planning Department was able to publish some tentative proposals for five-year building programmes at Droitwich and at Redditch, but was also able to argue that any further progress towards local commitment must depend on the negotiation of more realistic levels of financial aid. During this time, the Technical Committee continued to meet periodically, but its focus became largely confined to the discussion of particular cases of industrial firms displaced by redevelopment within the conurbation, which might be steered towards relocation in one or other of the prospective overspill towns in the region.

Thus, a state of stalemate persisted throughout most of the nineteen-fifties. Meanwhile, within Birmingham the problems of maintaining momentum in the City's programme of clearance and re-housing were becoming increasingly acute, as the reserves of available land within the city boundaries began to near exhaustion. Again, during this period, the Counties were faced with new demands to settle the areas for their respective sectors of the West Midlands Green Belt, in accordance with a Ministry policy directive of 1955. These two sets of pressures gave new urgency to the question of whether or not the negotiation of overspill agreements was to be regarded as providing a realistic and complete alternative to the peripheral growth of the conurbation. In Worcestershire, the County Clerk received a letter from the Ministry during 1958, urging early decisions to facilitate the implementation of the County's prospective overspill schemes. With an increased sense of immediacy, therefore the County staff began to address themselves to the processes of local consultation and detailed technical appraisal which formed a necessary prerequisite to the conclusion of viable town expansion agreements.

A case for decision

In early 1959, however, an event took place which was to change the whole context of relationships between Birmingham and Worcestershire from one of cautious moves towards mutual adjustment to one of public confrontation. Within the City Council the conclusion had been reached that the momentum of the municipal housing programme could no longer be maintained without some peripheral expansion in the fairly early future; accordingly, Birmingham submitted outline applications under the Town Planning Act for the development of an area of some ten square kilometres at Wythall, just outside the southern boundary of the city. About two-thirds of this land lay within Worcestershire and the remainder in Warwickshire, and it was proposed that the city would build some 14,000 houses to accommodate its own municipal tenants, with the effect of increasing the population of the area from 8,000 to 54,000. A proportion of the land concerned was to be developed for industry and playing fields, and it was envisaged that in due course steps would be taken to incorporate the site as a whole within the administrative boundaries of the city.

Formally, it was necessary for Birmingham to submit four separate planning applications to the two District Councils concerned, which at that time exercised local powers of development control by delegation from the two County Councils. However, it was clear that some major issues of regional policy were involved, and so the Land Planning Ministry exercised its discretion to 'call in' the application for central determination. As a prelude to decision, it was decided that a public inquiry should be held. At this inquiry objections were presented by both Worcestershire and Warwickshire Counties, by the two local District Councils, and by a number of more local interests including residents' associations, sports clubs, farmers, and other land owners. The City and the two County Councils were all legally represented – in the case of Warwickshire, by a future Lord Chief Justice – while a number of chief officers and elected representatives were called upon as witnesses. Further technical evidence was called by two independent associations – the Town and Country Planning Association and the Midlands New Towns Society – both appearing at the inquiry as independent pressure groups concerned with the wider issues of regional policy. These two groups were subsequently to join together in sponsoring an edited transcript of the proceedings under the title of *The Wythall Inquiry: A Planning Test-Case* (Long, 1961).

Although the problem for decision, as presented by Birmingham, concerned only one restricted site, the debate during the ten days of the inquiry was to range over a much wider set of inter-related issues of regional policy, exposing sharply many of the underlying pressures, uncertainties and conflicts. The edited transcript of the inquiry provides an important source document for understanding the major issues at stake. In the following two sections of this chapter, it will be used as a foundation for, first, analysing the process of public inquiry as a means of exposing issues and uncertainties, and second, interpreting the problem that faced the inspector in terms of weighing up the ways in which so diverse a range of uncertainties could in practice be managed.

The exposures of issues and uncertainties

In the edited transcript, no attempt is made to follow the actual sequence of submission, evidence, and cross-questioning at the inquiry; rather, the proceedings are covered in five main chapters, each of which is concerned with one major area of debate. The first chapter outlines the central issue of Birmingham's application to develop at Wythall, while those that follow focus on the wider issues of:

- Birmingham's population trends and housing construction policies
- issues of industrial and office location
- land-use policies, with special reference to the Green Belt
- accommodation of overspill through new and expanding towns.

It was submitted by Birmingham that their application for building at Wythall did not impinge significantly on such wider issues; rather, it was a case of once-and-for-all adjustment to Green Belt boundaries which would allow the city to cope with its immediate shortage of housing land, while at the same time satisfying all the city's demands for new municipal housing sites over the next twenty years. However, the County representatives contested this restricted view of the problem to be explored, and in so doing opened up to challenge a wide range of underlying assumptions, relating to long-term trends in population and employment within the conurbation and the extent to which these could be influenced by different aspects of central and local government policy.

Thus, the inquiry was to expose many latent uncertainties

impinging on the apparently simple question of whether Birmingham's proposals for Wythall should be accepted or rejected. These
uncertainties concerned not only aspects of the operating environment, but also matters of policy and assumptions about future
intentions in a variety of related fields of choice. The range of
uncertainties exposed can be illustrated most clearly in relation to
the most central piece of quantitative information submitted by
Birmingham in support of its case: a 'municipal housing balance
sheet' in which it was calculated that the houses to be built at
Wythall would be exactly sufficient to cover their estimated
deficiency of rented housing accommodation over the next twenty
years. This balance sheet is reproduced in graphical form in
Figure 18, together with an indication of the major assumptions
upon which doubt was cast at the inquiry.

One estimate which was contested more vigorously than most was
that of the 19,500 families expected to be added to the municipal
housing waiting list as a result of natural increase of population. On
behalf of Warwickshire it was argued that the order of uncertainty in
this estimate alone could be such as to invalidate the case for
short-term development at Wythall. Not only was there much
uncertainty about interpretation of the available statistical data and
about underlying trends in voluntary migration; there were also some
important questions of housing policy to be challenged. To what
extent, it was asked, had Birmingham a statutory obligation to make
publicly rented housing available to newly formed families according
to the particular criteria of need that were adopted in the immediate
post-war years? Also, how far was Birmingham justified in its
scepticism over the likely contribution of overspill schemes now
under negotiation, when the outcomes of these negotiations were
largely dependent on how far the city and other public agencies were
willing to adopt financial or other policies through which they might
be helped to succeed?

Through questions such as these, a rich variety of inter-related
decision problems began to come to light, involving fields of
individual or joint discretion for a number of different public
authorities, including some that were not directly represented at the
inquiry. In *Figure 19*, an attempt is made to illustrate the broad
structure of these related fields of decision through the conventions
of the strategy graph as described in Chapter 2, in so far as this
structure can be inferred from the transcript of the inquiry. Each of
the decision fields shown in the diagram appears as a subject of
contention in one or other of the five chapters of the transcript
which cover respectively the topics of the proposal itself, of city

Figure 18   Birmingham municipal housing balance sheet

Estimates as presented at Public Inquiry into
application to develop site at Wythall, 1959

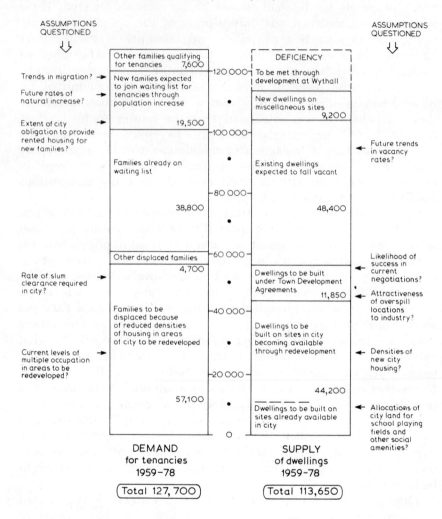

ASSUMPTIONS
QUESTIONED
⇩⇩

Trends in migration? →

Future rates of
natural increase? →

Extent of city
obligation to provide
rented housing for
new families? →

Rate of slum
clearance required
in city? →

Current levels of
multiple occupation
in areas to be
redeveloped? →

Other families qualifying
for tenancies   7,600

New families expected
to join waiting list for
tenancies through
population increase

19,500

Families already on
waiting list

38,800

Other displaced families
4,700

Families to be
displaced because
of reduced densities
of housing in areas
of city to be redeveloped

57,100

DEFICIENCY

To be met through
development at Wythall

New dwellings on
miscellaneous sites
9,200

Existing dwellings
expected to fall vacant

48,400

Dwellings to be built
under Town Development
Agreements
11,850

Dwellings to be
built on sites in city
becoming available
through redevelopment

44,200

Dwellings to be built on
sites already available
in city

ASSUMPTIONS
QUESTIONED
⇩⇩

← Future trends
in vacancy
rates?

← Likelihood of
success in
current
negotiations?

← Attractiveness
of overspill
locations
to industry?

← Densities of
new city
housing?

← Allocations of
city land for
school playing
fields and
other social
amenities?

120 000
100 000
80 000
60 000
40 000
20 000
0

DEMAND
for tenancies
1959–78

(Total 127,700)

SUPPLY
of dwellings
1959–78

(Total 113,650)

housing policy, of industry, of the Green Belt, and of prospective overspill solutions. However, it is only in the case of six or seven of these decision fields, such as that of response to Birmingham's application for development at Wythall, that the field can be regarded as a decision *area* in the more restricted sense of Chapter 2, in that the problems of choice within the field can be fully resolved by commitment to a specific option at a specific point in time.

In the submission of Birmingham, the proposals for Wythall were to be judged primarily as a means of coping with the city's immediate difficulties in maintaining the pace of its programme of slum clearance and municipal housing construction; in other words, the relevent fields of decision were mainly those concentrated towards the top of *Figure 19*. It was argued that the city had a statutory responsibility to re-house families displaced through slum clearance and also to make provision for the housing needs of a proportion of new families; the resulting issue of 'statutory' overspill could be seen as separate from the longer-term issue of 'planning' overspill, seen as relating to the total level of outward migration for use as a target in land-use planning. It was argued that the Wythall development would neither increase the city's total population nor involve any long-term loss of recreational land; indeed, accessibility to open spaces could eventually be increased by a strategy whereby new school playing fields would be gradually opened up on cleared land within the city, as opposed to being sited within the Green Belt. In the meantime, it was claimed that the availability of land for housing at Wythall would provide the 'extra square on the chess board' which was essential to allow the pace of housing clearance and relocation of occupiers to be maintained.

At the inquiry, the County Councils contended that the distinction between 'statutory' and 'planning' overspill was far from absolute. The field of exploration therefore gradually became extended much more widely, as indicated in *Figure 19*, to embrace such questions as the case for flexibility in drawing Green Belt boundaries, the longer-term targets for growth of population and industry in the city, the total level of overspill need, and the prospect of meeting this entirely through Town Development agreements. The issue of industrial growth led on to the argument by Birmingham that the City Council could not reasonably be expected to act as agent for execution of national policies for location of industry, in a situation where appropriate controls were directly available to central government through the agency of the Industrial Development Ministry (at that time, the Board of Trade).

Thus, the fields of decision emerging at the inquiry included

Figure 19   Field of exploration at Wythall inquiry in 1959

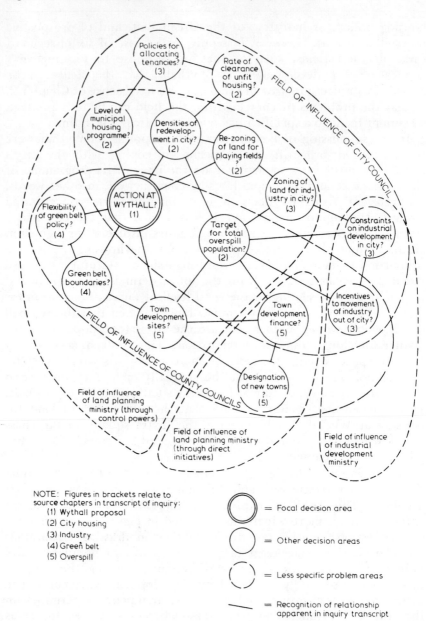

NOTE: Figures in brackets relate to
source chapters in transcript of inquiry:
  (1) Wythall proposal
  (2) City housing
  (3) Industry
  (4) Green belt
  (5) Overspill

◎ = Focal decision area

◯ = Other decision areas

( ) = Less specific problem areas

—— = Recognition of relationship
        apparent in inquiry transcript

several in which the responsibilities of different local authorities overlapped, and also several that involved powers of authorization or direct intervention by government departments. In many of these fields, the same broad conflicts of policy tended to recur; for instance, the balancing of the economic viability of Birmingham against the environmental gains from constraining peripheral growth, and the balancing of the immediate pressures for new housing in Birmingham against the longer-term principles of regional planning which many felt to be at stake.

Although the process of inquiry continually tended to force the debate about possible courses of action into wider terms of reference than those with which the inspector was officially concerned, the conventions of quasi-judicial procedure proved to be better adapted to the exposure of issues and uncertainties than to the systematic exploration of sets of feasible solutions. It therefore remained for the presiding inspector to do what he could after the close of the inquiry to weigh up the possible courses of action which might be considered, both in the more immediate future to deal with the specific issue posed at Wythall, and in the longer term to deal effectively with the various sources of uncertainty that had now been so publicly exposed.

The management of uncertainty

It was some two months after the close of the inquiry when the inspector submitted his final report, and a further six months before the Minister was to announce his decision. This interval could be explained by the convention within central government that a range of departmental interests should be consulted before a final policy judgement could be made.

The inspector's report, as quoted in an appendix to the inquiry transcript (Long, 1961), contains a number of passages that reveal clearly the problems that faced him in identifying the salient uncertainties of the situation, in assessing their relative importance, and in deciding what should be done about them. For instance, paragraph 440 of the report reads as follows:

'It is my own view that the mathematical assumptions are necessarily so inexact that the Corporation are not justified in their submission that if they can build exactly 14,050 dwellings at Wythall they will be able to meet their housing commitments for twenty years. On the other hand, they are quite correct in bringing the forecast of natural increase into their calculations. The simple arithmetic is only a way of expressing a complicated problem that

Figure 20 Analysis of sources of uncertainty identified by inspector at Wythall inquiry

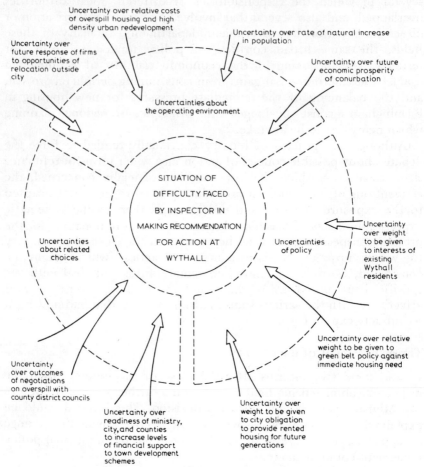

Uncertainty over relative costs of overspill housing and high density urban redevelopment

Uncertainty over future response of firms to opportunities of relocation outside city

Uncertainty over rate of natural increase in population

Uncertainty over future economic prosperity of conurbation

Uncertainties about the operating environment

SITUATION OF DIFFICULTY FACED BY INSPECTOR IN MAKING RECOMMENDATION FOR ACTION AT WYTHALL

Uncertainties about related choices

Uncertainties of policy

Uncertainty over weight to be given to interests of existing Wythall residents

Uncertainty over relative weight to be given to green belt policy against immediate housing need

Uncertainty over outcomes of negotiations on overspill with county district councils

Uncertainty over readiness of ministry, city, and counties to increase levels of financial support to town development schemes

Uncertainty over weight to be given to city obligation to provide rented housing for future generations

NOTE: CLOSENESS OF EACH ARROWHEAD TO CENTRAL CIRCLE REPRESENTS IMPRESSION OF SALIENCE OF THAT SOURCE OF UNCERTAINTY IN INSPECTOR'S REPORT

must be looked at as a whole. I do not think that any other mathematical equation could have produced a fairer expression of the problem and am content to accept the broad picture which it presents. As I have pointed out above, the really debatable figure is that of 11,850 houses to be produced by town development. I have noted also, that the Corporation base their housing need on the figure of 3.2 persons per dwelling although in 1951 they were thinking in terms of 3.77, reducing to 3.5 and in 1956 to 3.4.'

Bearing in mind these implied judgements on the relative importance of disparate sources of uncertainty, together with the doubts about other aspects of the municipal 'housing balance sheet' identified in *Figure 18*, it becomes possible to reconstruct an impression of the relative significance of the salient sources of uncertainty that faced the inspector in formulating his recommendations. Such a reconstruction appears in *Figure 20*, where the various uncertainties are classified broadly according to the three categories introduced in *Figure 10* of Chapter 2 — and where the more salient sources of uncertainty are located at least distance from the central circle representing the focal issue for decision.

The strategy recommended by the inspector for dealing with some of the more salient uncertainties can be appreciated from a reading of his final remarks before presenting his conclusions:

'Some development (at Wythall) will, however, be necessary unless town development can be speeded up. This speeding up depends primarily upon persuading industrialists of the advantages of moving out and upon all the authorities concerned co-operating still more closely to solve the financial problems by an equitable sharing of the burden of cost. If, as the Town and Country Planning Association claim, town development is cheaper than the subsidisation of in-city development, it might prove economical for central government to play a greater part in the matter than it has done so far.'

The judgement arrived at by the inspector was that Birmingham's proposal for development at Wythall should be refused in its present form, although a proposal for more limited development might have to be favourably considered at a later stage. Meanwhile, the feasibility should be explored of meeting the balance of Birmingham's immediate housing need through overspill at promising sites, among which special mention was made of Droitwich, Redditch, Kidderminster, and Coventry. At all these sites, it was suggested that the problems were more organizational than technical; in other words, the uncertainties were more of a type to be overcome by negotiation than by investigatory activities alone. In effect, the strategy proposed for management of uncertainty involved a partial solution only to the problem of the future of Wythall, coupled with steps to reduce the level of uncertainty in related fields of choice through more energetic activation of inter-agency decision networks. The implication of the final line in the above quotation was that this should include renewed attempts by the Land Planning Ministry to negotiate Treasury agreement to a higher level of financial assistance for Town Development schemes, with the support of new evidence on relative costs.

The formal decision authorized by the Minister a few months later largely accepted the recommendations of the inspector, and concluded by proposing that the Ministry should 'now arrange to meet the authorities concerned in order to discuss with them ways and means of accelerating provision of the movement of people and industry out of the city'. Thus, the initiation by Birmingham of its proposal for development at Wythall had finally induced a significant change in the pattern of pressures indicated in *Figure 17*, with the onus now clearly lying with Worcestershire to prove that it could produce viable counter-proposals to peripheral development in the immediate future, coupled with an implied onus on central government to inject fresh resources into the search for locally acceptable solutions. Some of the consequences of the shift in pressures will be followed through in the next chapter, where the focus of analysis turns to the course of local negotiations in Droitwich.

Some general inferences

This chapter has revealed the complex set of relationships between the various problems involved in planning the re-distribution of population and industry in the West Midlands during the post-war years, and has raised many issues which have a direct bearing on our central theme of decision-making across the boundaries of different public authorities.

Nevertheless, any general inferences which can be drawn at this stage can only be of a relatively modest nature. In analysing processes of decision more than ten years after the event, it has been necessary to draw primarily on information assembled from documentary sources, with only limited opportunities to supplement this through discussion with individuals who were directly involved at the time. Under such circumstances, it is not easy to determine with any confidence how far the train of events may have been influenced by the personal attributes of particular politicians or officials, especially where these qualities concern the presence or absence of skills in activating informal decision networks.

However, the existence of an extensive transcript of the Wythall inquiry (Long, 1961) does provide an indication of the way in which a formal public debate between opposing public authorities, each able to marshal considerable legal and technical skills, can provide a means of exposing a wide range of hitherto latent uncertainties. In this instance, the result was that the inspector in charge found himself faced not only with the limited question of casting judgement on a specific application for development, but with a much more complex task of assembling a package of proposals as to the ways in which the more dominant sources of uncertainty might be managed; in this sense, his position became a pivotal one in the activation of decision networks at both central and local government levels.

The edited transcript of the inquiry itself concludes with some broad interpretive comments, in the form of a 'Planning-Political Postscript' by David Eversley, then Honorary Secretary of the Midlands New Town Society but writing purely in a private capacity. In this postscript, Eversley criticizes both the performance of central government at the inquiry and that of the local authorities. He argues that it was unrealistic for the ministry to assume a passive role of impartial arbitrator between opposing interests in a case where important issues of national policy were involved. So far as the local authorities were concerned, Eversley singles out Birmingham for particular criticism because of an apparent lack of co-ordination between the evidence of the Chief Officers responsible for housing and for planning matters, together with the apparent state of dependence on their judgements demonstrated by the elected leadership of the Council.

Relating these comments to the mapping of organizational relationships presented in *Figure 17*, the picture becomes one of a complex pattern of interactions between different policy systems, both at the inter-organizational and to some extent the intra-organizational level. Of course, the formal authorizing powers of the Ministry did provide some element of central control over the actions of the local authorities, and indeed the search for solutions to the problem at regional level was largely initiated by the Ministry's original sponsorship of the Abercrombie and Jackson study. However, the conclusion of this study left something of a vacuum in terms of any continuing capacity to explore relationships between decision problems within the region. While it was hoped by some that the Joint Technical Committee of the Planning Authorities

Conference could have formed a nucleus for the evolution of a new multi-organizational policy system, the Committee's field of exploration in fact became constrained to comparatively narrowly defined issues, because of the reluctance of the individual authorities to relinquish their future bargaining power through concessions on finance or other major points of policy.

It is hardly surprising that the effectiveness of 'co-ordination' in such a situation should be inhibited by underlying divergences of constituency interest. However, it is clear from the inquiry proceedings that the structural complexity of the problem was such as to leave an unusual scope for misunderstanding and confusion. Until the various issues were gradually pieced together in the context of the Wythall inquiry, there appears to have been a lack of any framework within which the parties might have worked towards a common appreciation of the structural characteristics of the overspill problem, in order to put into perspective the divergences between their respective assumptions and policy positions, let alone work towards mutually acceptable solutions. Such a framework was revealed to be deficient even within the single corporate setting of the City Council; a point which prompts speculation as to the long-term effects of the explicit institutional separation between housing and strategic planning powers in the new Metropolitan County structure.

As Chapter 14 will indicate, the continuing evolution of regional processes in the West Midlands since the time of the original Wythall inquiry was ultimately to bring further infusions of exploratory skill to bear on the overspill issue, through the appointment of a joint local authority Study Team, the establishment of regional offices of government, and the formation of an advisory Council broadly representative of different regional interests. Throughout these changes, the underlying sources of conflict were to persist, and in later chapters we shall return to the question of the challenges which they pose to those who are concerned to bring about innovations in the organization and methodology of regional planning. However, at this stage, our immediate concern is to appreciate the historical background of one particular town development scheme; and, to this end, we must now begin to introduce some rather more local parties to the inter-agency planning processes.

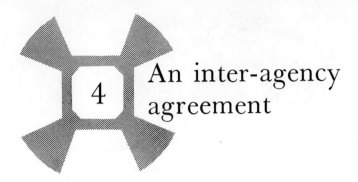

4 An inter-agency agreement

A problem of negotiation

In this chapter, our focus narrows from the regional perspective of the Birmingham overspill problem to the more local problems of negotiating a Town Expansion Agreement at Droitwich. The period of most intensive activity in this field extends over the three or four years immediately after the holding of the Wythall inquiry in 1959, which helped to give the search for local agreement a new degree of urgency.

The agencies with which we shall be most directly concerned in this chapter include two of those that have already figured prominently in our analysis of regional processes — Birmingham City Council and Worcestershire County Council. They also include a third local authority — Droitwich Borough Council — of very much smaller size but nevertheless of primary significance, both as 'receiving' housing authority for overspill and as the channel for direct representation of the collective interests of the existing local community.

Before discussing the relationships between these three bodies in the new context, it will first be necessary to introduce briefly some of the more significant features of the town of Droitwich and the interests represented by the elected Borough Council at that time. Subsequently, the reorganization of local government has had the

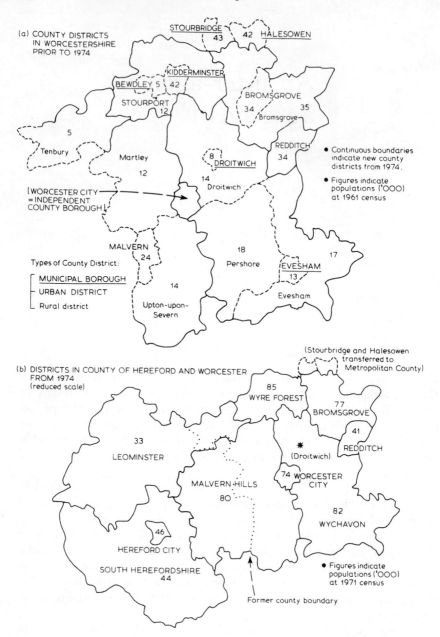

Figure 21   Droitwich in its county setting

(a) COUNTY DISTRICTS
    IN WORCESTERSHIRE
    PRIOR TO 1974

STOURBRIDGE 43   42 HALESOWEN

KIDDERMINSTER
BEWDLEY 5   42
STOURPORT 12

BROMSGROVE
34   35
Bromsgrove

5
Tenbury

Martley
12

8 DROITWICH
14
Droitwich

REDDITCH
34

• Continuous boundaries
  indicate new county
  districts from 1974.

• Figures indicate
  populations ('000)
  at 1961 census

[WORCESTER CITY
= INDEPENDENT
COUNTY BOROUGH]

MALVERN
24

Types of County District:

┌ MUNICIPAL BOROUGH
├ URBAN DISTRICT
└ Rural district

14

Upton-upon-
Severn

18
Pershore

EVESHAM
13

17

Evesham

(b) DISTRICTS IN COUNTY OF HEREFORD AND WORCESTER
    FROM 1974
    (reduced scale)

(Stourbridge and Halesowen
 transferred to
 Metropolitan County)

85
WYRE FOREST

77
BROMSGROVE

33
LEOMINSTER

41
REDDITCH

*
(Droitwich)

MALVERN HILLS
80

74 WORCESTER
   CITY

82
WYCHAVON

46
HEREFORD CITY

SOUTH HEREFORDSHIRE
44

• Figures indicate
  populations ('000)
  at 1971 census

Former county boundary

effect of reducing this Council from County District to Parish status, most of its executive functions being inherited by a new and larger district embracing also the town of Evesham and some of the County's most productive agricultural areas. Some of the broader implications of this kind of amalgamation for inter-authority decision-making will be explored further in later chapters.

Droitwich and its Council

The administrative map of Worcestershire, prior to its amalgamation with Herefordshire in 1974, is reproduced in *Figure 21*. The Borough of Droitwich can be seen to occupy a central position within the County, being encircled by the much more extensive area of the Droitwich Rural District Council, which served a somewhat larger population prior to the expansion of the town. Despite its independence from the Borough as a separate County District, the Rural District was also administered from a set of offices located within the town itself.

As one of the least populous of the eighteen districts of Worcestershire, Droitwich Borough owed its independent municipal status to historic rather than demographic qualifications, having been granted its original Royal Charter in the early thirteenth century. The history of the town can indeed be traced back as far as the Roman occupation of Britain, when the local discovery of valuable subterranean deposits of salt gave rise to a settlement by the name of Salinae. The exploitation of these salt deposits was to remain the central feature of the economy of Droitwich well into modern times; and indeed the prefix 'Droit', which became attached to the town's Saxon name of Wych during the middle ages, is believed by some to refer to the King's right to tax the output of the local brine springs in return for the grant of a municipal charter.

By the middle of the nineteenth century, Droitwich had become a thriving industrial town whose economy was dominated by the commercial pumping and evaporation of the brine formed by the passage of water over the subterranean salt beds. This method of salt production had however ceased to be economic by the close of the century, leaving a legacy of derelict industrial land close to the core of the mediaeval town, and also a marked liability to subsidence above those areas where the pumping of brine had ceased.

Fortunately for the prosperity of the town, its decline as an industrial centre was accompanied in the late nineteenth century by a growing reputation as an inland watering place. The Droitwich brine baths quickly acquired a national reputation as a centre for the treatment of arthritic complaints, and this led to the development of a small but elegant nucleus of curative establishments, hotels, pleasure gardens, and related amenities. As the cult of the inland spa receded during the twentieth century, the economy of Droitwich fell into a state of relative decline. However, the town remained popular as a residential area for retired people and, increasingly, for those able to contemplate commuting to and from work in the conurbation and other nearby centres of employment.

Thus, after the Second World War, the Borough Council of Droitwich found itself representing the interests of some 6,000 inhabitants, including significant numbers of elderly people and commuters, who tended to share a common concern to maintain the character of Droitwich as a quiet and dignified residential town. This dominant conservatism was largely reflected in the elected membership of the Council; but, at the same time, the local authority found itself facing some severe problems in maintaining viable local services on such a restricted base of population and rateable value. One especially difficult problem was that of financing the replacement of the town's sewerage system, which had become severely overloaded and was beginning to create dangers of flooding and risk to public health, particularly in those parts of the town centre that had sunk in level through the effects of brine subsidence.

Gradually, the problem of sewerage began to place the local Council in more and more of a dilemma. On the one hand, the capacity of the existing system was beginning to place an increasingly severe constraint on any form of residential or commercial development; on the other hand, however, the costs of the investment necessary to modernize it seemed more and more likely to impose an unacceptable burden on the existing local ratepayers, whose annual burden of local taxation was already higher than that of any other district within the County.

Such pressures came to dominate the annual municipal elections at Droitwich. Each May one-third of the twelve directly elected Councillors were required to retire and seek re-election, each candidate being obliged to treat the entire town as his constituency because its size was then insufficient to justify sub-division into electoral wards. The membership of the Council was brought up to a total of sixteen by the indirect election of Aldermen, while, in common with most other Boroughs, a new Mayor was elected each year, usually on a criterion of seniority of service.

It was not until the later sixties that party politics began to emerge openly in the local elections. As the local Labour party began to nominate its first candidates for the Council, some of the existing members began to respond by standing for re-election with official Conservative party support. It was not in fact to be until 1972, in the final annual elections prior to local government reform, that the Labour party was to gain its first three seats on the Council; an event explicable partly in terms of local reaction against the policies of the national government of the day, and partly in terms of the rising electoral strength of the overspill housing areas.

During the period with which we shall be concerned in this chapter, the members of the Borough Council were faced not only with financial and other local pressures from their electors, but also with an external threat to their independent status as a municipality. Following the work of a Local Government Commission, which was then engaged on a review of the main administrative boundaries in the West Midlands, the County Council was itself required to embark on a re-appraisal of District boundaries within its territory, and this could be expected to result in recommendations for amalgamating with neighbouring Rural Districts any Borough Councils whose population base was too limited to allow them to carry out adequately the full range of County District services. This threat provided a further motivation among Council members not to dismiss the idea of planned expansion out of hand; but, as it happened, the boundary review process was to be overtaken by the government decision in 1966 to investigate the opportunities for a much more radical reorganization of local government in England. This process will be described more fully in Chapter 15; in the meantime, it may be noted that even a much expanded town of Droitwich was unable to justify more than 'successor parish' status within a larger County District after the 1974 reorganization, indicated by the second map reproduced in *Figure 21*.

In this and the following chapters, Droitwich Borough Council will be referred to simply as the 'Borough Council'; however, in our more general interpretations, we will not be concerned so much with the historic Municipal Borough form of government, as with the patterns of relationships between city, county, and town interests within an evolving local government structure, through whatever agencies these respective constituencies of interest may be represented.

Relationships between the agencies

As indicated in *Figure 22*, the focus of this chapter is on a process of negotiation between city, county, and borough councils within a context provided by the powers of the Land Planning Ministry to provide assistance to approved Town Development schemes. In this

Figure 22   Main organizations involved in negotiation of town development
agreement for Droitwich, 1959-63

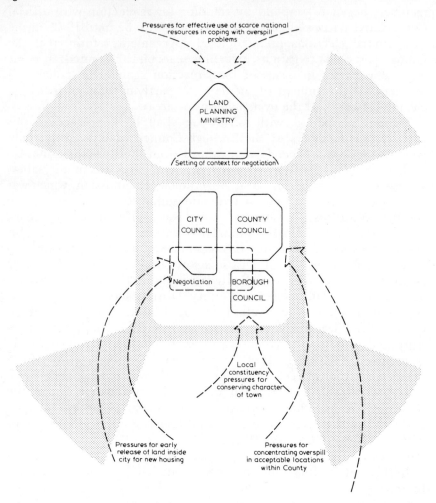

process, the dominant pressures reflected through the Borough Council were concerned with conserving the town's existing character, while also strengthening its viability as a municipal unit; as one public official was to put it, the local representatives 'wanted Droitwich to grow, but nicely'. The interests of the City and County Councils in the local negotiations were of course closely associated with their wider constituency interests (as discussed in Chapter 3 and reflected in *Figure 18*), but there were some significant changes in emphasis. In particular, the pressures generated by the Whythall debate now placed a more direct onus on the County Council to prove that it could negotiate at Droitwich a viable alternative to Birmingham's proposals for peripheral expansion; while the City Council's attitude had been revealed at the public inquiry as one of scepticism as to whether the Droitwich scheme could start in time to contribute towards solving their more immediate housing problems.

The parties to the negotiations differed markedly, not only in the ranges of interest which they reflected, but also in the nature of their mutual relationships at the time the negotiations began. So far as the County and the City Councils were concerned, the last chapter has already described the strained state of relations which had developed between them, as independent local planning authorities under pressure to co-ordinate their land-use policies within the external controls maintained by the Ministry. Between City and Borough Councils, direct relationships were virtually non-existent; even though the provisions of the Town Development legislation gave both authorities a more direct status in the negotiating process than the County, as prospective 'exporting' and 'receiving' authorities respectively, there was a strong reluctance among Borough Council members to meet Birmingham representatives face to face because of the great disparity in the level of their resources and the fear that the smaller authority might be out-manoeuvred. So it came about that, although the Borough Council had agreed to 'consider' the possibility of overspill as early as 1952, it was some seven years later before the County Council was able to act as intermediary in arranging a direct face-to-face meeting involving both prospective partners.

The relationship between Worcestershire and Droitwich, as a County and one of its eighteen constituent Districts, was of course a much more deeply rooted one, and one that was in fact to provide the primary axis of the negotiating process. As in all such relationships between tiers in England, each authority was essentially independent in terms of electoral accountability and financial budgeting, even though the machinery of local government finance required all County rate revenue to be collected through a 'precept' levied through the agency of the District Council, and there were always a variety of detailed adjustments to be negotiated between County and District Treasurers in relation to central government grants and other financial matters.

One form of relationship of special significance to the overspill negotiations was the arrangement for delegation of powers from the County to its constituent Districts in the field of development control. The arrangement which had evolved in Worcestershire was broadly similar to that in other English counties, and had the effect that the County retained responsibility for laying down general guidelines for land-use policy, while delegating to the Districts most powers of decision-making in relation to individual applications to develop by private interests. This arrangement was subject to a right of comment on proposals by the County's Area Planning Officer, and an agreed procedure for resolving any differences between his judgement and that of the District Council.

In consequence, the County Council could do much to exercise restraint over the rate of private housing and other commercial development at Droitwich, but little to initiate public housing development, whether for overspill or other purposes. The formal status of the Borough Council as the sole local housing authority was in fact to be one of the few resources that it could deploy in the negotiating process, with the County able to exercise only an indirect influence in the form of exhortations, offers of financial aid, and supply of technical expertise for any initial planning studies and survey work.

Thus, the forms of influence available to the County in relation to the powers of the Borough Council — as a source of veto power over land-use decisions on the one hand, and of financial and technical assistance towards desired policies on the other — were in many ways parallel to those powers of external control exercised at regional level by the Land Planning Ministry, through its access to reserve powers in relation to local development plans coupled with its ability to offer financial support to approved Town Development schemes.

The field of negotiation

Initially, the field of negotiation was an extremely open one, as the provisions of the Town Development legislation left open a wide range of options for administration and finance. As already discussed, the main responsibility for the implementation of the development programme could be taken on — according to local circumstances — by the exporting city, by the receiving district, by

the County Council for the receiving area, or by some form of joint
venture involving any two or more of these three parties. In the field
of finance, the only explicit commitment in the Act was the
provision of a special housing subsidy for each new dwelling assigned
to an overspill tenant, payable at the rate of £8 a year over a
fifteen-year period after occupation, providing this was matched by
at least the same level of subsidy from the exporting authority.
Although some central support was also promised towards the cost
of approved sewerage and water investments, the scope of this was
not made explicit at the time the Act was passed. It was not
surprising that members of Droitwich Borough Council, when first
faced with this extensive field of possibilities, were concerned about
the unpredictable impact on local ratepayers and were unwilling to
commit themselves to do more than 'consider' whatever further
proposals the County might wish to put forward.

   The field of negotiation in Droitwich was in time to range over
many issues: who should exercise control over the expansion, how
the costs and risks of the development should be shared, what the
overall scale and time-span of the expansion should be, in which
areas adjoining the town the new growth should be located, and what
the balance should be between public and private housing development. During the years which preceded the first tripartite meeting in
1959, the range of possible solutions within this field began to be
narrowed slowly through a process of incremental commitments
from each of the individual agencies concerned. In the financial field,
the Ministry made the extent of its aid towards infrastructure
development more explicit in the form of a 50 per cent grant
towards the cost of water and sewerage investments directly
attributable to overspill, while Birmingham announced its readiness
to provide the minimum housing subsidy required by the Town
Development legislation to match that of the Ministry. However,
these commitments were argued by the County to be still insufficient
to meet the financial difficulties of the receiving authority.

   At a technical level, the County attempted in 1955 to carry the
process forward by suggesting tentative programmes for building
approximately 1,000 houses each at Droitwich and Redditch between
the years 1957 to 1962, thus fulfilling the County's annual target
of 400 overspill houses, as agreed with the other Counties on the
Technical Committee, while also, in the case of Droitwich, keeping
broadly to the level of population increase originally envisaged in the
West Midlands Plan. However, the County Planning Committee had
subsequently to admit in a report to the Council (21 November,
1959) that, while Redditch Urban District had been persuaded to

enter into overspill negotiations with Birmingham on the basis of such a programme:

> 'Droitwich Borough Council are not yet prepared to meet Birmingham City Council and want to consider further the effect on the Borough of participation in this scheme. There appear to be two points which are worrying the Borough Council: (1) their financial position, and (2) the danger of the proportion of Council Houses to private houses getting out of balance.'

Indeed, there is evidence in the columns of the local press during that period (the *Droitwich Guardian*) that the Council was reflecting a much wider upsurge of anxiety in the town at the publication by the County of its first phased proposals for an overspill housing programme. Among other signs of local concern, a Droitwich ratepayers' association was re-activated, and began to lead demands for a local referendum on the overspill issue. These anxieties were subsequently to become quiescent, when the Borough Council issued assurances that their only commitment so far was to 'consider' more detailed proposals, and that a great deal of further financial and technical information would be required before a final decision could be reached. The onus therefore remained on the County Council to come forward with more specific proposals as to the physical form and financial implications of the proposed expansion.

Pressures and initiatives

It was early in 1959, not long after the County had been urged by the Ministry to come to early decisions on its overspill schemes, but just before it was to be presented with the threat of peripheral development at Wythall, that the County Planning Officer was able to report the results of a first comprehensive survey of the physical opportunities for expansion at Droitwich. The conclusion was that it would be technically feasible to expand the town from its then population of about 8,000 to an ultimate level of 30,000 over a period of ten to fifteen years. It was on the basis of this information that the financial and technical officers of County, City, and Borough Councils first met together to discuss the administrative and financial implications of an expansion that was now of significantly larger dimensions than had earlier been envisaged. For such a scheme it was suggested by the County that the most appropriate agency would be some form of joint committee with Droitwich represented but with the County and Birmingham sharing most of the initial costs and risks. However, provision could be made for ultimate repayment by the Borough Council, whose ratepayers might be expected to accumulate a substantial profit in the longer term.

Rumours about the content of these proposals led to renewed anxieties within the town, and the Mayor of the day attempted to allay these by convening a press conference at which assurances were given as to the lack of commitment 'even in principle' to the proposals which the County had now put forward. It was, however, not long after this reassurance that the County representatives at the Wythall inquiry were to find themselves countering Birmingham's arguments by public expressions of optimism about an early and successful outcome to the Droitwich negotiations. Thus, a complex set of pressures and counter-pressures was beginning to build up between the three local authorities involved.

When a full-scale meeting of elected members and officers from the three local authorities was convened to discuss the next steps, it was not surprising that the area in which agreement was most readily reached concerned the need for further assurances about various forms of support from departments of central government. These included assurances about the readiness of the Agriculture Ministry to release farming land, the co-operation of the Industrial Development Ministry in exercising its controls over industrial relocation, and the support of the Highway Ministry (then independent of the Land Planning Ministry) in its assessment of priorities for road construction. It was, however, becoming clear within the County Council that neither Birmingham nor the Land Planning Ministry was likely to move much further in the direction of support for expansion at Droitwich until a final decision had been arrived at in relation to peripheral expansion at Wythall; a process which in itself was likely to involve extensive consultation and bargaining between different departments of central government, possibly extending up to Cabinet level.

Meanwhile, the problem of sewerage at Droitwich was creating more and more acute difficulties for the Borough Council. A point had been reached where the shortage of sewerage capacity had led to a virtual moratorium on all forms of development within the town, and it was becoming evident that at least some temporary improvements to the existing system would be inevitable, whatever the outcome of the overspill negotiations. Within the local electorate, the prevailing state of uncertainty over the future of the town was beginning to lead to renewed demands for a local referendum on overspill; and the Borough Council agreed to accede to this request through the medium of a postal vote. A public meeting was convened shortly before this vote was held, so that both the County and Borough officials could put forward the technical arguments in favour of proceeding. Briefly, these were that overspill could be to the long-term advantage of ratepayers; that few of the initial financial burdens would have to be absorbed by the local rates; and that it was by no means settled that the majority of new residents of an expanded Droitwich should be Birmingham overspill tenants. The only real issue, it was claimed, was whether or not the negotiations should be allowed to continue.

As an added financial inducement, the County Council at this time undertook to meet half the residual costs of sewerage development after allowing for the central government grant, on the proviso that the Borough Council should agree 'in principle' to town development, and also undertake to delay any consent to major physical development in the town for a further two years while negotiations continued. However, when the postal vote was conducted, it revealed a majority of 1,522 to 1,104 against continuing negotiations, from a total local electorate of 5,054. The local elected members therefore found themselves in something of a quandary. The issue came to a head when one member moved at the next Council meeting that, in view of the results of the postal vote, all further negotiations be terminated. A majority of councillors cast their votes against this proposition, but not without a clear indication from several of them that they would only be prepared to proceed on the basis of a much smaller scheme than that prepared by the County.

On the wider front, the Land Planning Ministry had by now rejected Birmingham's application for development at Wythall, but implicitly accepted the need to play a more positive role in promoting alternative solutions to the overspill problem. In the long term, it was now estimated that something of the order of 200,000 to 300,000 people would have to be dispersed within the region over the next twenty years, and that, in order to achieve this, it would be necessary to concentrate on three or four schemes providing quick results, including one or two which might have to be of New Town dimensions. This strategy was put forward by the Ministry's Permanent Secretary at a meeting which included officials from Birmingham and an enlarged group of six Midland counties; and the Droitwich expansion scheme emerged as one likely candidate for inclusion in such a regional programme, provided local agreement could be reached.

In the event, the Ministry became involved in some difficult negotiations with other government departments in attempting to agree other sites for major urban developments in the region. This led to delays in the publication of what had been envisaged as a comprehensive solution to the regional overspill problem as a whole. However — as an interim measure — the Ministry was able to tell Worcestershire in 1961 that they had now been able to reach agreement, again 'in principle', to the proposals for Droitwich which had been formulated some two years earlier. So, the processes of exploring options at a national level had at last produced a degree of commitment to expansion at Droitwich which could allow local explorations to continue. It was therefore agreed between the County and Borough Councils that a joint committee should be set up to examine the problems further and 'if possible, prepare a scheme'.

Options for the expansion of Droitwich

The negotiating committee which was set up in Droitwich in 1961 excluded any representation from Birmingham; indeed, the City Council had a wide front of negotiation to maintain with other potential receiving authorities and was therefore content to wait and see what emerged in the case of Droitwich. The Committee was comprised of elected representatives from the County and Borough Councils, together with the adjoining Droitwich Rural District whose territory would clearly be affected by any proposals for expansion that might involve extensions to the area of the town.

In view of the sensitive attitudes to the negotiations within the town, the terms of reference of the Committee were deliberately left unconstrained, leaving a wide variety of possible arrangements to be explored in the fields of finance, organization, and scale of development. In particular, it was accepted, at the insistence of the Borough Council representatives, that explicit consideration should be given to an option involving a population increase of the order of 10,000 rather than 20,000.

The difficulties of the local members' position were promptly underlined at the next annual municipal elections, where two of the four vacant seats were won by candidates campaigning on an explicitly 'anti-overspill' platform; and, not long after this election, the Borough Council passed a resolution that any scheme to be put forward for consideration should incorporate provision for no more than 8,000 overspill population from Birmingham. Underlying this constraint was a continuing local fear of disturbance to the town's existing social and political balance; this is endorsed by a report in the local press that one member of Council argued for a reduction of the limit to 6,000, in order to avoid a 'take-over' of Droitwich by newcomers.

The technical expertise required to construct viable proposals for the expansion of Droitwich lay predominantly with the officers of the County Council. Accordingly, one of the first moves by the County representatives on the joint negotiating committee was to offer the services of their Planning Officer to prepare an 'outline plan', given a loosely worded assurance that a majority of Borough Council members would afford the necessary co-operation. It was conceded that such a plan should not necessarily follow the lines of that produced two years earlier, the details of which were still as yet unpublished.

Not long afterwards, the County Planning Officer was able to present to the Committee a preliminary report setting out what were seen as the main physical constraints to development, including those of drainage, brine subsidence, communications, and conservation of agricultural and green belt land. This survey pointed to eleven areas where housing development might be considered, and a population target of the order of 26,000 was postulated. It was, however, argued that a more exact target would depend on the proportion of housing development to be undertaken under Town Development powers, and that 'it might not be in the best interests of the Borough if this proportion were determined arbitrarily'. Rather, the balance should be influenced by such calculations as the Borough Council's need for financial assistance towards infrastructure investments, the phasing of development so as to avoid undue strains on local ratepayers in the shorter term, the level of expansion necessary to justify supporting investment from other public agencies, and the degree to which it was desired to create new employment opportunities locally.

Once again, wider considerations came to cast their shadow over the negotiating process. When the Ministry was finally able to announce a set of co-ordinated measures for dealing with the regional overspill problem, these excluded any assumptions about the expansion of Droitwich, in deference to the Borough Council's ambivalent attitude. They did, however, include a proposed marginal adjustment to the Green Belt at Wythall and an expansion of Worcester City, both of which involved prospective encroachments on the County Council's boundaries. Once more, at another public inquiry concerning the future of Wythall, the County representatives found themselves expressing optimism over the development opportunities at Droitwich, and thereby generating renewed suspicions among Borough Council members. In this climate, misunderstandings arose over the interpretation of the constraint imposed by the Borough Council of no more than 8,000 overspill population. Did this limit apply to all migration from the conurbation or only to tenants nominated by Birmingham for occupation of municipal dwellings? The possibility of a distinction between these interpretations arose from the prospect that some of the land publicly acquired within a designated area of Town Development might be sold or leased for private housing under some form of control by the local Town Development agency. Provided that any such housing could be shown to contribute to the Ministry's general aim of relieving population pressures in the conurbation, it might still qualify for the all-important central government subsidies towards sewerage and water investments.

It was through exploiting this possibility that the County was able to submit, in late 1962, a draft plan for the development of Droitwich which was broadly consistent with the aims of both the County and the Borough Council. This plan envisaged a total increase of 20,000 population through construction of a total of just over 6,000 houses, falling into three roughly equal categories. One category consisted of local authority dwellings, predominantly for letting to tenants nominated by Birmingham; one of private dwellings outside the designated area of Town Development; while the third was an intermediate category of private dwellings within the designated area, to be 'sponsored' by the parties to Town Development in such a way as to qualify for the government water and sewerage grants. The introduction of this intermediate category provided a means of reconciling the County's aim of demonstrating its ability to make a significant contribution to the regional overspill problem at Droitwich, and the Borough Council's stipulation that the reception of population from Birmingham should be limited to a figure of 8,000 or less.

The evaluation of alternatives

The proposals were supplemented by an extensive set of tables under the joint signatures of the County and Borough Treasurers, which, among other things, compared the costs of this scheme with those of a 'notional alternative' in which a more modest population increase of 14,000 was postulated. This assumed a rejection of overspill and a reliance on private development alone, with the implication that none of the forms of outside financial support available under the Town Development legislation would be forthcoming. One set of tabulations attempted to compare the effects of these two schemes on local ratepayers over a fifteen-year period. The results of this comparison are reproduced graphically in *Figure 23*.

In this way, numerical evidence was marshalled to support the

Figure 23   Comparison of effect on local ratepayers of alternative schemes for development at Droitwich

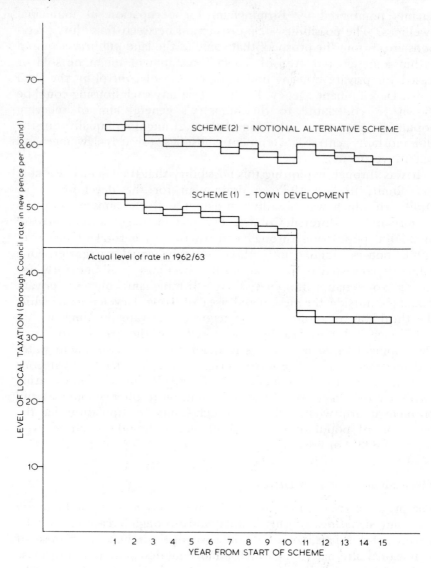

argument that the acceptance of overspill could be expected to have a beneficial effect on local ratepayers. In the more immediate future, this would be brought about through the provision of outside aid towards essential infrastructure investments, and later through a combination of the build-up of the local tax base and the inflow of revenue from investment in land for 'sponsored' housing and in industrial estate development. Of course, such a projection of long-term cash flows had to be based on a wide range of assumptions. These covered such factors as future levels of costs and interest rates, the expected profitability of different forms of investment, the relative phasing of the different types of housing development, and the means through which it might prove practicable to manage the implementation of the 'sponsored' sector of the programme. Not all of these assumptions could easily be tested, given the difficulty of making reliable predictions about future economic and social trends; and, not surprisingly, not all of them have been borne out by subsequent events. It is, however, likely that the differentials of local rate impact indicated in *Figure 23* provided as reasonable an estimate as could have been attempted at the time of the implications for local ratepayers, even though giving no direct indication of the risks underlying such an enterprise. In accordance with the normal local authority procedures for presenting recommendations to elected representatives, the uncertainties of the situation were dealt with through settling on a single set of intuitively reasonable assumptions; and the variety of available solutions to the problem was managed by the device of contrasting the recommended solution with a single alternative which was demonstrably inferior, at least when appraised in the light of the only consideration that could readily be presented in quantitative form, that of cost to the local Council.

Given this view of two alternative futures from which to choose, the members of the Borough Council finally voted to accept the Town Development option. However, this motion was passed only after an amendment to accept the 'notional scheme' had been lost by ten votes to four, and only on the members' insistence that a series of conditions should be observed. It was stipulated that the development should be managed through a joint committee of County and Borough Councils alone; that redevelopment in the central area of the town should leave scope for private investment; and that the Borough Council would reserve its position over acceptance of more detailed physical proposals and financial arrangements.

Despite these further constraints on the field of more detailed negotiation, a watershed of commitment to the expansion of

Droitwich had been passed. With the County officers again providing much of the necessary legal, financial, and town planning expertise, the two authorities entered into a process of negotiation over more detailed issues, which was to lead to the signature to a formal set of agreements late in 1963, and the establishment of a joint Development Committee to manage the expansion programme in April of the following year. In this process, Birmingham as exporting authority was again to play a comparatively marginal role. The Borough Council was still reluctant to enter into any form of direct bargaining with the City, and the County Council's hope that Birmingham might be persuaded to share some of the financial risks of the scheme quickly receded as it became clear to the City Council that only a comparatively modest number of houses were to be built for direct letting to tenants nominated from their own housing register; a mere 2,000 compared with the 14,000 that Birmingham had originally proposed to build at Wythall as an answer to its immediate housing problems. Thus, it became clear that the County on its own would have to underwrite most of the early risks of the scheme. Accordingly, the County and Borough Treasurers proceeded to discuss outline arrangements for a system of County advances with allowance for phased repayments as the financial viability of the expanding town increased.

The form and content of the agreements

Thus, the process of negotiating a Town Development Agreement for Droitwich drew towards a conclusion that was to impose certain obligations on each of the three parties but, inevitably, was also to leave a great deal of further scope for manoeuvre and mutual adjustment during the fifteen-year period over which the expansion programme was to be implemented. The balance between commitment and room for manoeuvre embodied in the formal Agreement is revealed by a broad analysis of the content of the set of contractual and statutory planning documents which together spelt out the understandings on which the development was to proceed. These documents were as follows:

(1) A *Town Map* for Droitwich, submitted as an official amendment to the Worcestershire County Development Plan, indicating the proposed boundaries for the designated Town Development Area, the zoning of land for housing, industrial, and other purposes, and a basic road layout for the town

(2) A *Written Statement* forming part of the formal Town Map submission, consisting of eight pages of text and tabular

matter setting out proposed population targets, housing densities, policies for development of various public services, and broad intentions for phasing in terms of an initial five-year period from 1963 to 1968 and a subsequent period up to eventual completion of the scheme in 1981. The Statement referred not only to the Town Map itself but also to a set of supplementary maps giving further information on programming and designations of land for particular public purposes

(3) An *Agreement Between County and Borough Councils* constituting the Droitwich Development Committee as agency for execution of the proposals contained in (1) and (2) above. This ran to seven pages of text and indicated the legal powers to be delegated to the Committee, together with undertakings of financial and other support from the parent authorities and provisions for arbitration in case of dispute

(4) A *First Schedule* appended to (3), in the form of a further Agreement between Birmingham and Droitwich Borough — the latter acting in association with Worcestershire — covering the arrangements for building and letting of overspill housing within the terms of the Town Development Act

(5) A *Second Schedule* to (3), setting out the formal constitution of the Droitwich Development Committee

(6) A *Third Schedule* concerned with the functions and finance of the Droitwich Development Committee.

With the exception of the maps, this set of documents was published as an Appendix to the first interim report of the joint Development Committee formed to implement the expansion programme (Droitwich Development Committee, 1964). The documents cover between them a wide range of fields of policy, which can be classified broadly into those concerned with aspects of physical development — set mainly in the context of formal town planning procedure, in documents (1) and (2) above — and those concerned with aspects of administration, procedure, or finance — cast mainly in the contractural setting of documents (3) to (6).

In *Figure 24*, an attempt is made to assess the content of each of the six main documents on a broad impressionistic basis, primarily according to the relative weight each document appears to give to each of eleven main fields of policy, represented in the diagram by the respective heights of the shaded blocks. Within each block, the relative proportions occupied by the dark, shaded, and unshaded areas represent a rough appraisal of the relative space given within the document concerned to expressions of firm commitment, expressions of comparatively ambiguous or 'soft' commitment, and

Figure 24   Droitwich Town Development: Contents of agreements

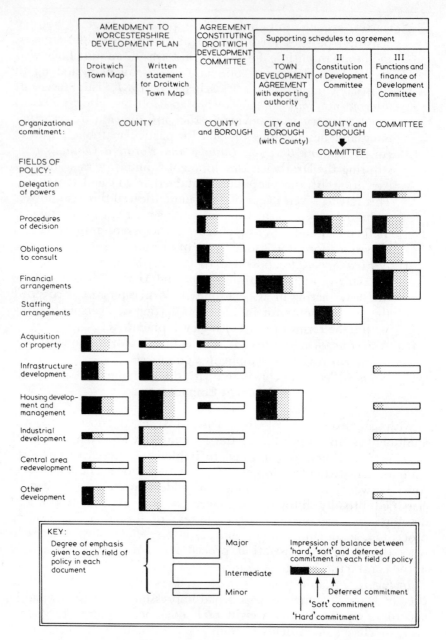

expressions of explicitly deferred commitment within each of the fields concerned.

For example, taking the field of housing, the comparatively large areas of dark shading in the first, second, and fourth columns reflect a dominant emphasis on statements of comparatively 'hard' commitment in such matters of location, density, and letting procedure, while the areas of intermediate shading indicate the space given to other statements of more 'soft' commitment in such areas as scheduling of development and degree of control over private housing, where there was seen to be a case for retaining more flexibility to respond to future contingencies.

A contrasting example is the field of central area redevelopment, where expressions of commitment were kept to a minimum, as the most important function of the documents was seen as that of giving explicit reassurance that all options remained open apart from a general designation of the area in question for some form of comprehensive redevelopment, in which as much scope as possible would be left for further exploration of design alternatives and detailed negotiations with the many local commercial and residential interests in the area.

General interpretations

The process with which this chapter has been concerned is essentially one of bargaining between independently elected local authorities within a context laid down by an agency of central government. The shared task was to attempt to design a set of contractual arrangements whereby each party might gain something that would further its own distinctive interests: the interest of a City Council in finding sites to house its expanding population, the interest of a County Council in resisting urban encroachment at its boundaries, and the interest of a small District Council in ensuring its future viability while resisting changes to its existing social mix. It was by no means assured, however, that the negotiating process would arrive at its intended outcome; this point was to be dramatized by events in the neighbouring town of Redditch, where the gap between the parties was to remain so wide that the Minister then responsible eventually decided to intervene personally and impose the alternative solution of a centrally appointed New Town Development Corporation.

The process described in this chapter conforms much more closely to Lindblom's concept of partisan mutual adjustment, as discussed in Chapter 2, than to that of centralized co-ordination. However, the leading role emerges as that of the County Council, which not only had the greatest incentive to intitiate the search for a mutually acceptable solution, but was also able to command the requisite resources of finance and of technical skill to put forward propositions which were viable and consistent in terms of the various physical, economic, and political constraints coming to bear on the local situation at Droitwich. Of the three parties to negotiation, it was the Borough Council whose electorate stood to be most deeply affected by the outcome of this exploratory process; yet their dependence on the technical skills of other parties was on several occasions to lead them to assert their interests by imposing constraints on the processes of search, rather than by formulating any constuctive counter-proposals of their own. Thus, at one critical point in the bargaining process, the County was able to confront the Borough Council with a stark choice of two alternative futures, from which it was difficult to avoid the conclusion that the rejection of overspill would imply unacceptable levels of increase in the burden of local taxation.

As the skills required to steer the decision-making process through all the technical and administrative complexities of town expansion lay predominantly with the larger authority, it was perhaps not surprising that the Borough Council should be drawn increasingly towards reliance on its only significant resource — that of its formal right of discretion as housing authority as to whether or not it should enter into an overspill agreement with Birmingham.

As the process of adjustment proceeded, the inter-relationships between the different types of issue at stake gradually became more and more central to the remaining scope for negotiation. Initially, it had been possible for each authority to make a series of incremental and largely disjointed commitments in such fields as the level of financial contribution, the scale of expansion, and the agency of development, each tending to reflect the external pressures to work towards a successful outcome under which that authority found itself at the time. Later, as the search narrowed, it became more difficult to evade the structural linkages between physical, organizational, financial, and timing options, with the result that the final set of agreements was to reflect a complex pattern of commitments on the part of the various agencies concerned which, overall, provided a mutually acceptable basis for future co-operation.

In the pattern of commitments eventually agreed, it has been seen that many options were still to remain open. Indeed, it can be argued more generally that, in any plan or set of agreements relating to a comparatively long-term joint enterprise, the freedom of manoeuvre allowed to respond to future contingencies can be just as positive an aspect of content as the degree of formal commitment to protect the various constituency interests concerned. Relating this point to the conventions used in *Figure 24*, it is possible to argue that the unshaded areas can represent as creative an outcome of the negotiating process as the darker areas, in so far as they reflect opportunities for creative adaptation to future uncertainties — whether these concern knowledge of the operating environment, unresolved policy issues, or unknown future intentions on the part of other agencies. Clearly, there must always be a difficult balance to be sought between this kind of flexibility and the level of commitment entered into to safeguard the many sectional interests on which such an enterprise must impinge. This is a consideration which applies equally to other levels and contexts of inter-agency negotiation, including, for example, the processes of negotiation which preceded the enlargement of the European Economic Community in 1973.

In any such situation, it can never be easy to judge whether the set of commitments expressed at the contractural stage is too restrictive or too permissive, either in total or in any particular field of policy. This will apply irrespective of whether the evaluation is being attempted from the partisan viewpoint of one of the contracting parties, or from a position of central co-ordination such as that occupied in this instance by the Land Planning Ministry. In later chapters, an attempt will be made to throw some further light on these fundamental questions of inter-authority planning, by tracing some of the subsequent events at Droitwich from the perspectives of the various fields of policy involved. In particular, we shall bear in mind the question of how far the sources of future uncertainty to be dealt with through such a joint enterprise can be realistically anticipated at the time of initial commitment, and how far the framework of co-ordination and control can be designed or adapted so as to encourage — or at least so as not to inhibit — the emergence of appropriate skills at the more crucial interfaces of the decision-making system.

5 Local arrangements

A problem of organizational design

The purpose of this chapter is to discuss some of the more significant aspects of the system of local management for the planned expansion of Droitwich, both in so far as this was specified through the initial agreement, and also in so far as it had evolved through less formal arrangements between the local agencies and actors by the time our opportunities for direct observation arose during 1969, 1970, and 1971. This chapter will therefore complete the setting for the discussion in Part II of a range of issues arising during the course of the development programme itself, and the analysis of the decision networks through which these issues were handled.

The focus at this stage turns in particular to the Droitwich Development Committee and its resources — its membership, staff, finances, and working procedures — all of which inevitably introduce issues of relations between this new body and its two parent institutions, the County Council of Worcestershire and the Borough Council of Droitwich. In terms of the broad breakdown of main fields of policy introduced in *Figure 24*, our concern will be with those at the top of the diagram which can be broadly classified as organizational — concerned with delegation of powers, procedures of decision and consultation, financial and staffing arrangements — as opposed to the remaining six fields concerned with specific aspects of developmental operations.

It will not be until the discussion of developmental issues in Part II that we shall be able to draw any very significant inferences about the effectiveness of the particular organizational configuration that was agreed at Droitwich, in relation to its allotted task of managing the planned expansion of the town. However, anticipating the discussion in Part III of alternative forms of organization for development, and of the implications of a reformed local government structure, it is possible to argue that the Droitwich arrangements — though in some respects unique — do expose in a particularly sharply defined form some of the more general problems of mutual adjustment between agencies which must be confronted in any major programme of planned local or regional change.

In *Figure 25*, the organizational structure for the development of Droitwich is interpreted as a special case of the general phenomenon of the multi-organization as defined by Stringer (1967); in other words, a set of parts of several organizations brought together through the interaction of individuals in the performance of a common task. In the case of Droitwich, the task was that of expanding the town from a population of 8,000 to one of approximately 30,000 over a fifteen-year period. In *Figure 25*, the two parent Councils are shown as only partly directed towards the execution of this particular task, while the third organizational unit — the specially recruited Development Group reporting to the two parent authorities through a joint Committee of their members — is shown located wholly within the broken line representing the task boundary, because of its exclusive concern with management of the local expansion programme.

The Droitwich Development Committee

Looking first at the formal structure of control by elected representatives, as shown on the right-hand side of the diagram, it will be noticed that the Committee was constituted by agreement to consist of an equal number of members from each parent authority; a number that had been increased from six to eight at the express request of the Borough Council during the negotiating process. It will also be noticed that this representation accounted for exactly half the membership of the Borough Council, although only a small minority of the total membership on the County Council side. On each side, the members of the Committee were nominated annually by the parent Councils; in practice, there was a considerable continuity of membership from one year to the next.

On the Borough Council side, nominations for the Committee

Figure 25   Multi-organizational structure of Droitwich town development

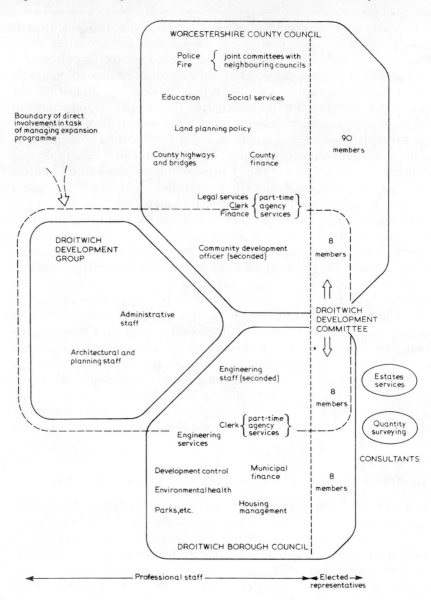

were determined initially by direct voting among the sixteen Council members, rather than by *ex-officio* appointment. In most years, the nominations from the Borough were in fact to include either the Chairman or Vice-Chairman (if not both) from each of the five standing committees of the Council. The responsibilities of these covered Planning and General Purposes; Finance; Housing; Parks and Open Spaces; and Estates and Public Works respectively; all of these were fields of responsibility on which the planned expansion of the town could be expected to have some impact.

Within the County Council, a practice had evolved of building in an element of *ex-officio* cross-membership between Committees, and, in the case of the Droitwich Development Committee, it was agreed that those nominated on this basis should include the Chairman of the County Planning Committee, the Vice-Chairman of the Finance Committee, and the Chairman of the County Council itself (who in practice was rarely to attend except at occasional moments of crisis in the relations between the parent authorities). Over and above these *ex-officio* links, it was significant that the County Council, with a total of ninety-eight elected members to choose from, as opposed to the sixteen of the Borough Council, also chose to appoint to the joint Committee some of its more important Committee Chairmen and Vice-Chairmen, representing such interests as Education, Highways, and the influential County General Purposes Committee. These nominations were to provide a visible indication of the high priority that the County attached to the execution of the Droitwich programme and, in the judgement of senior officers in the Development Group, were to contribute in a significant way to the fabric of co-ordination among the various County interests concerned.

It was also agreed, by convention, that the Chairmanship of the Droitwich Development Committee – and therefore the all-important casting vote in any situation of deadlock – should always fall to a Borough Council representative. As will be seen later, the role of Chairman was to prove an exacting one in practice, because of the need to reconcile a stance of leadership to the Development Committee with one of responsiveness to recurrent anxieties within the Borough Council about the directions in which some aspects of the expansion programme were to develop. Also by convention, the Vice-Chairmanship of the Committee fell to a County representative, who from 1969 onwards was in fact to be one of the town's two elected representatives on the County Council.

Sources of professional expertise

Any agency charged with the planned development of a community requires access to a variety of professional skills, including those of administration, finance, town planning, architecture, engineering, legal advice, and negotiation within property markets. In the case of Droitwich, the scale of development was such as to provide a clear justification for some — but not necessarily all — of these skills to be brought together within a local group directly accountable to the joint Development Committee. In fact, by the time the development programme had acquired its full momentum in the early seventies, the staff concentrated within the Droitwich Development Group amounted to just over forty in all, but with only a limited range of professional disciplines, as indicated within the left-hand block of *Figure 25*. However, the diagram also indicates that other types of expertise were contributed by officials of the parent authorities serving the Committee either on full secondment or on a part-time agency basis, or in some cases by outside consultants.

The first appointment to be made by the Development Committee was that of Chief Administrative Officer, to take responsibility for the general management of the local Development Group and to act as principal adviser to the Committee. A second step was to recruit a Chief Planner/Architect as leader of a technical design team, which would ultimately embrace a balanced range of skills in planning, architecture, and engineering.

While most of the newly recruited staff were to be treated for purposes of personnel administration as officers of the County Council, a more complex arrangement was agreed upon in the case of the engineers. In common with other County Districts, the Borough Council already employed an Engineer and Surveyor whose responsibilities embraced a variety of engineering and related services, and who, under the formal terms of the agreement, was to retain responsibility for development of the town's sewerage system. For this reason, it was decided that the team of engineering staff to be recruited for the new Development Group, to carry responsibility for local roads and associated works within the designated area of Town Development, should be regarded as serving on formal secondment from the Borough Surveyor's Department. In this way the Borough Council was able to maintain nominal responsibility at least for the provision of one form of technical service which, on the completion of the development programme, could be expected to take its natural place within the range of responsibilities of an enlarged County District.

A further post was created on the basis of formal secondment once the rate of immigration to Droitwich began to gather such momentum as to justify the appointment of a full-time Community Development Officer. This time the secondment was regarded as being from the County Council staff, on the argument that the individual concerned might be expected to move on later to play a similar role elsewhere within the County. Other skills which were more difficult to justify on a full-time basis were provided through agency agreements with the parent authorities. It had already been specified in the agreement that the County Clerk should act as legal adviser to the joint Committee and the County Treasurer as its accountant; the agreement also provided that the Clerks of the two parent authorities should act jointly as Clerks to the Development Committee. In practice, however, the responsibility for preparing all relevant agendas, minutes, and other documents was assumed by the Chief Administrative Officer and his own staff within the Development Group at Droitwich.

To complete the general picture of *Figure 25*, it is necessary to refer to certain other supporting skills which were secured by the Committee on a consultancy basis. The expertise of negotiation in the property market was provided by an Estates Adviser from a London firm which already acted in this capacity for the County, while another firm of consultants was retained to provide quantity surveying services to the architectural and engineering staff.

Further specialist skills were made available through the normal departmental structures of the two parent authorities; among these, special mention must be made of that of housing management. Because of the arrangement that all houses constructed for rent under the Town Development programme were to be handed over to the Borough Council immediately on completion, this became a matter for the Council's own housing staff, working under the direction of a newly appointed Housing Manager.

Relationships within the Development Group

In *Figure 26*, the internal structure of the Development Group is set out in greater detail, in order to identify certain individual roles with which we shall be especially concerned when it comes to the analysis of decision networks in subsequent chapters. In some cases, the designations introduced in this diagram differ from those formally in use in Droitwich; this is done in order to provide a set of descriptions for use in subsequent chapters, which will readily distinguish between officers of the Development Group and those of other

Figure 26   Management structure of Droitwich Development Group

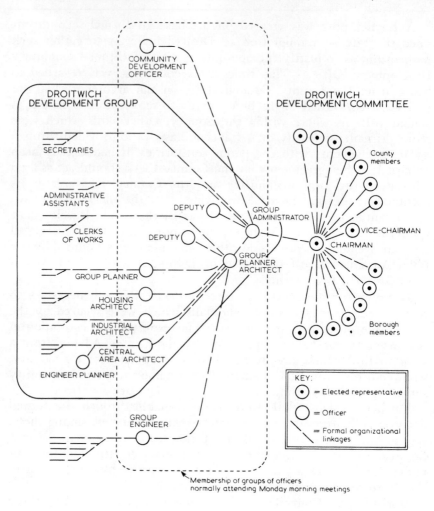

DROITWICH
DEVELOPMENT GROUP

COMMUNITY
DEVELOPMENT
OFFICER

DROITWICH
DEVELOPMENT COMMITTEE

SECRETARIES

ADMINISTRATIVE
ASSISTANTS

CLERKS
OF WORKS

GROUP PLANNER

HOUSING
ARCHITECT

INDUSTRIAL
ARCHITECT

CENTRAL
AREA ARCHITECT

ENGINEER PLANNER

GROUP
ENGINEER

DEPUTY

DEPUTY

GROUP
ADMINISTRATOR

GROUP
PLANNER
ARCHITECT

County
members

VICE-CHAIRMAN

CHAIRMAN

Borough
members

KEY:

⊙ = Elected representative

◯ = Officer

╱ = Formal organizational
linkages

Membership of groups of officers
normally attending Monday morning meetings

authorities. For instance, the Chief Administrative Officer will be referred to as Group Administrator, the Chief Planner/Architect as Group Planner Architect, and the Senior Engineer on detachment from the Borough Council simply as the Group Engineer, thus stressing his primary working allegiance.

Within this local group of officials, a number of influences were to combine to produce a marked degree of internal cohesion by the time the development programme had built up its full momentum. Most obviously, there was their common orientation towards achieving the stated aims of the development programme expeditiously and to high professional standards — an orientation which from time to time was to place them in opposition to some of the interests of existing local people as represented on their controlling Committee. Indeed, the Development Group officers at times found themselves taking on the role of representatives of the assumed interests of future newcomers to the town, in the absence of any representation on the joint Committee of Birmingham as exporting authority. Another factor making for cohesion within the Development Group was that several of the officers brought with them to Droitwich a background of experience in working for New Town Development Corporations, where they had been concerned in the management of similar development operations under the somewhat less exacting conditions of accountability to an appointed Board as opposed to a Joint Committee of elected local authorities. In fact, three of the senior technical staff had previously worked together in one particular New Town project in the South-East of England.

A third, if often taken for granted, influence towards cohesiveness of the Development Group was the opportunity to work together from a common location — a set of purpose-built temporary offices in the centre of Droitwich, shared with the Borough Engineer and Surveyor's Department — allowing frequent opportunities for casual social contact and for the convening of ad hoc meetings.

In this continuing pattern of communication between Group members, one focal point was a convention whereby some nine or ten of the more senior officers indicated in Figure 26 would assemble regularly each Monday morning in the Group Administrator's office to discuss any immediate topics requiring co-ordination or early decision. At a typical meeting, each officer in turn would raise two or three issues currently of concern to his own section, and other officers would comment in so far as these impinged on their own activities and interests. Sometimes, a more extended debate would be opened up on the strategy for dealing with some major issue before raising it at a forthcoming meeting of the Committee.

Figure 27 Seating arrangements at a typical meeting of Droitwich Development Committee

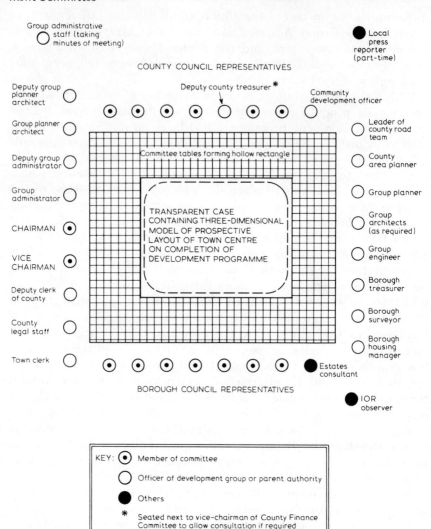

Group administrative staff (taking minutes of meeting)

Local press reporter (part-time)

COUNTY COUNCIL REPRESENTATIVES

Deputy group planner architect

Deputy county treasurer*

Community development officer

Group planner architect

Committee tables forming hollow rectangle

Leader of county road team

Deputy group administrator

County area planner

Group administrator

TRANSPARENT CASE CONTAINING THREE-DIMENSIONAL MODEL OF PROSPECTIVE LAYOUT OF TOWN CENTRE ON COMPLETION OF DEVELOPMENT PROGRAMME

Group planner

CHAIRMAN

Group architects (as required)

VICE CHAIRMAN

Group engineer

Deputy clerk of county

Borough treasurer

County legal staff

Borough surveyor

Town clerk

Borough housing manager

Estates consultant

BOROUGH COUNCIL REPRESENTATIVES

IOR observer

KEY: ⊙ Member of committee

○ Officer of development group or parent authority

● Others

* Seated next to vice-chairman of County Finance Committee to allow consultation if required

One significant feature of the pattern of local relationships was a sense of occasional frustration at the comparatively extended lines of communication between the local group of administrative and technical staff and their advisers on financial, legal, and commercial matters. Despite the evidence of a considerable degree of rapport between the local staff and some of those providing supporting services from the County offices in Worcester or the Estates Consultants' Headquarters in London, the barriers to quick communication were a recurrent theme in discussion with officers of the Development Group. Clearly, this could have negative consequences in so far as important professional perspectives were less fully represented than, for instance, in the case of a large New Town Development Corporation with its own finance, legal, and estates departments. Against this, however, was the positive consequence that the Group Administrator and his staff were themselves forced to develop a sufficiently rounded appreciation of costing, commercial, and legal considerations in order to be able to make broad managerial judgements on the more significant issues that arose for day-to-day decision.

The conventions of committee procedure

The formal pivot for decision-taking at Droitwich could readily be identified in the form of the monthly meeting of the Development Committee itself. At this the elected members would normally be attended not only by the more senior officers of the Development Group, but also by the full range of advisers from the parent authorities and elsewhere. The seating arrangement was itself of some significance. On a typical occasion, this took the general form indicated in *Figure 27*, with the Borough and County Council representatives sitting facing each other across a wide hollow table. In the centre of this, permanently on display, was a three-dimensional model representing a vision of the possible physical form of Droitwich town centre on completion of the scheme. Although rarely referred to during the course of a meeting, this model had the effect not only of symbolizing the task facing the Committee, but also of increasing the physical distance separating the Borough and County representatives across the table.

At each meeting, the agenda would be divided into a public section, at which a local press reporter would be present, and a subsequent private section. Normally, the public business would be confined to issues of factual information on such matters as progress of current development works, and would be rapidly despatched, while any items involving problem areas of any significance would be withheld until the private part of the meeting. The Chairman would retain control of business according to the normal conventions of committee procedure, and the Group Administrator would play the central role in the provision of background information and advice, calling on the Group Planner Architect or other specialists for supporting evidence where necessary. The meeting was normally preceded by a short agenda conference at which the Group Administrator and his colleagues would have an opportunity to brief the Chairman, and also the visiting officers of the County and Borough Councils, on the implications of some of the more significant agenda items.

Although most major issues were ultimately brought for decision to the Development Committee itself, there was a limited amount of delegation to specialist sub-committees concerned with housing, industrial development, sports and leisure, and other issues. These met irregularly and usually with only a few members present, except in the case of the Industrial Development Sub-Committee whose practice it was to meet briefly just before each meeting of the full Committee, to review the state of negotiations with any firms currently contemplating moving to the town.

Of rather more general significance was the role of a General Purposes Sub-Committee, which met regularly at the half-way point in the monthly Committee cycle. This included four members from each side, with the Chair taken by the Vice-Chairman of the main Committee. Originally, the role of this Sub-Committee was seen as one of relieving the full Committee of some of the less contentious issues for decision, at a stage of the development programme when its overall load of business was increasing, and also of dealing expeditiously with any urgent issues arising in the earlier half of the monthly cycle. In practice, however, one of its more significant functions was to become that of providing an additional sounding-board for the reactions of members to some of the more sensitive issues eventually to be brought up for decision in the full Committee; in terms of the model of *Figure 10*, it was to serve as a vehicle for policy-clarifying activities.

It was inevitable that most of the more difficult issues relating to the development of Droitwich impinged more intimately on the interests of the Borough Council than of the County Council, and it was noticeable that actual attendance at the Sub-Committee tended to be much more sparse on the County than the Borough Council side, despite the nominal equality of numbers. This contrasted with the situation at the full Committee meetings at which most of the more conclusive votes were taken. Here — apart from the infrequent attendances of the County Council Chairman — both sides would normally be represented virtually at full strength

Conventions of consultation with the parent authorities

Underlying many questions of Committee procedure at Droitwich was the delicate question of the degree of autonomy of the Development Committee itself in relation to the parent authorities. Although the formal set of agreements included several clauses relating to formal delegation of powers to the Committee, to its powers of independent action, and its obligations to consult the parent bodies, there were, nevertheless, a number of points of ambiguity, one of the most troublesome being the third clause of the schedule relating to functions and finance of the Committee, which read as follows:

'From time to time the Committee shall arrange for the preparation and submission to the parties hereto for approval of more detailed plans and estimates of individual projects forming part of the scheme and such detailed plans and estimates as may be agreed between the parties hereto shall thereupon be deemed to form part of the Agreement.'

This clause was far from specific as to the range of projects for which such external submissions would be required, or the stage of the decision process at which the views of the parent authorities should be sought. In the event, its effect was that the Borough Council, and in theory also the County Council, were to preserve extensive powers of veto, or at least of delay, in relation to the recommendations submitted to the Development Committee. According to the type of issue involved, this sanction could be invoked by Borough members through references either to the full Council, or to its Planning and General Purposes Committee, or to the local Housing Committee; or to the Finance Committee in the case of any project involving formal application to a government department to sanction the raising of a loan.

Each of these Borough Council Committees met on a monthly cycle bearing a more or less fixed relationship to that of the Development Committee. Understandably, some of the Borough Council representatives came to see their power to refer issues to one of their own Committees prior to decision as an important safeguard in protecting the financial interests of their electors and in maintaining democratic influence over changes in the physical and social structure of the town. Equally understandably, the officers of the

Development Group would come to look on the exercise of such powers as a frustrating source of delay in the efficient execution of the programme.

On the County side, the main powers of control over the actions of the Development Committee lay in the fields of finance — which will be considered later in this chapter — and in the field of land-use policy, in so far as any major departures from the guidelines outlined in the Town Map required the formal approval of the County Planning Committee. This power was usually exercised in practice not through the full Committee, but through its influential General Purposes Sub-Committee which met on a quarterly cycle.

Arrangements for development control

Within the general field of land-use planning, one of the most significant and sensitive problems resulting from the formation of the Droitwich Development Group concerned changes in the existing arrangements for control over private development. These arrangements had the effect that most decisions on the acceptance, deferment, or rejection of applications by private developers to carry out works within Droitwich were taken by the town's Planning and General Purposes Committee (which in fact consisted of all sixteen Council members sitting in Committee) on the recommendation of the Borough's Building Inspector. However, all such applications were open to scrutiny by an Area Officer of the County Planning Department, who would have the opportunity of submitting a report in writing where he judged that significant questions of County policy were involved. Any differences of opinion between this Officer and the Borough Council could then be referred to the County Planning Committee for adjudication, although this procedure was rarely invoked in practice.

In effect, the formation of the Development Group, with the task of implementing the town expansion scheme, introduced a third element into the policy system for this field of decision-making. The particular concerns of the Group were first to make sure that all private development would conform to the comparatively forward looking and exacting standards that were judged appropriate to the future expanded town, and second to avoid premature commitment to developments that might pre-empt future options of co-ordinated layout and design in particular areas. The Group planners saw this danger as particularly significant during the first few years, while they were still engaged in preparing the 'master plan' proposals which were to translate into more explicit policy guidelines the broad land-use proposals drawn up by the County planners at the time of the agreement. During this initial period of uncertainty, the Group planners had an interest in deferring any commitments to individual developments that could set undesirable precedents for the future; an interest which might not always be readily reconcilable with the responsibility of the Borough Council for giving speedy and fair consideration to proposals from developers that could help to advance the natural growth of the town and to enhance its rateable value.

The arrangement which was adopted as a means of maintaining mutual adjustment between these sometimes conflicting sets of interests was one whereby each application for private development within the town was submitted formally to the Group Planner Architect, who would have an opportunity to add any comments he might have to those of the County's Area Planner, and if necessary to ask for its submission to the Development Committee for further discussion. At a less formal level, it became the practice for the Borough Council's Building Inspector, the County's Area Planner, and the Group Planner Architect or his Deputy to meet weekly in the Development Group offices. This gave them an opportunity to debate the implications of any new planning applications, and where necessary engage jointly in discussion with the applicant over possible modifications to his proposals.

In the event, the technical staff of the Development Group found it in their interests to devote a considerable proportion of their time to this aspect of their work, and found themselves being looked upon as a source of expertise on architectural design matters which, in other circumstances, neither the local Building Inspector nor the County's Area Planner would have been able to supply. Thus, the weekly meetings of this informal group began to assume some importance in the search for mutual adjustment between a set of contiguous policy systems, each with an interest in the future physical form of Droitwich. However, the effort involved on the part of the Development Group was one which sometimes tended to impose a strain on their resources, in view of a continuing financial pressure to cost as much of their time as possible against specific projects within the development programme.

Arrangements for financial control

As in the case of other administrative aspects of the Droitwich development scheme, the arrangements for financial control were laid down in outline only at the time of the agreement, leaving considerable scope for subsequent adjustment and negotiation. This applied particularly to the respective contributions of the County and Borough Councils, as the two active partners in the development programme. The principle accepted by Worcestershire was that the County should be prepared to insulate the town against most of the early financial burdens and risks of expansion, but should make provision for ultimate repayment in the expectation that the Borough Council would become progressively more viable in its financial base, and that some types of investment within the programme would in time yield significant dividends for the local ratepayers.

The arrangement agreed upon for the financing of capital works had to respect the legal constraints on local authority borrowing, which required all loans to be repaid by instalments over a fixed period of years related to a nominal rate of depreciation for each type of asset — for instance, sixty years in the case of housing and thirty in the case of roads. It was agreed that all capital should be raised through the medium of the 'loans pool' already operated by the Borough Council, but that the annual loan charges incurred should be met during the early years from County sources, with the exception of those arising from highway, sewerage, and other infrastructure developments which would have been necessary even without an element of overspill in the scheme. These initial advances from the County would be free of interest, but the Borough would be expected to repay them over a ten-year period after the completion of each 'unit of development'. However, it was agreed that the County should cover directly all the costs of the initial planning work that could not be allocated to individual projects, such as the preparation of a Master Plan and a redevelopment scheme for the central area.

The administrative costs of the Development Group were to be regarded as 'oncosts' to be added on a percentage basis to the costs of time spent by the technical officers on specific capital projects or other planning exercises. At the end of each financial year, the accounts for the development scheme as a whole would be drawn up and the net costs of the year's operations would be apportioned between the Borough and County Councils — a process which often entailed some delicate negotiation over the interpretation of specific points of the agreement, in the light of the current financial circumstances of the Borough. The apportionment of costs was to become a matter of much political sensitivity for the members of the Borough Council, whose annual rate income amounted to only some 2 per cent of that of the County. Although the County Treasurer was able to claim that hardly any of the rapid rise in the level of local rates during the early years of development was attributable to overspill, it was by no means easy for ratepayers to appreciate the complex technical arguments involved in the apportionment process. Consequently, when the level of the local rate rose inexorably from year to year, there was a persistent local tendency to look upon the overspill commitment as the most obvious explanatory factor.

While the financing of the scheme was to remain a recurrent source of anxiety in Droitwich, both among ratepayers and within the Borough Council, the implications for the County Council were much more marginal. The handling of policy issues relating to the Droitwich expansion was therefore left largely to the Chairman and Vice-Chairman of the County Finance Committee, working inform-ally with the County Treasurer and his Deputy. Although the County was able to maintain that it handled the negotiations at all times in a generous spirit, the element of discretion in interpretation of the arrangements remained, so that the Borough Council was always faced with an implied threat of less generous treatment should they adopt too obstructive an attitude to any aspect of the development.

Patterns of cash flow between agencies

Figure 28 sums up the overall pattern of financial flows between the Borough Council, the County Council, and the Town Development Accounts, using graphical conventions that re-interpret the account-ing format used in presenting the annual Town Development accounts from 1964 onwards. The revenue transactions of the town development operation were presented in terms of a main revenue account reflecting the developmental activities of the Development Group itself, together with a 'net revenue account' through which were reflected certain other transactions such as the apportionment of loan charges between parent authorities, and the expenditures and incomes arising from property under the management of the Development Committee.

The division of amounts advanced by the County between its general rate account and a special recoverable account reflects an arrangement whereby all advances for non-revenue earning schemes carried out by the Development Committee were to be met from the County's annual revenue budget, while advances for those schemes with revenue earning potential were to be met from a special account with more explicit provision for recovery.

In contrast to the income and expenditure flows of a normal local authority, the tabulations included in *Figure 28* indicate that the

Figure 28 Financial arrangements for Droitwich Town Development

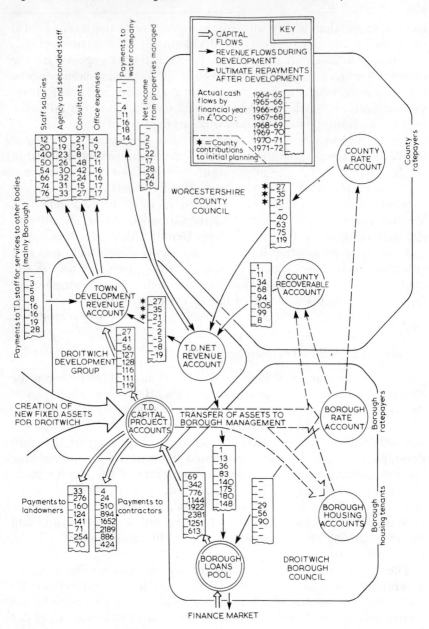

cash flows in and out of the Droitwich Town Development accounts were to change markedly from one year to the next, reflecting the gathering momentum of the programme and the changing pattern of operations. For instance, while the level of payments to landowners for land acquisition reached an early peak in the second year of the scheme, payments to contractors for construction work were then only just beginning to mount up. The fall in the latter payments from the year 1969/1970 reflects a series of obstacles that arose in maintaining the pace of development works, which we shall discuss in later chapters. Expenditure on salaries shows a comparatively stable pattern from the fourth year onwards, when the Committee's own staff was well-established and the need for reliance on outside consultants was correspondingly diminished. Transfers into the main revenue account from the net revenue account ceased to be significant in 1967 because of an agreed limitation on the period during which the County would support the Group's general planning activities. From that time onwards, the Group was under increasing pressure to become self-supporting through its work on specific projects. Because there were none of the continuing revenue accounts of a normal local authority through which to absorb administrative oncosts, any delays in the pace of development quickly became reflected in increasing difficulties in working within the budgeted levels of oncost percentage.

By the onset of the nineteen-seventies, a total of some half a million pounds had been advanced from the County's rate and recoverable accounts towards the loan charges on capital schemes, as can be seen by accumulating the sums appearing in the relevant tabulation of *Figure 28*. Another of the tabulations in the analysis indicates how the Borough began to make mounting contributions from its own rate fund at one period — reflecting in particular those proportions of highway and sewerage investments that had been judged as not attributable to overspill — though there was a respite in the following years. In later chapters, some of the implications of these financials transactions will be discussed from the perspective of particular forms of development; at this stage, our concern is merely to present a broad view of the financial aspects of the internal relations between the three main local components of the complex configuration of organizations and interests concerned with planned expansion at Droitwich.

The policy system for the expansion of Droitwich

This chapter has explored several dimensions of the new local arrangements that evolved to manage the expansion of Droitwich once the Town Development agreement had been signed. The set of actors appearing partly or wholly within the broken boundary of *Figure 25* can be viewed as working within a multi-organizational policy system, which can be described with some precision by reference to an action space constituting the class of all decisions about how to implement the development programme, within the written policy guidelines as accepted at the time of the agreement.

Seen as a case of a 'multi-organization', as defined by Stringer — a set of individuals from different organizations brought together in pursuance of a common task — some distinctive characteristics of the Droitwich arrangements emerge. First, one of the three contributing organizations — the local Development Group — is distinguished not only by being entirely rather than partially concerned with the defined task, but also by being primarily accountable to the other two agencies through a Joint Committee. Also, as shown by *Figure 26*, the Development Group differs from the two established local authorities in being based on the principle of a unified staff structure with hierarchical lines of accountability, backed up by several other attributes of a cohesive corporate organization — a common location, a shared orientation towards a recognized task, and a rich network of internal communication, which in this case focused on the Monday morning meetings in the Group Administrator's office.

Because the planned duration of the expansion programme was of the order of fifteen years, the arrangements which evolved at Droitwich can be interpreted as a significant borderline case between the building of a new permanent organization and the assembly of a more transient 'project-type' form of structure, as recognized by organizational theorists. The latter form is typical of many types of task in the field of construction — where *ad hoc* teams of architects, engineers, and other specialists may be assembled from independent consulting firms (Higgin and Jessop, 1965) — and of advanced technology, where major programmes may require formation of large teams which cut across several departmental and organizational boundaries (Miller and Rice, 1967).

However, a time-horizon of fifteen years is quite a long one for such a project-type organization — indeed, not far removed from the career horizons of many of the participants. The borderline status of the Droitwich organization in the distinction between project-type and permanent organizations is underlined by the fact that some of the staff were specially recruited from other authorities, others were serving on secondment or contributed on a part-time agency basis, while others again were working under consultancy terms. If the membership of the Droitwich policy system is defined to include all those attending the monthly meetings of the Development Committee, as shown in *Figure 27*, then representatives of each of these categories are included. For instance, the estates consultant, who attended these meetings regularly and was thereby provided with opportunities to communicate freely with all the officers and elected representatives present, could be considered more fully a member of the Droitwich policy system than the consultant quantity surveyor, who would not normally attend these meetings but would communicate through more specialized bilateral channels with particular technical officers.

During the period of the research, opportunities arose to talk individually to most of the main professional officers who attended the monthly meetings of the Development Committee. Personal interviews were also held with each of the Borough representatives serving on the committee of 1969–1970, with all but one of the County representatives, and with the first representative of the Labour Party who joined the committee after the Borough election of 1972. In this way, we were able to draw together a rich variety of different perspectives on the problems of the expansion, and the effectiveness of the organizational arrangements in dealing with those problems.

Perhaps predictably, one point on which the elected members from both the County and Borough Councils expressed virtually complete agreement was that the principle of control through a joint committee of existing local authorities was to be preferred to the alternative solution of control by a New Town Development Corporation. That alternative would have meant yielding the primary responsibility to an agency of central government, a solution which had in fact been imposed in the neighbouring town of Redditch on the breakdown of negotiations between the local authorities concerned. Also predictably, some of the officers of the Development Group would from time to time express a sense of frustration at the problems of working for a joint committee; under the more clear-cut arrangements of the New Town solution, they felt that they might have expected their controlling body to have developed a more consistent set of policies, less vulnerable to changing pressures from local councils and their electorates.

Within the three main organizational groups concerned, the most persistent stresses tended to be those between the officers of the

Development Group and the Borough Council representatives on the Development Committee — though these stresses would not usually emerge overtly in the committee meetings themselves because of the need to preserve the formal relationship of subordination between officer and member. Both these groups were much more intimately concerned in the execution of the Droitwich development programme than the County Council representatives, whose main concern was to see the programme carried out sufficiently expeditiously to demonstrate that they were making an effective contribution to the accommodation of Birmingham overspill, while maintaining their financial liability within tolerable limits. To the Borough Council members, however, almost any proposal put forward by the officers could be seen to impinge intimately on the physical and social fabric of their local environment, with a possibility also of adding directly or indirectly to a financial burden which was already a source of much concern to local ratepayers.

Of course, continuing processes of mutual adjustment were to take place over the years between the Development Group officers and the Borough Council representatives on the committee, both through the monthly committee meetings and through other less formal contacts. As the latter were gradually able to form a fuller appreciation of the various operational problems and constraints encountered in the management of a comprehensive development programme, so the former were gradually able to increase their understanding of the policy pressures to which the local representatives were subjected. It was significant, however, that exactly one-half of the Borough Council members did not have the opportunity of attending the meetings of the Development Committee, and so were less directly involved in this mutual adjustment process. Consequently, at the meetings of the Borough Council and its committees, where no officers of the Development Group were normally present, there were occasions when proposals emanating from the Development Group would be viewed with suspicion, and sometimes referred back or rejected. On such occasions, the apparently obstructive attitude of the Borough Council could add to the sense of frustration among the officers; while the Borough Council members would feel equally frustrated by their inability to challenge the technical basis of the officers' proposals.

The stresses involved in the processes of mutual adjustment between these groups came to bear most insistently on certain individuals occupying crucial positions at the interfaces between organizations, and therefore deeply engaged in the processes of 'boundary control' in the terminology used by Miller and Rice

(1967). One of these individuals was the Group Administrator, in his role as principal adviser to the joint committee; another was the committee chairman, whose role required him to strike a continuing balance between the sometimes conflicting tasks of providing leadership to the Committee and acting as a spokesman for the local interests of his parent authority. To a lesser extent, similar stresses had to be borne by the remaining seven Borough representatives on the committee, with their dual responsibility for representing their Council's local interests at the monthly committee meetings, and for imparting to their other colleagues on the local authority an appreciation of the complexities encountered in the management of the Town Development programme.

Such forms of stress can be seen as a consequence not so much of the particular organizational configuration at Droitwich, but rather of difficulties that are intrinsic to the task of managing a major transformation of an existing urban community in conformity with regional policy aims. This point will, we hope, emerge more clearly in the next few chapters, where the focus shifts to an analysis of the ways in which the multi-organizational policy system introduced in this chapter proceeded to deal with a range of fields of decision including highway construction, housing and industrial development, and central area renewal. In each of these fields, the role of the Development Group and its controlling committee was a central one, although, in each case, the processes of decision-making tended to range widely within networks of relationships with government departments, local community interests, private enterprises, and other bodies. However, we shall also be concerned in Part II with certain other fields, including those of neighbourhood improvement and provision of specialist community services, in which the role of the Development Group becomes more peripheral, and the focus of attention moves to the planning processes of other local and regional agencies.

Superimposing the main organizational relationships described in this chapter on the organizational base-map presented earlier, the broad picture becomes one of interaction between existing local authorities and an 'agent of local change' in relation to the management of an agreed developmental task, as indicated in *Figure 29*. The general situation is one which can arise in many different types of regional and national setting, and the choice of organizational configuration for any particular local operation will always have to reflect the existing institutional structure; but, within these constraints, a rich variety of organizational choice may still be open.

Figure 29   Main organizations involved in development of Droitwich from
1964 to local government reform in 1974

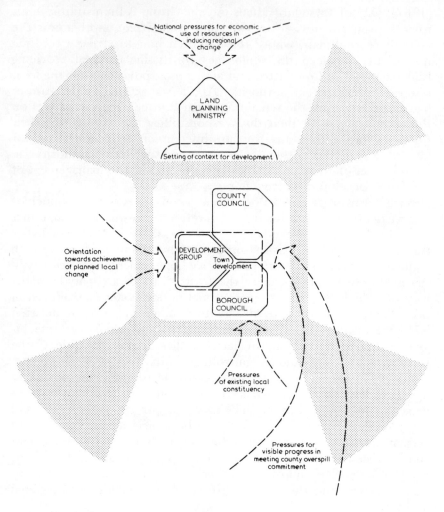

As will be discussed more fully in Chapter 15, the options open for local organization range from that where the 'agent of change' is located entirely within one existing local authority to that of the centrally-appointed Development Corporation. Other types of organizational solution for planned expansion may involve more direct involvement by the exporting authority than in the case of Droitwich; while again, the location of the principal 'agent of change' may shift into other quarters of the diagram in situations where the main developmental initiatives move towards the realm of private enterprise or that of voluntary community organization, as in some inner city areas.

Although, in most of the chapters of Part II, we shall be approaching the problems of managing local and regional change from the specific vantage point of Droitwich Town Development, our ultimate purpose will be to form more general propositions which can be interpreted and tested much more widely within the field of public planning, irrespective of the pattern of relationships between agencies which may have developed in any particular set of local, regional, and national circumstances.

Part II Networks

6   Planned expansion

The task of the development group

As has already been indicated in the preceding two chapters, the task
for which the Droitwich Development Group was set up was to
manage the planned expansion of the town according to the
guidelines laid down at the time of the Town Development
Agreement, working under the direction of the joint Development
Committee. As in any scheme of rapidly induced urban expansion,
this task involved the co-ordinated planning and implementation of
many interrelated aspects of development including housing, industry, roads, schools, public utilities, shopping, and recreational
facilities. Each aspect of development was subject to its own specific
set of external influences, and these will be further explored in
succeeding chapters. The purpose of the present chapter, however, is
to look more broadly at the pattern of relationships in space and in
time between different types of development project, and to
understand the implications for internal co-ordination among the
staff of the Development Group itself.

The policy context

The local policy context within which the officers of the Development Group first faced their task of managing the expansion of

Figure 30   Droitwich Town Map proposals: simplified presentation

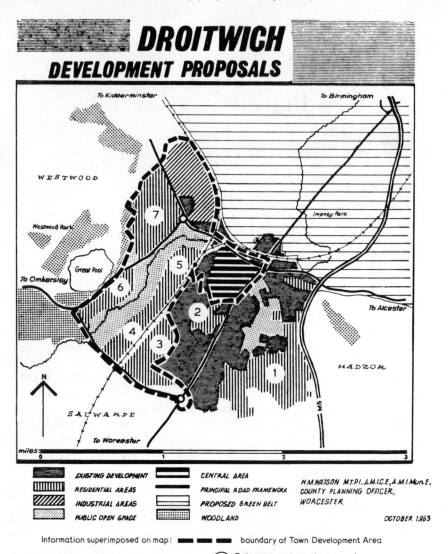

Droitwich was provided by the Town Map and accompanying written statement drawn up by the County Planning Department in 1963. A simplified version of the basic Town Map layout is reproduced in *Figure 30*. The map itself is taken from a leaflet produced for public information by the County Planning Department, but in *Figure 30* the designated boundaries of the Town Development Area have been shown superimposed to indicate the geographical extent of the responsibilities of the Development Group. Within the designated area, the map shows proposals for new housing on either side of the River Salwarpe — a local tributary of the Severn — with the lower-lying areas of the river valley reserved for use as public open space. Other main proposals included an industrial area in the north, forming an extension of a small existing industrial estate, and an area of comprehensive redevelopment covering most of the commercial core of the town. The map also indicated proposals for a roughly rectangular 'box' pattern for the main road network, with the A38 Birmingham-Worcester trunk route continuing to take most of the town's through traffic.

Between the A38 road and the M5 motorway, which formed a barrier to eastward expansion, some further land, outside the Town Development Area, was zoned for housing development by private enterprise, as part of the understanding that approximately one-third of the total housing construction programme would be carried out entirely within the private sector. Within the designated area, however, the exact allocation of sites between the rented and 'sponsored' housing sectors was left open for future determination.

The assembly of land

Of the proposed housing sites within the Town Development Area, there was one which was already in Borough Council ownership and readily accessible for early development. Even before the Development Group was formed, it was therefore possible to retain consultant architects to prepare layouts and make an early start on the housing programme. However, most of the land required for development in the designated area was not yet in public ownership. The Town Development legislation provided the Development Committee with powers of compulsory purchase at values determined independently by an agency of central government, on the basis of expected market price in the absence of town development; and in order that the processes of land assembly should proceed without delay, it was agreed that two compulsory purchase orders should be submitted to the statutory processes of public inquiry and

Figure 31   Droitwich Master Plan proposals

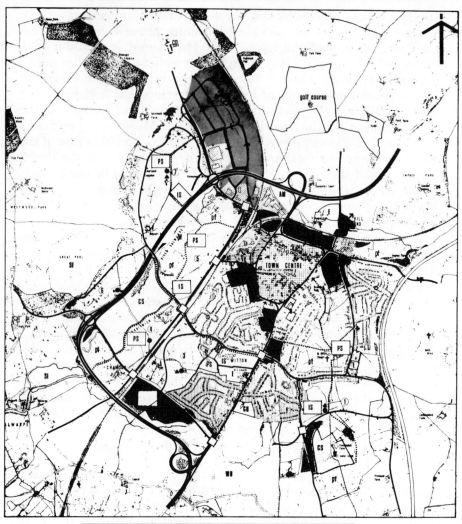

Primary distributor   District distributor
pf = Playing fields   PS = Primary school   IS = Intermediate school
CS = Comprehensive school
(Housing areas numbered as in Figure 30)

central government authorization at an early stage. One of these related to the industrial estate and the other to the remainder of the land required outside the central area; in both cases, most of the land concerned was then in agricultural use, so that only limited numbers of owners were affected. The more complicated and contentious problems surrounding the compulsory purchase of residential and commercial properties within the town centre were deferred for the time being, pending the drawing up of a comprehensive scheme for central area redevelopment.

The Master Plan

As a prelude both to the preparation of a central area plan and to the drawing up of a phased programme of development elsewhere, an initial task of the Development Group Officers was to translate the land-use proposals of the Town Map into a somewhat more specific 'Master Plan', in accordance with the conventions that were widely accepted in the planning of New Towns. The requirement to produce such a Master Plan had been set out formally in the initial agreement, which specified that the Plan should 'implement the principles' of the Town Map proposals, and should also 'act as a general guide to development during the progress of the scheme'.

Thus, the Group Planner Architect on his appointment was explicitly committed to certain guidelines in terms of physical form of the expanded town; but once he began to appraise the opportunities and constraints presented by the existing form of the town in the light of his earlier New Town experience, he found himself challenging certain key aspects of the design, especially the proposed road layout. Preliminary indications of future traffic flows appeared to indicate that the simple 'box' layout would have entailed the construction of split-level junctions close to the town centre, which would have been quite out of keeping with its intimate character and scale; while the proposed widening of the A38 trunk road would have created a physical barrier making it more difficult to achieve any social integration between the Town Development Area on its west side and the mainly private residential neighbourhoods to the east. Consequently, when the Master Plan proposals were published, some eighteen months after the formation of the Development Group, some radical changes in road layout were proposed, including the diversion of through traffic onto a new 'outer relief road'. The changes are indicated by *Figure 31*, which reproduces the basic map showing the Master Plan proposals. Comparing this to *Figure 30*, and allowing for the use of a more detailed

Figure 32 Phasing of capital expenditure in Droitwich town development programme (as estimated in 1966)

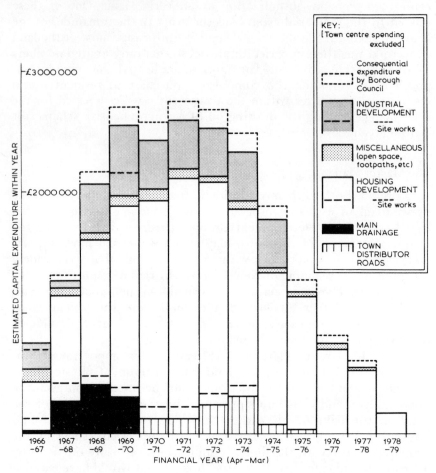

KEY:
[Town centre spending excluded]

- - - - Consequential expenditure by Borough Council

INDUSTRIAL DEVELOPMENT
- - - - Site works

MISCELLANEOUS (open space, footpaths, etc)

HOUSING DEVELOPMENT
- - - - Site works

MAIN DRAINAGE

TOWN DISTRIBUTOR ROADS

ESTIMATED CAPITAL EXPENDITURE WITHIN YEAR

£3 000 000

£2 000 000

1966 -67 | 1967 -68 | 1968 -69 | 1969 -70 | 1970 -71 | 1971 -72 | 1972 -73 | 1973 -74 | 1974 -75 | 1975 -76 | 1976 -77 | 1977 -78 | 1978 -79

FINANCIAL YEAR (Apr–Mar)

HOUSING PROGRAMME BROKEN DOWN BY AREA:

◄--AREA 3---► (374 dwellings)   ◄--AREA 5--► (450 dwellings)   ◄---AREA 3---► (230 dwellings)

◄----AREA 7----► (1500 dwellings)   ◄----AREA 4----► (920 dwellings)

◄-AREA 6-► (430 dwellings)

(Locations of numbered areas indicated in Figure 30: areas 1 and 2 excluded, as reserved for private housing outside Town Development Area)

notation, it may be noticed that there is little difference in the disposition of industrial or residential sites, although the areas of the latter appear as somewhat reduced in the Master Plan to allow for the siting of schools and other local amenities.

The scheduling of development

After the Master Plan proposals had been approved by the Development Committee and its parent authorities, and the necessary processes had been set in train for amending the statutory Town Map to allow for the modified road layout, the officers of the Development Group were able to begin drawing up a programme for the phased implementation of housing, industrial, and other related works. In this, they had to take into account the knowledge that they had so far gathered about the constraints affecting opportunities of early development in certain areas, such as difficulties of road access or lack of sewerage provision. Some broad assumptions had then to be made about the incidence of each form of capital expenditure over the years from 1966 to the planned completion date of 1979. The result was a long-term capital programme, costed at some twenty-two million pounds and phased over time in the way indicated in *Figure 32*; included within the total was an element of just over one million pounds of Borough Council expenditure directly associated with the town development programme.

In the two key sectors of housing and industrial development, the pattern revealed in Figure 32 is one of rapid rise to a peak level of activity during the years 1968 to 1975 inclusive, with the industrial programme then terminating and the housing programme continuing at a decreasing rate until the agreed completion of the scheme in 1979. So far as infrastructure is concerned, the pattern is one of concentration on main drainage works in the earlier years to enable the programme of housing and industrial development to build up, followed by construction of the internal road network to open up further housing areas to the west and south of the town. The proposed sequence of housing development by area is indicated at the foot of *Figure 32*, the numbers corresponding to those indicated on the maps of *Figures 30* and *31*.

This initial capital programme provided a basis from which the scale of forward commitments could be assessed by those departments of central government responsible for the sanctioning of loans for capital projects. The programme was also used by the County Treasurer's staff as a basis for bringing up to date their estimates of the revenue implications of the programme, which they had originally prepared in 1963 as supporting information for their negotiations with the Borough. By now, the expected financial impact in the earlier years of the scheme was appreciably higher than in the original profile (as charted in *Figure 23*). Accordingly, the Treasurer attached to his projections a report discussing alternative ways in which the costs might be more evenly distributed over the period of the programme.

Uncertainty in the capital programme: An experiment

During the years that followed the presentation of this long-term programme in 1966, it was not found worth-while to revise it in its entirety in the light of changing circumstances. However, every year a shorter-term programme was prepared on the basis of a rolling three-year planning horizon, and was submitted by the Group Administrator to the Development Committee as part of the annual review cycle, alongside the coming year's revenue estimates and a report of the past year's actual capital expenditure by projects.

During 1969 and 1970, when opportunities arose for us to follow the deliberations of the Committee as observers, and to discuss the problems of managing the expansion with its members and officers, it became apparent that the sources of uncertainty surrounding the programme were becoming so complex that the course of operations could not realistically be foreseen more than a year or two ahead. In view of the aims of our research, it seemed important that we should attempt a systematic analysis of these sources of uncertainty, and the ways in which they were perceived by officers of the Development Group with different professional and operational perspectives. Accordingly, in January 1970 we decided to invite the collaboration of officers in a short experiment, intended to assess the then current status of some of the main projects in the development programme, and to explore in a methodical way the sources of difficulty encountered in their scheduling.

For the purposes of this experiment, it was decided to exclude the industrial estate and the central area, both of which could be regarded as relatively independent — although internally complex — aspects of the total programme, at least so far as the scheduling and management of development operations was concerned. Discussions with officers of the Group indicated that the future programme of development in the remaining areas could be adequately described in terms of a set of thirty development projects in all. Nine of these were concerned with housing, four with schools, twelve with roads, and four with public open spaces. The remaining one was a footpath which was to form an important link between the large new housing estate in the north-west and the town centre.

The idea of the experiment was that different officers of the Development Group should be asked, for each of the thirty projects in turn, to give their individual judgements on the range of uncertainty surrounding the year in which construction work might be expected to start, and also on any necessary relationships of precedence between one project and another. The assessments of the individual officers could then be collated, and a round-table discussion held to establish what information each had taken into account in making his judgement, and what explanation there might be for any divergences between them.

This kind of approach was suggested by an acquaintance with the 'Delphi' method (Dalkey, 1969), a technique for combining different sources of individual judgement in the estimation of parameters which cannot readily be estimated by less subjective methods. The 'Delphi' method has mainly been used for forward estimation of aggregative measures, such as national population or income levels, in the comparatively long-term future, where intelligent speculation may become more appropriate than specialist knowledge. The process allows for several cycles of independent estimation by individuals, interspersed by a feedback of measures of the statistical distribution of the estimates made at the previous stage. The expectation is that those with least confidence in their assessments will be most likely to modify them between one round and the next. The final distribution of estimates can then be expected to reflect a collective judgement in which the more confidently held opinions have attracted more weight than others, so minimizing the type of distortion that can arise through the influence of dominant individuals in a group discussion process.

In the exercise at Droitwich, however, our aim was not so much to arrive at a set of single 'best' estimates for project starting times, but rather to explore the nature of the factors underlying any divergences between the judgements of different professional officers. With this in view, a more informal and less tightly structured form of experiment was felt to be appropriate. Three of the senior officers of the Development Group agreed to co-operate, each from a different professional background: the Group Administrator, the Group Engineer, and the Group Planner. (The position of these three officers within the Group organization structure can be located by reference to *Figure 26*.)

For each of the thirty projects, each officer was asked to indicate his judgement as to the range of possible starting dates, using a special form which included a separate box for each year between 1970 and 1980 inclusive, together with two additional boxes to indicate any possibility of a project starting either 'later' (than 1980) or 'never' (to allow for the possibility that some of the longer-term plans for road links or housing projects might never materialize at all). A separate form was provided for each project, and the officer was asked to strike out at either end those boxes corresponding to years that he believed to be outside the range of conceivable starting dates for the project in question. This approach through elimination was chosen deliberately, in preference to one in which the respondent was asked for a more direct indication of conceivable starting dates, as it was felt likely to give a more realistic reflection of the individual's current state of uncertainty. To give an example of the data obtained, the assessment of possible starting dates for one of the larger housing projects (Chawson Lane I) was as follows for each of the three participants:

Administrator		Engineer		Planner	
1970	x	1970	x	1970	x
1971	x	1971	●	1971	x
1972	x	1972	●	1972	x
1973	x	1973	●	1973	●
1974	●	1974	●	1974	●
1975	●	1975	●	1975	●
1976	●	1976	x	1976	x
1977	x	1977	x	1977	x
1978	x	1978	x	1978	x
1979	x	1979	x	1979	x
1980	x	1980	x	1980	x
Later	x	Later	x	Later	x
Never	x	Never	x	Never	x

x = years eliminated from range of feasible starting dates for this scheme

● = feasible years of starting remaining after elimination of others

Thus, the engineer was more ready to entertain the possibility of an early start on this particular scheme than either of his colleagues, while all three agreed that it was virtually inconceivable that a start on construction would be delayed beyond 1976, if not 1975.

When considering each project, the respondent was also asked to mark with a cross on a map any other related projects upon which he believed the current project to be dependent in terms of sequencing, indicating the approximate orders of time lag involved. Taking again the example of the housing area already quoted, the judgement of the planner was that the housing development could not start earlier than the construction of the proposed new primary school within its curtilage, and also that a start would have to be made on the adjoining sector of the new spine road at least two years before work on housing in this area could begin.

The judgements recorded by the three officers about the total set of precedence constraints for all thirty projects differed considerably, but there were not many outright inconsistencies between them. It was therefore possible to use the collated information on sequencing constraints to assign serial numbers from one to thirty to the projects, in such a way that no project with a lower serial number was likely to be constrained in its timing by the starting date of a project with a higher number. This provided a logical order in which to present the collated information on each of the thirty projects for discussion at a round-table meeting with the three officers concerned. This discussion was spread over two whole afternoons, and exposed a great deal of significant information about the factors that the officers had taken into account in making their individual assessments.

Figure 33 indicates the spatial relationships of the thirty projects in relation to an outline map of major roads and housing areas, abstracted from the Master Plan map of *Figure 31*. It also draws attention to the relationships of precedence between different pairs of projects, as identified by one or more of the officers. Then *Figure 34* on page 146 sets out a comparison, in tabular form, of the assessments by the three officers of the ranges of conceivable starting date for each of the thirty projects. The vertical strip appearing to the right of each set of estimates represents an interpretation by the IOR team of the range of conceivable starting years towards which the three officers were converging, following discussions on the causes for discrepancy between their individual judgements. It was not always easy to agree on a 'range of convergence' of this kind, given the limited duration of the exercise, the relatively unstructured nature of the discussion, and the tendency for debate to become diverted into other related issues. The indicated range of convergence does not therefore necessarily indicate a state of final consensus between the three officers, although in most cases it can be assumed to imply some degree of mutual adjustment in their initial perceptions.

Figure 33 Main development projects still to be started in Droitwich, January 1970 (excluding industry and town centre)

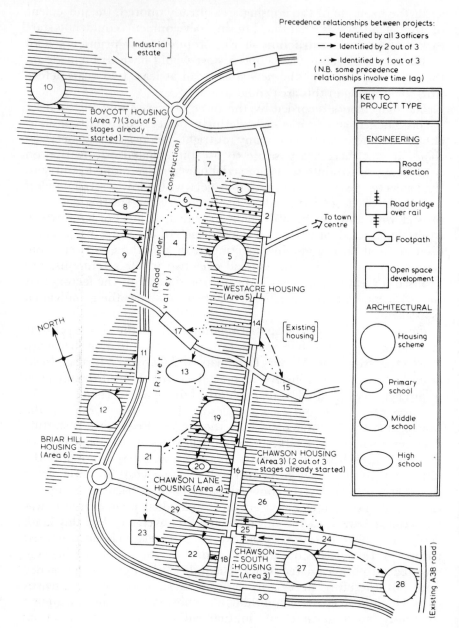

Precedence relationships between projects:
→ Identified by all 3 officers
- - ▸ Identified by 2 out of 3
· · ▸ Identified by 1 out of 3
(N.B. some precedence relationships involve time lag)

KEY TO PROJECT TYPE

ENGINEERING

☐ Road section

☒ Road bridge over rail

⬭ Footpath

☐ Open space development

ARCHITECTURAL

◯ Housing scheme

◯ Primary school

◯ Middle school

◯ High school

Industrial estate

1

10

BOYCOTT HOUSING (Area 7) (3 out of 5 stages already started)

(Road under construction)

7

3

6

8

2

4

To town centre

9

5

WESTACRE HOUSING (Area 5)

14

[Existing housing]

NORTH

17

[River valley]

11

13

15

12

19

BRIAR HILL HOUSING (Area 6)

21

20

16

CHAWSON HOUSING (Area 3) (2 out of 3 stages already started)

CHAWSON LANE HOUSING (Area 4)

26

29

23

25

24

22

18

CHAWSON SOUTH HOUSING (Area 3)

27

28

30

(Existing A38 road)

Development in the northern sector

Because of the sequence in which the thirty projects were arranged for review at the meeting, those covered in the earlier stages of the discussion tended to be at a more advanced stage of commitment than those discussed later, and there was therefore a lesser degree of discrepancy about conceivable starting dates. The first project, the northern section of the County's outer relief road (1), was agreed to be unlikely to start later than 1971 as it was already tightly programmed; also, after discussion, it was agreed that problems of completing the necessary documentation would make a start during the current year (1970) unlikely. The northern section of the proposed central spine road (coded 2, and discussed in detail in the next chapter) was readily agreed to be certain to start before the end of 1970 in accordance with the engineer's detailed schedule of operations in the area. Work on the adjoining primary school at Westacre (3) was seen to be almost certain to start during the following year; in the administrator's view, an earlier start was ruled out by procedural difficulties, and a later start ruled out by local pressures on school space and difficulties in transporting local children to other schools as an interim measure. The main housing area on the Westacre site (5), programmed for early construction of local authority rented housing, was also thought to be certain to start during 1971 — although, as Chapter 8 will discuss, this was one confident prediction that was to be confounded by subsequent events.

As the sequential linkages for project 5 in *Figure 33* indicate, the start of work in the Westacre housing area was thought to be closely interlinked with the timing of a number of other developments in the northern part of the Town Development Area, including certain works to be carried out towards the provision of public open spaces in the Salwarpe Valley (4 and 7). In particular, a footpath was urgently required (6) to give the rapidly growing population of the Boycott Estate a safe and direct means of access to the centre of the town. To the engineer, the footpath provided a key link in a network of related operations, involving demolition of an old sewage works which was rapidly becoming a public health hazard; the transfer of soil from one site to another to level the surface of future playing-fields; and the partial or total reclamation of the section of derelict canal which formed the western boundary of the Westacre housing area. The officers found some difficulty in assessing the timing of individual projects within this valley area, but came to the conclusion that 1970 was the most likely year for a start of work on

Figure 34   Range of possible starting years for construction of each of 30 development projects at Droitwich as assessed by 3 officers of Development Group, January 1970

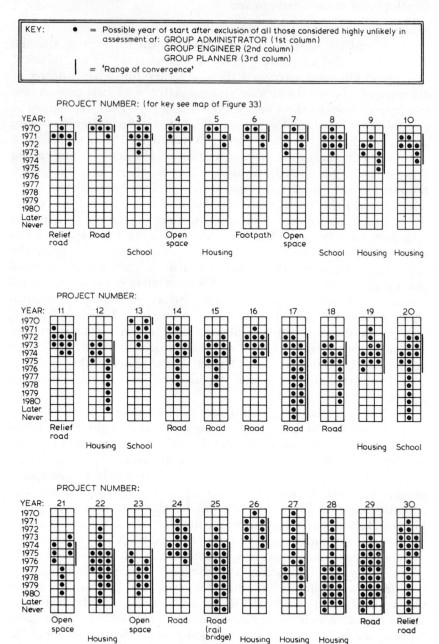

KEY: •   = Possible year of start after exclusion of all those considered highly unlikely in
                   assessment of: GROUP ADMINISTRATOR (1st column)
                                  GROUP ENGINEER (2nd column)
                                  GROUP PLANNER (3rd column)
            | = 'Range of convergence'

each of projects (4), (6) and (7). The possibility of deferment until 1971 could not however be excluded, because of uncertainties about the readiness of the Borough Council and the Land Planning Ministry to give early priority to those parts of the development to which they would be required to make a financial contribution: the provision of playing fields and the reclamation of derelict land, respectively.

Moving north-westwards to the large Boycott housing site, the building of a new 'Middle School' (8), catering for the age group between eight and twelve under the County's newly introduced three-tier structure of comprehensive education, was agreed almost certain to start during 1972, but with some possibility of a start before the end of 1971. Although the engineer had been ready to conceive of an earlier start, the administrator ruled this out on the argument that, because the school was designated to be managed under the auspices of the Church of England, there were the administrative procedures of the diocese as well as of the County Council to be allowed for before a start on construction could be made.

Turning to those sectors of the Boycott housing area on which work had not yet started at that time — represented by projects (9) and (10) — the range of uncertainty about possible starting dates began to widen significantly. Both areas were at that time under consideration as possible sites for 'sponsored' housing development, to be undertaken by private developers according to a planning brief to be laid down by the Development Committee as ground landlords. The situation was further complicated by a current threat of brine subsidence on the eastern side of Droitwich, affecting builders who had already bought land in that quarter but who might have to be offered alternative sites within the Town Development Area, if the momentum of the purely private element in the town's expansion programme was not to be lost. The complications encountered in maintaining a balance between sectors of the housing programme will be discussed further in Chapter 8; at this point, it is sufficient to note that there were appreciable differences in the officers' expectations of starting years for both the prospective new housing projects in the Boycott area. The discussion which developed in the meeting ranged widely over considerations of relative attractiveness to private developers, under either 'sponsorship' or direct sale agreements, of each of the three areas in the town where reasonable road access was already available — including not only the two Boycott sites but also a site adjoining the existing Chawson housing estate in the south.

Expansion towards the south

A further housing area at Briar Hill (12) lay on the far side of a section of the outer relief road (11). The scheduling of the latter was seen by each of the officers as uncertain at the time they completed their individual assessments; but, by the time the group exercise was held a few weeks later, confirmation of starting date had been received from the Highway Ministry. This was one of a number of instances in which the flow of new information from external sources led the officers to modify their predictions, almost on a day-to-day basis. Over the starting year for work in the Briar Hill housing area, which was believed to be especially suitable for the sponsored form of development, there was a considerable range of views. However, after discussion, a start later than 1975 was ruled out on the grounds that any further deferment would imply a virtual breakdown of the whole development programme.

The inclusion of the Briar Mill secondary school (13) as a single project in the exercise proved to have been misleading, in that the school itself was to be built in a number of phases, while engineering operations would also be required to level the surrounding land for the provision of playing fields. These, it was envisaged, might be used not only for school purposes but as part of the open space provision for the town as a whole. The interpretation of 'starting year' for the project had in fact differed between members of the team and, in default of an opportunity to repeat the experiment with a finer definition of the component development operations, the only possible starting year to agree upon was 1970, as certain preliminary stages of the development were already under way.

The next set of projects to be reviewed consisted of subsequent stages in the southward development of the new 'spine' road, with its distributory linkages to the remainder of the town's road system. The central section of the spine (14) could, in the engineer's opinion, conceivably be deferred until quite late in the programme because, if conditions of financial stringency were to persist, access to the new housing areas in the south could still be provided through other links in the network. However, the administrator argued that such an expedient could scarcely be publicly defensible in view of the modest cost of this stretch of road, as compared to the disruption entailed by leaving a missing link in the distributor road system; this would have meant a diversion of all traffic between the southern housing areas and the industrial estate through the congested central streets of the town. The engineer conceded this point; so, in this instance, the exposure during the discussion of some of the likely costs and benefits of alternative timing options had the result of bringing about a fairly specific and significant piece of mutual adjustment between the perceptions of the officers concerned.

Of the further proposed elements in the system of distributory roads, the link westwards from the spine road (17) involved improvement of an existing road rather than construction of a new one, and was therefore thought a possible candidate for deferment by both the planner and the engineer. However, the administrator conceded this possibility only with reluctance, after arguing that the prospective increase of traffic generated by the new secondary school was likely to make improvement an urgent priority, particularly if its facilities were also to be made available for general community use. The eastern link road (15) was a direct responsibility of the Borough Council and therefore thought liable to deferment, while the southern stretch of the spine road (16) was felt to carry significant implications for the opening up of all the southern housing areas, a process that could not be deferred too long if the basic aims of the town expansion were to be realised. However, there could also be disadvantages in opening up these areas too early, as the profitability of the town development scheme as a whole could be adversely affected should the housing areas in the south as well as those in the north be seen as providing options for short-term sale of land to sustain the pace of the private building programme while the uncertainty over brine subsidence remained. In contrast to the strategic implications of this road link, those of the short further extension of the spine road to the south (18) were seen as quite insignificant other than in terms of very localized housing access.

Turning to the first of the main southern housing areas (19), a prolonged and wide-ranging debate developed between the administrator and the engineer, starting from the apparently narrow question of whether or not a start as late as 1976 was conceivable. On the one hand, the engineer argued that a start by 1975 would be essential if the town expansion as a whole was to be completed on schedule by the end of 1979; in contrast, the administrator argued that the economic trends which were gradually slowing down the pace of housing development throughout the country were beginning to make the target of 1979 for completion of the programme look increasingly irrelevant.

As the debate developed, some of the underlying implications became more clear. The difference of opinion over the realism of the target completion year for the town development programme reflected not so much basic differences of attitude between the administrator and the engineer, as differences in the sets of organizational constraints within which each had to work. On the one hand, the engineer was required each year to submit claims for ministerial loan sanction covering the following five years, to be justified according to the plausibility of the assurances that could be given as to how far the roadworks were essential for sustaining an agreed programme of housing development. On the other hand, the administrator was in a position of having to keep under review a continually changing system of external influences on the pattern of housing development operations, all predisposing him at that time towards a strategy with a high premium on flexibility. Current sources of uncertainty included a fairly imminent prospect of changes in the system of central financial subsidies for local authority housing; an increasing element of doubt about the future supply of tenants from Birmingham in the face of divergent trends in levels of rents and of family incomes; a further doubt about the attractiveness to private builders of opportunities to participate in sponsored housing development in the prevailing market situation; and a possible need in the short term to divert private house construction from the east to the west side of town because of the current state of anxiety over the brine subsidence issue.

After eventually agreeing to leave open the possibility that the first stage of the Chawson Lane housing development (19) might conceivably be deferred until 1976, as well as the possibility that it might start as early as 1972, it was agreed that a similar range of conceivable starting years could apply to the new primary school (20) planned for a site — as yet undefined in detail — within that housing area, as there would be difficulties in finding school places elsewhere for the children of incoming residents. The proposed provision of playing fields in the adjacent valley area (21) was agreed to require phasing in conjunction with the construction of housing, first because of the need to transfer soil from the housing site, and second because of the likelihood of a serious deficiency in recreational provision in the southern sectors of the town. The value of open space development further down the valley area (23) was, however, seen to be much more dubious, in that it meant considerable expenditure to raise the land above flood plain level for a somewhat marginal return. Accordingly, this was agreed to be one 'project' that might never materialize at all.

Uncertainties in the southern areas

The officers were conscious that the remaining group of projects in the extreme south of the Town Development Area were related to certain questions of basic road layout which were as yet not fully resolved. The engineer expressed reservations as to how far it would be possible to justify a through traffic route along the east-west line of sections (29 and 24), requiring in particular the expense of an additional bridge over the railway (25), given that it was intended to run the southern section of the outer relief road (30) in a similar direction only a short distance away. At that time, however, a degree of uncertainty existed as to whether this stretch of the outer relief road might be realigned further to the south. This would have served in particular to increase the area available for housing in sites (22) and (27) at the southern end of the Town Development Area, and so to strengthen the case for bridging the railway as part of a separate through link within the internal network.

Even assuming the existing line of the relief road were to be retained, there was some uncertainty as to whether its proposed southern connection to the existing A38 trunk road might be combined with that of the internal link road (24) in a single gyratory interchange — an option that would have compressed the small housing site in the intervening area (28) to such an extent as to cast doubt on its viability as a unit of development, and therefore on whether it might ever be built at all.

The prevailing doubt over the justification for the new railway bridge in the south (25) implied a doubt over the ultimate justification of the proposed link to the outer relief road in the west (29). Even though the County Council had agreed to make a direct financial contribution to this road, the engineer was conscious that its traffic load might be comparatively light in relation to its costs, both in terms of finance and of disturbance to adjoining housing areas. The option of never building the link at all raised some practical difficulties, in that the County was well advanced with design work for the gyratory junction linking it to the other relief road. Nevertheless, the officers agreed that its omission could not be altogether ruled out at this stage.

The only area in the southern part of the Town Development Area where early housing development was thought feasible was the Chawson III site (26), the future of which the officers saw to be closely bound up with the uncertain future of adjacent parts of the road system. Both the planner and the engineer felt that the steeply sloping ground would present considerable difficulties of access unless this could be achieved by means of the proposed eastern link road (24). However, the administrator argued that construction of this road in order to provide housing access would entail changing the costs directly against the capital account for the housing scheme,

Figure 35 Overlapping planning perspectives emerging from exercise in assessing 30 town development projects, January 1970

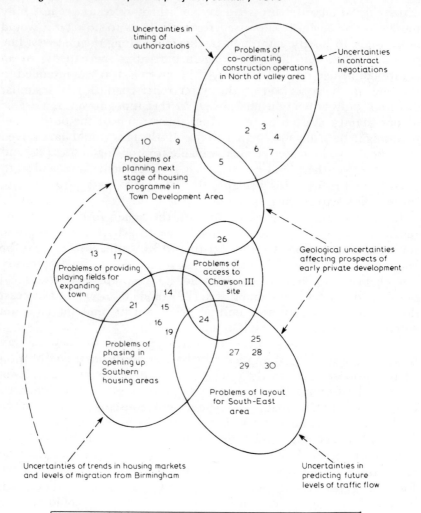

Uncertainties in timing of authorizations

Problems of co-ordinating construction operations in North of valley area

Uncertainties in contract negotiations

2   3   4
6   7
5

10   9
Problems of planning next stage of housing programme in Town Development Area

26

Geological uncertainties affecting prospects of early private development

13   17
Problems of providing playing fields for expanding town

Problems of access to Chawson III site

14
21   15
16
19   24

Problems of phasing in opening up Southern housing areas

25
27   28
29   30

Problems of layout for South-East area

Uncertainties of trends in housing markets and levels of migration from Birmingham

Uncertainties in predicting future levels of traffic flow

NUMBERS relate to project references as given on Figure 33

notes:
● projects 1, 8, 11, 12, 18, 20, 22, 23 not significant in terms of any of the perspectives defined above
● mapping is not intended to correspond to physical layout, but North/South and East/West relationships are preserved where possible in positioning of overlapping perspectives

which would almost certainly destroy its economic viability. If it should be decided to develop the area urgently as a means of maintaining the momentum of the total housing programme, then the difficulties of obtaining construction access through existing roads would have to be overcome. This in turn might restrict the options for housing on the site to one based on private development by a local builder whose construction techniques were not dependent on the use of heavy mechanical plant.

Planning perspectives in the Town Development Area

Despite the modest nature of this exercise, confined to the assessment of likely starting years for a set of thirty development projects, it had had the desired effect of providing a realistic cross-section at a particular point in time of the various sources of uncertainty and difficulty with which the technical and administrative officers of the Development Group had to contend in exercising day-to-day management of the implementation of the town development programme.

In *Figure 35*, the more difficult of the thirty schemes are shown grouped into overlapping sets which reflect some of the planning perspectives that were, at the time of the exercise, brought to bear on different parts of the Town Development Area. A notable feature is the geographical shift from a concern at the northern end with short-term problems in the co-ordination of construction operations, to a concern at the southern end with questioning some of the basic features of the Master Plan layout. The nature of the dominant sources of uncertainty varied accordingly. At the northern end, there were uncertainties on the one hand about the abilities of contractors to schedule their operations within the required sequential and seasonal constraints, and on the other hand about the speed of response of governmental bodies whose sanction was required before development works could be started. These included not only the (then separate) Transport and Housing Ministries, but also a financially hard-pressed Borough Council. Many of the uncertainties arising at the southern end, however, arose from inability to predict longer-term trends at a regional or national level. These included market influences which might affect the attractiveness of the proposed sponsored housing programme to investors, prospective changes in public housing finance, and the future readiness of Birmingham workers to move to Droitwich or any other of the regional overspill areas.

Figure 35 does not attempt to carry out an exact classification of the various uncertainties which had been exposed in terms of the three basic classes introduced in *Figure 10*. However, uncertainties of policy were clearly apparent in some of the debates that developed between the officers over whether certain technically feasible but politically undesirable timing options should be entertained; and several of the other sources of uncertainty indicated on the diagram included elements of uncertainty about related choices, any response to which would involve some form of co-ordination with other decision-makers, as well as elements of uncertainty in the operating environment, which could only be managed through surveys or predictive exercises. Even the uncertainty about the risk of brine subsidence in the eastern areas of the town, although at first sight clearly classifiable in terms of environmental knowledge, was in the event partly attributable to differences between one consultant geologist and his successor in the way the same physical evidence should be interpreted; so a case could be argued for classifying at least some of this source of uncertainty as concerned with fields of related choice. Some of the problems of management of uncertainty implied by the various planning perspectives highlighted in *Figure 35* will be dealt with more fully in the following two chapters, which focus on the distinctive planning processes for roads and for housing respectively.

The three officers and their organizational environments

Even though the three officers taking part in the exercise had worked together for several years as members of a cohesive group, sharing a commitment to a common task, the analysis presented in *Figure 34* and the ensuing discussion revealed several points of divergence in their appreciations of the state of the forward programme at the time in question. Although some of the divergences can be attributed to differing temperaments and professional backgrounds, the discussion revealed that one of the most important causes of divergence was the differing pattern of external influences to which each officer was required to be responsive.

Thus, the engineer, at the time in question, was required each year, to present a case to the Highway Ministry for a programme of expenditure stretching five years ahead, justified on the basis of necessity to meet housing construction deadlines. He was therefore reluctant to concede the possibility of delays in important housing projects which could jeopardize the whole progress of the scheme even though, as *Figure 34* shows, he was more ready than his colleagues to envisage a deferred start on some of the less essential projects. The administrator, on the other hand, was conscious above all of the fluid state of the housing market at that time, and the case for retaining a flexible stance for the time being on the scheduling of the major housing projects. This became most apparent in the extended argument that developed over the latest feasible start date of the Chawson Lane I housing scheme.

The contributions of the planner to the discussion process were rather more subdued; a reflection partly of temperament and partly of his role in the Development Group, which exposed him less directly to the immediate pressures of market forces or governmental control procedures than either of his colleagues. In general, however, his assessments as set out in *Figure 34* reflect an intermediate position between those of the other two. This supports the hypothesis that his patterns of interaction with them and other members of the group gave him a balanced, though not always very specific, general appreciation of constraints of both a technical and an administrative nature, through which to modify the longer-term orientations which he introduced as a member of the land-use planning profession.

Although the data presented in *Figure 34* can be subjected to various forms of further statistical analysis, any results must be treated with reserve because of the structural relationships between projects, and also because of the ambiguities in the questions posed in the experiment. For instance, any differences between the respondents in the criteria they implicitly adopted for judging earliest and latest 'conceivable' starting years could significantly affect the final distributions. However, one significant observation is that, in discussion, the officers were often prepared to concede that the range of uncertainty for a project was wider than they had allowed in their initial assessments, because of factors that they had not taken into account at the time. This illustrates the important general point that interchange of information between actors does not necessarily lead to a reduction in levels of perceived uncertainty. As suggested by the 'range of convergence' alongside each table of *Figure 34*, there may frequently be instances where the effect of new information on the recipient is to increase his awareness of 'latent' sources of uncertainty rather that to narrow down the range of uncertainties of which he was hitherto aware.

It is possible to argue that the exposure of new uncertainties can be just as creative a part of the mutual adjustment process as the reduction of sources of uncertainty which are already appreciated, especially if it helps in selecting immediate actions which are not too vulnerable to the choice of supporting assumptions. However, the

Figure 36 Some salient pressures bearing on officers of development group participating in project assessment exercise

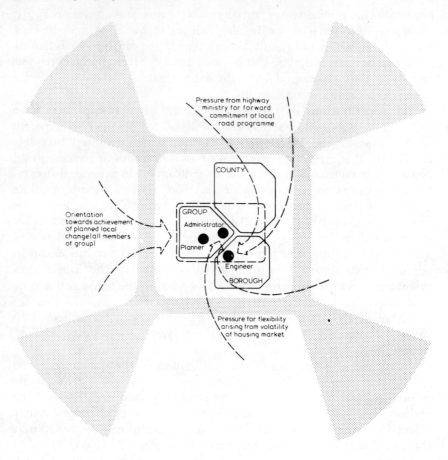

Pressure from highway ministry for forward commitment of local road programme

COUNTY

GROUP

Administrator

Planner

Engineer

BOROUGH

Orientation towards achievement of planned local change (all members of group)

Pressure for flexibility arising from volatility of housing market

engineer's problem of justifying his forward road programme to the Ministry illustrates that there may be political penalties to be incurred if the range of uncertainties affecting proposals for action becomes too widely exposed outside the protected setting of an informal decision-making group. In order to secure allocations of central resources in a situation of competition with other local claimants, it may be necessary to present a programme that represents only one optimistic scenario from a very complex range of future opportunities, over which the local decision-makers may have only a limited degree of control.

In the case of the Droitwich development programme, we made some tentative attempts to map out the overall 'opportunity space' for the timing of projects, through a computer program which sampled randomly from among the project starting years indicated in *Figure 34*, respecting the constraints of precedence shown in *Figure 33*. However, by this time it was becoming clear to us that any further analysis would have to take into account options other than those of timing alone, and also to consider the distinctive sets of external interests and influences impinging on roads, housing, and other sectors of the programme. These influences will be considered in the chapters that follow. For the time being, the types of external influence which we identified as salient in the case of the administrator, the engineer, and – to a lesser extent – the planner can be superimposed on our institutional base-map in the way shown in *Figure 36*, to indicate the kinds of factor that may create divisive forces even within the most cohesive working group.

Postscript

The results of the experiment can be evaluated not only as a means of exploring differences in perception between actors in the decision process, and inducing some mutual adjustment between them, but also as a contribution to our own learning processes as members of a research team, coming to the exercise with only a superficial understanding of the complexities of the local problem situation.

In reaching the broad appreciation of problem structure presented in *Figure 35*, we were made more fully aware of which of the thirty projects selected at the start of the exercise were important in terms of the overall programme, and which were of a more marginal significance. Indeed, this fuller awareness suggested that some of the projects would have been better split down for purposes of analysis into ·two or more component parts, while others could have been ignored altogether, had we felt justified in asking the officers to collaborate in a further round of the exercise.

One point of some wider significance concerns a matter of cartographic convention. We had approached the exercise without realising clearly that some of the internal roads we had marked on *Figure 33* were in fact existing roads to be improved rather than new links to be constructed. We had not found it easy, in effect, to develop a quick intuitive appreciation of the spatial relationships between the vision of the future presented by the Master Plan and the existing layout of Droitwich as set out, for instance, in the local town guide. What we lacked was a clear view of the problems of transition from the old to the intended new physical form of the town. To clarify this picture, we later found ourselves drawing up other forms of map, such as that reproduced in *Figure 38* of the next chapter, in which existing features were emphasized and projected future developments indicated in a less definitive way.

The question of cartographic conventions for the representation of uncertainty and indeterminacy is one that faces planners in most of the situations with which they deal, even though the devices adopted are not often viewed explicitly in this light. Indeed, several such devices were used in the Droitwich Master Plan reproduced in *Figure 31*, and we shall touch on some of them in later chapters. This suggests a case for recognising a general 'cartography of uncertainty', through which fields of indeterminacy can be made just as explicit as fields of intended commitment. As we shall see, the problem can become significant where the planner is concerned not so much with the creation of new structures on previously undeveloped land, as with achieving a gradual transition from an existing to an intended future state of a local community. In this situation, some conflict is only to be expected between the desire for purposive planning and the insistence of local people and their representatives on adequate room for future manoeuvre within a democratic process of government.

7 Roads

The extension of a road network

In turning from a broad survey of the relationships between highway, housing, and other capital projects at Droitwich to the more specialized planning context of highway engineering, we shall in this chapter be entering what is sometimes seen to be one of the more technical fields of urban and regional development. However, it is also a field in which the powers and interests of several different levels of government become involved, and is therefore of direct relevance to the theme of this book. This applies especially to the problems of introducing major extensions in existing urban road networks, as in the case of Droitwich.

The perspective which we shall adopt for most of the discussion that follows will be that of the Senior Engineer recruited to work within the Droitwich Development Group on terms of formal secondment from the Borough Council. Although he was directly responsible only for the construction of the more local roads within Droitwich, the Group Engineer (as we shall call him in accordance with the conventions established in Chapter 5) was also assigned a co-ordinating role in relation to all other engineering operations within the Town Development Area. We are grateful to the individual concerned, Mr Tony Hartshorne, for the considerable assistance he has given in compiling the picture of his activities and decision networks which

Figure 37 Division of highway responsibilities in English counties

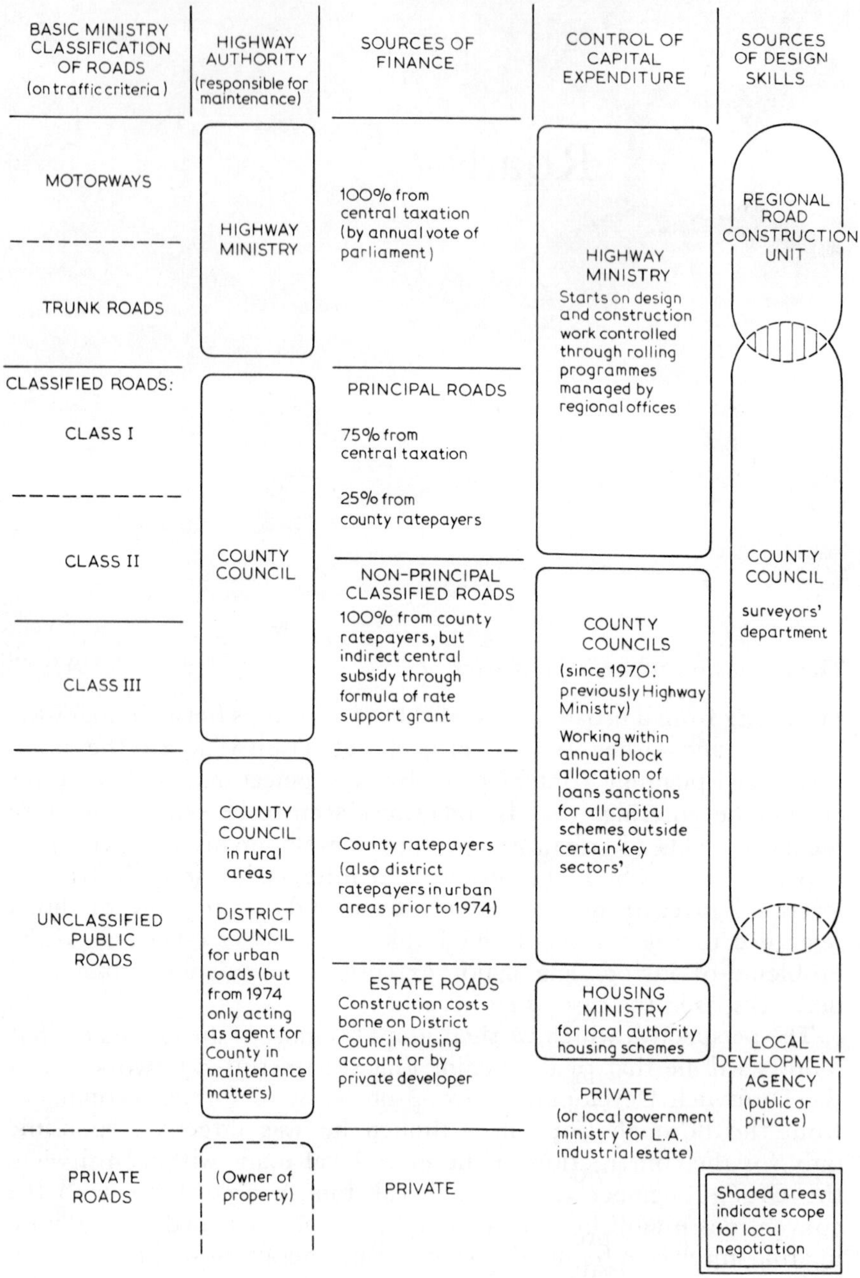

BASIC MINISTRY CLASSIFICATION OF ROADS (on traffic criteria)	HIGHWAY AUTHORITY (responsible for maintenance)	SOURCES OF FINANCE	CONTROL OF CAPITAL EXPENDITURE	SOURCES OF DESIGN SKILLS
MOTORWAYS - - - - - - - - - TRUNK ROADS	HIGHWAY MINISTRY	100% from central taxation (by annual vote of parliament)	HIGHWAY MINISTRY Starts on design and construction work controlled through rolling programmes managed by regional offices	REGIONAL ROAD CONSTRUCTION UNIT
CLASSIFIED ROADS: CLASS I - - - - - - - - CLASS II CLASS III	COUNTY COUNCIL	PRINCIPAL ROADS 75% from central taxation 25% from county ratepayers NON-PRINCIPAL CLASSIFIED ROADS 100% from county ratepayers, but indirect central subsidy through formula of rate support grant	(principal roads under Highway Ministry) COUNTY COUNCILS (since 1970: previously Highway Ministry) Working within annual block allocation of loans sanctions for all capital schemes outside certain 'key sectors'	COUNTY COUNCIL surveyors' department
UNCLASSIFIED PUBLIC ROADS	COUNTY COUNCIL in rural areas DISTRICT COUNCIL for urban roads (but from 1974 only acting as agent for County in maintenance matters)	County ratepayers (also district ratepayers in urban areas prior to 1974) - - - - - - - - - ESTATE ROADS Construction costs borne on District Council housing account or by private developer	HOUSING MINISTRY for local authority housing schemes PRIVATE (or local government ministry for L.A. industrial estate)	LOCAL DEVELOPMENT AGENCY (public or private)
- - - - - - - - PRIVATE ROADS	(Owner of property)	PRIVATE		Shaded areas indicate scope for local negotiation

follows later in this chapter: not only did he concede willingly to our various requests for information, but he often managed to keep one step ahead of us in interpreting it in a form relevant to the aims of our analysis.

The national policy context

As elsewhere, the provision of roads in England and Wales is subject to a set of procedures which allocate responsibilities between different types of agency according to criteria that relate mainly to the primary function of a road within a hierarchy of national, regional, and local communication linkages. At the national level, the government department carrying direct responsibility for highway matters was for many years the Ministry of Transport, but in 1970 this was brought together with the former Ministry of Housing and Local Government within the new Department of the Environment. It is significant that the highway functions of the transport ministry were at first brought within that part of the new department concerned with local government and development, rather than that concerned with other forms of transport, although this decision was later reversed. This reflects a continuing difficulty in judging whether it is more important to give formal recognition to the interdependence of highway and land-use policies, or to that of highways with other aspects of transport policy. Following the conventions introduced in *Figure 5* of Chapter 1, the term 'Highway Ministry' will here be used when referring to whichever department exercised statutory highway powers at any particular time.

During the years with which this chapter will be mainly concerned, the primary basis for allocating responsibilities for roads was the system of classification laid down by the Highway Ministry. As indicated in *Figure 37*, the most important roads within the national hierarchy, including the purpose-built motorways and other 'trunk roads' carrying substantial long distance traffic, were adopted for purposes of maintenance by the Ministry itself, which would insist on high design standards for any improvements or new construction works. Other stretches of road linking different local settlements were divided into three grades known as Classes I, II, and III, primarily on the basis of levels of traffic flow, and such roads would generally be provided and maintained by the County Councils. Most of the unclassified roads open to public traffic would also be maintained by local authorities. Prior to 1974, those within towns would generally be the responsibility of the Borough or Urban District rather than the County Council; after reorganization, it was ruled that County Districts could still claim maintenance responsibilities for all non-classified roads that could be described as 'urban', but that the County Council should be regarded as ultimate highway authority.

The level of contribution from central funds towards any proposed project of road construction or improvement was regarded at one time as a matter to be determined by the traffic classification of a road, but during the later sixties a separate type of classification was introduced for financial control purposes. All roads that were judged to make a significant contribution to regional communication networks would now be classified as 'principal' roads, attracting a fixed central grant of 75 per cent towards capital and maintenance costs; and it was understood that all Class I roads, but only some of those with a Class II traffic rating, would in time be designated as 'principal' according to this criterion. Motorway and trunk road projects would, as before, be wholly financed from central taxation, while non-principal classified roads would attract no central support, beyond an indirect subsidy arising from the inclusion of the total mileage of classified roads within a County as a parameter in the formula by which annual 'rate support grants' towards general County expenditure were calculated.

The assignment of priorities to future road construction projects in which central government had a strong financial interest — including motorways, trunk roads, and principal roads — was regulated through the Highway Ministry's forward capital programme procedures. Liaison with County Councils was maintained through the channel of regional representatives of the Ministry who were known for many years as Divisional Road Engineers. Later, as Regional Controllers in the Environment Ministry, their responsibilities were extended towards public transport investments through a new system of local 'Transport Policies and Programmes'.

Until 1970, priorities for other local authority road projects were regulated through central loan sanction procedures, operated again through the offices of the Divisional Road Engineers, but as a matter of purely financial rather than detailed design control. However, this procedure was superseded by one that gave County Councils greater freedom to determine their own capital priorities outside certain 'key sectors' of local government expenditure. One of the initial effects of this change was to increase the scope for local conflict between protagonists of different services and different District interests within a County, and there were many initial uncertainties as to the kinds of procedure through which the County Councils should exercise their new and difficult responsibilities for assigning relative priorities to different 'locally determined schemes'.

As *Figure 37* indicates, the division of responsibilities for design and supervision of road construction projects has always tended to be treated on a more flexible basis than the division of financial or maintenance responsibilities. The main design resources available for the larger projects were for many years those of the Surveyors' Departments of the County Councils; but, in recognition of the special pools of expertise required to handle design work on the motorway and trunk road programme, a decision was taken by the Highway Ministry in the later sixties to establish six new Regional Road Construction Units within its own departmental organization. However, there remained much scope for mutual adjustment in contracting work out on an agency basis where the local balance of skills and current commitments made this desirable.

The local context at Droitwich

The agreement between Worcestershire and Droitwich which constituted the joint Development Committee explicitly deferred any commitment to the future division of highway responsibilities, other than that for estate roads, until the shape and extent of the internal road network could be established. The relevant clause of the agreement read as follows:

> 'That any arrangements to be made between the parties hereto for or in relation to the construction, reconstruction, alteration, improvement or maintenance of a highway for which either party are the highway authority shall be the subject of a separate agreement or separate agreements under section 251 of the Highways Act, 1959 and may authorise the Committee, who under clause 3 hereof are responsible for estate roads only to undertake responsibility for other unclassified roads and also, if so agreed between the parties hereto, for such lengths of classified roads as may be agreed.'

So far as the physical form of the network was concerned, the Town Map prepared in 1963 specified only some limited changes to the existing pattern of roads in Droitwich, with the A38 road continuing to carry the through traffic from north to south, and other through traffic deflected into the 'box' pattern of roads as shown in *Figure 30*. However, the Land Planning Ministry, in approving these proposals, had advised that the A38 could not be expected indefinitely to carry the main flow of traffic through the town, and that alternative arrangements should be considered. Also, during the same year, a new policy perspective was beginning to emerge on the use of environmental as well as traffic criteria in transport planning,

Figure 38   Droitwich road network, with changes proposed in Master Plan

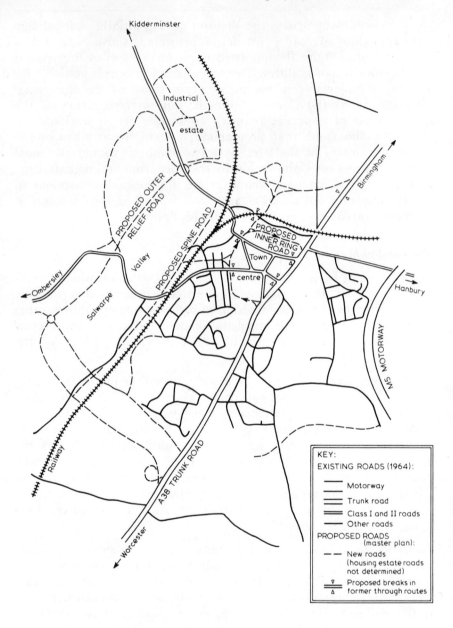

through publication of the Buchanan report on *Traffic in Towns* (Ministry of Transport, 1963). These two influences provided a justification for the comparatively ambitious modifications to the Town Map road pattern which were put forward in the Master Plan in 1965, following intensive discussions between the Group Planner Architect at Droitwich and the head of the County Highways Department, formally known as the County Surveyor and Bridgemaster.

Once the Master Plan proposals had been formulated, the field of potential negotiation over highway responsibilities at Droitwich became considerably easier to define. *Figure 38* superimposes the road proposals of the Master Plan on a map of the existing layout of streets and roads in the town at the time it was prepared, showing proposals both for new construction and for ultimate severance of certain existing road links. In the established pattern, the A38 road from Birmingham to Worcester was classified as a trunk route and therefore a direct responsibility of the Highway Ministry. However, much of the long distance traffic on the north-south axis was now being carried by the parallel M5 motorway, and there was always a possibility that the Ministry might ultimately propose 'de-trunking' the A38 for that reason. One or two other local roads had classified status, including those to Ombersley in the west and Kidderminster in the north-west, both of which were designated as principal roads once the separate system of financial classification had been introduced.

The main highway proposals in the Droitwich Master Plan were for the construction first of the new outer relief road, onto which the traffic on the A38 could eventually be diverted, and second of a new system of 'distributor' roads serving the Town Development Area. The principal features of this internal system were a one-way inner ring road encircling the town centre — so permitting the area enclosed to be restricted eventually to pedestrian circulation and access roads only — together with the new spine road already referred to in the previous chapter, running alongside the existing railway to connect the new housing developments to the west and south of the town with the town centre and industrial estate. Thus, the road system for which responsibilities were to be divided between the Ministry, the County, the Borough Council, and the Development Committee was significantly more complex than that envisaged in the earlier Town Map proposals.

Although the outer relief road was intended ultimately to replace the existing trunk route, the case for this replacement was not so immediate that it could be argued solely on the basis of the traffic criteria that governed the decision processes of the Highway Ministry at that time. Rather, the case had to be presented in terms of the present inadequacy of the two lesser classified roads, from Ombersley and Kidderminster, which joined the A38 within the town, both being of sub-standard width in places and passing under narrow railway bridges which were acute traffic hazards. These deficiencies were accepted by the Ministry as a justification for including the outer relief road within their principal road programme, so attracting a 75 per cent grant towards construction costs. Further, the Ministry accepted that, in due course, the relief road might qualify for reclassification as a trunk road, in which case they would take over full responsibility for maintainance. Such a reclassification would be required before the one-way inner ring road. system could be completed, as this would mean breaking the continuity of the existing A38 as a two-way traffic route. At this stage of the development programme, the central area of Droitwich would also effectively lose its existing external linkages to the national road network; and in compensation, the Ministry accepted the argument that the inner ring road itself should be given principal road status, together with the short stretch of road linking it to the outer relief road in the north. Among other conditions, this particular solution satisfied the Ministry's established constraint that any changes in classification should never be such as to increase the total length of trunk and principal roads already existing within an area.

Thus, the problems of assigning financial responsibilities introduced some subtle considerations of the transitional as well as of the final stages of the network, in which arguments about the environmental benefits underlying the form of the new network could not be deployed so overtly as those based on more traditional traffic criteria. Even though new procedures were at that time beginning to develop for closer consultation between the regional offices of the (then separate) Land Planning and Highway Ministries in the assessment of priorities for road construction works, difficulties were still being encountered in making these arrangements fully effective in view of the powerful professional and departmental interests involved.

Having clarified which parts of the Droitwich road network would attract principal road status, the County and Borough Surveyors — as the officers formally responsible within the town for principal and non-principal roads respectively — were in a better position to arrive at an understanding over their respective contributions of design resources. To work on the principal road system — the outer relief and inner ring roads, with the short connecting link between them — the County Surveyor set up a local design team in Droitwich (though after a few years this was moved back to headquarters at Worcester); meanwhile, all other roads in the Town Development Area were to become the responsibility of the Development Group's own Senior Engineer and his staff, working on secondment from the Borough Surveyor's Department. Before the formation of this group, however, the Development Group had already recruited to its technical team an Engineer Planner who was able to initiate much of the preliminary survey work, especially in the central area, and who was ultimately to become a member of the central area design team as indicated in *Figure 26*.

Within this accepted pattern of responsibilities, it proved possible to make a variety of local adjustments in accordance with considerations of mutual convenience. For instance, much of the early road design on the industrial estate was undertaken by the County Surveyor's Department before the Group Engineer's own team was assembled in 1965; while the Group Engineer was on occasion able to supervise certain projects for the Borough Council concerned with the improvement of roads outside the Town Development Area, making accessible a pool of technical staff which would not otherwise have been available within a local authority of that size.

The activities of the Group Engineer

During the first six or seven years following his appointment in 1965, the Group Engineer found himself involved in a succession of different kinds of activity directed towards the development of the distributor road system. He was able to express to us the changes over time in his focus of concern in the form of a diagram, which is presented in *Figure 39* in a somewhat modified and amplified form. Given the broad layout of the Master Plan from which to work, there were two interdependent types of process to be managed. One of these was concerned with the exploration of engineering design problems, while the other involved the estimation of expenditures and the initiation of the necessary administrative steps towards securing the required ministry and local authority authorizations.

Both types of process involved the Engineer in appraising different sources of relevant local information. So far as the design process was concerned, one of his first tasks was to review the form of the network as presented in the Master Plan, in the light of an improved set of traffic estimates which had now become available from the Group Engineer Planner. Also, his past experience indicated that one of his early priorities should be to identify any sources of

Figure 39   Changes over time in focus of decision processes for system of distributor roads in Droitwich

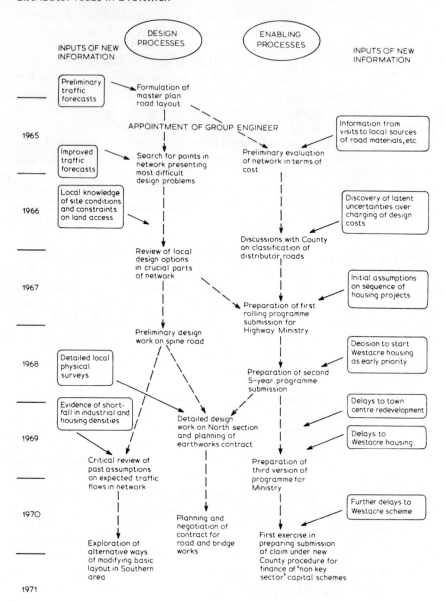

information on local site conditions which might be relevant to future construction problems. Potential difficulties of gaining access to land had to be identified, and attention had to be focused on any awkward points such as railway bridges where problems of a technical nature were likely to become enmeshed with constraints of conformity to external design standards and administrative procedures.

Among the inputs of information required for the activities indicated in the right hand stream of *Figure 39* were knowledge of local sources of road construction materials and skills, and estimates of the likely phasing of housing developments in different parts of the Town Development Area. It was while he was building up this body of local experience that the Group Engineer, through discussions with his colleague the Engineer Planner, became more fully aware of the ambiguities that existed as to the way in which the distributor road system, for the design of which he was responsible, would ultimately be financed. As yet, there was no clear understanding as to which costs would be met through the Town Development accounts — implying advances from the County to meet initial capital expenditure — and which costs would fall directly on the local ratepayers. Recognising the sensitivity of this issue while the financial base of the Borough Council remained slender, the Group Engineer and the Engineer Planner decided to raise with the County Surveyor the issue of whether some parts of the distributor network might ultimately attract classified road status, and therefore qualify for a 50 per cent government grant under the system of financial support which at that time applied.

The context of these negotiations with the County was in the event modified by the introduction of the new basis for determining ministry financial aid. Eventually, it was agreed that the County itself should bear 50 per cent of the construction costs of the main section of the proposed spine road, together with that link in the south (project 29 on *Figure 33*) which connected it to the outer relief road in the west. The expectation of Class III status could be justified for these particular links on the argument that ultimately they were likely to provide part of a public transport network linking the residential areas of Droitwich to other neighbouring centres. However, there still remained uncertainty as to whether the remaining 50 per cent of expenditure on these roads should be met through the Town Development or local rate accounts, as the County was able to argue that the traffic they carried in future would not be generated exclusively from within the Town Development Area. It was not until 1971 that a formula was agreed whereby these costs were to be divided between the two accounts according to the ratio of the current population of the town in any year to that envisaged at the end of the Town Development period.

From 1967 onwards, the Group Engineer became involved in a cycle of annual discussions, together with the senior administrative, planning, and architectural staff of the Development Group, to plan the sequence of construction of the distributor road programme over the next few years, with a view to securing authority from the Highway Ministry to raise the necessary loans. Although a programme was required each year to cover the following five years, the critical planning horizon was only two years ahead, so far as firm commitment to proceed with design work was concerned. The decision as to what level of work to plan for on this horizon was not an easy one, because of changing expectations about the likely starting date both for the housing developments adjacent to the proposed spine road and also for the nearby town centre redevelopment. Too ambitious a programme submission could be expected to lessen future credibility in the eyes of the Highway Ministry if it proved incapable of implementation; while too modest a submission could result in embarrassing constraints on the road programme at critical moments in the opening up of new areas to housing development.

The transfer of control over capital expenditure on the distributor road system to the County Council, under the new system introduced in 1970, meant a change in orientation on the part of the Group Engineer and his colleagues. Instead of having to justify rolling programmes to a government department concerned solely with highway expenditure, the Engineer found himself more concerned with supporting shorter-term claims on the County's total allocation for locally determined schemes of various different kinds. When the new system was first introduced, it was stated by the Ministry that allocations of capital spending for each County in each year would be calculated on the basis of average expenditure levels over the last three years, with the division between Districts, and between services, to be determined through local negotiation. However, it could justifiably be claimed that the circumstances of an expanding town justified some degree of special treatment. In the case of the distributor roads, the problem of securing adequate allocations of funds was further compounded by the prevailing uncertainty as to how costs were ultimately to be divided between the Town Development and local rate accounts.

The more technical activities of the Group Engineer and his section, having initially focused on the identification of key points of design difficulty in the distributor network as a whole, later began to divide into two parallel streams, as indicated in *Figure 39*. One of these was concerned with a reappraisal of the basic shape of the network, especially in the southern areas, for reasons which have already been discussed in the previous chapter. Before the end of 1971, this process was to lead to acceptance of some fundamental design changes, in which the southern end of the spine road was made to curl round to connect directly to the Outer Relief Road to the west, with improvements in terms of cost and housing layout. The other stream of activity was concerned with more detailed design work on the northern section of the proposed spine road, once it had been decided that the nearby Westacre housing site should be developed as an early priority. A review of alternative directions of access for housing construction traffic quickly indicated that the only feasible route was from the Kidderminster Road in the north, by way of the first section of the proposed spine road. Thus, it became essential to proceed rapidly to the negotiation of contracts, and the first stage in the implementation of the distributor system became a matter of considerable urgency to the Development Group officers.

The design options for Salwarpe Road

The problems of detailed design facing the Group Engineer and his colleagues in preparing for construction of the northern section of the new spine road — later to be named Salwarpe Road — involved a series of related decisions, of a kind which the Engineer felt to be in many respects typical of highway development within urban areas. Although the stretch of road concerned was to be only some 600 metres long, it nevertheless accounted, together with its junctions at either end, for over 30 per cent of the total capital cost estimated for the distributor system as a whole. This was because it would have to span the Salwarpe valley area, bridging both the river itself and the derelict Droitwich canal, which the Development Committee had agreed should not be severed in order to preserve the opportunities for ultimate reclamation for recreational use. The total capital expenditure for this section amounted to more than twice the annual rate income of the local Council, so economy of construction cost would clearly be a matter of some significance.

The starting point for design work was the Master Plan map, which indicated a line for the proposed road running not quite parallel to the existing railway, as shown in *Figure 40*. The approximate location of the junction at either end was also indicated on the

Figure 40   Design choices for northern end of Salwarpe Road

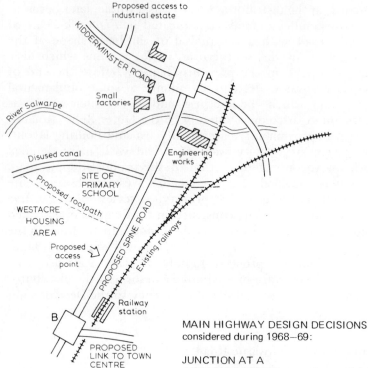

MAIN HIGHWAY DESIGN DECISIONS
considered during 1968—69:

JUNCTION AT A
- TRAFFIC DESIGN — gyratory or light controlled?
- SITING — move E or W of Master Plan position?
- CONTRACT — construct interim or final layout?

ROAD DESIGN BETWEEN A AND B
- WIDTH OF CENTRAL RESERVATION
  — enough to allow right turn from housing area?
- ALIGNMENT — move E or W of Master Plan line?

JUNCTION AT B
- TRAFFIC DESIGN — gyratory or light-controlled?
- SITING— location in relation to station?

OTHER RELATED AREAS OF CHOICE
- INDUSTRIAL ESTATE — access as shown or directly at A? ⎫
- SMALL FACTORIES — arrange for early relocation or not? ⎪ pattern of
- ENGINEERING WORKS — relocate or allow to stay? ⎪ perceived links
- UNIT FACTORIES — what priority for construction? ⎬ to highway
- LAND BETWEEN ROAD LINE AND RAILWAY — change ⎪ design decision
  zoning to allow for further industry? ⎪ areas changing
- ALLOCATION OF CONSTRUCTION COSTS — how to ⎪ gradually over
  split between Town Development and Borough rate account? ⎭ time
- FUNDING OF SECOND CARRIAGEWAY — make chargeable
  to housing account?

Master Plan map, although in each case the form was left open. This indeterminacy was indicated by means of a hollow square symbol, it being implied that either a gyratory layout or a simple intersection controlled by traffic lights might be considered.

It was such questions of traffic engineering which presented the Group Engineer with his first set of design problems. A related issue was that of whether or not breaks should be provided in the central reservation between the two carriageways of the road, a dual carriageway design being necessary according to current County design standards. The inclusion of breaks would only be needed if it was required to allow for traffic joining or leaving the road at intermediate points, to or from destinations which necessitated a right turn movement across the main traffic flow. Any such breaks would inevitably increase the width of the central reservation and therefore of the road as a whole; but the need for them could be avoided by the use of gyratory junctions providing U-turn facilities at either end of the road. The gyratory option could be most significant in the case of the northern junction, as the main intermediate access was at that time expected to be from the Westacre housing estate, from which southbound traffic would otherwise have to cut across the main northward traffic flow on the left-hand carriageway.

Before the detailed design work on the spine road began, the processes of detailed layout for the industrial estate to the north had led to the conclusion that the estate should connect directly to the top of the spine road, instead of joining the Kidderminster Road a little to the west of the northern junction as indicated on the Master Plan. In the view of the Group Engineer, this provided a fairly clear case for a gyratory junction at the north of the spine road, as opposed to the traffic light alternative. However, when the technical officers of the Group came to a detailed planning appraisal of the whole area, including the Westacre housing estate and the northern end of the spine road, questions arose as to how far the alignment of the spine road itself might be modified from that shown on the Master Plan map.

One problem was that the siting indicated for the Kidderminster Road junction implied the relocation of three small factories lying immediately to the south-west and also of a larger engineering works to the south-east, and it was at least conceivable that a re-siting of the junction a little to the west or to the east could reduce the total level of disturbance caused. The smaller industries had already been offered accommodation in a new group of 'unit factories' to be constructed by the Development Committee on its industrial estate to the north; but the programming of these units was already causing problems because of the constraints of designing within ministry cost and design standards. The larger engineering works had already been allocated a site of its own on the industrial estate; but the Group Administrator now raised the possibility that, if the northern end of the new spine road could be realigned slightly further to the west, the works management could be offered the chance of remaining and expanding on its existing site. This afforded a prospect of significant savings in compensation costs for the Development Committee, and also the possibility of ultimately allowing further industrial development in the wedge between the road and the railway. This land was designated on the Master Plan as 'incidental' open space, implying little opportunity of benefit, either economic or environmental, for the town. The potential gain in terms of productive land use would, however, have to be balanced against certain procedural complications, as such a change would require the express consent of the County as planning authority either as a 'departure' from the approved zonings or as a formal amendment to the Town Map.

Somewhat similar choices of layout and siting arose in respect of the southern junction, located close to the railway station; but it was the northern junction which presented the most immediate problems if contracts for the northern section of Salwarpe Road were to be drawn up as an early priority. Consultations with the management of the engineering works were beginning to indicate their interest in expanding on their existing site, provided that they could be assured of adequate road access and that a satisfactory basis of compensation could be negotiated for those peripheral parts of their existing site area that would have to be sacrificed for road building purposes. Thus, the technical problems of road design began to become connected to a variety of other choices, some involving interfaces with outside agencies, and the detailed planning of Salwarpe Road became a process of incremental commitment as various wider explorations were pursued.

Meanwhile, the Group Engineer began to question his earlier assumption that the form of the northern junction should be gyratory if it was to cope adequately with the traffic flows involved. If it were possible to design a simpler form of junction with traffic light control which would cope adequately with the expected traffic flows, this might possibly lead to less dislocation of existing industry: perhaps some of the smaller factories could be allowed to remain, as well as the engineering works. Also, there might be a financial saving in avoiding the acquisition of one particular piece of land to the north of Kidderminster Road which was not covered by compulsory purchase orders. However, a light controlled junction would mean the loss of U-turn facilities, and consequently a widening of the central reservation to provide a break for traffic turning south from the Westacre housing estate. This would mean an increase of some four metres in the total width of the road and the embankment on which it would have to be built, with consequential increases in construction cost and possibly a marginal sacrifice of land on the Westacre site, the housing capacity of which had already been effectively reduced by the County's introduction of new space standards for the primary school site adjoining it.

The evaluation of alternatives under uncertainty

For the Group Engineer, it was a finely balanced question whether or not the possible benefits of a light controlled junction in the north would be sufficient to outweigh these other disadvantages; but it was only a matter of a week or so's work on the part of one of his technical staff to produce a sketch layout for the light controlled alternative, and this he judged to be a worthwhile investment of resources in the light of the importance of the information that might be gained. In the event, the results of this design exercise showed quite clearly that there was virtually no saving of land acquisition costs to be realized through the light controlled alternative, so this option was once more rejected in favour of the gyratory form.

This brief episode in a continuing design process does, however, serve to illustrate the general types of judgement that repeatedly face a highway engineer, working in a context where traffic design and land-use choices are closely interrelated. In deciding whether or not to devote resources to the acquisition of different types of information, he must judge how far they are likely to contribute to increasing levels of confidence in the submission of design proposals. A discussion with the Group Engineer, two or three years after the events in question, led to a reconstruction of the factors entering into his consideration at the time, and this is set out in *Figure 41*.

The technique of AIDA (as introduced towards the end of Chapter 2, and illustrated in *Figures 13, 14,* and *15*) was used to discuss with the Engineer the relationships between the various areas of choice listed in *Figure 40*. This revealed that his attention at this time had become focused on two key decision areas concerning the form of the junction and the width of the proposed road, with his choice of feasible combinations restricted by certain incompatibilities. A light controlled junction could not be combined with a narrow central reservation on traffic grounds, while a gyratory junction combined

Figure 41 Analysis of alternatives and implications considered in making final commitment to design of Salwarpe Road

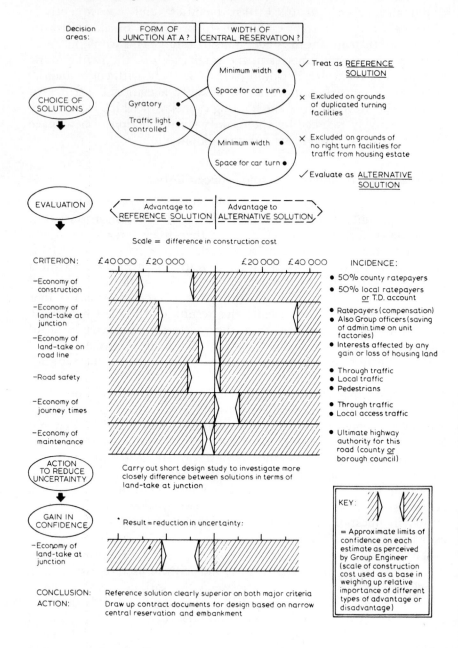

Decision areas:

| FORM OF JUNCTION AT A ? | WIDTH OF CENTRAL RESERVATION ? |

CHOICE OF SOLUTIONS

Gyratory ●
Traffic light controlled

Minimum width ●
Space for car turn ●

Minimum width ●
Space for car turn ●

✓ Treat as REFERENCE SOLUTION

✗ Excluded on grounds of duplicated turning facilities

✗ Excluded on grounds of no right turn facilities for traffic from housing estate

✓ Evaluate as ALTERNATIVE SOLUTION

EVALUATION

Advantage to REFERENCE SOLUTION | Advantage to ALTERNATIVE SOLUTION

Scale = difference in construction cost

CRITERION: £40 000 £20 000   £20 000 £40 000   INCIDENCE:

−Economy of construction
● 50% county ratepayers
● 50% local ratepayers or T.D. account

−Economy of land-take at junction
● Ratepayers (compensation)
● Also Group officers (saving of admin. time on unit factories)
● Interests affected by any gain or loss of housing land

−Economy of land-take on road line

−Road safety
● Through traffic
● Local traffic
● Pedestrians

−Economy of journey times
● Through traffic
● Local access traffic

−Economy of maintenance
● Ultimate highway authority for this road (county or borough council)

ACTION TO REDUCE UNCERTAINTY
Carry out short design study to investigate more closely difference between solutions in terms of land-take at junction

GAIN IN CONFIDENCE
Result = reduction in uncertainty:

−Economy of land-take at junction

KEY:

= Approximate limits of confidence on each estimate as perceived by Group Engineer (scale of construction cost used as a base in weighing up relative importance of different types of advantage or disadvantage)

CONCLUSION: Reference solution clearly superior on both major criteria
ACTION: Draw up contract documents for design based on narrow central reservation and embankment

with turning facilities between carriageways could be ruled out on
the grounds of extravagance, provided a U-turn facility was available
to the north. The choice was therefore reduced, as shown by the
simple decision tree at the top of *Figure 41*, to the comparison of a
solution based on a gyratory junction with a narrow central
reservation against a single alternative solution based on a light
controlled junction and a broader central reservation. The implications of this comparison are set out in the diagram, using a format
for the analysis of costs and benefits that permits the representation
of perceived orders of uncertainty as well as of expected orders of
magnitude.

Taking first the question of economy of construction cost, the
Engineer judged that the advantage of the 'reference' solution based
on a gyratory junction would be of the order of £20,000 — arising
mainly from a reduction in soil requirements for the embankment
and structural costs of bridgeworks — with approximate limits of
confidence of some £10,000 in either direction. In terms of economy
of land-take at the junction, there was an initial likelihood — but by
no means a certainty — that the light controlled junction would carry
a net advantage, and the Engineer's initial state of confidence in this
assessment is represented by the range between the arrows in the
second row of the analysis, using a scale implicitly related to that of
construction cost indicated in the row above. Other potentially
significant criteria in road design were reviewed in his discussion with
us, including economy of land-take along the road line itself, level of
road safety, economy of journey times, and economy of maintenance. In each case, the Engineer felt confident that the advantage
lay with the gyratory solution, although he expected the effects on
some of these criteria to be negligible when compared to the
construction cost differential.

Once the Engineer's technical staff had carried out their brief
design study into the light controlled alternative, any likelihood of
advantage from this solution became eliminated. This meant that the
gyratory form could now be seen to be 'dominant' in the sense of
possessing a clear advantage in terms of each of the more significant
criteria examined. This particular decision problem therefore proved,
in the light of further information, to be quite straightforward to
resolve. However, had the design studies indicated that there were in
fact significant economies of land-take to be gained from the light
controlled alternative, the Engineer and his colleagues could have
found themselves faced with some difficult judgements as to how the
remaining uncertainties of the situation should be managed.

Among these uncertainties, questions would have had to be faced about the implicit levels of trade-off between the different forms of cost and benefit indicated in *Figure 41*. Some of the policy considerations involved are suggested to the right of the 'balance sheet' of advantages and disadvantages, where the incidence of costs and benefits is analysed according to the different sectors of the community affected. To greater or lesser degrees, similar problems of trade-off between the interests of these various sectors could also be seen to underlie many of the other problems of judgement with which the Group Engineer and his colleagues were faced from time to time, including such issues, discussed in the previous chapter, as the choice of priority for the central section of the spine road and of possible design changes at the southern end of the network.

Taking the criteria set out in *Figure 41* in turn and exploring the various uncertainties of policy involved, the special circumstances of Droitwich made it more difficult even to weigh up the importance to be attached to differentials of construction cost, because of the prevailing uncertainty as to how much of this would fall directly on the politically sensitive local rate account. Furthermore, the cost of land-take was a factor that could not easily be evaluated entirely in monetary terms. For instance, at the junction, there was a need to attach some implicit weighting to the administrative difficulties likely to be encountered by the Development Group if the building of unit factories had to be accelerated to accommodate displaced industries. Also the extra land which would have to be taken to extend the width of the road could only be realistically valued in terms of gain or loss of intended housing opportunity, since it had already been acquired by the Development Group for this purpose. The land at issue corresponded roughly to that required for three or four local authority rented dwellings; however, policy questions arose in judging whether this should be implicitly valued in terms of loss of housing opportunity for Birmingham tenants, or in terms of some other indicator of the marginal sacrifice of opportunity involved to the local Development Group.

The analysis presented in *Figure 41* concerns a transient, and in many ways straightforward, incident in the continuing processes of design for Salwarpe Road; but it serves to illuminate some of the many sources of uncertainty which faced the technical and administrative staff of the Development Group in managing even the more tactical aspects of the expansion programme. Of the sources of uncertainty revealed by our simple reconstructed cost-benefit assessment, by no means all could be assigned to purely predictive factors of the type that could be resolved by technical survey work. Significant uncertainties of policy judgement can be identified both within and between the categories of impact identified in *Figure 41*, relating to different sectors of constituency interest; while other uncertainties emerge from the various fields of related choice identified at the foot of *Figure 40*.

The planning of road construction operations

Once the key decision on the width of the embankment had been finalized, the Engineer was able to proceed to the planning of construction operations and the prepartion of the necessary contract documents. Here, some further problems of design and negotiation began to arise. By this time, it had been formally agreed that the engineering factory located between the road and railway could remain, so it became necessary to preserve some means of access at all stages of construction work. Also, sources of soil had to be located for the construction of the embankment. Potentially, the closest such source was that provided by the intended excavation works for the new industrial approach road to the north of the junction; however, this was classified as an estate road, so that its construction was at that time subject to the loan sanction procedures of a different ministry to that of the spine road itself, and attempts by the Group Engineer to secure the necessary synchronization of timing proved unsuccessful. At this level of planning, which involved the scheduling of earth moving operations, seasonal factors also became significant; there were real advantages to be sought in completing the main transfers of earth before the winter months, while the soil was still comparatively light and dry.

In accordance with normal civil engineering practice, the preparation for construction work involved a procedure of drawing up formal invitations to tender, in which different elements of work had to be interpreted in terms of estimated inputs of materials and labour. Questions now arose of strategy for going to tender: whether or not the work should be assembled into two or more contracts, and whether contractors should be selected through open tender, through selective invitations to reliable local firms, or through direct selection from a list maintained by the County Surveyor. This was where the Group Engineer had to bring into play his accumulated experience of negotiation and on-site relationships with different types of civil engineering contractor. Each firm had to be assessed in terms of its known resources, including any specialist skills, its past record of reliability, and its current liquidity state, at a time when even long-established firms were becoming vulnerable to adverse trading conditions. Furthermore, some local contractors had to be regarded with caution because of the uncertainties generated by heavy dependence on sub-contracting, sometimes extending to individuals operating on a basis of 'labour only' contracting for reasons of tax avoidance. Thus, at this level, the processes of highway planning moved into a very different network of inter-agency relationships — one which might be peripheral in terms of relations between local authorities but, nevertheless, one whose intricacies had to be fully appreciated by the Group Engineering staff.

In the case of Salwarpe Road, physical and seasonal considerations indicated that a separate initial contract should be negotiated for the earthmoving operations, after which some time would have to be allowed for settling down before work could begin on the construction of bridges and the road surface itself. The process of going to tender for bridgeworks and road construction involved the Group Engineer in a complex sequence of procedural steps, for which he found it worthwhile to draw up a critical path diagram. Because the County Surveyor's specialist staff were acting as agents in the design of bridgeworks, the contract was a joint one; it therefore involved close collaboration with County staff, and had to be formally approved through the County Highways and Bridges Committee, as well as the Droitwich Development Committee and, for loan sanction purposes, the Borough Council.

The question of how much of the roadworks to put to contract initially, and how much to defer until later, meant a balancing of economies of scale in engineering operations against the known difficulties of meeting capital expenditure at a time when the division between Town Development and local rate accounts was still in dispute. Because of these short-term financial difficulties, the Group Engineer decided to recommend construction, in the first instance, of a temporary T-junction with Kidderminster Road only, together with a single carriageway to provide access to the housing site. The underlying hope was that the financial problems of constructing the second carriageway, and also certain associated works such as footpaths and pedestrian underpasses, could be better overcome at a later stage in the development programme. Indeed, one possibility envisaged by the Group Engineer was that the cost of the second carriageway might ultimately be absorbed within the cost of the Westacre housing site, by treating it as an estate road which would thus attract an element of subsidy from the Housing Ministry. However, as we shall see later, this prospect was to be ruled out by the course of subsequent events.

So, it came about that, by the summer of 1971, the first carriageway of Salwarpe Road had been opened to traffic, still

without any final decision as to whether it should be adopted for
maintenance purposes by either the County or the Borough Council.
Ironically, the construction of housing on the Westacre estate —
which had provided the initial justification for bringing forward the
construction of this stretch of road — had by then become subject to
indefinite delay for reasons largely beyond the control of the
Development Group. The result was that the local newspaper was
able to publish a photograph of a brand new road constructed at
considerable expense yet leading, for an indeterminate period of
time, only to one isolated residential property. Such a situation
could of course be condemned by the layman as simply one of 'bad
planning'; but, from the perspective of the development agency, this
sort of penalty is more realistically seen as a consequence of the risks
that must inevitably be borne in managing a complex set of
operational and organizational uncertainties. A further irony was
that, by 1971, shortfalls in the densities of housing and industrial
development in Droitwich, coupled with a continuing high incidence
of commuting to work in Birmingham, were making it increasingly
doubtful whether the construction of a second carriageway for
Salwarpe Road, together with the full gyratory junction, would be
justified until the comparatively distant future, if indeed then.

The Group Engineer and his decision network

So far, we have seen that the role of the Group Engineer involved the
management of several different types of inter-organizational relationships at successive stages in the process of planning the
distributor road system and managing its construction. In order to
build up a comprehensive picture of the network of relationships he
had developed up to 1971, we asked him to record the names of all
those other individuals with whom, in his recollection, he had
communicated either regularly or more intermittently, in relation to
those of his decision-making activities that concerned the distributor
road system. He was also asked to distinguish those individuals with
whom he communicated as an inevitable consequence of his task and
of the nature of the local organizational arrangements at Droitwich,
from those individuals where some element of discretion was
involved on either side. Finally, he was asked to identify any
individuals who exercised a significant influence in modifying the
pattern of communications in which he became involved at any point
in the sequence of activities set out in *Figure 39*; in other words, he
was asked to indicate those actors who had performed a significant
'reticulist' function in the activation of decision networks.

Figure 42   Network relationships of Group Engineer for development of distributor road system

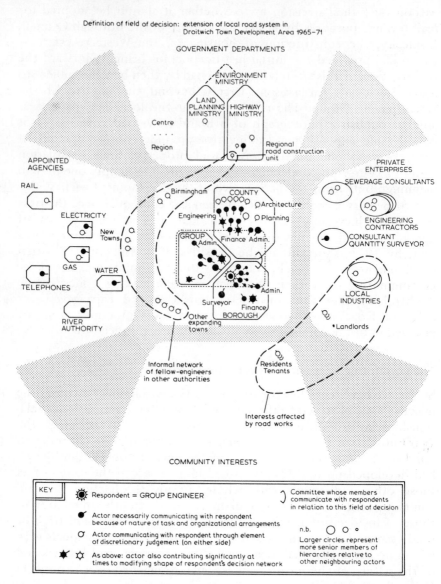

Definition of field of decision: extension of local road system in Droitwich Town Development Area 1965–71

GOVERNMENT DEPARTMENTS

ENVIRONMENT MINISTRY

LAND PLANNING MINISTRY   HIGHWAY MINISTRY

Centre
. . . .
Region

Regional road construction unit

APPOINTED AGENCIES

PRIVATE ENTERPRISES

SEWERAGE CONSULTANTS

RAIL

ELECTRICITY

New Towns

GAS   WATER

TELEPHONES

RIVER AUTHORITY

Birmingham

COUNTY

Engineering   Architecture

Planning

GROUP   Finance   Admin.
Admin.

Admin.

Surveyor   Finance
BOROUGH

Other expanding towns

ENGINEERING CONTRACTORS

CONSULTANT QUANTITY SURVEYOR

LOCAL INDUSTRIES

Landlords

Informal network of fellow-engineers in other authorities

Residents Tenants

Interests affected by road works

COMMUNITY INTERESTS

KEY	
☀ Respondent = GROUP ENGINEER	) Committee whose members communicate with respondents in relation to this field of decision
◗ Actor necessarily communicating with respondent because of nature of task and organizational arrangements	
◯ Actor communicating with respondent through element of discretionary judgement (on either side)	n.b. ◯ ○ ∘ Larger circles represent more senior members of hierarchies relative to other neighbouring actors
✸ ✧ As above: actor also contributing significantly at times to modifying shape of respondent's decision network	

The results of this analysis are summarized in *Figure 42*. At the centre of his network, the Group Engineer was able to identify the four or five other technical staff in his own section, and several other members of the Development Group, including most of those attending the Monday morning meetings. Other actors with whom his role inevitably brought him into contact included certain administrative, financial, and engineering staff of the two parent authorities; local engineers from statutory undertakings concerned with gas, electricity, and other services; and regional civil servants involved in the sanctioning of capital expenditure. Contacts with the members of the Development Committee and relevant committees of the parent authorities were important in procedural terms but not, in the engineer's view, very significant in terms of the exploration of the particular types of problem with which he had to deal.

Also among those with whom he found himself involved in exploratory processes, as a result of decisions made during the course of development, were the contractors and property interests involved in the planning activities concerned with Salwarpe Road, as well as certain other technical staff from various relevant public authorities and consultant firms. One civil servant from the Town Development Policy section of the Ministry appears because he occasionally served as a useful source of informal information on the progress of loan sanction applications through the central administrative procedures, during the period before the responsibility for assigning priorities to 'non-key sector' projects was devolved to the County Councils. Of particular interest are the set of fellow engineers from other public authorities, including neighbouring New Town Development Corporations and the Ministry's Regional Road Construction Unit, with whom the Group Engineer found it useful to keep in informal contact, in order to compare experience on ways of overcoming technical or procedural difficulties which arose from time to time. Most but not all of these individuals were known personally to the Engineer from earlier stages in his career.

The Group Engineer was able to amplify the information appearing in *Figure 42* by indicating which actors had been involved in the exploratory processes for each of the successive stages of decision-making plotted in *Figure 39*. Not unexpectedly, those activities described as 'enabling' tended to involve more financial and administrative actors than those concerned with design. Among the latter, activities concerned with review of the form of the road network as a whole tended to involve a much 'tighter' network of colleagues than those involved with the detailed planning of construction operations. The informal network of fellow engineers was activated mainly when questions of road classification arose in the early years, and later when it came to a critical review of the traffic predictions originally used in planning the configuration of the distributor road system.

Those whom the Group Engineer identified as playing a significant role in modifying the shape of his networks included the Group Administrator, who had first suggested the option of avoiding relocation of the engineering factory; the Engineer Planner, who had first raised the possibility of negotiating classified status for some of the distributor links; and the Assistant County Surveyor responsible for bridgeworks, who had initiated discussions with the railway authority over some difficult issues of procedure in the re-placement of existing railway bridges. The Treasurer of the Borough Council and Deputy Treasurer of the County were identified as having affected the form of his decision networks in a more negative sense, because their influence was such as to add to the range of uncertainties with which the Engineer had to contend, and thus cause him to seek clarifications of his own through various forms of investigatory or co-ordinative activity.

The management of uncertainty under financial constraints

Viewing the network of *Figure 42* as a whole, it was significant, though not unexpected, that the most heavily constraining influences on decision-making should have been seen by the Group Engineer to have arisen from the finance departments of the two parent authorities, with the degree of negative influence exerted by an officer tending to increase in accordance with his departmental seniority. To some extent, this judgement could be interpreted as simply reflecting proximity to pressures for economizing on the local rate accounts. However, discussion with the Group Engineer revealed that much of the constraining influence in his view arose from the specific difficulties of working within the somewhat unusual finan-cial structure of the Town Development accounts, which lacked any explicit provision for expenditure other than that which could be offset against specific capital projects. This difficulty was aggravated by the persistent state of uncertainty as to which agency would ultimately pay for different elements of the distributor road system, and the difficulty of obtaining information on whether particular parts of the road network had been specifically provided for in the forward budgetary estimates.

Because the shape and extent of the system of internal roads had remained undefined at the time of the agreement, the construction of this system had gradually emerged as one of the most sensitive areas of financial bargaining between the two parent authorities; and the uncertainties of this situation came to bear increasingly on the Group Engineer as his activities moved from broad design work through to practical implementation of the first road construction schemes. With increasing frequency, he would find himself called upon to produce detailed justification for the basis on which his staff costs had been charged against past projects. Usually, such requests would arrive after a considerable lapse of time, because it was normally not until six months or so after the end of a financial year that that annual Town Development accounts would be completed, allowing for the apportionment falling on the sensitive local rate account to be negotiated between the Treasurers.

In order to provide a basis for answering any queries that might arise, the Group Engineer found himself having to keep detailed personal records of the ways in which staff spent their time, and also having to make difficult judgements as to how to account for the high proportion of his own time that he spent in internal meetings and in managing his external relationships. Such network managing activities, forming a central part of the continuing processes of learning through which the Engineer endeavoured to enlarge his initial appreciation of the range of physical, organizational, and political constraints pertaining to the Droitwich situation, were clearly instrumental in allowing him to play his full role in the decision processes of the Development Group. This was especially so in view of the structural linkages between road development and other fields of decision which have been explored in the present and preceding chapters. However, the time he spent in such activities could not so easily be justified in retrospect, especially in relation to the externally determined norms of 'reasonable' proportions of design to construction cost.

Judgements as to how much time should be spent in searching for better solutions to highway planning problems, and how extensively the available networks of communication with other relevant parties should be activated, enter to some extent into the role of any road engineer, especially when working in an urban environment containing significant concentrations of local community and commercial interests. At Droitwich, however, the nature of the Town Development operation introduced additional complexities of both a technical and an organizational nature. This meant that the engineer was called on to exercise his skills of network management under more stringent financial constraints than if he had been working for an established local authority, where most recurrent management costs could have been met through annual revenue budgets.

The continuing state of uncertainty about how far the financial impacts of the highway programme would fall directly on local ratepayers had, in practice, the effect of adding to the bargaining resources that the County Council could deploy in its continuing negotiations with the Borough Council, many of whose electors were still far from reconciled to the goals of the town expansion scheme. However, the field of negotiation over roads could be claimed to involve so many technicalities that the processes of adjustment required to be handled almost entirely at officer rather than elected level. This observation goes some way to explain the low salience of elected representatives in the Engineer's decision processes, and the marked constraining influence of financial officers. In such circumstances, it was not surprising that he should have found himself subject to difficult stresses in judging how to divide his time between his more technical responsibilities and others of a network managing nature.

The policy system for local roads: a general appraisal

This chapter has attempted to explore some of the main problems facing professional officers carrying responsibility for what is ostensibly one of the more technical aspects of a planned expansion scheme. The salient sources of uncertainty which have emerged include those concerned with the demarcation of responsibilities between different highway agencies; with the interactions between highway problems and other fields of local decision; and with the incidence of costs and risks in a field where the need for complex technical calculations can tend to obscure the underlying political implications. The result is that abnormal financial pressures can be brought to bear on the senior professional staff, tending to accentuate the continuing problems of how far, and in what directions, to activate networks of decision-making activity beyond the members of the local policy system which is explicitly concerned with decisions of road provision within the defined area.

For the design centred activities of local road development, the nucleus of the policy system at Droitwich can be identified as consisting solely of the Group Engineer and a few of his colleagues, but with ready opportunities for enlarging the decision network through continuing contacts with the other senior officers of the Development Group, and with County engineering staff. For the 'enabling' activities identified in *Figure 39*, the nucleus of the policy system in effect expands somewhat to include certain senior administrative, architectural, and planning staff of the Development Group. The dominant local political pressures appear as being largely channelled through senior financial staff of the parent authorities; and also through regional civil servants specializing in highway matters so far as the interplay of local and national policies is concerned. Of course, one would expect the definition of the policy system, and also of the corresponding action space, to differ somewhat when seen from the viewpoint of any of these other actors.

Like the earlier processes of regional planning and local negotiation leading up to the launching of the Droitwich expansion scheme, the processes of executing the programme have emerged, at least in the specialized aspect here considered, as generating commitments to action which are essentially incremental when compared to the wider fields of choice explored. New sets of uncertainties come into prominence at each successive stage of commitment, and difficult judgements have to be made as to how much effort to devote to coping with them either through specialist professional or more general network managing skills. The stereotype of a highly technical process of engineering design, leading to a clear-cut subsequent stage of implementation, has proved far from adequate to interpret the problems facing the professional officers in such circumstances. This is a point which has wider implications for the management of local and regional change, and one to which we shall wish to return in later chapters.

8 Housing

Housing development as a problem field

The field of housing development differs from that of highway development in a number of ways, two of which will be of particular relevance to our theme of inter-agency planning. First, while the provision of roads is generally recognised as a public responsibility, the extent to which governmental bodies should intervene in the operation of housing markets is a more politically controversial issue. A second but related point is that people occupy houses in a less transient and a more exclusive manner than they occupy roads, so that, given any element of participation by public agencies in the supply of housing, greater opportunities exist for the application of social policies in assigning specific types of occupier to specific units of development.

In the English counties, the provision of public housing has traditionally been a responsibility of the District Councils, amounting to some 1,100 in number before the 1974 reforms and a total of just over 300 thereafter. The diffusion of executive responsibilities among such comparatively localized authorities in turn led to the introduction of some stringent procedures of central government control. The department concerned will be referred to here as the Housing Ministry, remembering that, since 1970, it has formed a part of a much larger Environment Ministry as shown in *Figure 5*.

Because of the difficulties involved in any attempt to maintain a flexible negotiating stance with such a large number of peripheral bodies, the Housing Ministry has developed a tendency to try to exert its influence through formalized rules. Among the points we shall examine in this chapter are the distorting influences which such controls can have on the local processes of decision, and also the tendency for local policy problems to become caught up in wider questions of regional and national politics.

The two individuals most intimately concerned in the problems of housing development and allocation at Droitwich, who will form the twin foci of the decision processes to be discussed, were the Development Group's Housing Architect and the Borough Council's Housing Manager. However, the wider 'policy system' for housing also involved various other members of the professional staff, rather more closely than in the case of roads; furthermore, the involvement of elected members was in this instance more direct.

The national background

Chapter 3 has already discussed some of the problems of housing shortage in Britain during the post-war years, from the vantage point of one of the major cities where these problems were most acute. Throughout the country in general, a consistent trend in the development of housing policies since the late nineteenth century had been the growth of a significant sector of publicly constructed dwellings for rent, to meet the difficulties experienced by lower income families in finding accommodation on the open market. At the beginning of the century, a high proportion of the nation's housing stock was controlled by private landlords; but as these houses progressed towards the end of their useful life, and became increasingly deficient in the light of rising standards of amenities and environment, so they became subject to policies of clearance and redevelopment. The steady decline of the privately rented sector was accompanied by a growth both in the local authority rented sector and in the number of owner-occupied houses, which by the end of the nineteen-sixties had come to account for over half the national total.

The field of national housing policy has proved a fertile one for party political controversy, with the Labour party tending to derive a significant proportion of its electoral support, locally and nationally, from the votes of local authority tenants. Patterns of central subsidy and control have been frequently debated and modified while, under the conditions of persistent economic constraint during the nineteen-sixties, ways were sought to reduce the level of public investment — and also to increase the active involvement of community interests — through the encouragement of voluntary housing associations and through new incentives towards the improvement of existing houses and their surroundings. However, the question of improvement of older housing areas is one which we shall leave to discuss more fully in Chapter 11.

The management of the local authority rented housing sector has become an endemic source of political debate in Britain, both locally and nationally. One of the main areas of local authority discretion has been the allocation of tenancies, based on locally determined criteria of family need. In many authorities, a degree of demonstrable objectivity was introduced by placing reliance on a scale of 'points', in which various different indices of need were added together to determine the priority to be assigned to each family on the waiting-list. For many years, another significant field of local authority discretion was the setting of rents, subject to the important constraint that the local 'statutory' housing revenue account should be kept separate from the accounts concerned with general rate expenditure, so as to avoid any hidden subsidies from ratepayers to tenants. One effect of this constraint, under the conditions of persistently rising construction costs which followed the Second World War, was that those authorities with substantial stocks of older housing were better able than other authorities to keep down the levels of rental for newly-constructed housing, by operating policies of rent equalization between newer houses and older properties of similar size and standards. Consequently, marked differentials in rents began to arise between some of the older towns and those that had grown more recently, where rent levels had to be geared much more tightly to current construction costs. Meanwhile, the political debate became extended to the question of whether local authorities should be allowed (or indeed encouraged) to sell off houses from their existing stock to sitting tenants. Underlying this controversy was the policy issue of whether the tenant's stake in a home in which he might have been living for much of his life should be judged to outweigh the local authority's stake in an asset created to meet a wider social need.

During 1972, the level of political controversy was sharply increased, both locally and nationally, by the new Housing Finance legislation enacted by the Conservative Government, changing the whole basis of central government support for the public sector of housing. The principle was to become one of subsidizing the tenant rather than the property, by comparing the tenant's ability to pay against what was judged to be the 'fair rent' level for the house in question. The assessment of 'fair rents' was to follow a method already introduced to the private rented sector by the earlier Labour government, of estimating a hypothetical market value on the assumption that local supply and demand were in a state of approximate balance. Scales of rent rebate based on income and family responsibilities were determined nationally, and central subsidies were to be calculated at 75 per cent of the difference between income and expenditure on the housing revenue account after such rebates had been met. Any surplus on the account was to be returned to the central exchequer to help pay for rebates, and it was this provision, together with the introduction of a means-testing procedure, for rebates, that attracted continuing opposition from the Labour party both nationally and locally.

These political developments took place against a background of continuing technical advances in housing construction, coupled with increasing shortages of building land. In response, local authorities in many of the larger towns found themselves, during the nineteen-fifties and sixties, devoting much of their attention to the construction of blocks of high rise flats. However, evidence began to accumulate that severe social stresses could arise among those living in such blocks, particularly in the case of families with young children; and architects began to concern themselves increasingly with alternative means of building to comparatively high densities in areas where land for new development was scarce.

Although many of the events we shall describe in Droitwich preceded the implementation of the new provisions for housing finance in the 1972 Act, an air of uncertainty as to future directions of national housing policy had been progressively building up, compounded by the pressures of economic and technological change. Such uncertainties were to exercise an increasingly significant influence on the climate within which the local decision-makers were operating, as has already been illustrated by the exercise described in Chapter 6. However, before looking at the local context of housing at Droitwich in more detail, it will be useful first to review the various mechanisms of external control within which the local decision-makers were required to operate.

The mechanisms of government control

The range of controls which had developed by the early nineteen-seventies to exercise public influence within the general field of housing provision included:

- an intricate pattern of central and local powers in the field of land-use planning (which has already been encountered in earlier chapters);
- a system of national and local building regulations, designed to prevent construction of houses of inferior materials and design standards, especially by speculative builders in the private sector;
- central controls over the purchasing powers of would-be private occupiers, through fiscal and other measures affecting the lending powers of building societies, and through provision of funds to local authorities with which to provide mortgages according to social rather than purely economic criteria;
- central controls over levels of rent in the private sector, through the system of 'fair rent' assessments by appointed local rent officers (extended in 1972 to the local authority housing sector, assessments made initially by the local council's own staff);
- a central power to regulate the implementation of local authority housing programmes, through a requirement that all loans raised on the finance market for new construction should be backed by official 'loan sanction' from the Housing Ministry (also, local authorities were required by statute to repay such loans by regular instalments over a period of sixty years);
- a system of cost control designed to ensure economy of design and construction by local authorities. Until 1962, this was exercised through a 'Housing Manual' which prescribed norms of cost broken down according to detailed elements of construction expenditure. However, the difficulty of operating this system fairly when levels of costs were continually changing led to the introduction of a new — and ostensibly simpler — system of aggregative 'cost yardsticks'. These yardsticks used only two basic parameters of a proposed new housing scheme — the average number of persons (i.e. bed spaces) per dwelling, and the average density of persons per unit of site area — to determine permitted levels of cost for superstructure, substructure, and external works respectively;
- a system of standards of interior space and facilities for local authority houses, derived from a report issued in 1962 entitled *Homes for Today and Tomorrow*, and usually known as 'Parker Morris standards' after the chairman of the committee responsible. These standards were made more demanding than those adopted by many private builders, because of an argument that investment in public housing should anticipate the living standards of future as well as present generations.

For central government, the national programme of public housing development was to provide one of the most readily available instruments for the restriction of public spending when the economy was under pressure, because it was regulated through comparatively short-term loan sanction controls rather than longer-term rolling programme arrangements as in the case of roads and schools. Meanwhile, local authorities in general found it increasingly difficult to design and launch new schemes that conformed to the twin constraints of cost yardstick and Parker Morris standards. In Droitwich, as we shall see, these difficulties were exacerbated by the circumstances of the overspill scheme, which introduced the need to offer rents which could be expected to attract prospective tenants away from the exporting city.

The local context at Droitwich

For reasons discussed in earlier chapters, the programme of expansion set out in the written statement which accompanied the Droitwich Town Map covered three sectors of housing development, each of approximately 2,000 dwellings. In descending order of public control, these were the rented, 'sponsored', and private sectors. The intermediate sector of sponsored housing had been specially devised as a means of reconciling the Borough Council's desire to maintain the town's existing social balance with the Land Planning Ministry's desire that the majority of new housing should contribute to the relief of congestion in the West Midlands conurbation. The relative sizes of the three sectors in relation to existing housing stocks are shown in *Figure 43*, together with an indication of the forms of influence over each sector exercised by different public authorities.

As *Figure 43* indicates, the proposed programme of new local authority housing corresponded to almost three times the local authority stock already existing in 1964; and, by the end of 1971, approximately two-thirds of the intended total had been completed. At that time, no new houses had yet been completed in the 'sponsored' sector. In the purely private sector, outside the Town Development Area, the number of new houses to be built was of the same order of magnitude as the town's existing stock but, because of a combination of national economic circumstances and local physical difficulties, only about 200 of these had been completed.

As the lower part of the diagram illustrates, public influence over the course of development in the purely private sector was limited to normal planning powers and building regulations exercised through the agency of the Borough and County Councils. However, in the

Figure 43   Analysis of Droitwich housing programme by sector

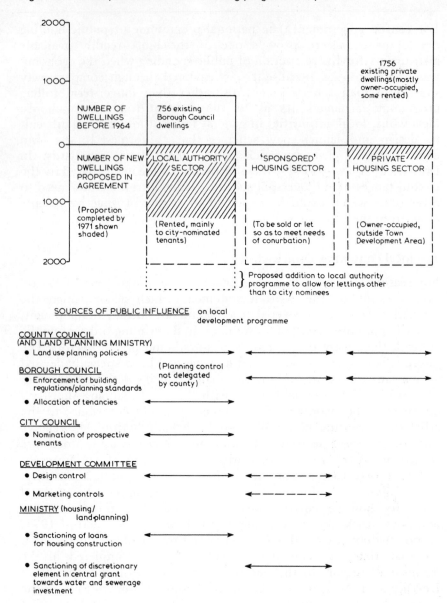

2000—

1000—

0—

NUMBER OF DWELLINGS BEFORE 1964

756 existing Borough Council dwellings

1756 existing private dwellings (mostly owner-occupied, some rented)

NUMBER OF NEW DWELLINGS PROPOSED IN AGREEMENT

(Proportion completed by 1971 shown shaded)

LOCAL AUTHORITY SECTOR

(Rented, mainly to city-nominated tenants)

'SPONSORED' HOUSING SECTOR

(To be sold or let so as to meet needs of conurbation)

PRIVATE HOUSING SECTOR

(Owner-occupied, outside Town Development Area)

1000—

2000—

} Proposed addition to local authority programme to allow for lettings other than to city nominees

SOURCES OF PUBLIC INFLUENCE   on local development programme

COUNTY COUNCIL
(AND LAND PLANNING MINISTRY)
• Land use planning policies

BOROUGH COUNCIL
• Enforcement of building regulations/planning standards
• Allocation of tenancies

(Planning control not delegated by county)

CITY COUNCIL
• Nomination of prospective tenants

DEVELOPMENT COMMITTEE
• Design control
• Marketing controls

MINISTRY (housing/ land planning)

• Sanctioning of loans for housing construction

• Sanctioning of discretionary element in central grant towards water and sewerage investment

local authority sector, there were many fields of possible influence, involving the powers of several different authorities. The sponsored sector occupied an intermediate position between these extremes, but the exact extent of public influence was to remain for many years a matter of considerable uncertainty. This was because some basic policy decisions still had to be confronted. Among the options were that the sites concerned could be sold undeveloped subject only to certain forms of covenant entered into by the purchaser; could be sold or leased at a higher price with all main services provided by the Development Group; or could be built upon by the Development Group itself, which would subsequently sell the houses with or without the retention of public ownership of the land.

Despite an initial scepticism in some quarters as to whether it would ever be feasible to make much progress in the sponsored sector, events in the early nineteen-seventies were to combine to bring about a marked change in the field of concern of the Development Committee, away from the comparatively familiar field of rented housing, and towards the much more uncertain opportunities for progress offered within the field of sponsored development.

Before discussing more fully the involvement of the Development Committee in the fields of rented and sponsored housing, a brief mention must be made of its more indirect interest in events within the private housing sector. At most times, this interest was limited to the professional concern of some of the Group's technical staff with the implications of developments outside the Town Development boundaries for the generation of traffic, shopping, and other demands within the town as a whole. However, there was a period between 1969 and 1971 when decisions about private housing came to impinge rather more intimately on the concerns of the Development Group. As already mentioned in Chapter 6, at this time there was a sudden rise in anxiety over the effects of brine subsidence on any new housing development to the east of the A38 trunk road, and a consequent concern to explore whether alternative sites within the Town Development Area could be released, so that private building could proceed in the immediate future. Meanwhile, the necessary technical and administrative procedures were set in train to identify possible new sites for longer-term housing development in the surrounding rural areas, as an insurance against the contingency that all prospects of new development east of the A38 might have to be finally abandoned.

In the event, however, the climate of uncertainty which had begun to spread among local people, and among the building societies whose capital would be at risk in brine subsidence areas, began to recede as further information accumulated about the likely scale of the problem and the ways in which it might be overcome. Much of the risk arose from the operations of a large company which was pumping brine from the subterranean salt beds to a factory a few kilometres away. In 1971, however, the firm decided to close the works on commercial grounds. Also, evidence became available to the Borough Council that the residual risks could be countered by ensuring that any new houses built were equipped with special types of foundation, of a type which would not involve exorbitant cost on the part of the developer.

This whole climate of anxiety had in fact stemmed from the interpretation of technical data from boreholes by a consultant geologist, who differed from his predecessor in advising that, unless the pumping of brine was to cease, there was a risk of catastrophic collapse. The word 'catastrophic', it was subsequently remarked by one of the local officials, appeared to relate more to geological than to human timescales; but, from this judgement, there developed a complex situation in which the local authorities, the private builders who had already invested in land, the prospective purchasers, and their potential financial backers all suddenly found their local investment decisions surrounded by new orders of uncertainty. Because the relationships between these various bodies were determined more by market interactions than by procedures of inter-agency co-ordination, there were few readily available channels of communication through which they could become more aware of each other's intentions. Although incidental to the main thread of this chapter, this episode is one not without relevance to the wider problems of inter-agency relationships in a loosely controlled market economy, where the requirements of free competition may inhibit the scope for mutual adjustment between agencies.

Arrangements for the allocation of rented housing

Turning to the local authority rented sector at Droitwich, with its much more extensive involvement of public agencies, we shall focus first on those processes concerned with the allocation of tenancies. The arrangement set out in the Town Development agreement was that Birmingham would supply the names of nominees who would qualify for the agreed annual overspill subsidies of £12 per annum each from the City Council and the Ministry, payable for a period of fifteen years from the date of occupation. Tenants from other designated 'exporting authorities' in the West Midlands conurbation could also be nominated on similar terms.

The actual allocation of tenants to dwellings would be a matter for the Borough Council, working through its Housing Manager, as also would be the drawing up of conditions of tenancy and the setting of rents. On the question of rents, the Borough Council made an informal undertaking that it would maintain separate compartments of its 'statutory' housing revenue account for its existing houses and for those built under Town Development powers, at least until the two parts of its stock had become approximately equally balanced. This undertaking reassured existing tenants that they would not be expected to cross-subsidize the rents of newcomers who had been channelled to Droitwich as a result of decisions taken to alleviate wider regional problems. However, the effects of this policy were to become a matter of increasing concern to the Town Development officers as they found the costs of new development escalating from one year to the next.

The coming of town development to Droitwich saw a marked increase in the level of activity of the Borough Council's Housing Committee, with lettings increasing from a rate of only about ten per year to some seven or eight a week as work on the large new Boycott estate gathered momentum. Whereas housing powers had previously been exercised by the Borough Surveyor's Department, a separate Housing Manager was appointed in 1966, bringing with him experience from one of London's first town development schemes. Although formally responsible solely to the Borough Council through its Housing Committee, he was also given opportunities to attend the monthly meetings of the Development Committee and, on occasion, the informal weekly meetings of senior development group officers, to give his judgement on the expected marketability of different housing forms and rent levels to prospective tenants.

Figure 44 depicts the Housing Manager's view of his network of relationships when dealing with issues in the field of allocation of town development houses. His main source of nominations was the head of the overspill section of Birmingham's Housing Department, who had latterly been assisted by a peripatetic overspill liaison officer. Discussions with Birmingham at a policy level had taken place only rarely, intitially over the payment of subsidies, and then over the nomination for tenancies of employees from the first industrial firm to move to Droitwich. On both these occasions, the City Housing Manager became personally involved, along with a member of the City Clerk's department, and the Group Administrator from Droitwich.

The normal procedure for nomination was for Birmingham to supply names of prospective tenants in batches shortly before the expected completion dates of new housing, with the Borough

Figure 44   Network relationships of Borough Housing Manager for letting of town development houses

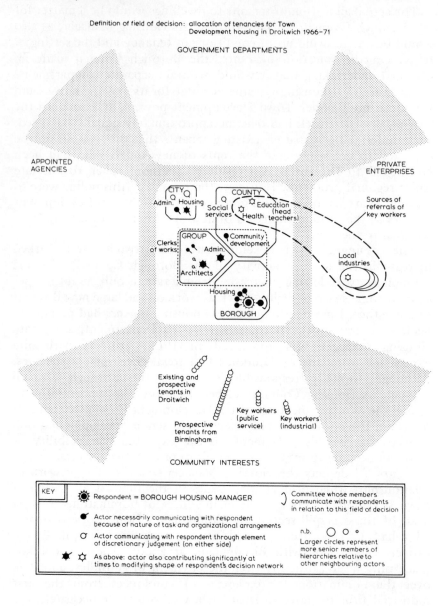

Definition of field of decision: allocation of tenancies for Town
Development housing in Droitwich 1966–71

GOVERNMENT DEPARTMENTS

APPOINTED
AGENCIES

PRIVATE
ENTERPRISES

CITY
Admin. Housing

COUNTY
Social   Education
services (head
Health   teachers)

Sources of
referrals of
key workers

Clerks
of works

GROUP
Admin.
Architects

Community
development

Local
industries

Housing

BOROUGH

Existing and
prospective
tenants in
Droitwich

Prospective
tenants from
Birmingham

Key workers
(public
service)

Key workers
(industrial)

COMMUNITY INTERESTS

KEY

☼ Respondent = BOROUGH HOUSING MANAGER

◖ Actor necessarily communicating with respondent
because of nature of task and organizational arrangements

◯ Actor communicating with respondent through element
of discretionary judgement (on either side)

★ ☆ As above: actor also contributing significantly at
times to modifying shape of respondent's decision network

⟩ Committee whose members
communicate with respondents
in relation to this field of decision

n.b.   ◯ ○ ∘
Larger circles represent
more senior members of
hierarchies relative to
other neighbouring actors

Housing Manager keeping a batch in hand in order to retain a margin of flexibility. Some 90 per cent of nominees were existing city tenants, many of them families in post-war high rise blocks who were motivated to move by the prospect of better living conditions for young children, even at a cost of changing employment or commuting long distances to work. It was claimed in Birmingham that there was little demand for overspill housing from other classes of prospective tenant, such as those identified on the 'Housing Balance Sheet' of *Figure 18*. This was recognized in Droitwich as a point with significant implications for the demographic and social structure of the expanding town.

Each nomination was accompanied by a report by a Birmingham housing visitor, recording preferences for type of accommodation and acceptable level of rent, and also including an assessment of the tenant's record in payment of rent and treatment of property. From these assessments, Droitwich applied rules of thumb in classifying tenants into four grades, with the Housing Manager paying direct visits to a sample of those nominated to satisfy his committee that there were no discrepancies between the Birmingham and Droitwich criteria. Nominees in the upper two grades could be allocated dwellings on the Housing Mananger's own discretion, while any other applicants had to be referred for committee decision. The committee also retained discretion over the allocation of tenancies to other categories of applicant, including some families from the Borough's own housing register and any incoming 'key workers'. These included skilled employees nominated by industrial firms or by public service agencies with an important role to play in the expansion of the town, including the County Education, Health and latterly Social Service departments, as well as members of the Development Group staff itself. Such key workers were required to pay a slightly higher rent unless qualifying for a nomination by Birmingham or one of the other designated exporting authorities, entitling them to the agreed Town Development subsidies.

The Housing Manager's responsibilities in the field of housing allocation thus involved him in more or less continuous contact with his committee, and especially its chairman, and more intermittent communication with other sources of referral, such as managers of firms and officers of County departments. Such actors are indicated as nodal points in the network of *Figure 44*, because they exercised a network-forming role in the somewhat restricted sense that they influenced the Housing Manager's processes of exploration over prospective lettings with certain types of tenant. Other relationships which were formed by the Housing Manager as development proceeded included a link with the Group's Community Development Officer who, on appointment, took over the primary concern for the provision of community facilities on housing estates, and a link with the County Social Services staff who were concerned with modifying dwellings to meet the needs of the handicapped.

The Housing Manager made a point of seeking access to the Group architectural staff at an early stage of design, to pass on information which might help to reduce the incidence of tenants' grievances after completion. A useful channel for such information was found to be the four Housing Assistants who visited the local authority estates regularly for the collection of rents. Problems in the handover of new houses from the Development Group to the Borough, which under the terms of the agreement took place immediately on completion, involved the Manager in local negotiations with the Development Group Clerks of Works. This transfer of responsibility could raise local difficulties of inter-agency relationships whenever there was any defective work to be remedied, and the Development Group staff felt there was a strong case for deferring the handover until a year or two after completion.

Generally, the Housing Manager emerges as having a linking role to play between the processes of housing development and management, and between the close-knit team of the Development Group and the much more loosely structured set of prospective tenants introduced through different channels of referral. As an officer of the Borough Council, however, the Manager had to reconcile his primary accountability to the Borough Housing Committee with the demands made on his time if he were to assist the Development Group officers as fully as possible in providing judgements about the rent paying abilities and design preferences of prospective tenants, through attending the Monday morning meetings and involving himself in other activities within the province of the joint Development Committee.

The design and appoval of new schemes

The individual most closely concerned with the design of new schemes for rented housing was the Group Housing Architect, with a small section of three or four design staff reporting through him. During the years when his involvement in the rented sector was at a peak, his patterns of communication involved a range of other officers in the Development Group and its parent authorities, as in the case of the Group Engineer. However, because rented housing was more a matter of concern for the Borough than the County, his

contacts with County staff were much less extensive, except in
relation to matters of financial calculation and control. As will be
seen later, the level of policy concern in housing issues was such as to
involve the group administrative staff rather more closely than in the
case of roads, and also to bring members of the Development
Committee more directly into the exploratory process.

At the professional level, the role of the Housing Architect
required him to maintain contacts with two officials from the
regional office of the Housing Ministry, the Regional Architect and
the Regional Quantity Surveyor, through whom the machinery of
central control over the design and costing of new housing schemes
was operated. At the County level, each new scheme required the
formal approval of the County Planning Committee, as a unit of
development for which the Borough did not possess delegated
powers of approval; and more locally, the design would have to be
approved both by the Borough's Housing Committee and by the
joint Development Committee, usually on the advice of its special
Housing Sub-Committee.

Before seeking formal authorization, however, proposals would
usually be discussed informally with representatives of these various
bodies in order to take soundings on matters of policy. An important
part of the skill of the Group Housing Architect was the ability to
predict likely reactions to different design solutions before formal
submissions were made, especially at the three levels of endorsement
where there was greatest concern with evaluation of the dwellings
from the viewpoint of future occupiers: the Development Committee, the Borough Housing Committee, and the Housing Ministry.

When asked to rank these three sources of authority according to
the relative predictability of their reaction to proposals, the Housing
Architect's response was as follows:

most predictable   :   Housing Ministry
next most predictable   :   Development Committee
least predictable   :   Borough Housing Committee.

In other words, the architect saw the uncertainties in policy which he
faced in making design choices as arising more from the local
representatives than from the ministry officials. This could be
explained by the fact that the latter were continuously concerned in
their professional capacity with appraisal of the housing schemes of
different local authorities, and so were known to have developed
clearly defined sets of ground rules. On the other hand, members of
the local Council were called on to make such judgements much more
intermittently, and therefore had less opportunity to form a

consistent policy stance, although clear preferences would be
expressed for attributes such as low density which were not always
easy to reconcile with costing constraints. In the observation of the
architect, local members tended to become more predictable in their
attitudes over time; this applied especially to those Borough
members who had the opportunity to attend the Development
Committee, and so learn about the various facets of the Town
Development operation and the technical complexities involved.
Sometimes, members would be able to criticize specific design
features in new proposals from experience of tenants' reactions to
previous schemes; but such inputs tended not to be offered until it
came to the stage of formal submission to committee. With
experience, the group technical staff were in time able to counter
these difficulties by setting up informal meetings of committee
members at a pre-design stage, where creative contributions to
questions of design policy could be actively encouraged.

Many of the early differences of opinion between Development
Group staff and local elected members concerned departures from
traditional principles of housing design, and, in this field, the process
could be seen as one of gradual mutual adjustment in attitudes over
time. Whereas the officers could claim that the local members had
sometimes been unreasonably reluctant to agree to certain accepted
modern design features such as single-pitch roofs, the local members
for their part could claim that their insistence on rejecting the few
high rise buildings which were indicated in early three-dimensional
models of the town had helped to avoid a form of living environment
that experience elsewhere had since demonstrated to be both
unpopular and socially undesirable.

The first step in the design process for a new housing area was the
preparation of a brief by the Development Group's Planning Section,
setting out the population to be housed, the area available for
residential development within the curtilage of the site once other
local facilities had been taken into account, and the provisions
required for internal circulation and open space. It would then be the
responsibility of the Housing Architect, in consultation with his
colleagues in the Group, to make proposals as to the way in which
the brief could best be met, keeping in mind the various cost, design,
and layout constraints within which he had to work and also the
social purposes of the scheme.

In 1969, when we were first given access to decision processes at
Droitwich, the officers were at an early stage of this process for the
third of the main sites that were proposed for rented housing
development. This was the site at Westacre, which has already

entered into the discussion of Salwarpe Road in Chapter 7, and which can be located as project 5 on *Figure 33* (and coincidentally as housing area 5 in the system of reference introduced on the Town Map). It so happened that the preliminary exploration of design possibilities for this site was to raise difficulties that were to have far-reaching implications for the housing programme as a whole, and the pattern of events that followed will therefore be pursued in some detail in the next two sections.

Design alternatives at Westacre

Over the years, the planning brief for Westacre was to be amended several times. By 1969, the total site of fifty-three acres (twenty-one hectares) as shown on the Town Map had become whittled down to a mere twenty-two acres (nine hectares) available for housing, because of the inclusion of other local land uses and the proposal to run a distributor 'spine' road between the housing site and the railway. If this area was to accommodate the specified population of 1,610, it would be necessary to build to a high residential density of seventy-three persons per acre (180 per hectare). This was thought to be acceptable in terms of traffic generation because the proximity of the site to the town centre would encourage pedestrian movement; but at the same time, it could be expected to cause some difficult design problems if high rise buildings were to be avoided.

The basic problem faced by the architect was to find ways of manipulating certain key design variables in such a way as to reach a solution that was consistent with the design standards of the Parker Morris report, with the Ministry's cost yardstick criteria, and with the levels of rent that might be expected to attract overspill tenants from Birmingham. Several successive sets of calculations were produced by the Housing Architect for different sets of alternative choices for the key design variables. These were subsequently passed on for further evaluation by the County financial staff, working in association with the Deputy Treasurer of the Borough Council. The individual most closely concerned from the County side was the officer who in effect served as accountant to the Development Group, and will therefore by referred to here as the Group Accountant.

A broad view of the factors taken into account in this kind of assessment appears in *Figure 45*, which concentrates on inputs and outputs of information without setting out in full the elaborate sequence of steps involved in bringing together the various elements of input to produce the required outputs. However, there was only

Figure 45   Process of assessment of alternative design solutions for a rented housing estate

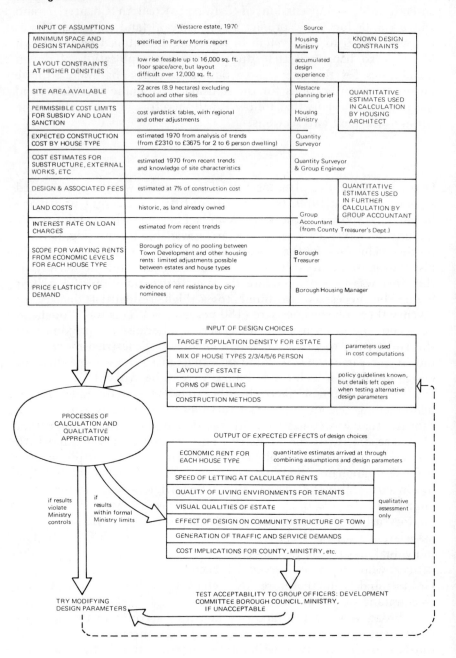

INPUT OF ASSUMPTIONS	Westacre estate, 1970	Source	
MINIMUM SPACE AND DESIGN STANDARDS	specified in Parker Morris report	Housing Ministry	KNOWN DESIGN CONSTRAINTS
LAYOUT CONSTRAINTS AT HIGHER DENSITIES	low rise feasible up to 16,000 sq. ft. floor space/acre, but layout difficult over 12,000 sq. ft.	accumulated design experience	
SITE AREA AVAILABLE	22 acres (8.9 hectares) excluding school and other sites	Westacre planning brief	QUANTITATIVE ESTIMATES USED IN CALCULATION BY HOUSING ARCHITECT
PERMISSIBLE COST LIMITS FOR SUBSIDY AND LOAN SANCTION	cost yardstick tables, with regional and other adjustments	Housing Ministry	
EXPECTED CONSTRUCTION COST BY HOUSE TYPE	estimated 1970 from analysis of trends (from £2310 to £3675 for 2 to 6 person dwelling)	Quantity Surveyor	
COST ESTIMATES FOR SUBSTRUCTURE, EXTERNAL WORKS, ETC	estimated 1970 from recent trends and knowledge of site characteristics	Quantity Surveyor & Group Engineer	
DESIGN & ASSOCIATED FEES	estimated at 7% of construction cost		QUANTITATIVE ESTIMATES USED IN FURTHER CALCULATION BY GROUP ACCOUNTANT
LAND COSTS	historic, as land already owned	Group Accountant (from County Treasurer's Dept.)	
INTEREST RATE ON LOAN CHARGES	estimated from recent trends		
SCOPE FOR VARYING RENTS FROM ECONOMIC LEVELS FOR EACH HOUSE TYPE	Borough policy of no pooling between Town Development and other housing rents: limited adjustments possible between estates and house types	Borough Treasurer	
PRICE ELASTICITY OF DEMAND	evidence of rent resistance by city nominees	Borough Housing Manager	

INPUT OF DESIGN CHOICES

TARGET POPULATION DENSITY FOR ESTATE	parameters used in cost computations
MIX OF HOUSE TYPES 2/3/4/5/6 PERSON	
LAYOUT OF ESTATE	policy guidelines known, but details left open when testing alternative design parameters
FORMS OF DWELLING	
CONSTRUCTION METHODS	

PROCESSES OF CALCULATION AND QUALITATIVE APPRECIATION

OUTPUT OF EXPECTED EFFECTS of design choices

ECONOMIC RENT FOR EACH HOUSE TYPE	quantitative estimates arrived at through combining assumptions and design parameters
SPEED OF LETTING AT CALCULATED RENTS	
QUALITY OF LIVING ENVIRONMENTS FOR TENANTS	qualitative assessment only
VISUAL QUALITIES OF ESTATE	
EFFECT OF DESIGN ON COMMUNITY STRUCTURE OF TOWN	
GENERATION OF TRAFFIC AND SERVICE DEMANDS	
COST IMPLICATIONS FOR COUNTY, MINISTRY, etc.	

if results violate Ministry controls

if results within formal Ministry limits

TRY MODIFYING DESIGN PARAMETERS

TEST ACCEPTABILITY TO GROUP OFFICERS: DEVELOPMENT COMMITTEE BOROUGH COUNCIL, MINISTRY, IF UNACCEPTABLE

one of the outputs indicated that could realistically be put forward
for appraisal as a clear quantitative estimate: the economic rent that
it would be necessary to charge for each type of house in the scheme
in order to defray costs, bearing in mind the subsidies that could be
earned through working within limits of expenditure related to the
cost yardstick tables. Other criteria for the assessment of a given
design solution could only realistically be appraised in qualitative
terms, by the various interests involved at Development Committee,
Borough Council, and Ministry levels.

Among the wide variety of assumptions brought together to
estimate economic levels of rental were several based on quantitative
estimates from different sources, and others where more reliance was
placed on judgemental factors. In particular, broad professional
judgements were used at this stage in weighing up in advance the
likelihood of being able to find acceptable design solutions at
different densities, and in predicting the resistance of Birmingham's
nominees to different levels of rent. It appeared relevant to our
research interests to explore further the sources of uncertainty
underlying as many as possible of the types of assumption indicated
in *Figure 45*; and this we did through discussion with the Group
Housing Architect and the Group Accountant, applying methods
similar to those previously used in an analysis of shopping proposals
for Coventry (Friend and Jessop, 1969: Chapter 4).

The discussions with the Architect revealed, for instance, that
there still remained some uncertainty as to the total site area
allowable for cost yardstick purposes. Negotiations with the Ministry
might allow the western boudary of the site to be drawn at the canal
bank rather than the adjoining footpath, yielding an extra acre for
the purposes of yardstick calculations, though not affecting layout
options. To take another example, discussion with the Group
Accountant indicated that the level of design and associated fees
might vary either way from the estimated 7 per cent, especially as
new scales of quantity surveying fees were then under negotiation.
Questioning revealed that the Accountant would be surprised only if
the total fees went above 9 per cent or below 6 per cent, thus giving
an indication of his overall limits of confidence. Neither of these
uncertainties emerged as having a very significant influence in
relation to the outputs shown in *Figure 45*; nevertheless, they can be
seen as fairly typical of those sources of uncertainty that must be
managed, implicitly or otherwise, as part of even the most technical
process of appraisal of alternative design solutions.

At this early stage in the considerations of design variables, the
Group Housing Architect and his team carried out some tentative

Figure 46 Search for acceptable design solution for Westacre housing estate plotted according to cost yardstick parameters

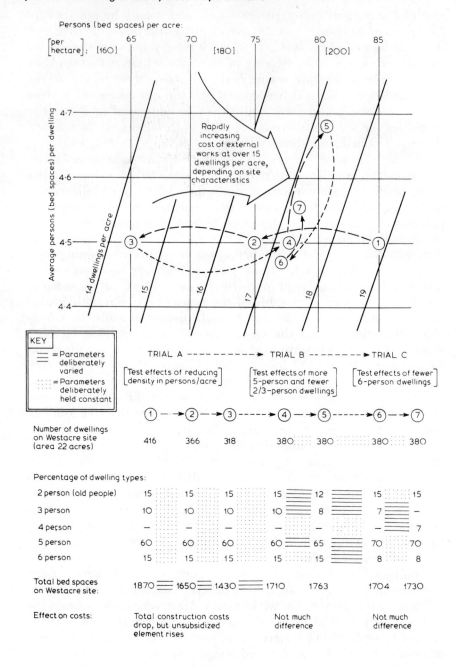

Persons (bed spaces) per acre:

[per hectare]:	[160] [180] [200]

Average persons (bed spaces) per dwelling

14 dwellings per acre

Rapidly increasing cost of external works at over 15 dwellings per acre, depending on site characteristics

KEY

≡ = Parameters deliberately varied

⋮ = Parameters deliberately held constant

TRIAL A - - - - - - - - ► TRIAL B - - - - - - - - ► TRIAL C

[Test effects of reducing density in persons/acre] [Test effects of more 5-person and fewer 2/3-person dwellings] [Test effects of fewer 6-person dwellings]

① — ►② — ►③ - - - - ► ④ — ►⑤ - - - - - ►⑥ — ►⑦

Number of dwellings on Westacre site (area 22 acres)	416	366	318	380	380	380	380

Percentage of dwelling types:

2 person (old people)	15	15	15	15	12	15	15
3 person	10	10	10	10	8	7	–
4 person	–	–	–	–	–	–	7
5 person	60	60	60	60	65	70	70
6 person	15	15	15	15	15	8	8

Total bed spaces on Westacre site:	1870	1650	1430	1710	1763	1704	1730

Effect on costs:	Total construction costs drop, but unsubsidized element rises	Not much difference	Not much difference

explorations in layout with the aid of sketch plans and models; but it was mainly the first two of the design variables set out in *Figure 45* – those of target population density and mix of house types – that provided the focus for discussion of alternatives with his other colleagues in the Development Group. Because these variables between them determined the levels of the two primary parameters used in the cost yardstick tables, they affected both the eligibility of a scheme for loan sanction and the level of subsidy attracted. The Ministry's regulations at that time were that tenders from contractors for housing development could only be accepted if they fell within 10 per cent tolerance of the allowable costs under the cost yardstick limits (with similar but separate arrangements for garages). Also, any excess costs above the yardstick limit but within the tolerance figure would not qualify for the Ministry's standard housing subsidy. This in itself was a serious matter, because the formula for calculating subsidy at that time was designed to make good the differential between current market rates of interest and a 'base rate' of 4 per cent. This differential had been steadily rising, and the effect of losing subsidy even on a small proportion of the total contract cost could well be serious in terms of the level of rents which would have to be charged to recover costs.

Figure 46 illustrates a few of the successive steps made by the Architect and his colleagues in the search for an acceptable solution for Westacre within these cost yardstick constraints. First, the effect was tested of varying the density in persons per acre from the target of seventy-three set out in the design brief, keeping the mix of house types constant, with 60 per cent of dwellings of the standard five-persons, three-bedroom type and the remainder reflecting a combination of local and national policies for accomodation of older people on the one hand, and larger families on the other. Four-person dwellings were omitted because the Architect's experience showed they could be just as costly to build as the standard five-person type. Calculations on this basis showed that as the density was decreased from eighty-five through seventy-five to sixty-five persons per acre, there were decreases in both the total estate costs and the average costs per dwelling, but at the same time there was an increase in the proportion of cost that was unsubsidized. This was because of the structure of the cost yardstick table, which operated generally to increase the allowable costs per dwelling (composed of superstructure, sub-structure, and external works components) as the density in persons per acre rose.

However, as the Housing Architect, the Group Engineer, and the Group Administrator were keenly aware, one effect of moving towards the right of *Figure 46* was to increase the level of the more basic parameter of dwelling per acre. This took the field of search into an area of local policy dispute, which was also one in which design solutions became progressively more difficult to achieve and external works costs tended to rise sharply, in ways which could, however, vary markedly from site to site according to local topography. When it appeared that none of the three solutions based on an average of 4.5 persons per dwelling — solutions 1, 2, and 3 of *Figure 46* — was likely to lead to readily acceptable levels of costs and rents, the Group officers obtained agreement from the Development Committee that the Housing Architect should begin exploring whether any improvements could be made by modifying the mix of dwelling types. The most promising modification he felt able to make in this direction, within known policy constraints, was to increase the percentage of five-person dwellings from sixty to sixty-five, with corresponding reductions in three-person and two-person dwellings. The latter were intended primarily for old people, and it was recognized that there would be significant implications for the future social structure of the estate. This step in the exploratory process is indicated by the shift from solution 4 to solution 5 in *Figure 46.* However, this change turned out to have only a marginal effect on the ability to attract subsidy, as also did a subsequent reduction in the number of six-person dwellings (solutions 7 and 8).

Consequently, at one of the officers' Monday morning meetings where the results of the various calculations came up for appraisal, sustained attention was directed to the range of other ways in which it might be possible to come up with an acceptable design solution. At this stage, almost a year had passed since the drawing up of the original Westacre design brief:; and *Figures 45* and *46* give only a broad impression of the prolonged and complex processes of exploration which had taken place. The process of generation and evaluation of alternatives had been made arduous, and the feedback cycle extended, by the division of the process of estimating economic rents into two stages carried out separately by the Housing Architect and Group Accountant, working from Droitwich and Worcester respectively with only intermittent opportunities for face-to-face contact.

Extending the context of the decision process

At this stage, the Group Aministrator decided to report to the Development Committee that there were three alternative courses of action which could be pursued. The first was to defer all further action on Westacre; the second was to try and negotiate additional 'ad hoc' cost allowances with the regional officers of the Housing Ministry; and the third was to proceed with detailed design work based on the best available set of cost yardstick parameters, accepting the adverse indications of the cost appraisals so far attempted.

The argument in favour of the first option was that Droitwich was not alone in its difficulties; national housing policy was rapidly becoming unworkable, under changing economic circumstances, and early revisions were to be expected at least at the technical level of cost yardstick limits, if not also at the level of basic principles. Thus, events in the next year or so could be expected to clarify some of the uncertainties about whether a viable scheme could be produced, and assist in judging whether or not the site should be abandoned as one for rented housing, and considered for the 'sponsored' form of development. The second option, of negotiating 'ad hoc' cost allowances, relied on the hope that ministry officials might be prepared to exercise more latitude than usual in the exercise of their discretionary powers, ostensibly to allow for the abnormal physical conditions of the site but with an underlying recognition that it was becoming more and more impracticable to keep within rigid yardstick limits now that the currently approved levels had been overtaken by cost inflation. The third option, of proceeding with detailed design work on the existing cost assumptions, involved accepting the risk that it might be difficult to let the dwellings quickly at the rent levels to be charged; however, it was always possible that, during the two-year period before the first houses of the estate could be ready for occupation, levels of income and of rentals in the exporting authority might have risen sufficiently to reduce the level of tenants' resistance to the rents which would have to be charged, estimated to range between £4.20 per week for a two-person dwelling to £5.90 for one capable of accommodating a family of six.

The committee members found the choice between these options a difficult one to make, especially when comparing the strategy of playing for time implicit in either of the first two options with the higher risks presented by the third. To play for time would have meant a temporary pause in the entire housing programme for Droitwich, at a time when there was no imminent prospect of progress in either the sponsored or private sectors. This would have meant for the Borough a corresponding retardation in the growth of population and of local rateable value; and for the housing design staff of the Development Group, a serious interruption in their work programme, with consequent problems in allocating salaries against capital projects. Further, it would mean some loss in the credibility of Droitwich as an actively expanding town in the eyes of industrial and commercial investors.

In the event, the debate in committee ranged over a number of other possibilities for exerting influence on other parties to overcome the financial problems at Westacre. Could not the Ministry be approached, not only through technical channels to explore the scope for 'ad hoc' cost allowances, but also through political channels to make representations on the need to introduce more basic policy changes, such as a relaxation of Parker Morris standards, on behalf either of Droitwich alone or of all overspill towns? Significantly, the Group Planner Architect was a founder member of the Technical Officers' Committee for Expanding Towns, a national representative body through which information could be exchanged on problems arising in different Town Development programmes, and arguments could be presented to the Ministry on the local effects of current central policies. Alternatively, as one Borough Council member suggested, might not approaches be made to Birmingham, either directly or through the collective channel of the Regional Conference of Planning Authorities? Could the City Council be persuaded that it could be in its own long-term interests to increase its annual overspill subsidy of £12 per house to a more realistic level in the light of current costs, if this would allow the overall momentum of overspill to be maintained? Such an approach was, however, argued by one County representative to be both unrealistic and unwise; it could become entangled with many other aspects of the delicate relationship between Worcestershire and Birmingham. As it happened, the County was at that time in the course of presenting objections to a new planning application by Birmingham for peripheral expansion, at a public inquiry which paralleled in many respects that held some ten years earlier into the proposals for development at Wythall. Implicitly, representations for increased finance from Birmingham could have weakened the County's case at a time when it was arguing that the progress of overspill schemes made any peripheral expansion at the city boundary unnecessary.

Now that the committee members had begun to discuss policy constraints which might be removed through negotiations with other parties, one of the County officers seized the opportunity to mention one other such constraint involving delicate policy considerations of a more local nature; the separation of the housing revenue accounts for Town Development from that for other local tenants. Such a constraint, it was suggested, could be overcome by a simple decision of the Borough Council to pool the two accounts. However, the Borough representatives countered this suggestion by reference to their past pledges that Town Development would not bring a rise in rentals for tenants of the Borough's older housing estates.

We have now discussed three successive levels of search for a solution to the Westacre problem — a level of technical design calculations, a level of tactical moves proposed by the officers to the committee, and a more strategic level emerging during the committee debate itself. The relationships between these levels are shown diagramatically in *Figure 47*, along with some of the criteria of judgement that emerged most clearly at different levels of discussion. At the strategic level, it was significant that the options involving negotiation with Birmingham were unacceptable to the County members, while the option of negotiating with the Borough Council was unacceptable to the local representatives at the meeting. It was only the strategy of exerting pressure on the Ministry that was generally acceptable to all those present, whatever opinions they might have had as to its probable success. Accordingly, it was decided that the Group Planner Architect should investigate how far such representations might be made jointly with other bodies, while also exploring at regional level the question of *'ad hoc'* allowances, this being one form of exploratory action that could be undertaken at little cost but with at least some realistic hope of gain.

However, not long after this meeting, the state of uncertainty about the future of Westacre was increased still further by a combination of other factors, which we shall now proceed to discuss. These factors included doubts as to how much longer Birmingham would be prepared to continue the nomination of tenants; expectations of major changes in the system of central support for local authority housing following the election of a Conservative government; and an increasing local urgency to make a start on the sponsored sector of the Town Development housing programme.

The swing to sponsored housing

The arrangements for siting, programming, financing, and marketing of the proposed 2,000 'sponsored' houses had been deliberately left open at the time of the Town Development agreement. For the purposes of long-term financial projections, the County Treasurer's Department in 1966 had worked on the assumption that construction would begin in 1971, and that disposal would be through the leasing of sites on which all engineering services had been provided to private developers. These developers would then sell the houses to

Figure 47   Extensions to field of search for acceptable solution to problem of Westacre estate

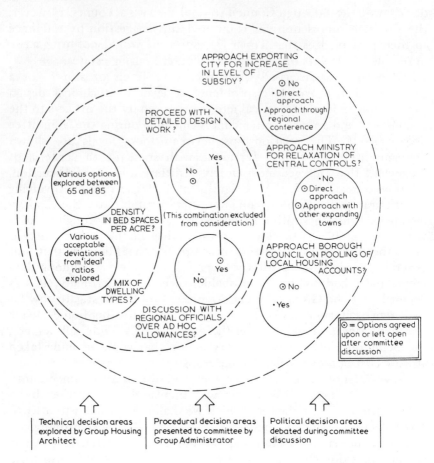

APPROACH EXPORTING
CITY FOR INCREASE
IN LEVEL OF
SUBSIDY?

⊙ No
• Direct
  approach
• Approach through
  regional
  conference

PROCEED WITH
DETAILED DESIGN
WORK?

Yes

No
⊙

(This combination excluded
from consideration)

APPROACH MINISTRY
FOR RELAXATION OF
CENTRAL CONTROLS?

• No
⊙ Direct
  approach
⊙ Approach with
  other expanding
  towns

Various options
explored between
65 and 85

DENSITY
IN BED SPACES
PER ACRE?

Various
acceptable
deviations
from 'ideal'
ratios
explored

MIX OF
DWELLING
TYPES?

⊙
Yes

No

DISCUSSION WITH
REGIONAL OFFICIALS
OVER AD HOC
ALLOWANCES?

APPROACH BOROUGH
COUNCIL ON POOLING OF
LOCAL HOUSING
ACCOUNTS?

⊙ No

• Yes

⊙ = Options agreed
upon or left open
after committee
discussion

Technical decision areas explored by Group Housing Architect	Procedural decision areas presented to committee by Group Administrator	Political decision areas debated during committee discussion

Main criteria introduced at each stage:

• Effect on expected construction cost	• Effect on momentum of town development	• Effect on relationships between county and city
• Effect on unsubsidized element of cost	• Effect on borough and county ratepayers	• Effect on relationships between Development Committee and Borough
• Effect on flow of overspill tenants	• Effect on ability to charge salaries of technical staff against schemes	
• Effect on social mix of town		

prospective purchasers, providing a fair level of return on investment to the Development Committee, and allowing them to retain some powers of control over the place of origin of occupiers, in accordance with the statement in the agreement that the sponsored sector was intended to contribute to the relief of congestion in the West Midlands conurbation generally.

The deferment of sponsored housing during the earlier years could be justified in terms of the argument that the initial urgency of the Droitwich programme arose from Birmingham's short-term difficulties in finding sites on which to maintain the momentum of its programme of building houses for rent. Moreover, it was the experience of other overspill schemes which involved a planned provision of new employment opportunities that the early demands were predominantly for rented accommodation. During these early years, a lack of commitment to the exact form of marketing arrangement for sponsored housing could be justified because of the sensitivity of the market to changing economic circumstances. Conceivably, future circumstances might at one extreme allow the Development Committee themselves to build houses for leasing to unsubsidized tenants outside the terms of the Birmingham agreement or, at the other extreme, might force them to sell off plots to speculative builders, whether serviced or not serviced, to produce immediate capital gains.

In 1969, when the development of the proposed local authority rented housing scheme at Westacre was first beginning to assume high priority, the Group Administrator presented a report to the Committee arguing that this scheme would leave only a small element of the total rented programme uncompleted, and that the time was now ripe to test the market for sponsored housing, perhaps launching small pilot schemes under different arrangements on different sites. The extreme solution of building sponsored housing for rent had then emerged as impracticable, even allowing an option for subsequent purchase, so the main options remaining were:

— the sale or lease of undeveloped land to developers;
— the sale or lease of plots to developers after provision of roads and sewerage;
— the building of houses for sale by the Development Committee.

Any solution involving the outright sale of plots was open to objection as an unjustifiable disposal of land that had originally been acquired through compulsory purchase powers. However, it was agreed that all these options merited further exploration, and the Committee's Estates Adviser was asked to undertake a study of their implications, with particular reference to potential sources of capital funding. One possibility under the third option was the use of conventional local authority loan finance; but it was thought that the necessary Ministry sanction for this was unlikely to be forthcoming, because of the stringency with which the central government was then attempting to exercise control over local authority spending. Other possibilities for funding under this option involved building societies, merchant banks, or leaseback arrangements with institutions such as insurance companies or pension funds. However, the Estates Adviser concluded that such bodies were unlikely to be very interested in financing publicly sponsored housing development during a period when more attractive outlets for investment were available in the commercial, industrial, and private housing fields. Underlying this assessment was a belief among potential private investors that local authority architects and planners were not sufficiently well attuned to commercial considerations for them to design schemes that would be competitive in the open market. The Estates Adviser thought it possible that such attitudes might change if ever the relative profitability of other investment outlets began to decline, but in the meantime the most practical opportunities for making a start on the sponsored programme appeared to lie within the first and second options, involving the sale or lease of sites to private developers.

In exploring further lines along which potential developers should be approached, and in particular in assessing what degree of *control* they should attempt to retain over both design and marketing, the Development Committee had to bear in mind three potentially conflicting aims. These were:

Design quality	The aim of maintaining the high standards of design and layout so far achieved in the Town Development Area
Regional benefit	The aim of ensuring that as many of the houses as possible should be seen to go to residents of the West Midlands conurbation to meet the terms of the original agreement
Return on investment	The aim of achieving as high a net income as possible to the Town Development accounts.

The first aim (reflected primarily in the attitudes of the technical staff of the Development Group) favoured the retention of as much control as possible over design standards; the second aim (reflected especially in the policies of the Land Planning Ministry) favoured retention of as much control as possible over marketing; while the third aim (reflected particularly in the attitudes of the County Treasurer's department, which was carrying most of the initial costs of the Droitwich expansion) favoured the sale of developed plots to the highest bidders without too much regard to the retention of design and marketing controls. One of the major uncertainties in reconciling these aims concerned the way in which the policies of the Land Planning Ministry were likely to come to bear in the assessment of regional benefit. This was important because the Town Development Policy Section of the Ministry was in a position to advise on the release or otherwise of the substantial grants payable towards water and sewerage investments. The agreed formula was that these grants should only be payable towards that proportion of development contributing towards overspill need; but this formula was open to differing interpretations according to the strength of the evidence that could be produced as to the place of origin of those coming into the town other than by direct nomination of the exporting authority.

The opening of negotiations with developers

The degree to which it would be feasible to retain marketing and design controls in practice, and the means through which they could be exercised, could not easily be judged except through entering into negotiations with prospective developers. Accordingly, initial discussions were opened with a selected set of builders, including some who had already made approaches to the Committee and appeared to the officers to have the kind of resources and experience necessary to participate in this kind of development. Also, on the recommendation of local elected members, approaches were made to one or two more local firms which could be capable of handling smaller schemes within the available sites.

These negotiations were pursued on a commercial front by the Estates Adviser, and at the same time on a technical front by the Group Housing Architect and his colleagues. However, the Group architectural staff found themselves faced with a certain amount of initial doubt as to how far they should set out to fulfil a detailed design function, as in the earlier rented housing, and how far they should be content with exercising a development control function as for normal private development. In confronting this problem, they became aware of a contrast between those smaller building firms which relied largely on outside architectural skills and were only too glad to find these made available to them without payment, and the larger firms which had their own teams of architects accustomed to problems of overall estate design, and therefore tended to resist advice from the Group that could conflict with their own commercial judgements. The Group Architect therefore found himself in a state of some uncertainty about his role, during a stage of transition from relatively clearly defined to much more loosely controlled forms of development. In this situation, his whole network of relationships with other parties was shifting significantly towards the private sector.

The outcome of the parallel processes of commercial and technical negotiation was that 'heads of agreement' were finally drawn up for the sale of certain limited plots of land to builders, on a ninety-nine year lease with provision for periodic revisions of ground rents. As agent of the Borough Council, the Development Committee was able to retain a degree of landlord control which gave it power to specify layout and design constraints within an initial planning brief. Another condition was that 80 per cent of the houses should be sold in such a way as to 'show regional benefit', with the Group Administrator retaining the right to scrutinize the original addresses of potential purchasers for this purpose. Such controls might not have proved so acceptable to the builders, had it not been for some marked changes in the national housing market during 1971 and 1972, which caused demand for private houses to rise rapidly and supplies of available land to become correspondingly diminished.

One of the problems exposed by these negotiations with private builders was that of conflicting criteria when it came to the location of sponsored housing in relation to local authority rented estates. On social grounds, it could be argued that the segregation of areas of rented and privately occupied housing was highly undesirable; but on commercial grounds it could be argued that the proximity of rented houses reduced market prices and thereby the level of profit to both the builder and the landlord. This conflict arose at an early stage when sponsored development was under discussion in those peripheral parts of the Boycott estate not already occupied by rented housing; and it was also to arise at a later stage in the long and difficult history of the Westacre site.

The impact of external changes

Shortly after the committee discussions on Westacre in 1970 which are analysed in *Figure 47*, the future of the site became a subject of even wider speculation when a letter was received from the Town Clerk of Birmingham, giving a first indication that the city might find itself unable to nominate further tenants for Droitwich housing after the two-hundred or so houses currently under contract had been let. It was argued that the original target of 2,000 nominations did not impose any explicit obligation on the city under the terms of the agreement, and that Birmingham's main problem was now one of how to re-house people displaced by slum clearance schemes and who were generally reluctant to move to areas remote from their existing places of work. The advice in the letter was that it would be 'unwise' for Droitwich at this point to enter into any further housing contracts for city-nominated tenants. This was interpreted by local officers as something of a holding action pending the outcome of the public inquiry into Birmingham's latest proposal for peripheral development in North Worcestershire.

Whatever political inferences could be drawn from the letter, the immediate practical implication for the Development Comittee was to force them to direct early attention towards the option of switching the Westacre site to sponsored housing development. When the implications of a sponsored scheme were investigated, a dispute developed with the Borough Council's Housing Committee, which expressed a wish to see at least some part of the site retained for rented housing to meet the town's own local needs. At a special joint meeting of the two Committees, it was now the turn of the local members to present the case for avoiding social segregation, and the Development Group officers to argue the advantages of keeping the site intact to maintain its profitability to a prospective developer. A further argument for the latter course, it was suggested, was that the demand for local authority tenancies, even from local sources, might dwindle once the full impact of the new housing legislation, then being debated in parliament, became clear.

During 1972, a further external event of some significance was a change of political control on Birmingham City Council, raising the possibility that the flow of nominated tenants might not after all be terminated. Also, the County Council published its first draft structure plan under the new planning legislation, suggesting that, as a means of accommodating future regional growth in population, Droitwich should be planned to increase beyond its existing population target of 30,000 to a new target of 46,000 by 1986. Such influences, combined with the imminence of local government reform, presented still further uncertainties to be confronted by those concerned in managing the housing programme at Droitwich;

Figure 48　Network relationships of Group Housing Architect for provision of town development housing

Definition of field of decision: provision of Town Development housing in Droitwich, 1966–71 (rented and sponsored)

GOVERNMENT DEPARTMENTS

ENVIRONMENT MINISTRY

HOUSING MINISTRY

Centre

Region

● Quantity surveyor
● Architect

APPOINTED AGENCIES

PRIVATE ENTERPRISES

CONTRACTORS

CONSULTANT ARCHITECTS
(first estate only)

CONSULTANT QUANTITY SURVEYOR

Q
City housing architect

COUNTY

Planning

ELECTRICITY

Clerks of works

GROUP

Finance Legal

PRIVATE ARCHITECTS

GAS

Planner

Chairman

WATER

Engineers

Housing

ESTATES ADVISER

Architects in other expanding towns

Surveyor

ESTATE AGENTS

Building surveyor

BOROUGH

PRIVATE BUILDERS

Boundary of network for rented housing development

Boundary of modified network after shift of emphasis to sponsored housing

COMMUNITY INTERESTS

KEY

◉ Respondent = GROUP HOUSING ARCHITECT

☽ Committee whose members communicate with respondents in relation to this field of decision

● Actor necessarily communicating with respondent because of nature of task and organizational arrangements

Ơ Actor communicating with respondent through element of discretionary judgement (on either side)

n.b. ◯ O ∘
Larger circles represent more senior members of hierarchies relative to other neighbouring actors

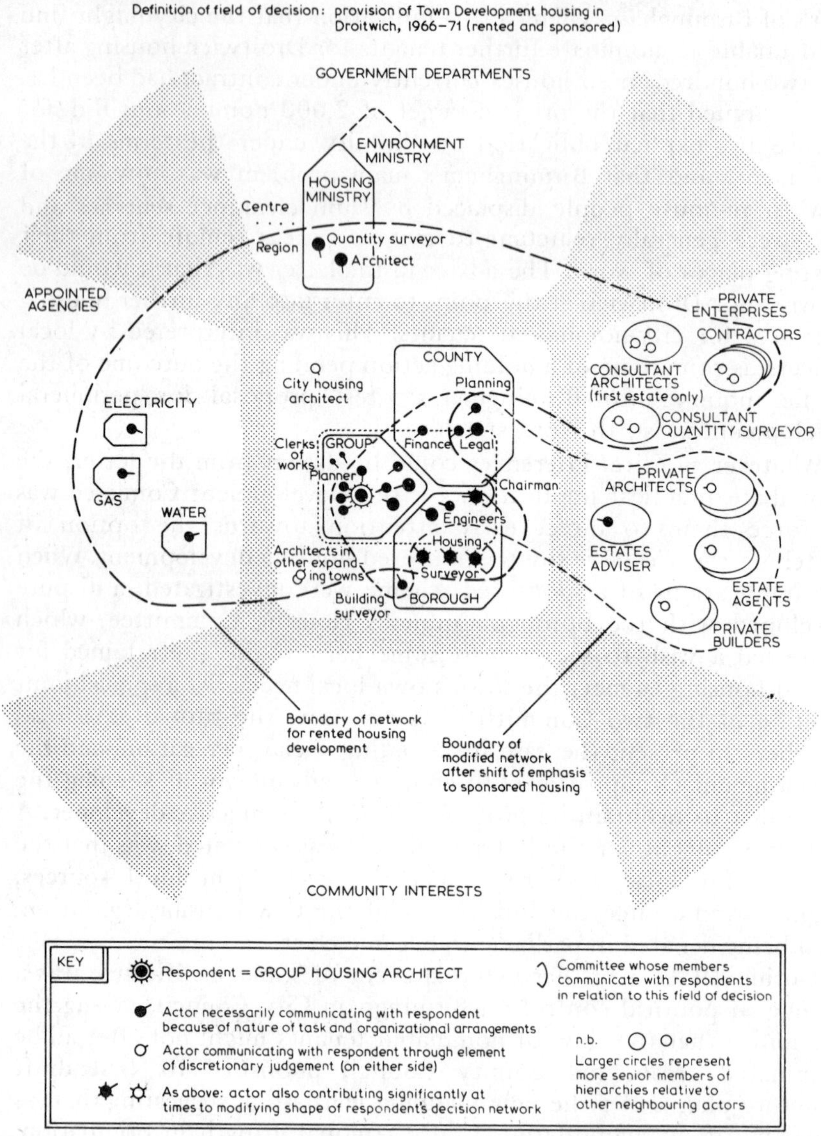

✸ ✩ As above: actor also contributing significantly at times to modifying shape of respondent's decision network

but, meanwhile momentum was beginning to build up in both the sponsored and private sectors, and the period of retardation in the planned expansion of the town appeared at last to be nearing an end.

Policy systems in the housing field

Figure 48 indicates a structure for the decision network of the Group Housing Architect in the field of housing development which is, in many respects, similar to that of the Group Engineer for roads, at least prior to the switch to the sponsored element of the programme. As housing was designated a 'key sector' when the procedures for delegated capital control of locally determined schemes were introduced in 1970, the detailed machinery for external control through regional offices of the Ministry was retained: and, as the case of Westacre demonstrated, it proved too rigid either to adapt rapidly to accelerating trends in costs, or to respond with sensitivity to variations of local circumstance. The formal system of control through cost yardsticks, devised to be both simple and fair in dealing centrally with large numbers of relatively small local authorities, proved in cybernetic terms to lack the *requisite variety* to cope with the intrinsic variety of the operations to be controlled. The result was that the regional civil servants tended to become increasingly drawn in to the local exploratory processes, rather than to act merely as a source of external policy constraints; and the Technical Officers' Committee for Expanding Towns emerged as an important forum for the exchange of local experiences and the expression of views to central government on the difficulties of operating within the formal control system.

The case example of Westacre has also indicated the way in which the problems of working within external policy constraints made it more difficult for the local decision-makers to arrive at an acceptable balance between social and economic criteria. Here, it was significant that the policy system for housing development at Droitwich was strongly connected to another policy system for the letting of dwellings, reflected in the Housing Manager's network as set out in *Figure 44*. Decisions on lettings had an important potential influence on the future social structure of the town, but were formally a matter of responsibility for the Borough Council, acting within the terms of the agreement, rather than for the Development Committee itself. Consequently, some of the differences of primary motivation indicated in *Figure 29* were therefore to emerge especially clearly in the housing context.

The Housing Manager's role became crucial in the transmission of information about the preferences of prospective tenants and their likely response to differing levels of rent; while, because of the policy uncertainties involved in alternative ways of overcoming the constraints imposed by the Ministry control system, elected members became more closely involved in the exploratory processes than they did in the case of roads, with the Group Administrator playing a crucial role as intermediary between the technical and political processes.

Major uncertainties arose not only at the policy interfaces with the Borough Council, the exporting City, and the Ministry, but also at the interface with the private housing market. Although, by the end of 1970, a successful start had been made in the comparatively unfamiliar sponsored sector of housing, there had been continuing doubts over its viability for many years. It was only when faced with the specific economic circumstances of scarcity of land for private housing and retrenchment in the public sector, that the local decision-makers were able to exploit to the full the flexibility which had been built into the original plan by leaving open the basic questions of finance for the intermediate 'sponsored' sector, and thereby to maintain the momentum of the entire development programme during an especially difficult period.

9 Industry

Decision-makers in industrial development

Along with housing, the provision of employment opportunities is usually considered to be one of the most basic tasks involved in the development of a new or expanding town. In Britain, at least, the dominant sector of employment has for long been that concerned with industrial production, although in recent years the automation of many manufacturing operations has brought a steady increase in the proportion of the working population employed in shops, offices, and social services of various kinds.

In an expanding town, the provision of new industrial employment is a field in which the local development agency – in the case of Droitwich, the joint Development Committee – tends to play a less central role than in other primary aspects of urban growth. As an industrial estate operator, the agency can of course exercise some degree of influence in the attraction of new industry to the town, acting essentially in an entrepreneurial capacity in the face of competition from other rival centres. However, in Britain at least, its entrepreneurial freedom is heavily constrained by the controls over industrial location exercised by central government. These controls were for many years exercised by a department known as the Board of Trade, the responsibilities of which were in 1970 brought within a powerful new Department of Trade and Industry after a brief period within a Ministry of Technology. In this chapter, we shall use the term Industrial Development Ministry throughout, in accordance with the conventions established in *Figure 5*.

Essentially, there are four types of primary decision-maker in the field of industrial development and relocation, which can be described as follows:

- *central government*, operating mainly through the Industrial Development Ministry;
- the *local estate operator* (in our case, Droitwich Development Committee);
- the *firm* that contemplates new development or relocation;
- the individual *worker*, especially where he or she faces a prospective change of workplace.

Of these four groups, we shall see that it is the firm which forms the nodal point of communication network involving the others. However, before attempting to look at the problems of inter-agency planning from this perspective, it will first be important to outline rather more fully the types of process in which each kind of decision-maker is engaged.

Central government and industrial location policy

Since just after the Second World War, the primary aim of the industrial location policy of successive British governments has been to channel employment into those regions, predominantly in the north and west, which have experienced levels of unemployment persistently above the national average, and where material standards of living have suffered accordingly. This aim has been pursued through a system of control over the location of new industrial developments, combined with an increasing range of inducements to encourage firms to move to these disadvantaged regions. The main form of control over location has been through the granting or withholding of an Industrial Development Certificate, generally known as an 'IDC', to any manufacturing firm contemplating a change of location or an extension of premises over a certain minimum floor area. This form of control is exercised by the Industrial Development Ministry, but enforced by being treated as a prerequisite for the granting of planning permission by the appropriate local authority.

The use of governmental incentives to steer firms towards desired locations began in the thirties, with the provision of ready-built factory premises for leasing on advantageous terms. However, as the local mobility of workers increased so the emphasis tended to shift from alleviation of unemployment in local 'black spots' towards the support of regional centres of growth; and incentives increasingly took the form of more general financial inducements such as investment grants or tax allowances, loan facilities, contributions towards removal and training expenses and regional premiums geared to the. number of employees on a firm's payroll. Meanwhile, continuing restrictions were placed on the granting of IDCs outside the areas where these forms of assistance were available.

As *Figure 49* indicates, the boundaries of the areas where incentives to investment were in force in 1967 — the Development Areas — coincided fairly closely with those of the regions of high unemployment. However, the simple demarcation between develop- ment and other areas was highly unselective, and rising levels of national unemployment led to much lobbying for further extensions of development area status by Members of Parliament and pressure groups representing the interests of particular towns. In subsequent years, an increasing element of selectivity was added to the system by the designation first of 'Intermediate Areas', which attracted lesser ranges of incentives and were situated mainly in the North West and Yorkshire and Humberside regions, and later of 'Special Development Areas' where problems of local employment were especially acute within the Development Areas themselves.

All three types of area were known collectively as the 'Assisted Areas', or, for the purposes of publicizing incentives, as the 'Areas for Expansion'. In 1972, a further step was taken towards the introduction of finer levels of discrimination in industrial develop- ment policy through a new Industry Act. This was designed to encourage the regeneration of existing local industries in the assisted areas as much as to promote the movement of new industries into them, recognising that only limited success had been achieved through past inducements to relocation. Special forms of selective assistance were to be made available through a new Industrial Development Executive within the Ministry, working largely through the staff of its regional offices. In Scotland, Wales, and the three Northern regions of England, Regional Industrial Directors were appointed, advised by specially appointed Regional Industrial De- velopment Boards. Through this facility for taking a selective approach to the circumstances of individual firms, it was hoped to counter some of the criticisms of misuse of resources that had been made in the past, more especially in the cases where central government funds had been channelled into capital-intensive rather than labour-intensive industries in areas of high unemployment.

Figure 49 Areas of government aid to industrial development in Great Britain

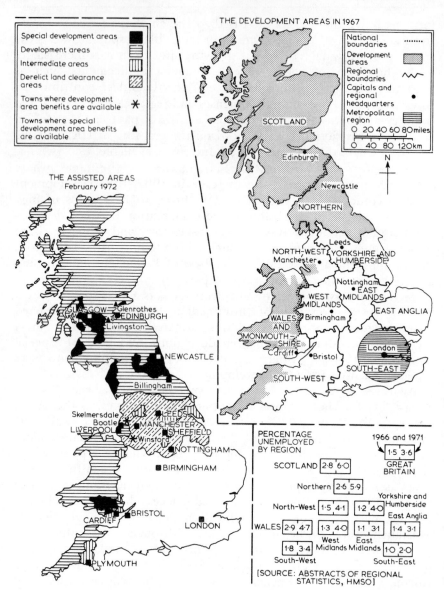

Special development areas

Development areas

Intermediate areas

Derelict land clearance areas

Towns where development area benefits are available ✳

Towns where special development area benefits are available ▲

THE DEVELOPMENT AREAS IN 1967

National boundaries ....
Development areas
Regional boundaries
Capitals and regional headquarters •
Metropolitan region

0 20 40 60 80 miles
0   40   80 120 km

N

SCOTLAND

Edinburgh

Newcastle

NORTHERN

Leeds
NORTH-WEST YORKSHIRE AND
Manchester • HUMBERSIDE

Nottingham
EAST MIDLANDS
WEST MIDLANDS
Birmingham   EAST ANGLIA
WALES AND
MONMOUTH-
SHIRE
Cardiff • • Bristol
SOUTH-WEST
SOUTH-EAST
London

THE ASSISTED AREAS
February 1972

GLASGOW Glenrothes
EDINBURGH
Livingston

NEWCASTLE

Billingham

Skelmersdale LEEDS
Bootle MANCHESTER
LIVERPOOL SHEFFIELD
Winsford
NOTTINGHAM

BIRMINGHAM

BRISTOL
CARDIFF
LONDON

PLYMOUTH

PERCENTAGE UNEMPLOYED BY REGION

1966 and 1971
1·5 3·6
GREAT BRITAIN

SCOTLAND 2·8 6·0

Northern 2·6 5·9

Yorkshire and Humberside
North-West 1·5 4·1   1·2 4·0
East Anglia
WALES 2·9 4·7   1·3 4·0   1·1 3·1   1·4 3·1
West   East
1·8 3·4 Midlands Midlands 1·0 2·0
South-West   South-East

[SOURCE: ABSTRACTS OF REGIONAL STATISTICS, HMSO]

However, new uncertainties were cast on this developing pattern of regional incentives to industry when it became certain that Britain would join the European Economic Community at the beginning of 1973, and would have to subscribe to supranational agreements controlling the forms of regional assistance that were permissible within member countries. Thus, the question of national policy for industrial location now began to depend on wider processes of international bargaining, raising new uncertainties about the future prosperity of the assisted areas of Britain.

Movement within and between regions

As the momentum of national economic growth became more difficult to sustain during the nineteen-sixties, so firms became less ready to plan and finance relocations over either long or short distances, and the government's policies for encouraging movement to the assisted areas tended to come into increasing conflict with its policies for planned overspill within the more prosperous regions. Most of the New Town and Town Development schemes which had been initiated to relieve congestion in the London and West Midlands conurbations had been planned on the basis of generalized assurances that the development of employment opportunities would be allowed to proceed in step with housing development, in order to realise as far as possible the ideal of the 'balanced' local community. Increasingly, therefore, policies for dispersal within regions, for which the Land Planning Ministry was primarily responsible, became difficult to reconcile with the Industrial Development Ministry's policies for steering new industry towards the areas of persistent unemployment.

As indicated in the second map of *Figure 49,* this kind of conflict could be resolved in the special circumstances of Liverpool and Glasgow, as cities qualifying for more generous assistance than other locations in their surrounding regions, by the device of designating any overspill towns as carrying the same status as the exporting authority. However, those concerned with the success of overspill schemes for the London, Birmingham, and Manchester conurbations continued to feel that policies for helping the assisted areas persistently worked in opposition to policies of dispersal within regions. The general policy commitment of the Industrial Development Ministry was that applications for industrial development should only be sanctioned in a location outside an assisted area if the firm could show convincing arguments in terms of its own pattern of operations; but, given such arguments, development in an overspill town was likely to be permitted much more readily than in its exporting city.

A recurrent criticism of the Ministry's policy was that there appeared to be no agreed guidelines on the proportions of IDC applications to be channelled to Assisted Areas, and the corresponding proportions to be permitted to remain within the more prosperous regions, either in overspill towns or elsewhere; essentially, policy was built up on a basis of case-law. The IDC policy was further criticized on the grounds that it relied solely on negative constraints on movement and could therefore only be enforced insofar as firms were either motivated to relocate or forced to move, for instance under urban redevelopment plans. No machinery was normally available for preventing a firm, refused an IDC, from staying put and foregoing expansion, which might be undesirable in terms of national policies for stimulating economic growth (Barbara Smith, 1971).

The Ministry's standard procedure for dealing with an IDC application from a firm was first to require completion of a standard form specifying floor space requirements, intended employment levels, and justification for moving to the proposed site. The firm would then be visited by an inspector from the regional office of the Industrial Development Ministry, experienced in weighing up the operational problems of that kind of industry. His report would form the basis for written recommendations to be circulated informally among regional officers of other government departments – the Land Planning Ministry, the Transport Ministry, the Employment Ministry, and the Agriculture Ministry. It was only rarely that any officer other than those representing the Land Planning Ministry would have any comment to make that was directly relevant to the granting or refusal of the IDC.

If any serious disagreement appeared likely, a meeting would be called. Usually, the source of any disagreement would lie in the continuing conflict between the policies of dispersing employment opportunities within and between regions. Cases which could not successfully be resolved at regional level would have to be referred for judgement at headquarters, together with those of a size exceeding the limit of regional discretion. Very large applications or important test cases would, from time to time, have to be resolved at ministerial or cabinet level. Here, judgements had to be made against a background of vocal pressures from the many Members of Parliament representing assisted areas, as well as any counter-pressures from the representatives of the proposed relocation site.

Often, the system of IDC control could be used as a means of striking bargains with firms, whereby some expansion could be allowed near existing sites, provided it was balanced by other development in the Assisted Areas. Certain conditions might be attached to the granting of an IDC, either concerning the future use of an existing factory in a congested urban area, or specifying a limit to employment levels on the new site. However, the former condition was only legally enforceable if both new and old premises fell within the same planning authority, which was clearly not the case for moves to overspill or assisted areas. The latter condition was also a very difficult one to enforce; indeed, the problems arising from such attempts to constrain the level of growth permitted after an IDC had been granted were to be a recurrent source of difficulty in Droitwich and other overspill towns.

Estate development at Droitwich

As an entrepreneur in the provision of industrial sites and associated services, Droitwich Development Committee had as its primary resource a single site of 107 acres (43 hectares) in the extreme north of the Town Development Area, acquired through compulsory purchase of agricultural land and forming a natural extension of a smaller industrial zone in which several of the town's primary employers were already concentrated. The competitors of the Development Committee in attracting new industry were a variety of estate operators in other towns — some of them local authorities and some private — and, most directly, other new and expanding towns both within the region and in the assisted areas. Among competing locations for Birmingham overspill, the New Town Corporations at Telford and Redditch and the expanding town of Daventry were all, during the later nineteen-sixties, engaged in vigorous policies for the promotion of industrial growth, each having more than one industrial estate either under development or planned.

Figure 50 shows the layout of the single Droitwich estate as envisaged in the Master Plan, indicating the overall area within which sites were to be offered, and also the broad division into two successive phases of planned development. As the sponsoring agency, the Development Group was responsible, through the Group Engineer, for laying out roads and car parks and for co-ordinating the provision of water, sewerage, gas, electricity, and telephone networks through the relevant specialist agencies. Also, the Group assumed full responsibility for the construction, on sites within the estate, of two blocks each consisting of four small 'unit factories', which could accommodate small local firms that would be displaced by road works or other developments in other parts of the town.

Figure 50   Layout of industrial estate at Droitwich

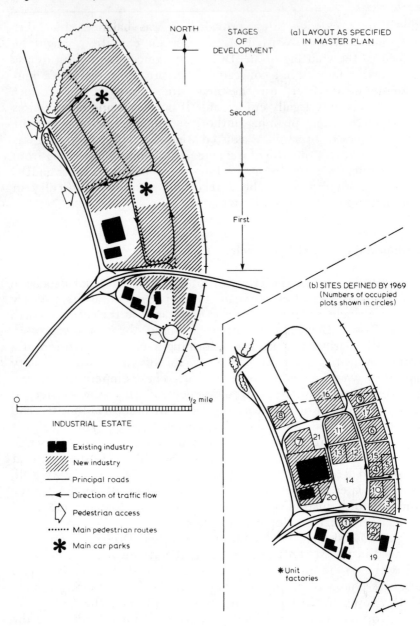

NORTH

STAGES
OF
DEVELOPMENT

(a) LAYOUT AS SPECIFIED
IN MASTER PLAN

Second

First

(b) SITES DEFINED BY 1969
(Numbers of occupied
plots shown in circles)

0 ————————————————— 1/2 mile

INDUSTRIAL ESTATE

Existing industry
New industry
Principal roads
Direction of traffic flow
Pedestrian access
Main pedestrian routes
Main car parks

*Unit
factories

All capital works on the estate by the Development Committee required governmental loan sanctions; these were issued through the regional estates division of the Local Government Ministry, until the introduction in 1970 of the new procedures of block allocations to counties for 'locally determined schemes' outside key sectors of expenditure. When it came to the second block of unit factories in particular, difficulties were encountered in finding acceptable design solutions within ministry financial and technical constraints, in much the same way as in the case of the Westacre housing estate. Because of the perceived urgency of relocating the small industries affected by the construction of Salwarpe Road, this issue came to absorb much time on the part of both the technical and the administrative staff.

The technical staff of the Group — especially the Group Planner and the Group Architect responsible for industry together with miscellaneous projects — also became heavily involved in discussions over design matters with firms that were intending to build their own factories on particular sites within the industrial estate. Some of these firms would draw on the services of consultant architects, while others would rely on specialist contractors operating on a 'package deal' basis. *Figure 50* shows that, by the middle of 1969, some 21 plots had been defined, covering rather more than half the total area of the estate, and concentrated in the southern area where roads and other infrastructure had so far been provided. Excluding the two sites for unit factories, six were already occupied or being built upon, four or five were under active negotiation, and the remainder were vacant. In three or four cases, negotiations with interested firms had recently fallen through; in some cases, marginal scope remained for re-drawing the boundaries of the sites in response to the requirements of new applicant firms. By 1972, only some 20 per cent of the available site area remained unallocated, and most of this was under active negotiation.

The constraints of IDC policy, coupled with the strategic location of Droitwich in relation to the M5 motorway, had the effect that the firms most easily attracted to the estate were those engaged in distributive rather than manufacturing operations; and this yielded a density of employment that was significantly lower than that originally predicted at the start of the Town Development pro-gramme. Accordingly, the Development Group became increasingly concerned that further land should be zoned for industrial develop-ment, and the search for possible additional sites became a significant local policy issue, to which we shall return later in this chapter.

Figure 51 Network relationships of Group Administrator for industrial development

Definition of field of decision: letting of sites and factory buildings on Droitwich Industrial Estate, 1968–72

GOVERNMENT DEPARTMENTS

ENVIRONMENT MINISTRY

LOCAL GOVT. MINY.

LAND PLANNING MINISTRY

INDUSTRIAL DEVELOPMENT MINISTRY

Centre

Region

APPOINTED AGENCIES

PRIVATE ENTERPRISES

CITY
Redevelopment
Housing

COUNTY
Planning
Finance   Legal

GROUP
Admin.
Planner

Architects

BOROUGH

CONSULTANT QUANTITY SURVEYOR

ESTATES ADVISER

FIRMS CONSIDERING MOVING INTO TOWN

EXISTING LOCAL FIRMS CONSIDERING EXPANSION or requiring relocation

Town Development executives committee

COMMUNITY INTERESTS

KEY

Respondent = GROUP ADMINISTRATOR

Actor necessarily communicating with respondent because of nature of task and organizational arrangements

Actor communicating with respondent through element of discretionary judgement (on either side)

As above: actor also contributing significantly at times to modifying shape of respondent's decision network

Committee whose members communicate with respondents in relation to this field of decision

n.b.
Larger circles represent more senior members of hierarchies relative to other neighbouring actors

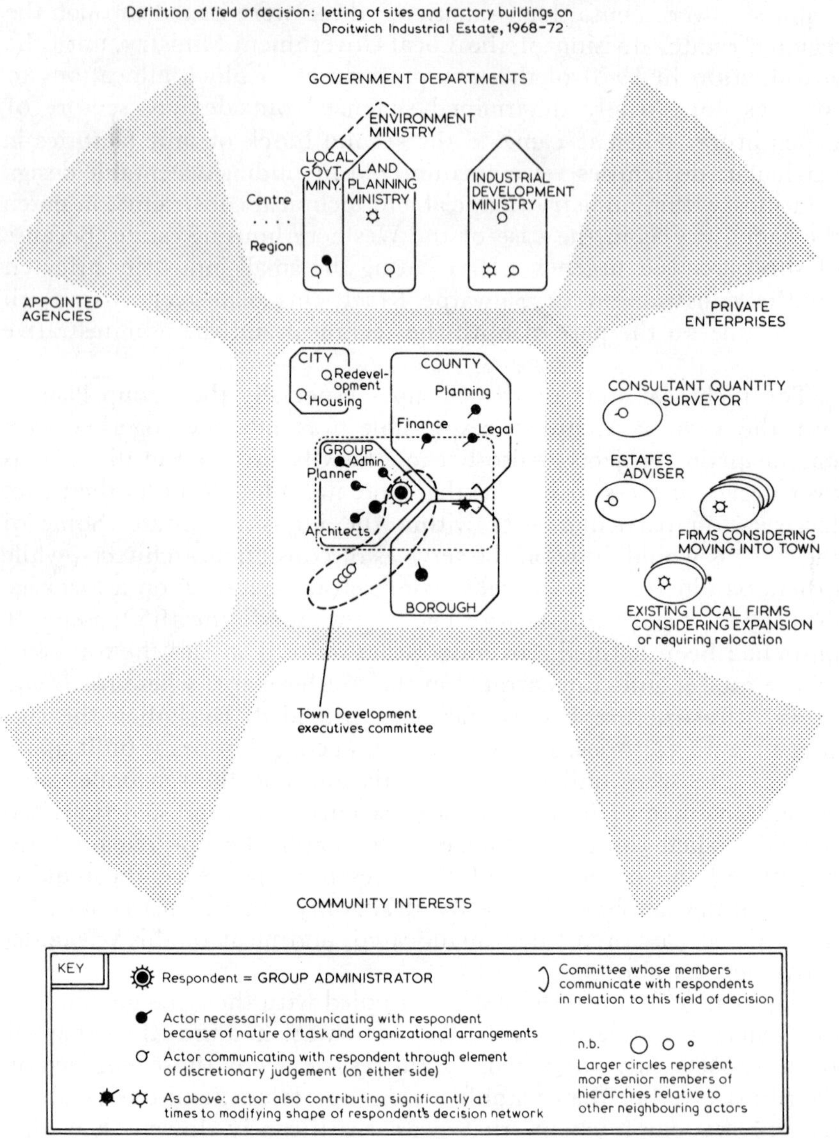

The Group Administrator as Entrepreneur

The most significant decisions in the field of estate development at Droitwich were those which came within the scope of the administrative rather than the technical staff, with the Group Administrator himself playing a prominent role in the processes of negotiation with prospective industrial tenants. *Figure 51* represents his view of some of the more important linkages in his network of relationships within this field of decision. Despite the involvement of a number of the technical staff of the Development Group in matters of design and layout, the Administrator saw these staff as less central to the crucial fields of promotion and negotiation than the firms themselves and the representatives of central departments concerned with questions of industrial location policy.

Among the channels through which firms were first referred to Droitwich as a prospective site for relocation or expansion were the redevelopment section of Birmingham City Council and the Technical Committee of West Midlands Planning Authorities, both of which had a nominal responsibility to steer displaced firms from the conurbation towards agreed overspill centres within the region. However, as at the time of the Wythall inquiry discussed in Chapter 3, it was felt in the overspill towns that Birmingham was not pursuing policies to promote the movement of its industry out of the city with a sufficient degree of vigour, for the understandable reason that its council had a direct interest in preserving and expanding the city's economic base. A more significant channel of referral to Droitwich was provided by the regional officials of the Industrial Development Ministry, who would persuade firms wishing to develop within the conurbation to contact overspill towns within the West Midlands, but only after they had produced evidence that they had made a realistic examination of the opportunities offered by Assisted Areas.

During the difficult early years of the Droitwich industrial estate, the Group Administrator made a series of representations within the region about the need for stronger support for industrial expansion at Droitwich. In Birmingham, those approached included not only the Redevelopment Section but the Housing Department, over the question of housing nominations for employees of the first incoming firm. Representations were also made to the Land Planning Ministry through the Principal Planning Officer in the regional office, and to the planning official at headquarters within whose geographical field of responsibility Droitwich was included. Regional civil sevants at the Industrial Development Ministry were also approached, in order to argue the case that firms were being presented with unnecessary difficulty by being forced to make lengthy investigations of opportunities in assisted areas, even where experience indicated that such a move would almost certainly be impracticable for the type of business concerned. A wider channel for presenting this kind of argument at national level was offered by the committee of chief executives of all Town Development schemes, of which the Group Administrator was secretary. This committee formed a special working party for IDC matters, which acted as a collective pressure group in representations to the headquarters staff of the Industrial Development Ministry.

Direct methods of promoting the Droitwich industrial estate included judicious advertising in the regional press and, on one occasion, participation in a joint exhibition in Birmingham city centre along with other overspill towns. On another occasion, some success was achieved through direct mailing to firms in the conurbation within the size range which was likely both to be attracted to Droitwich and to qualify for an IDC for such a move. As soon as a tentative inquiry was received at Droitwich, whether by telephone or letter, an administrative assistant of the Development Group would normally send out a standard letter setting out rental terms for sites, accompanied by a batch of publicity material giving background information on Droitwich and its expansion programme. Also, a short form would be sent requesting details from the firm about type of business, size and use of existing site, reasons for moving, prospective demands for space on the new site, present and expected employment levels, any training schemes, likely traffic generation and car parking requirements, and levels of demand on the statutory services.

Discussion would then follow between the Group Administrator and a representative of the firm's management — often a director, sometimes accompanied by an estate agent or architect — to elaborate on this exchange of information and to probe any wider policy issues on either side. If there was agreed to be a reasonable basis for further negotiation, more technical discussions with the Group's planning and architectural staff would follow.

The standard commercial terms were for the disposal of sites on a ninty-nine-year lease, allowing close landlord control over design, with levels of rental per unit of site area determined on the basis of market assessments by the Development Committee's Estates Adviser. Provision was made for rent reviews at one-third and two-third points in the lease, and there was some scope for negotiating deferments of rent over the early years of the lease for firms wishing to undertake development in two or more stages. A further provision was for the purchase of options on land over periods of up to five years, at progressively increasing levels of rent, for firms that felt unable to gauge at first whether or not they might wish to expand beyond the level planned on first coming to Droitwich. In the event, such arrangements for coping with the uncertainties of industrial growth were concluded with only a small proportion of incoming firms.

It was the Group Administrator who provided the focal point for all such commercial negotiations, and for submission of progress reports and policy issues to the Development Committee, which for this purpose operated mainly through a special Industrial Development Sub-Committee. Unlike other specialist sub-committees, this committee was convened on a regular basis, normally meeting for half-an-hour immediately before each monthly meeting of the full committee. Much of the information which the Group Administrator would present for discussion concerned progress in the processes of negotiation with individual firms; often, there were developments to report which were too recent to have appeared on the agenda paper. While the day-to-day management of the negotiating process was very much in the hands of the Group Administrator and his colleagues, the formal conclusion of negotiations involved the participation of the Committee's Estates Adviser in drawing up 'heads of agreement' in such a way as to prove acceptable to the legal staff or advisers of the firm concerned.

The decision problems of the firm

In the field of industrial relocation generally, one of the most significant points about the position of the firm in the negotiating process emerges clearly from the extensive surveys carried out by Townroe (1971). Townroe argues that there are few firms that have to consider relocation decisions sufficiently frequently for any clear policy guidelines to be formulated. Essentially, the firm's key decision-makers tend to be very much in a learning situation as soon as a move to a new location is contemplated, and to have to rely heavily either on the advice of consultants or (more frequently) on their own intuitive appreciation of factors that may be quite outside their normal working experience.

The simplified view that a firm can always base its locational decisions primarily on a criterion of expected future profit ignores the multiplicity of uncertainties which managers may have as to the ways in which different aspects of their operating environment may change in future, or may respond to any given option for change of geographical location. Within any firm, different assessments of these factors may be made by staff who are concerned with different aspects of the firm's external relations — sales managers, purchasing officers, and those who deal most directly with employee relations, whether line managers or personnel officers. Even assuming that the firm's accountants are able to attempt any quantitative assessment of the costs of moving, the general management may find itself having to weigh up in a more intuitive way, and under considerable uncertainty, the implications for relations with suppliers, customers, investors, and any 'key workers' whom it is especially wished to retain in the new location. In such a situation, there may often be much truth in the cynical view that the main determining factor is the attractiveness of the new living environment to the firm's senior management and their wives.

In the case of larger firms with many existing sites or subsidiaries, the assessment of the merits of different locations may often differ appreciably between more local and more central levels of general management. In the case of international firms, there is evidence that the incentives to locate in the assisted areas of Britain exert a substantial influence on decision-making, often dominating considerations of relative distance from markets or sources of supply. On the other hand, many industrialists based in the London or Birmingham areas adopt a more parochial perspective, in relation to which a location in Scotland or the North of England may appear too remote to be seriously considered.

Whatever the circumstances of a company — whether it be a small firm contemplating complete removal to a new site, or a larger business seeking an additional location in which to expand, or a major corporation concerned with the strategic siting of several points of production and distribution in relation to changing markets — the processes of search for prospective sites must involve some degrees of selectivity. The choice of search method may vary from the purely intuitive to the most sophisticated mathematical programming exercise; but in no case can it be feasible to draw upon all available sources of local information about all possible sites. In the case of the smaller firms at least, attention is likely to focus on certain locations to which notice has already been attracted by advertising, by contacts with referring agencies, or by prejudgement of desirable residential environments.

The information sought about these selected locations is likely to vary according to the nature of a firm's operations. Location in relation to markets and national motorway linkages — a point on which Droitwich scores highly — is likely to weigh especially heavily with distributive industries, while certain types of manufacturing industry may be more concerned with the local availability of pools of labour with appropriate forms of skill — a field in which Droitwich has scored rather less highly, at least during the early years of the expansion scheme. Some industrial managers, when contemplating a move to an expanding town, would also seek out information on the planned programme of future development of roads, housing, service industries, recreational opportunities, and shopping and school facilities. The more wary of them would seek to look beyond the intentions expressed in the published plans, and form some appreciation of their credibility in terms of likely future fulfilment, from whatever local indicators of confidence or of difficulty might be currently available.

One salient point about the decisions of the industrial manager is that any assessment of the effects of moving to a remote location will inevitably raise a wider range of uncertainties than will the comparative assessment of the likely effects of staying put or moving only a short distance from an established base, because his appreciation of operating conditions in a new local environment will have to be made on the basis of a much less comprehensive body of information and experience. Often, this may predispose the industrialist towards remaining on his existing site as long as possible, or alternatively moving within a reasonable commuting distance. This has wider implications for the incremental character of industrial relocation decisions generally; it also has implications for the decision problems of the individual worker, to whose policy perspective we shall now briefly turn.

The decision problems of the worker

Among the many types of decision situation that face the individual in relation to his work — whether unskilled, skilled, professional, or managerial — there are two that will concern us directly here. First, there is the worker who has to choose whether or not to move with his (or her) existing empoyer to a new location if asked; and second, there is the worker who is considering changing his (or her) place of residence for reasons not connected with a move by his existing employer, and contemplating whether to accompany the change of home with a change of job, either at the time of moving or perhaps later, especially if the distance is such that a period of commuting is feasible. We shall be less directly concerned with the case of the worker who faces a decision as to whether to change jobs locally without a change of address; but clearly the prospect of later opportunities of this kind may enter into the worker's calculations in facing an initial decision on migration to an expanding town.

In a majority of cases, the individual worker's review of options as to whether or not to move to a new work location will take place within a context of family relationships — or, in anthropological terms, of kinship networks. While this is most obviously true of workers within a 'nuclear' family of husband, wife, and children, it will also usually apply to some extent to workers in other circumstances, whether male or female, whether married or unmarried, whether close to retirement or making the initial transition from school to employment.

Another form of allegiance which may influence the decisions of the worker is that to a trade union or professional association. Although this allegiance may be very important to the individual in his relationships with the management at his existing place of employment, it tends to be less significant in relation to choices of movement to a new site, except in the case of comparatively large-scale employers who must negotiate any major relocation to a new site with the representatives of their employees' collective interests.

In Droitwich, the procedures already discussed for the nomination of overspill tenants by Birmingham, in conjunction with the various economic and other forces coming to bear on prospective migrants, had the effect that a very high proportion of newcomers to the town in the earlier years of the expansion scheme were married couples with young children. In moving, such families faced prospects of multiple changes of allegiance, with little opportunity to form a clear appraisal of the risks involved; the change of home would bring with it a need to adjust to new school environments for the children and new informal social networks for the family as a whole, as well as a prospective change in workplace by the husband and any other working members of the family.

A survey of residents in old and new local authority housing estates at Droitwich, carried out for the Community Development Officer in 1970, revealed that no less than ninety per cent of husbands who had recently taken up tenancies in the new Boycott estate were then commuting to work in the conurbation, with a majority of these working at the large British Leyland car factory on the southern fringes of Birmingham, readily accessible from Droitwich on the M5 motorway. Many of these workers travelled to work in their own cars or those of neighbours, the remainder taking advantage of a special works bus service. This heavy incidence of commuting could be explained to some extent by differentials in pay between the Birmingham motor and engineering industries and the local industries in Droitwich; but also to some extent by a reluctance by migrant families to burn their boats by making simultaneous changes of home, social, and work allegiances, under conditions of considerable uncertainty as to whether the overall effects of the move would turn out to be beneficial in the long run.

As in the case of the firm, one response of the worker to uncertainty was to take decisions incrementally, 'decoupling' the decision to change employment from that to move to a new place of residence. Such a strategy for coping with uncertainty helps to explain the difficulties experienced by other overspill schemes outside easy commuting range of Birmingham, such as those at Telford and Daventry, in realising their planned rates of growth during the early years of their development. It also casts some doubt on the ideal of maintaining a fully 'balanced' community by matching housing and employment growth at all stages in the development of a new or expanding town. Whatever the social disadvantages of commuting in the longer term, in the shorter term it can provide a means for the worker to keep important options open in his overall pattern of family living.

In Droitwich, the Development Committee was able to draw some satisfaction from a survey in 1971 which showed that the proportion of overspill families returning to Birmingham was significantly lower than in other comparable schemes. The hope was that the dependence on commuting would eventually drop as more and more husbands transferred to local jobs, and as their children grew up and began to look for employment locally, whether in industry or in the office or public service sectors.

Even at the purely economic level, the set of factors entering into the decision processes of the family can become extremely subtle. To assess the balance of economic advantage or disadvantage, the would-be migrant must attempt to balance the effects of moving not only on pay levels but also on rents, travel costs, and other expenses such as fuel bills; the overall implications of such changes have been demonstrated in studies of family budgets before and after moving from Liverpool to the expanding town of Winsford (Ministry of Housing and Local Government, 1967). Looking beyond the economic level, complex changes in social networks and psychological pressures may be set in train; but at both levels, the management of uncertainty is a central— if sometimes unrecognised – aspect of the family decision process.

Government and the mobility of labour

Recognising the difficulties faced by families in contemplating simultaneous changes of home and workplace, and the importance of trying to balance the skill requirements of incoming firms with the policies of exporting authorities for nominating overspill tenants, various forms of 'Industrial Selection Schemes' have been initiated involving a degree of joint working between the Employment Ministry and the exporting City Council. These have been investigated in some detail at the Centre for Urban and Regional Studies at Birmingham University (Ruddy, 1969). The first such scheme was established on local authority initiative in the Greater London area. More briefly and less successfully, a similar scheme was attempted in Birmingham, where it was run by the regional office of the Employment Ministry, in association with the City Housing Department. The aim was to bring to the notice of prospective employers in the receiving area the names of workers possessing required skills who were also eligible for overspill housing. In practice, however, it proved of little help to the circumstances of towns such as Droitwich, within commuting distance of Birmingham, and difficult to operate elsewhere because of the very limited numbers of workers satisfying both the exporting authority's criteria of housing need and the employer's requirements for specific forms of skill.

In the West Midlands, the original attempt at an Industrial Selection Scheme was therefore abandoned; but two schemes of a more modest nature were introduced subsequently, one for New Towns, and later, another for expanding towns. In the latter case, the City Housing Department rather than the Employment Ministry accepted the responsibility for the collation of information; but again discrepancies between city criteria of housing need and the skill requirements of employers served to limit the practical effectiveness of the arrangements. In practice, employers in overspill towns found that they achieved better results through advertising vacancies in the Birmingham press, with a footnote indicating that applicants meeting the City's known criteria for the allocation of municipal tenancies could expect to qualify for overspill housing accommodation.

The role of the Employment Ministry, as the government department primarily concerned in the regulation of employment markets, therefore tended to become a somewhat marginal one when it came to matters of employment policy for overspill towns. At a strategic level, of course, the ministry was deeply involved in national policies for reducing differences in unemployment levels between regions; but it was a matter for the Industrial Development Ministry, with its fuller capacity to investigate the operational problems of firms, to implement these policies through IDCs and related policies. Although the Employment Ministry maintained a local Employment Office in each main town — with a branch of its Worcester office in Droitwich – its main local operational responsibility was to find work for the local unemployed of the area. In times when job opportunities were limited, the inclination was therefore to place the interests of people from the immediate locality before those of prospective immigrants from exporting cities.

The primary decision-makers

Four primary types of decision-maker have now been introduced in the processes of industrial relocation and expansion: the officials of the Industrial Development Ministry, the estate developer, the management of firm, and the individual worker. In *Figure 51* a view was presented of the resulting decision network from the perspective of the local estate developer in the particular case of Droitwich. The pattern is in many ways typical of networks concerned with industrial development in overspill towns; but, in the assisted areas, it should be noted that further influences may appear in the shape of Development Associations set up to pursue a general promotional role in the region, and Industrial Development Boards set up to advise the Ministry on the application of its selective assistance policies.

It will be noticed further that *Figure 51* includes no indication of the part played by the individual worker, because he does not normally come into direct contact with the estate developer in relation to decisions about the prospective migration of the firm. It is the firm's management which provides the main pivot of communication with the other three types of primary decision-maker, and in this sense becomes the primary centre of network-managing or reticulist activity. At this point, we shall therefore discuss two particular cases of industrial firms moving to Droitwich from the point of view of the local management, before returning to the perspective of the Development Committee as estate operator in order to analyse the characteristics of the local policy system for estate development. We are very grateful to the two managers concerned for their ready agreement to talk to us about their firms' operations and their experiences before and after they made the move to Droitwich.

The manager's perspective: a case example

Firm A, a specialist manufacturer of office machinery, was the first employer of all to take up a lease on a plot on the new Droitwich Industrial Estate. Having originated as a family engineering business, founded in Birmingham in the nineteen-thirties, the firm was operating from three separate sites in the city when, in the early sixties, it was decided to apply for an IDC to carry out a local expansion. The firm was advised by senior regional officials of the Industrial Development Ministry to consider moving to a development area; but, after an extensive investigation of the opportunities afforded, the management ruled them out as impracticable. The main problem was one of dependence on materials and supplies from within the West Midlands, although the prospect of resistance to moving by key personnel was also seen as significant. The Ministry accepted this case and indicated that a move to a local overspill area would be accepted, given an undertaking by the firm's parent group that any subsequent relocations should go to an Assisted Area. This undertaking was, in fact, fulfilled in 1972 when another member of the group moved to South Wales.

In his review of possible overspill locations in the West Midlands the Managing Director of Firm A at first found none that appeared to meet his requirements for accessibility to suppliers and markets, and to accord with the preferences which his staff had recorded in a questionnaire survey, for a location to the south of Birmingham rather than to the north. A situation of stalemate therefore remained until he happened to learn, in 1964, of the recent agreement on a town expansion scheme at Droitwich.

The Managing Director therefore made a direct approach to the Group Administrator, who was the only officer in post at the time. There were some subsequent difficulties with Group technical and County planning staff over choice and layout of site, at a time when there had been as yet little investment in site services, but these were overcome and an IDC was readily obtained for a site of about one hectare, with an informal understanding that a somewhat smaller adjacent site could be made available for further expansions. This understanding was subsequently put on a contractual basis, through purchase of an option; and an unexpectedly rapid achievement of growth targets led in time to a series of four successive stages of expansion on the two sites, financed through the resources of the parent group.

Of the original 100 workers whom the firm had hoped to attract from Birmingham to Droitwich, about 80 per cent had in fact come, assisted by the provision by the firm of a special bus service to make commuting possible during the transitional period, and by contributions towards removal expenses. The Group Administrator proved helpful in resolving doubts about the eligibility of these employees for nomination by Birmingham for tenancies of overspill houses, at a time when the rented housing programme was in its early stages and there were no established precedents to follow. By 1971, the total number of employees of firm A at Droitwich was some 200. No difficulty was experienced in recruiting skilled male workers, especially since redundancies had arisen in engineering firms in Worcester. However, one field in which Droitwich contrasted adversely with Birmingham was the availability of a pool of trained female machine operators. This made it necessary for firm A to train such workers from scratch; a problem which had indeed led one other engineering firm to withdraw from Droitwich after becoming established on the estate, but which the Managing Director of firm A was inclined to discount as by no means insuperable.

One of the positive features of Droitwich, not fully appreciated by the Managing Director at the time of his original decision to move, was that the delivery of materials by motorway was actually simpler than to the firm's previous city location. However, he did not find it easy, in retrospect, to evaluate the overall financial implications of the move, because comparisons were inhibited by the many changes in the firm's operating environment since the original relocation decision.

The status of firm A as the first employer to be attracted to Droitwich helped in developing good relations with local officials and provided some useful publicity for the Development Committee in its early entrepreneurial efforts. Subsequently, the Managing Director was to become Chairman of a new Droitwich Industries Association, formed to represent the collective views of both new and established local firms. This had made successful representations to such bodies as the Post Office Corporation on standards of postal and telephone service, and the Borough Council on street lighting. Also, collective pressure had been maintained on the Borough Council over the continuing escalation of local rate demands; though the Managing Director of firm A expressed an awareness both of the underlying need to invest in new facilities for the future, and of the limited control that the Borough Council could exercise over the rising levels of costs.

Speaking more generally, the Managing Director volunteered the view that he had no regrets at all over the move to Droitwich. His only anxiety for the future concerned his ability to lease further land within the local industrial estate, since he had exhausted his options on all adjoining land and could not predict whether or not he might be granted an IDC for expansion on other parts of the estate. This latter question is one which loomed larger in the case of firm B to which, at this point, we shall turn.

Another case example: an International Company

Firm B presents a similar case to firm A in being engaged in a specialized field of engineering, but differs in its status as the sole British subsidiary of an American company, and in having its sales and finance as well as production activities directed from its Droitwich site. As a base for its UK operations, the parent company in 1968 bought out a small machine tool firm in the West Midlands conurbation, employing only nine people, and then began looking for a site for a major expansion. This expansion was to involve a significant change in the firm's production operations, from tool-making for aircraft production to machine tool assembly for the plastics industry. Like firm A, firm B was able to convince the Industrial Development Ministry that it could not reasonably move to a development area, because of the need for close access to suppliers of specialist parts for machine tools, who were concentrated within the West Midlands conurbation.

The original IDC which was granted for the firm's move to Droitwich involved occupation of the shell of an abandoned factory building within the curtilage of the industrial estate, the application having been lodged under the original name of the small firm rather than in the name of the American parent. A year later, a further IDC was granted for construction of a new building within the firm's existing site area. Later again, an application was made to expand further and to concentrate all the firm's activities on a larger site in another part of the Droitwich estate, reserving the existing site for possible future expansions. At this stage, the Ministry decided to refuse an IDC and advised a move to a development area, on the grounds that the nature of the firm's business had changed from that specified in the original application under the firm's previous name.

Following this judgement, a director of the American parent firm paid a visit to make strong representations to the Regional Controller of the Industrial Development Ministry, arguing that most of the firm's production went to export markets and therefore made an important contribution to Britain's balance of payments. It was suggested that the logical response of the parent firm to a decision that made its British operations much less economic would be to move to an alternative location on the continent of Europe. With the help of the Group Administrator, representations were made to the local Member of Parliament. The advocacy of the wider national implications of the loss of this small but fast-expanding multinational firm was in this way taken to a high policy level, and was sufficiently successful to produce a revised decision in late 1971. It was agreed that the firm should be permitted to build on half the proposed new site at Droitwich, while continuing to work from its existing premises, on condition that any future expansion should take place within a development area. For the firm, this decision meant a separation of machine shop and assembly operations between different locations on the same estate; but the resulting loss of efficiency was much more acceptable to the Manager than if he had been forced to work from locations in different parts of the country.

In the aftermath of this hard-won decision, the local Manager of firm B found himself faced in 1972 with some difficult strategic decisions. A temporary recession had now arisen in the machine tool industry, and he had to weigh up its possible implications for his expansion plans. In particular, he had to judge quickly whether to commit himself to architectural design costs for the expansion on the new site at Droitwich before the currency of his IDC lapsed in twelve months' time. When he decided on balance to proceed with this commitment, he did so largely on the grounds of the rapid expansion of markets he foresaw after Britain's entry to the European Economic Community in 1973. Significantly, however, he was very conscious of the many sources of uncertainty inherent in the prediction of future sales levels in his specialist field, and sceptical of the practical possibilities for reducing the uncertainties through systematic forecasting methods. His approach to planning was therefore essentially one of making successive incremental commitments while preserving his future room for manoeuvre.

In some markets, the company and its American parent were in direct competition, even though the British subsidiary was responsible for the network of sales representatives within Europe. In other parts of the world, the question of which firm could sell at the most competitive prices was sometimes influenced quite strongly by differentials in tariffs and trade preferences. Because the firm was foreign owned, the local Manager found himself involved in periodic dealings with the Bank of England over questions of capital funding for new construction work. These contacts were handled largely through experts in the regional office of one of the clearing banks in Birmingham, who also dealt with problems of arranging credits for overseas sales.

In expanding his local work-force, of about eighty in all, the Manager of firm B — like his counterpart in firm A — looked more to the local pool of unemployed engineering workers in nearby Worcester than to migrants from Birmingham, and often recruited through the Worcester area office of the Employment Ministry. The securing of rented houses under 'key worker' arrangements brought him into occasional contact with the Borough Housing Manager. He had also found the Group Administrator and his colleagues to be generally helpful at all stages in his relationships with the Development Committee. Among his employees, there was some criticism of the inadequacies of social and other facilities of Droitwich. In particular, the limited local shopping facilities, generally uncompetitive in terms of stock and prices, led many of his employees to travel to Worcester or Birmingham for many of their needs, while the firm itself tended to look to these centres when purchasing its own general sundries. Indeed, the recurrent delays in the redevelopment of the town centre had led to an air of scepticism as to whether the new facilities would ever be built at all.

The policy system for industrial development at Droitwich

To firms such as those just considered, the problems of relocation in Droitwich and of subsequent expansion required decisions of a rather different nature from those concerned with the management of their normal production and marketing operations. By contrast, the officers and members of the Droitwich Development Committee faced a steady stream of such problems from which to build up a general body of experience, relating both to firms already in Droitwich and also to those considering a move from elsewhere. During an average week, the Group Administrative staff would expect to receive about four tentative inquiries from new firms; while the monthly agenda of the Committee's Industrial Development Sub-Committee would normally include three or four cases of firms at different stages of negotiation, with perhaps a further two or three other cases brought up at the meeting as a result of developments since the agenda was drawn up.

From this pattern of experience, certain policy guidelines for the Development Committee gradually evolved. The Group Administrator, as the most central individual in the negotiating process, was able to learn from experience that any firms that employed less than twenty workers initially were unlikely to be worth considering except in special circumstances, while those employing over 100 could usually expect to be diverted elsewhere by Ministry IDC policy. Although the estate could successfully accommodate one or two larger firms with over 200 employees, experience indicated that many of the larger firms tended to be deterred by the limited size of the labour pool. Ideally, the Group Administrator preferred to attract firms with a high ratio of employment to site area, especially because the Committee was experiencing much difficulty in achieving the level of employment within the estate as a whole which had been hoped for at the time the Town Development agreement had been drawn up. Because of a combination of IDC constraints on manufacturing industry and the attractiveness of Droitwich as a centre for distribution, by 1970 a high proportion of the sites on the industrial estate had been let for different forms of storage, employing small numbers of workers with comparatively modest types of skill and levels of wages. The result was that the distribution of milk, tobacco products, mail order goods, and parcels joined light engineering industry among the major economic activities within the estate.

A significant development during the early seventies was the onset of negotiations with two firms concerned with the refrigerated storage of food. At first, the Group Administrator and his Committee were inclined to treat these approaches with no great enthusiasm, looking on them as further instances of the type of distributive activity that was likely further to depress the employment densities of the estate. Hwever, it then became apparent that the basic cold storage facility could provide a nucleus which would quickly attract associated food processing operations, both within and outside the premises. Not only could these operations help in generating local industrial employment, but they could also give a boost to local farming communities by providing an outlet for their products. Accordingly, the Committee came to adjust its policy stance so as to regard cold storage as a type of activity to be strongly encouraged within the local industrial estate.

The Industrial Development Sub-Committee, chaired by the Chairman of the Development Committee itself, included both County and Borough representatives among its members, and although they shared a common concern in the success of the estate, there were some variations in emphasis between them. One pressure which tended to encourage rapid expansion of the estate — even at the cost of low employment densities and limited provision of opportunities for skilled workers and prospective apprentices — was the County's concern to see an early return through rentals on its initial advances for investment in estate development. Also, the Borough Council had a continuing concern both to see a steady build-up of rateable value from the estate, and to see its new rented housing developments occupied as soon as possible by workers from incoming firms.

A further important criterion for the Borough Council was the environmental impact of firms; the avoidance of noise, of the visual impact of tall chimneys, of air pollution, and of the effects of noxious effluents on the local sewerage system. The Borough Surveyor regularly attended the meetings of the Industrial Development Sub-Committee to advise on such matters. One move which was only agreed after considerable discussion concerned a very small firm engaged in the metal finishing business, which nevertheless placed a disproportionately heavy load on the local water and sewerage systems. This was because the Severn River Authority, as the body then responsible for controlling the discharge of effluent into the river system, insisted on a very substantial dilution of the water that carried away the fine metal shavings resulting from the firm's operations.

Among the sources of shared concern in the Sub-Committee was the question of the local effects of government IDC policy. In particular, there were two or three cases similar to that of firm B, where a company, after being given initial permission to move to Droitwich, was subsequently advised to move again to a development area as soon as it wished to to expand its scale of operations. Clearly, if firms making the initial move could not rely on future permission for further expansions, the general effect could be one of sapping the confidence of employers in the opportunities afforded by overspill schemes outside the development areas. This could have wider detrimental effects on the realization of regional policies for dispersal from the London and West Midlands conurbations, and continuing local representations on this issue were made through the networks of influence on central policy making indicated in *Figure 51*.

The Group Administrator and the members of the Sub-Committee also found themselves faced with various other sources of uncertainty in predicting whether negotiations with particular firms could be brought to a successful conclusion. Often, they had to speculate whether an apparent cooling of interest on the part of one firm or another might be attributable to adverse trends in specialist markets, prospective takeover deals, or risks of imminent bankruptcy. There was, however, rarely any conflict on the Sub-Committee over the Group Administrator's proposed methods of coping with such uncertainties; and, despite the comparative lack of success in achieving planned employment levels, a situation had been reached by the early seventies where there would soon be no further sites available on the existing industrial estate. Accordingly, it was agreed to explore the possibilities of acquiring additional land for industrial development, with the primary aim of providing additional local employment which could ultimately help to reduce the local residents' dependence on commuting into Birmingham and other accessible centres.

A search for possible locations was therefore undertaken by the County planning staff, relying largely on the local expertise of the Development Group technical officers. The upshot was a recommendation for a further northward extension of the existing estate, rather than a separate industrial area in another sector of the town. This solution was opposed by members of Droitwich Rural District Council, for whom it meant a further loss of territory to the Borough, and a public inquiry therefore became necessary into the required amendment to the County Development Plan.

However, during 1972, a completely new factor arose: the publication of a preliminary draft of the County's first structure plan proposals under the new development plan system. In this, the preferred solution to the problem of accommodating the County's future population growth relied to a considerable extent on a further expansion of the size of Droitwich to a population of some 46,000. Clearly, therefore, the question of further industrial land would now have to be related to a rather broader policy context.

Summary

The picture emerging from this chapter is one of four very different types of decision-maker — the Industrial Development Ministry, the local estate developer, the firm, and the individual worker — all making successive incremental commitments relating to the general field of industrial development, under conditions of persistent uncertainty about each others' intentions as well as the future effects of market and other external forces. Although it is the firm which serves as the main pivot for communications between the various parties, it is the estate developer who bears the main responsibility for developing local policy guidelines, to provide a context for individual negotiations with industrial managers. Outside the assisted areas, however, these local policies are severely constrained by the IDC policies of central government, which can only be influenced indirectly through the separate and collective pressures of would-be areas of expansion.

This broad picture is summarized in *Figure 52*, which indicates the many subtle influences that can come into play in the processes of

Figure 52 General characteristics of decision-making in field of industrial relocation

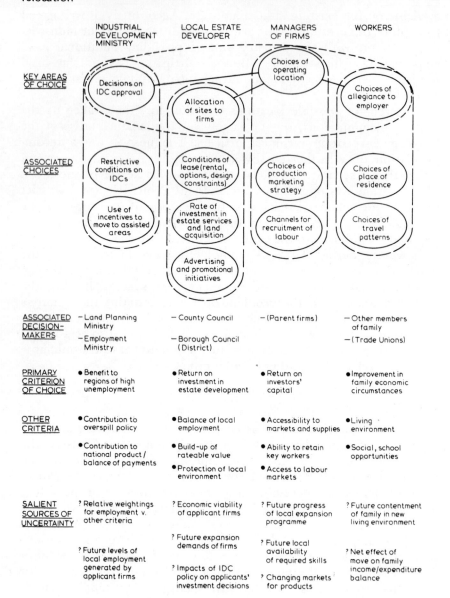

	INDUSTRIAL DEVELOPMENT MINISTRY	LOCAL ESTATE DEVELOPER	MANAGERS OF FIRMS	WORKERS
KEY AREAS OF CHOICE	Decisions on IDC approval	Allocation of sites to firms	Choices of operating location	Choices of allegiance to employer
ASSOCIATED CHOICES	Restrictive conditions on IDCs	Conditions of lease (rental, options, design constraints)	Choices of production marketing strategy	Choices of place of residence
	Use of incentives to move to assisted areas	Rate of investment in estate services and land acquisition	Channels for recruitment of labour	Choices of travel patterns
		Advertising and promotional initiatives		
ASSOCIATED DECISION-MAKERS	– Land Planning Ministry – Employment Ministry	– County Council – Borough Council (District)	– (Parent firms)	– Other members of family – (Trade Unions)
PRIMARY CRITERION OF CHOICE	• Benefit to regions of high unemployment	• Return on investment in estate development	• Return on investors' capital	• Improvement in family economic circumstances
OTHER CRITERIA	• Contribution to overspill policy • Contribution to national product / balance of payments	• Balance of local employment • Build-up of rateable value • Protection of local environment	• Accessibility to markets and supplies • Ability to retain key workers • Access to labour markets	• Living environment • Social, school opportunities
SALIENT SOURCES OF UNCERTAINTY	? Relative weightings for employment v. other criteria ? Future levels of local employment generated by applicant firms	? Economic viability of applicant firms ? Future expansion demands of firms ? Impacts of IDC policy on applicants' investment decisions	? Future progress of local expansion programme ? Future local availability of required skills ? Changing markets for products	? Future contentment of family in new living environment ? Net effect of move on family income/expenditure balance

each of the four types of decision-maker, helping those involved to form strategies for managing their salient uncertainties and in particular for selecting what level of commitment is appropriate at any point in time. The industrial manager has to choose the appropriate level of commitment both during negotiations and, subsequently, in his incremental capital investment decisions, often relying on a parent company to provide the necessary finance. The estate developer faces similar problems, but with the difference that most of the key investment decisions must precede the negotiations with tenants. The worker has to decide whether or not to risk committing himself and his family to simultaneous changes of working and residential environment, while the Ministry has to decide how far commitments to the approval of small-scale industrial developments in overspill areas can be justified, in the light of political pressures from areas of high unemployment. None of these types of decision are ever likely to be free of difficulty for the public and private agencies concerned; and, taken together, they exert some powerful cumulative influences on the processes of local and regional change.

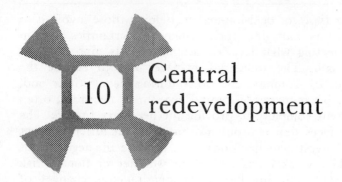

10 Central redevelopment

The problems of central area redevelopment

In turning from industrial development to another field in which commercial interests are closely involved — that of town centre redevelopment — we are beginning to make a transition, which will be continued in the following chapter, from the processes of creating new assets to those of introducing physical change in existing areas of urban development. Because this kind of change can induce intricate patterns of disturbance to established local patterns of social and economic activity, the transition from the previous chapter also involves a move away from a field where the interests of the County Council, the Borough Council, and the Development Group at Droitwich largely coincided, towards one in which some serious areas of conflict emerged.

In many ways, the difficulties can be seen as a continuation of those which preceded the signing of the Town Development agreement, and which were analysed in Chapter 4. Significantly, the agreement itself included very little specific commitment so far as the future of the town's central area was concerned. This flexibility recognized not only the difficult design problems which were involved, but also the considerable variety and intensity of commercial and residential interests concentrated within this very compact geographical area, with which much more detailed negotiations would have to be pursued if the provision of central facilities was to keep pace with the expansion programme in the rest of the town. In the event, the search for agreement on central redevelopment proved so difficult that it was not until 1972 that any firm commitments to building work could be entered into. In many ways, the bargaining processes of this period could be seen as an extension in time of those which preceded the signature of the Town Development Agreement in 1963, translated to a yet more localized and intimate scale.

In this chapter, we shall focus initially on two primary actors, concerned with the twin aspects of design and negotiation respectively: the Development Group's Chief Planner/Architect and its Consultant Estates Adviser. The former, who, in accordance with our conventions, will be referred to more briefly as Group Planner Architect, joined the Development Group shortly after its formation to head its technical team and therefore found himself becoming heavily involved in the difficult design problems of the central area from the beginning. The latter, a partner in a London firm, was at that time already acting in a consultant capacity to the County. He had therefore already been able to follow some of the early negotiations between the County and the Borough, and to proffer some advice on the commercial aspects of the scheme even before the agreement had been signed. A further important actor, the Group Central Area Architect, entered the scene in 1967; and it is his perspective that we shall use to present a view of the decision network for central redevelopment at a later point in this chapter.

The national context

Because the field of central area redevelopment is such a complex one, involving the co-ordination of so many different activities, it is one in which a wide range of governmental powers have gradually become involved, with a corresponding growth of concern that these should be deployed in ways that are mutually consistent with each other.

Traditionally, one of the most significant forms of involvement by public agencies in systems of central area activities has been the provision of roads, sewerage, and water supply networks; largely, in the British context at least, by local authorities acting under statutory powers laid down during the nineteenth century. Other public utilities have followed, while a further body of legal provisions, steadily increasing in volume, has been concerned with regulating the activities of private bodies in accordance with considerations of public interest. Such provisions include those for the control of development under town planning powers, for the regulation of traffic movement and car parking, for the control of street advertising, for enforcing specified standards of hygiene and of fire protection in commercial premises, and for the conservation of historic buildings.

Although many of the more prominent buildings in a town centre are usually devoted to commercial uses, there are also certain forms of public building which have traditionally been agreed to require a central location — notably town halls, police and fire stations, post offices, law courts, libraries, and, at least until lately, hospitals. Also, there has been a growing acceptance that local authorities may sometimes be justified in becoming directly involved in the field of commercial property development. In Britain, as elsewhere in Europe, it was the bomb damage of the Second World War that provided the initial impetus to some large-scale programmes of redevelopment in the central areas of cities, prompted largely through local authority initiatives.

Scarcity of national resources led to such investments becoming tightly controlled through central government loan sanctions, at first tied to individual projects but later released to local authorities in annual bulk allocations through the 'non-key sector' arrangements. In the interests of comprehensive rather than piecemeal redevelopment during the post-war years, local authorities began to make increasing use of compulsory purchase powers, recourse to these being preceded by the declaration of 'Comprehensive Development Areas' under the 1947 Town Planning Act. Such declarations could, if necessary, be sought for the whole of a town's central area; but the case for comprehensive redevelopment would first have to be justified at a public inquiry presided over by an official of the Land Planning Ministry, wherever a sufficiently large volume of objections were lodged by the existing commercial and residential interests. In its submission to the Ministry, the local authority would have to include a plan showing intended land uses and circulation patterns, and giving some evidence of their economic feasibility and conformity to accepted planning principles. However, the rules applied by central government were inevitably less specific than they would be, for instance, in the case of local authority housing schemes. There were real difficulties in attempting to reduce the complex interactions of central area activities to a few simple parameters for purposes of central government approval, and consequently it became important to demonstrate to affected interests, through the public inquiry system, that each local scheme was being dealt with according to its intrinsic merits.

A feature of the nineteen-fifties and -sixties was the increasing volume of vehicular traffic moving into or through town centres, using street patterns that had usually been laid down well before the coming of the internal combustion engine. Tighter controls over street car parking aften had to be accompanied by local authority investment in off-street car parks, and — as land became increasingly scarce and valuable — authorities found themselves often resorting to multi-storey construction. A landmark in national policy was the publication in 1963 of the Buchanan Committee's report on 'Traffic in Towns', advocating various measures to exclude vehicular traffic from major shopping streets, as part of a more general concern to introduce wider environmental criteria into the planning of urban transport systems. At about the same time, the Land Planning and Highway Ministries jointly produced a series of advisory *Planning Bulletins* for the guidance of local authorities in central area renewal.

These bulletins argued the need for a comprehensive approach to the analysis of town centre problems; advocated the segregation, wherever possible, of vehicular and pedestrian movements; and stressed the importance of realistic financial evaluation. Also, in the interest of flexibility, the bulletins recommended the principle of 'partnership' between local authority and private developers; indicated that the declaration of Comprehensive Development Areas was not necessarily the only way of controlling implementation; and introduced a new form of 'Town Centre Map', as an instrument of planning which carried statutory status but would nevertheless form a practical guide to the Ministries in the appraisal of local authority proposals.

Later in the nineteen-sixties, national economic difficulties led to increasing constraints on local authority spending, and the Land Planning Ministry found it necessary to follow up this guidance with another circular which went somewhat further in advocating compromise with economic necessity in applying the principles of comprehensive planning advocated in the earlier advisory bulletins. In particular, it was indicated that total segregation of vehicles and pedestrians might not be either necessary or desirable in every local situation within the immediately forseeable future, and that there might often be a great deal to be said for evolutionary rather than revolutionary changes. It was therefore suggested that planning proposals should be concentrated in those sectors of a central area where there were more immediate pressures for change, and options explicitly left open in other sectors. Also, the Land Planning Ministry introduced new provisions by which whole groups of historic buildings rather than individual listed premises could be nominated

Figure 53   Droitwich town centre before redevelopment

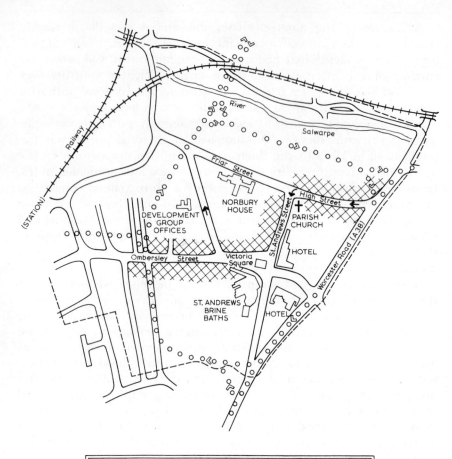

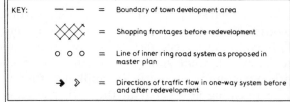

KEY:	- - - -	=	Boundary of town development area
	✕✕✕	=	Shopping frontages before redevelopment
	o o o	=	Line of inner ring road system as proposed in master plan
	➤ ❯	=	Directions of traffic flow in one-way system before and after redevelopment

as 'Conservation Areas' in which especially stringent policies of development control should be applied.

It was against the background of these successive developments in national policy that the proposals for town centre renewal in Droitwich had to be formulated, evaluated, and eventually acted upon.

The central area of Droitwich

The town centre at Droitwich, having evolved to serve a population of little more than 5,000 with only a limited rural hinterland, underwent much less physical change during the nineteen-fifties and -sixties than most comparable shopping areas. This was primarily because of the state of uncertainty over the future of the town which arose at the time of the first tentative proposals for town development, and was to continue for several years after the Development Committee was formed in 1964. Pending any agreement on proposals for comprehensive redevelopment, it could be argued that the only realistic policy was one of extreme restraint in the sanctioning of private development in the central area; and so a state of 'planning blight' became more and more evident in the commercial core of the town. Indeed, by 1972 Droitwich still preserved much of the appearance of a town centre surviving from an earlier generation, with many small shopkeepers still operating who, in other comparable towns, would have gradually been driven out of business by the advent of supermarkets and of branches of the specialist multiple stores.

Figure 53 indicates the basic layout of Droitwich town centre prior to redevelopment, with the proposed line of the inner ring road — measuring some 500 metres in diameter — superimposed to show its relationship to the Master Plan layout for the town as a whole as indicated earlier in *Figure 31*. The main concentration of historic buildings in Droitwich — several of mediaeval origin — lay on either side of the narrow High Street. This was a street of small shops having much visual attraction as a group; it had, however, suffered badly through brine subsidence, which had caused structural damage to many of the buildings 'listed' as being of special architectural interest. During the nineteenth century, the development of the town had been influenced by the siting of the railway station to the west. This had led to an extension of the shopping area in a south-westerly direction, first along the line of St. Andrew's Street and then along that of Ombersley Street, so that the resulting pattern of shopping was essentially of a broken linear form, with occasional short breaks in continuity which tended to accentuate the division between the High Street and Ombersley Street facilities.

Something of a focus was provided by the comparatively modern Victoria Square with a disused cinema building in its centre. This square, which also served as the town's main bus terminal, was flanked by three large buildings comprising the nucleus of what had become known to the planners as the town's 'Spa Quarter'; the St. Andrew's Brine Baths, together with two major hotels which had built up a prosperous trade during the peak of the town's reputation as an inland watering-place in the later nineteenth and earlier twentieth century. One other large hotel building further to the north — Norbury House on Friar Street — had been built too late to profit from the cult of the inland spa, and had subsequently been converted into flats. Later, it was to pass into Borough Council ownership, and provide an important focus for various local authority and voluntary activities.

Despite the intimate scale of the town centre, there were unusually large quantities of unused land behind the principal shopping streets. In particular, much of the land on either side of High Street and Friar Street had earlier been occupied by salt workings, and so presented an appearance of industrial dereliction. The temporary offices of the Development Group were located on one such site, the remainder of which had been laid out as public open space and car parking.

Preliminary steps in central area planning

During the period when the provisions of the Droitwich Development agreement were being negotiated, local traders were beginning to become concerned over the loss of trade to competing local centres, such as Worcester and Bromsgrove, resulting from the prolonged moratorium on planning permissions for extensions to premises. They were also concerned, in a rather more immediate sense, over the possible threats to their property interests which the town development proposals seemed likely to present. These anxieties led the Droitwich Spa Chamber of Trade, as the collective pressure group for local commercial interests, to ask for a meeting with the County Planning Officer at the time the proposed Town Map was first published in 1963. The published proposals for the central area were at that time confined to the demarcation of boundaries for a Comprehensive Development Area within the designated Town Development Area, and to the following statement of policy contained within the Written Statement:

'The scale of the Town Map is too small to show proposals for expanding and redeveloping the present town centre. The intentions of the Planning Authority for the central area will, therefore, be shown in a separate Comprehensive Development Area Scheme. This will provide for the shopping needs of the enlarged population and will allocate sites for public buildings of various kinds. In order to provide a proper balance of local employment, it is intended to encourage the movement of commercial undertakings from the West Midlands Conurbation to Droitwich and for this purpose, provision will be made in the central area for the building of offices and other commercial premises. The redevelopment scheme will be designed to overcome present traffic problems and provide for the considerable increase of traffic consequent on town development. The whole operation of redevelopment is so complex that it will be essential for it to be directed jointly by the Borough Council and the Planning Authority and for the central area to be included in the area defined under the Town Development Act, 1952.'

At the meeting requested by the Chamber of Trade, the County Planning Officer was able to respond to pressures to expand upon these very general guidelines by putting forward some sketch plans and suggesting some broad principles for central redevelopment based on work carried out by his own staff. As a step towards allaying local anxieties, it was agreed at the meeting that these principles should be presented in a brochure and publicized through the medium of the local press.

The brochure which was produced included a nine-point policy statement. Three of the points concerned environmental planning principles which were beginning to be generally accepted at the time, relating in particular to the segregation of vehicles and pedestrians; another three points presented general policy perspectives on the form and extent of shopping, office, and civic development required to meet the specific local purposes of the Droitwich expansion scheme; and the last three points provided reassurance to local interests about the preservation of historic and spa buildings, the relocation of any disturbed traders, and the provision of some housing development within the central area. The first and most significant of the nine points was the statement that:

'There is a useful nucleus of shopping in High Street, St Andrew's Street and Ombersley Street. There are suitable sites and opportunities here for additional shops and some development in depth. This should be sufficient for future needs.'

Following the formation of the Droitwich Development Committee, the next step in clarification of the future of the central area came with the formulation of the Master Plan proposals. These introduced one significant new element, in the form of the distributor road system designed by the Group Planner Architect in collaboration with the County Surveyor. In the Master Plan report of 1965, the case was first presented for an inner ring road on the line indicated in *Figure 53,* with one-way traffic circulation because of its restricted diameter and with the area inside reserved for pedestrian circulation, apart from access roads for car parking and servicing of shops. Thus, at this stage, a compact traffic-free zone was in effect demarcated to enclose most of the major central area facilities, within the comparatively regular boundaries determined by the line of the inner ring road.

The Town Centre Report

The more detailed proposals for the central area of Droitwich were not to be published until early 1967, some fifteen months after the Master Plan. However, the Group Planner Architect had in fact begun to appraise the potentialities of the central area soon after his appointment in 1965, against a background of his earlier experience in New Town Development. He had soon become convinced that something more positive would be required than the comparatively modest infilling of the exisiting linear pattern of shopping facilities which had been implied by the County Planning Officer's preliminary design work; and this judgement was reinforced by the Group Estates Adviser's view that the economics of shopping development in a motorized age demanded concentration around a clearly-defined focus with off-street parking provision, rather than the development of a more extended linear form. Therefore, an early choice was required concerning the location of a central shopping focus in relation to the two main groupings of existing facilities, in High Street and Ombersley Street respectively. Inevitably, such a choice would have implications for the future trade — and perhaps even the survival — of some existing shops either at the western or the eastern extremity of the established shopping area. In retrospect, the Group Planner Architect felt he could conceivably have opted for a design that allowed fuller retention of shopping facilities in the western part of Ombersley Street at the expense of those at the eastern end of the High Street, with a corresponding westward shift in the line in the inner ring road. However, there would have been a serious penalty in the loss of historic buildings in High Street, whereas the option based on the road line shown in *Figure 53* allowed these to be retained, in conjunction with a new central shopping focus to be established in the area north of Victoria Square and west of St. Andrew's Street.

It was around this latter concept that a more detailed design for the Droitwich central area was worked out, to be presented in 1967 in a copiously illustrated Town Centre Report, forming a companion volume to the Master Plan Report. The case for the recommended layout was argued from a set of nineteen 'basic principles', which had earlier been proposed by the Group technical staff and formally approved by the Development Committee. Generally, these principles could be claimed to be compatible with the set of nine principles enunciated earlier by the County Planning Officer. Among the points emphasized were the importance of comprehensive planning, of designing to modern environmental standards, and of relating new to existing premises in both economic and visual terms. Of course, the enunciation of such statements of principle as policy guidelines could not necessarily give any clear guidance where questions of balance arose between potentially conflicting aims — for instance, between comprehensiveness and flexibility, between short-term and longer-term impacts, between environmental and economic values, or between the interests of traders and those of consumers. However, the Group Planner Architect was able to argue that, because of the constraints of the local site, the type of proposals he put forward followed almost inexorably from the acceptance of the nineteen principles as set out in the report.

The detailed proposals of the Group Planner Architect were set out in the form of a series of maps, the most comprehensive of which is reproduced in *Figure 54*. Because of the local contours, a pattern of pedestrian circulation on two levels was proposed; and to make the nature of the design more clear, the two-dimensional plans were supplemented in the report by a photograph of a three-dimensional model and by a series of sketches illustrating the pedestrian's perspective from various key vantage points. Although the narrative accompanying the plans gave some prominence to the need for phased implementation, the plans and sketches themselves were essentially directed towards the end-state of the redevelopment, and included a level of architectural detail considerably beyond that to which commitment was at that stage required. This was in accordance with accepted practice in civic design, where inevitably a dilemma arises in deciding how far to fire people's imagination by presenting an attractive visual image of a potential end state, and how far to emphasize flexibility of design so as to accommodate the

Figure 54   Droitwich central area proposals (central section of plan reproduced from 1967 Town Centre Report)

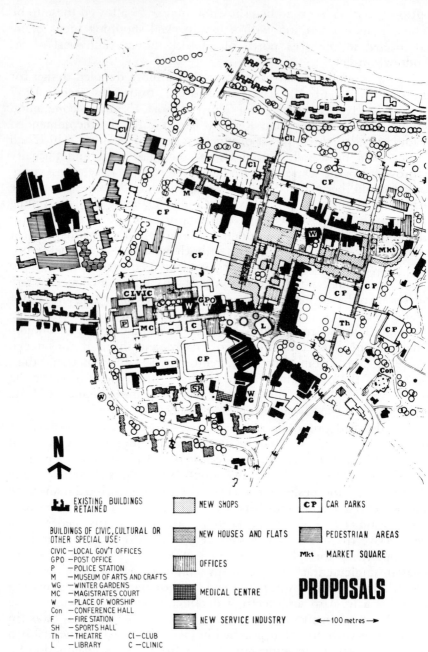

N

EXISTING BUILDINGS RETAINED

BUILDINGS OF CIVIC,CULTURAL OR OTHER SPECIAL USE:

CIVIC —LOCAL GOV'T OFFICES
GPO —POST OFFICE
P   —POLICE STATION
M   —MUSEUM OF ARTS AND CRAFTS
WG   —WINTER GARDENS
MC   —MAGISTRATES COURT
W   —PLACE OF WORSHIP
Con   —CONFERENCE HALL
F   —FIRE STATION
SH   —SPORTS HALL
Th   —THEATRE   CI—CLUB
L   —LIBRARY   C—CLINIC

NEW SHOPS

NEW HOUSES AND FLATS

OFFICES

MEDICAL CENTRE

NEW SERVICE INDUSTRY

CP CAR PARKS

PEDESTRIAN AREAS

Mkt   MARKET SQUARE

PROPOSALS

◄—100 metres—►

interests of affected parties and permit adjustments to the uncertainties of future economic and policy trends.

In the Droitwich Town Centre Report, the proposals presented were justified not only by reference to statements of broad principle, but also by reference to the results of various local surveys concerned with such factors as the risks of flooding and brine subsidence, and the predicted levels of traffic flow. Also, the Estates Adviser contributed an extensive section to the report presenting estimates of shopping floor space required for different stages of population growth, while acknowledging the many sources of uncertainty involved in such calculations. These sources were essentially similar to those which have been analysed elsewhere in the case of the much more extensive shopping provisions of Coventry (Friend and Jessop, 1969, Chapter 4). In the light of these uncertainties, the consultants stressed the need for flexibility in translating floor-space estimates into specific land allocations, and concluded that economic factors would have to be given due weight when it came to reviewing such future areas of decision as the provision of access facilities, the disposition of ancillary land uses, the methods of servicing shops, the phasing of different aspects of the redevelopment, and the choice of agencies for implementation.

Reactions to the proposals

The publication of the town centre proposals was accompanied by the mounting of a public exhibition, at which many models, plans, photographs, and sketches were placed on display. Some five thousand visitors attended, while leading members and officers of the Development Group also held meetings with twenty-four of the local organizations affected including the Chamber of Trade, the principal religious denominations, and several clubs and voluntary associations.

A variety of comments and criticisms were registered during the exhibition. An analysis by the Group officers showed that a majority of the criticisms took the form of objections to acquisition or demolition of particular properties, although a significant number reflected a more general view that the scheme was too ambitious or expensive for a town of the character of Droitwich. Where the proposals impinged most directly on particular commercial interests, the reaction was sometimes one of considerable shock. One instance was the owner of a flourishing store, who had repeatedly been refused planning permission for extension pending production of the Town Centre Plan, and who now found his existing site designated

for future civic offices, with a prospect of having to sacrifice the
security of his freehold for a tenancy in another central site. The
individual concerned was left with a profound sense of grievance,
because he had spent most of his working life building up a viable
business from scratch, and introducing other members of his family
into its management with a view to ultimate succession.

As in any small town, there tended to be numerous social linkages,
as well as some degree of direct overlap, between the memberships of
the elected Borough Council and the local trading community. It was
therefore not surprising that the local members of the Development
Committee should have found themselves directly exposed to the
anxieties created by publication of the central area proposals, both
within the membership of the local Chamber of Trade and also
among the more old-established residents of the area.

Accordingly, when the various comments and criticisms were
collated by the Development Group officers and submitted to their
Committee, it proved possible to do no more than agree that the
report containing the proposals be accepted as a 'framework' to pass
forward for the comments of the Borough and County Councils. In
advocating this move, the Borough representatives were able to
invoke the clause in the agreement constituting the joint Committee
which required that 'from time to time' detailed plans and estimates
should be submitted to the parent authorities for approval. Meanwhile, the Chamber of Trade resolved to commission an independent
firm of shopping consultants to produce a reasoned alternative to the
proposals formulated by the Development Group Officers, with a
view above all to finding ways of retaining more of the exisiting
shopping facilities intact and lessening the need for compulsory
purchase of existing freeholds.

When the Borough Council met to discuss its attitude to the
Development Group proposals, it was agreed that a list of six points
be submitted to the next meeting of the Development Committee, to
the effect that:

(1) the principle of a ring road with pedestrian shopping within it
    should be accepted;
(2) the amount of demolition involved should be substantially
    reduced;
(3) the proposed civic development should be re-sited, especially
    with a view to preserving vehicular access to the parish church
    of St. Andrew by way of Ombersley Street;
(4) the proposal for a new open market at the eastern end of High
    Street should be rejected;

(5) more private development should be permitted, both by individuals and by property companies;
(6) before a final decision, a year-by-year forecast should be submitted showing the impact of any revenue expenditure or loan charges on local ratepayers.

A few days later, the General Purposes Sub-Committee of the County Council's Planning Committee considered these six points, accepting the first and last but expressing disagreement with the remainder. Thus, when the joint Development Committee next met, each of the points (2) to (5) had to be put to a formal vote, with the County members aligned on one side and the Borough Council members, apart from a few who were strongly committed to the progress of the Town Development scheme, aligned on the other. The Chairman of the Committee in particular found himself placed in a difficult and invidious position, as both a local representative and a central figure in the structure that had been set up for the implementation of the expansion programme. On each point of disagreement, the voting went narrowly in favour of the published proposals and against the majority view of the Borough Council; but the situation was strained and, when the full Borough Council next met a week later, its members resolved by a substantial majority to ask for a meeting with County Council representatives at the first opportunity to agree new 'instructions' to the Development Committee.

Thus, the most serious crisis had arisen in the relationships between the parent authorities since the signature of the agreement setting up the joint committee. If no way out could be found, it remained a possibility that the County could adopt the course of going ahead with a unilateral submission of the town centre proposals to the Land Planning Ministry, with the Borough Council joining the Chamber of Trade as an objector at the ensuing public inquiry. The outcome of such an inquiry was recognised to be unpredictable; and, at least, there could be serious delays to the development programme both in the town centre and in the associated road construction projects. The officers did not see any practical prospect of meeting the local objections through piecemeal modifications to the design proposals; while it was claimed that the preparation of a completely new scheme could have been very costly in staff time. As a basis for assessing the likely order of cost involved, the County financial staff were able to claim that the original survey and design work for the central area had involved a total expense of some £30,000 in the salaries of Development Group staff and the fees of their external advisers.

There followed a series of informal meetings between leading elected members and officials of the two Councils, in an attempt to find ways of overcoming the state of impasse that had arisen. The result was an understanding that the Development Committee should ask its officers to look into the possibility of an alternative central area scheme, based on a new brief suggested by the Borough Council. This would aim to retain more of the existing shopping facilities, especially in that part of Ombersley Street zoned for civic buildings. To this end, the officers would be asked to examine the possibility of locating the proposed civic offices outside the area enclosed by the inner ring road. However, part of the bargain accepted by the local members was that, if such a scheme should be shown to be less viable economically than the original proposals, then the latter should be allowed to proceed to the detailed design stage without further dispute.

It took a period of two months for the officers to investigate the possibilities of an alternative scheme as instructed, and to report on its implications. The Group's Estates Adviser and the Group Planner Architect were able to point out the disadvantages of additional cost in the alternative proposal; the physical difficulties presented; and the dangers of failing to establish a clear focal point to make the new centre attractive from the outset. This advice left the Borough Council representatives with no alternative but to agree to the original scheme in principle, 'subject to further discussion of details taking place before implementation'. Some local members were subsequently to express to us the view that it had been unrealistic to have required the same officers who had prepared the original proposals, and in the process had built up a considerable degree of professional commitment to them, to have embarked with equal enthusiasm on the preparation and evaluation of an alternative scheme based on a radically different brief. On the other hand, the officers were able to contend that they had already investigated thoroughly a wide range of alternative solutions in their original design exercises, and had found convincing reasons for rejecting all that differed significantly from that eventually put forward.

The processes of statutory submission

By early 1968, therefore, a sufficient degree of commitment had been secured from the parent authorities for the officers to proceed with the further work involved in preparing their statutory planning submissions to the Land Planning Ministry. These submissions involved the declaration of a Comprehensive Development Area

(CDA) covering Droitwich Town Centre, along with a draft order for the compulsory purchase of those properties within that area that were required in order to carry out the first of the three proposed four-year stages of implementation. This first stage embraced the establishment of a new pedestrian shopping square to the west of St. Andrew's Street, the construction of the first of the new civic buildings, and also most of the work required to bring the inner ring road into operation. The second phase would complete the main shopping development, would close existing traffic routes and would allow the pedestrianization of the High Street; while the third phase would be confined to the development of a peripheral area for service industry, coupled with the construction of offices and town housing to complete the overall balance of central area activities.

One choice facing the Development Committee was that of whether to make the initial Compulsory Purchase submission in parallel with the wider CDA submission or subsequently. The latter option would mean holding two consecutive public inquiries, with corresponding legal costs and delays in implementation, at a time when it was becoming important for the Development Group work programme that an early start should be made in the central area. However, some of the Borough Council members continued to resent any indications that the scheme was being pushed through irrespective of their reservations. This led them to oppose the idea of simultaneous submission, and it was only on the strength of a single vote that the committee finally agreed that the officers should go ahead on this basis.

When it came to the annual Borough elections the following spring, there was a new manifestation of the frustration on the part of some of the members at their apparent inability to influence the course of important events in the centre of the town they represented, when the two Borough representatives who had voted for simultaneous submission were not nominated for a further term on the Development Committee. One of these was the Committee Chairman himself who, it was agreed, should exchange roles with the Chairman of the Borough Planning Committee. The following year, his nomination for the Development Committee was in fact renewed; but the Borough Council had now demonstrated the extent of its concern to maintain a greater measure of unanimity and consistency in voting patterns within its own ranks. For the Group officers, the effect was to underline further the operational uncertainties of working within a system of decision-taking through an evenly balanced joint committee, at least in relation to issues that involved underlying conflicts of interest between the parent authorities.

Later in 1968, initial drafts of the two parallel statutory submissions had been prepared. The CDA submission, including a formal map of proposed land zonings, together with a supporting written statement, in fact included a significant measure of flexibility in some of the more crucial decision areas. By the device of a 'use zone table', it was made clear that certain parts of the central area zoned primarily for one purpose, such as shopping, might also be considered for other compatible types of development, such as offices or car parks; while it was also stated that the broad proposals for phasing within the three successive four-year periods might be varied because of the intricate problems of acquisition, relocation, and maintenance of access likely to be encountered during the implementation process. The accompanying draft compulsory purchase order, specifying the properties to be aquired during the first phase, involved almost a hundred different ownerships in all. However, the land areas involved were not extensive, as a high proportion of the land and property within the central area had already been aquired in a single transaction from the local company which had owned the St. Andrew's Brine Baths and several related assets.

By the time these documents had been prepared, the County and Borough Treasurers were nearing the completion of a detailed appraisal of the financial implications of the scheme, in conjunction with the Committee's Estates Adviser. The assessment was prepared in two parts, of which the first was designed to estimate the attractiveness of the commercial elements to a prospective developer, leaving open the question of whether this should be the Development Committee itself, or a commercial organization, or some form of partnership. The second part was designed to examine the impact on Borough and County ratepayers, bearing in mind that the Borough had insisted on a detailed appraisal of this kind when agreeing in principle to go ahead with the scheme.

In the second stage of this process in particular, the Estates Adviser played a key role by presenting the financial implications first in the form of assessments of the short-term costs and returns, and second in the form of a DCF or 'discounted cash flow' rate of return, over a time horizon of sixty years. This latter method rests on the principle that incomes and expenditures expected to arise in the earlier years of a scheme should be given greater weight than those expected later, in recognition of the costs involved in borrowing capital or sacrificing competing investment opportunities. The DCF rate of return derived by this method can thus be taken as at least an approximate indicator of the prospective attractiveness of a scheme, judged against prevailing long-term interest rates.

A fuller discussion of the method appears in the book by Merrett and Sykes (1966). However, the DCF approach remains a source of some controversy in investment appraisal circles (Adelson, 1965), on the practical grounds that any estimation of long-term cash flows involves somewhat speculative assumptions in relation to the many underlying sources of risk and uncertainty, as well as on more theoretical grounds concerned with the conditions under which a single-valued DCF rate of return can be computed.

In the case of Droitwich, the estimated DCF rates of return did provide a convincing case for the economic viability of the proposals, given an acceptance of the various assumptions on which the computations were based. One of the most crucial of these concerned the levels of income from the rental of shopping premises to prospective central area traders. Inevitably, the rents charged for modern purpose-built shop units would have to be set at levels considerably higher than those to which many established local traders were accustomed. Experience in other towns provided evidence that higher rentals could usually be recouped readily by the trader in the form of higher turnover and profit levels, given efficient trading methods; but this evidence provided little reassurance to the smaller traders in Droitwich. To these people, the prospect of exposure to competition from the larger multiple stores presented a serious threat. This was a threat that was by no means peculiar to Droitwich, but it was one from which local shopkeepers had been protected for many years by the moratorium on new shopping development in the central area.

The two parts of the financial appraisal were presented not only to a meeting of the Development Committee but also to the relevant committees of both parent authorities; and the most sensitive issue that arose during these processes of consultation concerned whether or not the results of the costing exercises should be made public. On the one hand, the existing traders of Droitwich could claim a legitimate concern to know the assumptions on rent levels for new shop units on which the calculations of returns to a prospective investor were based; but, on the other hand, the Group officers and Estates Adviser could claim with equal cogency that such disclosures could seriously prejudice their stance in subsequent negotiations with developers. This, it was argued, could be to the ultimate disadvantage of local ratepayers; even a minimal disclosure of financial information at a public inquiry would merely open the gates to further pressures, and would be contrary to established practice in similar town centre redevelopment submissions elsewhere.

It was only after a prolonged debate over these conflicting

arguments, both within and outside the setting of the Development Committee, that the Borough representatives reluctantly came to accept the arguments for confidentiality. This left the local Chamber of Trade as the main focus of continuing pressure for disclosure. It also implied that the town centre proposals would have to be defended at the forthcoming public inquiry on the basis of town planning rather than economic criteria, supported by assurances that the necessary economic investigations had been carried out but without an opportunity for its results, and the underlying assumptions, to be subjected to any form of critical public scrutiny. Such a situation, by no means unique to Droitwich, raises some basic issues of public involvement in the planning process to which we shall later wish to return.

The Town Centre Inquiry

The public inquiry into the Droitwich town centre proposals, held in late 1969 in accordance with statutory town planning procedures, provided a formal climax to the decision processes of central area redevelopment. An inspector was appointed by the Land Planning Ministry to preside over the quasi-judicial proceedings, while a distinguished Queen's Council, with a national reputation in the specialized field of town planning law, was retained to advocate the joint case of the Development Committee, the County Council (as planning authority formally responsible for the CDA submission), and the Borough Council (as the public body in whose name the compulsory purchase order was formally submitted).

In opposition to the local authority interests were ranged some seventy objectors to the CDA proposals and a further hundred to the Compulsory Purchase Order. A majority of these were objecting specifically to impacts on their individual commercial or residential property interests, and many were represented individually or collectively through the services of local lawyers or estate agents. While some hoteliers and shopkeepers had specific objections of a kind that they wished to present separately, the collective case of the local traders was put forward by the Droitwich Spa Chamber of Trade, whose members had been called upon to subscribe funds in order to secure legal representation, and also to call evidence from the same firm of shopping consultants which they had retained some two years earlier to advise on alternatives to the proposals presented in the Development Group's Town Centre report.

In the interests of our research, we decided to attend the opening stages of the eight-day inquiry, and cover as many of the subsequent stages as possible. On the first day, the advocate for the Development Group and the parent authorities — whom we shall refer to as the Group Advocate — opened his case by outlining the various stages of the decision process which had led up to the Town Development agreement, and the progress that had so far been achieved in implementing the housing, industrial, and other aspects of the programme. This led on to the argument that progress on the town centre had now become urgent, and that the Development Group's proposals represented a realistic solution to the specific local problems presented by Droitwich. It was fully consistent with the policy guidelines contained in a circular issued by the Land Planning Ministry in 1965, which was concerned with central area redevelopment generally and stressed the need for segregation of pedestrian and vehicular traffic. Four witnesses were then called upon to present written and verbal evidence; the Group Planning Officer on the background of local planning policy, the Borough Surveyor on sewerage problems, a representative of the County Surveyor's Department on the case for the inner ring road, and a partner from the Group Estates Consultants on questions of estimation of future shopping demand.

The Group Advocate went on to stress the distinction between the CDA submission — concerned with an ultimate layout whose details could be subject to much modification in the light of trends and events over the period up to the proposed completion date of 1981 — and the Compulsory Purchase Order, required to enable certain immediate steps to be taken towards the implementation of the comparatively limited initial four-year programme. While arguing that the inquiry was essentially concerned with land-use rather than financial implications, the Advocate maintained that most of the public investment projects required, including the drainage alterations, the inner ring road, and the various civic buildings, derived directly from the earlier commitment to town expansion at Droitwich and were not closely related to the specific question of central area layout. Indeed, many of these projects had already attracted provisional loan sanction from relevant government departments. The only substantive financial question left open was whether or not the shopping developments proposed would be economically viable from the standpoint of the Borough Council as prospective landowner, so that they would not become a burden to local ratepayers. The answer to this question, it was argued, depended first on the Development Committee's freedom to adopt a realistic negotiating position with prospective developers and traders, unhampered by advance disclosures of financial assumptions, and second on the power to assemble the necessary land speedily through the machinery of compulsory purchase. At this point, the Group Advocate gave a formal assurance on behalf of his clients that compulsory purchase powers would not in practice be invoked where owners could demonstrate a readiness to develop on their own in accordance with the Development Committee's plans and timetable, and a further assurance that suitable relocations would be arranged for all trading interests that might have to be disturbed.

The Advocate for the Chamber of Trade opened by claiming to represent a total of fifty-six business and professional interests in Droitwich, of which all but twelve would be affected by the central area proposals. The decision that the Chamber should oppose the proposals was endorsed by a large majority at a well-attended public meeting, and was based not on opposition to change as such but on a deeply held fear that the proposals would prove too costly both for individual traders and for the ratepayers of the local council. Traders who had long provided personal service to local residents would, it was claimed, be driven out by excessive rents, while the ability of an expanded town of 30,000 inhabitants to attract any major influx of multiple stores or supermarkets was extremely questionable, giving rise to a prospect of stagnation and continuing diversion of trade to other neighbouring centres.

Although the Chamber did not have the resources to prepare a full alternative scheme, it was claimed that the feasibility of a simpler and more viable solution could readily be demonstrated. Following the studies which the Chamber had earlier commissioned, one alternative could include replacing the proposed new shopping square by a pedestrian 'mall', while retaining most of the existing shops in Ombersley Street through a re-siting of some of the proposed civic buildings outside the confines of the inner ring road. The retention and expansion of shopping facilities in Ombersley Street would, it was claimed, be more compatible with the general westward shift of the centre of gravity of the town which was implied by the location of the Town Development housing areas. The Chamber's advocate proceeded to cast doubt on a number of the assumptions underlying the local authorities' proposals. These included the projected future volumes of trade in the town; the realism of the plan's claim to flexibility when the physical design appeared to be so highly integrated; the ability to predict pedestrian flows within the complex multi-level 'figure eight' circuit which was ultimately envisaged; the amount of space needed for civic offices at a time when the future of local government was highly uncertain; and the practical feasibility of achieving full segregation of vehicular and pedestrian traffic.

Indeed, it was argued that the Ministry circular to which the Group Advocate had referred had since been superseded by a later circular giving guidance to local authorities seeking loan sanction. This reflected conditions of increased economic stringency and advised a more cautious combination of limited redevelopment with other types of management scheme in local policies for central area renewal. Thus, both sides were able to draw on official Ministerial policy statements, published at different times and implying different levels of trade-off between environmental and financial criteria, in support of their conflicting claims.

Following the presentation of these two opposing cases, one of the most significant, and indeed dramatic, points in the inquiry came with the cross-examination by the Group Advocate of the Chamber's principal witness, in the person of the shopping consultant who had been retained some two years earlier to carry out a brief survey of the possibilities for drawing up an alternative and less ambitious scheme. The cross-examination began with a series of searching questions relating to the amount of time devoted to this earlier survey — implying an unfavourable comparison with the effort so far expended by the officers of the Development Group — and went on to question the extent of the witness's agreement or otherwise with the basic principles of the scheme, to which commitment had already been secured at earlier stages of the decision-making process. In this way, the area of overt disagreement was progressively whittled down to two comparatively narrow areas of choice where it was possible for the Group Advocate to demonstrate elements of apparent inconsistency in his opponent's argument. This strategy of progressive reduction in the area of overt disagreement between the two sides can be represented diagrammatically, as in *Figure 55*.

During his cross-examination, the Group Advocate successively obtained from the witness his agreement to the approved principles of the Town Map on which the original expansion programme was based; to the proposed line of the inner ring road, already sanctioned by the Highway Ministry; and to the proposed zoning of all but one of the five areas into which the CDA proposals had divided the land within this inner ring. He was then able to confine his interrogation to two highly specific areas of decision: the choice of an alternative use for the area under dispute — that part of Ombersley Street where it was proposed to replace existing shops by civic buildings — and the choice of an alternative location for the civic buildings concerned.

In both these areas of choice, the Group Advocate was able to suggest an element of inconsistency in the witness's arguments. The only possible alternative zoning for the land in Ombersley Street

Figure 55 Reduction of field of decision during cross-examination at Droitwich town centre inquiry

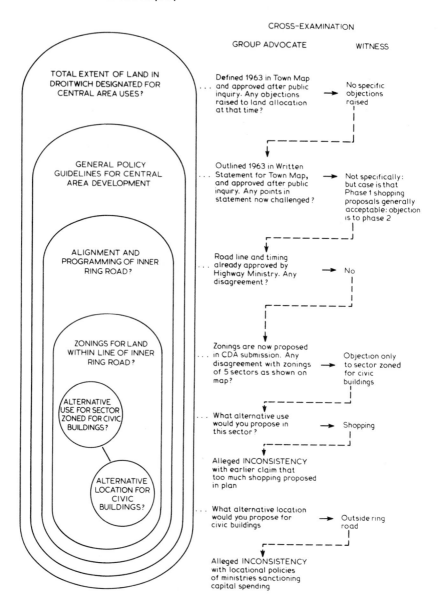

CROSS-EXAMINATION

GROUP ADVOCATE   WITNESS

TOTAL EXTENT OF LAND IN DROITWICH DESIGNATED FOR CENTRAL AREA USES?

... Defined 1963 in Town Map and approved after public inquiry. Any objections raised to land allocation at that time?

→ No specific objections raised

GENERAL POLICY GUIDELINES FOR CENTRAL AREA DEVELOPMENT

... Outlined 1963 in Written Statement for Town Map, and approved after public inquiry. Any points in statement now challenged?

→ Not specifically: but case is that Phase 1 shopping proposals generally acceptable: objection is to phase 2

ALIGNMENT AND PROGRAMMING OF INNER RING ROAD?

... Road line and timing already approved by Highway Ministry. Any disagreement?

→ No

ZONINGS FOR LAND WITHIN LINE OF INNER RING ROAD?

... Zonings are now proposed in CDA submission. Any disagreement with zonings of 5 sectors as shown on map?

→ Objection only to sector zoned for civic buildings

ALTERNATIVE USE FOR SECTOR ZONED FOR CIVIC BUILDINGS?

... What alternative use would you propose in this sector?

→ Shopping

Alleged INCONSISTENCY with earlier claim that too much shopping proposed in plan

ALTERNATIVE LOCATION FOR CIVIC BUILDINGS?

... What alternative location would you propose for civic buildings

→ Outside ring road

Alleged INCONSISTENCY with locational policies of ministries sanctioning capital spending

which he had been able to suggest was for shopping, and it was suggested that this conflicted with the Chamber of Trade's submission that the estimates of future shopping space were over-ambitious; while the only alternative location for the civic buildings could be outside the inner ring road, and it was suggested that this would conflict with the stated locational policies of those government departments responsible for supervision of local fire, police, ambulance, health, and judicial services. It was therefore argued that, in all likelihood, locations outside the inner ring road would disqualify the construction projects concerned when it came to obtainining the necessary central loan sanctions.

After this cross-examination, the inquiry moved on to deal with other objectors who were more concerned with the impact of the proposals on their own individual interests than with the overall assumptions behind them. But the cross-examination of the Chamber of Trade's expert witness had served above all to demonstrate the imbalance between the resources that the two main sets of protagonists — the local authorities and the traders — had been able to muster in order to conduct an informed debate about the principles of central area redevelopment. As it later transpired, the cost of the legal representation secured by the local authorities was several times greater than the sum that had been subscribed to retain counsel by the membership of the Chamber of Trade as principal objecting body. Furthermore, the Development Committee had been able to draw on the various civic design, engineering, and economic skills that had contributed to the formulation of its proposals, over a continuous period of several years, whereas the expert witness called by the Chamber of Trade had had to base his arguments on a much briefer survey of the problem mounted some two years earlier. The extent to which the outcome of such an inquiry is likely to be influenced by disparities in resources is of course a debatable point: and a view expressed by one of the Development Group officers was that the presiding inspector can usually build up a sufficient feel for the merits of the case to form a sound judgement whatever the quality of advocacy on either side may be.

One point which the strategy of *reductio ad absurdum* adopted by the Group Advocate had demonstrated clearly was the way in which broad policy commitments undertaken in earlier years could have the effect of constraining the range of more concrete design options remaining at subsequent stages. As in many other types of planning situation, it is inherently more difficult for a coherent challenge to be presented against statements of broad intention than against specific proposals which impinge directly on individual interests. As one of the Group officers suggested, one effect of the choice of a solution which involved the displacement of shops in Ombersley Street was that the resistance mounted by the local traders tended to be dominated by trading interests in that part of town; had an alternative scheme been substituted which impinged more on the traders at the High Street end, then the balance of pressures from the trading community might have shifted in the other direction. This raises the general point that the traditional legal processes of public inquiry and objection always tend to encourage the adoption of adversarial postures which attempt to discredit the arguments of opponents (Wraith and Lamb, 1971). The problems of moving from such a process towards more open styles of exploration are difficult ones, which have been of much concern to those concerned in introducing the new types of statutory planning procedure that we shall touch upon in Part III.

The continuing processes of adjustment

After the formalities of the public inquiry, more than two years were to elapse before the Minister concerned, the Secretary of State for the Environment, gave his final consent to the CDA proposal and associated Compulsory Purchase Order. During this period, the climate in Droitwich remained one of considerable uncertainty, verging on anxiety, both among the affected trading interests and among the Development Group officers whose work programmes were becoming more and more disjointed; but, at a more informal level, a great deal of mutual adjustment was taking place between the various interests concerned, both locally and nationally.

At the national level, the Ministry's Inspector had to prepare and submit his formal written report and, before the Minister could give his final judgement on the case, extensive processes of consultation had to be carried out within central government, allowing different departments and divisions to make known their specialist views, in accordance with normal civil service practice. Of course, such processes could be only dimly perceived by the local representatives and officers at Droitwich. A first formal indication of the verdict on the CDA proposal was 'received by the County Council some twelve months after the inquiry, in the form of a 'comment letter' setting out the Minister's readiness to proceed towards confirmation subject to a number of qualifications and proposed amendments of detail. Some points of general principle were raised, concerning the importance of making sure that the proposals for shopping were financially viable, and the need for flexibility in reviewing requirements for additional shopping space after the proposed first phase had been completed. There were also a number of more detailed points, on most of which the officers felt that appropriate adjustments to the proposals could be made without too much difficulty. Accordingly, further discussions were intiated with relevant local interests to allow mutually satisfactory design compromises to be found.

Meanwhile, the Group Estates Adviser proceeded to investigate alternative means of financing the commercial elements of the first stage programme, given that there had been significant changes in the state of the property market since the earlier appraisals. The main options considered were either to involve a development company, which would take out a lease for the land concerned and carry out the actual development and letting of shop units itself, or alternatively to work through a financial institution which would then arrange a return lease to the Borough Council; in this case, the development and management of the properties would be undertaken by the Droitwich Development Committee. While the latter alternative should ultimately produce a better expected rate of return to the Borough Council, it was pointed out that it also carried a somewhat higher financial risk. Apart from this, there were possible consequences to be evaluated when making the final choice in terms of degree of public control, speed of decision-making, sources of 'know-how', and effort to be devoted to negotiations with individual traders. The approach through a financial institution was agreed to be the more attractive on balance and so, on receiving the Ministry's final sanction to proceed in 1972, a brief for the initial shopping development was drawn up as a basis for negotiations with prospective institutional investors.

The policy system for central redevelopment

Among those who were most continuously involved in the early development of central area policies in Droitwich were not only the Group Planner Architect and the Group Estates Consultant — who, as already mentioned, carried most of the initial responsibilities for the design and commercial aspects of the scheme respectively — but also the Group Administrator, who had the difficult task of judging the way in which the more delicate issues which arose should be presented to the members of the Development Committee. The Committee Chairman also had an exceptionally difficult role to play, in view of the continuing tensions between the local representatives and the other participants at Committee meetings on fundamental

Figure 56   Strategy graph for a set of central area scheduling problems at Droitwich (as seen in 1971)

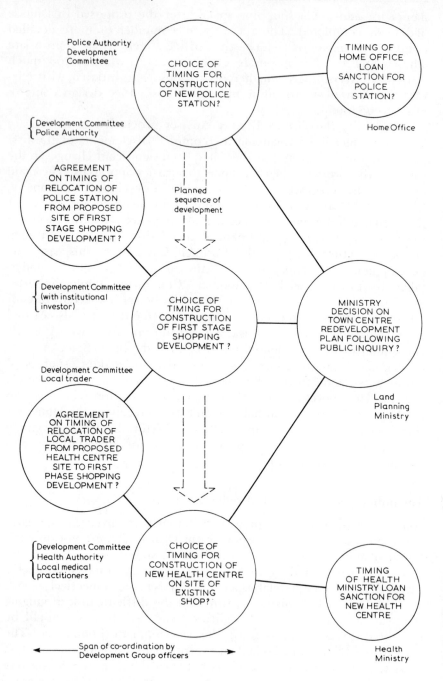

matters of central area policy. One significant complication was that no less than four of the eight representatives of the Borough Council on the Committee had commercial or professional interests of their own within the central area, and were therefore obliged to retire from the Committee meetings whenever sensitive issues of town centre redevelopment came up for discussion. This led to open expressions of unease among the members concerned. It was only to be expected that a proportion of local representatives would be concerned both publicly and privately in matters relating to the hub of the town's social and economic life. Yet the effect of the national rules and conventions that concerned withdrawal from meetings when matters impinging on private interests came up for discussion was that the Borough representatives at Droitwich could be repeatedly and heavily outvoted by the County members on matters of this kind. In these circumstances, problems of confidentiality and dissemination of information could become not only delicate but intrinsically complex, in view of the intricate relationships between different central area issues and actors. There were many issues on which there were good commercial grounds for maintaining secrecy, yet it was very difficult to judge where the limits of dissemination of information could be drawn, when relating to a close-knit local community where social networks and public decision networks tended to become tightly interwoven.

Even though the thread of this chapter has been primarily concerned with the public inquiry and the various events that preceded it in the evolution of general town centre policy, there continued both before and after the inquiry a network of inter-actions between Development Group staff and affected local interests in relation to various specific facets of central redevelopment. In particular, these concerned detailed design exercises for particular sites or elements of infrastructure, and bargaining over relocation with particular property interests. In such activities, the most central role was taken over, after publication of the Group Planner Architect's initial Town Centre proposals in 1967, by the leader of a specialist Central Area design team — referred to in *Figure 26* as the Group Central Area Architect. One important member of his team was the Engineer Planner, who has also figured as a key actor in earlier decision networks.

As in other aspects of development, the delays encountered in the implementation of the central area programme raised recurrent anxieties as to how the continuing costs of design work, and time spent in associated negotiations with property interests, would ultimately be absorbed within the agreed accounting framework. The

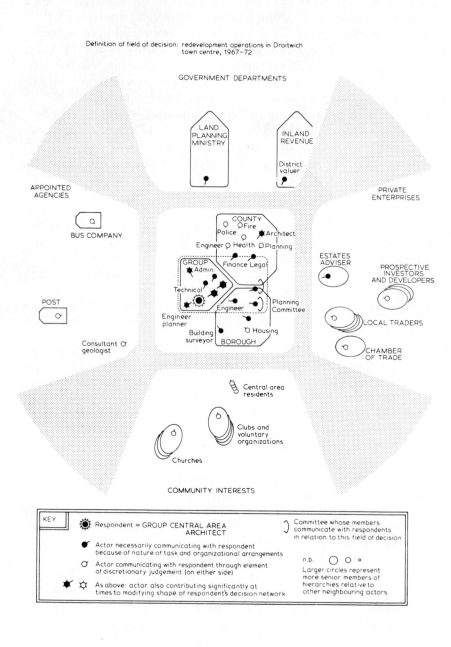

Figure 57   Network relationships of Group Central Area Architect for redevelopment of Droitwich central area

Definition of field of decision: redevelopment operations in Droitwich town centre, 1967–72

GOVERNMENT DEPARTMENTS

LAND PLANNING MINISTRY

INLAND REVENUE

District valuer

APPOINTED AGENCIES

PRIVATE ENTERPRISES

BUS COMPANY

COUNTY
Fire
Police
Engineer   Health   Planning
Architect

GROUP
Admin
Finance Legal
Technical
Engineer
Planning Committee
Engineer planner
Building surveyor
Housing
BOROUGH

ESTATES ADVISER

PROSPECTIVE INVESTORS AND DEVELOPERS

POST

LOCAL TRADERS

Consultant geologist

CHAMBER OF TRADE

Central area residents

Clubs and voluntary organizations

Churches

COMMUNITY INTERESTS

KEY

Respondent = GROUP CENTRAL AREA ARCHITECT

Actor necessarily communicating with respondent because of nature of task and organizational arrangements

Actor communicating with respondent through element of discretionary judgement (on either side)

As above: actor also contributing significantly at times to modifying shape of respondent's decision network

Committee whose members communicate with respondents in relation to this field of decision

n.b.
Larger circles represent more senior members of hierarchies relative to other neighbouring actors

County's general undertaking to finance initial planning activities had come to an end in 1967, and the successive postponements and revisions in the expected timetable for central redevelopment generated recurrent uncertainties of work scheduling for the small core of technical staff concerned.

At different points during 1970 and 1971, we were able to discuss with the Group Administrator and the Group Central Area Architect their current perceptions of the complex patterns of structural interdependence between the various problems with which they were grappling within the central area. *Figure 56* illustrates one of the more difficult instances encountered of the general problem of the 'relocation chain', where a number of different activities within a central area have to be moved to new sites in a particular sequence, which may be subject to a complex set of external uncertainties. In this case, the uncertainties were associated both with the outcomes of bargaining processes with local property interests, and also with the timing of central government approvals. At the time of discussion the dominant anxiety of the Group Administrator was over the decision processes of the Home Office, as the government department responsible for approving the new police station building. Later, when the timing of the official verdict on the inquiry began to become the most crucial source of uncertainty, a dominant local concern became the achievement of a satisfactory compromise with the proprietor of one of the two main central area hotels over his future car parking provision.

Similar interfaces of negotiation had to be managed with many other trading interests, voluntary associations, residents of the central area, departments of the County Council, and other statutory agencies such as the Post Office Corporation. *Figure 57* represents a broad interpretation on the resulting decision network, based on the perspective of the Group Central Area Architect. It will be noticed that certain actors and agencies who have been referred to as important in the course of the chapter have been omitted, because contacts with them were managed by other members of the local team. For instance, it was the Engineer Planner who handled the interface with the electricity, gas, and water undertakings, while policy discussions with local elected members and with civil servants were usually conducted at the level of the Group Administrator and Group Planner Architect. This point emphasizes the difficulty of regarding a central area redevelopment programme as anything but a complex team operation in which a considerable degree of diffusion of management responsibilities becomes inevitable.

Summary

The events recounted in this chapter raise some crucial questions about planning processes in general – in particular, the potential conflict between the arguments in favour of a cohesive and comprehensive physical layout for an area which must accommodate many interrelated activities, and those in favour of flexibility to respond to unforeseen circumstances and adapt to individual requirements. This question leads into some other basic questions, already raised in Chapter 3, about the formal procedures of public inquiry and their tendency to cast the processes of reviewing alternatives into a quasi-judicial framework, in which a lack of objection to comparatively abstract policy commitments can be held to invalidate any later objections to more specific action proposals. Another related question, to be explored in the next chapter, concerns the feasibility of mobilizing hitherto unorganized interests to participate actively in decision-making without first presenting the spur, or threat, of explicit planning proposals. This may lead into a further issue of how much time the members of a technical planning team should be encouraged to devote to managing the processes of exploring design alternatives in a spirit of search for mutual adjustment with the various local interests affected.

As a case history, the story of Droitwich town centre up to 1972 emerges as one of persistent conflict of interest within a very compact local area. Had it not been for the town expansion scheme, much of the conflict might have been resolved gradually through market forces, with established local traders steadily losing ground – for better or for worse – to more aggressive competitors in the form of supermarkets and multiple stores. But the commitment to town development in effect shifted much of this conflict from an economic to a political arena, in which a great deal came to depend on a few crucial decisions at the interfaces between the local authorities and within the Land Planning Ministry. The resulting stresses were to put the delicately balanced organizational machinery of the joint Development Committee to its most exacting – and indeed traumatic – test since the original commitment to the town development programme.

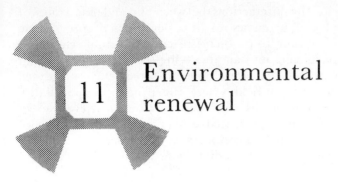

11 Environmental renewal

Problems in the use of existing assets

Problems relating to the future treatment of established features of the local environment – buildings, roads, and other elements of infrastructure – have emerged at several points in the preceding chapters. They became particularly salient in our discussion of redevelopment in the town centre, with its historic buildings and richly connected patterns of economic and social activity.

Such problems are a pervasive matter of concern to local authorities in all established urban areas, whether or not faced with programmes of externally induced expansion as in the case of Droitwich. In a climate of rapidly changing technologies and material standards of living, established structures can quickly become obsolescent in terms of their original uses, and the combination of functional obsolescence with straightforward physical deterioration can present the local decision-makers with difficult problems in selecting appropriate forms of response. Not only may it be difficult to reach clear decisions as to whether different forms of investment in renewal or rehabilitation can be justified; there may also be uncertainties as to how readily the requisite resources can be mobilized, often against a background of some ambiguity about the powers and responsibilities of different public agencies.

Such problems tend to be exacerbated in the circumstances of an expanding town by the interactions between the endemic issues of rehabilitation and the urgencies of the development programme itself. However, in turning to problems of environmental renewal in Droitwich, we are moving into an area lying outside those fields of policy covered in the original Development Agreement, as analysed in *Figure 24*, and into a field where the primary responsibility remained with the Borough as local District Council. Nevertheless, the Development Group represented a significant local source of relevant skills, and we shall therefore now be concerned with the relationships between the two bodies from a somewhat different perspective.

In this chapter, we shall focus on two contrasting case histories in the renewal of the built environment at Droitwich, both of a kind that have also been encountered widely in the older industrial areas of the West Midlands and of Britain generally. One concerns the future of a neighbourhood of nineteenth-century housing immediately to the west of Droitwich town centre, while the other concerns the derelict canal running through the Salwarpe valley just to the east of the river itself. Both problems raise issues considerably wider than that of the rehabilitation of physical structures. The former leads into consideration of the consequent impact on the social environment of a well-established urban neighbourhood, and thereby into questions of community participation in the decision-making process. The second case impinges on many other questions, including one of conserving the natural environment in an area designated as of 'special scientific interest' just outside the boundaries of the town. Such implications mean that, in both our case studies, we shall encounter the formation of informal 'working parties' and other forms of *ad hoc* organization within which the various relevant interests become mobilized to deal with comparatively unfamiliar tasks. Each of the cases will have to be discussed within a differing context of evolving national policies, in which the roles of local authority, development agency, and voluntary organizations are subject to various types of ambiguity, uncertainty, and constraint.

Housing improvement: the national context

Chapter 8 has already outlined some of the major trends in British housing policies since the Second World War, indicating the gradual shift of emphasis from slum clearance and redevelopment towards investment in the rehabilitation of the existing housing stock. To successive governments, such policies became increasingly attractive on economic grounds, as the worst of the nation's slum housing was cleared and priorities shifted towards 'twilight' areas where the choice between redevelopment and rehabilitation became more marginal, with the latter course holding out the promise of substantial savings in public investment (Needleman, 1969). Of course, any attempt to base national housing policies on purely economic criteria was always open to challenge: but the case for rehabilitation gained further strength from the social argument that such action could help to avoid the kind of damage to the fabric of community that had become a widely criticized feature of many comprehensive clearance and redevelopment schemes.

At first, national policies for rehabilitation focused specifically on the problems of equipping older dwellings with those 'standard' amenities, such as hot water and internal toilets, now considered essential to physical health. Owners who undertook to provide all such standard amenities were entitled by statute to public grants covering half their cost, subject to a defined upper limit. However, during the nineteen-sixties, further forms of assistance were introduced, on a more discretionary basis, first to help prolong the useful lives of individual houses in ways that were not so directly related to physical health, and subsequently to help local authorities in improving the amenities of whole residential neighbourhoods where a sufficient degree of commitment to rehabilitation could be demonstrated among the local people.

The foundations for this more ambitious policy of neighbourhood improvement were laid in the Housing Act of 1969, which followed the report of an official committee in 1966 (Ministry of Housing and Local Government, 1966). Among various other provisions, the new legislation introduced the new concept of a 'General Improvement Area' (GIA). Each local housing authority was given authority to designate any predominantly residential area as a GIA, provided proposals had been prepared demonstrating how a comprehensive improvement of the local environment could improve living conditions for the residents, and that evidence could be produced that the residents had been adequately consulted. At that time, the principle of public participation in decision-making was beginning to become increasingly topical and to gain a measure of official support (Ministry of Housing and Local Government, 1969); and accordingly, the new legislation placed stress on the need for the residents to become actively involved in the preparation of a GIA scheme.

Given sufficient evidence of agreement between local authority and residents, the legislation required the Housing Ministry to provide new levels of assistance towards the improvement of individual properties, matched by an equivalent local authority

Figure 58   Newtown: the neighbourhood and its changing planning context

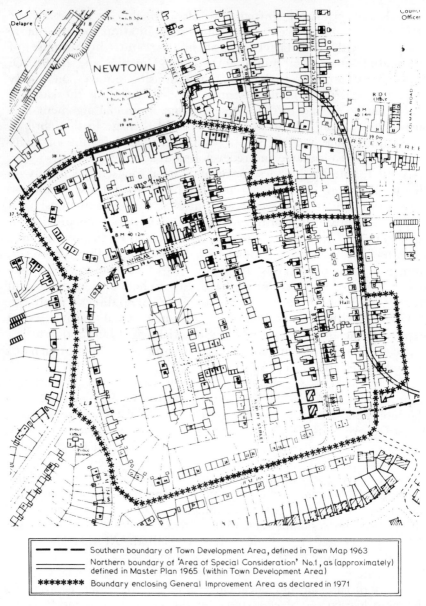

— — —	Southern boundary of Town Development Area, defined in Town Map 1963
———	Northern boundary of 'Area of Special Consideration' No.1 , as (approximately) defined in Master Plan 1965 (within Town Development Area)
*******	Boundary enclosing General Improvement Area as declared in 1971

Based upon the Ordnance Survey Map with the sanction of the Controller of Her Majesty's Stationery Office, Crown copyright reserved.

contribution. It also provided for a grant to the local authority of £50 per property towards the cost of general environmental works such as road diversions, tree planting, footpaths, and play spaces. Later, as a result of working experience and changing levels of cost, the levels of assistance were increased, with some special inducements applying in the Development Areas.

The problem presented to the local authorities was thus one of how best to exploit new powers and procedures, the practical effects and implications of which were initially highly uncertain. Although the emphasis was very much on achieving voluntary agreement between the local authority and the residents, the unfamiliarity of the process meant that the Housing Ministry found itself playing an indirect, but nevertheless influential, role through the provision of informal advice, information, and exhortation. The problems of the management of uncertainty which this situation presented to a comparatively large all-purpose local authority – the City of Coventry – have been analysed elsewhere, in the report of a study undertaken by IOR for the Home Office Community Development Project (Carter, Friend, Luck, and Yewlett, 1972). The problems that confronted Droitwich were in most respects similar, though overlaid by some special complications arising from the commitment to the town expansion programme.

Newtown: the future of a neighbourhood

The particular residential area in Droitwich with which we shall be concerned was built in the latter half of the nineteenth century, primarily to house workers in the local salt industry, in what was then a strategic location between the town centre and the railway station. It therefore represents an outcome of an earlier kind of town expansion process, designed primarily to support industrial growth. Somewhat ironically, the area had been given the name of 'Newtown', like many other such districts now becoming ripe for rehabilitation in various parts of England.

The layout of the area in the early nineteen-sixties is illustrated in *Figure 58*, showing a mixture of terraced and semi-detached housing with later infilling, including even a few comparatively modern detached properties. Tenure was mixed, with many of the older properties owned by private landlords but also a considerable element of owner-occupation, while a substantial estate of inter-war local authority housing abutted the area to the south-west, lying outside the boundary of the Town Development Area. The area possessed a cohesive, relatively stable social structure, with a high proportion of elderly and long-established residents. Unlike some physically similar neighbourhoods in inner city areas within the West Midlands Region, it had not served as a reception area for immigrant workers from the Commonwealth or elsewhere. Thus, in Droitwich, the problem of physical deterioration was not compounded by problems of changing social structure, and subsequent tension between different community groups, as in Birmingham and some of the Black Country towns.

In the Town Map proposals of 1963, most of the Newtown area was included in the Town Development Area, because of its strategic location linking the town centre to the area of new development to the west, even though its future remained largely undetermined. When the Master Plan was published in 1965, the choice of a specific line for the inner ring road and its westward link led the planners to designate the remaining part of Newtown immediately to the south and west as one of several 'Areas of Special Consideration' in different parts of town. This device allowed the options for its future to be kept open pending more detailed study at a later stage in the development programme. At that time, no machinery had yet begun to emerge at a national level to make the comprehensive improvement of entire neighbourhoods of older housing possible. It was therefore expected by the Development Group staff that any design studies carried out in the area would lead to a substantial element of clearance and redevelopment.

Much of the housing in the Newtown area was believed to be structurally sound, and there were not many houses which at that time remained deficient in terms of the standard interior facilities. However, a serious problem was presented by the extremely narrow streets and the lack of space for the parking or garaging of cars; over the years, this had led to a situation in which parked cars severely restricted circulation and access both for pedestrians and for other vehicles. From time to time, planning applications had been submitted by owners for extensions to properties and also for the provision of garages, but the state of uncertainty about the treatment of Newtown in relation to the Town Development programme had obliged the Borough Council, acting on the advice of the Development Group architects under the agreed consultation procedure, to adopt a policy of deferment until the future of the area was settled.

Consequently, pressures began to emerge for the speedy resolution of the state of uncertainty about the future of Newtown, and these came to bear predominantly on the Borough Council through the representations of residents and landlords. Once the new provisions of the 1969 Housing Act became known, it was therefore not surprising that local elected members began to show a good deal of interest in the new opportunities that might be created for comprehensive improvement as a solution to the problems of the area. Such an improvement, it was hoped, might be much more acceptable to local people than the extremes either of wholesale clearance or of continued stagnation. The readiness of the Borough Council to be among the first to explore the possibilities of the new legislation was promptly welcomed by the regional officials of the Housing Ministry, who carried a general responsibility for encouraging and advising local authorities in the use of the GIA machinery. To them, the Newtown area was of particular interest because it appeared to combine in a single neighbourhood many of the practical problems that they expected to confront much more widely in the West Midlands Region.

However, at that time, the administrative and technical officers of the Development Group took a much more cautious attitude to what had been designated as the first of their 'Areas of Special Consideration' on the Master Plan map. To us, they expressed considerable doubt as to whether improvement policies were likely to prove economically justifiable within 'ASC No. 1', since the tightly constrained street pattern provided only very limited room for environmental improvements. Consequently, they believed that traffic circulation and living conditions could not be brought up to anything like the standards that were being planned in the adjacent central area redevelopment scheme.

Setting up an exploratory process

The situation was therefore one of agreement between the Borough Council and the Development Group that the Newtown area would indeed require some form of 'special consideration', but initial uncertainty existed as to what that consideration should entail, and consequently which agency should be primarily responsible for the initiation of exploratory processes. While the area lay within the boundaries of the Town Development Area, and so within the field of planning responsibility of the Development Group, the powers to declare a General Improvement Area lay explicitly with the Borough Council as local housing authority. It would clearly make sense to utilize the technical skills of the Development Group staff in any surveys or design studies, but it was by no means clear whether the costs of such exploratory work should be borne by the Town Development accounts or by the local ratepayers. Moreover, although it was the Borough members who were most keen to see the

Figure 59   Network relationships of Group Engineer Planner for improvement of local environment in Newtown

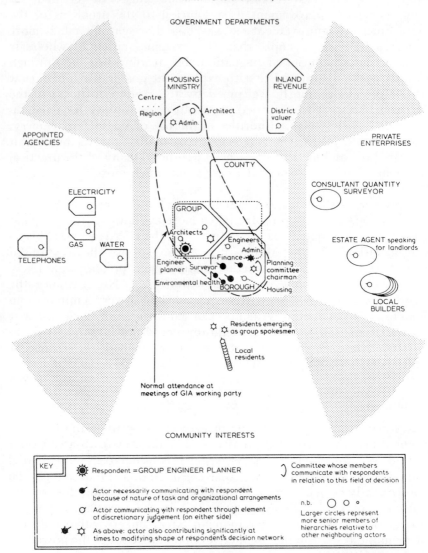

Definition of field of decision: design of environmental improvement proposals for
Newtown area of Droitwich, 1969–72

GOVERNMENT DEPARTMENTS

APPOINTED
AGENCIES

HOUSING
MINISTRY

Centre
Region   Architect
        Admin.

INLAND
REVENUE

District
valuer

PRIVATE
ENTERPRISES

CONSULTANT QUANTITY
SURVEYOR

COUNTY

ELECTRICITY

GAS   WATER

TELEPHONES

GROUP

Architects

Engineer
planner   Surveyor
Environmental health

Engineers
Admin.
Finance
BOROUGH

Planning
committee
chairman

Housing

ESTATE AGENT speaking
for landlords

LOCAL
BUILDERS

Residents emerging
as group spokesmen

Local
residents

Normal attendance at
meetings of GIA working party

COMMUNITY INTERESTS

KEY

● Respondent = GROUP ENGINEER PLANNER

● Actor necessarily communicating with respondent
because of nature of task and organizational arrangements

○ Actor communicating with respondent through element
of discretionary judgement (on either side)

● ☆ As above: actor also contributing significantly at
times to modifying shape of respondent's decision network

) Committee whose members
communicate with respondents
in relation to this field of decision

n.b.   ○ ○ °
Larger circles represent
more senior members of
hierarchies relative to
other neighbouring actors

exploratory work proceed, there was an initial reluctance to commit local funds without some estimate of the likely magnitude of the costs involved.

In order to reduce these uncertainties sufficiently to make a start, the Development Committee agreed that their staff should make some initial assessments of the feasibility of proceeding further and, on the basis of this, the Borough Treasurer should prepare a financial report for his Council's Planning Committee. The Treasurer's report, submitted in mid-1970, stressed the difficulty of producing reliable costings in view of a range of uncertainties, most of which arose from two main directions. First, there was the uncertainty surrounding the cost to the authority of the local environmental improvements; while second, there was the uncertainty surrounding the rate at which residents would apply for grants towards housing improvements, part of which were payable from local authority sources. Despite these uncertainties, the Borough Council agreed to proceed with a first step towards further commitment; the setting up of a working party on which both its own officers and also the Development Group technical staff would serve. The work would be funded by a modest initial budget from the local rate account, and the brief would include the preparation of a timetable for the administrative procedures leading up to the early declaration of a General Improvement Area by the Borough Council, assuming that the further technical studies showed this to be a feasible proposition.

The working party and its activities

The pattern of participation in decision-making which gradually developed around the GIA working party is illustrated in *Figure 59*, from the perspective of the Development Group's Engineer Planner who was a member from its inception and provided much of the expertise for the formulation of alternative layouts. In this, he worked closely with another member of the Group's town centre design section, an architect-planner, and also with the Deputy Group Planner Architect. The Deputy Town Clerk served as secretary to the committee, and other Borough officers normally in attendance included the Treasurer, the Surveyor, and a public health inspector from his department. The Chairman of the Borough's Planning and General Purposes Committee also attended, officially as an observer; but because of his status as a senior elected member with a long-standing personal concern with the future of the area, he tended to be regarded as the focal point of the meetings. This became especially evident when, at one meeting, his enforced early departure

Figure 60   Process of decision-making for Newtown area improvement scheme, Droitwich

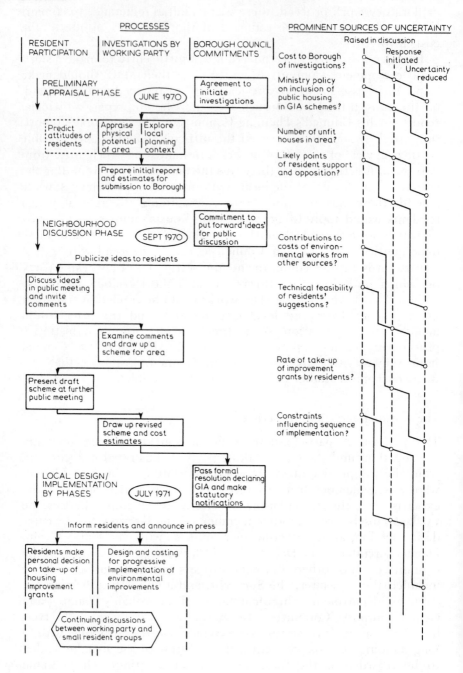

led to temporary confusion as to who should take over the control of proceedings; and eventually his status was clarified by his official recognition as chairman of the working party.

At most meetings of the working party, the Housing Ministry was represented by two senior regional officials — an administrator and an architect — who were able to offer advice on procedural and technical points, as well as demonstrating by their presence the extent of the Ministry's interest in Droitwich as a test case for the new GIA provisions. However, they were insistent that they should take a back seat when it came to any consultations with the local public, as the whole principle of the new legislation was one of voluntary collaboration between the local authority and the residents of the neighbourhood concerned.

As *Figure 59* indicates, the network of those involved in the decision process eventually extended well beyond the confines of the working party to include a wide range of local interests, both residential and commercial. In terms of the conventions of the diagram, it is of course debatable whether a small local landlord, perhaps an elderly widow owning only three or four houses of low market value, should be classified within the 'commercial' rather than the 'community' sector of social organization. In keeping with the experimental and permissive spirit of the GIA procedures, it will be noted that few actors are shown in the diagram as *necessarily* involved in the decision-making process by nature of their responsibilities. It is indeed only a small group of Borough officers, including those concerned in housing, public works, and environmental health, who justify this status, if the field of decision is defined simply as the choice of environmental treatment for the selected residential area.

The involvement of residents and other community interests built up gradually over the period between 1970 and 1972, during which we were given the opportunity to follow actively both the discussions of the working party and the processes of public consultation. A view of the successive stages of decision-making over this period is presented in *Figure 60*. They divide into a first phase of preliminary explorations confined largely within the working party itself; a second phase of widespread general involvement of neighbourhood interests; and a third phase of more detailed consultation over the future of particular streets and groups of houses. While it was the members of the working party who carried most of the responsibility throughout for the management of the exploratory process, it was necessary for them to maintain at all times a sufficient level of authorization or legitimation both from the local authority and from the residents, in proceeding towards each successive step in commitment towards future action within the neighbourhood.

At each stage, the working party members found themselves confronted with new sources of uncertainty to be overcome. The right-hand margin indicates broadly the points at which some of the more salient among these were first raised in discussion, were subsequently tackled by various forms of exploratory or consultative action, and were finally reduced to more manageable proportions. As *Figure 60* indicates, this process of incremental commitment was by no means concluded with the formal declaration of a GIA by the Borough Council, and many options remained open to be settled only gradually over the years through detailed discussion on a street-by-street basis.

The preliminary exploration of options

In the early stages of the working party's existence, one of the more salient decision areas was how widely the boundaries of the proposed area of survey should be drawn, and in particular whether or not the adjacent council estate of some 150 dwellings should be included within the proposed GIA boundary. Being just outside the Town Development Area, this estate was clearly the responsibility of the Borough Council in planning as well as proprietorial terms. So far as interior improvements were concerned, the Borough had already initiated a policy of remedying the most outstanding deficiency, that of space heating provision; but, externally, the estate still fell below currently accepted standards in terms of traffic circulation and garaging. The working party members agreed that inclusion of the estate in the GIA would be desirable for reasons of urban design; moreover, the fact of council ownership would provide a guarantee both of improvement to individual dwellings and of co-operation in environmental improvements, and this might well set a standard for the adjoining areas of private housing.

However, a significant uncertainty arose in that the 1969 Housing Act was not specific as to whether publicly owned as well as private dwellings would qualify for the special 'amenity' grant of £50 per house, payable by the Ministry to the local authority towards general improvements in the local environment. In this instance, the difference was highly significant in terms of the cost to the Borough of the local roadworks, estimated at £17,000 and expected to form the major element of local authority expenditure. The response to this uncertainty was to request clarification from the Ministry representatives, who proceeded to seek policy guidance from their more senior colleagues. For the Housing Ministry, the underlying policy issue was whether environmental improvement was to be seen primarily as an inducement to owners to modernize their individual properties, or as a desirable form of public expenditure in its own right. The verdict which was reported back to the working party was that the inclusion of the council estate would indeed be welcomed, and that it would qualify for full amenity grant.

A further salient uncertainty concerned the amount of clearance of 'unfit' housing that should be considered either inside the GIA boundary, or in adjoining areas. Although there were statutory criteria of 'unfitness' to be followed, these depended on the inspection of dwellings under public health powers, and involved elements of judgement on the part of the local authority inspector. Wherever examination showed a dwelling to be unfit, the local authority was immediately under an obligation to take early action; so, during the early exploratory phase of the GIA process, there could be advantages in being content with only a brief external appraisal of the condition of dwellings. In fact, some houses thought to be unfit on this basis were later discovered, on detailed internal inspection, to be in a sound state; this had financial implications in that, if they were to be demolished to make room for environmental amenities within the GIA, they would have to be purchased at full market valuations. This information led in turn to a decision to minimize the amount of clearance within the GIA boundary and, ultimately, this boundary was so adjusted to exclude certain properties in the more peripheral locations, as indicated in *Figure 58*.

In order to conform to the spirit of public participation, the members of the working party agreed that, as a basis for their first discussions with residents, they should put forward not a single proposed plan but a set of alternative 'ideas' which might encourage people to be forthcoming with their own suggestions. At first, three such 'ideas' were drawn up by the engineer planner and his colleagues. The most ambitious of them illustrated the effects of full pedestrianization of existing streets, with road access to properties now provided from the rear. A second indicated a balance between rear access and retention of existing streets, while a third used existing streets exclusively, but proposed their closure to through traffic. In the working party, it was agreed that the first and second 'ideas' should both be presented to the public in outline plan form, withholding the third as it was so close to the status quo that residents might be tempted to settle for it prematurely, without being encouraged to express their views on which aspects of the two more ambitious schemes appealed to them most.

An experiment in public participation

Following the decision to present two sets of 'ideas' to the residents for simultaneous consideration, the working party fixed on a date in November 1970 for a public meeting to discuss the proposals. Preparations for the meeting included the sending of an invitation to attend to every resident and landlord; the mounting of a public exhibition; the holding of a press conference for local journalists; and the arrangement of a series of preliminary meetings with small groups of people having a more specialized or intensive concern in particular aspects of the scheme, including local builders and people affected by the redevelopment proposals. The latter group would require particularly sensitive treatment, and it was therefore agreed to set up a series of four separate meetings, distinguishing both between tenants and owners, and between the properties to be acquired inside and outside the proposed GIA boundary.

The organization of the open meeting for residents also presented the working party with some difficult procedural problems. For the first time, the attitudes of residents were to be regarded as a matter for direct consultation rather than prediction. In effect, the residents were to be introduced into the decision process as actors within contiguous policy systems rather than as elements in the operating environment, even though there was as yet no representative organization through which their collective views could be articulated. There was some anxious discussion within the working party as to how the extent of local commitment to a GIA solution could realistically be gauged; and the advice of the Ministry representatives was that any kind of formal voting procedure should be avoided, as it could lead to polarization of attitudes rather than considered reactions to the specific ideas floated. From experience elsewhere, they were able to predict that the meeting itself could well become somewhat unruly, even though discussions with individuals before and after might reveal that underlying attitudes were much more favourable. A good working guide was that the declaration of a GIA could reasonably go ahead if no more than 20 per cent of residents ended up by registering opposition in writing at the end of the consultation process, provided the objectors were not too closely concentrated within any part of the neighbourhood that was essential to the success of the improvement programme. As a preliminary step in the appraisal of local attitudes, it was agreed that a comment sheet should be sent out to each resident with the invitation to the meeting, requesting either general comments on the principle of GIA declaration or more specific views on possible environmental improvements.

The public meeting itself was presided over by the Mayor and attended by some 200 people in all, including about sixty owners or tenants of affected properties. The scene was set by the Chairman of the Borough Planning and General Purposes Committee, who gave a general résumé of the problems of the area and the history of the working party's investigations. He stressed that the success of a GIA depended essentially on co-operation between Council and residents; indeed, they were all involved in what was very much an 'experiment in organization' of a rather novel kind. The Group Planner Architect was then introduced to explain the two alternative sets of ideas, indicating that some combination of the two might in the end be found most acceptable. A Ministry film was then shown, introducing in non-technical terms the main features of the new GIA policy and demonstrating how it had already been successfully applied in a district of Exeter, attracting strong support from local residents there.

An open discussion followed, at which the first — and most closely argued — contribution came from one of the town's estate agents, speaking on behalf of the local landlords. Some of these, he argued, owned several properties in the area and would find themselves faced both with substantial sums of capital to raise to pay their share of the improvements costs, and also with the necessity to recoup these costs through higher rents. Experience elsewhere indicated that this could lead to protracted negotiations over 'fair rents' with the local Rent Officer, and the outcome could be one of severe economic difficulty from the point of view of the landlord. In reply, the Borough Treasurer revealed that these points had already been covered in previous informal discussions with the questioner, and gave assurances that any personal financial difficulties could always be discussed on an individual basis. However, the estate agent had succeeded in giving public expression to his point about the economic implications of a GIA for the group of landlords whose interests he was unofficially representing; and the discussions then moved to questions raised by individual residents.

These questions covered such points as changes in garage access; the risks of vandalism on pedestrian routes; and the possibilities of assistance towards the cost of exterior decoration. One resident raised a specific suggestion for the creation of a new pedestrian short cut for schoolchildren, and this was greeted by the Group technical staff in attendance as a positive contribution to their thinking. A further idea put forward was that of a one-way system of traffic circulation, so as to leave open more existing streets and avoid the problems of some residents whose drives or garages would otherwise be left facing in the wrong direction. However, the Group Planner

Figure 61   GIA plan as submitted for resident discussion, June 1971

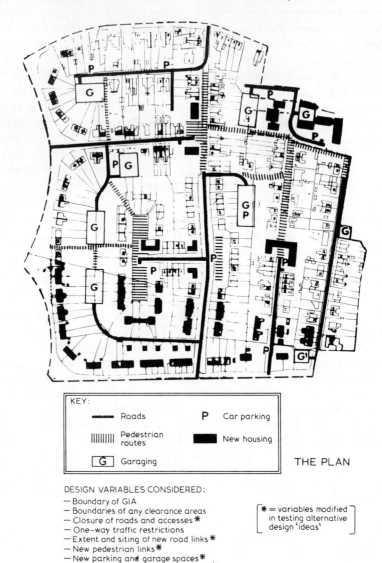

KEY:

——— Roads   **P**   Car parking

|||||||| Pedestrian routes   ▬ New housing

[G] Garaging

THE PLAN

DESIGN VARIABLES CONSIDERED:
— Boundary of GIA
— Boundaries of any clearance areas
— Closure of roads and accesses ✱
— One-way traffic restrictions
— Extent and siting of new road links ✱
— New pedestrian links ✱
— New parking and garage spaces ✱
— New pedestrian spaces/play areas ✱
— Siting and layout of any new housing ✱

[✱ = variables modified in testing alternative design 'ideas']

Architect explained that this particular kind of solution had been thoroughly investigated and found impracticable within such a constrained area.

After a couple of hours in all, the meeting was brought to a close. By this time, the atmosphere appeared to be one of general goodwill and enthusiasm to proceed with the scheme, and the expected element of opposition had largely failed to materialize. A period of two weeks was then allowed for further individual comment, either verbally or through the return of the comment sheets which had been distributed beforehand. Of the 300 residents, some 20 per cent submitted written comments in some shape or form; those expressing outright dissent were outnumbered almost four to one by those expressing general agreement, even if sometimes qualified in respect to points of detail. For instance, one group of twelve residents came together to sign a joint letter presenting a detailed case, complete with sketch map, in favour of an alternative solution in which as much of the existing street pattern as possible was kept open to facilitate access by service vehicles.

The evaluation of residents' views

To the working party, the results of this first exercise in participation therefore provided both a measure of general encouragement and also some more specific indicators from which to work towards an acceptable design solution. Following the agreed success of the public meeting, it was decided that the Borough Council could be recommended to endorse a six-month programme of further design work and consultations by the working party, with a view to incorporating as many as practicable of the requests and suggestions received in a new draft scheme. This would be submitted at a further public meeting, before asking the Borough to make a formal declaration of a General Improvement Area in early 1971.

Before long, the Group technical officers were able to put forward a draft 'Master Plan', which is reproduced in *Figure 61*. In this, they could claim that the reactions of the local people to the alternatives put forward at the public meeting had been reflected as far as possible. Some of the residents had also presented suggestions about the phasing of the work, as well as desirable design features. However, the further exploratory discussions within the working party revealed that decisions about the rate and sequence of implementation were likely to be strongly influenced by uncertainties about the allocation of financial responsibilities, in a situation where there were severe limitations on the levels of expenditure that could be met through the Borough rate account. Among the uncertainties exposed at this stage were doubts about how far those called upon to sacrifice parts of their gardens for road widening would require to be compensated financially, when it could be argued that they were obtaining environmental benefits in exchange; how far the water, gas, electricity, and telephone authorities might be persuaded to modify their local distribution networks at their own expense, rather than at that of the local authority; and how far expenditures ancillary to the limited proposals for housing redevelopment within the GIA might qualify for loan sanctions under the new 'key sector' arrangement or, alternatively, would have to be met through the statutory housing account, therefore impinging on the town's existing tenants.

Viewed in combination, these sources of uncertainty created a problem of deciding what financial estimates to lay before the Borough Council to enable an assessment to be made of the implications for ratepayers of a commitment to a GIA solution. One possible approach was to attempt to estimate the costs of the environmental improvement works alone. However, the Treasurer advocated a 'total costing' approach, which would also incorporate an estimate for the Council's share of improvement grants to individual dwellings, and would attempt to offset the additional municipal revenue accruing through increases in rateable value following the proposed rehabilitation of the area. Furthermore, allowance could be made for the costs of inaction in the area, in terms of maintenance and ultimate redevelopment expenditures. Such an approach could be expected to stengthen the case for the GIA, but, at the same time, to involve so many and such varied uncertainties as to invalidate precise comparisons.

Ultimately, it was agreed that the various financial uncertainties could not realistically be resolved before a formal GIA declaration was made, and therefore the working party should proceed to make its recommendations to the Council on the basis of the best set of working assumptions that could currently be put forward. Consequently, preparations were put in hand for the second public meeting, at which the new draft scheme was to be presented for the approval of local residents. A second exhibition was mounted and a small booklet was produced, setting out the basic proposals for the area, along with a sketch of the 'Master Plan' layout as reproduced in *Figure 61*.

At the second public meeting, the Chairman of the Borough Planning Committee presided, and the Group Planner Architect explained how the scheme had evolved in response to the wishes previously expressed by residents. However, he mentioned that there were some local wishes — such as the preference for individual rather than grouped garages — that it had not been feasible to incorporate within the physical constraints of the area. He stressed that not all the proposals shown in this 'Master Plan' would necessarily be carried out; the scheme would have to evolve gradually over time in accordance with the demands expressed through more detailed processes of group and individual discussion with residents of particular streets. Questioned about the costs of implementation, the Borough Treasurer mentioned the difficulties of assessing these where the principle was one of partnership between local authority and residents. However, he quoted a rough estimate of £180,000 overall expenditure, of which £110,000 would be met by the Borough Council, although there would be rental incomes for provisions such as garages to offset against some of this. Central government grants would cover £40,000 of the remainder, so that private owners would have only a limited proportion to pay.

In contrast to the previous occasion, there was vocal opposition at the meeting to some of the specific design proposals, so that the local press was able to report the meeting as a 'rowdy' one. Nevertheless, the consensus of the working party members was that the objections had arisen from very localized quarters only. Moreover, many of these objections had been effectively answered at the meeting itself, and it was felt confidently that the remaining points of difference could be dealt with through more detailed discussion with the residents of particular streets. Accordingly, the working party advised the Borough Council, through its Planning Committee, that the time was now ripe to make a public commitment to the GIA solution. Consequently, the Council set in train the various required procedures, including the issue of a formal GIA declaration, its advertisement in the press, and the depositing of a copy with the Ministry. At the same time, it was agreed that the working party should be reconstituted, with more or less the same membership, but with a new brief directed towards the detailed problems of implementation.

The transition to implementation

Thus, the Borough Council had successfully passed a major point of commitment to the future treatment of the Newtown area; but there remained many details of layout to be settled, and there were still many uncertainties to be tolerated by both the local authority and the residents. The expertise of the Group technical staff remained in demand when it came to the more detailed exploration of design options in such fields as modifications to the access arrangements for particular properties. At this scale, the process tended to become one of negotiation between the technical staff and residents, either individually or in smaller groups representing the interests of particular streets. While the problems might appear of limited significance when compared to the wider issues of the town development programme, it was at this level that the choices of individual residents and of the public sector could be seen to impinge on each other most directly and immediately. Modifications to road widths, for example, involved direct bargaining over the territorial rights of home owners and local authority; and both parties could be seen as having similar status as 'planners', in that each had to confront similar orders of local investment decision under uncertainty. On each side, the problem was one of what level of resources to commit to the improvement of existing property assets, in a state of some uncertainty about the future intentions of the opposite party, as well as of other neighbouring interests.

For the technical officers of the Development Group, one problem requiring careful treatment was raised by differences in time horizons. For instance, some of the older residents were reluctant to make concessions over the provision of new garage space as they saw little likelihood that such improvements could be of any value to them in their lifetime. Their primary concern was to conserve a familiar home and street environment, with a minimum of disturbance. However, the officers had to look ahead over a time horizon of at least the thirty years for which GIA policies were intended to guarantee the future life of the housing. Such a period could be expected to see many changes in occupancy of the property, and create a level of demand for garage space which many of the present occupiers were unable to appreciate.

An underlying problem for the officers, and for the Borough Council which was meeting the costs of their work, was that of how much time they could justify spending in detailed negotiations with individual citizens over matters of limited public significance. In fact, because the early stages of discussion over implementation coincided with the continuing delay over town centre work, the officers of the central area team, and other specialists such as the Group Engineer, were able to devote much more effort to the GIA than they would have been able to do had the main programme been proceeding to schedule. In terms of working relationships, this situation was not without its benefits. Not only were the Group technical officers able to acquire some valuable working experience of public participation at a scale where the opportunities for interaction were extremely concrete; they were also able to develop a harmonious and constructive working relationship with members and officers of the Borough Council, so helping to counterbalance, to some degree at least, the tensions that had been generated over the issue of central area redevelopment.

Another environmental issue: the Droitwich canal

Another contrasting issue concerned with the treatment of existing assets, which again gave rise to some difficult challenges in the management of inter-agency decision processes, was presented by the existence of the largely derelict Droitwich canal. This we have already encountered as an obstacle in the construction of Salwarpe Road, and also as a western boundary for the Westacre housing site. As *Figure 62* indicates, its line followed closely the contours of the Salwarpe valley. It had been constructed during the late eighteenth century to sustain the local economy of Droitwich by facilitating the import of coal and the bulk export of salt. Later, the short Droitwich Junction Canal was also constructed, with a separate system of water supply. The Droitwich waterway system was therefore now linked not only to the River Severn in the west but also to the Worcester and Birmingham canal in the east, so making the town accessible to an extensive regional network. However, commercial usage declined with the growth of the railway system, and the Droitwich canals fell into disuse. This position was formally recognised by an 'Abandonment Act' in 1939, under which ownership of the land along their length was transferred to the Borough Council, which subsequently sold off some sections to private interests.

In terms of the Town Development programme, the canal was recognised as an asset the future of which was open to several possibilities. At the foot of *Figure 62*, the conventions of AIDA are used to present the options for the four different sections of canal shown on the map, as seen by the Group Engineer who was commissioned to carry out some preliminary studies into the feasible courses of action and their costs. For the canal as a whole, there was only a limited range of combinations of these options which could realistically be considered. At one extreme, the entire length might be imaginatively rehabilitated to create a through facility for motor cruising as well as other recreational uses; indeed, the model of the central area produced in 1965 indicated a new marina close to the town centre dotted with brightly coloured cruising craft. At the other extreme, the state of 'abandonment' could be maintained over most of the canal length at little or no cost.

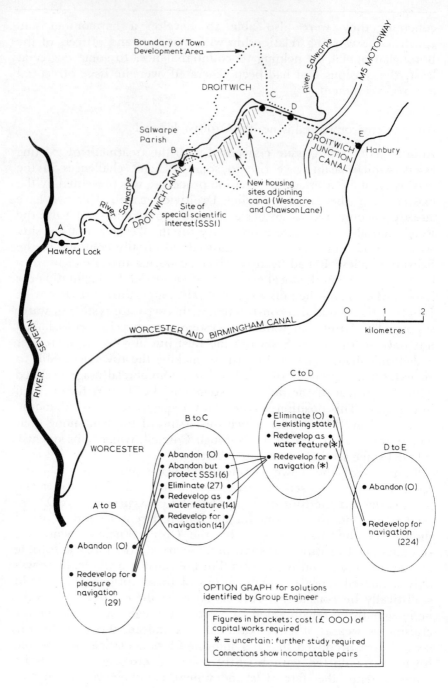

Figure 62 Options for the future of the Droitwich canals

Boundary of Town Development Area ⟶

DROITWICH

River Salwarpe

M5 MOTORWAY

C

D

Salwarpe Parish

B

DROITWICH JUNCTION CANAL

E

Hanbury

DROITWICH CANAL

River Salwarpe

New housing sites adjoining canal (Westacre and Chawson Lane)

Site of special scientific interest (SSSI)

A

Hawford Lock

RIVER SEVERN

WORCESTER AND BIRMINGHAM CANAL

0   1   2
kilometres

WORCESTER

C to D
• Eliminate (O) •
  (= existing state)
• Redevelop as •
  water feature (✳)
• Redevelop for •
  navigation (✳)

B to C
• Abandon (O) •
• Abandon but •
  protect SSSI (6)
• Eliminate (27) •
• Redevelop as •
  water feature (14)
• Redevelop for •
  navigation (14)

D to E
• Abandon (O)

• Redevelop for
  navigation
  (224)

A to B
• Abandon (O) •

• Redevelop for
  pleasure
  navigation
  (29)

OPTION GRAPH for solutions
identified by Group Engineer

Figures in brackets: cost (£ OOO) of
capital works required
✳ = uncertain: further study required
Connections show incompatable pairs

However, stretches of the canal did in fact perform a residual role as part of the town's surface water drainage system. In the town centre, the canal had already been officially 'eliminated' through past expenditure on alternative surface drainage arrangements, but considerable expenditure would still be required for 'elimination' in the areas to the west of the Westacre and Chawson Lane housing estates. The other options were either that the canal should be left as an eyesore in this part of the Town Development Area, or that it should be restored to provide an attractive 'water feature', with or without navigational uses. Either solution would involve lower costs than the works required for complete elimination, which legally required the Borough Council to restore the land and its drainage arrangements to their original state before the canal had been cut. Although the Abandonment Act released the Borough from its obligations to maintain locks and water levels, it still remained liable by the original laws under which the canal was built to maintain satisfactory drainage and avoid nuisance through leakage or damaged fences.

National and local policy influences

The context of national policy within which these local options had to be considered was one of a reawakening of interest in the recreational potential of the canal system, after generations of neglect. Both voluntary and governmental bodies had become active in searching for ways of exploiting this potential; this was especially so in the West Midlands, where the existence of a substantial and relatively affluent urban population, without easy access to coastlines or mountainous areas, led to compensatory demands for canal cruising, coarse fishing, and other water-based recreations. Thus, a restoration of the Droitwich canals for through navigation could provide an attractive circuit in a rehabilitated regional network for pleasure cruising, which could conceivably justify the very considerable cost of re-opening the Droitwich Junction section in the east, where much of the land had already been sold off and where the M5 motorway presented a formidable barrier.

Another external policy influence was the emergence of a growing national concern with the conservation of natural environment. In order to protect natural habitats, certain areas throughout the country had been graded by the national Nature Conservancy as requiring special protection; and the most modest in the hierarchy of classifications adopted was that of the local 'Site of Special Scientific Interest' (SSSI), where consultation with local conservation societies was required before any adjacent developmental action

Figure 63 Network relationships of Group Engineer for restoration of Droitwich canals

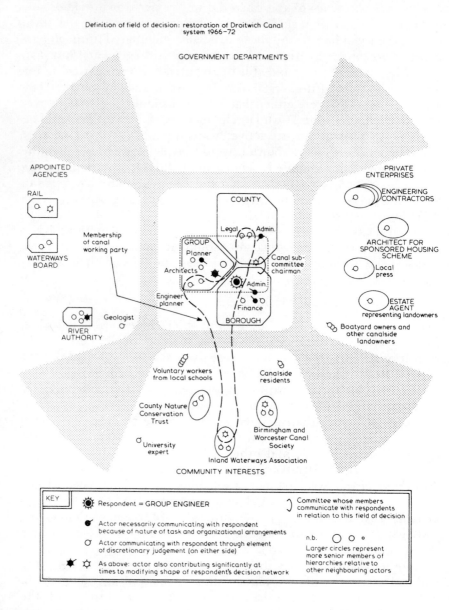

Definition of field of decision: restoration of Droitwich Canal
system 1966-72

GOVERNMENT DEPARTMENTS

APPOINTED
AGENCIES

RAIL

WATERWAYS
BOARD

Membership
of canal
working party

RIVER
AUTHORITY

Geologist

Engineer
planner

GROUP
Planner
Architects

Legal   Admin.

COUNTY

Canal sub-
committee
chairman

Admin.

Finance

BOROUGH

PRIVATE
ENTERPRISES

ENGINEERING
CONTRACTORS

ARCHITECT FOR
SPONSORED HOUSING
SCHEME

Local
press

ESTATE
AGENT
representing landowners

Boatyard owners and
other canalside
landowners

Voluntary workers
from local schools

Canalside
residents

County Nature
Conservation
Trust

University
expert

Birmingham and
Worcester Canal
Society

Inland Waterways Association

COMMUNITY INTERESTS

KEY

○ Respondent = GROUP ENGINEER

● Actor necessarily communicating with respondent
because of nature of task and organizational arrangements

○ Actor communicating with respondent through element
of discretionary judgement (on either side)

✦ ☆ As above: actor also contributing significantly at
times to modifying shape of respondent's decision network

) Committee whose members
communicate with respondents
in relation to this field of decision

n.b. ○ ○ ∘

Larger circles represent
more senior members of
hierarchies relative to
other neighbouring actors

was initiated. In the case of Droitwich, such a site had been designated alongside a length of canal in the parish of Salwarpe immediately to the west of the Town Development Area. In this marshy area, seepage of brine into the canal bed had led to the presence of some forms of plant life usually found only in coastal areas: and, furthermore, one of the few colonies of reed warblers in that part of the country migrated each year to nest in the local reed beds.

To confront the various policy issues raised by the future of the canal, the Development Committee resolved in 1966 to appoint a small canal sub-committee, including not only members of the Borough and County Councils but also a representative of Droitwich Rural District, in whose territory much of the canal lay. The Chairman of the County Planning Committee, who had a personal interest in canal restoration, was elected to the Chair and representatives were invited to join from two voluntary bodies: the Worcestershire Nature Conservation Trust and the Inland Waterways Association. The latter Association provided a national focus for those concerned with canal resoration; it was fortuitous that one of its leading activists happened to live locally, and so was able to play a prominent policy role on the sub-committee along with the County Planning Chairman.

To produce technical appraisals of the situation for the sub-committee, a small 'working party' was established including two officers of the Development Committee – the Group Engineer and the Engineer Planner – along with the representative of the Inland Waterways Association (IWA). Other officers of the County and the Development Group contributed on an occasional basis, and the working party's explorations brought them into contact with a variety of other actors and institutions from time to time. The general pattern is indicated in the network chart of *Figure 63*, as seen from the perspective of the Group Engineer. As in the case of the Newtown GIA, there were few roles in the network that were clearly ordained by the existence of the field of decision about the future of the canal or by the formal relationships of the organizations concerned; much, therefore, depended on the network-forming judgements of certain key actors identified as nodal points in the diagram. Among the few organizations which inevitably had to be consulted was the Severn River Authority which, prior to the comprehensive reorganization of public agencies concerned with water resources in 1974, was responsible for all matters of regulation of water flows within the catchment area of the Severn and its tributaries.

Obstacles and opportunities

The first crucial point of decision encountered by the sub-committee concerned whether or not the existing road bridges over the canal, some of which the County Surveyor wished to replace at an early priority, should be rebuilt in such a way as to keep open the ultimate option of through navigational facilities. There was some doubt over whether the Canal Abandonment Act obliged the County to secure the consent of the Borough, as owners of the canal, before reducing the height of bridges; but, in the event, the policy influence of the Canal Sub-Committee was instrumental in ensuring that all bridges were rebuilt to full clearance, so keeping future options open at some cost to the County highway budget. Similar problems arose over the question of rebuilding a rail bridge over the canal, where financial compensation would be payable towards the rail authority from the Town Development Accounts.

Another technical problem concerned the amount of water that the Severn River Authority might allow to be extracted from the River Salwarpe to maintain the level of the restored canal, given an insistence on a sufficient flow in the river itself to provide adequate dilution of effluents from the town's new sewage works downstream. However, recordings of river flows provided reassuring evidence that the problem could be overcome, so the working party were able to conclude that there were no severe technical obstacles to restoration of the canal, at least in the length between the town centre and the Severn where there were no difficulties of land acquisition to be confronted.

When it came to discussion of the impact of canal resoration on the Site of Special Scientific Interest, discussions with the representatives of the County Nature Conservation Trust indicated at first that there was unlikely to be much disturbance to the habitats concerned beyond that already resulting from other development works. Among these were works directed towards a reduction in levels of brine concentration, as brine was regarded as an undesirable pollutant by the River Authority. In fact, it emerged that the restoration of the canal might bring positive benefits to nature conservation through opening up further extensions in the area where the reed warblers and maritime plants could flourish. However, it would be necessary to avoid the programming of engineering works during the Spring, when there was a risk that the colony of reed warblers could be so disturbed on their return from their annual migration to Africa their established nesting habits were entirely disrupted. Not entirely frivously, the reed warblers might be regarded as one set of relevant decision-makers which could not conceivably be regarded as part of the decision network in *Figure 63*, because of a lack of any communication channels for joint exploratory processes.

The organizational issues

When it came to considering ways and means of mobilizing the necessary resources to restore the canal, the IWA representative helped in establishing contacts with bodies such as the British Waterways Board, a governmental agency which operated most of the major canals still in navigable use, and also with the voluntary interests concerned with the restoration of other regional waterways, including the Worcester and Birmingham Canal Society and the National Trust, which had taken over two other derelict waterways in the Avon valley area. Also, the Chairman of the Salwarpe Parish Council played a prominent role in setting up meetings to discuss the future of the canal within the parish area.

A working party report produced in 1971 set out the various possible advantages of opening the canal, recommended a policy of restoring as much as possible of its length, and indicated that the difficulties of proceeding were mainly of an organizational nature. The benefits were seen as many different kinds: canal cruising facilities with associated opportunities for local revenue from mooring sites and ancillary services; towpath opportunities for angling, walking, and horse-riding; the enhancement of the urban environment; the gains in nature conservation; the additional capacity available for the town's surface drainage system in times of flood; and even the opportunities provided by the restoration programme to mobilize voluntary labour in a worthwhile local cause.

So far as the costs were concerned, it was envisaged that much of the expense of dredging and restoration within the Town Development Area could be met through the capital accounts of housing or other development projects; indeed, there could be a net saving as against the costs of alternative drainage provisions. The restoration of the towpath as a pedestrian route could well be treated in a similar way, although the re-assignment of the Westacre estate to sponsored development raised an additional element of uncertainty in this respect. The general conclusion was that the restoration of that part of the canal within the Town Development Area should be treated as a direct responsibility of the Development Committee, generating mutual benefits for the wider town development and canal restoration programmes.

For the stretches of canal outside the Town Development boundary, the problem of organizing and financing restoration works became more difficult and the working party identified various possible solutions. These included direct local authority management; a partnership arrangement between the local authority and a voluntary organization; creation of a special trust; and adoption by the British Waterways Board. Two further options which were quickly excluded were those of restoration by a commercial body, since the proposition was unlikely to be economically attractive; and by a voluntary organization alone, as there would be legal difficulties in handing over the Borough Council's statutory responsibilities. After much debate, both in the working party and the sub-committee, a clear preference emerged for the establishment of a special trust, on the governing body of which might be represented such interests as the County and Borough Councils (or their successors after local government reform), and the Inland Waterways Association. The charitable status of such a trust could both bring financial advantages in the opportunity to utilize free military and prison labour, and advantages of goodwill when negotiating with local landowners.

These recommendations were submitted by the Canal Sub-Committee to the full Development Committee in 1972, and accepted with a good deal of enthusiasm, reflecting the sense of commitment shown by most of the members and officers who had been concerned in the wide-ranging, though intermittent, explorations over the preceding five years. There still remained daunting uncertainties over the formation of the proposed trust, and the practicability of ever raising the resources to open the Droitwich Junction section to achieve the ultimate goal of through navigation. But a clear commitment to proceed had now been attained, not so much on the basis of a careful balancing of expected costs and benefits, as from a belief that voluntary community effort could readily be mobilized in pursuance of an ambitious and imaginative piece of renewal of the local environment.

The two case studies: an appraisal

The two case studies, of the Newtown Improvement Area and the Droitwich canals, contrast with each other in that one primarily concerned the residential environment of a close-knit local community, while the other concerned a potential environment for recreational pursuits which might attract a much wider range of users. However, both raised opportunities for environmental renewal of a kind that has been receiving increasing attention in cities as

well as smaller country towns; and both became matters of priority
in Droitwich primarily because of their interaction with other forms
of change induced by the Town Development programme. Significantly, neither the field of housing rehabilitation nor that of canal
restoration had been touched upon in the Town Development
agreement, and most of the statutory responsibilities remained with
the Borough Council. However, in each case, the technical skills of
the Development Group provided a useful resource in the exploration of alternative solutions; and one of the leading sources of
uncertainty which was encountered concerned the way in which the
body of available legislation might best be exploited, in pursuit of
forms of action for which there was as yet little body of established
precedent in other towns.

Both cases can be regarded as local experiments in forms of *ad hoc*
organizations designed to deal with decision problems where the
prospect of success depended on the mobilization of commitment
and voluntary effort among the community interests concerned. In
each case, the core of the decision network which evolved was a
small working party with relevant skills, and with policy support
from a formally constituted local authority committee — respectively
the Borough Planning Committee and the Droitwich Development
Committee through its Canal Sub-Committee. Each of the working
parties was able to draw informally from a range of outside sources
of advice, ranging from the Housing Ministry in the case of the GIA
to the IWA and the Nature Conservation Trust in the case of the
canal. In each case, it may be noted that a leading elected member
came to play a salient role in the exploratory process, combining a
strong policy commitment to the cause concerned with an ability to
exercise influence in the extension of decision networks. In the case
of the GIA, the Borough Planning Chairman became a focal point in
the mobilization of resident involvement; while, in the case of the
canal, the sub-committee chairman and the IWA representative were
able to bring the working party into contact with several relevant
voluntary interests.

In both cases, the process of commitment was once more a
cumulative one, demanding sensitive political management in leading
up to certain crucial points of formal commitment, while leaving
important options open for future discretion. The retention of this
freedom of manoeuvre served not only to protect the future action
space of some of the parties whose interests were most closely
involved, such as the residents of the Newtown community, but also
to allow any new and unforeseen opportunities to be exploited
within an evolving framework of national legislation and central
policy guidance.

12 Contributions to community

The planning of supporting services

In this chapter, we shall conclude our extended case history of Droitwich by reviewing the planning problems of a range of specialized public services; by discussing the catalytic role of the Community Development Officer; and by a brief case example which cross-cuts many of our earlier heads of analysis. The theme will be — to adopt a term from aerospace technology — that of the planning and co-ordination of 'life-support systems' for a changing community. We shall recognise that many of the topics already covered, including roads, housing, and industry, can themselves be considered as basic elements in the life-support systems of any local community; but we shall also recognise that there are many other supporting services — from health care to policing and energy supply — which must be taken into account to some degree at least in any programme of planned urban development.

Many of these services must be planned with a view not only to the demands of the local residential community, but also to those of other more specialized working communities based within the local area, such as factories and schools. Some intricate patterns of interdependence can therefore be expected between different forms of 'life-support system', however disparate their primary purposes may appear. In the situation of a local community such as Droitwich, which is undergoing a rapid expansion to several times its previous size, the problem then arises of avoiding any severe imbalances between the states of development of these various systems, not only after the expansion programme is completed but at all stages during its execution.

In *Figure 64*, our standard organizational base-map is used to plot some of the more important community services, other than housing, employment, and highways, according to the form of public or private agency that was primarily responsible for their local provision in 1972 within the English Counties. The allocation of responsibilities was by no means a static one; there had been many changes in the pattern and extent of public involvement since the end of the nineteenth century, and the arrows in the diagram indicate a number of further changes to which the government was publicly committed over the few years from 1972 onwards.

Most of the forms of service indicated in *Figure 64* will be found to have equivalents in other societies — even in those which have attained a much lesser degree of economic development or, to express the point in a different way, have remained more locally self-sustaining. One characteristic of highly developed economies, such as that of Britain, is the pervasiveness of centralized control structures, especially for those services such as energy supply which have become dependent on regional and national grid systems sustained through large-scale capital investment. Even such services as education and social welfare have become subject to centralizing tendencies because of the controversial issues of national policy which they involve; and there has also been a gradual increase in the range of contextual and fiscal controls over private business transactions, in the interests of more sensitive management of the national economy. Meanwhile, moves have been made to 'hive off' some of the activities of government, either to autonomous public agencies (as in the case of the Post Office or employment services) or to private operators. Significantly, the only major local service that remains to be managed directly through local offices of central departments — apart from those 'services' concerned with tax collection — is the payment of social security benefits, where it is important that the same set of impartial central rules should be seen to operate equitably in all parts of the country.

Although *Figure 64* classifies services according to the primary form of agency at the local 'point of supply', the relationships between the various agencies at local level must evolve within a framework of other relationships between agencies that operate at a regional, a national, or indeed in some cases, an international level.

Figure 64   Range of main forms of community service, indicating the types of organizations through which provided locally in English Counties in 1972

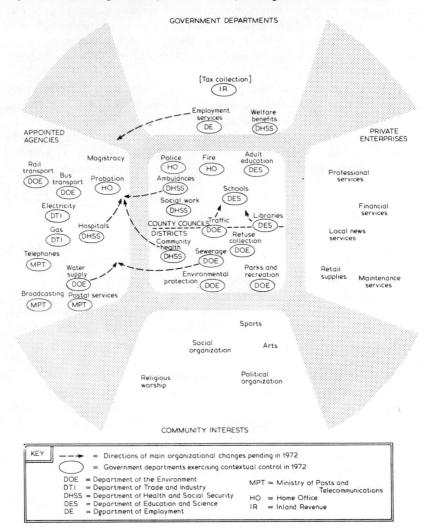

GOVERNMENT DEPARTMENTS

[Tax collection]
IR

Employment services
DE

Welfare benefits
DHSS

APPOINTED AGENCIES

PRIVATE ENTERPRISES

Rail transport
DOE

Bus transport
DOE

Magistracy

Probation
HO

Police
HO

Fire
HO

Adult education
DES

Professional services

Ambulances
DHSS

Schools
DES

Electricity
DTI

Social work
DHSS

Financial services

Hospitals
DHSS

Gas
DTI

COUNTY COUNCILS
DISTRICTS

Traffic
DOE

Libraries
DES

Local news services

Community health
DHSS

Refuse collection

Telephones
MPT

Water supply
DOE

Sewerage
DOE

Parks and recreation
DOE

Retail supplies

Maintenance services

Environmental protection
DOE

Broadcasting
MPT

Postal services
MPT

Sports

Social organization

Arts

Religious worship

Political organization

COMMUNITY INTERESTS

| KEY | - - - ► | = Directions of main organizational changes pending in 1972 |
| | ⬭ | = Government departments exercising contextual control in 1972 |

DOE = Department of the Environment
DTI = Department of Trade and Industry
DHSS = Department of Health and Social Security
DES = Department of Education and Science
DE = Department of Employment

MPT = Ministry of Posts and Telecommunications
HO = Home Office
IR = Inland Revenue

These agencies include a number of departments of central government, as listed earlier in *Figure 5*. During the later nineteen-sixties and early seventies, their number became reduced through the creation of some larger and more powerful departments headed by Secretaries of State of Cabinet rank: the Department of Health and Social Security, the Department of Trade and Industry, and the Department of the Environment. While such amalgamations could be justified on the grounds of increasing the effectiveness of policy formation in the Cabinet and reducing the problems of inter-departmental co-ordination at other levels, the problems of intra-departmental co-ordination became correspondingly more formidable, and it was by no means easy to evaluate the overall impact of the changes. The span of contextual control over local affairs for each of the larger specialized ministries is indicated in parenthesis in *Figure 65*. This shows the dominant position of the three enlarged departments mentioned above, together with the Department of Eduction and Science and the Home Office, which bore a more long-standing range of responsibilities in the field of internal affairs.

In this chapter, we shall concentrate on a selected range of local community services, which raise some widely differing problems in the organization of planning processes. We shall begin in the capital-intensive field of energy, comparing and contrasting the planning processes for electricity and gas supply. We shall then move to the provision of schools, as one major form of social provision, the planning of which follows well-established rules. This will be followed by discussion of the contrasting field of community health care, in which the organization of the planning processes had by 1972 become a subject of far-reaching structural change, with corresponding short-term uncertainties. We shall then briefly discuss the provision of passenger transport, where government policies had placed a new onus on local financial support, before turning to the field of outdoor recreation, by tradition largely a responsibility of the local district councils and of voluntary organizations. This will lead us into a discussion of the co-ordinating activities of the Community Development Officer, first in expanding towns in general and then in the particular case of Droitwich.

The planning of energy supply

By beginning our review in the field of electricity and gas supply, we are introducing two forms of community service that reach the consumer directly through the impersonal media of networks of overhead conductors, underground cables or pipes. Their distribu-

Figure 65   Patterns of organizational relationships in energy supply (England and Wales, 1973)

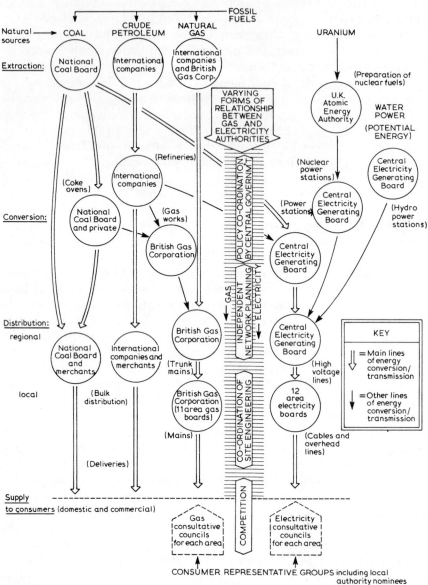

FOSSIL FUELS

Natural sources

Extraction:

Conversion:

Distribution:
regional

local

Supply to consumers (domestic and commercial)

COAL — National Coal Board
CRUDE PETROLEUM — International companies
NATURAL GAS — International companies and British Gas Corp.
URANIUM

VARYING FORMS OF RELATIONSHIP BETWEEN GAS AND ELECTRICITY AUTHORITIES

(Preparation of nuclear fuels)
U.K. Atomic Energy Authority
WATER POWER (POTENTIAL ENERGY)

(Coke ovens)
(Refineries) International companies
(Gas works)
British Gas Corporation
National Coal Board and private

(Nuclear power stations)
Central Electricity Generating Board
Central Electricity Generating Board
(Power stations)
(Hydro power stations)
Central Electricity Generating Board

POLICY CO-ORDINATION BY CENTRAL GOVERNMT
INDEPENDENT NETWORK PLANNING
GAS   ELECTRICITY
CO-ORDINATION OF SITE ENGINEERING

National Coal Board and merchants
International companies and merchants
British Gas Corporation
Central Electricity Generating Board
(High voltage lines)

(Bulk distribution)
(Trunk mains)
British Gas Corporation (11 area gas boards)
12 area electricity boards

(Deliveries)
(Mains)
(Cables and overhead lines)

KEY
⇊ = Main lines of energy conversion/ transmission
↓ = Other lines of energy conversion/ transmission

Gas consultative councils for each area
COMPETITION
Electricity consultative councils for each area

CONSUMER REPRESENTATIVE GROUPS including local authority nominees

Forms of ultimate energy use: heating (space, water, process)
motive power (transport, machine tools, appliances....)
lighting, refrigeration, electrolysis, etc.
[Diagram adapted from a model by John Stringer, 1968]

tion to the local level involves more integrated processes of planning than those of other fuels such as oil and coal, which can be stored locally and delivered on demand through competing systems of commerical supply. The public authorities concerned with gas and electricity distribution, like those concerned with the planning of water, sewerage, and telephone systems, have already been encountered in the networks of communication of the engineering and architectural staff at Droitwich. Taking a wider view, it is only within the last hundred years that the provision of energy to the consumer through electricity or gas points has become accepted as essential to the support of any urban community in a nation with a developed or developing economy; and it is only since the late nineteen-sixties that widespread concern has developed over the long-term implications of a continuing and increasing reliance on non-renewable resources of fossil fuels, in whatever forms these may be converted for ultimate supply to the consumer.

The supply of electricity and gas therefore raises issues ranging from those of detailed local engineering to those of national energy policy, as indicated in *Figure 65*. At the national level in Britain, the policy issues which arise include those of levels and directions of investment in alternative forms of energy supply technology; of political relations with oil-producing countries; of pollution and countryside conservation; and of local employment opportunities. Conflicts between questions of conservation, of employment, and of the technical efficiency of different energy sources can become especially critical in localities close to the indigenous sources of fossil fuels, ranging from the declining coal-mining communities of the North of England, the South of Scotland, and South Wales, with their status as Special Development Areas (*Figure 49*), to the rural communities in the coastal areas of North-East Scotland, for which the recent discovery of North Sea oil and natural gas fields implies both the benefits and disbenefits of new sources of economic wealth.

Although the co-ordination of policy for different sources of energy supply had been brought within a single division of the Department of Trade and Industry, the social, environmental, and international aspects of national energy policy began to become so pressing that many strategic issues would be referred for processes of interdepartmental exploration and ultimate Cabinet decision. Thus, circumstances began to prevail in which, justifiably or otherwise, critics could frequently complain that governments were failing to develop a comprehensive, unified energy policy for the nation as a whole; and the question of energy policy was among those referred for exploration by the government's Central Policy Review Staff.

Within the ambit of the Department of Trade and Industry, as successor to the earlier Ministry of Power, operational responsibility for both the gas and electricity industries lay in 1973 with specialized appointed agencies, organized hierarchically at national and regional levels, and possessing a large measure of internal management autonomy. In the case of gas, distribution to consumers in England and Wales lay in the hands of eleven Area Boards, one of which covered an area approximating to that of the West Midlands Region. These Boards were subject only to loose contextual controls from a central Gas Council until 1973, when they were reincorporated as operating units within a new statutory authority, the British Gas Corporation; a change introduced because of the increased case for centralized planning presented by a transition from reliance on locally-manufactured town gas to a national grid of natural gas supplies piped ashore from the North Sea fields.

In the case of electricity, the pattern in England and Wales in the early seventies was again one of distribution through Area Boards, co-ordinated through a central Electricity Council; but an additional central authority existed in the form of the Central Electricity Generating Board (CEGB) responsible for generation and transmission of bulk power supplies. As the most capital-intensive of the nation's industries, the CEGB had become responsible for one of the public sector's largest programmes of capital expenditure.

The CEGB itself was organized on regional lines, with its Midlands Region — covering both the West and East Midlands of England — serving as a major exporter of power to other parts of the country. Of necessity, its operations involved working on some widely different planning perspectives. Because electricity is a non-storable form of energy, regional control centres must be capable of minute-by-minute responses to local demand fluctuations, while, at the other extreme, capital programmes must be based on anticipation of levels of demand ten years and more into the future. At an intermediate level, seasonal fluctuations in demand generate a cycle to which regional overhaul and construction processes must be geared; and the difficulties of responding effectively to the uncertainties which must be faced within this planning cycle have led to some extensive innovations in systems of information management and control (Kidd and Morgan, 1968).

At an early stage of our Droitwich research, in 1969, discussions were held with senior planning staff of the two Area Boards responsible for local distribution of energy to the town — the West Midlands Gas Board and the Midlands Electricity Board. Neither regarded Droitwich as presenting them with any difficult problems at a strategic, as opposed to a tactical, level; the town was well located in relation to existing supply networks, while the scale and pace of expansion were modest compared with other regional schemes with which they were concerned at the time. These others included Birmingham's rapidly growing housing development at Chelmsley Wood, just outside the city's eastern boundary, and the New Towns of Redditch and Telford. In the last case, both boards had encountered difficulties because the original growth target had been superseded by a second, much more ambitious one, and because of a failure to achieve the projected rates of growth in practice. The outlying location of Telford in relation to the West Midlands conurbation had meant considerable investment in new trunk mains by the Gas Board and in high voltage transmission lines by the Electricity Board. In each case, the technical solution chosen, in the light of the best assumptions of growth rate that could be made at the time, had proved to be much less economic, once these assumptions were invalidated.

In their planning processes, the Area Boards were constrained by statutory requirements that they should maintain supplies within given limits of pressure or voltage at all times, and also that they should plan to yield a fixed long-term rate of return on capital advanced from Treasury funds. Responses to changing levels of local demand were planned through formal procedures involving approval of long-term development plans and review of 'rolling' capital programmes, while explicit Ministry approval was required for many of the forms of capital project that impinged on local community interests. In the case of gas, the statutory obligations to provide supplies to all would-be consumers were – at that time – less stringent than in the case of electricity, and the method of DCF rate of return (as briefly discussed in Chapter 10) was used to assess the priorities for competing projects designed to improve local supply networks. One important but transient problem during the late nineteen-sixties and early seventies was the scheduling of the conversion of supply networks and appliances from manufactured to natual gas. In this programme, expanding towns such as Droitwich tended to be given special priority because of the diseconomies involved in leaving conversion until after the initial investment had been made.

Both Boards based their planning processes on predictions of changes in local demand, estimated separately for domestic and industrial consumers. In the industrial field, different types of business had widely differing patterns of energy usage, and this created difficulties for the Electricity Board not only in the planning of levels of local supply but also in the siting of grid supply points. On a new industrial estate, for instance, factories carrying out welding operations could both create heavy loads and cause interference for other users, so should, wherever possible, be sited close to grid supply points. On the other hand, cable-laying operations could become uneconomic for the Board if the first factories coming into operation were both remote from supply points and low consumers of electricity, so some difficult judgements of priority and location sometimes had to be made at the local planning level.

In the domestic field, predictions of consumption were somewhat more staightforward except in the rapidly expanding field of central heating, where the two Boards were in direct competition with each other. One problem was that developers of large public housing estates could, at a late stage in their design processes, create abrupt changes in predicted load for either form of energy – and thus in the profitability of either Area Board – by a decision to standardize on either gas or electric space heating systems. Indeed, one official of the Area Electricity Board saw Droitwich as something of a 'black spot' on his map because of a Development Committee decision to standardize on gas. In their attempts to gain customers, both Boards were able to bargain with developers to some extent over the payment of connection charges – although the opportunity to do so was later reduced after a report by the government's Monopolies Commission.

At the interface with the consumer, the competitive stance of the two industries was maintained through large-scale and sustained advertizing campaigns. Meanwhile, each Board maintained its own channels of consumer contact through local sales offices and district or regional procedures of meter-reading, billing, and servicing of appliances. Each also had its own system of consultative councils, including some members nominated by local authorities, intended to provide a channel for consumer pressures and the airing of any grievances. It was, however, argued by some that their effectiveness was much reduced by their purely advisory status, and by their dependence on the officers of the Board itself for technical expertise.

Within the consumer's own premises, though, the separation of gas and electricity supply systems was by no means so complete, because of the increasing use of complex technologies which required the four basic 'piped' services of gas, electricity, water, and effluent disposal to óperate in some degree of combination. These ranged from the domestic central heating boiler and automatic washing machine to the most sophisticated systems of industrial production engineering. There was also some local contact between the human agents of the competing energy systems, through the participation of distribution engineers in site meetings such as those convened periodically by the Group Engineer at Droitwich, to co-ordinate local trenching operations. At this level, there was an obvious common-sense case for co-ordination to minimize the repeated digging up of roads and pavements. However, despite much national advocacy of 'common trenching' methods, the practical opportunities were always constrained by the problems encountered by each public agency in managing its own intricate internal scheduling problems, under conditions of persistent uncertainty about labour availability and completion dates in different local sites.

Overall, the fields of gas and electricity supply can both be seen as the province of powerful, self-contained, and specialized public authorities, subject to various external pressures towards competition or co-ordination at different levels of operation. Over the spectrum indicated in *Figure 65*, their mutual relationships vary from a degree of strategic co-ordination within a central framework of national energy policies, through a virtually complete independence in questions of bulk grid supply, to a state of open competition at the consumer interface, but often with an element of voluntary local co-operation at the site engineering level, co-ordinated through the channel of the site developer.

The planning of school facilities

Among the community services provided through local authorities in England, the education service is clearly dominant in terms both of the expenditure borne by ratepayers and of manpower. The range of services provided cover the established sectors of primary, secondary, and further education, with additional arrangements for nursery schooling and the education of handicapped children. In order to gain an appreciation of the problems arising in relation to Droitwich, we arranged in 1970 to talk to a senior officer of the Worcestershire County Education Department who had a special responsibility for planning the provision of school facilities.

Although most of the local powers in the planning of school buildings lay with the County Council, working through its statutory Education Committee and a set of specialist sub-committees, the management of individual schools was supervised through a system of district committees, one of which covered the area of Droitwich Borough and Rural District Councils. Many matters of internal school organization were in fact left to the discretion of head teachers, acting within constraints laid down by the national school inspectorate and the external examination syllabi. However, the County officer consulted felt that the district committees did sometimes provide a useful channel for the feedback of local opinions and pressures on matters of concern to the County as a whole.

In Worcestershire, as in other Counties, a matter of overriding policy concern had been, for several years, the reorganization of the secondary education system along comprehensive, as opposed to selective, lines. This had become a matter of much controversy nationally; while both leading political parties claimed to accept the long-term desirability of abolishing selection for different forms of secondary education on the basis of tests of ability, there was disagreement over the rate at which national resources should be channelled in this direction, as also over the extent to which the preservation of long-established grammar schools could be considered compatible with the comprehensive principle.

This conflict was reflected in two successive circulars from the Education Ministry, the first — in 1967, under Labour — requesting all authorities to prepare immediate plans for early reorganization, and the second — in 1970, under the Conservatives — taking a more gradualist line and assigning firm policy priority to primary rather than secondary school building. In Worcestershire, a policy commitment had already been made as early as 1964 to the introduction of a novel education policy, involving introduction of an additional 'middle' tier between the primary and secondary levels, accompanied by the elimination of selective admission procedures. Following Ministry approval in 1966, the system was introduced first of all in the Droitwich district in 1969. Because of the extensive school building programme required for the town expansion scheme, and the lack of an existing grammar school, this was an obvious area in which to start; thus, as in the case of conversion to natural gas, Droitwich attracted some priority in the introduction of a major programme of national innovation through its status as an expanding town. In other parts of the County, however, controversy remained. Following the election of the Conservative government in 1970 and its publication of the revised policy circular, a resolution was formally moved in the Council Chamber that Worcestershire's plans for comprehensive reorganization be 'reconsidered'. This was only outvoted by a narrow majority, and one of the senior officers attending the meeting admitted that he had been quite unable to predict the outcome in advance.

Even in Droitwich, the transition to a three-tier system of

education raised some complex administrative problems, involving the re-assignment of existing buildings, the transfer and recruitment of staff and the phasing of changes so as to avoid excessive disturbance to the 'cohorts' of children passing through successive stages of their education. On some issues, agreement had to be reached with the Diocesan authorities responsible for management of Church schools aided or controlled by the local authority; a point that has already been touched on in Chapter 6 in discussing the scheduling of the new Boycott Church of England middle school. The national agreement was that the Church could always opt to maintain its existing share in the total school provision in an area, given evidence that the necessary 20 per cent contribution to any such 'voluntary maintained' school could be mobilized through Diocesan funds. One source of uncertainty for the County officials concerned the question of how far such schools should be regarded as specialized facilities having their own comparatively far-flung catchment areas, or alternatively how far the policy should be one of siting them as part of the general distribution of schools within the local area.

In contrast to many other local authority services, the prediction of demand for local school places was a comparatively straight-forward matter. Only a minority of children could be expected to go forward to private schools, to Roman Catholic Church schools, or to schools for handicapped children; the majority could be expected to go forward to mainstream County schools on reaching pre-determined ages, and in an established town a knowledge of the existing community structure usually provided a reliable guide to the future demand for education within the time horizon required for school building programmes. In the case of overspill towns, however, a need arose to predict the age structures of incoming families and the proportion expected to require places in Roman Catholic schools, which was often significantly higher than that in the existing local population. In the case of Droitwich, parameters derived from experience in earlier overspill schemes proved to be sufficiently accurate for the County's purposes.

As schools were classified as a 'key sector' of local authority expenditure, a system of close control over building programmes was maintained by the Education Ministry, broadly similar to that for principal roads discussed in Chapter 7. At least three years before a new school was likely to be required within the County, it would have to be submitted for inclusion in a 'preliminary' list, going forward the following year to a 'design' list and then to a 'starts' list, provided the case for early construction could still be substantiated by evidence of need from the local authority. One of the County's problems in presenting such evidence arose from uncertainty over how soon private housing developments already planned would actually be built and occupied, in an economic climate where the buoyancy of the housing market was very sensitive to fluctuations in the supply of mortgage finance.

Although the Master Plan for Droitwich indicated one proposed college of further education for school leavers, the projected size of the town was somewhat marginal for a facility of that kind. The County's strategy was therefore to postpone any commitment either to a full-scale local college or to a more modest centre until a later time, when more of the children of the incoming families would be approaching the age for this kind of provision.

The planning of community health services

In the school services we encountered a field of social provision where, despite changing policies on organization, patterns of demand were clearly predictable and planning processes well established. By contrast, the field of health care presented a much more fluid situation at the time in 1970 when we arranged a discussion with the Worcestershire County Medical Officer. Even though most of the population were dependent for health care on the National Health Service, first established by the government in 1948, there were at the time a series of organizational changes pending. These included the transfer of non-medical services managed by the Medical Officer, such as home help services, to the new County Social Services Department which, by law, was to be set up during the following year to integrate all the authority's main functions in the field of social welfare. Also, a reconstruction of the entire National Health Service was then under active discussion nationally, with a view to bringing together, under the aegis of unified Area Health Authorities, the three main branches of the Service: the hospital service, the work of independent local contractors such as general and dental practitioners, and the various community health care services hitherto run by the County Medical Officers.

Thus the situation for the County Medical Officer in 1970 was one in which he expected his post to disappear in a few years' time, and his various responsibilities all to be transferred to new kinds of agency which would be expected to develop new forms of planning processes within their respective spheres. Ideally, these would work in close co-ordination with each other, as it was by no means easy to define a clear-cut boundary between community health and welfare services.

Figure 66 provides a broad view of the wide range of provisions for community health and welfare — some based primarily on types of building equipped for various different purposes, and others based on people with various forms of specialized skill, whether operating primarily within buildings, through domiciliary visiting or from vehicles, as in the case of ambulance staff. Also indicated in the diagram are some broad divisions of the population most at risk, including infants and the elderly, with a high proportion of the physically and mentally infirm to be found in the latter category.

Whatever the organizational structure of health care, the problems confronted in the planning of future facilities are intrinsically more difficult than in the case of school places, because of the element of uncertainty as to whether or not any particular individual may require any of the range of possible forms of health care in future, and also because of the existence of many different channels through which the condition of an individual may be diagnosed and the course of any further treatment or care determined (Spencer, 1971). An individual who feels unwell might, according to circumstances, come into contact in the first instance with either a general practitioner, or a social worker, or a health visitor, or a hospital casualty department, or a works doctor. Each type of specialist may in turn be in contact with some limited set of individuals or centres to whom the patient might be referred. The course of subsequent care may be much influenced by the shape of such 'referral networks', which can indeed be considered as special cases of the general phenomenon of the decision network with which this part of the book is concerned.

The planning of different forms of provision for institutional or domiciliary care may often be sensitive to implicit assumptions both about the way such referral networks operate, and about the extent to which they can be influenced by changes in the local or national policy framework. For example, the provision of homes for the elderly by district Housing Authorities, of alternative forms of institutional or domiciliary care facilities by county Social Service Departments, and of long-stay geriatric or psychiatric facilities in hospitals are all dependent on assumptions of policy about the care of elderly people who can no longer lead independent lives within the community. The very definition of a state of dependency on the part of an individual, in a social climate of gradual change concerning the acceptance of responsibilities within the extended family, itself generates uncertainties in the planning of facilities for the elderly and other dependent groups — uncertainties of a considerably greater order than arise in the planning of school facilities.

Even after the completion of its expansion programme, Droitwich

Figure 66 Patterns for provision of community health care

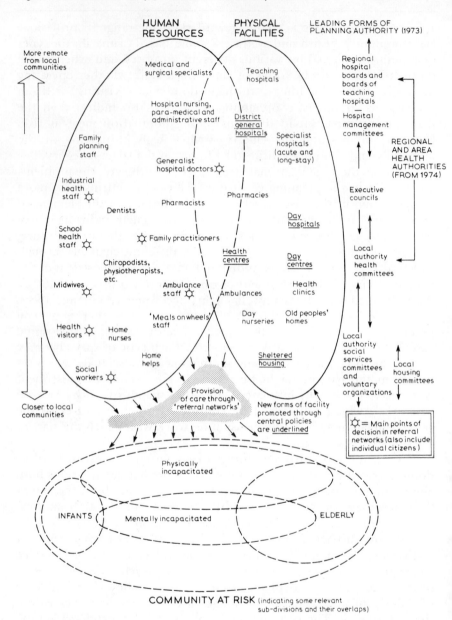

would clearly be too small to justify any general hospital facilities, in the light of the Health Ministry's policy guidelines for the catchment areas of District General Hospitals. Therefore, the question of priority for hospital building did not become a local issue, as it had done in the nearby New Town of Redditch. For the County Medical Officer, the main local planning problem was the provision of new health centres, to conform to the Health Ministry's current policy of encouraging family medical practitioners to come together in new purpose-designed buildings where a wide range of supporting facilities and staff could be made available. The problem was essentially one of negotiation with the general practitioners, whose status was that of independent contractors to the National Health Service. Many of them were wary of the loss of independence that might be implied in a move from their own local surgeries to premises owned by a public authority, despite a strong inducement in the form of financial aid from the government towards rental expenses.

In Droitwich, the town centre proposals envisaged a single health centre stategically sited within the inner ring road — although, as discussed in Chapter 10, the siting of this and other civic facilities was to become a matter of dispute at the public inquiry. A context for negotiations with the established local doctors was established in the form of an *ad hoc* consultative committee on which were represented the doctors, the County Medical Officer, and the local Health Executive Council, as the organ of the National Health Service through which relationships with local contractors were managed. However, this was to meet only twice in five years while the fate of the town centre was uncertain. In the County Medical Officer's experience, any detailed bargaining over layout and facilities could only realistically begin after a firm decision on a site had been reached; any advance commitments on such points were always subject to changes of mind on the part of the local doctors. At Redditch, the corresponding negotiations were made more complex because the size of the New Town was such as to justify construction of two or more health centres, at least in the longer term. It also meant that some new practices would have to be established through the Executive Council, and some sensitive points arose in planning the areas to be served and the location of the buildings, form the point of view of their effects on existing practices.

Many of the community health services operated by the County until 1974, and by the Area Health Authorities thereafter, could be planned in conjunction with new health centre buildings; and here again, as in the case of gas supply and education, expanding communities such as Droitwich tended to attract priority because of the comparative ease with which technical or organizational innovations could be introduced. A somewhat different case was provided by the ambulance service, operated until 1974 through a special joint committee covering both the County and City of Worcester. Here, community demand for a local station at Droitwich to meet emergency needs was quickly mobilized following one serious local accident, raising in an acute form the pervasive problem of balancing improvements of operating economy against the value of human life.

In Droitwich itself, as in other County areas, matters of environmental health were the concern of a District Medical Officer, who held part-time appointments as a member of both the County and Borough staffs, and also served two nearby Rural Districts. Although we have already encountered him playing a direct role in the planning of the Newtown General Improvement Area, his role in the planning of community care services was largely confined to the provision of occasional advice, based on detailed knowledge of the personal health risks implicit in different aspects of the local environment of Droitwich and its surroundings areas. After 1974, environmental health was destined to remain a local authority function at the level of the new County District; but, in the preceding years, the question of reorganization was one that clearly overshadowed the planning processes of all those concerned in the provision of health care, at all levels from the highly specialized facilities provided by the teaching hospitals to the most modest local environmental services.

The planning of local bus routes: a service in decline

In the early seventies, the provision of local passenger transport had become another field in which traditional organizational responsibilities were becoming increasingly subject to challenge. Many local rail services had been withdrawn, leaving the maintenance of local passenger transport networks increasingly to the bus operators. In the rural areas, most services were operated by local subsidiaries of the government-controlled National Bus Company, including the 'Midland Red' Omnibus Company, whose network covered most of the West Midlands Region. However, with the spread of car ownership, their services had become increasingly poorly patronized and uneconomic, and frequent applications for the withdrawal of particular routes were made to the regional Traffic Commissioners – a public body responsible for ensuring that local interests were taken into account in changes of operating policy.

Recognising the social costs of any run-down of public transport services for reasons of operating efficiency, the Transport Act of 1968 had introduced new forms of encouragement towards the maintenance of routes in both urban and rural areas. In four main conurbations, including that of the West Midlands, new Passenger Transport Executives were introduced for the co-ordinated planning of road and rail services, and for the direct operation of urban bus routes hitherto run by municipal undertakings. These agencies were required to work within the policy guidance of Passenger Transport Authorities whose members would be appointed by the local authorities in the area. In the rural areas, the government announced a readiness to encourage County and District Councils to pay operating subsidies towards those bus routes providing a local social benefit, by undertaking to repay half the amount of any local subsidy that could not be recouped in the form of increased revenue from fares.

To County Councils such as Worcestershire, the operation of public transport undertakings was a much less familiar field than it was to the large urban local authorities. To formulate a County policy, the County's General Purposes Committee appointed in 1970 a special Public Transport Sub-Committee, which was able to report in the following year the results of a County-wide survey of local bus operations, and to put forward to the Council three possible strategies. The first was to pay no subsidies and allow the decline of local services to continue; the second was to discover how far local services might be taken over by small private operators who were sustained mainly by coach touring and school contracts, perhaps at a comparatively modest level of subsidy; while the third was to provide subsidies directly to the Midland Red Company. It was suggested that this last solution should require joint contributions from the County and from the District Councils which benefited from each route, working according to a carefully devised set of rules for apportionment. The Sub-Committee judged this third approach the most practicable in current circumstances and it was recommended for adoption on a trial basis; but, in the Council Chamber, it was endorsed only after a wide-ranging debate on its social, financial, and organizational implications. As the Chairman of the County Council concluded, the situation was one in which the County could proceed only in short steps, keeping options open until further experience could be accumulated.

In Droitwich, the question of operating subsidies arose over the build-up of services to link the new Chawson and Boycott housing areas to the industrial estate and the town centre respectively. The Midland Red Company had at first shown little interest in the provision of such town services, which could be expected to be unprofitable in the earlier years of development. Later, however, they agreed to provide services when presented with the threat of these being initiated by a local private operator. After some two years of operation, however, the company applied to withdraw the Boycott service, and the County and Borough Council were unable to agree on a basis for joint subsidization. The deadlock was resolved when again the local private operator agreed to take over the service, at a reduced frequency. But the economics of bus operation remained such that there persisted a state of continuing uncertainty over the future of these arteries in the town's internal communication system which, although short, were nevertheless highly significant for those who did not have ready access to private car transport.

The planning of physical recreation facilities

The provision of facilities for physical recreation — including the upkeep of recreation grounds, playing fields and swimming baths, and the mobilization of relevant team or club activities — is a field that has always depended heavily on local initiative, so that any public involvement has usually been regarded as a matter of primary concern for District Councils. However, it also impinges on the County Education Committees as providers of school playing fields and indoor sports facilities. In addition, it has become accepted that many of the more modern or specialized forms of recreational provision, such as swimming pools, athletic stadia and indoor sports halls, can serve a sub-regional or regional catchment area.

During the nineteen-sixties, the government introduced a policy for the provision of financial aid towards local facilities through the machinery of a national Sports Council, wherever there was a local willingness to support for such facilities through public funds. In the West Midlands, as in other regions, a regional Sports Council was appointed to advise the government on strategy for the provision of grants and the dispensation of loan sanctions for local authority projects, especially where there was a risk of duplication of facilities between neighbouring centres.

In Droitwich, one of the Borough Council's five standing committees was concerned with Parks, Open Spaces, and the Droitwich Lido, while the Development Committee also established a Sports and Leisure Sub-Committee to concern itself with new facilities in the Town Development Area. Although both committees were chaired by the same Borough Councillor, there were problems to be resolved of relative priority for open space schemes in the Salwarpe Valley in the west and in the expanding areas of private housing outside the Town Development Area to the east. Such problems were exacerbated by uncertainties over sources of finance for open space development in the Town Development Area, similar in nature to those affecting local road building discussed in Chapter 6. In addition to the question of allocation of costs between the Town Development and local rate accounts, there were questions to be negotiated of the possible eligibility of projects for support through a special amenity grant for expanding towns, which was introduced only in 1970 after some sustained advocacy through the Town Development Executive Committee.

A further difficult interface of negotiation, in Droitwich as in many other towns, concerned the availability of school playing-fields for general community use. As indicated in *Figure 31,* the playing fields of the large new Droitwich High School at Briar Mill covered a strategic cross-section of the Salwarpe Valley area, in which the main open space provision for the new housing estates was to be located. A report prepared by the Group Planner in 1969 demonstrated that the question of whether or not 'dual use' of the school playing fields was to be permitted could make a crucial difference to the adequacy or otherwise of local open space provision according to currently accepted standards.

The issue of dual use also arose over the school's proposed provision of a swimming pool, a gymnasium, and hard open spaces such as tennis courts, with a possibility that the gymnasium might be extended so as to meet the anticipated demands in the town for a multi-purpose sports hall. However, the loan sanction regulations of the Education Ministry required that the local District Council should show a readiness to make a direct contribution, in capital and manpower, to any developments of this kind; and ultimately, it was only found possible to negotiate over the provision of very limited changing-room and storage facilities to meet the demands of general community use. This left the external use of the school facilities primarily within the discretion of the youth and community service of the County Education Department; a solution, which in the experience of the Development Group officers, was not likely to encourage a high level of participation by local voluntary groups. As in the issue of dual use generally, the underlying problem was one of demarcation of management responsibilities, extending to matters of fine operational detail. For the school caretaker or groundsman, some stressful uncertainties could arise over such questions as the responsibility for any damage done, which could not easily be resolved through prior arrangement at the level of negotiation between local authority departments and any voluntary bodies concerned.

The co-ordination of services for expanding communities

At this point, a sufficient range of community services has been reviewed from a functional perspective to allow us to turn to the general question of avoiding imbalances between them during the implementation of a local expansion programme. The experience of the early New Towns had soon demonstrated the kinds of physical imbalance that could arise through the difficulties of co-ordination between the agency responsible for housing and industrial development and those responsible for basic elements of infrastructure such as electricity, gas, sewerage, and water networks. However, it was not until the immigration of new residents had built up some momentum that another kind of imbalance became apparent; that between the provision of housing and the various types of social and recreational facility that were required to foster a sense of community among the newcomers. In some New Towns in particular, the high priority attached to housing, and to any clearly essential services such as schools, left the population without access to 'many of the opportunities for the use of leisure time to which they had been accustomed in their previous urban environment; and the phrase 'new town blues' began to acquire common currency throughout Britain.

In the New Towns, the importance of making special provision for the development of social facilities was recognised by means of a provision whereby central grants could be obtained towards the provision of such amenities as community meetings halls and recreation grounds, at a level of up to £4 per head of planned population. The problems of expanding towns were not quite so straightforward to deal with on the basis of a simple formula; but the importance of the problem was demonstrated in two reports sponsored by a governmental advisory group, the Central Housing Advisory Committee. The first of these, *The First Hundred Families* (Ministry of Housing and Local Government, 1965) concentrated on the problems of new arrivals; while the second, *The Needs of New Communities* (Ministry of Housing and Local Government, 1967) turned to the problems of co-ordination in the later stages of development.

Among the recommendations was a proposal for the provision of specific but discretionary 'amenity grants' towards projects that could be demonstrated to be important in terms of social development, with each case negotiated on its merits. Also, it was recommended that each expanding town should appoint a Social Relations Officer, following a precedent that had already been established in some New Town Development Corporations. This could provide an organizational focus both for the infusion of an element of social planning into the local development programme, and also for building up the various networks of voluntary community activity which it was important to encourage during the crucial early stages of expansion.

The Community Development Officer at Droitwich

At Droitwich, the Group Administrator had been conscious since the early years of the expansion programme of the value of adding to his staff an officer concerned with the broad field of social relations or community development, as discussed in *The Needs of New Communities*, even though there had been no explicit provision for such a post in the agreement.

It was during 1968, when the build-up of population on the Chawson and Boycott estates was beginning to gather momentum, that a basis for setting up such a role was finally agreed. A post of Community Development Officer was created on the staff of the County Clerk's Department, on the understanding that the occupant would be seconded initially to the Droitwich Development Group on a full-time basis, with an expectation of re-assignment later to other expanding communities within the County. The individual appointed was a retired army officer who had previously been responsible for the County's civil defence organization, only recently disbanded. Upon taking up his new post he gained some initial experience in community development work through a short attachment to the noted pioneering group at Telford New Town.

Working largely on his own, with the advice and encouragement of the Group Administrator, the Droitwich Community Development Officer found himself faced with wide-ranging terms of reference. In a series of discussions with us during 1971 and 1972, he identified his main functions as falling within four broad areas. The first and most demanding task was the mobilization and support of voluntary community groups. The other tasks, which had to be fitted in as time permitted, were concerned with the public relations of the Development Group at a more personal level; with the commissioning of some modest exercises in the collection and analysis of survey information on the changing characteristics of communities within the town; and with the forward planning of social and sporting facilities. For instance, he contributed a section on local voluntary organizations and their future requirements to the comprehensive report on the planning of social and recreational facilities for Droitwich, which was submitted by the Group Planner Architect in 1969 to the Sports and Leisure Sub-Committee of the joint Development Committee.

More explicitly than in the case of any other officer of the Group, the role of the Community Development Officer was concerned primarily with the management of informal decision networks. During his first year or so, one of his primary concerns lay in the use of part of the large Norbury House building in the town centre (*Figure 53*) as a community centre within which the activities of voluntary community organizations could be accommodated. Here, he encountered difficulties over such questions as rentals and priorities for the hire of rooms; such problems were complicated by the differing perspectives of the Borough Council as landlord, and the Development Committee as management agency with an interest in stimulating forms of use that could attract the newer residents of the town. Eventually, the difficulty of resolving such disputes led the Group Administrator to propose that the Community Development Officer should withdraw from active involvement in the Norbury Community Centre, leaving its management exclusively in the hands of the local Borough Council.

With the development of the new Chawson and Boycott housing estates, attention turned towards the provision of social facilities at the neighbourhood level. On the first estate at Chawson, the Community Development Officer played a catalytic role in the formation of a new Droitwich Community Association and in the provision of a meeting hall, after some extensive negotiations over finance between the Development Group Officers and the Housing Ministry. Here again, differences emerged within the Development Committee over the extent to which rentals should be subsidized; and a formula was eventually agreed whereby the support would be provided on a decreasing scale during the early years. For the Community Association, this created a problem of meeting running expenses at a level that would be difficult to afford through voluntary contributions alone; and one solution advocated within the Association was the provision of a bar which could become a source of direct profit. However, the experience of the Development Group Officers indicated that this solution would reduce the availability of the meeting hall to some of the sections of the community among whom they were most anxious to encourage social activity, including the youth of the neighbourhood. Once again, when the decision to install a bar was taken against his advice, the Community Development Officer found it necessary to withdraw from an active promotional role in a centre of community activity which he had helped to foster, although he continued to maintain informal contacts and provide advice as and when required.

The problems of the Boycott Estate

In the larger housing estate at Boycott, the physical provisions for community activity were more ambitious, including a meeting hall provided by the Roman Catholic Church as well as one for general neighbourhood use. Here, the Community Development Officer was instrumental in achieving the formation of a variety of voluntary neighbourhood groups — a process which involved making contact with the national and regional organisers of several established voluntary organizations, in the attempt to persuade them that there was a sufficient level of support in the expanding population at Droitwich to justify the giving of immediate priority to the formation of new local branches.

One of the more vigorous groups established at Boycott was a branch of the Townswomen's Guild, which became active in pressing for such facilities on the estate as a doctor's surgery, a resident nurse or midwife, a pharmaceutical chemist, and a library service. These pressures highlighted the considerable degree of isolation of the Boycott estate from the remainder of the town, accentuated by the delays which had been encountered in developing the intervening Salwarpe Valley area and Westacre housing estate. At one stage, the local press was able to draw attention to these problems under the headline 'Boycott, a World on its Own', alleging a high rate of petty criminal offences compared with other parts of the town, and attributing this to a lack of leisure facilities comparable to those to which the residents had been accustomed within the conurbation.

A survey commissioned by the Community Development Officer, and executed by a student interviewer, compared the social structures and perceived needs of residents in Boycott, Chawson, and two of the older-established areas of the town. Among the early residents of the Boycott estate, the analysis indicated a high level of car ownership, coupled with an initial dependence on commuting to Birmingham for work. Among both Boycott and Chawson residents, the main deficiencies were felt to be in the fields of shopping facilities, social activities, and local bus services; and the dearth of

social facilities was taken up as a primary theme by the Droitwich
Labour Party in the annual municipal elections.

During the survey exercise, the interviewer reported having
encountered a variety of signs of lack of contact between older and
newer residents, at times degenerating into antagonism. Several cases
of social discrimination were quoted, as well as occasional instances
of deliberate overcharging of newcomers by shopkeepers in the town
centre. However, a more optimistic picture was presented by a later
survey which indicated that the proportion of incoming families who
later opted to return to city life was appreciably lower than in most
comparable new and expanding towns at a similar stage in their
development. To the Community Development Officer, one of the
most rewarding moments came in early 1973 when it was agreed to
reconstitute the local Boycott Club as the Boycott Community
Association, embracing a wide range of activities and opening up a
new channel for representation of local views, which might well
increase in significance with the impending transfer of powers to new
and more remote local authorities.

The decision network of the Community Development Officer

A further initiative with which the Community Development Officer
became associated was the establishment of an Information Centre at
a strategic point in the centre of town. Staffed mainly through
volunteers on a rota basis, this centre became for him a valuable
means of making contact with new residents of the private housing
areas as well as of the Town Development estates, and fostering
activities that could help in breaking down the social and geographical barriers between them. A major part of the work of the centre
concerned the distribution of directories of local recreational clubs
and facilities; but, where in doubt, the volunteer on duty could
always refer a caller to the Community Development Officer for
answers to queries, and he in turn could pass these on to the
appropriate officer of the Development Group or Borough Council.

As a means of maintaining informal liaison with the whole range
of statutory and voluntary agencies concerned in community work in
Droitwich, the Community Development Officer decided to institute
a series of monthly lunch-time meetings, the declared purpose of
which was to hear a talk by an invited speaker on some aspect of
community relations. In practice, the meetings provided the more
general function of allowing personal relationships to develop
between local authority social workers, clergy, probation officers,
and representatives of voluntary and charitable groups working in

Droitwich. In the belief of the Community Development Officer, this opportunity for informal contact made an important contribution to the development of effective co-ordination among the various social services operating within the town.

Figure 67 indicates the Community Development Officer's view of his total network of relationships in relation to his overlapping tasks of mobilization of voluntary activities, of co-ordination between social service agencies, and of provision of information to incoming residents. As in the case of the networks considered in the previous chapter, the relationships that could be considered a necessary part of the role of the Community Development Officer were comparatively few, focusing on the Group Administrator, to whom he was directly accountable, the Deputy Group Administrator, the Borough Housing Manager, and the County Social Services Department. At the same time, the effectiveness with which the role could be performed in practice depended on the maintenance of close relationships with such diverse actors as community leaders in the new housing areas, local press reporters, representatives of the Droitwich Industries Association, and civil servants involved in various forms of grant aid and encouragement to local community activities.

Thus, to a more evident degree than in the case of any other officer at Droitwich, the ability of the Community Development Officer to play his role in the expansion of Droitwich depended on the cultivation of network-managing or 'reticulist' skills, from an organizational base of very little formal power or authority. However, his status as a member of the Development Group staff, on secondment from the County Council, did provide him with the support of other members of a close-knit local working team. It also provided him with a context within which to weigh up some difficult tactical problems, such as that of whether to continue playing a direct operational role in the Norbury Community Centre and, later, the Community Association on the Chawson estate, after decisions had been taken that were judged not to be in the wider interests of community development within the town.

Local co-ordination of external agencies

The problem of maintaining a local co-ordinative influence over the operations of external agencies, many with powerful internal motivating forces and well-developed planning processes of their own, was one which had already been confronted in a number of other guises at Droitwich before the role of the Community Development Officer had become clearly established.

Figure 67 Network relationships of Community Development Officer for co-ordinating responsibilities in Droitwich

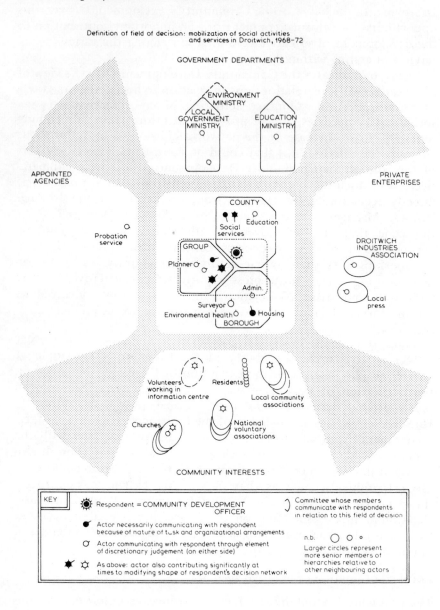

Definition of field of decision: mobilization of social activities and services in Droitwich, 1968-72

GOVERNMENT DEPARTMENTS

APPOINTED AGENCIES

PRIVATE ENTERPRISES

ENVIRONMENT MINISTRY

LOCAL GOVERNMENT MINISTRY

EDUCATION MINISTRY

COUNTY

Social services

Education

Probation service

GROUP

Planner

Admin.

DROITWICH INDUSTRIES ASSOCIATION

Surveyor

Environmental health

Housing

BOROUGH

Local press

Volunteers working in information centre

Residents

Local community associations

Churches

National voluntary associations

COMMUNITY INTERESTS

KEY

Respondent = COMMUNITY DEVELOPMENT OFFICER

Actor necessarily communicating with respondent because of nature of task and organizational arrangements

Actor communicating with respondent through element of discretionary judgement (on either side)

As above: actor also contributing significantly at times to modifying shape of respondent's decision network

Committee whose members communicate with respondents in relation to this field of decision

n.b.

Larger circles represent more senior members of hierarchies relative to other neighbouring actors

From the time of the early negotiations over the expansion scheme discussed in Chapter 4, it had fallen to the County Planning staff to maintain communications with other county departments and with water, gas, and electricity undertakings, over questions of the implications for specific services of alternative rates of growth for the expanding town. However, the written statement prepared in 1963 as a basis for the Town Development agreement included only the most general of guidelines relating to the scale of provision of public utility networks, education, open spaces, churches, and places of assembly and entertainment, reflecting the difficulty of attempting to commit the various agencies concerned to precise undertakings at such an early stage.

After signature of the agreement, relationships with other public agencies were placed on a somewhat more formal plane by letters from the County Clerk to the gas, electricity, telephone, and water authorities, officially notifying them of the town development commitment and asking them to give due priority to the expansion of their respective services so as to avoid any delays in implementation of the overall programme. Similar letters were also sent to the Chief Officers of specialist departments of the County Council. However, the difficulties of extracting precise commitments in response were highlighted by a reply from the County Education Officer, saying that he would do his best to collaborate but would give no firm guarantee of his ability to do so. He pointed out that the programming of school building was subject to rigorous control by the Education Ministry, and was liable to unpredictable fluctuations from year to year because of the attempts of central government to control the performance of the economy through restrictions on local authority capital spending.

As the staff of the Development Group began to build up, so there began to develop a variety of *ad hoc* arrangements for maintaining local co-ordination over the activities of external agencies. Many of these have already been discussed in this and preceding chapters: the Group Engineer's co-ordinating role in relation to the public utility undertakings, the work of the central area team in reconciling complex relocation problems, as indicated in *Figure 56*, and the review of leisure activities initiated by the Group Planner Architect. Also, instances arose from time to time where the loan sanction procedures of different government departments had to be co-ordinated on the basis of local information if inconvenience or diseconomy was to be avoided in the planning of development operations, as again in the relocation problem analysed in *Figure 56* and also in the case of securing local sources of soil for the Salwarpe Road embankment.

Such instances indicate the inadequacy of any model of 'co-ordination' which views the process entirely as one of maintaining consistency between various sectional activities from the vantage point of a central body within which superior resources of authority or financial control are concentrated. Within the field of local and regional change, an equally necessary element of 'management' is the ability of local actors to perform a role of 'inverted' co-ordination over the operations of external agencies, working from a position of little or no formal authority in order to modify procedures of corporate planning and control which may often have been developed to a high pitch of internal effectiveness. No matter how effective such procedures may be, they are inevitably tailored primarily to sectional aims. It is thus not realistic to expect them to respond equally quickly to the complex local interactions between decision problems in their own and other specialist fields, without the stimulus provided by other actors who are steeped in knowledge of the structural characteristics of the local planning situation, and who can utilize this knowledge through the largely informal deployment of reticulist influence and skills.

At the local level, it is significant that the patterns of interaction between different services can be very different from the patterns that are recognized as important at the level of national policy formation. For instance, gas and electricity supplies are clearly linked at the national policy level as alternative forms of energy supply dependent largely on fossil fuels, as indicated in *Figure 65*. However, at the level of trenching operations on a building-site, the strongest connections are those between gas and water supply, as services dependent on pipe-laying operations, and between electricty and telephone systems, as services dependent on cable-laying operations, providing two different (though by no means independent) foci of co-ordination for the local engineer which cross-cut the national policy fields of energy, communication, and water resource systems.

The general point about differences between local and national foci of co-ordination can be further illustrated by a final case example from Droitwich. This will bring together several of the topics considered in Part II in a rather unexpected way, and will also bring us back to the distinctive local resource of Droitwich from which much of its history derives — the subterranean salt deposits.

The future of the Droitwich brine baths

The St Andrew's Brine Baths were built in 1887, occupying a focal position in the centre of Droitwich, as indicated in *Figure 53*. To the officers of the Development Group and to the Borough Council, the baths provided a form of existing asset whose future was by no means clear, as in the cases of the Newtown residential neighbourhood and the Droitwich canal discussed in Chapter 11.

The Brine Baths had for many years provided a somewhat unusual but wide-ranging set of facilities for the treatment of rheumatic and orthopaedic conditions, based on the extreme buoyancy of the local brine solution. These included a large brine pool open to the general public, a smaller remedial pool, immersion and aeration baths and douches. In attendance was a permanent staff of physiotherapists, some with specialist qualifications, and management was provided through a non-profit Droitwich Medical Trust, including both medical and lay representatives. Patients were regularly referred for treatment under the provisions of the National Health Service, until in 1968 the Birmingham Regional Hospital Board came to a decision to withdraw their support, as it was argued that alternative outpatient facilities could be provided at a specialized hospital already within their management only a short distance from the centre of Droitwich.

This threw into doubt the whole future of the Brine Baths building, but the West Midlands Sports Council agreed to recommend the government to give loan sanction for its purchase by the Borough Council, on the grounds that a major part of the building might well be converted for sports and social use. Acquisition was speedily completed just before the end of the financial year 1970/71 for which the loan sanction had been approved, but there remained many possible combinations of uses to be considered, offering different levels of recreational benefit to the local community, of attractiveness to commercial operators, of return to the ratepayers, and of facilities for the nucleus of local medical specialists who had earned a living by providing treatments for private patients under the administrative umbrella of the Droitwich Medical Trust.

As in the case of the GIA and the canal, an *ad hoc* working party of officers was set up, reporting to the Development Committee, as the baths were sited inside the Town Development boundary. One possibility foreseen by the Borough members was the conversion of the building for use as a health centre, thus resolving one of the more contentious points over siting of civic buildings in the new central area redevelopment; but technical studies quickly showed this not to be a feasible solution. Other ideas submitted by various interested persons and organizations included provision of sauna bath facilities, a health food restaurant, a sports hall, and a youth centre to be managed by the youth and community service of the County

Education Committee. So far as future medical use was concerned, one of the more difficult problems concerned the practicalities of continuing to combine orthodox medical treatments with others such as osteopathy, which were not approved by the General Medical Council.

In the management of this complex network of interests, the Group Administrator assumed a leading role. After a steadily increasing level of activity during 1971 and 1972, the Working Party was able to reach agreement only on the elimination of some of the more extreme options, and recommend that further external discussions should still be maintained on a variety of fronts, with a view to ultimate joint use by some or all of the Borough Council as landlord, the County Youth Service, the local medical practitioners providing 'ethical' forms of treatment, and one or more commercial undertakings providing restaurant, sauna, or other recreational facilities. Among the more prominent difficulties encountered by the Development Group staff were those of ensuring the continuing operation of the various activities in the building while the changes were planned and implemented, and of keeping local Councillors adequately briefed on the intricate organizational and financial issues which were encountered. Such difficulties were exacerbated by uncertainties in the split of responsibilities between the Development Committee and the Borough Council, and, as the date of local government reorganization approached, questions of allocation of expenditures and distribution of assets among the successor authorities began to loom increasingly large over the discussions. Thus, the particular local issue of the Brine Baths, involving a somewhat unusual conjunction of external and local interests, came to add a further complexity to the already intricate relationships between the Borough and the Development Group, and to tax to the full the reticulist skills of the Group Administrator and some of his colleagues.

Droitwich as a base for generalization

In Part II, the circumstances of Droitwich have been used as a reference point in considering a wide range of problems and organizational relationships, many of which we believe to have close counterparts elsewhere. In Part III, this extended case example will be used as a basis for the articulation of some more general propositions, leading to discussion of some opportunities for future evolution in the management of local and regional change. Like all case histories, that of Droitwich of course has its atypical features:

the role of the salt deposits in its economic history, the (politically controversial) commitment to a fourfold expansion of population with an element of planned immigration from an overcrowded city, and the unusual organizational arrangements for joint working between District and County Councils.

As we have seen in this chapter, the status of Droitwich as an expanding town itself meant that it attracted special priority in the introduction of new technologies or organizational forms in the fields of gas supply, education, and health. In Part III, we shall wish to concern ourselves also with communities whose problems are those of decline rather than expansion, as in the inner city areas where the less mobile and economically self-sufficient sectors of the population tend to become more concentrated, with the consequence that any investment in the renovation of local services tends to become a more difficult matter, and to assume a lower priority in the programmes of service-providing agencies.

Running throughout the Droitwich case history has been a continuing volatility in the political, economic, and technological environment within which the local actors have had to work, placing a premium on flexibility in the processes of decision-making, as opposed merely to competence in working within a pre-arranged organizational framework. In Part III, we shall be similarly concerned to retain flexibility in looking beyond the specific types of circumstance that prevailed between 1964 and 1973 in the management of expansion schemes under the Town Development Act — itself in all probability no more than a transient form of organization for the achievement of planned local and regional change. We shall therefore seek to address ourselves to more far-reaching problems of government and social organization for exercising influence over an environment which, in the words of Schon (1971), had passed beyond the stable state; but, in facing this ambitious task, we shall find it helpful from time to time to return to the local perspective of Droitwich and the regional perspective of the West Midlands, as the constituencies of public interest concerned confront the new contextual changes and uncertainties introduced by the 1974 reforms of local government in England.

Part **III** Outlooks

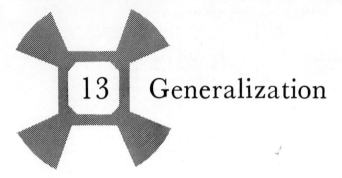

13　Generalization

Retrospect and prospect

Taken together, the case studies of Part II provide a body of evidence that demonstrates the many dimensions of complexity to be understood in any attempt to appreciate fully the processes of public intervention in local and regional change. In Part III, our concern will be to use the evidence so far assembled as a point of departure in developing some general arguments and hypotheses relating to the future evolution of public planning, and subsequently in suggesting certain forms of innovation and experiment through which some realistic progress might be achieved.

The relationship of the present chapter to those that precede and follow it is outlined in *Figure 68*. In the course of this chapter, a series of linked propositions about public planning will be presented, leading towards the articulation of some general guidelines addressed to all those who share a concern to bring about changes in the decision-making processes of public and private agencies. As *Figure 68* indicates, the most direct influence on the framing of the propositions has been the body of evidence accumulated through the Droitwich case studies, as interpreted through the approach to analysis presented in Chapter 2. However, a further indirect influence has been the experience of a number of other research projects in which the authors have become involved at certain times during the

Figure 68   The process of generalization in context

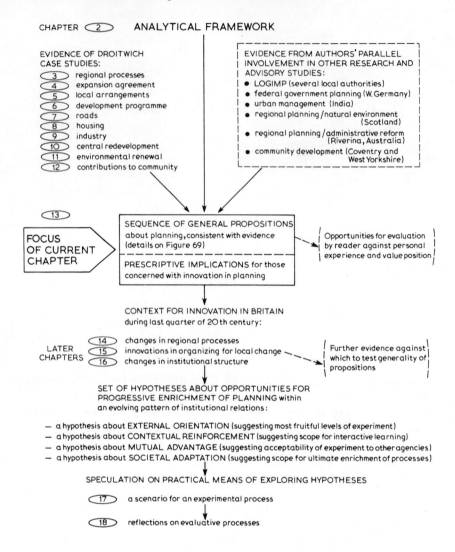

CHAPTER ⟨2⟩   **ANALYTICAL FRAMEWORK**

EVIDENCE OF DROITWICH
CASE STUDIES:
- ⟨3⟩ regional processes
- ⟨4⟩ expansion agreement
- ⟨5⟩ local arrangements
- ⟨6⟩ development programme
- ⟨7⟩ roads
- ⟨8⟩ housing
- ⟨9⟩ industry
- ⟨10⟩ central redevelopment
- ⟨11⟩ environmental renewal
- ⟨12⟩ contributions to community

EVIDENCE FROM AUTHORS' PARALLEL
INVOLVEMENT IN OTHER RESEARCH AND
ADVISORY STUDIES:
- LOGIMP (several local authorities)
- federal government planning (W. Germany)
- urban management (India)
- regional planning / natural environment
  (Scotland)
- regional planning / administrative reform
  (Riverina, Australia)
- community development (Coventry and
  West Yorkshire)

⟨13⟩

FOCUS
OF CURRENT
CHAPTER

SEQUENCE OF GENERAL PROPOSITIONS
about planning, consistent with evidence
(details on Figure 69)

PRESCRIPTIVE IMPLICATIONS for those
concerned with innovation in planning

Opportunities for evaluation
by reader against personal
experience and value position

CONTEXT FOR INNOVATION IN BRITAIN
during last quarter of 20th century:

LATER
CHAPTERS
- ⟨14⟩ changes in regional processes
- ⟨15⟩ innovations in organizing for local change
- ⟨16⟩ changes in institutional structure

Further evidence against
which to test generality of
propositions

SET OF HYPOTHESES ABOUT OPPORTUNITIES FOR
PROGRESSIVE ENRICHMENT OF PLANNING within
an evolving pattern of institutional relations:

— a hypothesis about EXTERNAL ORIENTATION (suggesting most fruitful levels of experiment)
— a hypothesis about CONTEXTUAL REINFORCEMENT (suggesting scope for interactive learning)
— a hypothesis about MUTUAL ADVANTAGE (suggesting acceptability of experiment to other agencies)
— a hypothesis about SOCIETAL ADAPTATION (suggesting scope for ultimate enrichment of processes)

SPECULATION ON PRACTICAL MEANS OF EXPLORING HYPOTHESES

⟨17⟩ a scenario for an experimental process

⟨18⟩ reflections on evaluative processes

Droitwich work, and also the earlier experience in Coventry, in Australia, and elsewhere, through which the analytical framework of Chapter 2 first began to evolve. Clearly, it would be rash for us to formulate general propositions in such a form that we did not believe them to be at least broadly consistent with these various experiences relating to other contexts and levels of public planning, some of which have involved our working in an advisory or catalytic role rather than merely as observers.

In succeeding chapters, we shall explore the particular context for innovation in planning that exists in Great Britain (and more specifically in England) upon entering the last quarter of the twentieth century. We shall look first at developments in regional planning networks, then at changing forms of organization for inducing local change, and finally at some important changes in institutional structure. This will provide some further evidence from beyond Droitwich against which to evaluate the wider validity of the propositions formed in the present chapter, and will lead us in Chapter 16 to formulate a set of four more specific hypotheses which, we shall argue, can be explored through programmes of conscious experimentation involving participation at several different levels of community and government organization. In order to give a sense of direction to the argument that follows, a preliminary glimpse of the content of these hypotheses is given near the foot of *Figure 68*.

Such hypotheses are clearly not of a kind that can realistically be tested under laboratory conditions. Indeed, following the arguments of Popper (1968), they must be regarded as open to falsification through experience, but not as verifiable in any conclusive sense. Like the more general propositions that precede them, the hypotheses are offered first for evaluation by the reader in the light of his or her personal experience and values, and second, as prospective guidelines to the mobilization of societal or governmental action.

A sequence of general propositions

Figure 69 sets out, in as compact a form as possible, the sequence of general propositions that we shall develop in this chapter, relating each successive proposition to the type of evidence from our Droitwich case studies through which it can be supported. Our starting point is the definition of public planning that was first presented at the end of Chapter 2, in the following terms:

Public planning is the domain of all processes wherein people acting on behalf of publicly accountable agencies take part in the

Figure 69   A sequence of general propositions

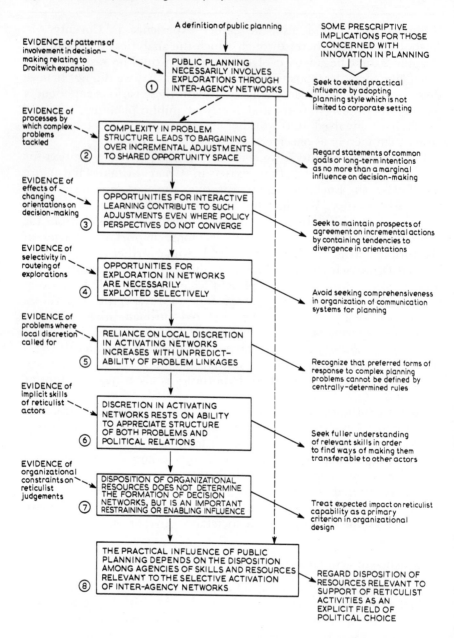

A definition of public planning

SOME PRESCRIPTIVE IMPLICATIONS FOR THOSE CONCERNED WITH INNOVATION IN PLANNING

EVIDENCE of patterns of involvement in decision-making relating to Droitwich expansion

① PUBLIC PLANNING NECESSARILY INVOLVES EXPLORATIONS THROUGH INTER-AGENCY NETWORKS

Seek to extend practical influence by adopting planning style which is not limited to corporate setting

EVIDENCE of processes by which complex problems tackled

② COMPLEXITY IN PROBLEM STRUCTURE LEADS TO BARGAINING OVER INCREMENTAL ADJUSTMENTS TO SHARED OPPORTUNITY SPACE

Regard statements of common goals or long-term intentions as no more than a marginal influence on decision-making

EVIDENCE of effects of changing orientations on decision-making

③ OPPORTUNITIES FOR INTERACTIVE LEARNING CONTRIBUTE TO SUCH ADJUSTMENTS EVEN WHERE POLICY PERSPECTIVES DO NOT CONVERGE

Seek to maintain prospects of agreement on incremental actions by containing tendencies to divergence in orientations

EVIDENCE of selectivity in routeing of explorations

④ OPPORTUNITIES FOR EXPLORATION IN NETWORKS ARE NECESSARILY EXPLOITED SELECTIVELY

Avoid seeking comprehensiveness in organization of communication systems for planning

EVIDENCE of problems where local discretion called for

⑤ RELIANCE ON LOCAL DISCRETION IN ACTIVATING NETWORKS INCREASES WITH UNPREDICT-ABILITY OF PROBLEM LINKAGES

Recognize that preferred forms of response to complex planning problems cannot be defined by centrally-determined rules

EVIDENCE of implicit skills of reticulist actors

⑥ DISCRETION IN ACTIVATING NETWORKS RESTS ON ABILITY TO APPRECIATE STRUCTURE OF BOTH PROBLEMS AND POLITICAL RELATIONS

Seek fuller understanding of relevant skills in order to find ways of making them transferable to other actors

EVIDENCE of organizational constraints on reticulist judgements

⑦ DISPOSITION OF ORGANIZATIONAL RESOURCES DOES NOT DETERMINE THE FORMATION OF DECISION NETWORKS, BUT IS AN IMPORTANT RESTRAINING OR ENABLING INFLUENCE

Treat expected impact on reticulist capability as a primary criterion in organizational design

⑧ THE PRACTICAL INFLUENCE OF PUBLIC PLANNING DEPENDS ON THE DISPOSITION AMONG AGENCIES OF SKILLS AND RESOURCES RELEVANT TO THE SELECTIVE ACTIVATION OF INTER-AGENCY NETWORKS

REGARD DISPOSITION OF RESOURCES RELEVANT TO SUPPORT OF RETICULIST ACTIVITIES AS AN EXPLICIT FIELD OF POLITICAL CHOICE

exploration of patterns of related choices which are of recognised concern to more than one constituency of public or private interest.

Beginning from this definition, we shall argue that exploratory activities which transcend agency boundaries form an inescapable part of public planning; that the more complex becomes the perceived structure of problems, the more likely it is that commitments to action will emerge as incremental adjustments to the shared 'opportunity space' of the participants; and that the influence of the exploratory process over these commitments to action depends on the opportunities created for continuing mutual adjustment of perspectives between the actors concerned. It will be argued that communications within the network of possible participants in the decision process are necessarily initiated on a selective basis, in a way that depends not only on judgements introduced from positions of central authority but also on the reticulist skills of actors at a rich variety of more peripheral points; and it will be postulated that such skills are necessarily founded on a capacity to appreciate both the structure of decision problems and the corresponding structure of organizational and political relations. We shall then postulate that the development and deployment of reticulist skills can be inhibited or encouraged, but cannot be automatically assured, by decisions about the distribution of organizational resources among different publicly accountable agencies; so that the practical influence of public planning activities on decision-making can be enhanced through a more conscious consideration of the opportunities for deployment of reticulist skill within any projected structure of formal organizational relations.

For those who have a concern to bring about changes in the processes of public planning, for whatever reason, the implication of these propositions is that they should look on the disposition of reticulist resources among agencies as an explicit field of organizational choice, and, to this end, they should explore whatever opportunities for innovation or experiment may be found in the specific set of environmental and institutional circumstances within which they are currently working.

The limitations of the corporate frame of reference

The sequence of propositions in *Figure 69* begins with a statement that exploratory activities which cut across the boundaries between agencies form an inescapable feature of public planning. Even if our own chosen definition of public planning is accepted – with its emphasis on fields of choice which are of recognised concern to more than one constituency of public and private interest – this first proposition is not an automatic consequence. Rather, it rests on a body of evidence from the Droitwich case studies to the effect that, at several different levels of the planning process, sets of pressures emerge which of necessity bring together parties who are accountable to different sets of interests in some form of joint exploratory activity.

Even when an attempt at joint planning broke down – as in the case of the early Birmingham overspill negotiations – the County's resistance to the city's application to develop on a peripheral site led to a wide-ranging exploration of related areas of choice within the ritualized adversarial contest of the Wythall inquiry (Chapter 3, *Figure 19*) – a procedure designed to arrive at a fair arbitration between divergent sets of public and private interests. In most of the succeeding chapters, instances can be found of inter-agency exploratory processes in a rather more informal setting, introducing different groupings among the various actors who are identified within the decision network charts. Even where the opportunities for joint exploration are clearly limited, as in the case of relationships between individual local authorities and government departments which are required to operate formal systems of external control over the activities of many such bodies, we found that a significant degree of informal exploration of alternatives sometimes took place.

Etzioni, in *The Active Society* (1968), has drawn a distinction between systems of prescriptive and 'contextuating' control, the latter allowing freedom of action within certain agreed limits. In theory, the latter form of control releases the central body from the requirement of detailed knowledge of the activities and circumstances of each of the local agencies it seeks to influence, and is thus more economical in terms of the level of communication between them. However, the more stringent such contextual controls become, the more they may in practice be challenged by the local agency, which will seek to establish that special local circumstances make the rules inapplicable in its own case. Referring to Lindblom's typology of modes of co-ordination, the central body seeks to exercise 'unconditional manipulation' over the choices of the peripheral bodies, which must respond through 'adaptive adjustment'. However, as illustrated most clearly by the example of cost yardsticks discussed in Chapter 8, severe distortions can arise from any attempt to apply controls that do not match the complexity of local problem situations. The pressures acting upon the local agency are then such as to change the relationship into a more symmetrical one, typically involving some form of bilateral negotiation. Of course, if all such requests from local agencies are acceded to, this can quickly create a situation of information overload for the superordinate agency. The trick of effective 'contextual control' is therefore to design generalized forms of 'unconditional manipulation' which limit the pressures on subordinate agencies to establish symmetrical relations with the superordinate, while not stifling their capacity to exercise initiatives in desired areas. However, the complexity of many of the problem situations encountered at Droitwich suggests that such an ideal is unlikely to be fully realisable in practice. Therefore, some degree of joint exploratory activity remains inevitable even in the context of highly centralized systems of co-ordination and control. In these circumstances, we sometimes found it necessary to look on certain actors from central departments as themselves forming a part of the local policy system, rather than simply as an external source of recognised policy guidelines.

Turning to the question of interaction between agencies that are not linked by any relationships of hierarchical control, it is possible to distinguish those inter-agency explorations that take place in the setting of some form of contractual agreement from those initiated outside any such formal context. The position of public agencies differs from that of private entrepreneurs in that their freedom of action is usually circumscribed by well-defined functional and territorial boundaries; and an incentive to inter-agency explorations arises wherever the perceived complexity of relationships between decision problems transcends these boundaries. Thus, the problem of coping with growth and urban congestion in the West Midlands became recognised as transcending the territorial boundaries of Birmingham and the surrounding Counties (Chapter 3) and also the functional boundaries between Counties and County Districts (Chapter 4). Both before and after the negotiation of a contractual agreement with Droitwich (Chapter 5), extensive joint explorations took place, though it may be noted that the level of involvement by Birmingham in the exploratory process was much less than in the case of the other two contracting parties. In effect, the city had less to gain or lose by subsequent choices in Droitwich than had either the County or the Borough, or indeed had the staff of the Development Group once this became established.

There were many issues at Droitwich where the three parties locally concerned shared incentives to engage in some level of joint exploratory activity, whether or not this was clearly demanded under the terms of the agreement. In Chapters 8, 9, 10, 11, and 12 in

particular, various issues were encountered where there were pressures to extend the processes of decision-making across the boundaries between public and private agencies: the switch to sponsored
housing, the attraction of new industry, the relocation of traders in
the town centre, the involvement of residents in the Newtown
improvement scheme, and the mobilization of social activities by the
Community Development Officer. In each case, there were external
policy influences — arising either from central government or from
the terms of the local agreement — which provided some incentive to
engage in inter-agency explorations; but these influences were more
salient in some cases than in others, and in many instances the
incentive towards interactive decision-making arose more from a
perception of mutual interest on the part of the actors locally
concerned.

Whether the organizational context for an inter-agency exploratory process is one of contextual control, of contractual obligation,
or simply of a perception of mutual gain by independent parties, it
is the recognition of complexities in the relationships between
present and anticipated problems that creates the essential spur to
actors to engage in any form of connective planning activity, and will
therefore form the theme for our next proposition. Before moving
on, however, we shall note that many of our arguments for the
inevitability of interactive exploratory activities may be found to
apply not only to public planning but equally to 'private' planning
within the single corporate context, where there may still be a
variety of sectional responsibilities and motivations involved. Indeed,
some writers (Mack, 1972) have argued that even the single
individual can be regarded as having many of the characteristics of a
diffused or pluralist planning system.

Forms of response to complexity

The second proposition of *Figure 69* argues that, in a situation where
actors become jointly engaged in the exploration of complex
decision problems, it is possible to see the response to complexity in
terms of a process of bargaining over incremental adjustments to
their shared 'opportunity space', defined as the perceived field of
possible present and future influence of the policy system or systems
within which they are operating, whether that influence is exerted
through direct action or through negotiation with other decision-
makers. In effect, the more complex the structure of the problem at
issue is seen to become, the more difficult it becomes to resolve it in
total at any point in time. Therefore, the more the actors will be

driven to seek mutual agreement on commitments to action only in certain limited parts of the overall field, with each actor attempting to anticipate his opportunities for the future choice as clearly as may be possible in his current stage of knowledge, so as to assess the implications of any bargains which may be struck in terms of his own partisan freedom of action.

There is much evidence in the Droitwich case examples to support this view of the response to complexity. The early history of the scheme is one of successive incremental commitments by the various parties, first to general financial and other measures for dealing with the Birmingham overspill problem, and then to the specific content of the Droitwich scheme. Even at the moment when the most important single step of joint formal commitment was taken − in the form of the Town Development agreement − the commitment was of a very limited or ambiguous nature in many of the crucial fields of policy, as indicated in *Figure 24*. This point is highlighted in the successive chapters of Part II, where the subsequent processes of negotiating further increments of commitment within each field are discussed. Both before and after the signature of the agreement, the actors in the various agencies concerned could often be seen to be negotiating from highly partisan positions. This was especially so over issues such as the town centre, where the constituency pressures bearing down on the parties to the agreement were most clearly in conflict. In such situations, what might appear as a desirable increment of commitment to one party could often be seen as a threat to the future 'action space' of the other, with a corresponding attenuation of the decision-making process.

The preservation of freedom of future manoeuvre may, of course, be seen as advantageous, not only from a partisan viewpoint, but also from that of agencies or actors who share a common interest in preserving a capacity to adapt to future changes in overlapping sectors of their respective operating environments, some aspects of which may be not so much unpredictable, in a statistical sense, as unforeseeable in structural terms. This point emerged most clearly from the experimental group exercise in Chapter 6, where some of the central actors in the Droitwich Development Group were asked to predict the range of possible starting dates for a set of interdependent construction projects. In the individual assessments and the discussions that followed, not only was it difficult to make realistic predictions more than a year or two ahead, but it was often difficult for the officers to appreciate in advance what degree of control they or other actors might expect to exercise in the face of a variety of external influences. For instance, whether a given housing project could be started by some particular year was sometimes seen to depend not merely on the provisions of the agreed capital programme and the will of the parties to the town development agreement to implement it, but also on the future behaviour of the housing market and the pressures of government policy under future national circumstances about which none of those present could do other than speculate. In fact, the threatened withdrawal of nominations by Birmingham was soon to introduce a new factor upsetting one of the most basic common assumptions of the group.

In effect, the more distant the time horizon, the more difficult it became for the actors to draw a distinction between the controllable and the uncontrollable. Even given a willingness of each actor to view his own sectional 'action space' within the context of a shared 'opportunity space', the boundaries of this opportunity space were far from clear cut. In many dimensions — physical, financial, administrative — it tended to become entangled with uncertainties in the operating environments of the actors within a wider 'indeterminancy space', of a form whose structure was often so obscure that it could only be appreciated in an extremely intuitive way by each of the individuals concerned.

Opportunities for learning through continuing interaction

Given the complexity of problem structures and the incremental nature of the resulting decision processes, a third proposition can now be articulated. This says that the processes of adjustment within a shared opportunity space are facilitated by whatever cumulative opportunities exist for actors to learn from each other by penetrating each others' appreciations of situations in the course of combined exploratory activities. Such processes of interpenetration, or interactive learning, do not necessarily imply that the actors steadily converge towards a common policy perspective. Indeed, if they are primarily responsible to different constituencies of interest, any such convergence could be regarded as a negation of democratic principles. Nor, indeed, can the processes of interactive learning be assumed to lead towards a steadily increasing degree of confidence in their appreciations of their shared operating environment, especially where the texture of that environment is so unstable over time as to fit the description of 'turbulence' put forward by Emery and Trist (1972).

Given these caveats, the proposition that the processes of adjustment are facilitated by cumulative opportunities for interactive learning can be supported by a variety of illustrations from

Droitwich. For instance, on appointment, each of the officers of the Development Group had to immerse himself in the processes of learning about his local operating environment. In the case of the Group Engineer, this involved building up an appreciation of local sources of materials and contract skills, while, in the case of the Community Development Officer, it involved the cultivation of relationships with local community leaders and external organizers of voluntary associations. Over the years, we saw that a high level of continuing adjustment could be maintained between the orientations of the different specialist officers at Droitwich through the medium of the Monday morning meetings and numerous informal contacts in the Development Group offices. However, as the exercise described in Chapter 6 demonstrated, even the high level of communication and consensus which existed among the members of this group did not entirely eliminate differences in perception about such crucial questions as the realism of the target completion date for the development programme.

Further processes of interactive learning could be seen taking place during the monthly meetings of the Development Committee, where the elected members would be brought up against a fuller realization of the technical complexities of development, and the officers in turn would be brought up against a ruller realization of local political pressures. At these meetings, the information transmitted by the local politicians was often enriched by the multiple roles that many of them played in different representative institutions. Because we have avoided identifying individual elected members in our case studies, except where they held relevant committee chairmanships, this is not an aspect that has emerged explicitly in the preceding chapters. However, it became evident through the series of interviews that we conducted with committee members during 1970 and 1971. Indeed, it is a matter of common observation in Britain and elsewhere that leading local politicians often provide a rich pattern of cross-connections between different representative bodies. Among the other roles held by the eight County representatives on the Development Committee were leading positions in the West Midlands Planning Authorities' Conference, in other District Councils throughout the County, in Parish Councils and school management boards, in voluntary organizations, and in relevant professions such as law and accountancy. On the Borough side, some of the representatives held leading positions in such institutions as the local magistracy, in the Chamber of Trade, and in industrial firms in the conurbation, as well as playing prominent roles in the normal range of social and commercial activities within the local community.

Thus, the spread of relevant experience was wide, even though the political complexion of both Councils at that time was such that certain sectors of community interest were by no means fully represented. Indeed, each of the elected representatives could himself — or herself — be plotted as occupying a number of different positions in different parts of our institutional base map, and therefore as providing a set of informal channels for mutual adjustment between decision-making agencies, so further enriching the overall processes of 'reticulation of knowledge' (Power, 1971b).

One type of situation where the opportunities for learning were not cumulative was encountered in our discussion of industrial development in Chapter 9. Although the officers and members of the Development Committee did share the opportunity to develop a common appreciation of their problems over time, the focal point of the decision process was the manager of each incoming firm, who often approached the problems of relocation from a basis of comparatively meagre experience. This brings us up sharply against a practical problem implicit in the concept of reticulation of knowledge: that it is extremely difficult to devise a system that ensures that the information or experience which is most relevant to decision-making is speedily disseminated to all points where it can be utilized. Some recognition must be paid to the natural limitations in the capacity of the human brain and its sensory and effectory mechanisms — and also, we should perhaps add, the limitations of the electronic computer as a means of manipulating those kinds of information that are most relevant to human decisions in a complex socio-political environment.

Selectivity in the activation of decision networks

The fourth proposition in *Figure 69* states that, because resources for decision-making are finite, communications between actors concerned in complex problem situations are necessarily initiated on a selective basis. As an aid in elaborating this proposition, we shall at this point introduce a diagrammatic representation of a continuous process of interactive learning through exploration of a shared opportunity space, which takes a stage further the series of general models first developed in Chapter 2 (*Figures 8 to 12*).

In *Figure 70*, a series of successive stages is indicated in a continuing exploratory process. At each stage, some decision problem is explored by a set of actors connected within a decision network, usually in relation to certain other areas of present or anticipated choice which may be recognised as related by some, if not all, of the actors. As a result of this exploration, there will often be an incremental output of commitments to certain agreed lines of action, even if only to the action of putting on paper certain recommendations that still require the formal endorsement of some further authorizing body before any executive steps can be set in train. Whatever direct outputs of commitment there may be, the exploratory process will usually have a further indirect output, in the form of a degree of mutual adjustment between the perceptions of at least some of the actors involved. This is indicated to the right of *Figure 70*, which shows a process of modification in the actors' initial appreciations of relevant characteristics of their shared environment, according to the three facets first introduced in *Figure 9*.

Each actor begins with some appreciation of the operating environment, of the contiguous policy systems, and of the constituency pressures in relation to the set of problems currently at issue. He will also begin with some set of personal relations to other actors in the network, which may affect his contributions to the discussion. Such orientations may be changed as a result of the communications that pass during the current stage of decision-making. *Figure 70* assumes, as is usually the case, that at least one of the actors in each stage is also present to provide continuity when it comes to the subsequent stage, where the composition of the decision network and the structure of the problem may have changed; but, in the meantime, such actors may of course have taken part in other exploratory activities which, whether or not directly related, may bring about some further changes in their orientations.

As illustrated again through the exercise described in Chapter 6, such modifications can often bring an enlargement rather than a decrease in the areas of uncertainty perceived by any of the actors. Even where this is so, the learning process will still usually tend over time to take each actor in the direction of a more realistic appreciation of the difficulties of decision-making in a complex operating and political environment. An integral part of this learning process is the modification of actors' perceptions about what might best be done to counteract perceived uncertainties. Indeed, it may be only through reaching a measure of adjustment in this field that the actors are able to agree to translate the decision process into a different context, as indicated between the successive phases of *Figure 70*.

Accordingly, the actors who perform the linking roles between one stage of decision-making and the next may face some crucial problems of *selection* both in judging how the problems should be

Figure 70   Problem-solving and learning in decision networks

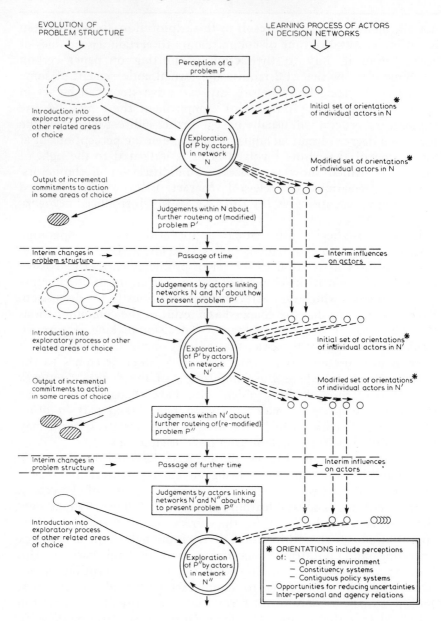

EVOLUTION OF
PROBLEM STRUCTURE

LEARNING PROCESS OF ACTORS
IN DECISION NETWORKS

Perception of a
problem P

Introduction into
exploratory process of
other related areas
of choice

Initial set of orientations *
of individual actors in N

Exploration
of P by actors
in network
N

Modified set of orientations *
of individual actors in N

Output of incremental
commitments to action
in some areas of choice

Judgements within N about
further routeing of (modified)
problem P′

Interim changes in
problem structure   →

Passage of time

← Interim influences
on actors

Judgements by actors linking
networks N and N′ about how
to present problem P′

Introduction into
exploratory process of other
related areas of choice

Initial set of orientations *
of individual actors in N′

Exploration
of P′ by actors
in network
N′

Modified set of orientations *
of individual actors in N′

Output of incremental
commitments to action
in some areas of choice

Judgements within N′ about
further routeing of (re-modified)
problem P″

Interim changes in
problem structure   →

Passage of further time

Interim influences
on actors

Judgements by actors linking
networks N′ and N″ about how
to present problem P″

Introduction into
exploratory process
of other related areas
of choice

Exploration
of P″ by actors
in network
N″

✱ ORIENTATIONS include perceptions
of: – Operating environment
     – Constituency systems
     – Contiguous policy systems
  – Opportunities for reducing uncertainties
  – Inter-personal and agency relations

'routed' through the various available channels of communication, and also in deciding in what ways the information which has now emerged about the problem should be presented to those involved at the next stage, given practical limitations in the demands that can be made on the 'interaction time' of busy people. In Droitwich, a good example of the types of judgement indicated in *Figure 70* appears in the instance of Westacre housing, as analysed in *Figure 47*. In this case, at each stage of the exploratory process, certain suggested extensions to decision networks were accepted or rejected, in the light of an exchange of information about their costs in terms of such factors as delay to the housing programme or possible damage to existing political relationships between agencies.

Another example is that of the successive stages of exploration of the future of the Newtown neighbourhood, analysed in *Figure 60*. Here, the Working Party had to make a series of decisions, with little precedent to guide them, about the points at which they should present the results of their explorations to two different sets of people from whom some kind of policy endorsement was required: the Borough Council and the local residents. Especially in the case of the residents, difficult judgements had to be made about the variety of alternative solutions that should be put forward and the way in which supporting information should be presented, given a desire to reconcile the principles of public participation with a minimal risk of inconclusive or tangential discussion.

The early difficulties in approving the town centre proposals, as discussed in Chapter 10, provide an instance of the kind of judgement that arises in the more familiar situation where courses of future action require the endorsement of two or more formally constituted public agencies (in this case, the County and Borough Councils). Here, there is a risk that contradictory commitments to action will emerge, especially if sets of proposals are submitted to both agencies more or less simultaneously. This means that those presenting the results of an exploratory process may face some difficult tactical judgements not only about the sequence of presentation, but about the range of alternative solutions to be carried forward at each stage, and the way in which any supporting information should be presented. One common strategy may be first to test the policy stance of the least predictable group, by putting forward a range of possible alternatives, to allow some pre-selection before presenting a single recommendation or a more limited range of options to other groups.

In general, the choice is one of how the variety perceived to exist in a' situation of choice should be presented at a particular organizational interface, between the extremes of a single recommendation (with a risk of rejection) and a much more open projection of the structure of the total action space — extremes that correspond broadly to those of 'negative' and 'positive' coordination, as defined by Scharpf (1972). The question of selectivity can therefore be seen to enter, of necessity, not only into the activation of communication channels but also into the transmission of information through them, if only because it is quite impracticable to envisage a situation in which each actor transmits his complete mental mapping of the problem situation to every other actor. For linking actors of the kind indicated in *Figure 70*, the judgements required can be interpreted in terms of both the 'management of uncertainty' (relating the choice of channels to the view of uncertainty in decision-making presented in *Figure 10*) and the 'management of variety' (concerning choices about the presentation of information through any given channel). Both can be seen as aspects of the general field of *reticulist judgement*, through which successive changes in the context of decision are effected in practice, as indicated between the successive phases of exploration in *Figure 70*. In turning to the next in our sequence of propositions, we shall seek to discuss more fully the ways in which such reticulist judgements appear to be made in practice.

The diffusion of reticulist opportunities

Because particular actors may be involved in many different exploratory processes in parallel, the type of 'chain' process indicated in *Figure 70* does not itself provide a sufficient model of the kind of complex multi-dimensional environment within which reticulist judgements are called for and decision networks are formed, activated, and modified. Our fifth proposition returns to this more multi-dimensional perspective by stating that, in a turbulent environment, the shifting patterns of linkage between problems limit the opportunities for relating reticulist judgements to a framework of agreed rules or precedents, and place a premium on the use of discretion at many dispersed points of decision. In the terms introduced by Burns and Stalker (1961), there will be pressures generated for a shift from a 'mechanistic' towards an 'organic' management system.

There may, of course, be instances where the sequence of steps in an exploratory process can realistically be pre-programmed at some central point. Where the structure of a problem is comparatively well defined, prior specification may be possible of the points at which formal endorsement should be sought from authorizing groups, or consultations should be held with affected parties; and it may even be possible to specify how many alternatives should be carried forward from one stage to the next, together with the form that any supporting information should take. However, this assumes an ability to classify clearly in advance the various types of problem situation that may arise. Furthermore, it assumes a level of policy co-ordination from some central point which is far removed from the evidence of our Droitwich case studies.

The changing structures of the problems encountered during the course of the first few years of the Droitwich expansion are perhaps brought out most graphically by the example of the sequence of decisions on the distributor road network, as set out in *Figure 39*. However, similar patterns of change in the focus of decision-making over time can be recognized in the narrative accounts presented in the succeeding chapters concerned with the planning of housing, industrial development, central redevelopment, environmental renewal, and community services. Among the influences which prevent the laying down of rules to guide the formation of decision networks in these fields are the frequent changes in the policy framework laid down by departments of central government, often themselves a reflection of technological trends or shifting economic forces as much as of changes of political control.

At the level of Droitwich itself, the classification of problems in such a way as to provide clear rules for the mobilization of decision networks was inhibited by the intricate patterns of local linkage which became recognised between different areas of choice faced by the Development Committee and its staff — patterns that often cut across a variety of established fields of local responsibility. A broad view of some of these patterns of linkage was presented in *Figure 35*, indicating also some of the salient sources of external uncertainty as perceived at that time. A more localized picture of the varied set of problems associated with the design options for Salwarpe Road was presented in *Figure 40*, while some examples of patterns of local linkage between the choices of different agencies which do not normally have the opportunity to develop patterns of recurrent communication with each other appeared in *Figures 52* and *56*, concerned with the fields of industry and central redevelopment respectively. In the cases of the canal and the brine baths, discussed in Chapters 11 and 12, the scope for local discretion in activating decision networks was even further enlarged because the patterns of problems which were then encountered lay largely beyond the experience, not only of the local decision-makers, but also of their counterparts in any other similar local situation.

At Droitwich, there were many actors who exercised discretion on occasion in the activation of decision networks. This is indicated in the main sequence of network charts presented in Part II (*Figures 42, 44, 48, 51, 57, 59, 63,* and *67*). In these charts, it will be noticed that the symbol representing an actor who sometimes contributes significantly to a modification of the respondent's decision network appears in many different sectors of the general organizational 'map', reflecting variations in those who are in the best position to make judgements about the routeing of exploratory processes in different parts of the broad field of decision with which the chart is concerned. In providing this information, doubts often arose in the mind of the respondent as to whether or not this kind of status should be attributed to particular actors. For instance, certain financial staff are given the status of network-shaping (or reticulist) actors in the network diagram of the Group Engineer for the local road system, not so much because they brought the engineer directly into contact with other decision-makers but because he saw them as introducing constraints or difficulties, which he had to find ways of overcoming through activating communications with other actors who could provide information relevant to the operating decisions he faced.

In the networks of the Housing Manager and the Group Administrator, concerned with housing allocation and industrial development respectively, a network-forming status has been assigned to certain actors who performed the role of 'broker', in referring to the respondent prospective tenants for town development housing and industrial sites. Such processes of referral of individual cases involve a relatively clearly-defined type of reticulist judgement, as do the referral decisions of the various types of actors identified in *Figure 66* as concerned with services in the field of community health and welfare. It is in relation to relatively discrete problem situations of this kind that opportunities are most likely to arise for relating network activating judgements to centrally determined rules or policy guidelines. However, the element of local discretion is always likely to be significant where it becomes difficult to classify the full circumstances surrounding each 'case' without a loss of significant information. This factor has created considerable difficulty for those concerned to introduce centralized planning procedures in some of the personal social services, notably in the integrated local authority Social Service Departments which were first established in England in 1971.

The case for local discretion in the mobilization of decision networks becomes even stronger in terms of actors concerned with shifting patterns of related problems, the focus of which may change repeatedly and unpredictably over time, as in the case of the officers at Droitwich concerned with interdependent issues of design, finance, scheduling, and division of responsibilities during the course of the development programme. Similar shifts of focus may of course take place at a less local scale. As indicated in Chapters 3 and 4, the complex set of related regional issues explored at the Wythall inquiry (*Figure 19*) were seen as requiring network-shaping initiatives from actors in many central and local agencies. This emerges clearly from the recommendations for further action which were eventually put forward by the presiding inspector.

These illustrations bear out the point argued by Ozbekhan (1971), among others, that the order of complexity of a problem is not necessarily a function of its physical scale. This is because, at any scale from the nation or the region to that of the local neighbourhood, any representation of problem structure must necessarily be related to the order of complexity of the decision mechanisms that may be available in working towards a solution. In cybernetic terms, this point relates to Ashby's law of requisite variety (Ashby, 1956): that a control system can only be effective to the extent that it can succeed in matching the inherent complexity — or variety — of its environment. Thus, the design of an improvement scheme for the Newtown neighbourhood may demand as high an order of reticulist judgement as the design of a set of responses to problems of regional congestion and population growth. For this reason, we were able to identify actors with a significant reticulist role not only at central points in the County, the Borough, and the Development Group, but also at comparatively modest points in local, regional, and national hierarchies. Examples of such actors, in the case of the Newtown improvement network presented in *Figure 59*, include the regional administrator from the Housing Ministry and the Group Engineer Planner. Both of these operated at different levels of government, in positions giving them little formal authority over others, yet important measures of access to other relevant actors and forms of experience. Indeed, it will be noticed that the Group Engineer Planner was also identified as playing a significant reticulist role in a number of the other network diagrams of Part II, despite his modest position in the Development Group's formal organization structure (*Figure 25*).

Because our respondents in charting the sequence of decision networks — with the exception of the Borough Housing Manager —

were all officers of the Droitwich Development Committee, the picture that emerges may well differ significantly from that which might have been built up had those asked to participate included a wider range of Borough or County officers, or of elected members from either parent authority. It is therefore to be expected that our identification of reticulist actors within the multi-organizational policy system at Droitwich — and also of those operating in relevant sectors of private enterprise, community interest, and appointed agencies — is somewhat biased towards the under-representation of certain network-shaping opportunities and roles with the decision networks with which we have been concerned. Nevertheless, we have been able to assemble sufficient evidence to feel some confidence in arguing the general proposition that, in a turbulent environment, the selection of information channels and the transmission of information through them are not so much influenced by conformity to sets of rules or precedents determined by a prior classification of problem situations, as by the discretion of actors working in a widely-diffused range of both peripheral and central roles.

The characteristics of reticulist skill

At this stage, we can proceed to a sixth proposition, to the effect that the making of reticulist judgements — in other words, the mobilization of decision networks in an intelligently selective way — depends on a capacity to appreciate both the structure of problem situations and the structure of organizational and political relations that surround them. The actor concerned, whatever his formal status, must first be able to appreciate the patterns of interdependence between those present and future problems which may impinge significantly on his own current field of concern, so that he can weigh up the alternative ways in which the focus of exploration might be extended. At the same time, he must be able to appreciate the structure of relationships, formal and informal, between roles in the decision process, so as to understand the political costs and benefits of activating alternative forms of communication with other relevant actors, both in his own and in other organizations.

Such capabilities may be regarded as providing a necessary foundation for the cultivation of reticulist skills, yet other personal attributes will clearly enter into the success or failure of an actor in maintaining and exploiting relevant channels of communication. This question may indeed be one which merits more widespread and far-reaching research, with an orientation towards social psychology. More systematic attempts might be made to learn from the differences in 'reticulist style' between actors who occupy similar organizational roles in a variety of comparable local situations — for instance, between the political leaders of different District Councils, between the Chief Executives or Planning Officers of different Counties, between leaders of social work teams for different areas, or between engineers who must co-ordinate the site operations of contractors and public utility authorities for different local projects. Social scientists have of course already given much attention to developing frameworks for understanding differences of style both in management and in politics (Davies, 1972, 1973). It could be fruitful to discover whether the concept of reticulist judgement throws any additional light on this general area — for instance in helping to appreciate differences in decision-making style between those who have become drawn into political, administrative, technical, or community service roles. Returning to our main proposition, however, the evidence of our case studies suggests strongly that the understanding of both problem structures and political structures, at however intuitive a level, is a necessary foundation for the development of network-shaping skills, whether the primary role of the actor concerned appears to be essentially technical or political in its orientation.

The basic problem facing the would-be reticulist can be seen as that of initiating and cultivating a network of human relationships, in such a way as to maintain access to information about changing problem situations which he expects to interact in a significant way with those particular types of decision over which he wishes to be able to exert some practical influence. As argued by Faludi (1973) in his discussion of planning strategies, actors in such situations often adopt the kind of approach that Etzioni has described as *mixed scanning*, moving between different levels of strategic and tactical exploration so as to develop an appreciation of how the one influences the other. Seen in this light, the cultivation of human relations can be seen as instrumental to the reticulist's ultimate aim of influencing decision-making; though, of course, it would be unrealistic to suppose that he is not sometimes guided by other motives at the more personal level such as the desire to be liked or esteemed by his associates.

One of the main difficulties for the reticulist arises from the limited time at his disposal to cultivate relationships on different fronts, given that on each front he may have a different expectation of gaining knowledge of practical use to him, and also that he may encounter different costs of communication, whether in terms of time spent in interaction or travelling or of potential threats to valued political relationships. Sometimes, he may find that one strategy with a high level of 'cost-effectiveness' is to mobilize or participate in some group discussion process not directly related to the exploration of specific decision problems. Thus, in the case of Droitwich, we saw the Community Development Officer mobilizing the lunch-time meetings of voluntary community workers and, at another level, the Group Administrator helping to found a national Town Development Executives Committee. In either case, a number of relevant communication links could be maintained at comparatively low cost — though with correspondingly reduced control by the individual over the nature of the information transmitted (at least during the course of the formal meeting itself) to ensure its relevance to his current problems.

   This general type of skill, concerned with questions of how much time and effort to give to opening up and maintaining different opportunities for communication, was indeed one that we found essential to our own research mission at Droitwich, where the opportunities for individual discussion and committee attendance were often embarrassingly wide. Choices of allocation of resources between the available interfaces of communication can be seen as one particular aspect of the more political dimension of reticulist skill, where the strategy to be adopted can only realistically be reviewed in the light of local circumstances. For instance, we saw how most of the Borough Council representatives on the Droitwich Development Committee's General Purposes Sub-Committee judged it worth-while to attend regularly, but not the County representatives. This meant that the Group Administrator was able to use this interim occasion between meetings of the full committee to prepare the ground on locally controversial issues. Also, the Group Administrator, the Committee Chairman, and others had to weigh the potential gains in influence against the costs in political relationships in deciding whether to pursue an apparently irresolvable problem by activating *ad hoc* communications with particular actors representing different organizational or political interests. This emerges most clearly in the case of Westacre housing analysed in *Figure 47*. On that occasion, different actors at the meeting showed that they had their own partisan appreciations of the political costs and benefits involved, and, in arriving at a practical compromise, a great deal depended on the reticulist skills of the Chairman and the Group Administrator, as the two actors playing the most prominent roles at that particular stage of the decision-making process.

   As argued elsewhere (Power, 1971b), the political skills of the reticulist must include a sure grasp of modes of behaviour relevant to different types of relationship between agencies and between actors. He must appreciate when to bargain, when to seek to persuade, and when to confront, in situations varying from those where there is a high degree of consensus to those of inherent conflict between different constituency interests, as typified by the case of Droitwich town centre. In this process, he must learn to work within the context of formal role relationships which vary from that of servant to master — as in the case of the Group Administrator and his committee — to that of manager to line staff — as in his relationships with other officers within the Group. The political aspect of reticulist skill, as Power argues, must be considered essentially as a *craft*; but it is a craft which cannot realistically be viewed without taking into account also those other elements of skill that are concerned with the appreciation of problem structures.

Although the skill of probing the structure of problems is one that is itself usually exercised at a highly intuitive level, we have attempted to make it more explicit through the various diagrams we have presented interpreting aspects of problem structure by means of the AIDA conventions. Unless the actor has at least an intuitive appreciation of the relative salience of different problems and relationships between problems, and the range of feasible options available, then his understanding of the current 'opportunity space' will be correspondingly diminished, and he will not be able to make judgements about either the management of variety or uncertainty in an intelligently selective way, nor will he be able effectively to challenge the judgement of others. Perhaps the aspect of reticulist skill which concerns the understanding of problem structure can be most neatly summed up by quoting one of the maxims of the Group Administrator at Droitwich, that if a problem appears to be insoluble, then the problem itself must be changed. In the terms introduced by de Bono, the search process may in these circumstances become dependent on a well-developed capacity for lateral thinking (de Bono, 1968).

The reticulist and his organizational environment

Moving on from our concern with the nature of reticulist skills, our penultimate proposition states that the opportunities for an actor to develop and deploy skills of this nature are influenced by the configuration of organizational resources that are at his disposal. As a qualifying statement, it is necessary to add that the disposition of organizational resources within and between agencies cannot by itself be expected to guarantee the development of any required patterns of exploratory activity, or any required level of reticulist skill on the part of particular actors. Rather, it can only serve as an enabling or, often, an inhibiting factor, but one which, as we shall argue, can be highly influential in practice.

One significant organizational resource, especially in the light of our discussion about the role of 'mixed scanning' in the mobilization of decision networks, is the granting to an actor of formal rights of *access*; that is, the opportunity to attend meetings of relevant decision-making groups, or to approach individuals in order to ask them questions about current problems, or to have access to documents which are not generally available. Such a resource must, however, often be skilfully utilized and husbanded if it is not to become dissipated through the fears of other parties concerned that they may lose control over politically sensitive or valuable information. Here, it may be important that the rights of access should be supported by the *political authority* that stems from the actor's formal accountability to a representative group which is recognised as reflecting some constituency interest — or set of constituency interests — that is relevant to the problem in hand. Such an accountability carries the implicit threat that, unless that interest is adequately represented in the way the exploratory processes are managed, recourse may be made to opportunities for formal expressions of dissent. Such expressions might take the form of public protests after a decision has been irrevocably taken, or possibly of objections at a public inquiry, where the commitment might not be quite so final, yet the opportunites for effective intervention may still be severely constrained.

In the years prior to the Droitwich town centre inquiry, for instance, there was always an implicit threat that the Borough Council could, in extreme circumstances, appear as an objector, carrying considerable political authority as the body elected to serve the collective interests of the town's population; while the Chamber of Trade, which in the end carried its opposition to these lengths, presented its case at the inquiry in a way which placed much emphasis on the cohesion of the constituency of local traders whose interests it could claim to represent.

However, if an actor is to be made accountable specifically for his achievements in mobilizing networks of exploratory activity, as well as in performing any more clearly defined tasks he may have, then another important organizational resource has to be considered. This resource concerns the degree to which the organization to which he owes primary allegiance gives explicit recognition to those aspects of the role that involve the exercise of reticulist skill, together with the marginal costs of developing such aspects more fully and the kinds of marginal benefit that may ensue. This point can be illustrated in the case of the Group Engineer at Droitwich, who — like many of his fellow-officers — felt constrained by an accounting system geared almost exlusively to the implementation of specific capital projects. Any time spent in group meetings or other activities offering reticulist opportunities had then ultimately to be accounted for either as part of the design expenses of individual projects or as general administrative 'oncosts'. Both these heads of account were subject to external pressures for economy, despite the persistent demands from Borough representatives for more information on the choices open to them. Of course, it would have been by no means easy to design a formal accounting system that was sensitive enough to assist rather than inhibit the seeking of those levels of exploratory activity most appropriate to each of the tasks in hand. Nevertheless, even an agreement to provide, and to keep under review, some continuing budgetary estimate for general planning activity (such as indeed existed in the early years of the Droitwich programme) could have formed a significant resource to assist the search for appropriate levels of exploration within and beyond the Group.

Figure 71 presents a general model of any actor in an organizational environment that demands the exercise of reticulist skills, as a background against which questions of these and other organizational resources can be further explored. The actor in question is shown first as owing a working allegiance to some employing agency, which may or may not be under the full control of the representative group to whom he is most directly accountable and from whom he draws his political authority. For instance, the officers reporting to the Droitwich Development Committee all held formal appointments on the payroll of one or other parent authority, serving under different kinds of contractual arrangement to the Development Committee, which was intended to represent two of the salient constituencies of interest involved. Among other leading actors in the exploration of developmental options, the Estates Adviser served the Committee as a consultant in the employment of a private organization. In this, as in the other cases, the employing agency served to provide the individual with a resource of security of income and opportunities for career advancement, within which to develop his reticulist and other skills in the service of the Development Committee.

A pre-requisite in such cases is the existence of some form of contractual agreement, or at least an informal understanding,

Figure 71　The reticulist role in context

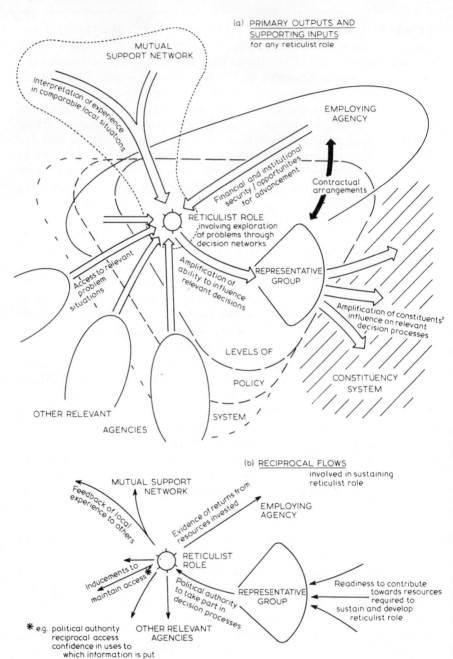

(a) PRIMARY OUTPUTS AND SUPPORTING INPUTS for any reticulist role

MUTUAL SUPPORT NETWORK

Interpretation of experience in comparable local situations

EMPLOYING AGENCY

Financial and institutional security / opportunities for advancement

Contractual arrangements

RETICULIST ROLE involving exploration of problems through decision networks

Access to relevant problem situations

Amplification of ability to influence relevant decisions

REPRESENTATIVE GROUP

Amplification of constituents' influence on relevant decision processes

LEVELS OF

POLICY

CONSTITUENCY SYSTEM

OTHER RELEVANT AGENCIES

SYSTEM

(b) RECIPROCAL FLOWS involved in sustaining reticulist role

MUTUAL SUPPORT NETWORK

Feedback of local experience to others

Evidence of returns from resources invested

EMPLOYING AGENCY

RETICULIST ROLE

Inducements to maintain access *

Political authority to take part in decision processes

REPRESENTATIVE GROUP

Readiness to contribute towards resources required to sustain and develop reticulist role

* e.g. political authority reciprocal access confidence in uses to which information is put

OTHER RELEVANT AGENCIES

between the employer and the representative group through which
any costs to the one can be related to the services provided to the
other. This point also relates albeit in a different way, to the elected
representative, who may be constrained in the degree to which he
can develop an exploratory role in relation to the affairs of one or
more representative groups by the readiness to grant time off work of
an employer who may have little or no direct interest in the
problems under review. It is here that the retired or self-employed
representative can be at a real advantage — especially when it comes
to operating through informal channels, rather than through media
such as formal committee meetings where the time demanded can be
more clearly justified to an employer.

Another, comparatively informal, organizational resource indicated in *Figure 71* may be the linkage of the actor concerned to
some set of people who fulfil similar roles in other local situations:
an informal network as in the case of the Droitwich Group Engineer
(*Figure 42*), or an organized association holding periodic meetings as
in the case of the Administrator (*Figure 51*). Such a grouping can
allow the exchange of mutually useful information on reticulist as
well as other aspects of the actor's role, as instanced by the Group
Engineer's use of his informal network in relation to certain
problems he faced of a procedural rather than a technical nature.
Also, we saw how a more formal voluntary association such as the
Town Development Executives Committee could serve as a collective
pressure group to persuade government departments to modify the
policy context within which the local decision-makers had to
operate.

As *Figure 71* indicates, the various actors with whom an individual
may seek to cultivate relationships may vary from those who clearly
operate within the same policy system to those who clearly operate
in other and possibly conflicting policy systems, with various
intermediate categories of actor who can be regarded as either inside
or outside the bounds of the relevant policy system, according to the
field of decision currently under review. In relation to the representative group to which the actor owes primary allegiance, we shall, in
the chapters that follow, find it useful to distinguish between those
actors whose reticulist judgements are exercised mainly in an
outwardly connective as opposed to an *inwardly connective* mode.
The former mode, which is dependent on seeking contacts with
actors over whom the representative group has little or no formal
authority, was perhaps most clearly typified at Droitwich by the
case of the Community Development Officer. The performance of
his role depended almost entirely on the cultivation of relationships

with actors in many different voluntary organizations and service agencies where, in his opinion, success could often only be realistically evaluated in terms of an awareness of potential crises which had been avoided. Such an observation might also apply to the Group Administrator or, perhaps to a lesser extent, the Group Planner Architect, each of whose roles we saw to demand frequent judgements of a reticulist character, operating in both the outwardly and inwardly connective modes. In this respect, their roles were perhaps not too dissimilar from that of any other senior executives in any semi-autonomous organization, public or private, which is dependent on maintaining complex sets of relations with its environment.

However, the preceding chapters contain much evidence of the additional challenges presented by the multi-organizational nature of the policy system relating to their primary task of expanding Droitwich. As already argued, the formation of a joint agency can be interpreted as simply a rather more explicit expression than usual of the complex relationships that arise more generally in the management of local and regional change, as a field within which decision-makers must always remain responsive to multiple constituencies of public interest. It follows that operation in the outwardly connective mode becomes integral to the role of the would-be reticulist actor, who must seek to maintain access to relevant problem situations mainly by bargaining across the boundaries between agencies subject to different and probably conflicting constituency pressures, as indicated in *Figure 71*. Sometimes, the resource of political authority may be one of the few bargaining counters available. Instances can, of course, be quoted of exceptionally skilled actors who can operate freely across the interfaces between organizations as virtually autonomous agents, without such a resource at their disposal. However, such instances can hardly be regarded as providing an adequate foundation for any attempts to encourage a wider spread of reticulist capabilities among the various constituencies of community interest that are concerned in the processes of public planning.

The influence of reticulist activities on public planning

In the final proposition in the sequence set out in *Figure 69,* we bring together much of the preceding argument to state that:

> the practical influence of public planning activities on decision-making depends on the disposition among publicly accountable

agencies of skills and resources relevant to the selective activation
of inter-agency networks

This proposition does not rest on any further evidence from
Droitwich; rather, as suggested by the layout of *Figure 69,* it
represents a more explicit interpretation of propositions *2* to *7* in the
specific context of public planning. In the form in which they appear
on the diagram, it will be noticed that none of the six intermediate
propositions makes any explicit reference to public planning or to
the inter-agency context. This is to facilitate their testing in other
contexts, including that of purely 'private' planning where decisions
within a single corporate framework are assumed to impinge on no
more than a single constituency of interest.

In the chapter so far, we have attempted to frame our propositions
in such a way as to exclude — as far as possible — any specific value
content. However, at the stage we have now reached, it becomes
more difficult to retain a detached stance of this kind. For instance,
the final proposition, as stated above, clearly implies a view that it is in
some sense a 'good thing' that public planning should indeed have an
influence on decision-making — though how far this influence should
extend may remain a matter of dispute, both in general and in
particular fields of decision. Such a proposition, it may be noted,
does not necessarily carry the same implications of value if translated
to the context of inter-agency explorations in the purely 'private'
planning field. For instance, any joint explorations between independent entrepreneurs competing in a limited market can conjure up
connotations of practices such as price-fixing which are generally
regarded as unethical, even where not expressly forbidden by law.

In any field involving relationships between agencies which can
claim to represent different constituencies of community interest,
the contention that planning processes should exercise an effective
influence on decision-making becomes a much less controversial one.
In the view of one civil servant with considerable experience in
regional planning, the primary aim of planning should be to 'secure
agreement on action'. Indeed, the demand for effective public
planning tends to arise most strongly from situations where there is
overt disagreement between public authorities over proposed actions,
as at the Wythall inquiry discussed in Chapter 3, so that — to the lay
observer at least — the processes of government may appear to be in
a state of evident disarray. Indeed, it may be contended that the best
practical index of effective planning is the avoidance of such states of
crisis in which there is a clear lack of effective mutual adjustment
between the decisions of different governmental agencies. However, a

counter-argument can be advanced, to the effect that occasional crises can serve a constructive purpose if they serve to maintain the public pressures for effective planning processes. It can then be argued that the aim should be to ensure that such crises come to a head before rather than after irrevocable commitments have been made. Consequently, it is the incidence of overt dispute over past decisions that perhaps provides the clearest indicator of success or failure in the processes of inter-agency adjustment.

Some guidlines for the innovator

It would be contrary to most of the accumulated experience of the social and political sciences to suppose that a value position could ever be defined in relation to the evolution of public planning, such that it could be subscribed to equally by any individual or set of constituency interests. Recognising this, we shall at this point turn to consider what some of the prescriptive implications of our analysis could be for any actor who is concerned to bring about innovation in the way planning is done, whatever his organizational role or set of guiding motivations may be. We shall therefore seek to articulate some guidelines which could apply equally to the situation of an actor in a local change agency such as the Town Development Group at Droitwich; or to that of a representative of specific community interests affected; or to that of people who may be concerned — whether as civil servants, politicians, or laymen — with designing structural changes in the organization of governmental institutions.

Some general implications of our sequence of propositions for the would-be innovator — conditional, of course, on his acceptance of the content of the propositions as in accord with his own experience — are set out to the right of *Figure 69* and we shall briefly expand on them here. One inference from the first proposition — that inter-agency explorations are an inescapable feature of public planning — is that the innovator can enlarge his own area of influence if he does not constrain his thinking by the assumption — common during the late nineteen-sixties and early seventies — that the corporate frame of reference should always be his dominant concern. Thus, we return to the opening statement of our book, that corporate planning is not enough. In making this point, we must recognise that actors in certain roles — especially those occupying positions of central co-ordination in corporate bodies with several quasi-autonomous departments — will have a natural motivation to place the corporate emphasis before all others. Nevertheless, we would suggest that even such actors can benefit from looking beyond the corporate frame of reference in searching for conceptual frameworks that will help them to .exercise more effective influence over the way decisions are made.

Our second proposition interpreted the question of response to complexity in terms of bargaining over incremental adjustments within a shared opportunity space. This suggests a reduction in the status accorded in decision-making to the concept of the comprehensive plan, the grand design, or the hierarchy of agreed long-term objectives as advocated, for instance, by some proponents of programme budgeting systems. For the would-be innovator, it becomes more realistic to regard such instruments as exercising only marginal influences over a continuing process of mutual adjustment between divergent interests, than as providing reliable guidelines for coping with the inevitable difficulties of decision-making in a complex and changing environment.

Our third proposition concerns the element of interactive learning in the continuing processes of adjustment between decision-makers. For the innovator, one inference is that he should recognise the potential value of 'talking shops' which may appear to lead to little in the way of clear decisions, but may nevertheless promote gradual changes in the orientations of influential actors in the decision-making process. It is also important to recognise, however, that this learning process cannot be assumed to be a convergent one. Not only must the actors continually adjust to changing environmental influences; they must also recognise that it is not realistic to expect that they can ever reach agreement on definitive statements of shared policies, goals, or objectives, in so far as each must remain responsive to divergent constituency pressures. The problem is more one of containing such divergence in orientations while securing mutual agreement on action, than of seeking to converge on positions where all conflict may appear to have been eliminated.

The fourth proposition, relating to the necessarily selective way in which exploratory processes are mobilized, implies that the innovator should come to an explicit realization that the goal of imposing a comprehensive solution to the organization of planning activities is bound to be illusory. Given limited resources, any actor will always have to face practical problems of selecting between many available channels of communication, each of which may appear desirable in itself. As the next proposition indicates, such choices must be expected to depend heavily on the use of local judgement at many different points of discretion, peripheral as well as central in terms of any given organizational frame of reference. If this is so, then the innovator should recognise the limitations of what he can achieve through the medium of central control systems, of a kind that rest on explicit ground rules for dealing with clearly-defined classes of situation.

Moving to the last three propositions of *Figure 69,* the prescriptive implications begin to become somewhat more constructive, though still by no means easy for the would-be innovator to follow through in practice. If, as the sixth proposition indicates, the critical factor in responding to complexity can be expressed in terms of what we have called 'reticulist skill', combining the abilities to appreciate both problem structure and political structure, then the question arises of how far such skills can be sufficiently understood to provide a basis for the development of explicit techniques, through which the fruits of experience can be transmitted from person to person. This question recognises that there is always likely to be a scarcity of actors who combine the requisite personal attributes with the opportunities to develop and deploy them in practice. Further, if these opportunities depend on the disposition of organizational resources (proposition 7), then it can be inferred that the innovator should explicitly consider the ways in which reticulist capabilities might be enhanced through the exercise of any influence he may have over the design and adaptation of organizational structures and relationships.

Returning more specifically to the context of public planning, as in our eighth proposition, the final and most central inference of a prescriptive nature is the injunction to *regard the disposition of resources relevant to the support of reticulist activities as an explicit field of political choice.* The interpretation of such a statement as a guideline for action will depend on many aspects of the political environment of the would-be innovator; not only his relationship to other influential actors, but the wider currents of change, or resistance to change, which allow him to identify his opportunities for intervention in an ongoing political situation.

In the next three chapters we shall consider, as a context in which to illustrate the implications of our set of guidelines for practical action, the currents of change which can be identified in Britain as it enters the last quarter of the twentieth century, with a new set of institutions of local and regional government. We shall consider first a succession of significant changes in the organization and technology of regional planning; then some innovations in organization at a more local level, concerned with inducing change not only at selected points of expansion, as at Droitwich, but also in inner city areas facing crises of economic and social deprivation. Finally, we shall consider some implications of the exceptionally sweeping series of institutional reforms introduced in Britain during the mid-seventies. In this, we shall take England as our main point of reference — allowing us to maintain continuity with our earlier case material — but we shall also make some reference to the parallel developments in Scotland and Wales, with their differing patterns of social geography, culture, and governmental institutions. This recognition of the influence of contextual differences will, we hope, make it easier for readers from other countries to relate our arguments to their differing institutional frameworks, and to evaluate the more general implications of the type of wide-ranging experimental strategy upon which we shall speculate in Chapter 17.

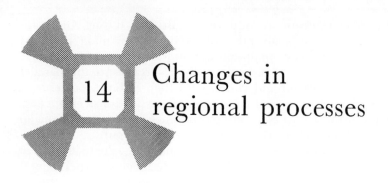

Changes in regional processes

14

Evolution in the processes of regional planning

In this chapter, we shall begin to explore the practical implications of the guidelines that have now been articulated, by examining some important processes of innovation which have been taking place since the early nineteen-sixties, in the organization of regional planning in Britain. Although these processes have often been hesitant and sometimes controversial, we shall argue that the new forms of skill and of organizational relationship which have been emerging at the regional level are of considerable importance for the evolution of public planning in general, and offer some significant opportunities for future experiment.

Throughout most of this chapter, we shall find it convenient, for reasons of continuity, to retain the perspective of the West Midlands Region of England, which was first introduced in Chapter 3 and which provided the regional context for the planned expansion of Droitwich. Similar processes of change to those that we shall trace have also been developing in other regional divisions of England, though not always in the same way or at the same pace. Towards the end of the chapter, we shall extend our focus towards the problems of these other regions; we shall also briefly refer to certain parallel developments in Scotland, in order to illustrate the way in which the processes of regional planning may have to adapt to differing national patterns of social geography and governmental structure.

As in our case studies of Droitwich, the events upon which we shall focus most closely in this chapter took place over the years between 1968 and 1971, before the main priorities of our research shifted from observation to written interpretation. These were years of considerable flux in the organizational arrangements for regional planning in England; but they saw a momentum established which culminated in the formation of more clearly-defined structures during 1972 and 1973. Of necessity, therefore, our emphasis here is on a transitional process, in which the roles and relationships of the actors could change rapidly from one year to the next. However, it is a process which, in our belief, yields some important lessons for the evolution of inter-agency planning in general, upon which we can build further in the chapters that follow.

Ministry initiatives in the West Midlands

In Chapter 3, the processes of regional planning in the West Midlands were traced from the publication of the original West Midlands Plan in 1948 — as a first attempt to provide a cohesive analytical base for land-planning decisions in the region — up to' the public inquiry at Wythall in 1959, which exposed a state of open conflict between Birmingham and two of its adjoining counties over a wide range of strategic issues. This inquiry was to be only the first in a series of such confrontations over the future of Wythall, and later of other sites on the fringe of the West Midlands conurbation. However, it was the first to focus public attention on the complex patterns of relationship between different planning issues within the region, and had a corresponding effect in stimulating pressures for the exploration of such issues through wide-ranging regional planning studies.

In Chapter 4, we saw how a Ministry commitment to the Droitwich expansion proposal emerged from a wider process of review of possible sites for overspill development in the West Midlands, following the inconclusive outcome of the first Wythall inquiry. The political priority given to this process is indicated by the fact that much of the intricate negotiation which followed was conducted in person by the Ministry's Permanent Secretary, Dame Evelyn (later Baroness) Sharp. The search now was for three or four substantial development schemes that could yield quick results, including possibly one or two where the use of New Town powers could be justified. This meant conducting explorations, individually and collectively, with a wider range of Midland planning authorities than had hitherto been involved, extending from Herefordshire in the west to Northamptonshire in the east. It also meant approaching the

Treasury over possible financial inducements to ease the path of overspill negotiations, and arguing the merits of alternative New Town sites with other government departments, most notably the Agriculture and Industrial Development Ministries.

Meanwhile, anxieties as to what was happening began to build up within the region until, in 1961, the results of the Ministry's explorations were announced, having been given political sanction at Cabinet level. Support was to be given to major overspill schemes then under discussion at Worcester, at Redditch, and at Daventry, just outside the region's eastern boundary in Northamptonshire. A marginal adjustment to the green belt was to be permitted at Wythall, and investigations were to be pursued as a matter of urgency into the designation of a New Town at Dawley in Shropshire.

None of these various outcomes could be seen as irrevocable decisions, but rather as significant increments in political commitment at national level to schemes which, in many cases, would still require painstaking processes of negotiations or challenge at the interfaces with the local interests affected. As it happened, the schemes for the New Town at Dawley and the expansion of Daventry were duly launched in the years that followed. However, the negotiations at Worcester were to remain inconclusive, while in 1963 events at Redditch took a dramatic turn with an announcement by the then Land Planning Minister that he was to seize the initiative by imposing a New Town solution, because of a breakdown over financial questions in negotiating a voluntary town expansion agreement. Such difficulties, accentuated by a continued resistance from Warwickshire and Worcestershire to any further erosion of the proposed green belt boundaries, combined to increase the pressure from Birmingham for short-term solutions to its search for sites for municipal housing development, through peripheral expansion on the southern and eastern fringes of the city.

During this period, none of the Ministry's staff concerned with land planning problems were based in the region itself. However, pressures were beginning to mount towards a more explicit regional devolution of ·central government activities, particularly in response to the chronic problems of economic deprivation in the northern parts of the country. In 1962, the Industrial Development Minister was given the new title of Secretary of State for Industry, Trade and Regional Development, with an immediate assignment to investigate the economic problems of the north-east corner of England, supported by a new regional office of the Ministry in Newcastle, covering both land planning and housing functions.

A further initiative in the direction of more explicit concern with regional planning came in 1964, when the government decided to launch wide-ranging studies of the three regions of England dominated by major conurbations — the South East, the West Midlands, and the North-West — and assembled special inter-departmental teams of civil servants for this purpose. The study group for the West Midlands proceeded to collate as much relevant information on the problems of the region as could be obtained through the analysis of the data already available to central government on demographic, employment, and other trends, and to supplement this information through a programme of discussions with local planning authorities and other regional interests, thus adding a dimension of more localized appreciation to their search for acceptable regional strategies.

The introduction of an economic planning framework

Shortly before the West Midlands Study Group was due to report its findings, the growing commitment to regional planning activities in Britain was given an additional impetus by the election of a Labour government, publicly committed to policies of more extensive intervention by central government in the management of the economy. One of the first actions of the new government was to set up a new Department of Economic Affairs, which was intended to provide a positive lead in sustaining progress towards faster economic growth, and to act as a counterweight to what were seen as the financial orthodoxies of the Treasury. One of the tasks with which the new Ministry was charged was the formulation of a first 'National Plan', setting broad targets for economic growth which could be interpreted in terms of planned levels of achievement for different sectors of the national economy. Such an exercise could, it was hoped, provide a framework for more realistic planning activities at a regional level, where uncertainty over future rates of economic growth had been identified as one of the inhibiting factors in drawing up realistic capital investment programmes.

   In 1965, a more explicitly defined basis for the administration of regional planning was established by the sub-division of England into the eight Economic Planning Regions indicated earlier in *Figure 3*. In most but not all parts of the country, their boundaries corresponded closely to those of the 'standard regions' which, for some years previously, had been used to provide a common framework for the presentation of departmental statistics. At this time, several government departments already exercised some of their local responsibilities from offices in the regions, but most of the land plannning and housing functions of the Ministry of Housing and Local Government were still exercised from London, except for the two most northerly regions of England. As a step towards fuller co-ordination between the regional activities of the various ministries concerned in the new economic planning framework, a decision was taken that, in each region, the activities of all the relevant ministries should, wherever possible, be grouped together in a single building. In every case, this new centre should include a regional office of the Ministry of Housing and Local Government, while a central co-ordinating role was to be taken by a senior official of the new Department of Economic Affairs, who would serve as Chairman of a new Regional Economic Planning Board. This Board was to consist of senior civil servants representing all the various ministries concerned in regional affairs, including those responsible for housing and land planning, transport, employment, industry and technology, education, agriculture, and investment in public utility services.

In order to provide a body of informed regional opinion to which the Regional Economic Planning Board could refer, a new Regional Economic Planning Council was appointed for each region by the Secretary of State for Economic Affairs. This Council was to consist of about twenty-five people selected for their knowledge and experience of the region concerned. Although it was stressed that the members of each Council were to be appointed for their individual qualities, rather than as representatives of particular sectional interests, some care was taken to select a set of people for each region who could be seen to reflect a fair balance of territorial interests, and of important sectors of regional influence, such as industry, the trade unions, the universities, agriculture, and local government.

On their formation, the Economic Planning Councils were given the following terms of reference: first, 'to assist in the formulation of regional plans, having regard to the best use of the region's resources'; second, 'to advise on the steps necessary for implementing the regional plans on the basis of information and assessments provided by the economic planning boards'; and, third, 'to advise on the regional implications of national economic policies'. Further, they were encouraged to take an active initiating role in bringing matters to the attention of the Boards where they felt this to be necessary. Given these responsibilities, it was accepted that the proceedings of the Councils would have to be treated as largely confidential. If sensitive information on current issues of central government policy was to be freely discussed, then even a full disclosure of the items covered on the agenda could make the Council members uncomfortably vulnerable to their sectional constituency interests.

The new regional structure drew some immediate criticism from those who had been advocating bolder moves towards the establishment of elected regional assemblies equipped with 'teeth' in the form of specific executive powers. However, even the limited functions envisaged for the Economic Planning Councils and Boards raised some difficult questions of demarcation with existing agencies of planning and co-ordination, not least of which was the then Ministry of Housing and Local Government with its established role in land planning and related fields. It was largely to avoid the appearance of trespassing on the Ministry's statutory responsibilities in such areas – concerned largely with processes of contextual control over the activities of local planning authorities – that the prefix 'Economic' was attached to the new Planning Councils and Boards. However, as we shall see, the relationship of 'physical' to 'economic' planning was to prove at first a difficult one to define, giving rise at times to much uncertainty about the institutional relationships between the Land Planning Ministry and the Department of Economic Affairs. These uncertainties were reduced to some extent when the DEA was disbanded in 1969 after five years of independent existence – largely because of national political pressures and difficulties in defining its role in relation to the all-pervading influence of the Treasury. Significantly, the DEA's small nuclei of economic planning staff in the regions were retained, later to be integrated with the physical and transportation planners in the new Department of the Environment. Gradually, the relationships between these various forms of planning skill began to become more clearly established, in a context of exploratory activities that varied somewhat in their emphasis from region to region, but which we shall now discuss more fully from our perspective of the West Midlands of England.

The growth of regional processes in the West Midlands

The broad discussion, which follows, of the evolution of regional planning in the West Midlands rests largely on information gathered in discussions with civil servants and others who played central roles in the processes of physical and economic planning in the region during the period from 1968 to 1971; on a review of documents published by the Economic Planning Council and other relevant agencies; on published discussions of the role and influence of the Council (Cadbury, 1968; Painter, 1972); and on our own participation in various activities of the West Midlands branch of the Regional Studies Association. We did not seek opportunities for more continuous observation of the kind we were afforded in

Droitwich, and to that extent our picture of regional relationships will inevitably be less complete than that of local relationships at Droitwich, though we hope no less balanced in its emphasis.

The most readily visible outputs of the new regional machinery were a series of published planning studies, the first of which, entitled simply 'The West Midlands: a Regional Study', appeared in 1965 under the auspices of the DEA. This reported the work of the inter-departmental team of civil servants which had been commissioned the previous year, shortly before the DEA had been formed or the new regional structure had been established. Much of the information assembled fits the description of 'regional stocktaking' suggested by Cullingworth (1970), in that it brought together various forms of data from the records of different ministries, on the region's demographic, economic, and employment structure, as a background against which to review existing and potential commitments for the future distribution of population and public services.

Like others of its generation, this study can be viewed as reflecting a comparatively early stage in the process of learning about relevant approaches to the appraisal of regional options. The Director of one subsequent regional study team has described much of the work of this period as being conditioned by the traditional administrator's response of focusing on specific topics rather than broader issues, seeking to tackle each exhaustively rather than selectively, and extrapolating from the present to the future without the help of any explicit methodology for coping with uncertainties either internal or external to the region. However, despite the paucity of systematic techniques with which to reach beyond the level of stocktaking and qualitative appraisal, the authors of the 1965 study found themselves inexorably focusing on the still-pervasive issue of Birmingham overspill. The conclusion they reached was that the commitments so far negotiated still left a substantial population increase to be accommodated in new locations, in a manner that — at least in the medium term — would have to take into account constraints in industrial location arising from inter-regional employment policies.

The overall problem was diagnosed as one of striking a balance between the peripheral expansion of the conurbation, the growth of 'satellite' communities within commuter range, and commitments to major new centres of growth further afield. One such centre already existed at the time in the newly designated New Town at Dawley in Shropshire (Salop), and one of the team's more specific recommendations concerned the possibility of locating additional population in this area. If, as then mooted, other centres of expansion were eventually to be established in the neighbouring regions to the north and south — around the Dee and Severn estuaries respectively — then it was argued that an attractive long-term strategy could be to establish a new 'axis of national growth' extending along the full length of the border between England and Wales, and serving to relieve much of the pressure from the West Midlands conurbation and its immediate environs.

In a preface to this report, the government expressed itself as yet uncommitted to its findings, and referred it to the newly formed West Midlands Economic Planning Council to provide a considered appraisal, after consultation with local authorities and other relevant agencies. Some eight months later, the Council submitted its first interim reactions. These added support, with varying degrees of qualification, to the specific proposals that the study team had made for further expansion in the Dawley area and elsewhere. However, the view was also expressed that the areas of study for possible longer-term growth should not be confined in an 'arbitrary' way to the north/south axis recommended in the earlier study, and three other alternative axes were suggested for further evaluation.

A year later, a more comprehensive review of the region's problems was published by the Council (*The West Midlands: Patterns of Growth*, West Midlands Economic Planning Council, 1967), with the staff work this time carried out by the civil servants in the new regional office. While still accepting the 1965 study as a source of basic data, some of the group's assumptions were modified in the light of subsequent information, and a revised set of overspill proposals was put forward for meeting the modified estimates of growth over the next fifteen years. A map and table showing the main elements of these proposals is reproduced in *Figure 72*. One of the Council's main arguments was that the provision of new housing and social services for an expanding population depended on vigorous action to exploit more fully the region's economic potential. To this end, a variety of initiatives were suggested in the fields of further education, industrial training, and research; and it was argued that governmental controls over the movement of industry should in future be applied in a more positive and more flexible way.

When the national government issued its formal reply to the points raised in the report, several of the recommendations were accepted without demur. However, those relating to the more vigorous support of industrial dispersal within the region were rejected, as being incompatible with the national priority attached to reducing the differentials of unemployment between regions. Accordingly, it was argued that — at least in the shorter term — more attention would have to be focused on the promotion of overspill schemes within reasonable commuting distance of the conurbation.

Figure 72   Agreed and suggested overspill schemes in West Midlands (from *Patterns of Growth* report, 1967)

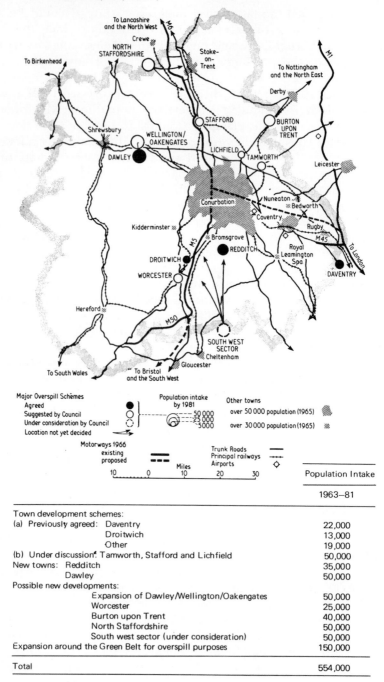

Town development schemes:		Population Intake 1963–81
(a) Previously agreed: Daventry		22,000
Droitwich		13,000
Other		19,000
(b) Under discussion: Tamworth, Stafford and Lichfield		50,000
New towns: Redditch		35,000
Dawley		50,000
Possible new developments:		
Expansion of Dawley/Wellington/Oakengates		50,000
Worcester		25,000
Burton upon Trent		40,000
North Staffordshire		50,000
South west sector (under consideration)		50,000
Expansion around the Green Belt for overspill purposes		150,000
Total		554,000

Initiatives by local authorities

While this kind of debate was taking place between the central government and the new Regional Council, the question arose of what part the local authorities in the region should seek to play in the evolving planning process. At this time, relations between particular county and city authorities were continuing to impede progress towards the relief of the problems of congestion within the conurbation. Warwickshire and Worcestershire continued to resist incursions by Birmingham into the proposed green belt — although some private housing development was conceded at Wythall — while progress in the New Town at Dawley was held up by the high cost of infrastructure development.

One interest that the local authorities clearly had in common was that of retaining some capacity to work towards their own solutions, rather than of allowing all initiative to pass to central government and the new Regional Council. With active encouragement from central government, Birmingham and Worcestershire therefore agreed to initiate a joint study of possible locations for peripheral development which could contribute to the city's short-term housing problem, on the understanding that other local planning authorities would join in a wider review process of other future locations for expansion within the region. Here, the emphasis would be on schemes that might avoid both the continual erosion of the prospective green belt boundaries, and the heavy investment costs of distant New Town development.

In 1966, those local authorities with a clear concern in this wider review process therefore came together to form a new permanent multi-organizational structure, known as the West Midlands Planning Authorities Conference or, more informally, the 'Standing Conference'. Subsequently, the membership of this was extended to embrace all five Counties and eleven County Boroughs within the Economic Planning Region. In some ways, this Conference was a successor to that established some fifteen years earlier in response to the 1948 Abercrombie and Jackson Plan. Although this earlier Conference had established one piece of permanent co-ordinating machinery in the form of a 'Technical Committee' of Chief Planning Officers, the meetings of this group had lost much of their significance through being consistently steered away from politically controversial issues.

This time, the local authorities, with encouragement and occasional advice from the regional civil service, agreed to form a joint study team, to be steered through a new 'Technical Officers Panel' on which the delicate question of Chairmanship would be settled through a rotation system. Also, an administrative panel was appointed to take decisions on budgeting and staffing matters. A senior planning officer was seconded from Birmingham to lead the study team, while most of the other posts were also filled by secondment from among the contributing authorities. Consultants were appointed to deal with a number of specialist aspects of the study, and it was agreed that civil servants from the regional office and headquarters would provide skills relating to demographic, social, and economic analysis, either on a full or a part-time basis.

The new study team took its place in an office in Birmingham, adjoining that of another joint local authority team which had already been recently established, concerned with transportation planning over the conurbation and adjoining areas. The origins of the transport study were somewhat different, in that it had been initiated as a second phase in an ongoing process of transportation planning, the first phase having already been completed by a team of specialist consultants. The consultants had set out many of the major issues and some tentative conclusions, with the aid of some of the sophisticated processes of mathematical modelling that were then becoming accepted in the transportation planning field; and it was accepted that the next step should be for the local authorities themselves to form a joint team which would be directed more explicitly towards the complex fields of executive decision that would be involved. As with the Regional Study Team, the joint transport study team was assisted by central funds and reported formally through a 'technical committee of relevant officials from the sponsoring local authorities. However, the staff differed in being appointed on a permanent basis, with a view to creating a permanent competence which, after the impending reorganization of local government, could be handed on to any metropolitan or regional agency of government which might be established within the conurbation area.

Meanwhile, another initiative towards inter-agency planning was crystallizing in the east of the region. In Coventry, a review of the City's Development Plan was disclosing the dimensions of a future problem of shortage of housing land after the mid-seventies, at a time when the Land Planning Ministry was beginning to encourage the experimental formation of sub-regional planning teams in a few carefully selected parts of the country. After settling some delicate problems of political balance which have been touched on elsewhere (Friend and Jessop, 1969), it was agreed that a study team should be appointed under the joint auspices of Coventry, Warwickshire, and Solihull, with a limited two-year life.

Also, within the main West Midlands conurbation, another sub-regional planning process was being mobilized at a more informal level. The 1968 Town and Country Planning Act introduced the new concept of the 'Structure Plan' as the primary instrument of strategic land use policy, intended to overcome the procedural and other rigidities of the established development plan system by concentrating on broad statements of policy rather than specified land zonings. More localized options were to be dealt with through a system of 'Local Plans' at the level of districts, including plans for selected local 'Action Areas' of various kinds. Here, planning authorities would have an increased degree of local discretion, leaving the Land Planning Ministry free to concentrate its formal powers of scrutiny at the broader policy level. Among the group of authorities invited to take part in the first wave of structure plan preparation were the seven County Boroughs in the West Midlands conurbation, and an *ad hoc* preparatory group was established with encouragement and technical assistance from the Ministry's regional planning offices.

Thus, a number of joint study teams were established during the late sixties, working in overlapping but by no means identical territorial boundaries. These boundaries are indicated in *Figure 73*, in relation to a mapping of the then planning authorities in which spatial relationships are preserved but areas are distorted in order to make them proportional to population. Thus, the map reflects the relative political weightings of different local constituency interests. Also superimposed on this map is the 'political territory' of the West Midlands Metropolitan County as later settled by the 1972 Local Government Act. Another new executive agency referred to in *Figure 73* is the West Midlands Passenger Transport Authority (PTA), which was first established in 1969 with an area slightly wider than that covered by the transport study team. This authority represented a further addition to the set of *ad hoc* joint local authority agencies established in the years prior to local government reorganization, to overcome problems of fragmentation in the planning of specific executive functions. In the case of the PTA, the joint agency was equipped with an explicit statutory role in relation to the provisions of the 1968 Transport Act, and a strong executive arm of its own in the form of a new Passenger Transport Executive (PTE), bringing together the municipal bus undertakings of Birmingham and the County Boroughs within the conurbation.

Figure 73   Political map of inter-agency planning activities in West Midlands, 1965-73

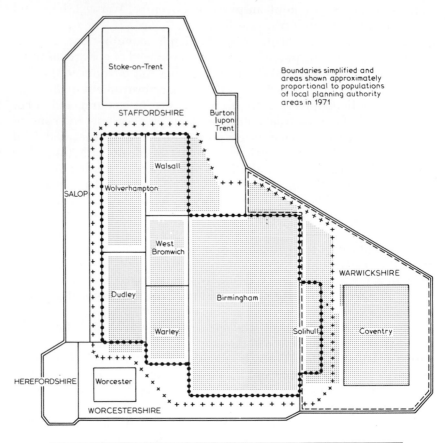

Boundaries simplified and areas shown approximately proportional to populations of local planning authority areas in 1971

Stoke-on-Trent

STAFFORDSHIRE

Burton lupon Trent

Walsall

SALOP

Wolverhampton

West Bromwich

WARWICKSHIRE

Dudley

Birmingham

Solihull

Coventry

Warley

HEREFORDSHIRE

Worcester

WORCESTERSHIRE

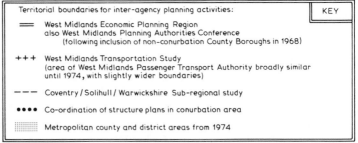

Territorial boundaries for inter-agency planning activities:

KEY

══ West Midlands Economic Planning Region
also West Midlands Planning Authorities Conference
(following inclusion of non-conurbation County Boroughs in 1968)

+++ West Midlands Transportation Study
(area of West Midlands Passenger Transport Authority broadly similar until 1974, with slightly wider boundaries)

– – – Coventry / Solihull / Warwickshire Sub-regional study

●●●● Co-ordination of structure plans in conurbation area

▒▒▒ Metropolitan county and district areas from 1974

Activities in the economic planning field

While these developments were taking place in the local government field, the economic planning staff of the government departments within the regional office were also engaged on a somewhat different front, in association with members of the Economic Planning Council. Following publication of the *Patterns of Growth* report in 1967, adverse trends in the national economy threw an increasingly sharp light on the vulnerability of the region's traditional industrial base. The members of the Planning Council therefore resolved to set up a working party from among their numbers to carry out a deeper appraisal of the economic potential of the region, and the actions that might be considered to stimulate further growth. Most of the eleven members of the working party were leading figures in the region's industrial life, who undertook between them to carry out a wide-ranging series of interviews to gather both impressionistic and other information about economic conditions, trends, and perceived conditions for future prosperity in various relevant sectors of industry.

The approach adopted was to analyse employment trends both by type of industry and by the territorial sub-divisions of the Employment Ministry, and then to pick out for further exploration by interview methods certain selected types of industry believed to be of special significance either because of a high existing concentration within the region, or because of an apparent deficiency of employment when compared to other regions, or because of future potential in terms of national economic growth. The results of the surveys and interviews carried out were presented in the second full report of the Economic Planning Council, entitled *The West Midlands: an Economic Appraisal* (West Midlands Economic Planning Council, 1971). This set out an ambitious set of proposals for governmental action to stimulate economic growth, with a less pronounced emphasis on spatial distribution within the region than had the proposals of earlier regional studies.

The main argument was for more positive support by government for growth within the region, including relaxation of IDC constraints. It was argued that such growth could serve to produce a 'spin-off' for other regions, as well as to reduce the level of unemployment in the West Midlands, which (as indicated by the comparisons presented at the foot of *Figure 49*) was now showing itself more sensitive than most other regions to fluctuations in the state of the national economy. At a meeting of the Regional Studies Association in Birmingham, the report was exposed to some criticism on the grounds that it represented a piece of special pleading on behalf of a set of predominantly industrial interests whose members shared the same implicit assumptions about the beneficial effects of continued economic growth (Herson, 1972), and that there was little evidence of any systematic planning process underlying the choice of recommendations advanced (Barbara Smith, 1972a). In the defence of the approach adopted, a leading member of the working party argued that the exercise had been carried out under intense time pressures, depending heavily on the accumulated expertise of individuals with long experience in the region's industries. Even when seen as a piece of informed regional advocacy, it was argued that the study could only help to improve the background against which central government confronted their major decisions of national economic policy.

Such a view is supported in the article by Painter (1972), in which the 'Economic Appraisal' report is seen as setting a seal of regional approval on a more diffuse set of representations by various regional interests, led by Birmingham's City Council and Chamber of Commerce, for modification of government industrial development policy in the West Midlands. Painter suggests that the report was in fact influential in bringing about certain changes in government IDC policy during 1972, which distinguished for the first time between the conditions of the West Midlands and those of the less vulnerable South East. He argues that the formation of the Council and working party helped to institutionalize the existing informal relationships between a variety of commercial, managerial, and trade union groupings in the region, as well as the more influential individual firms, to produce a new and more effective pressure group for effective regional development.

One of the intended functions of the Economic Planning Council was to participate in the strategic planning of public investment, through an annual review of the five-year projections of capital expenditure in the region by the ministries concerned with housing, transport, education, health, and other relevant sectors. In the West Midlands, these projections were scrutinized by a sub-committee of the Regional Council, with regional civil servants acting as technical assessors. They were then co-ordinated nationally through the Public Expenditure Survey Committee, a new piece of governmental machinery which had been established to increase the effectiveness of national economic management. At first, it proved by no means easy for the Regional Economic Planning Councils to intervene effectively in this national process of adjustment between the interests of different ministries, each with a powerful hierarchical

organization built around the principle of ultimate political accountability to the Minister. In the West Midlands, the opportunities for
effective regional influence were especially limited, because of the
continuing policy of steering as much as possible of the limited
national potential for public investment towards the assisted areas of
the North and West.

The new projections of regional expenditure were carried out and
evaluated on a confidential basis. Nevertheless, they were found
helpful by the regional civil servants in appreciating more clearly the
economic dimension of their planning task, and the process of
regional scrutiny was felt to work more effectively in the West
Midlands than in some other regions. Although Painter (1972)
suggests that it may have had no more than a marginal effect on the
allocation of public resources, he does attribute one important
decision of investment priority to the influence of the Council
through its annual review cycle: the early programming of a strategic
link between the New Town at Telford and the national motorway
system. Although other pressures may well have been involved in this
and other similar programming decisions, it would be surprising if the
exploratory processes of the Regional Council during this period did
not have a much more important influence in terms of mutual
adjustment between different decision-making agencies than their
publicly visible outputs might suggest. In the West Midlands, as
elsewhere, there has been much criticism of the limited practical
influence of the Economic Planning Councils, not least from those
invited to serve as members during the early years; but, in terms of
the gradual evolution of networks of decision-making activity at the
regional level, it appears likely that their contribution may have been
a comparatively subtle one, with indirect influences at many
different points in the total machinery of government.

An evolving pattern of inter-agency explorations

In *Figure 74*, the various regional and sub-regional planning studies
described in the last two sections are brought together to present a
picture of an evolving pattern of exploratory processes in the West
Midlands during the late sixties and early seventies — some of them
based primarily on co-ordinative activity among local authorities,
while others were initiated under central government or Economic
Planning Council auspices.

As we have already discussed, each of these exploratory processes
was initiated in response to a somewhat different set of pressures —
national, regional, or local. Accordingly, they differed in terms of

Figure 74   Pattern of main regional and sub-regional studies in West Midlands, 1964-73

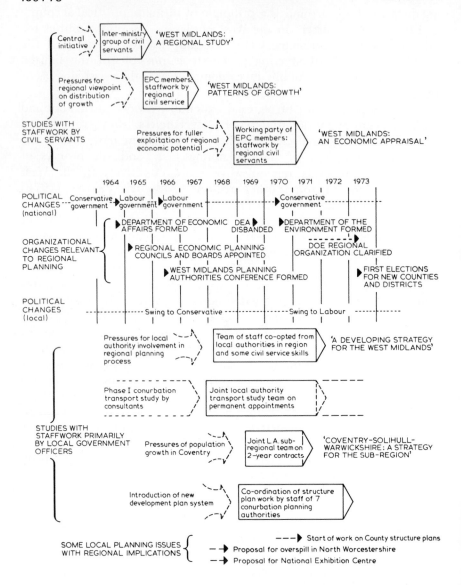

reference, pattern of accountability, management structure, and sources of exploratory skill. As indicated in *Figure 74*, the arrangements for assignment of staff varied from permanent recruitment to the formation of *ad hoc* working parties, backed by differing levels of financial support from central government. Inevitably, these different organizational settings led to differences of exploratory style, leading the teams concerned towards different planning horizons, different approaches to the gathering of relevant survey information, and different practices of consultation with relevant outside interests.

In the case of the regional study team sponsored by the Planning Authorities Conference, the management of the exploratory process posed some particularly exacting problems. It was launched at a time of rising professional concern to adopt a comprehensive 'systems approach' to regional planning studies, and specialist firms of consultants were retained both to analyse communications aspects and, once the range of locational solutions had been narrowed down to four 'fine options', to carry out a systematic evaluation of these using the Planning Balance Sheet method of cost-benefit analysis. Meanwhile, many specialist officers from the local authorities became involved in working parties for detailed exploration of such topics as population, employment, leisure, and financial resources. The outside consultants themselves related to two influential working parties concerned with communications and with 'strategy', which brought some of the most powerful local officials of the constituent authorities into direct round-the-table confrontation.

Thus, mechanisms were built up to extend the field of exploration beyond that which the study team could hope to cover through its own resources alone. This made the problem of co-ordination a formidable one for the team's Director and for the Administrative Committee of the Conference, which controlled the flow of resources. Because of the underlying conflicts of interest between the contributing local authorities, there was a lack of clear political guidance to the team, and also a tendency for the authorities continually to reclaim key staff who had been seconded to it, so creating a climate of instability and inhibiting and opportunities for interactive learning within the study team. Because of these difficulties, the team's reporting horizon was repeatedly delayed; and it became clear that the choice of recommendations would be a matter of some delicacy, in which the results of the team's analytical work was likely to be subjected to political challenge from one direction or another, however systematic their exploratory process and however clearly stated their assumptions.

When the report finally appeared, under the title of *A Developing Strategy for the West Midlands* (West Midlands PAC, 1971), it advocated a solution based on a main axis of growth extending north eastwards and south westwards from Birmingham, with three new centres of short-term population growth and five centres of new employment on the fringes of the conurbation. These recommend-ations were immediately subjected to public criticism from the political leadership of Birmingham City Council, on the grounds that they would mean a further erosion in the economic viability of the city. Subsequently, the City Council voted by a narrow margin to revoke its membership of the Conference, withdrawing the Director and other seconded members of the team.

A further criticism of the study, based on its methods rather than the content of its recommendations, came some months later in the publication of an informal letter of comment from the regional planning staff of the Environment Ministry. It was argued that there had been inconsistencies in the logic leading up to the choice of proposals, and that the team had failed to make use of much of the survey material on the region which other people had accumulated over the last few years. This criticism was underlined by the local reaction of the officers of the Development Group at Droitwich, who were able to point out that the modest 'additional' population growth recommended for the town was in fact less than the target to which the partners to the agreement were already committed. Despite these criticisms, the chairman of the Conference — a position at that time held by the Chairman of Worcestershire County Council — was able to argue that the study process was intended to be a developing one, so that the published results could be 'amended to make room for change' by the remaining members of the study team, which had been kept in being for this purpose. By this time, new economic and demographic trends were beginning to reduce quite markedly the size of the expected regional population increase and therefore the size of the political problem involved and, following a change of political control within Birmingham, the city duly re-opened its membership of the Conference. So another crisis in the relations between neighbouring authorities had been successfully overcome, but only at a time when relations between the cities and counties were becoming increasingly overshadowed by the impending reorganization of local government in 1974.

The influence on decisions in the region

The reports of most other parallel planning studies were received with rather more equanimity within the region. Taken together, the flow of outputs generated by the various exploratory processes provided inputs of information and policy guidance to a variety of other ongoing processes at different levels of governmental organization, including the modest influences already discussed on the economic planning activities and capital expenditure programmes of central government. Among the other major political concerns in the region at this time were two important planning applications, carrying major strategic implications yet surrounded by urgent pressures for commitment. One of these again concerned a proposal for expansion on the boundaries of Birmingham and Worcestershire, and this raised similar issues and conflicts to those of the earlier Wythall application discussed in Chapter 3. The other application, promoted jointly by Birmingham's City Council and its Chamber of Commerce, was for a National Exhibition Centre strategically sited in the rural belt between Birmingham and Coventry. This proposal, justified essentially through the 'central place' advantages of the West Midlands within England, was fiercely contested by rival interests in the London area and became a major national policy issue. Painter, in his paper on the West Midlands Economic Planning Council (1972), argues that this was an issue where the Council was only marginally involved, because the initiative lay very clearly with what he calls the 'Birmingham lobby' in arguing its case to the central government in London.

Because of the difficulty of synchronizing the outputs of the various regional planning processes with the more urgent pressures for taking specific decisions within the region, there were many other local planning issues during this period that had to be confronted in a state of uncertainty about future regional strategies. This applied in particular to the land-use options faced by some of the County Councils in the West Midlands, all of which during 1971 and 1972 were in the process of preparing their first draft Structure Plans. In Warwickshire, the County planners were able to work largely within the framework of the report published in 1971 by the Coventry/Warwickshire/Solihull sub-regional team, which had already been approved at political level. In Worcestershire, however, the planners faced a more open situation, in view of the lack of a similar commitment to the results of the West Midlands Conference study.

In its initial response to the regional team's report, the County Council asserted firmly its right to exercise its own discretion in deciding the pace and direction of the proposed future growth of Redditch, Droitwich, and any other prospective growth centres within its territory. Later, in their draft Structure Plan, the county planners put forward seven alternative strategies for growth within its area. As mentioned earlier in Chapters 8 and 9, the preferred alternative advocated, among other measures, an increase from 30,000 to 46,000 in the population target for Droitwich. So, once more, as in the late nineteen-fifties, the processes of regional exploration were beginning to impinge directly on the future prospects of Droitwich and other local communities in Worcestershire. Again, however, many further processes of local consultation and central government appraisal lay ahead before such proposals could form the basis of specific local actions. In this instance, the uncertainties appeared likely to be exacerbated by the imminence of local government reorganization in 1974. Not only could new political groupings be expected to emerge in the West Midlands Metropolitan County and its constituent districts, but also in the new Hereford and Worcester County Council, and in the county district of Wychavon, of which the town of Droitwich would form only one constituent part.

The emergence of regional decision networks

The achievement of some degree of co-ordination and consistency between these various regional and local activities inevitably became a matter of direct concern to those senior civil servants in the regional office most directly involved in physical and economic planning. Over the years, some complex networks of influence began to evolve, resting largely but by no means entirely on the formal responsibilities that had been created by the developing pattern of institutional relationships within the regional planning framework.

The Economic Planning Board provided an obvious focus for mutual adjustment between senior civil servants from the various ministries operating within the region. However, after its first few full meetings — involving representatives of some ministries that had no more than a marginal interest in regional economic policy issues — the Board met only infrequently in full session. Its place was taken in effect by a smaller 'steering committee' which met every Monday morning and was attended by representatives of the four or five ministries most directly concerned in economic planning matters. At this level, the policy interests originally represented were those of economic planning, industrial development, employment, transport, housing, and agriculture.

At a less senior level, the same departments were all represented on a Research Committee, which was set up under the chairmanship of the Principal Planning Officer of the then Ministry of Housing and Local Government. Although, at that time, this officer occupied a crucial position as the main point of contact with the local planning authorities, he was not automatically entitled to representation of the Economic Planning Board, as he was not the most senior officer in the regional organization of his department. However, his role as Chairman of the regional research committee earned him a place on the Board and, more importantly, on its steering committee. At a time when relations with local authorities were developing rapidly through the various joint study processes, but most local planners preferred to relate to the regional machinery through their own professional channels, linking these to civil service decision networks was clearly important.

As argued by B.C. Smith in his study of regional planning in the South West (1969), the Chairmanship of the Economic Planning Council was another potentially crucial position, as it allowed its occupant to play an active role in establishing communications between the regional planning organization and other regional interests. As Smith suggests, an energetic Chairman could become a 'natural initiator of a co-ordinated regional effort'. This point is endorsed by Painter (1972) with particular reference to the role of Mr. Adrian Cadbury, as Chairman of the Economic Council in the West Midlands between 1967 and 1970. In such a position, important linkages could be formed with representatives of industrial and other economic interests in the region, drawing where possible on the knowledge and influence of his fellow members of the Council. For the Chairman, the range of alternative strategies in the mobilization of regional decision networks could therefore become exceptionally wide, demanding – in our terms – a high order of reticulist judgement.

A third major node in the formation of decision networks was that provided by the senior regional official who acted as Chairman of the Economic Planning Board, and who carried direct accountability to the central government in London for the operation of the overall regional economic planning machinery. We were able to gain some insights into this role, at one stage of its development, through a discussion with the civil servant holding this position in 1971, who had initially been appointed to the regional office as an Under-Secretary in the Department of Economic Affairs. He had retained the role of Chairman of the Board after the disbandment of that Ministry and upon his re-assignment to the Environment Ministry during the following year. At the time of interview, a further step in the development of the regional planning machinery had just brought him to the position of Regional Director within the enlarged Ministry, although he was in fact due to retire a few months later. He likened his new position to one at the centre of an hourglass, as he was now placed more clearly in a position of central responsibility

Figure 75 Regional planning: network relationships of Principal Planning Officer

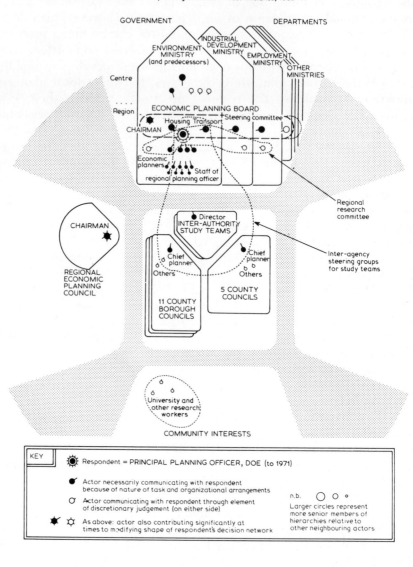

Definition of field of decision: oversight of physical and related planning activities in West Midlands, 1965–71

GOVERNMENT   DEPARTMENTS

INDUSTRIAL
DEVELOPMENT
ENVIRONMENT MINISTRY
MINISTRY   EMPLOYMENT
(and predecessors)   MINISTRY
                                        OTHER
                                        MINISTRIES
Centre

ECONOMIC PLANNING BOARD

Region   Housing Transport   Steering committee
        CHAIRMAN

Economic
planners
            Staff of
regional planning officer

                                        Regional
                                        research
                                        committee
CHAIRMAN   Director
                    INTER-AUTHORITY
                    STUDY TEAMS

                Chief   Chief
                planner   planner
REGIONAL   Others   Others
ECONOMIC
PLANNING   Inter-agency
COUNCIL   steering groups
                                    for study teams
            11 COUNTY   5 COUNTY
            BOROUGH   COUNCILS
            COUNCILS

University and
other research
workers

COMMUNITY INTERESTS

KEY	
☀	Respondent = PRINCIPAL PLANNING OFFICER, DOE (to 1971)
●	Actor necessarily communicating with respondent because of nature of task and organizational arrangements
○	Actor communicating with respondent through element of discretionary judgement (on either side)
✸ ✩	As above: actor also contributing significantly at times to modifying shape of respondent's decision network

n.b. ○ ○ ∘
Larger circles represent more senior members of hierarchies relative to other neighbouring actors

within the regional office of his Ministry, yet remained accountable upwards to some five or six Deputy Secretaries at headquarters, where responsibilities at that time remained organized primarily on functional lines. His own view was that such a position called for quick and confident judgements, often with little opportunity for hesitation, whenever issues arose for which the choice of channels was not clear-cut. In our own terminology, the role could be seen as one calling for a high order of reticulist judgement, especially in the routeing of exploratory processes within the civil service structure itself.

In the following years, further changes in the internal organizations of the Environment Ministry were to bring a more clearly-defined pattern to the management of the regional office. The responsibilities for statutory Development Plan functions, as well as the advisory functions of the Principal Planning Officer, were decentralized to the region under a Regional Controller (Plans and Planning), reporting to the Regional Director alongside parallel Controllers for Housing and Environment and for Roads and Transportation respectively. The primary channel of accountability of the Regional Director now lay through a single Deputy Secretary at headquarters, and it was envisaged that the new structure would endure at least until after the forthcoming report of the Royal Commission on the Constitution, which might conceivably point the way to further proposals for regional devolution of central government powers.

The Principal Planning Officer and his network

During the period we have been discussing, the three main interfaces of the regional planning organization could be regarded as that with regional industry and related interests, that with the central government, and that with the local planning authorities. We have now seen that the actors occupying the most crucial reticulist roles in relation to each of these interfaces, in the transitional form of the regional planning structure, could be identified respectively as the Chairman of the Economic Planning Council, the Chairman of the Economic Planning Board, and the Principal Planning Officer of the Land Planning Ministry. The network diagram presented in *Figure 75* indicated the broad pattern of communications in which the Principal Planning Officer became involved over the period from the formation of the regional office in 1965 until his retirement in 1971. This diagram identifies, among his primary points of contact, both the Chairman of the Economic Planning Board and of the Economic

Planning Council. Indeed, he had first been brought closely into contact with both in the course of the early explorations that had preceded the publication in 1967 of *The West Midlands: Patterns of Growth*, a document that can be regarded as the first major contribution by the new regional organization to the formation of regional policies.

During this period, the Principal Planning Officer was able to build up a team of some ten planners and research officers, most of whom were in fact recruited from local authorities in the region, and therefore provided ready access to networks of information on local planning issues. Such information could be drawn on extensively when contributing to, or advising upon, strategic planning studies; and it could also provide a regional context against which to advise on 'casework' applications, for instance relating to applications for Industrial Development Certificates. The structure of this regional planning team was so designed as to provide cross-connections between territorial and functional lines of delegation, backed by a small 'strategic group' to provide a broader and more forward-looking exploratory capacity. Although many of the external relationships of the office could be managed by other members of the team, the Principal Planning Officer considered it important to act in person as Chairman of the regional research committee. Also, he was invited to join the technical panel of the West Midlands Regional Study team and the equivalent steering groups of the two other joint planning teams which were operating during that period. In this way, he could act directly as a custodian of his Ministry's interests, speaking with additional authority in so far as there was any contribution of Ministry finance or manpower to the work of the study team concerned.

While such roles in group processes inevitably brought the Principal Planning Officer into contact with a variety of local authority officers and other public servants, his general responsibility for the dissemination of new planning methods and procedures required him to develop more direct individual relationships with the Chief Planning Officers of the local authorities within the region. Among his other significant relationships was that with research workers in outside institutions, as developed through his chairmanship of the Regional Research Committee and his involvement in the activities of the regional branches of the Royal Town Planning Institute and the Regional Studies Association. Indeed, it was through the interests he expressed in the kind of research into planning processes reported in this book that we were first directed to Droitwich as a potentially fruitful site for our work.

The linkages which the Principal Planning Officer had to maintain with his departmental headquarters in London included the administrators who were formally responsible for statutory planning functions — not at that time delegated to the regional office — and also certain professional scientific colleagues who could provide advice or information on a variety of specialized topics. The Principal Planning Officer in Birmingham therefore found himself in a position of little formal authority, yet potentially of considerable influence at the intersection of several types of exploratory network. As indicated in *Figure 75*, these included not only the evolving networks of activity within governmental departments, the local authorities, and the Economic Planning Council, but also those within the multi-organizational structures of the overlapping regional study teams and the Economic Planning Board with its steering and research committees. Later, the pattern of communication was to evolve further through the delegation of statutory land planning responsibilities from headquarters, the appointment of the three Regional Controllers under the Regional Director, and the establishment of closer working linkages with the Chief Executives as well as the Chief Planning Officers of the leading local authorities in the region.

Often, in the late sixties and early seventies, the argument was put forward that the development of a cohesive regional planning activity in England was being inhibited by the absence of the kind of political authority that might be provided by an elected regional assembly, and also by the pressures arising from the hierarchical structure of government departments, built around the principle of final accountability through a single Minister of the Crown (Mackintosh, 1968). This view was indeed supported by discussions held with the Chairman of the Economic Planning Board in a neighbouring region during 1968, when the regional machinery was still at an early stage of development. The Civil Servant concerned saw his only possible role in terms of attempting to extend the breadth of evaluation applied to proposals for action that had been generated elsewhere. However, the Principal Planning Officer in the West Midlands believed that a considerably more creative role was possible in his own particular set of regional circumstances, even given the constraints of the very limited degree of formal authority which he and his colleagues had at their disposal. Furthermore, he believed that a spirit of genuine co-operation was evolving both among the officials of different government departments within the regional office, and also between regional and central officials within his own departmental establishment.

The region as a centre of innovation

Viewed in the perspective of the various regional activities indicated in *Figure 74,* and the networks of relationships between actors set out in *Figure 75,* the regional organization of government in England, as it was evolving during the late sixties and early seventies, emerges as an important focus for processes of mutual adaptation and learning, at least in the case of the West Midlands. In the planning and management of the various regional and sub-regional studies, and also in the search for mutual consistency between those studies, methods of reconciliation had to be discovered between the very different traditions of economic, physical, and transportation planning. The problems of this reconciliation process were brought out by one planner on the staff of the Principal Planning Officer for the West Midlands in a paper presented to the annual Town and Country Planning Summer School (Bird, 1968). Using the imagery of social anthropology to discuss relations between the two 'tribes' of economic and physical planners, Bird argued that both had now prospered to the extent that they were competing for the same territory, located at the regional level of government where traditional boundaries were ill-defined. The economists, approaching this territory from an established base in central government, brought with them tools and attitudes concerned with the projection of highly aggregated measures of activity on comparatively modest time horizons. On the other hand, the tools and attitudes of the physical planners were rooted in their traditional ties with local planning authorities. Members of this profession had been accustomed to looking towards more distant time horizons, while reviewing choices of a much more localized character where considerations of imaginative design had traditionally taken precedence over those of quantitative evaluation. Bird speculated that the key to a gradual fusion of these very different traditions of planning might lie in the development of new types of systems approach to the planning process, in which the contributions of each type of discipline could ultimately become much more fully integrated.

Meanwhile, new disciplines, ranging from sociology to operational research, were being slowly introduced into the field of regional planning in the West Midlands and elsewhere. and the staff of the regional office in Birmingham became actively involved in the encouragement of experimentation with new techniques to assist the formulation and evaluation of alternatives and the handling of uncertainty and flexibility (Coventry/Solihull/Warwickshire, 1971).

In Britain and elsewhere (Alonso, 1971), speculations have been voiced about a trend towards the emergence of new 'meta-disciplines' in the urban and regional fields, through which the barriers of communication between such disciplinary frameworks as those of economics, sociology, and physical and transportation planning can ultimately be broken down. Although such an erosion of professional barriers was clearly discernible in many of the activities we have been reviewing in the West Midlands, our own evaluation suggests that perhaps the most powerful integrative force may be that generated by the pressures to achieve mutual adjustment between a multitude of political forces, each emanating from a different type of local, regional, or national constituency. As we have already indicated, the management of relationships between these various interests calls for highly developed reticulist skills from certain actors who occupy strategic roles in the regional planning structure. They must be able both to penetrate the conceptual frameworks of different types of planning expert, and also to choose their points of intervention at different levels of decision-making with a shrewd awareness of any underlying political implications.

In a broad sense, this tends to make the role of the administrator an increasingly political one, the less routinized and clearly structured his field of responsibility becomes. This is a point which emerges rather more directly at another emergent level of public planning – that of the supranational agency. In the case of the European Community, for instance, the role of the Commissioner is explicitly recognised as being intermediate between that of the politician and the civil servant, with a high degree of responsibility for the initiation of proposals for political action, which must be steered through many complex channels of further exploration and authorization before they can be translated into specific executive decisions.

Innovations in other regions

So far in this chapter, we have maintained our focus on one region of England, with its own particular set of strategic problems and organizational relations, which may have had a distinctive influence on the forms of innovation that we saw emerging at the regional level. Before drawing any more general conclusions, it is now fitting to look quickly at some other regions of Britain and to comment briefly on some of the similarities and differences in the development of planning processes over the same period of time.

As indicated earlier in *Figure 3*, the largest region of England in terms of population is the South East of England, containing some seventeen million people but treated as a single regional unit because of the dominance of the Greater London metropolitan area. Although the region contains a high proportion of national wealth and maintains comparatively low levels of unemployment (*Figure 49*), severe social and economic problems have persisted in inner London, while pressures of population on land resources and transportation systems have remained intense throughout and beyond the metropolitan area. For this reason, the evolution of the regional planning process in the South East has many points of similarity with that in the West Midlands. A succession of regional studies were carried out during the late sixties, the first by a working party of civil servants, the second under the auspices of the Regional Economic Planning Council, and the third through a joint conference of local planning authorities. In this instance, the study team reporting to the conference consisted mainly of experts drawn from central government, working under the leadership of the Ministry's Chief Planner. With the aid of a comparatively strong inter-agency steering group, it proved possible to contain the kinds of conflict that had materialized in the case of the West Midlands. As in the West Midlands the practical outcomes of the successive studies took the form of incremental shifts of commitment to particular overspill locations or 'corridors of growth' within the region, which were to impinge in subtle ways on a variety of processes of political negotiation at a more local level.

Among the pressing strategic issues within the South East during this period, the most widely debated were those of the Greater London Development Plan and the third London Airport, both of which became celebrated test cases for the use of sophisticated planning technologies in situations of conflict between powerful political interests. In the case of the third London Airport inquiry, a far-reaching cost-benefit analysis was carried out of four pre-selected alternative sites; but the results were widely challenged by other experts (Lichfield, 1971), on grounds concerned as much with questions of problem formulation as with evaluation of the given options. Many such questions were also raised at the inquiry into the Greater London Development Plan, which lasted for two years in all. The most contentious of the many issues which arose concerned a proposed new system of urban motorways, with far-reaching implications in terms of investment, land use, and social disturbance. Before the inquiry drew to a close, there was much mutual adaptation between the contending parties, and much adjustment of assumptions in relation to new information on demographic and economic trends. In both this case and that of the third London airport, the more important among the recommendations put forward were later reversed at a political level; but the processes of exploration involved could still be regarded as making a general contribution to the advancement of knowledge about ways of handling strategic issues of much technical complexity, in a climate of increasing concern to make adequate provision for participation by all the various community interests affected.

In the remaining regions of England, with the exception at one time of the North West, the strategic studies which were initiated after the regional economic planning structure had been established had a less clear physical planning focus in problems of congestion and metropolitan overspill, and tended to concentrate instead on the advocacy of the general economic interests of the region concerned. In some of these regions, the more significant innovations in planning methodology were made at the level of sub-regional study teams. The experiences of these teams have been evaluated by Cowling and Steeley (1973), who were themselves closely involved in the Nottinghamshire/Derbyshire sub-regional study. Among the authors' main concerns is the difficult problem of relating in a satisfactory way to the complex organizational and political environments within which such teams must operate.

In the early seventies, some further innovations were introduced in the organization of regional planning by the setting up of new strategic teams in the North West, East Anglia, and the Northern region of England, based explicitly on a principle of accountability to the Secretary of State through the triple channels of the Regional Economic Planning Council, the Environment Ministry, and the regional conference of local planning authorities. The management of such a process inevitably becomes a complex matter and, in some regions, it was by no means easy to see in advance where the points of most likely influence on executive decisions would lie. The spirit was essentially an exploratory and experimental one, recognising that the definition of crucial policy issues was itself by no means an easy matter, and much of the justification for each study would lie in its contribution to wider knowledge about practical methods of mediation between different constituency interests within an evolving regional process.

In concluding this brief review of other processes of regional innovation in Britain, some mention must be made of parallel events in Scotland. Here, differences of national history, of government organization, and of social geography create a contrasting context for regional planning activity, closer perhaps to that of some other countries — such as Australia — that do not share the high population densities and centralized parliamentary structure of England (Power, 1974b). A series of regional studies were initiated for different parts of Scotland during the nineteen-sixties, in response to predictions of a high level of long-term population growth over Britain as a whole. One favourable location for such growth was identified in the Tay estuary, for which a regional study was completed during 1970 by a civil service team with extensive university and consultant support (Scottish Development Department, 1970). However, in the succeeding years, population projections were adjusted downwards and the latent pressures for growth receded, while concern built up over the ecological consequences of new development in a part of Britain endowed with many natural resources. The discovery of oil and natural gas off the Scottish coast added to this concern, creating a new set of planning priorities and highlighting the shifting patterns of political pressure to which any evolving process of regional planning must be responsive (Carter, Friend, and Hickling, 1972).

Implications for connective planning

In evaluating the lessons of this chapter, it is appropriate to refer back to the structure of general propositions and prescriptive implications presented in *Figure 69*. Most of the evidence of the present chapter can be seen as lending further support to the main sequence of eight propositions, but from a very different vantage point to that of the Droitwich expansion scheme. In particular, the evolving multi-organizational structure of the regional office in the West Midlands emerges as an important interface for interactive learning between central and local governments, and between those contributing diverse skills in such fields as economic, physical, and transportation planning. The structural complexity of the problems faced, compounded by the complexity of political relationships at the regional interface, creates a situation in which the success or otherwise of regional explorations can only be gauged in terms of the degree of influence exercised over incremental commitment at many diverse points of decision. This means that much comes to depend on the reticulist skills of certain actors, occupying crucial positions in regional networks, who operate through processes of mediation that do not often attract much public attention, but can sometimes radically modify the context of the mutual adjustment process.

Despite the low profile of the regional structure in terms of public political debate, we conclude that the processes of innovation and interactive learning which have been developing in Britain in recent years — and which we believe may have their parallels in a number of other countries — are of much potential significance, in terms of the long-term challenge of creating processes for effective participatory planning in an increasingly disturbed and unpredictable environment. It is, of course, not only at the regional level of planning that motivations towards connective planning across agency boundaries may be found to dominate the motivation to organize and contain the planning process within the boundaries of a single corporate agency. Nor is it only at the regional level that a tendency can be found towards innovation in patterns of inter-agency relations, as we shall see in the next chapter. However, the regional level of government, at least as it has been developing in England since the mid-sixties, has, in our belief, a special significance which can be further exploited in future. It combines a climate of strong motivation towards the formation of inter-agency decision networks with a scale of operation that supports the formation of an important type of organizational resource, in the shape of inter-disciplinary teams which are oriented specifically towards explora-tory rather than executive activity. Within such a setting, experi-mentation becomes possible with new forms of evaluative and exploratory techniques, through which those concerned in the shaping of inter-agency networks can be assisted to adapt more consciously to the changing problem situations they confront. This is an argument we shall develop further in Chapters 16 and 17, where we shall consider further the potential role of the region within the wider spectrum of public planning processes extending from the supranational to the local neighbourhood level.

15 Organizing for local change

Experiment in local organizational relationships

At this point, we shall return from a regional to a local perspective to examine a wide range of organizational innovations in the management of processes of change within specific local communities. The case of Droitwich is only one example of many situations in Britain during the same period where, for one reason or another, processes of planned local change were induced which could not easily be managed through the established structure of local government alone. In response, a number of different organizational configurations were evolved, often in an openly experimental manner and involving significant elements of local initiative. A broad evaluation of these initiatives will be important to our purposes in this book, first because it will provide some limited further opportunities for testing the generality of the propositions formulated from our Droitwich experience, and second, because it will provide some indicators of the scope for further experimentation in the organization of planning during the rapidly changing conditions of the late twentieth century, at a more local scale than that considered in the previous chapter.

Many of the situations of induced local change which we shall consider, like that of Droitwich, developed initially in response to problems of spatial distribution of population and employment first formulated and explored at the regional level. However, among the more significant trends with which we shall be concerned has been a shift of emphasis, emerging in many regions of Britain over the last few years, from questions of organization for physical development beyond the boundaries of the main conurbations to problems of organization for the alleviation of poverty and the expansion of opportunities for those less mobile sectors of the population who remain concentrated within the inner city areas. This is a trend that we have observed from time to time in the case studies of Part II, and it is one that has led to a series of recent innovations in organization for local community development. Towards the end of this chapter, we shall comment on some of the limited experience that has accumulated in this field so far, with special reference to the Home Office Community Development Project in Coventry and the Shelter Neighbourhood Action Project in Liverpool. First, however, we shall review a selection of Town Expansion and New Town schemes which differ from Droitwich in terms of scale, regional context, or choice of organizational arrangements. In so doing, we shall find ourselves beginning to shift our focus increasingly from problems of new development to problems of renewal of existing physical and social fabrics — as indeed we did in the course of Part II — encountering on the way increasingly difficult problems of inter-authority relations.

A comparative review of planned expansion schemes

Figure 76, adapted from the government publication *Social Trends* (Central Statistical Office, 1972), indicates the location of all British New Towns designated up to mid-1970 and also all the larger expansion schemes negotiated on a voluntary basis between exporting and receiving local authorities under the provisions of the Town Development Act. Arrangements were made for the authors to pay brief visits to thirteen of these locations in all, meeting either the General Manager or another senior official who was in a central position in dealing with problems of inter-agency relations. We are grateful to the individuals concerned for their willingness to see us and provide us with much useful information. However, our experience over the years in Droitwich made it clear that the information relating to any other scheme, which we could hope to gather from a single discussion with a single officer (or, in some cases, a small group of officers), was bound to be incomplete and impressionistic in many respects. Suffice it to say that we encountered little in our series of visits that we could consider incompatible with the generality of the propositions expressed in Chapter 13 — though these propositions had not in fact been fully formulated

Figure 76 Locations of New and Expanding Towns in Britain

Adapted from 'Social Trends', HMSO, 1972.

at the time these visits were held. Our questions on each visit focused on four main fields of discussion. These were the identification of difficult local problem areas, the review of other salient organizations in the environment of the actor concerned, the internal organization of the primary agency of change, and the processes of co-ordination with other salient organizations. It is on the last of these fields that we shall concentrate most closely in the brief comparative discussion that follows.

In selecting towns for our visits, the criteria we attempted to follow were to concentrate more on schemes at a comparatively early stage of development rather than those, such as the early New Towns in the London area, which were already well advanced; to pay special attention to those with a substantial element of planned population growth in absolute terms; and to seek variety both in organizational arrangements and in regional circumstances. We sought in particular to cover a range of different types of scheme within the West Midlands, where we had explored the regional background in greater depth than elsewhere. This led us to the eight New Towns and five expanding towns underlined in *Figure 76*, and it is the latter which we shall consider first.

Organizational arrangements under the Town Development Act

As mentioned earlier in discussing the Droitwich negotiations, the Town Development Act of 1952 permitted a wide variety of forms of voluntary arrangement for development in 'receiving' County Districts to cater for the emigration of population from 'exporting' cities. By 1971, some sixty-eight agreements had been negotiated in all, but only a few further schemes were still under active discussion. National responsibility for the review of progress under such agreements lay with a small Town Development Policy section within the Environment Ministry. However, the Ministry could exercise little direct influence over the activities of the local authorities concerned. Although the section could seek to maintain the priorities given to expanding towns in the expenditure programmes of the relevant functional ministries and divisions, and could serve as a point of reference for the Town Development Executives Committee over any general difficulties that arose, its only direct executive responsibility related to the approval of the special grants towards water and sewerage investments available under the Town Development Act and, later, the provision of amenity grants towards specific social facilities judged necessary to keep pace with the housing construction programme. Both these forms of aid provided some

Figure 77 Scale and organization in the planned expansion of British towns

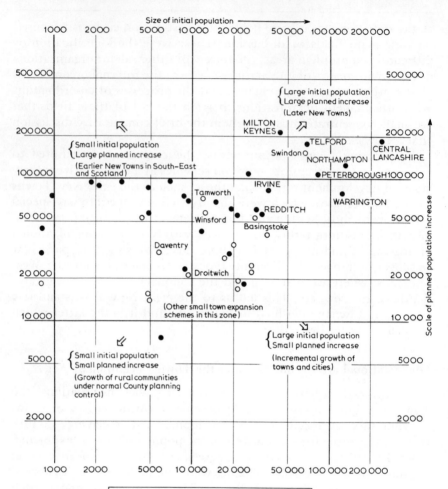

Size of initial population →

Scale of planned population increase →

- ● Expansions under New Town legislation
- ○ Expansions under Town Development legislation

(Named towns are those where senior officers were visited during course of research)

limited leverage to central government in demanding evidence that town development schemes were maintaining an acceptable level of progress towards the achievement of agreed targets; but progress was often fitful for a variety of reasons, some of which can be inferred from our exploration of the complexities of decision-making at Droitwich. Indeed, in addition to the many prospective receiving towns where negotiations ended in failure, there were many where formal agreement was reached but little progress subsequently achieved in terms of development. This suggests that Droitwich can be counted among the more successful schemes in terms of practical implementation, despite the many difficulties and uncertainties which we discussed in Part II.

More than half the sixty-eight agreements concluded by 1971 involved the Greater London Council as exporting authority, and many of the receiving authorities were comparatively small towns where the GLC was able to act directly as the primary agency of development. Not only was the GLC able to put the skills of a specialized technical group at the disposal of the receiving authority, but it was also prepared to grant financial help of a more generous order than that provided by Birmingham. Also, by establishing a special Town Development Committee, the GLC provided a means through which relatively clear precedents could become established in negotiation with small towns not only within the South East region itself, but also in some instances far beyond its boundaries.

The five town development schemes we shall consider here were all comparatively large in scope and thus involved complex problems of negotiation and adjustment between exporting and receiving authorities. In the cases of Basingstoke and Swindon, the Greater London Council was involved as exporting authority with large-scale overspill programmes in towns with substantial existing populations and resources. In the cases of Daventry, Tamworth, and Winsford, the scale of planned expansion was again substantial, but the receiving town was initially of a more modest size, and the exporting Council was less explicitly geared to the task of town development than in the case of the Greater London Council.

Figure 77 locates these and other schemes on a scatter diagram relating the scale of planned population growth to that of initial population, both plotted on a logarithmic scale. This indicates that most of the larger schemes under the Town Development Act occupy a central zone where the scale of planned growth is of the order of 20,000 to 70,000 and is broadly comparable with the scale of existing population. In general, larger increments than this tended to be managed through New Town powers, although the dividing line was far from clear cut. Smaller increments were generally managed through the normal planning and housing powers of existing local authorities, sometimes with the aid of the Town Development Act.

Some larger town development schemes: Daventry, Tamworth, and Winsford

In reviewing our five selected town development schemes, we shall begin by making brief reference to Daventry in Northamptonshire, because it shares some of the historical background of Droitwich, as a centre for Birmingham overspill development which emerged through a protracted process of regional exploration and bargaining. It differs from Droitwich in being situated just outside the boundaries of the Economic Planning Region in Northamptonshire, as shown in *Figure 72*, and in having had most of its initial development costs financed by Birmingham City itself, with provision for ultimate repayment at full economic rates of interest. The incentive to reach an agreement had come, in the case of Daventry Borough Council, from the members' own desire for an expansion of the town's modest and vulnerable economic base.

The Daventry scheme was co-ordinated through a joint committee with some delegated powers, as at Droitwich, but included representatives of Birmingham as well as County and Borough Councils. The City agreed to provide many of the technical skills required for the planning and implementation of the expansion, within the framework of a local Development Group, but — unlike Droitwich — the Borough Council retained responsibility for administrative matters. Its clear support for expansion meant that there was less of the kind of tension between the partners that emerged in the case of Droitwich. However, one recurrent source of difficulty was that the progress of housing and industrial development had to be much more finely synchronized than in the Droitwich situation because the town was situated beyond easy commuter range of the exporting city. Although the location between Birmingham and London was an attractive one to industry, it proved difficult to match the skill requirements of incoming firms to the attributes of those families on the Birmingham overspill register who were prepared to move to housing estates in such a distant location, leading to a situation in which newly built houses could often remain unoccupied for considerable periods of time.

The case of Tamworth, to the north east of Birmingham, introduces another situation where a small Borough Council was actively committed to the aim of town development, in order to bring new employment and wealth to a community with an established industrial tradition. In this it was typical of a number of other towns in Staffordshire which entered into overspill agreements with Birmingham in the mid-sixties. However, it quickly became one of the most successful, and, for this reason, it was ultimately agreed by central government to steer most of its investment in town development in Staffordshire towards this one town development scheme, slowing down the projected rates of growth elsewhere so as to increase the likely viability of its major commitment to a New Town at Telford, lying further to the west.

At Tamworth, the Borough Council built up its resources for town development largely within its own organizational base, contracting much technical work out to consultants and relying on the services of the County Council for physical planning studies. Although there were changes of political control on the local council, the commitment to town expansion never emerged as a politically controversial issue. In consequence, commitments to development were made with a minimum of financial or technical appraisal, and a rapid rate of expansion was quickly built up. This inevitably placed strains on the Council's established departmental organization. In response, the Town Clerk felt that considerable emphasis would have to be placed on the need for effective processes of corporate management. Among other innovations, he introduced the role of Project Co-ordinator to his staff. This officer found that much of his time became concerned not merely with the use of systematic methodologies such as network analysis, but also with the exercise of more informal skills in the steering of issues through various internal and external communication channels.

Moving outside the West Midlands, some very similar experiences were encountered in the expanding town of Winsford in Cheshire. Here again, the organization for the promotion of town development was built up within the existing structure of the local authority — this time an Urban District Council — in a situation where there was a high degree of local consensus about the desirability of town development. The Clerk of the Council again assumed a major initiating role and acquired the additional title of Director of Town Development, building up an internal technical team and, as at Tamworth, recruiting a management services specialist in the role of project co-ordinator. Once more, a strong emphasis was placed on the restructuring of committees and departmental organization in order to achieve more cohesive corporate planning.

At Winsford, external relations were made more complex by its location at approximately equal distance from Manchester and from

Liverpool. Of these cities, only the latter attracted governmental incentives for industrial development under the arrangements applying at the time *(Figure 49)*. Initial negotiations with Liverpool encountered difficulties, but a chance encounter of the Clerk of Winsford with Manchester representatives led to a first Town Development agreement with Manchester in 1960. Progress was slow, until a later agreement with Liverpool allowed Winsford to claim some (but not all) of the incentives to industrial movement that applied within the city itself. However, later legislative changes meant that the full range of incentives could be claimed through an undertaking that the town would expand to an increased population target of 60,000, with at least two-thirds of the increase drawn from the Liverpool area. Thus, as at Droitwich and elsewhere, national policy changes came to exercise an important influence on the course of the local development programme.

Town Development and the corporate perspective

The remaining two town development schemes which we shall briefly consider — at Swindon and Basingstoke — provide some further evidence of the interplay of corporate and inter-corporate perspectives in the expansion of existing urban communities. In organizational terms, Basingstoke provides the most direct parallel to Droitwich of all British town expansion schemes. It represents one of the few other instances in which extensive executive powers were delegated to a joint committee with its own specially recruited development group. In this case, the exporting authority — the Greater London Council — was represented on the Committee as well as the County and Borough authorities, and various arrangements for more informal communication at officer level evolved around this formal structure. As at Droitwich, there was some initial difficulty in reconciling local people to the existence of a development group that was not directly controlled by their elected Borough Council. However, there was a fuller measure of local agreement than at Droitwich on the desirability of town development, and the joint committee structure helped in achieving mutual adjustment between the various constituency interests concerned, although it rarely served directly as a channel for the resolution of contentious issues.

At Basingstoke, as at Droitwich, external changes in the housing market brought about a gradual shift of emphasis from rented overspill housing to private development. The long-term effects of this trend on the local organizational structure remained uncertain, in a climate of increasing governmental concern about alternative solutions for retaining a measure of public control over the development of private housing, especially under the conditions of intensive market pressure that persisted in the South East.

Swindon, an important railway town some 130 kilometres to the west of London, was the largest of all English towns to become a receiving centre for overspill under the Town Development Act. The passage of the Act in 1952 was seen by the Borough Council as providing a new opportunity to diversify its employment structure, at a time when the future of the local railway workshops was becoming increasingly uncertain. When visited during 1971, the Borough Council was in the process of concluding its third successive town expansion agreement with the Greater London Council, designed to double its existing population of almost 100,000 in accordance with the second of the successive strategic studies in the South East region concerned with the definition of major centres for long-term population growth.

As one of the largest towns in England without independent County Borough status at that time, Swindon had acquired extensive delegated powers in such fields as education and health. It therefore had responsibility for almost the entire range of local authority functions, while the local responsibilities of the surrounding rural county of Wiltshire were correspondingly limited. Experience of difficulties arising in earlier programmes, combined with a local tradition of self-help, led to a determination in Swindon to carry out as much as possible of the work in the new programme through the internal resources of the Borough. As a vehicle for this, a central system of corporate management had just been introduced, with the Town Clerk designated as Chief Executive and all services grouped under five broad directorates. These included a Directorate of Development and Corporate Planning, within which a system of programme budgeting was to be developed as a central co-ordinating influence. To complement this central structure, attention was also being directed to the encouragement of local community councils in the newly developed areas, formed wherever possible in such a way as to encourage involvement by owner-occupiers as well as local authority tenants.

In this brief review of some other town expansion schemes, we have found the degree of local commitment to town development to be generally stronger than at Droitwich. Consequently, except in the case of Basingstoke, the responsibility for managing the expansion programme lay more directly with the existing district authority. The commitment to expansion had thus tended to throw into relief the problems of co-ordination between quasi-autonomous departments and committees which are a recognised feature of local authority decision-making in Britain (Friend and Jessop, 1969) and has led those responsible for initiating development to seek a solution in terms of new philosophies of corporate planning. While the need for outwardly connective skills is implicitly recognised, much of the formal emphasis has been on the problem of internal connectivity between the parts of the district council itself, and on the introduction of new machinery and techniques of corporate management as a means of overcoming this problem.

In Droitwich and Basingstoke, on the other hand, the recruitment of a new professional team, outside the established local authority departmental structure, could be seen as providing a new kind of corporate focus within which specialists of different disciplines could address themselves towards a common task without necessarily subscribing to new management philosophies or techniques. The cost becomes one of uncertainty in the operation of the joint committee structure, with a risk of paralysis or open conflict where there is a strong divergence of views between the parent authorities. In the case of Droitwich at least, such a structure of joint control was a necessary condition for the successful conclusion of a town development agreement in the first instance, in circumstances where none of the agencies concerned was sufficiently committed to expansion, nor regarded by the others as having a sufficiently dominant interest in its outcome, to be allowed to assume a leading corporate role.

Such a situation, where political pressures are such that the leading role of change agent cannot easily be assumed by any one elected authority, seems likely to occur with increasing frequency in the new two-tier system of local government in England, and not only in respect of the management of overspill arrangements between exporting and receiving authorities. Both the new Counties and the Districts will have at their disposal considerable resources of town planning, technical, administrative, and financial skill. Also, as we shall discuss in the following chapter, the use of agency agreements and joint committee structures is likely to become widespread in several fields of operation. Therefore, as at Droitwich, we can expect that decision networks will become more and more outwardly connective in character with respect to any particular corporate frame of reference. In such circumstances, philosophies of corporate management are likely to become more and more insufficient as a guide to the organization of planning activities. Therefore, whether explicitly recognised or not, we can expect the problem of disposition of reticulist opportunities and skills among different types of public agency to become an increasingly salient one.

The New Town Solution

The organizational device of the New Town Development Corporation was introduced in England as early as 1946, as an instrument of governmental initiative in the creation of new communities. It followed earlier voluntary initiatives in the development of 'Garden Cities' at Welwyn and Letchworth near London. The experience in these schemes had highlighted the difficulties of achieving co-ordination between the various public agencies on which the development companies were dependent for the provision of supporting services, and a more direct involvement by central government was seen to be necessary in the conditions of acute housing stress existing immediately after the Second World War. The 1946 Act allowed the Land Planning Minister to designate any area of land for the development of a New Town, after the hearing of objections at a public inquiry, and to appoint a Corporation of not more than nine individuals to recruit the necessary technical and administrative staff. They would then prepare a 'Master Plan' as a framework for executing the development programme, funded by advances from the national exchequer. Within a few years, this legislation had been applied to designate eight New Towns lying just beyond the London Green Belt, two near Glasgow, one in Wales and two in the North of England. In these latter cases, the aim was not so much to meet demands for overspill from cities as to provide new centres of employment around which the populations of scattered mining communities could be regrouped as their original economic base fell into decline.

Most of the London New Towns turned out in time to yield very satisfactory rates of return on the government capital advanced, in the form of rents from housing and commercial property. They therefore came to be regarded as a clear economic success, even though attempts to evaluate their success or otherwise according to social criteria have, inevitably, been more controversial (Thomas, 1969). By 1971, there were four of the original London New Towns in which the programme of planned development was to all intents and purposes completed and the Development Corporation disbanded, its assets being transferred to a central 'Commission for the New Towns' rather than to the local elected Council. Such a step, though locally controversial, could be justified in order to ensure a continuing return to the central exchequer from investments originally funded through national taxpayers' money.

The later New Town Corporations subsequently set up in other parts of the country, with which we shall be more closely concerned in this chapter, generally involved grafting large-scale development of housing and industry onto larger existing settlements; the trend was broadly from the top left to the top right corner of the mapping indicated in *Figure 77*. Although the procedure for designation was very different from that of agreement on voluntary town expansion schemes, similar forms of conflict sometimes emerged, with established local authorities often appearing as objectors at public inquiries into draft designation orders issued by the Land Planning Ministry. Often, draft designation orders drew their main justification from regional planning exercises of the kind discussed in the previous chapter, and were preceded by feasibility studies commissioned from planning consultants. As has been pointed out by Levin (1969), the Ministry would sometimes find itself in a difficult position in reconciling its role as original sponsor of a designation order with its quasi-judicial role in relation to the public inquiry process.

The political problems arising at this stage of the New Town designation process were highlighted to us in discussion with one firm of consultants who, in their written report, had produced a persuasive set of arguments of an apolitical nature for recommending a particular set of boundaries for a proposed New Town area. At the informal level, however, they had also had to satisfy themselves that their proposals contained sufficient features that would be seen as attractive to each of the main elected Councils within the area, to minimize the risk that their political leaders would be forced into a position of overt objection at the public inquiry stage.

After the designation stage, another area of local political concern would often be the appointment of local elected members to the nine-member Development Corporation. As with the Regional Economic Planning Councils, members were formally selected by the Minister solely for their qualities as individuals. However, the provision of inbuilt linkages between the appointed Development Corporation and the one or more elected Councils serving its area could in practice be extremely useful in terms of the opportunities created for informal mutual adjustment between them.

The staff appointed by a Development Corporation would consist, typically, of a General Manager, a Secretariat, and departments concerned with finance, architecture, planning, engineering, estates, housing management, and — sometimes — social or community development. The range of skills would therefore correspond roughly to those available to the Droitwich Development Committee as indicated in *Figure 25*, although concentrated within a single corporate structure. In most of the New Town schemes, the scale and nature of the task was such that any resort to consultancy or agency arrangements became purely an optional matter.

Central responsibility for the financial and technical supervision of the implementation of New Town development programmes was vested, in the early seventies, in a separate directorate of the Environment Ministry reporting to the Minister of Housing and Construction. This alignment with the housing rather than the planning side of the Ministry's work tended sometimes to generate problems of adjustment between the executive processes of New Town development and the processes of regional planning through which programmes and targets were agreed and adjusted. For the General Manager of a New Town Corporation, the normal lines of communication with the Ministry would be almost entirely with the New Towns Division at the centre, creating little direct opportunity for informal contact with the civil servants in the regional office.

New Towns in the West Midlands: Redditch and Telford

In reviewing a few cases of individual New Towns, it is appropriate to begin with the case of Redditch, as it shares the same regional and county background as Droitwich; indeed, as indicated in Chapters 3 and 4, it shares much of the same history as a prospective site for the reception of overspill from Birmingham. However, at Redditch, negotiations on a town development agreement broke down in 1963. Among the many stumbling blocks, the most intractable was the resistance of members of the Urban District Council to the politically embarrassing prospect that, in order to qualify for Town Development housing subsidies, they would be required to withdraw an established subsidy from their general rate account to their housing revenue account, so raising the rent levels of all their existing tenants.

The impasse was broken, somewhat dramatically, at a meeting where the then Minister of Housing and Local Government suddenly informed the local authority representatives present that he intended to proceed towards the designation of Redditch as a New Town. Despite some financial advantages to the local authorities, they were confronted with an immediate threat to their autonomy, and both County and District Councils appeared as objectors at the ensuing public inquiry.

When a Development Corporation was appointed the following year, relations were somewhat strained with the town's Urban District Council, in which a significant Liberal element then held the balance between the Labour and Conservative parties. One source of discontent was the lack of any local elected representative among the members of the Development Corporation, although three of these were in fact resident within the town. As the implementation of the scheme progressed, however, procedures for co-ordination began to become established, resting partly on periodic consultative meetings between Development Corporation and District, and partly on professional and political contacts at a more informal level. Within the Corporation itself, responsibility for co-ordinating and monitoring the activities of project teams was vested in a formal group of Deputy Chief Officers.

The second New Town in the West Midlands was situated well to the west of the conurbation, at Telford in Salop, and grew from a re-designation in 1968 of the New Town of Dawley first established in 1963. As a result of the regional appraisals discussed in the last chapter, the designated area was now much increased, to accommodate an estimated population of 220,000 by 1990, as opposed to the original 90,000 for Dawley. The site was of much historic interest, containing iron-working settlements from which could be traced the origins of the industrial revolution during the eighteenth century; indeed, the name of Telford was chosen after the noted engineer who had left his mark on many local bridge and canal construction projects. However, the area had long been in a state of economic decline, and among the tasks of the new Development Corporation were not only the attraction of new residents and industries but also a vigorous programme of environmental renewal to deal with the extensive legacy of derelict industrial sites.

The designated area for Telford included a group of three existing towns, and the officers of the Development Corporation found themselves involved in managing relationships not only with an established County Council but with four separate County Districts, three urban, and one rural. Negotiations with each of these elected bodies tended to be bilateral rather than multi-lateral, and to be influenced by changing developmental priorities. For the members and officers of the local councils, there was a problem of adjusting their outlooks from dealing with a situation of decline to one of expansion. In the early years, problems of local competition tended to arise in relation to such issues as the siting of a new major shopping centre, and the distribution of sports and social facilities.

Considerable difficulty was encountered in the early years in attracting population and industry to Telford, partly because of its poor road communications with the conurbation and partly because of the wider economic circumstances then prevailing. However, the rate of attraction increased considerably in subsequent years, and these changes of fortune had significant regional implications, because of the scale of expansion proposed. This is a point we have already encountered in Chapter 12, in discussing the planning processes of the regional gas and electricity boards. It was also encountered in Chapter 14, when we discussed the influence of the Regional Economic Planning Council in pressing for an early priority for a new motorway link.

Variety in the organization of planned expansion programmes

The regional context of the West Midlands provides an appropriate one in which to pause at this stage to review the range of alternative configurations available for the management of any planned local expansion scheme. In *Figure 78*, the basic configuration of organizational relationships at Droitwich is compared, within the framework of our basic institutional map, with those at Daventry, Tamworth, Redditch, and Telford. In addition, we have included Birmingham's own large overspill housing estate at Chelmsley Wood in Warwickshire, combining to give a comparative picture of the organizational forms adopted in the six most important developments in progress in the region during the late nineteen-sixties and early seventies.

The main point of initiative in the management of the development process is shown as lying, variously, with the exporting city, with a local district council, with an appointed Development Corporation, or — in the case of Droitwich — with a jointly sponsored Development Group, with both County and District interests represented. Although none of the other schemes involved the same degree of formal delegation to a multi-organizational agency as in the case of Droitwich, each involved its own pattern of arrangements for inter-agency co-ordination and adjustment, both at the formal and informal levels. Although we could not hope to evaluate the relative strengths and weaknesses of such arrangements on the evidence of a single round of visits, it was clear to us that each pattern created demands for sensitive reticulist judgements on the part of the more strategically placed local actors, whether operating within the primary development agency or elsewhere.

Of course, the six types of configuration encountered in *Figure 78* by no means exhaust the range of possibilities for the management of local expansion programmes. For instance, in the North of England, the Northumberland County Council was able to exploit the provisions of the Town Development Act to initiate 'New Towns' in two rural districts each with a very low initial base of population and

Figure 78   Patterns of organizational relations in main planned expansion programmes for West Midlands (prior to 1974)

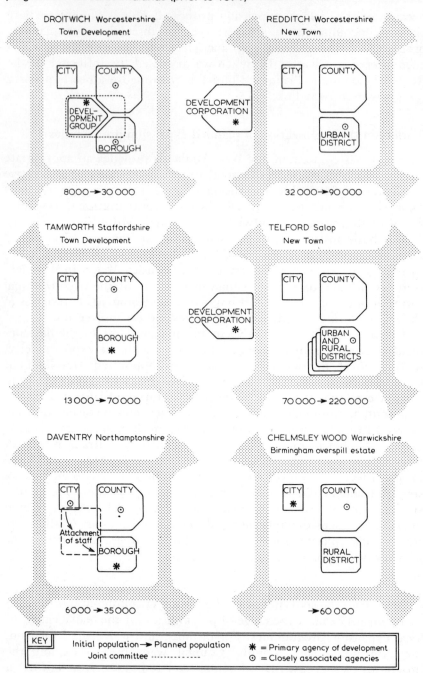

rateable value, working in partnership with private enterprise developers. Although the solution of the private enterprise New Town has found no place in Britain since the Second World War, it has been extensively employed in other sets of national circumstances. Also, in 1971 a significant test case arose in England with an application by a consortium of private developers to build a 'new town' on a site near the small village of Catthorpe, which was strategically situated in relation to the national motorway network, but straddled the boundaries of three counties and of two Economic Planning Regions, the West and East Midlands. In this instance, the motivation for the proposed new town was purely economic rather than social. At the public inquiry, all the counties involved objected on regional policy grounds, and much of the debate turned on the significance to be attached to the developers' assurances of large-scale financial support towards the provision of schools and other public amenities.

The 'partnership' New Towns

One of the more significant organizational developments during the late sixties was the designation of three 'new' towns using the provisions of the New Towns Act as a means of grafting major expansion schemes onto the large existing settlements of Warrington, Northampton, and Peterborough. The former two were already represented by independent County Borough Councils, and the third by a strong District Council situated within a small County with few resources at its disposal. Each had emerged as a strategic location for planned growth within its regional context, at a time when general issues of the disposition of future population were emerging as more important than specific agreements to provide rented housing for the residents of exporting cities.

For such towns, the provisions of the New Town legislation could provide some valuable forms of financial aid, and the concept of 'partnership' was introduced in recognition of the argument that a strong existing local authority could hardly be expected to surrender all its control over local development issues to a centrally appointed agency. The practical implications of this partnership principle varied between the three towns. In Northampton, it was agreed that the County Borough would act as agent for the Development Corporation in respect of all its legal and engineering work, and should act as the primary agent of change within the existing urban areas, including the town centre, while the Development Corporation should take primary responsibility for development on the more peripheral sites. Such arrangements were facilitated because an adjustment of the County Borough's boundaries had made the territories of the two agencies co-extensive. In the opinion of the General Manager of the Development Corporation, the successful running of the scheme hinged largely on the close informal working relationship he had established with the Town Clerk, together with a series of parallel relationships between heads of professional departments. However, he saw the 'partnership' arrangement as being highly vulnerable to accidents of personal incompatibility between key actors, and generally ill-fitted to the entrepreneurial stance that he was required to adopt in attracting industry in competition with competing local growth centres.

In Peterborough, the situation was broadly similar, although the General Manager was faced with the additional problem of maintaining liaison with two partner authorities, the County and City Councils, whose own relationship had been marked more by disagreement than by co-operation. The City Council had accepted from the outset that the Development Corporation should also be deeply involved in city centre planning and redevelopment, but the Corporation had declined to move into the field of slum clearance and housing rehabilitation, seeing this as the proper responsibility of the elected Council because of the social and political problems involved. The Corporation's territory impinged on three adjoining District Councils, relations with which were more distant because of their non-partner status, though still time consuming. Care was taken to discuss local plans for development with all the affected Councils at as early a stage as possible. Also, as a practical expression of the partnership principle, the Master Plan for the expansion as a whole was formally submitted in the joint names of the County and City Councils and the Development Corporation, even though most of the work had been undertaken by the Corporation's own professional staff.

The case of Warrington was made more complex by the fact that almost all the new development by the Corporation was planned to take place beyond the boundaries of the County Borough Council, despite its status as formal 'partner' in the scheme. It had been expected that this anomaly would be removed by boundary adjustments, but these had been shelved because of the national commitment to more sweeping local government reforms. Warrington was situated in a densely urbanized part of Lancashire, with an existing population of some 120,000 and a target increase of 80,000, and the case for a Development Corporation had been by no means an obvious one. However, the status of a New Town did provide access to important sources of external finance, upon which the existing local authorities would not have been able to draw even had they been able to agree on a means of executing the programme on their own.

Although it had originally been intended that at least half the new housing at Warrington would be built for renting to overspill population from the Greater Manchester area, re-assessments of demand led to a reduction of this component, with the majority of houses being built for eventual private sale. Drainage and other physical constraints meant that the first sites to be developed were scattered in several different locations on the periphery of existing urban areas, involving high costs of purchase and also creating diseconomies of programming which – during the early years – combined to depress the apparent economic viability of the scheme.

Uncertainty and flexibility within the New Town framework

Not only at Warrington but in the other 'partnership' schemes, difficulties arose in developing an accounting framework that could provide an adequate guide either to decision-making within the Development Corporation itself or to central government in evaluating the rates of return that it was deriving from its investment of taxpayers' money. It was by no means easy to apply the same criteria of success as had been found adequate in the earlier, more self-contained New Town schemes at a time when there was a strong unfulfilled demand for public rented housing and new industrial sites. Therefore, the new generation of New Towns could readily be construed as poor investments unless more sensitive processes of evaluation could be evolved, with fuller recognition of social criteria and varying local circumstances.

In the early seventies, considerations such as these led the Ministry to introduce a new system of management accounting for New Towns. This attempted to assess the economic returns yielded by their land acquisition, site development, and building activities within an output budgeting framework. In the opinion of one General Manager, however, the usefulness of this system as a local management tool was limited by the lack of a ready means of making systematic variations in the various assumptions underlying the calculations, so as to test their sensitivity to different types of external contingency. As had become clear from all our discussions at New Towns, the General Manager and his staff had to pursue their task of development under circumstances of considerable external uncertainty. So far as the operating environment was concerned, there were uncertainties about the rates of immigration of new residents and employers in times of changing demographic and economic trends. Also, there were uncertainties of policy in weighing up the interests of the constituency of national taxpayers against those of established local residents and, sometimes, an exporting city, while further kinds of uncertainty arose over the actions of decision-makers in other local agencies, especially the established local authorities. These authorities could often be classified more realistically as separate but contiguous policy systems than as part of a well-developed multi-organizational policy system, even in cases where a formal 'partnership' arrangement applied.

The strategies devised for managing such uncertainties can be illustrated with reference to two other major New Town developments initiated during this period, those at Milton Keynes, mid-way between London and Birmingham, and at Irvine on the Scottish coast south west of Glasgow. Both were strategically, if controversially, situated; the former in a mainly rural location where it was claimed by some that it could provide an undesirable reinforcement to the tendency for wealth to become concentrated along the London-Birmingham axis, and the latter near an area of considerable industrial potential, where a combination of steelmaking, oil refinery, and deep water port facilities were envisaged but as yet uncommitted.

The location of Milton Keynes was first identified as a major growth point in the South East study of 1964 and — unlike some of its contemporaries — survived to be designated as a New Town in early 1967, with an ultimate target population of up to 250,000, including a significant element of London overspill. The outline plan for the new 'city' attracted public attention as it was based on a flexible grid pattern of roads and a comparatively low housing density, accepting that the future residents should be able to exercise a high degree of freedom of choice in life-style and choice of transport mode. In effect, many of the design details were to be allowed to evolve later, responding to processes of market as much as political choice. Exploiting the flexibility of the plan, the Development Corporation began to experiment with new concepts of management and social planning, based on the monitoring of social indicators and the use of a framework of objectives formulated through application of programme budgeting principles. One of the practical problems, in the years preceding the reorganization of local government, was that the designated area impinged significantly on the territories of three District Councils, varying quite widely in their attitudes and socio-geographic features. Indeed, one of these had previously been designated as an expanding town under an earlier London overspill agreement. However, it was accepted that a new centre for Milton Keynes as a whole would have to be developed in a location quite distinct from any of the established small towns, and much of the corporation's initial effort was devoted towards establishing this new strategic focus as early as possible in the course of the development programme.

At Irvine, the first of the Scottish New Towns to be launched without a strong overspill housing commitment, the outline plan was also based on a flexible design concept, with an open-ended chain of neighbourhoods linked through a public transport circuit, permitting the population target of some 120,000 to be increased to one of 200,000 or more for an enlarged 'city region', should future national policy decisions on port and industrial development allow. However, as at Droitwich, some radical changes of road layout were introduced between the first design studies and the preparation of a master plan by the locally recruited staff. Relations with local authorities required considerable attention, as there were several within the designated area, some of them significantly smaller than the typical County District in England. Together with the various statutory undertakings, these local authorities were represented through a Joint Consultative Committee, which met regularly over the years, and provided a formal context in which various problems of local significance could be debated.

One particular problem which exercised the officers of the Corporation at the time of our visit concerned relations with the South of Scotland Electricity Board, which had laid claim to a site for a power station at Irvine before the commitment to New Town Development had been reached. Because of the potential attraction of Britain's first New Town on a coastal site, the Development Corporation was especially sensitive to questions of environmental protection, and in due course the difference of opinion between the two appointed agencies was resolved by a re-siting of the power station well outside the designated area.

Central Lancashire: organization for expansion and renewal

The most ambitious of all development programmes under the New Towns Act was initiated in 1971 in Central Lancashire, with a designated area embracing the County Borough of Preston and the two nearby towns of Leyland and Chorley, and a target of taking the existing population of 250,000 up to an ultimate level of 430,000 over a twenty-year period. The final commitment had been preceded

Figure 79   Initial organizational structure proposed for Central Lancashire
New Town Development Corporation, 1971

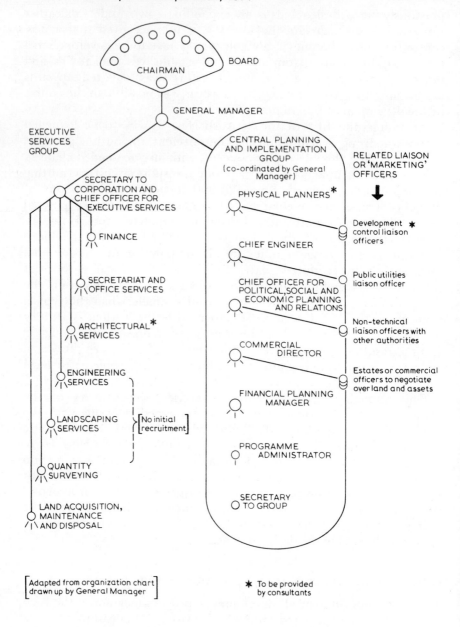

BOARD

CHAIRMAN

GENERAL MANAGER

EXECUTIVE
SERVICES
GROUP

CENTRAL PLANNING
AND IMPLEMENTATION
GROUP
(co-ordinated by General
Manager)

RELATED LIAISON
OR 'MARKETING'
OFFICERS

SECRETARY TO
CORPORATION AND
CHIEF OFFICER FOR
EXECUTIVE SERVICES

PHYSICAL PLANNERS*

Development *
control liaison
officers

FINANCE

CHIEF ENGINEER

Public utilities
liaison officer

SECRETARIAT AND
OFFICE SERVICES

CHIEF OFFICER FOR
POLITICAL, SOCIAL AND
ECONOMIC PLANNING
AND RELATIONS

Non-technical
liaison officers with
other authorities

ARCHITECTURAL*
SERVICES

COMMERCIAL
DIRECTOR

Estates or commercial
officers to negotiate
over land and assets

ENGINEERING
SERVICES

LANDSCAPING
SERVICES

[No initial
recruitment]

FINANCIAL PLANNING
MANAGER

QUANTITY
SURVEYING

PROGRAMME
ADMINISTRATOR

LAND ACQUISITION,
MAINTENANCE
AND DISPOSAL

SECRETARY
TO GROUP

[Adapted from organization chart
drawn up by General Manager]

* To be provided
by consultants

by a period of much uncertainty and controversy over the justification for such an investment at a time when predictions of population growth were falling; and it was feared that a new growth centre of this kind could have adverse effects elsewhere in the densely populated North West region, especially in the declining cotton towns to the east.

The final political commitment was made against a background of a reduction in the designated area, an assurance of continued investment in the nearby cotton towns, and a recognition that development in the Central Lancashire New Town would have to be accompanied by a much more extensive programme of rehabilitation to existing housing and environment than in most other 'New' Towns, if the legacies of past urbanization were not to detract from its attractiveness to potential new residents.

The General Manager of the Development Corporation was interviewed on the eve of his departure from a similar post at Skelmersdale. He was conscious in setting up his new management structure first of a need to establish a realistic division of functions with existing authorities in relation to problems of environmental renewal, and second of the uncertainties of programming arising from the lack of a closely controllable element of rented overspill housing development. In the light of this appreciation, he proposed to make some radical innovations in organizational design, the effect of which was to draw a clear distinction between the range of specialist functions concerned with the normal execution of a large-scale development programme, and a more compact 'planning and implementation group' under his own leadership. In this group, these and other specialist skills would be represented by another set of senior officers working in parallel, in a more strategic and forward-looking spirit unimpeded by routine responsibilities. This concept is illustrated in *Figure 79*, which derives from an initial organization chart drawn up by the General Manager himself.

Within different sections of the central planning group would be located a number of related liaison or 'marketing' officers explicitly concerned with maintaining strategic relationships with external agencies, local authorities, public utilities, industrial and commercial firms, and other forms of public or private agency. Thus, in the proposed organization for Central Lancashire, we encountered an unusually explicit set of arrangements for the development of functions concerned with the management of inter-agency planning networks. In effect, the 'outwardly connective' dimension of the planning process appeared to be more explicitly recognised in the internal structure than in any of the other towns we had visited.

Of course, the separation between executive services and other functions which we have identified as primarily of a reticulist nature — both inwardly and outwardly connective — might be expected to create its own problems of management and mutual adjustment, which would have to be confronted as they arose in the course of the development programme. However, in the light of our final argument in Chapter 13 — that the disposition of resources relevant to the support of reticulist activities should be regarded as an explicit field of political choice — the proposals for organization in Central Lancashire appeared to offer a particularly promising field for future experiment. As *Figure 79* suggests — when related to the more detailed network diagrams presented in Part II for different fields of decision at Droitwich — the problem is one that extends beyond the confines of the Development Corporation, to questions about the existence of matching 'outwardly connective' capacities in the various related agencies. Significantly, Central Lancashire was the only New Town, the area of which was destined to extend over the administrative boundaries of several County Districts even after the local government reorganization of 1974. The relatively large size of these districts would clearly make the problem of maintaining external relations an especially challenging one.

Changing priorities: innovation in the inner cities

By the outset of the nineteen-seventies, the surge of New Town designations during the previous decade, followed by a steady downward revision of national population projections, had led to a sharp fall in the number of further New Town proposals under discussion. One of the few exceptions was for a New Town Development Corporation to serve the proposed third London Airport development at Maplin in Essex, in association with a parallel appointed agency to manage the airport programme itself and associated industrial developments. However, even this ambitious scheme was subject to much uncertainty, and, following the commitment to the Central Lancashire scheme, it was becoming recognised that the whole problem of exercising public control over the development of new and existing centres of population and employment was becoming steadily more complex. Increasingly, the trend was towards intervention in existing urban areas, often demanding more subtle forms of action and inter-agency relationship than in the early post-war years of acute housing shortage, when the driving force of a development programme would usually stem from an arrangement for the nomination of housing tenants between an exporting city and a New Town Corporation or receiving district council.

During the sixties, concern had been steadily mounting over social and economic problems in the inner cities themselves, where the worst of the former slum areas had now been redeveloped, but where there remained other areas of nineteenth-century 'twilight' housing which had as yet benefited little from the public investment programmes of the post-war years. Many of the more mobile and self-sufficient of the residents of these areas had moved out to the New Towns or the suburbs, leaving behind the elderly, the low-income families, and — increasingly — immigrants from less economically developed countries. In the case of Britain, immigrants from Ireland were joined by those from the West Indies and South Asia, who often found that the inner cities offered the only realistic opportunities for employment and housing available to them. As such immigrant communities grew in number, so inter-communal tensions began to develop, and there was rising public concern that Britain might find itself drifting into the type of social conflict and breakdown that was at that time erupting in many cities of the United States.

In response to the deteriorating conditions of the inner areas of London, Birmingham, and other cities, a number of pioneering voluntary groups began to emerge, sometimes taking their lead from the advocacy planning movement in the United States, and experimenting with the politics of neighbourhood action to discover ways of assisting urban communities to articulate their demands more clearly to relevant government agencies. Also, a series of experimental initiatives was set in train during this period at the national level. One of the earliest of these was taken by the Education Ministry, in association with the Social Science Research Council, following a concern with the poor schooling opportunities that persisted in many of the older urban areas. It was decided to explore the opportunities for 'positive discrimination' to improve the educational opportunities in four selected urban areas in England, which were designated as 'Educational Priority Areas'. The national programme which was mounted in 1968 combined elements of action and research, focusing especially on questions of pre-school provision and the concept of the 'community school' as a means of bridging social and cultural barriers between parents as well as children in inner city areas (Department of Education and Science, 1972).

The Urban Programme and the Community Development Projects

Also at this time, the government of the day decided to move ahead on another related front by setting up a new Urban Aid Programme (since renamed the Urban Programme) through the medium of the Home Office, in association with other relevant government departments. The aim was to channel central funds — generally in the form of 75 per cent grants — into any projects submitted by local authorities, or by voluntary bodies through the medium of local authorities, which could be justified in terms of response to problems arising in localities of 'acute social need'. The programme attracted many claims for financial aid towards projects ranging from adventure playgrounds to neighbourhood advisory services. However, it also revealed some of the procedural difficulties involved in attempting to assess priorities outside the normal processes of contextual control by government departments over the expenditure claims of competing local authorities. One observation was that the number of claims submitted tended to vary widely between local authority areas, according to the differing abilities of officers, members, and voluntary agencies to diagnose local problems of acute social need and to formulate initiatives for appropriate forms of response.

Accordingly, the question arose of how local diagnostic capacities could be more systematically developed, and, as an experimental step, the government agreed to set up a number of Community Development Projects in selected areas, within the wider context of the Urban Programme. In each of the twelve urban areas selected, a small Action Team was to be recruited, with a parallel Research Team attached to a local university or polytechnic. The aim of the project would be to discover, through interaction with residents, public authorities, and voluntary agencies, how the needs and aspirations of local people could be more fully expressed, how appropriate forms of governmental response could be mounted, and what the ultimate prospects might be for involving the local communities concerned in a wider social planning process.

Among the first four local teams to be established during the pilot stage was one in the West Midlands Region — in Coventry, where the City Council had long prided itself on its receptiveness to innovation. We shall here concentrate on a brief discussion of this particular case, partly because of the involvement of two of the authors in some of the work of the project (Carter, Friend, Luck, and Yewlett, 1972) and partly because of the project team was one of the first to publish an interim evaluation of the progress achieved and the difficulties ecountered during the early years of their work (Benington, 1972).

The work of the first two years in Coventry was largely at a broad diagnostic level. In order to establish local interfaces, a shop-front Information and Opinion Centre was established, a 'Fieldwork Forum' was established involving different statutory and voluntary agencies, regular discussions were initiated with local authority officials and ward councillors, and various forms of support and expertise were offered to local residents and community groups. Thus, networks were established of a roughly similar character to that of the Droitwich Community Development Officer — as presented in *Figure 67* — though with some important differences arising from the inner city context and the differing structure of accountability. In Coventry, the formal structure agreed upon consisted of a Project Management Committee set up through the City Council's administrative machinery. This included chairmen and vice-chairmen of relevant local authority committees, elected members from relevant inner city wards, representatives of voluntary organizations, and a liaison officer from the sponsoring government department.

It had originally been suggested that the team should concentrate its efforts on the neighbourhood of Hillfields, an area to the east of the City Centre with a culturally mixed population and a local reputation for social stress and deviance. However, much of the area was rapidly being redeveloped, and the team therefore decided to concentrate on a wider area of 'Greater Hillfields' with some 20,000 population in all. From the initial learning experiences of the team, one of their first conclusions was that the processes generating the conditions of relative deprivation in Hillfields were city-wide rather than purely local in character. This implied that they should regard their constituency not so much in terms of territory on the map as of the population groups who then happened to live within the area, many of whom might later shift elsewhere under the influence of market forces or of redevelopment operations.

In defining the second phase of its work, the project team formulated six more specific programmes of activity to assist in moving towards their eventual aim of increasing the capacities of service-providing agencies to respond to inner city problems, and creating more effective processes of local community planning. The general pattern of management for these six programmes is set out in *Figure 80*, which is adapted from diagrams presented in the team's own progress report (Benington, 1972).

The management of the various external relationships generated

Figure 80 Structure of inter-agency accountability for Coventry Community Development Project

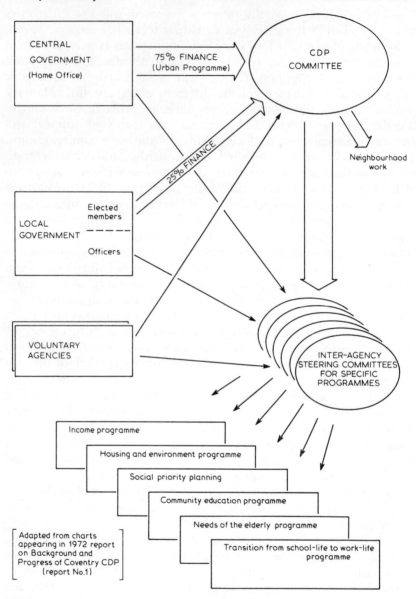

CENTRAL GOVERNMENT (Home Office)

75% FINANCE (Urban Programme)

CDP COMMITTEE

Neighbourhood work

25% FINANCE

LOCAL GOVERNMENT

Elected members
— — — —
Officers

VOLUNTARY AGENCIES

INTER-AGENCY STEERING COMMITTEES FOR SPECIFIC PROGRAMMES

Income programme

Housing and environment programme

Social priority planning

Community education programme

Needs of the elderly programme

Transition from school-life to work-life programme

Adapted from charts appearing in 1972 report on Background and Progress of Coventry CDP (report No.1)

by this pattern of organization was a task requiring a high order of reticulist skill on the part of the Project Director and his associates. Some of the team's initiatives placed him in opposition at times to various departmental and political interests within the City Council. Referring back to the model of *Figure 71*, much of his difficulty in developing the reticulist capabilities of his team lay in maintaining a sufficient level of access at the same time to local pressure groups and to departmental officers. His only realistic course was to move forward slowly but strategically on the basis of claims to be promoting the interests of relevant sectors of his local constituency – from which he could of course claim no direct electoral mandate – relying where necessary on the formal political commitment of the Home Office and the City Council to the original initiative in setting up the project.

One of the most difficult problems encountered by the team concerned its position in relation to the new corporate management system that had been recently introduced by the City Council. This used a programme budgeting structures as a framework within which hierarchies of broad objectives could be derived, and new forms of inter-departmental exploration could be stimulated within defined programme areas. A centralized approach of this kind contrasted with the CDP focus on more immediate local issues, which often had complex differential effects among members of local communities. In the team's progress report, it was argued that the tension between the 'top down' approach of corporate planning and the 'bottom up' approach of community development could be an important and creative one, though it was still not clear how a constructive equilibrium could be developed.

The Community Development Project in Coventry soon came to be regarded as one of the more successful within the overall programme, although in his progress report the Director remained cautious about its long-term effect in influencing the capacities of local and central agencies to respond to inner city problems. In some of the sister projects, there was much instability in staffing and much difficulty in forming research teams with a clear appreciation of the position they should take in relation to the ongoing initiatives of the action team. One of the problems which emerged as increasingly important was that of providing for the mutual exchange of experiences among the twelve local projects that ultimately became established. Although informal networks of contact had developed among the action teams, and had helped in defining common attitudes towards some of the difficult tactical problems of relations with other agencies which emerged, the problems on the research side were to remain a matter of some concern to the Home Office, which in 1973 decided to entrust a central co-ordinating role to the Centre for Environmental Studies in London.

A voluntary initiative and its repercussions

Among the many types of inner city experiment initiated during this period, one of the most fully and imaginatively documented was the Shelter Neighbourhood Action Project (SNAP) in Liverpool, which issued its final report in late 1972 after the conclusion of its agreed three-year term, under the title *Another Chance for Cities* (Liverpool SNAP, 1972). Shelter had been founded as a voluntary national pressure group to combat the problems of homelessness, but those concerned had soon come to the conclusion that, in addition to dealing with individual cases of homelessness as they arose, they should undertake investigations in some depth into the complex causal factors that led to conditions of chronic deprivation in the inner city areas. In seeking a site for a wide-ranging neighbourhood project with this aim in view, the attention of Shelter turned to the port of Liverpool, where conditions of poor housing and unemployment were especially deeply entrenched. However, they were by no means the only group to concern themselves with problems of deprivation among the residents of the city's inner areas. A number of local community councils were already active; a part of the city had already been selected by the Education Ministry as a site for an experimental Educational Priority Area; and a Community Development Project was later to be established by the Home Office in a different part of the city.

Concentrating on the Granby neighbourhood of the city, in which there were many symptoms of acute multiple deprivation, the Shelter team secured the formal blessing of the City Council but, as recounted in their final report, encountered much difficulty in constructing a coalition of relevant local interests through which they could create some form of local political accountability, clearly independent of any party allegiances, to give a degree of external authority to their interventions. The primary focus for their initial learning experience was the mobilization of residents' involvement in the achievement of neighbourhood renewal through the General Improvement Area provisions of the 1969 Housing Act, already discussed in Chapter 11. In this field, the SNAP team was able to secure much practical progress. However, they encountered many difficulties and frustrations in forming relevant relationships within the complex network of statutory and voluntary agencies operating within their chosen area, each of which was organized to provide a different form of community service with a different set of political, social, or economic aims in view.

As in Coventry, the City Council had recently become committed to a drastic reorganization of its management structure, with the philosophy of programme budgeting very much to the fore. One of the suggestions put forward by the SNAP team was for a parallel process of district budgeting, designed especially with a view to overcoming the problems of co-ordinated allocation of resources to inner neighbourhoods such as Granby. Although the idea of any form of special 'inner area agency' along New Town Corporation lines had been dismissed as simplistic and impractical, the image of 'Granby New Town' was invoked to discuss more subtle methods of mounting a relevant planning process at district level, which might make constructive use of supplementary resources from central government in breaking through the cycle of multiple deprivation, while recognising that ultimate responsibility for executive action would have to remain with the elected City Council. However, partly because of the 'New Town' imagery adopted in stimulating public interest, such ideas were not received with unqualified enthusiasm either by the local authority or by central government. The SNAP project therefore ended with some modest achievements to its credit, but with a renewed conviction on the part of its Director that much more far-reaching initiatives were needed to come to grips with the problems of inner city deprivation. He was aware in particular of the overriding problem of building a source of authority for making interventions in the decision processes of departmental bureaucracies within and beyond the local authority, having been concerned in particular to avoid the creation of a 'spurious constituency' for radical action on an extra-constitutional platform.

However, the work of SNAP had succeeded in attracting the attention of the then Secretary of State for the Environment, who took the initiative in 1972 of sponsoring a set of six local studies designed to discover ways of developing what was called a 'total approach' to the problems of deprived urban areas. To avoid any appearance of direct competition with the established Home Office Community Development Programme, the emphasis was specifically placed on environmental problems. Liverpool again featured as one of the six towns selected for these 'Urban Guidelines Studies', and for each town a firm of management or planning consultants was appointed to provide an element of external problem-solving expertise. The former Director of SNAP was appointed to fulfil a central advisory role; and so another important experimental programme, with elements of both central and local commitment, was launched to add to the experience that had already been accumulated by those working in the Educational Priority Areas and the Community Development Project teams.

Concluding remarks

In this chapter, we have shifted gradually from a perspective of the planned expansion of country towns to one of the rehabilitation of the decaying inner areas of cities, encountering on the way a variety of structures for inter-agency decision-making involving different combinations of central and local initiative. The shift of focus in this chapter corresponds broadly to a progressive shift of concern in Britain during the third quarter of the twentieth century, as the immediate post-war problems of overspill from the conurbations have receded in significance, and social tensions of the inner cities have become more acute. This changing problem focus makes it important that any constructive proposals which we attempt to formulate, on the strength of our detailed appraisal of problems at Droitwich should not be limited to any particular type of problem situation or framework for action such as that of the 1952 Town Development Act.

The complexities of the problems of inducing planned urban change — whether dominated by aims of physical, economic, or social development — have been shown to lead to some significant modifications in the existing patterns of relations between established public agencies. Often these modifications were of an openly experimental nature, requiring much skill in the mobilization of decision networks at the informal as well as the formal level. While the deployment of reticulist skills is an implicit feature of all such situations, some significant differences can be recognised in the relative attention given to inwardly and outwardly connective planning activities by leading actors in the primary agencies of change. In towns such as Swindon, Tamworth, and Winsford, where there was a strong commitment to change on the part of an existing local authority, the dominant emphasis was on processes of corporate planning designed to overcome inherited problems of internal departmental fragmentation. Indeed, a similar emphasis could be found in major cities such as Coventry and Liverpool, with a strong innovating tradition and — at least until 1974 — a unified responsibility for all local government services. In contrast, where the primary initiating role lay with a specially created development agency, whether appointed by central government as in the case of the New Towns or formed by local agreement as in the cases of Droitwich and Basingstoke, the problems of internal co-ordination were correspondingly reduced, but some difficult judgements had to be made in mobilizing exploratory processes across the boundaries with other agencies.

The problems of developing outwardly connective capabilities tended to become particularly salient in the case of the 'partnership' New Towns of Warrington, Northampton, and Peterborough. Also, the proposed organization chart for Central Lancashire, reproduced in *Figure 79*, indicates an unusually explicit recognition of the need for a set of outwardly connective roles relating directly to an ongoing planning process, in a situation where decision-making is of necessity incremental, and refuge cannot easily be sought in the formulation of long-term goals or strategies because of the very complex range of community interests involved. However, it is in the case of the emergent centres of innovation in the inner cities, such as the Community Development Projects, that the would-be initiators of change are most exclusively dependent on the development of outwardly connective skills which must be deployed in building up relations across the boundaries with established executive agencies. With only limited resources of political authority at their disposal, such actors may be dependent for their very survival, in a changing local situation, on the discovery of ways of maintaining sufficient access to other agencies to exert some ultimate influence over their decisions, drawing on whatever internal or external resources they can muster.

As we have now seen, therefore, the period of our work in Droitwich was one of widespread experiment throughout Britain, both at the regional and at the local levels, in the search for new forms of organizational relationship in the exploration of public policy issues. It was also, however, a period when some important changes were impending in formal institutional structures. In the next chapter, we shall turn to a fuller appraisal of these changes. In this way, we shall provide a context within which to speculate more widely about the prospects for future evolution in the processes of public planning, with special reference to the crucial question of inter-agency relations.

16 Changes in institutional structures

Institutional reform and its opportunities

We have now described some trends towards innovation and experiment at both the regional and local levels of inter-agency planning in Britain. In our belief, such trends combine to create a promising setting in which to explore the practical implications of the general propositions and guidelines formulated in Chapter 13, allowing them to be translated into somewhat more specific and concrete forms. However, we must also recognise that, during the last quarter of the twentieth century, the institutional context of local and regional planning in Britain will itself differ radically from that which has provided the setting for the case histories of the preceding chapters, because of the introduction during the nineteen-seventies of a sweeping programme of far-reaching structural reforms.

Most of these structural reforms can indeed be interpreted, in whole or in part, as responses to problems of co-ordination among established agencies, the responsibilities of which were regarded as too fragmented, either in territorial or in functional terms, to permit the emergence of effective processes of planning and control. However, the processes of intended rationalization themselves led to the creation of new institutional boundaries and new problems of inter-agency relations. We shall argue that these circumstances combine to create a fresh set of challenges to be confronted, and of opportunities to be exploited, when seeking ways in which the concepts developed in this book can be made of practical value to people directly concerned with the management of local and regional change, at whatever level of decision and in whatever capacity they may operate.

The recent processes of institutional reform in Britain can be interpreted, in terms of our general analytical approach, as ranging over a number of linked fields of decision, as indicated in *Figure 81*. Perhaps the most central and complex of these fields is the structural reform of the local government system, in that it impinges directly on a number of the more specialized reform processes that preceded it, concerned with such matters as the amalgamation of police forces, the formation of integrated local social service departments, and the establishment of new passenger transport authorities in metropolitan areas. Also, some far-reaching changes in the management of health services and water resources were arranged to take place simultaneously with the English local government reform of 1974. Meanwhile, other related innovations were either impending or in progress in the structure of central government departments and in the extent of political devolution between different parts of the United Kingdom.

It is this combination of interacting processes of change that makes the circumstances of British government during the nineteen-seventies somewhat exceptional. Nevertheless, in all societies, the re-structuring of formal aspects of organization is one of the most readily comprehended and frequently applied methods of attempting to improve the machinery of public planning. For this reason, we hope that the analysis of the processes and implications of structural reform which we shall present in this chapter will have some wider relevance outside the British context. We shall, however, argue that structural changes cannot be regarded as sufficient in themselves, but must be exploited for the opportunities they provide to overcome entrenched obstacles to innovation, and to encourage widespread experiment and adaptation at a much more local level. It is in this spirit that, towards the end of the present chapter, we shall form some practical hypotheses which might form a guide to the mounting of experimental initiatives within the evolving British situation.

Local government reform in England: the appointment of a Royal Commission

Prior to the reforms of 1974, the structure of local government in England had altered little since the basic pattern of County, District,

Figure 81 Related processes of reform in structure of British institutions, 1965–1975

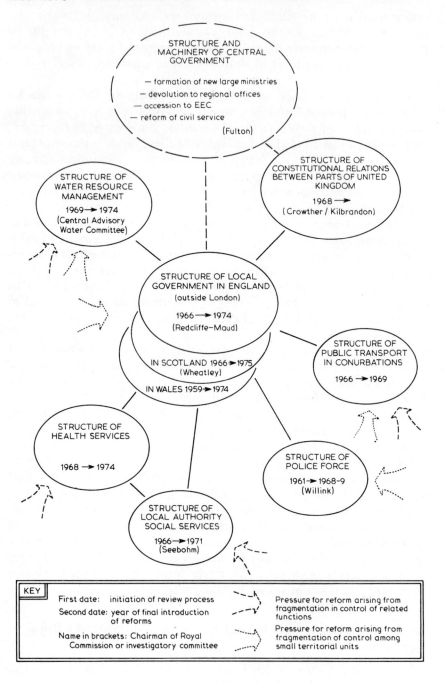

STRUCTURE AND MACHINERY OF CENTRAL GOVERNMENT

— formation of new large ministries
— devolution to regional offices
— accession to EEC
— reform of civil service

(Fulton)

STRUCTURE OF WATER RESOURCE MANAGEMENT

1969 → 1974
(Central Advisory Water Committee)

STRUCTURE OF CONSTITUTIONAL RELATIONS BETWEEN PARTS OF UNITED KINGDOM

1968 →
(Crowther / Kilbrandon)

STRUCTURE OF LOCAL GOVERNMENT IN ENGLAND
(outside London)

1966 → 1974
(Redcliffe–Maud)

IN SCOTLAND 1966 → 1975
(Wheatley)

IN WALES 1959 → 1974

STRUCTURE OF PUBLIC TRANSPORT IN CONURBATIONS

1966 → 1969

STRUCTURE OF HEALTH SERVICES

1968 → 1974

STRUCTURE OF POLICE FORCE

1961 → 1968-9
(Willink)

STRUCTURE OF LOCAL AUTHORITY SOCIAL SERVICES

1966 → 1971
(Seebohm)

KEY

First date: initiation of review process

Second date: year of final introduction of reforms

Name in brackets: Chairman of Royal Commission or investigatory committee

Pressure for reform arising from fragmentation in control of related functions

Pressure for reform arising from fragmentation of control among small territorial units and County Borough Councils had become established in the late nineteenth century. The main exception was to be found in Greater London, where a totally new structure had been imposed in 1965 in response to the growing extent of the metropolitan area and the increasingly difficult problems arising in its government. Outside London, a somewhat cumbersome machinery of continuing review by an official Boundary Commission had succeeded in bringing about some local changes and amalgamations in particular parts of the country, one instance being the 1966 amalgamation of local authorities in the Black Country, as shown in *Figure 16*.

However, the processes of local boundary adjustment came to a halt when Richard Crossman, one of the more vigorous, if controversial, members of the 1964 Wilson government, was appointed as Minister of Housing and Local Government. Before long, he came to the conclusion that a much more sweeping reform of local government would be necessary to adapt the system to the challenges created by contemporary patterns of living and the progressively increasing range of services and responsibilities with which local authorities were now required to contend. Accordingly, the government resolved in 1966 to establish a Royal Commission, with a remit:

> 'to consider the structure of local government in England outside Greater London, in relation to its existing functions; and to make recommendations for authorities and boundaries, for functions and their division, having regard to the size and character of areas in which these can be most effectively exercised and the need to sustain a viable system of local democracy; and to report.'

Although the implementation of the Commission's recommendations was eventually to be overtaken by developments and pressures on the political front, it is, nevertheless, relevant to our aims in this chapter to consider the way in which the Commission went about its task, and the kinds of argument that emerged. In general, the device of the Royal Commission represents a significant form of decision-making machinery at the level of national policy formation, to which many of the general propositions of Chapter 13 relate no less than to the local and regional processes we have so far considered. More specifically, the debate on the Commission's findings raised some general questions, relating, for instance, to the concepts of 'Unitary' and non-executive 'Local' Councils, which we shall find useful in articulating hypotheses about the scope for experiment within the rather different institutional structure that has in fact emerged.

A simplified view of the process of local government reform in

Figure 82 Sequence of exploratory processes leading to the re-organization of local government in England, 1966—74

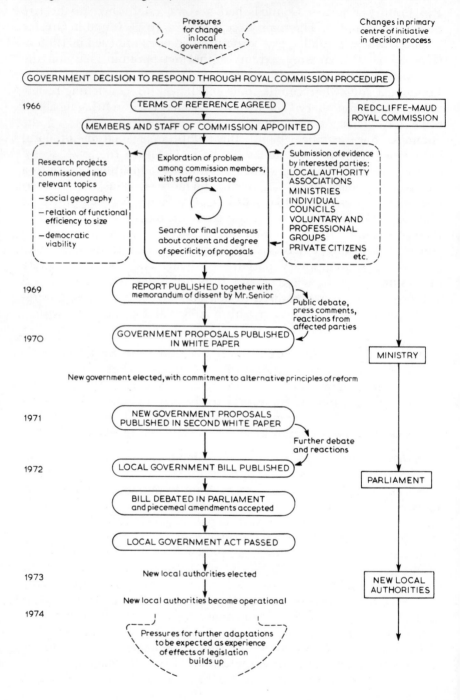

England, from the initial decision to appoint the Royal Commission to the eventual hand-over of power to the new authorities, is presented in *Figure 82*. The first problem for the government, after agreeing the Commission's terms of reference, was to select a set of members whose qualifications would command public confidence on the grounds of their depth and diversity of experience. Not only had the membership to cover a cross-section of the more important political and professional perspectives within local government, but a range of external viewpoints had also to be represented. Accordingly, those selected to serve included a former Permanent Secretary of the Ministry of Housing and Local Government, as well as prominent figures from the universities, business, the trade unions, and journalism. The Commission's Chairman, Lord Redcliffe-Maud, was already well known as the Chairman of an earlier committee of inquiry into the internal management structure of local authorities.

The work of the Commission has been discussed in some detail elsewhere (Morton, 1970). As *Figure 82* indicates, early decisions had to be reached as to how far the exploratory activities of the members themselves should be supported, on the one hand by directly commissioned research studies, and on the other hand by invitations to interested parties to submit their own representations in the forms of either written or verbal 'evidence'. In terms of the general decision model of *Figure 11*, the problem can be interpreted as one of how far the members of the Commission — seen as an *ad hoc* though clearly-defined policy system, relating to the specific 'action space' of local government reform — should seek to extend their exploratory processes across the interfaces both with their operating environment and with other contiguous policy systems, in order to increase their collective confidence as to the form their ultimate recommendations should take. So far as the seeking of evidence from outside bodies was concerned, it was clearly politic to make formal approaches to a number of relevant government departments, and to the five main associations which reflected the collective interests of different forms of existing local authority affected: the County Councils Association, the Association of Municipal Corporations (covering both County and non-County Boroughs), the Urban District Councils Association, the Rural District Councils Association, and the National Association of Parish Councils. It was also expedient to issue a more general invitation to submit written evidence. The result was a total of over 2,000 individual submissions from local authorities, interest groups, and private citizens. Such a volume of evidence inevitably presented difficult problems of selection and assimilation for the Commissioners and their staff, and, at a later stage, they had to use their discretion in asking 'a number of people to submit their views informally on questions on which we thought they would be particularly able to help us' (Royal Commission on Local Government in England, 1969: 20).

Meanwhile, the Royal Commission itself initiated a programme of research on a scale that was unprecedented for national inquiries of its kind. The topics selected as most relevant for research were structured under three main headings, the first of which concerned the changing social geography of England, and its implications for local government structure. The second heading concerned the relationship between the size of an authority and its effectiveness in performing different types of function, while the third concerned the problems of democratic viability in relation to different kinds of local community structure. The research programme as a whole was co-ordinated through a Director of Intelligence, Mr L.J. Sharpe, who was given the special status of Assistant Commissioner. This allowed him to play an active part in the Commission's internal deliberations, which extended to a total of 181 meetings over the three-year span of its existence.

The recommendations of the Commission

Within the Commission itself, the central task was one of reaching as much consensus as possible among the members about a preferred general approach to the restructuring of the local government system, and also about a specific pattern of local boundaries in accordance with this approach, throughout the various regions of England with their differing socio-geographical characteristics. The difficulty of reaching a full consensus on matters of such importance and complexity was underlined when the final report was published in 1969, with one member appending a closely-argued 'memorandum of dissent' which virtually amounted to a full alternative prescription for reform, and two others putting their names to disagreements of a somewhat more marginal nature.

In constructing a rational exposition of the arguments that had led them towards their recommendations, the signatories of the majority report enumerated four basic faults in the existing system. First, there was an increasing mismatch between local authority areas and modern patterns of life and work; second, the fragmentation of powers among independent Counties and County Boroughs created major problems in the planning of development and transportation; third, responsibility for closely related personal services was divided between levels of authority; and fourth, the smaller authorities were not sufficiently viable in economic terms to perform effectively the functions required of them. Such structural weaknesses had been progressively eroding the capabilities of local government in England, on the one hand through a proliferation of central government controls and on the other hand through an increasing loss of public interest in local government affairs.

To most of the members of the Commission, it appeared that the problems of functional interdependence between services, and territorial interdependence between town and country, could best be overcome by seeking to move towards a more unified form of local government structure. They could find little clear guidance either from their research findings or from the evidence submitted by other bodies as to the optimum size of unit for different forms of local service. However, it was eventually agreed that a population level of 250,000 could be regarded as a reasonable minimum for the effective organization of both the 'personal' and 'environmental' forms of service, with a population of 1,000,000 as an upper limit for the former category, though not necessarily for the second.

Several different maps were drawn up in the attempt to apply broad policy guidelines of this kind to the definition of alternative structures covering England as a whole. The proposal finally accepted by the majority divided the country into fifty-eight 'Unitary Authorities' with populations ranging from just over 200,000 to just over 1,000,000, together with three 'metropolitan areas' covering the Birmingham, Manchester, and Liverpool conurbations. In these areas, it was suggested that the general guidelines could only be followed by introducing a new form of two-tier system, in which the more personal services would be operated at a more local level than the 'environmental' services.

Although the Commissioners felt that such a structure should be sufficient for the performance of most of the executive functions of local government, they became convinced that there was also a need for two further types of representative institution: one at the regional or 'provincial' level to handle the broader issues of physical and economic planning, and the other at a much more local level to meet the need for a meaningful 'organ of community at grass roots level'. Thus, the pattern recommended compared with the structure then existing as indicated broadly in *Figure 83*, where different types of local authority are plotted against a logarithmic scale of the level of population served. The area of each circle represents an impression of the relative concentrations of functional powers at different levels of the local government system, using the concentration of powers in

Figure 83   Changes in English local government proposed by Royal Commission in 1969

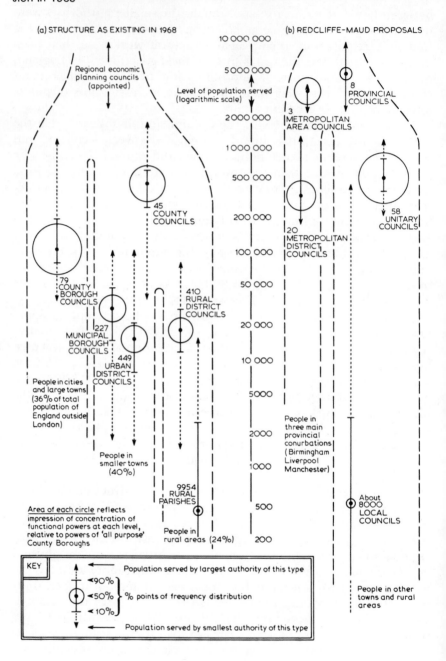

(a) STRUCTURE AS EXISTING IN 1968

(b) REDCLIFFE-MAUD PROPOSALS

10 000 000

5 000 000

Regional economic
planning councils
(appointed)

Level of population served
(logarithmic scale)

2 000 000

3
METROPOLITAN
AREA COUNCILS

8
PROVINCIAL
COUNCILS

1 000 000

500 000

45
COUNTY
COUNCILS

200 000

20
METROPOLITAN
DISTRICT
COUNCILS

58
UNITARY
COUNCILS

100 000

79
COUNTY
BOROUGH
COUNCILS

50 000

410
RURAL
DISTRICT
COUNCILS

227
MUNICIPAL
BOROUGH
COUNCILS

20 000

449
URBAN
DISTRICT
COUNCILS

10 000

People in cities
and large towns
(36% of total
population of
England outside
London)

5000

People in
three main
provincial
conurbations
(Birmingham
Liverpool
Manchester)

2000

People in
smaller towns
(40%)

1000

9954
RURAL
PARISHES

About
8000
LOCAL
COUNCILS

500

Area of each circle reflects
impression of concentration of
functional powers at each level,
relative to powers of 'all purpose'
County Boroughs

People in
rural areas (24%)

200

People in other
towns and rural
areas

KEY

⟵ Population served by largest authority of this type

<90%
<50% } % points of frequency distribution
<10%

⟵ Population served by smallest authority of this type

the established 'all-purpose' County Boroughs as a point of reference. For instance, *Figure 83* reflects acceptance of the general view that, for most County residents, those executive functions operated at the County level in the established system were rather more significant than those operated at the District level — if only because of the salience of the education service — while those operated at the Parish level in rural areas were considerably less significant again. Under the proposed system, the division of functional powers between 'tiers' within the metropolitan areas was intended to be a relatively even one.

It will be seen in *Figure 83* that the general effect of the Redcliffe-Maud proposals was to reduce drastically the number of executive authorities and to increase their median size, while the spread of population about the median level also tended to become less variable at the main executive levels. However, a much more flexible pattern was envisaged at the level of the proposed 'Local Councils', which it was suggested should be elected not so much to provide specified services as to 'promote and watch over the particular interests of communities in city, town and village throughout England'. While their primary duty would be to represent local opinion, they could also be granted certain rights of consultation, and also discretionary powers to mobilize local action; in the larger towns, they could perhaps be allowed to contribute to the management of certain services, given the consent of the Unitary Council.

The essence of the concept of the Local Council was an absence of constraint as to what things it was or was not expected to do. Initially, it was suggested that such Councils could be set up to succeed each County Borough, Municipal Borough, Urban District, and Parish already served by an elected Council, although there could be wide-ranging adjustments as the new system settled down. In the Metropolitan Areas, the establishment of such Councils might be less important except in the less urbanized fringes, and could be treated as a matter of local discretion. The concept was therefore far from a rigid one, with the constituencies of Local Councils varying in size from a few hundred to half a million or more, as indicated in *Figure 83*. It was intended that the system should allow much scope for local discretion in choice of titles, patterns of staffing, levels of initiative in providing local amenities, and channels of communication with other service-providing agencies.

The debate on the reform proposals

On its publication, the report of the Redcliffe-Maud Commission was welcomed in many quarters, including the government of the day, as a bold stroke in simplifying the tangled structure of local government which had developed over the years. In other quarters, however, some trenchant criticisms were heard. A rallying point for criticism was provided by the very detailed memorandum submitted by the dissenting Commissioner, Mr Derek Senior, who argued that his colleagues had adopted an unduly theoretical approach, which paid too much attention to population norms and too little to patterns of social geography. Mr Senior recommended as an alternative a two-tier pattern of 'regional' and 'district' authorities covering most of the country, and submitted a specific set of proposals for their functions and for a new administrative map of England.

Among the more important reactions awaited to the main report were those of the five main local authority associations. Although the urban authorities encountered much difficulty in arriving at an agreed collective view, the representatives of the County Districts became united behind a demand to see the unitary pattern replaced by a viable two-tier system in which the dangers of remote administration could be avoided. From the Counties, there came a claim that the boundaries of the new metropolitan areas should be more tightly drawn. In the case of Worcestershire, the County Council supported this argument by the suggestion that the problems of the West Midlands were such that solutions had to be sought either at the conurbation or the regional scale, rather than at any intermediate level.

After assessing these various reactions, the Labour government of the day set out its views in a White Paper (HM Government, 1970). This accepted most of the Royal Commission's basic proposals, excepting that for Provincial Councils, as this impinged on the field of study of the recently created Commission on the Constitution. Some changes were suggested in the number of Metropolitan areas and in the distribution of services within them, and so far as the proposed Local Councils were concerned, it was argued that more careful thought was required to establish how they could best play a constructive role in relation to other parts of the new local government system. This last comment reflected a widespread feeling of scepticism that had emerged in public discussion of the Redcliffe-Maud proposals. Many people were doubtful as to whether the concept was indeed equally applicable at all levels from the city to the small rural community, and whether a body with such limited executive responsibilities could be expected to attract Councillors of sufficient calibre to play a useful representative role. Accordingly, it was suggested by the government that perhaps the members of Local Councils could play an active part in the committee structure of the Unitary Authorities, especially if the administration of services was to be decentralized on an area basis. Within the cities, it was argued that Local Councils might better be established on a neighbourhood rather than a city-wide scale, quoting a finding by the Commission's research staff that most city dwellers tended to think of their 'home area' in terms of comparatively compact neighbourhoods at the scale of small clusters of adjoining streets.

The legislative stage

Although the Labour government was committed to early legislation on the basis of the 1970 White Paper, the situation was quickly changed by the return of a Conservative government in the general election later that year. The Conservative election manifesto had included a public commitment to introduce alternative proposals for local government reform based on a two-tier principle. This acknowledged the increasing resistance that had built up against the threat of remoteness implied by the unitary principle, especially in the more rural areas where Conservative influences tended to predominate.

When the new government produced its own White Paper in 1971, it proposed a different structure of new Counties and Districts throughout England. Six 'metropolitan counties' would be created to cover the main conurbations; these would be broadly similar to the Royal Commission's metropolitan areas, but with more closely drawn boundaries and a more limited range of powers. In particular, the crucial service of education was now to be managed at District level. The remainder of the country was divided into thirty-eight non-metropolitan counties, most of them following traditional County boundaries, but now increased in population and resources by the inclusion of the hitherto independent County Boroughs. The range of functions retained at District level was more limited than in the case of the metropolitan Districts, but included all housing and development control responsibilities. To provide a viable base for the management of such functions, it was proposed that the normal population for such a District should be in the range of 80,000 to 100,000, although the figure could be lower in the more thinly populated regions.

At this stage, several important issues still remained to be resolved, including those concerned with the boundaries of the non-metropolitan districts and the allocation of various particular responsibilities between the county and district levels. Therefore some further intensive processes of discussion ensued between the government and the various professional and local authority associations concerned. The upshot was the publication in 1972 of a Parliamentary Bill in which some of the proposed local boundaries were modified, while the functional responsibilities of District Councils were increased by the allocation of further powers or rights in such fields as urban road maintenance, environmental health, and the preparation of local plans under the new development plan system.

Many of these modifications had the effect of increasing the level of uncertainity about how the new system would work in practice, by extending the number of specialist interfaces across which the new County and District Councils would have to bargain with each other to arrive at a more precise agreement over the sharing of their various related responsibilities. Recognising that professional and other resources would be unevenly distributed, especially during the earlier years, the Bill provided for either the County or the District to act as 'agent' for the other in the execution of particular services. The division of land planning functions became a matter of especially acute professional concern (Royal Town Planning Institute, April 1972), as it was by no means easy to determine precisely where the scope of the County's 'Structure Plan' should end and that of the District's 'Local Plan' should begin. Nor was it clear that the same level of professional expertise could be deployed at each level, and it was eventually decided that, in each County, an early task would be for the two levels to agree on a formal 'development plan scheme', specifying the exact distribution of plan-making tasks between County and District staffs over the next few years.

A further uncertainty concerned the extent to which the smaller towns which were to be absorbed in larger districts would be able to retain their distinctive identities within the new system. In the rural areas, the government was pledged to retain the established rural parish system, and so it was agreed that certain towns previously served by Borough or Urban District Councils might apply for the status of 'successor parishes'. This would allow them to retain such civic dignities as the office of Mayor, and to elect a 'Town Council' in order to watch over specifically local interests where these might not otherwise be adequately represented at the County District level.

As the more basic uncertainties about the form of the new system were progressively resolved, so other uncertainties began to emerge about the problems of operating it in practice. In particular, many local authority officers began to profess anxieties about the way in which a bold act of simplification of local government structure, as had been proposed by the Royal Commission, had gradually given way to a more untidy administrative framework, in which all the familiar problems of divided responsibility between tiers could be expected to arise again, in new and by no means clearly predictable forms. But the commitment to reorganization had by now acquired a political momentum which could scarcely be arrested. Indeed, even had the unitary principle not been formally abandoned through a change of power at the centre, it was perhaps only to be expected that its deceptive simplicity should have become increasingly compromised, as the moment of implementation approached and the practical problems of transition loomed larger for the whole vast range of different professional and political interests concerned. In many ways, the passage of the Act itself could be regarded as only one of the more significant increments in a continuing and highly diffuse decision process, covering a very complex field of structural change in the most deeply entrenched of English governmental institutions. The flavour of this continuing process can perhaps best be appreciated by reverting briefly at this stage to the more localized perspective of our earlier case studies, and considering some of the specific problems of the transition within the West Midlands Region, from the particular view points of the historic County of Worcestershire and the local community of Droitwich.

Some more local impacts and processes

Within the West Midlands, there was little surprise that the Conservative White Paper proposed a reduction of the new metropolitan area, by excluding several towns in North Worcestershire and some other districts just beyond the immediate conurbation boundary. There was, however, considerable surprise when it was proposed to extend the area eastwards to embrace Coventry and the intervening green belt territory. This proposal met with the approval of most elected members in Coventry in that, as a metropolitan district, the city would retain loc l control of the crucial service of education and also of its new Social Services Department, established in 1971 in accordance with national legislation for the unification of local authority welfare services. However, it was difficult to reconcile with the recommendations for a corridor of growth to the north and south of Coventry which had recently been endorsed by Warwickshire, following the report of the sub-regional study described in Chapter 14. Also, it meant an unscrambling of the joint Warwickshire and Coventry police force, itself only recently created through a painful process of forced amalgamation. Among other consequences was a significant shift in the territory covered by the West Midlands Passenger Transport Executive, which now became an agency of the new Metropolitan County. Thus, the reform of local government meant some drastic modifications in a number of earlier structural reforms which had only recently been introduced in the more specialized areas of decision appearing in the lower part of *Figure 81*, each of these having itself been triggered off by more specialist arguments about administrative efficiency and the need for more co-ordinated planning and control.

Turning to Worcestershire, the principles of both the Labour and Conservative White Papers had pointed towards the solution of combining the County with the more sparsely populated County of Herefordshire to the west and with the County Borough of Worcester at its core. However, both Counties resisted the government's proposal to name the new unit 'Malvernshire', after the dividing range of hills, and settled for the more unwieldy, though less exceptionable, title of Hereford and Worcester County Council. Within the County, the designation of District boundaries was a matter not for legislation but for resolution through the machinery of a new national Boundary Commission specially appointed for the purpose. This Commission was required to take into account the government's basic criteria of size, but also to be guided wherever possible by local opinion. The solution finally chosen for Hereford and Worcester had already been indicated in *Figure 21*.

As it happened, the future of Droitwich became one of the most controversial matters within the new County. Faced with a require-ment to avoid breaking up existing County Districts wherever possible, the Boundary Commission considered options of bringing together Droitwich Borough and the surrounding Rural District as a separate unit, falling well below the preferred population level for a new District, or linking this combined area with Bromsgrove in the north, or again with Evesham and Pershore to the south east. In terms of the County as a whole, the last option was judged the most acceptable. However, for the members of Droitwich Borough Council, largely preoccupied with the local implications of the town development programme, it meant they now became a minority interest in a much larger district of over 80,000 population, with only seven elected representatives on a total Council of forty-three members in all. They shared few common interests with the residents of the district's other main urban centre at Evesham, which was indeed less accessible to local people than the County Town of Worcester. This meant that, as at the County level, there was much difficulty in selecting an appropriate name for the new Council. Eventually, the hybrid title of 'Wychavon' was imposed, combining the historic name of Droitwich with the name of the river that linked the two towns of Evesham and Pershore.

Thus, so far as Droitwich was concerned, neither the new County nor the new District was by any means a natural unit of community. There was some consolation when the Borough Council succeeded in an application for the retention of a Town Council and Mayor under the 'successor parish' provisions of the new local government system, though it was understood that this could claim few direct executive powers. Meanwhile, the local members and officers settled down to the exacting but urgent processes of preparation for the various transfers of responsibility which would be required on the transition date of 1st April 1974.

The problem of management structures

As uncertainties over the new County and District boundaries were resolved, so, throughout England, networks of Joint Consultative Committees became established to pave the way for the many mergers of authority that would be required, and to set up specialist working parties concerned with the organization of particular departmental services. One of the most central preoccupations was with the overall management structures of the new authorities, and the main local authority associations therefore agreed to set up a joint working group, with secretarial assistance from the Department of the Environment, to produce some practical guidelines in this field which could be of value to all the new County and District authorities.

This working group, which became known as the 'Bains Committee' after the name of its chairman, worked with a considerable sense of urgency. Its report (Department of the Environment, 1972), made a systematic appraisal of several recent experiments in local authority corporate organization, and endorsed certain principles of management which, although outside the historic traditions of British local government, had been gaining widespread acceptance in recent years. These included the principle of appointing a Chief Executive as leader of a management team of chief officers, and that of forming a small central Policy Committee to which the Chief Executive and his team would report. One more novel suggestion was for the appointment of a 'performance review sub-committee' with a free-ranging inquisitorial mission, somewhat akin to that of the Public Accounts Committee in Parliament.

Less than 5 per cent of the 130 pages of the Bains Committee's report was devoted to considering the inter-agency as opposed to the corporate dimension of local authority management and structure. However, endorsement was given to the idea, already widely discussed during the legislative process, of forming a District Joint Committee to cover each County District area, on which representatives of both District and County Councils could meet. Such committees would expect to play a deliberative and advisory rather than an executive role, and their primary task would be 'to facilitate joint discussion, joint action and the exchange of information between the two spheres of local government'. Such District Committees could be complemented by a county-wide Joint Committee on which all districts would be represented, meeting perhaps two or three times a year. In making these suggestions, the Bains Committee recognised the many complexities that would have to be confronted in the precise demarcation of responsibilities and the negotiation of agency agreements, especially during the early years after the election of the new authorities.

In the area of the new Hereford and Worcester County, such problems were confronted through an Officers' Management Structure Project Group which reported late in 1972 (Hereford and Worcester New County Committee, 1972). In this report, as in those of other similar groups throughout the country, the main concern was to establish a clear corporate framework for the activities of the new County Council, and most — though not all — of the recommendations of the Bains report were accepted as a reasonable basis from which to develop more specific local proposals. One area of special concern was the management of the environmental group of local government services, where it was recognised there was a particularly close pattern of interaction between County and District responsibilities. In an informal paper to the Project Group, the then Deputy Clerk of Worcestershire, who had been closely involved with the Droitwich Development scheme, argued that the device of a joint committee, with a range of delegated powers, had proved workable in practice despite the obstacles that had arisen from time to time. Referring to the interim conclusions of our research in Droitwich as then published (Friend and Yewlett, 1971), he argued that there might be much scope for further use of the kind of inter-corporate working arrangements that had been adopted in Droitwich, though recognising that the delegation of executive powers to a joint committee might only be justifiable where large-scale programmes of development were envisaged. Indeed, he suggested there could be considerable scope for local variation in the arrangements made for joint working between the County and the Districts, and for encouraging the emergence of appropriate forms of outwardly connective skill.

Recognising such possibilities, the report of the Project Group built further on the recommendations of the Bains Committee on District Joint Committees by suggesting that each should be served by one or more working teams of officers, concerned with environmental and possibly also other issues. Such a team would bring together skills from both the County and the District staffs, preferably with an officer of the latter authority serving as the primary point for submitting the results of their explorations through the District Joint Committee. However, detailed arrangements could clearly only begin to emerge once the new authorities had begun to become operational.

Meanwhile, the recommendations of the Bains Committee were receiving general acclaim from officers throughout the country, though encountering some criticism from politicians and journalists who felt that they gave too little recognition to the role of the political process in local government. In particular, it was argued that the recommendations did little to provide the elected leadership of the new enlarged authorities with resources that were matched to their exacting task of formulating, questioning, explaining, and justifying policy decisions of major local importance.

One more specific criticism was raised by Professor John Stewart of Birmingham University, at a conference held to discuss the role of the new West Midlands Metropolitan County Council a few days before its first members were elected in 1973. He argued that the Bains Committee had assumed that the Metropolitan County would require the same type of basic management structure as any other of the new authorities, whereas in fact its executive responsibilities would remain very limited in relation to those of the Districts, and the Metropolitan County could only expect to make its mark by exercising the considerable degree of freedom it possessed to choose the issues to which it wished to direct its initiatives. The political strength of the Metropolitan Counties would ultimately depend on how far they could succeed in marshalling and deploying the complex of planning capabilities at their disposal in the pursuit of causes that coincided rather than conflicted with the collective aims of the powerful District Authorities. For instance, pressures could be exerted on central departments and appointed agencies in relation to such complex issues as that of environmental pollution. One

Figure 84 Changing boundaries of responsibility in health and water management in England

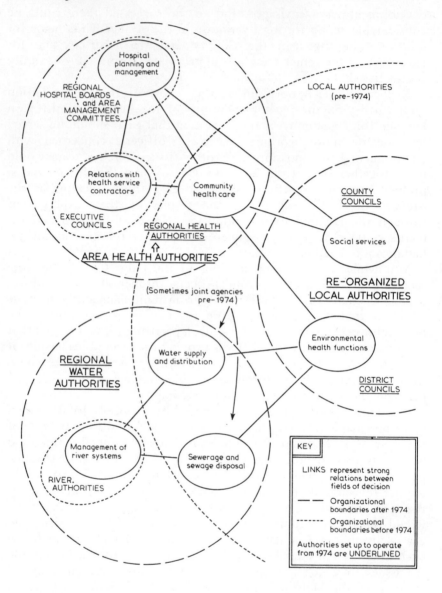

implication for internal organization could be that, at the Metropolitan County level, planning should not be regarded as a separate departmental service, as the Bains Committee had implied. Rather, it should be regarded as an integral part of the chief executive's responsibilities, so that an appropriate blend of physical, economic, and social planning skills could be mobilized to confront whatever range of policy issues the members might decide to focus upon from time to time.

New appointed agencies: the cases of health and water

The problems of local government reorganization were made no less difficult by parallel commitments on the part of central government to carry out two other reforms, also becoming operational on 1st April 1974: the first in the pattern of health services management, and the second in the management of water resources. Both these reforms involved a transfer to new appointed agencies of certain responsibilities that had previously been vested in elected local authorities, as indicated in *Figure 84*. However, both were the outcomes of initiatives and inquiry processes which were largely independent of the processes of local government reform initiated with the formation of the Redcliffe-Maud Royal Commission.

In the field of health, both the Labour and Conservative governments were committed to a radical restructuring of the National Health Service, first established in 1948. The main aim was to bring about closer integration between its three main branches: the hospital service, managed through its own structure of regional boards and area committees, the community services provided by local authority health departments, and the various professional services provided locally by independent medical and para-medical practitioners, under contracts to the National Health Service which were negotiated through special area Executive Councils.

The aims of reorganization had been neatly stated in terms of unification, co-ordination, local participation, and effective central control. However, there remained some difficult conflicts to be resolved between these aims. One of the most delicate problems, as at the time the National Health Service had first been established, was that of determining the position of the medical profession in the new management system, and satisfying its representatives that the proposals for reform could not erode their jealously guarded clinical freedom, rooted in the principle that the physician must always regard his primary accountability as being to the health needs of the individual patient.

Both political parties were broadly agreed on a pattern of fourteen Regional Health Authorities based on the former hospital planning regions, and about ninety Area Health Authorities as the primary units of management, with boundaries coinciding as far as possible with those of the proposed new local authorities. The main political debate was over the balance between an emphasis on local democratic influence and an emphasis on professional management skills. When the Conservative government modified the proposals of its predecessor, the latter emphasis was given additional prominence (HM Government, 1972), and, during the passage of legislation in 1972 and 1973, the implied loss of democratic control became the primary focus of pressure from the opposition. It was, however, agreed that about one-third of the members of each Area Health Authority be appointed on the recommendation of the elected local authority within the area. Also, at a district level within each Area Health Authority, a system of 'Community Health Councils' would be established as a channel for the transmission of constituency pressures, with a 50 per cent local authority representation. Although this step was generally welcomed, some concern arose over the likely effectiveness of the new Councils as watchdogs of community interests, as they would be dependent for staff services on the Area Health Authorities themselves.

The reorganization of water systems management had its origins in a national concern with the increasing difficulties of meeting rising levels of demand for water throughout England and Wales. Responsibilities for the control of hydrological cycles were divided among several different kinds of agency. These included some 200 water supply undertakings, mainly but not exclusively controlled by local authorities, acting individually or jointly; over 1,300 local authorities and joint agencies exercising sewerage and sewage disposal functions; and twenty-nine River Authorities, which had been established as recently as 1965 to control the overall discharges of effluent and extractions of water supplies within the main river catchment areas, in order to contain pollution and to safeguard overall levels of supply.

In 1969, a Central Advisory Water Committee was formed to recommend a new pattern of organization. After examining options for closer integration of responsibilities either on a territorial or a functional basis, the committee came out in favour of a small number of multi-purpose Regional Water Authorities based on the catchment areas of the main rivers, and taking over almost all the traditional powers of local authorities in the fields of water supply and sewerage. These proposals were accepted in principle by the government of the day, but, once more, it became apparent that the desired simplification of organizational responsibilities could only be achieved at a cost in terms of the creation of new boundaries elsewhere. One of the most difficult issues concerned the system of canals which had deliberately been created to cross-connect the main river catchments, and fears were expressed that their exploitation for leisure and commercial purposes was hardly likely to be regarded as a pressing priority by the regional authorities. After a sustained campaign by the various interest groups concerned, some significant concessions were made in the appointment of a new 'Water Space Amenity Commission' and the retention of the British Waterways Board as the primary public agency concerned with management of the national canal network.

The new system of Regional Water Authorities was also viewed with some concern by the local authority associations, as it implied a further erosion of local democratic control over the provision of basic community services, following the earlier loss of the electricity and gas networks to specialist appointed agencies, and the changes currently proposed in the field of community health. For the municipal engineering profession in particular, the prospect was one of the fragmentation of responsibilities which, at the local level, it had previously been possible to treat as a co-ordinated whole. Another implication was that the new water authorities would have to become closely involved in land-use planning processes at a wider strategic level, because problems of water and sewerage investment had repeatedly been shown — as at Droitwich — to impose important constraints in negotiation over prospective programmes for the planned expansion of towns. The anxieties of local authorities were only partly assuaged when, during the passage of the legislation setting up the new water authorities, it was announced that each would have a majority of its members appointed directly by the main local authorities in its area.

Increasingly, it became recognised, as the upheaval of 1974 approached, that the concepts of corporate management and planning, which had formed the linchpin of many of the attempts to restructure the decision-making processes of local government, would no longer be sufficient to handle the new situation, in which four new types of powerful executive agency would have to reach some form of continuing working relationship in the planning of local community services within any given geographical area: the new County Council, the new District Council, the new Area Health Authority, and the Regional Water Authority. As Professor Stewart argued (Stewart, 1971), it would therefore become necessary to look beyond the concept of corporate planning to a wider co-operative process of 'community planning', but, in interpreting this concept in a political environment, it was clear that there remained many further practical and conceptual problems to be overcome. In addressing ourselves to the future problems of local and regional planning in England, it therefore becomes important for us to consider how the general propositions of Chapter 13 might relate to the challenges presented by this particular set of evolving institutional relations. However, in so doing, it is also important not to lose sight of the wider implications for other systems of government. For this reason, we shall now briefly turn — as indeed we did at a similar point in Chapter 14 — to a consideration of some parallel developments in Scotland.

Parallel processes of organizational change: the case of Scotland

Although many of the underlying pressures for institutional change that we have described in the case of England were also making themselves felt concurrently in Wales and in Scotland, there were some significant differences of emphasis associated with more scattered patterns of community life, with differing national cultures and, in the case of Scotland, with a distinctive system of law, local government, and devolution of civil service responsibilities. For such reasons, the processes of local government reform followed a different path in each country. In Wales, proposals for the merger of traditional counties into larger units had already been published and debated by the time the Royal Commission for England had been formed, with the result that it proved possible to include Wales along with England in the provisions of the 1972 Local Government Act, with only marginal differences between the two countries in the general pattern of County, District, and Parish Councils — or 'Community Councils' as these last were designated in the case of Wales. In Scotland, the process of reform had begun with the appointment in 1966 of a parallel Royal Commission to that working in England (Royal Commission on Local Government in Scotland, 1969). However, keeping in mind the scattered social geography of Scotland, the Commission itself rejected the solution of the 'unitary authority' in favour of a two-tier system of seven new elected 'regional councils' and thirty-seven districts. Thus, the principle of a two-tier division of functions was never really in dispute in Scotland as it was in the case of England, although — inevitably — similar conflicts arose over the drawing of local boundaries and the allocation of specific functions.

A separate legislative process was set in train to bring the new Scottish authorities into existence in 1975, a year later than their English and Welsh counterparts. The resulting pattern of local accountability was broadly compatible with that south of the border, though the territories of some of the new regions (their number now increased to nine) were more extensive than any of the English and Welsh Counties, and their populations varied widely from the 2,500,000 of the Strathclyde Regional Council — centred on Glasgow, and comparable in resources with the largest of the English Metropolitan Counties — to the 100,000 or less of some of the more thinly populated regions. Also, there were three outlying island communities — Shetland, Orkney, and the Outer Hebrides — where unitary 'Island Councils' were chosen as the most appropriate solution. As in Wales, the concept of the 'Community Council' was adopted in Scotland to provide an equivalent to the English Parish as a channel of local opinion and influence in the rural areas. As in England and Wales, however, there remained much uncertainty and conflict of opinion as to how effective such channels could be made in practice when pitted against the resources of the new and enlarged units within which operational responsibilities would in future be concentrated.

Meanwhile, the constitutional relationships between England, Scotland, and Wales had become the subject of review by another Royal Commission, announced in 1968 at a time when pressures were rising for greater measures of political devolution, and when both the Scottish and Welsh Nationalist parties were encountering some dramatic successes in parlimentary by-elections. The terms of reference were

'To examine the present functions of the central legislature and government in relation to the several countries, nations and regions of the United Kingdom:

To consider, having regard to developments in local government organisation and in the administrative and other relationships between the various parts of the United Kingdom and to the interests of the prosperity and good government of our people under the Crown, whether any changes are desirable in those functions or otherwise in present constitutional and economic relationships:

To consider also, whether any changes are desirable in the constitutional and economic relationships between the United Kingdom and the Channel Islands and the Isle of Man.'

Figure 85   Institutions of public planning in England from 1974

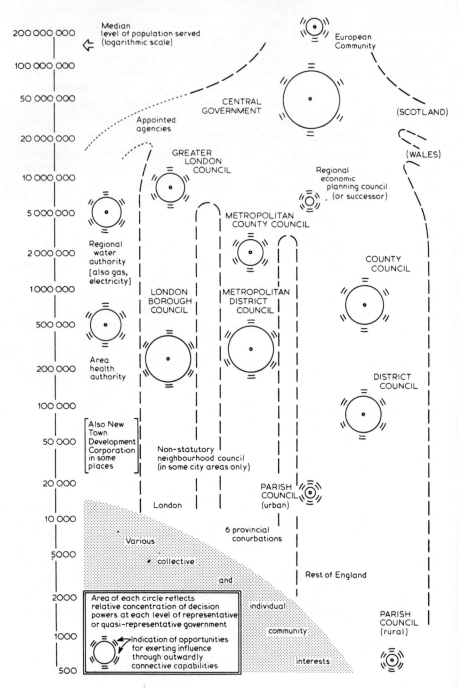

Meeting under the chairmanship first of Lord Crowther and later, upon his death, of Lord Kilbrandon, the Royal Commission on the Constitution encountered considerable difficulty in reaching an agreed recommendation. Meanwhile, the troubled political situation in Northern Ireland was leading to a separate process of constitutional reform in that part of the United Kingdom. In addition, the government became pledged to introduce a further degree of political devolution to an elected assembly in Scotland, recognising the rapidly changing situation presented by the discovery of oil under the North Sea and the consequent problems of control over large-scale international investment with far-reaching social and economic implications.

A new pattern of inter-agency relations

At the time of writing, one of the few issues of institutional structure in Britain which remained open to the prospect of early change concerned the future degree of regional devolution of central government powers, not only in Scotland and Wales but possibly also within England. Uncertainty remained not only over the nature of the recommendations to emerge from the Kilbrandon Commission, but also over the likelihood that any such recommendations would ultimately be accepted as a basis for governmental action. Although some observers were prepared to argue that the advisory Economic Planning Councils should be replaced as soon as possible by democratically accountable regional assemblies, there were others who maintained that, within England, the introduction of any form of elected body at an intermediate level between central and local government would only serve to complicate further an already difficult pattern of inter-agency relations, especially if any direct executive functions were envisaged, and could hardly be made politically acceptable either to central or local government interests.

The new pattern of inter-agency relations emerging in England after 1974 is summarized in *Figure 85*. This adopts – with some extensions – the same conventions as used earlier in *Figure 83* to compare the Redcliffe-Maud proposals with the traditional local government structure in England. The area of each circle has again been drawn so as to give an impression of the relative concentration of functional powers wielded by each level of representative government serving the population of England – this time extending from the rural parish council to the central government of Britain, and beyond to the European Community. In addition, the diagram includes the new Regional Water and Area Health Authorities, with their limited local authority representation. As reflected by analyses of local voting behaviour (Green, 1972), the areas of the circles indicate a view that central government wields powers of greater aggregate importance to most constituents than those of all levels of local government combined. It also shows the overall powers of decision of local government as concentrated most heavily at the lower tier in the Greater London and the new Metropolitan Counties, but being more evenly distributed between County and District outside these metropolitan areas. The concentration of direct powers of decision at the parish level is shown as very much smaller, as also, at another scale, is the direct power of the Regional Economic Planning Council and of any prospective successor. Indeed, the direct power of decision-taking of the Economic Planning Council — as opposed to any indirect influence it may have on decision-*making* — may be considered non-existent, unless publication of the results of regional studies or appraisals is considered as a form of direct executive action.

In *Figure 85*, the 'ripple' marks around each circle present the view that each level of representative or quasi-representative government for England inevitably has influence not only over decisions within its own recognised field of decision or 'action space', but also less directly over decisions taken elsewhere, through the exercise of whatever skills of an outwardly connective nature those working within that institution may be able to develop and deploy. Further, the conventions used in *Figure 85* have been designed to project a view that the pressure to exert influence through outwardly connective capacities is not necessarily any less in those bodies with very limited concentrations of executive power than in those with much greater concentrations. Indeed, in some circumstances, it may conceivably be greater: the less able a representative body is to absorb constituency pressures through its own internal decision-making processes, the greater may be the motivation to transmit those pressures elsewhere, by engaging in exploratory processes across the interfaces with other agencies.

The question of how far this potential for influence through outwardly connective capabilities may be realised in practice is one that takes us back directly to the sequence of general propositions and guidelines presented in *Figure 69*. If, indeed, it is believed to be desirable that capacities to shape and work within inter-agency decision networks should be dispersed widely through the institutional fabric of public planning, at the more peripheral as well as the more central nodes, then it becomes possible at this stage to transform our advocacy of a wide-ranging experimental approach to innovation in planning into some rather more specific hypotheses, designed more directly to indicate opportunities for experimentation within a specific institutional framework such as that set out in *Figure 85*.

The opportunities for experiment: some hypotheses

The four hypotheses with which we shall conclude this chapter combine to suggest a set of opportunities for working towards the *progressive enrichment* of planning processes within an evolving set of institutional relations — the concept of enrichment being itself one that we must seek to clarify in the way these hypotheses are expressed.

The first of our hypotheses relates to the *external orientation* of agencies, and pursues a little further the argument developed in the previous section. We shall hypothesize that:

the more limited the powers of decision that a representative agency commands in relation to the interests of its constituents, the more those acting within it will be motivated to develop outwardly connective styles of planning.

The most obvious implication of this hypothesis for any prospective experimentation in England is that the introduction of a two-tier local government structure throughout the country can be expected to increase the motivation to experiment with outwardly connective styles of planning at both County and District levels, at least in those areas that were previously dominated by unitary County Borough Councils. However, the pressure for more effective inter-agency planning may well be masked somewhat during the early years of the new system, especially in those Counties and Districts that bring together several previously separate territorial units, where there may be a strong motivation at first to overcome parochial attitudes by forming a strong and cohesive corporate focus. One particular context in which an especially strong motivation to exert influence through outwardly connective activities can be expected to materialize will be that of the 269 'successor parish' councils which inherit the traditions of former Boroughs and Urban Districts, mainly of populations between 10,000 and 20,000 but which must operate in a situation in which they are deprived of virtually all direct executive powers. However, whereas such Councils can be expected to have the motivation to play a leading role in any experimental process, it may be doubted whether they can muster the necessary resources of exploratory skill, or succeed in maintaining the requisite level of access to other relevant agencies. It might be argued that the idea of a vigorous outwardly connective role at this level lacks credibility, just as did the Redcliffe-Maud proposal for grass roots 'Local Councils' with a purely deliberative and advisory role. But this is a point which we can develop further by moving forward to our next two hypotheses.

Our second hypothesis relates to the possibilities of *contextual reinforcement* in the development of outwardly connective capabilities, and will be stated as follows:

> the advancement of outwardly connective styles of planning can be reinforced by creating a context wherein opportunities exist to compare systematically a variety of local experiences, and thereby to discover how far the relevant personal skills can be made transferable through the articulation of relevant techniques.

Such a context might be created through initiatives at a national, a regional, or a more local level. However, we argued in Chapter 14 that it was especially at the regional level of planning — presenting, in England, a crucial interface between local and central government but commanding comparatively few direct powers of decision — that there could be found a combination of a motivation to operate in an outwardly connective style and a concentration of resources of analytical and political skill through which more explicit technologies relating to the connective mode of planning could be developed and disseminated. We shall expand in the next chapter on the concept of the regional level of government as a centre for the interpretation of more local experiences and the reinforcement of local capabilities. However, we must, at this stage, also recognise that the concentrations of skills in both central government departments and the new County Councils may be equally relevant to any experimental process. Also, as we have already argued, the Counties and Districts will themselves have a direct motivation to engage in outwardly connective processes, even though the pressure to do so may be less dominant over other pressures — such as the pressure for cohesive corporate planning — than at the regional level. This brings us on to a third hypothesis relating to a question of *mutual advantage*:

> it is ultimately to the mutual advantage of those working in the more powerful as well as the less powerful institutions of representative government to encourage the emergence of more explicit processes of connective planning at the inter-agency level.

This hypothesis is by no means self-evident. In the language of the theory of games, it implies that relations between different levels of representative government are not necessarily those of a 'zero-sum game', in which a gain to the one implies a corresponding loss to the other. While rejecting a model of inter-agency co-operation based on consensual thinking as incompatible with the reality of divergence between differing constituency interests, the hypothesis does suggest that it is far from inevitable that attempts to develop more conscious patterns of inter-agency explorations will automatically be frustrated by those agencies that may appear to have least to gain or most to lose. Indeed, even the chequered histories of the Birmingham overspill problem and the Droitwich Development scheme provide grounds for optimism about the mutual advantage of working towards more conscious processes of connective planning in the long run, if only because of the public pressures that can come to bear on any agency that may appear to be adopting a deliberately obstructive stance.

Thus, our first three hypotheses, provided they can be sustained through experience, provide some grounds for optimism about the possibility of working towards a progressive enrichment of public planning through the more conscious development of outwardly connective capabilities across a wide spectrum of representative institutions of government. Our last hypothesis relates this general concept of enrichment to the wider question of *societal adaptation to change*, by stating that:

> cumulative experience in the more explicit development of connective styles of planning will generate increasing political pressures to channel resources towards the support of those forms of inter-agency network that are most necessary to sustain the processes of societal adaptation to turbulent environmental forces.

This is a far-reaching hypothesis, which itself rests on a degree of optimism about the stability of social and political institutions within the immediately foreseeable future. It interprets the idea of progressive enrichment of planning in a somewhat more tangible sense than hitherto, by relating it to the question of whether conditions can be created in which it will be accepted within a society that a higher proportion of that society's finite resources of human intelligence should be diverted into exploratory activities directed towards a particular field of human action, albeit one whose limits are by no means easy to define. This is the field of all forms of societal response to changes in a global environment which, as many would argue, is showing more and more symptoms of passing 'beyond the stable state' (Schon, 1971).

To summarize, we have now put forward four hypotheses which will help us in speculating about some opportunities for future experimentation in connective planning, taking as our frame of reference the particular institutional context set out in *Figure 85*. These hypotheses were introduced respectively as:

- a hypothesis about *external orientation*;
- a hypothesis about *contextual enrichment*;
- a hypothesis about *mutual advantage*;
- a hypothesis about *societal adaptation.*

Unlike the eight propositions of Chapter 13, these hypotheses can all be regarded as making assertions which are to some extent of a 'counterfactual' nature. In other words, they cannot be tested through observation alone; their validity can only be explored through processes of experimental intervention in the systems to which they relate. Nevertheless, they will form a set of implicit guidelines to us in building up the highly speculative narrative to which we shall turn in Chapter 17.

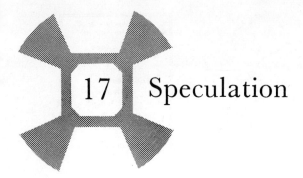

17 Speculation

A scenario for an experimental process

To provide a vehicle for some free-ranging conjecture about the opportunities for further experiment in the development of outwardly connective styles of planning, we shall now find it convenient to introduce a set of fictitious agencies and actors, operating within a hypothetical region of England some years after the reorganization of local government in 1974. We hope that the scenario which we shall unfold is one that the reader outside England will not find too difficult to translate into terms relevant to other sets of national circumstances. At this point, we shall have to adopt the standard fiction writer's disclaimer that none of our actors in this chapter will be based on actual individuals. All our characters will be purely imaginary, as will the various localities within which they operate.

Although the four hypotheses put forward at the end of the previous chapter were all expressed in terms that supported a belief in the scope for innovation, we shall try to be realistic in recognising the likelihood that there will be many stumbling blocks and setbacks in any wide-ranging innovatory process. Indeed, this was observed in our discussions of the innovatory processes which have already been initiated in the regions, in the new and expanding towns, and in the deprived inner city areas. However, it will be assumed that both the successes and failures which we shall encounter will hold their lessons

Figure 86   A map of Outland Region

KEY to names of towns
within County Districts:

Bo	Boxleywood
Br	Brawley New Town
F	Fluxton
Gr	Grumwich
GS	Great Shingle
LS	Little Shingle
Lu	Lulsworth
P	Pitsdale
W	Wuthering

Gr●   Lu●

North
Bound

NEWBOUND

Upmoor

Adminster

FRESHIRE

Br●   East
Bound

Brawley
Greenward   Fluxton
●F

●Bo
Patchover   West Freshire   Churn Bay

●W   GS●

●P   LS●

Dormiton   ●Dockport

GREATER WENCHESTER
METROPOLITAN COUNTY   Wighton-
super-Mare

Wenchester   ESTUARY OF RIVER SPENT

Checkham   Blakemills

COUNTIES in capitals
Districts in lower case

✱ =OTHER COUNTIES
NOT REFERRED
TO IN TEXT

for further advancement. In the long term, therefore, our scenario will be an optimistic one. Whether it is credible in its optimism is a matter on which the reader must be left to make a personal judgement; but, of course, a single scenario can by no means encapsulate all the opportunities for experiment that might be seized in different sets of local, regional, and national circumstances. Indeed, this chapter will have fulfilled its purpose if it encourages the reader to speculate on other alternative ways of initiating processes of experiment in the more conscious development of inter-agency planning activities and skills.

An introduction to the Outland Region

The Outland Region, we shall suppose, differs from the West Midlands of the nineteen-sixties in being comparatively remote from the main centres of economic prosperity in England or the neighbouring countries of the European Community. Despite successive infusions of regional economic aid, its mixed industrial and agricultural economy remains stagnant. High levels of unemployment tend to aggravate conditions of increasing deprivation and unrest in the inner city areas. However, conditions of comparative prosperity can be found elsewhere in the region, and the recent discovery of oil in nearby coastal areas has brought a new interest in large-scale industrial development in some locations well away from the established industrial towns.

One County of the Region, Newbound, will already be familiar to readers of *Local Government and Strategic Choice* (Friend and Jessop, 1969). *Figure 86* shows its location within the region as a whole, showing that the effect of the 1974 reorganization has been to divide it into five County Districts, the most populous of which is based on the former County Borough of Adminster, with a population approaching the half-million mark. Another district is based on the medium-sized town of Fluxton and its hinterland, while a third includes the New Town of Brawley — brought together, after a bitter political struggle, with the predominantly agricultural small towns and villages of the Greenward Valley, under the hybrid name of Brawley Greenward. The two remaining County Districts, of North Bound and East Bound, are each dominated by rural interests. though the former does include one sizable urban centre in the declining industrial town of Grumwich.

To the south of Newbound County lies the Metropolitan County of Great Wenchester, made up of six Metropolitan Districts which form a continuous conurbation with the regional capital of

Wenchester at its heart. Wenchester itself is by no means a homogeneous community, while the adjoining Districts all differ in their salient social characteristics. Dormiton has grown rapidly as a residential suburb with a reputation for exclusiveness, while Blakemills is a densely populated area with a poor physical environment and many symptoms of economic deprivation. The District of Checkham is becoming subject to increasing social and political stresses because of an influx of families from neighbouring Blakemills, many of them forced out by changes in the local housing market and bringing with them unfamiliar cultural influences. The future of Dockport is overshadowed by uncertainties as to whether or not the extensive port facilities will continue to provide a primary source of employment, or can be replaced by new types of industry. The final Metropolitan District, Patchover, stems from an uneasy amalgamation of three previously independent Boroughs: the unpretentious suburban Boxleywood, the proud hill town of Wuthering with its literary associations and ancient castle, and the former mining settlement of Pitsdale in the valley below.

There is only one other county of the Outland Region that will appear in our scenario: the much-visited county of Freshire, spanning the area between the Upmoor national park and the coastal towns of the Spent Estuary, with some rich agricultural areas in between. The coastal parts of the county are coming under intensive developmental pressures, both from recreational interests and from international companies attracted by the recent discovery of oil further out to sea and the prospects of constructing a new deep water port. There is, however, a growing concern over the consequences in terms of environmental pollution, especially among the small resort towns in the new County District of Churn Bay, which have already been losing their former reputations because of an accretion of effluents from industries further up the estuary.

The pressures for connective planning

For several years, a nucleus of regional civil servants has been working from offices in Wenchester. Although they owe formal allegiance to several different ministries, well-established practices of inter-departmental working have evolved, in association with some form of regional representative council. This, we may suppose, began its existence as a Regional Economic Planning Council, but may possibly since have been transformed to include an element of elected membership. Its exact status is a question that we shall discreetly leave open, in view of the controversy surrounding the

divided report of the Kilbrandon Commission on the Constitution
(1973), and the associated uncertainties over possible governmental
initiatives in response, at the time of writing.

Within the regional office is a rich variety of skills, including
economists, town planners, engineers, and other specialists, a strong
core of administrative civil servants. Over time, they have all – in
varying degrees – adjusted their individual orientations through
continuing contact with each other and with various political
interests within the region. Most of them will be subject in some
degree to departmental policy guidelines, but may have come to
regard themselves as primarily accountable to a regional constituency, the interests of which are represented – though not always
in a well-articulated way – by what we shall simply call the 'Regional
Council' for Outland.

We shall begin our story with one in a series of encounters
between an administrative civil servant in the regional office and
a lecturer from the University of Wenchester, who is engaged in a
research project in which the regional office has a close and
continuing interest. The civil servant, an up-and-coming figure who
surprised some of his contemporaries by opting for a posting in
Outland, has played a crucial catalytic role in a number of regional
planning studies and decisions over the last few years, though his
position requires him to work largely behind the scenes, and he is
little known in the region at large. The academic has a background in
economics but now lectures in public administration, having been
attracted towards that field through an acquaintance with the work
of his fellow-economist Lindblom – in particular, *The Intelligence of
Democracy* (1965) on which he based his doctoral thesis. He is also
something of a political activist himself, having been elected the
previous year to Patchover Metropolitan District Council – though
some views which he frequently propounds in the weekly political
journals have brought him into occasional disfavour with his local
party leadership. Both men, as may be inferred from these brief
sketches, have cultivated skills in the management of informal decision
networks. We shall call them Nettlefold and Webster respectively.

At this particular meeting, Nettlefold, the civil servant, begins
to expand on his current anxieties about the stresses that have been
building up between the various local authorities with which he must
deal. For instance, there is a bitter conflict over planning powers
between Wenchester District Council and the Metropolitan County.
The former, retaining its historic status as a city, maintains its own
large planning department, and its leaders insist that they must keep
responsibility for all aspects of central area development. However,

the County is engaged in preparing a draft Metropolitan Structure Plan, in which central area policy is regarded as a crucial element. Other conflicts simmer just below the surface both within and beyond the conurbation area, emerging at structure plan level mainly as issues about the location of housing and industry, but also carrying economic and political undertones which tend to be suppressed within the context of the formal structure plan debate.

In one of the more congested and physically run-down parts of Blakemills a Community Development Project team has worked for some years on problems of acute social deprivation, and has argued publicly for more concerted and imaginative programmes of investment of central government resources to arrest a gradual tendency towards the formation of ghetto areas. Some land which might be developed quickly for public housing has been identified by the County planners on the fringes of Dormiton and Checkham, but the leaderships of the District Councils concerned, responding to constituency pressures, contend that this land is only suitable for recreational use, or in some areas for low density private housing. For several years, the predecessors of the Greater Wenchester and Newbound Counties were locked in dispute over problems of planning for population growth. Although the New Town of Brawley has provided public housing for many years, for tenants nominated both by Adminster and by Wenchester, the agreed population target has now almost been fulfilled, and proposals have been formulated by a regional study team for the planned expansion of a number of small towns, including Lulsworth on the fringe of East Bound District. There remains much uncertainty over whether such proposals will eventually prove locally acceptable. This question depends on current negotiations over the level of external financial support for water and sewerage investments, and over a proposition that central government approval may be conditional on the acceptance of an element of public housing for tenants nominated by the Metropolitan County Council.

Meanwhile, a tense situation is building up in Freshire, and in other planning authorities which flank the estuary of the River Spent, where both members and officers have been forced to come to grips rapidly with an unfamiliar set of pressures from developers, both public and private, in the conflicting fields of industry and recreation. A proposal to site a new power station midway between the small resort towns of Great and Little Shingle is emerging as a critical test case, and a powerful grouping of conservationist interests has been putting forward increasingly cogent arguments against the proposal both at County and Regional levels. Among the assumptions which they challenge are the current national predictions of long-term growth in the demand for electrical energy, which they feel do not show sufficient awareness of an accelerating crisis in the availability of fossil fuels.

The disposition of reticulist skills

In reviewing such problems, Nettlefold expresses anxiety about how the various current sources of conflict within the region — some of them with deep historical origins — can be handled within the recently created local government structure without degenerating into a series of acrimonious and obstructive tactical battles between the interests concerned. This leads Webster to expound some views about ways of improving the disposition of network managing skills within the region. We shall develop these views in terms of our own concepts of reticulist capabilities and opportunities, although it may be that Webster himself has other related concepts or images in mind.

Nettlefold is able to relate much of what Webster says to the types of intuitive skill that he himself is continually called upon to exercise. Also, they find it possible to identify a number of other regional actors, known to them both, who possess reticulist skills of a high order, and have been able to deploy these skills to bring about some crucial adjustments across the interfaces with other agencies. Such actors range from the Mayor of the Town Council at Great Shingle (the successor to a long-established Borough Council) to the Director of Intelligence Services within the Metropolitan County. The former has already played a crucial mediating role in an earlier phase of the dispute over the siting of the power station; while the latter has a nominal responsibility for developing management information systems to inform the policies of both the County and District Councils. Even though he has a powerful computer under his command, he finds the creation of any form of central information 'bank' continually obstructed by the suspicions of other departments and authorities over the uses to which particular kinds of data could be put, and the interpretations to which they might lead. He therefore spends much of his time attempting to strike bargains that will keep open his lines of access to current policy issues, even if the information he gains may often be 'soft' in character and may be irrelevant to the expansion of his formal data processing system. Through taking this kind of line and remaining sensitive to political implications, the Director has succeeded in attracting the grudging respect of members of all three main parties on his Council.

Other successful reticulist actors in the region, it is agreed, include the former leader of the Community Development team in Blake-mills, who has remained active since the conclusion of his project at an informal level of neighbourhood grass-roots organization, both in Blakemills and neighbouring parts of the conurbation; the Chief Executive of Brawley Greenward District, who has had to discover practical ways of handling a series of wrangles between his elected members and the Brawley New Town Development Corporation; and the project co-ordinator from the planning department of Newbound County, who has had to act as mediator between different sectional interests in the County itself and its constituent districts, so as to arrive at agreed capital investment priorities. There are, however, other officials who, on reflection, have shown themselves much less successful in developing and deploying reticulist capabilities, even though they occupy crucial interface positions. Webster argues that the root problem may in some instances be one of inadequately developed reticulist opportunities, and in other instances of lack of relevant personal skills. In either case, the effects are detectable in the form of a succession of breakdowns in the processes of mutual adjustment at the inter-agency level.

Nettlefold finds this diagnosis not completely convincing, if only because so many political conflicts have structural or ideological roots, and are therefore likely to persist even in the face of reticulist skills of the highest order. However, he finds Webster's argument sufficiently plausible to merit some serious attention, and he responds with considerable interest when Webster suggests that a new kind of inter-agency experiment might be initiated, directed towards a more conscious disposition of outwardly connective capabilities throughout the region. Such an experiment, he recognises, could be fraught with difficulties but, viewed against the existing situation of endemic conflict and misunderstanding between agencies at many different levels, Nettlefold begins to feel there could be little to lose. He remains a little uneasy about the implications of association with such a venture for his own career progression; but if the experiment succeeds, he feels it could further enhance his growing reputation as an innovator.

The genesis of an experiment

By the next time Webster and Nettlefold meet, we shall suppose that Webster has been able to develop some more specific ideas for an experimental process. Whether he recognises it or not, we shall suppose that these ideas relate closely to the four hypotheses that we formulated at the end of Chapter 16. First of all, he argues that the most promising level at which to concentrate the experimental process could be just below that of the County District Council, where there exist a number of 'successor parish' councils and other less formal representative groups which are highly motivated to exercise influence over decisions affecting their constituents, but have few if any direct powers themselves. He sees the possibility that explicity designated 'community reticulists' could be placed at the disposal of a limited set of local representative groups operating at this level, who could be offered technical and other forms of support from the regional office, with the blessing of the Regional Council. Forestalling Nettlefold's next question about the danger that such an innovation might be considered subversive by the County and County District Councils for the areas concerned, Webster argues that he knows a number of officers and members personally whom he believes would probably welcome any move that helped the representatives of the smaller communities to participate in decision-making in a less erratic — and at times obstructive — way than they do at the moment. In some, at least, of the Counties and Districts of the Outland Region he believes that a majority of members could be won round to this view, given some evidence or assurance that such an unfamiliar being as a 'community reticulist' could be a stabilizing rather than a disruptive influence. He concedes, however, that there will probably be some Counties or Districts that he would expect to remain implacably opposed to this kind of experiment. This might well place a stringent limitation on the number of communities that could be involved in the experimental process, at least in the first instance.

Provided that many of the initial costs of this kind of experiment could be underwritten by central or regional funds, Webster sees an exciting possibility, in the longer run, that many of the communities served might come to see the continuing retention of at least one full-time 'community reticulist' as something well worth supporting through the local rate account, as a means of enhancing the collective influence of citizens on more remote yet powerful public agencies. Indeed, the whole success or failure of the experiment would depend on whether this point of take-off could be reached in some at least of the localities taking part. This in turn could depend on whether or not a number of necessary supporting conditions could be maintained. On the one hand, the community reticulist would have to relate to his constituents in a sufficiently open way to demonstrate that his services were directly useful to local people. On the other hand, he would have to work through a representative group who would expect him to amplify rather than usurp their powers; and he would have to maintain sufficient trust among officers and members of other authorities to prevent them obstructing his channels of access to their ongoing decision processes. In maintaining this difficult balance, the existence of a 'mutual support network' of some kind — as indicated in our general model of *Figure 71* — could be a crucial factor, and it is in this respect, argues Webster, that the regional office could provide a very important reinforcing influence. Further, it could in this way ultimately perform a vital connective role in the wider processes by which local experiences are diffused throughout wider social networks, and appropriate forms of societal adaptation are induced in changing environmental circumstances.

Nettlefold is attracted, but wary. Webster has now touched on the ground of each of the four hypotheses that we framed at the end of Chapter 16 — relating to questions of external orientation, of contextual reinforcement, of mutual advantage, and of societal adaptation respectively. But how credible is the whole proposition in terms of the practical politics within Outland? Also, how likely is it that Nettlefold will be able to mount a case to central government to release the necessary resources and provide the official endorsement to get such an experiment off the ground? Webster reminds him that government departments have already been prepared to back such experiments as the Community Development Projects and the Urban Guidelines Studies, and quotes parallel innovations in a number of other countries, ranging from India to the United States. He argues that the cost required to support one 'community reticulist' in each of half a dozen localities could be a comparatively modest one. Indeed, a quick calculation shows him that, for a 'successor parish' council of, say, twenty thousand population, the annual expenditure would work out at only a small fraction of the permitted expenditure limit for discretionary parish purposes. He believes it would be necessary for most of this cost to be met externally for a period of two, three, or perhaps four years, while each local community reticulist built up his basic knowledge of the locality and its problems. After that, he believes the parish council or other representative group should be in a position to make a judgement for itself as to whether or not the services of a full-time (or possibly part-time) officer of this kind should continue to be borne as a direct charge to the local rate.

A process of mobilization

Nettlefold remains non-committal, but shortly after the encounter he has to attend a meeting with Underwood, a senior civil servant in the head office of his department, and takes the opportunity to float the possibility of the experiment. He is careful not to mention the word 'reticulist', as Underwood is somewhat suspicious of what he regards as high-flown terminology. However, he finds Underwood receptive to any suggestions about ways of bringing a greater degree of order into the new local government structure, the complexities of which are beginning to drive him to despair. Nettlefold's diagnosis of this problem, in terms of inadequately developed capabilities to manage inter-agency decision networks, strikes a receptive chord in Underwood, whose own role in central government requires him to operate more through ingrained reticulist skill than through reliance on formal lines of authority. Nettlefold is mildly encouraged when Underwood breaks off the meeting by quoting one of his favourite stories, about President Kennedy's reaction whenever buttonholed by the proponent of a worthy cause demanding instant presidential attention: 'I agree with you that something should be done, but I don't know if the government will'.

Meanwhile, Webster has been taking every opportunity that arises to test the likely reactions of his fellow-members of Patchover District Council, and also of officers of other neighbouring authorities with whom he has come into contact during the course of his research activities. Some of these are markedly sceptical; but an unexpected chord of enthusiasm is struck in the Chief Planning Officer of Newbound, who has become seriously worried by the tendency of his own department and the planning departments of the Districts to work in more and more divergent directions, using different types of methodology which tend to mask incompatible assumptions. He is inclined to welcome any move that could increase the quality of communication between officers and members at county, district, and parish levels, and declares himself willing to try to persuade his Council and fellow-officers to collaborate in any experimental programme that may be set up, mentioning two or three of the five Districts within the County which he believes might also be receptive.

In this way, Webster and Nettlefold between them are able to develop a feel for the kind of support which they might be able to expect for what they have come to explain as a 'Policy Network Development Programme' for the Outland Region. Underwood has secured enthusiastic support from a Junior Minister, but has encountered many searching questions from fellow civil servants. The Chairman of the Regional Council is sounded out, and reacts in a non-committal though not openly hostile way, and there seems to be a good prospect that co-operation can be secured from a sufficient number of local authorities in the region to give the experiment a reasonable chance of success. The next step is therefore for Nettlefold to try to cast the proposal in a rather more concrete form, in order to allay some of the doubts and objections that have arisen during the processes of informal sounding, and then to write formally to the Chief Executives or Clerks of all local authorities in the region, informing them of the proposed 'Policy Network Development Programme' and inviting them to send representatives to a special one-day meeting where the aims of the exercise will be elaborated and the practical problems discussed.

On the day of the meeting, about fifty officers are present, and a few elected members. It is suggested by Nettlefold that the experiment should be confined to a total of between four and eight localities within the region. In each of these, an individual should be appointed to serve in the role of 'community reticulist', serving on short-term contract to a local representative group. According to the type of area, this group could be an urban 'successor parish' council, a joint committee of smaller rural parish councils, or a committee of members from adjoining wards of a metropolitan district, serving as a form of 'neighbourhood council' which would carry the political authority of the official electoral process. In each case, the community served would preferably be within the population range of ten to forty thousand. The salary and associated costs of each appointee would be paid for in the first instance through a central programme budget, but the parish or district council would be expected to make a direct annual contribution after the first year on a scale that would steadily increase until the fourth year, when it would be up to the local authority to choose whether to continue paying the full costs of a reticulist service indefinitely, at whatever level it judged appropriate, or to withdraw. The representative group would have the right, in certain circumstances, to withdraw from the contract earlier; it would also have the final say in the initial selection process. Appointments could only be made in communities where the County and District Councils were prepared to give official support to the experiment and provide reasonable assurances over access to information, in return for reciprocal assurances that such information would not be used in an irresponsible way.

After Nettleford has outlined these and other administrative points, Webster takes the floor to outline the kinds of technique that the proposed 'community reticulist' might use to open up the exploration of problem situations at the interfaces with other organizations. He indicates how the use of certain simple methods of analysis could help in increasing the opportunities for effective influence by the representative group to whom this individual reported, while also creating prospects of benefit for the other agencies involved, by diverting situations of potential conflict into more constructive channels. While Webster admits that the reticulist might be able to do little where the conflict takes on an ideological, non-negotiable character, he suggests that there could be many opportunities in other circumstances either for discovering latent areas of consensus where none were believed to exist, or for discovering areas of potential bargaining where conflicts were recognised as unavoidable. The exchange of experience during the experiment, both on technical matters and on other problems that arose, could — suggests Webster — be much facilitated by establishing a special 'regional forum' on which all the participating interests could be represented.

The experiment is launched

The reactions of those present at the meeting is, not surprisingly, very mixed, varying from enthusiasm through confusion to hostility. Nevertheless, Underwood — who has remained silent at the back of the room — is able to report back to headquarters that the level of apparent support, and the qualities of those organizing the experiment, are such as to justify a formal commitment by his Ministry to sanction the required expenditure. From this point, events move rapidly to the stage of setting a target launching date for the programme, though there are many further local arrangements to be negotiated, and reassurances to be given, through the regional and local networks to which Webster and Nettlefold have access.

The upshot is that selection panels are set up for the appointment of 'community reticulists' in each of the five localities indicated in *Figure 87*. In Lulsworth and in Pitsdale, the representative group is a single Town Council with successor parish status; in the Greenward Valley, it is a joint committee on which a set of nine contiguous rural parish councils are represented; in Shingle, the two small towns of Great and Little Shingle are equally represented despite some disparity in their populations; and in Checkham, a special neighbourhood committee is established comprising all councillors representing the four eastern wards of the Metropolitan District. These five localities have emerged through a process in which other communities were considered, but regarded as less promising because of insufficient assurances of support from the County or District Councils concerned. The case of East Checkham, we shall suppose, is one that still raises some anxieties on the part of Nettlefold and Webster. The changing character of the area makes it subject to a

Figure 87   The policy network development programme for Outland Region:
A political map

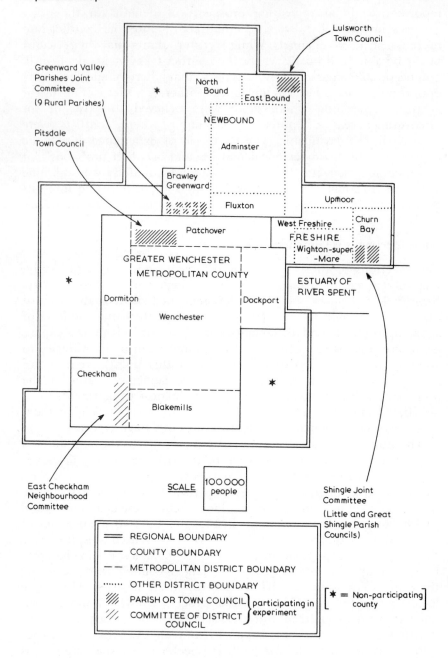

Lulsworth
Town Council

Greenward Valley
Parishes Joint
Committee
(9 Rural Parishes)

Pitsdale
Town Council

North
Bound

East Bound

NEWBOUND

Adminster

Brawley
Greenward

Fluxton

Upmoor

Churn
Bay

West Freshire

FRESHIRE

Wighton-super-
-Mare

Patchover

GREATER WENCHESTER
METROPOLITAN COUNTY

Dormiton

Dockport

Wenchester

ESTUARY OF
RIVER SPENT

Checkham

Blakemills

East Checkham
Neighbourhood
Committee

SCALE

100 000
people

Shingle Joint
Committee
(Little and Great
Shingle Parish
Councils)

REGIONAL BOUNDARY
COUNTY BOUNDARY
METROPOLITAN DISTRICT BOUNDARY
OTHER DISTRICT BOUNDARY
PARISH OR TOWN COUNCIL } participating in
COMMITTEE OF DISTRICT } experiment
COUNCIL

[✱ = Non-participating
county]

certain amount of inter-communal tension, and the political balance on the District Council is a delicate one, in which a centre party holds a crucial bargaining position. The leader of this party makes involvement in the regional experiment a condition of participation in a ruling coalition, so the role of the appointed reticulist may well be a somewhat uneasy one.

Advertisments are launched, asking for applicants with experience of local policy problems and with good professional or academic qualifications in any relevant field, combined with evidence of the ability to work outside their basic discipline and to operate in an imaginative way in a complex organizational environment. The response is surprisingly wide, and among those interviewed are several impressive candidates, most of whom have become highly dissatisfied with the conventional wisdoms of their respective professions.

Nettlefold represents the regional interest on each selection panel, and Webster attends to offer more technical advice. He finds that each panel tends to look for qualities that are directly relevant to the salient local planning problems as these are currently conceived. Therefore, when it comes to discussion of the relative merits of candidates, he finds he repeatedly has to play the part of advocate for other, less clearly perceived, forms of exploratory skill of a more general reticulist character.

Some compromise between these perspectives is possible, and the first upshot of the selection process is that Taplin, a town planner who began his career in local government but has since been working in another regional office, is appointed to the post for the Greenward Valley, where there is a concern to counter the planning skills of the nearby Brawley New Town Development Corporation. Orme, an operational research scientist who has been working for a large firm of engineering contractors, is appointed to the post at Shingle where the main problem is seen as being the environmental threats posed by industrial development proposals. Pitsdale, where traditional industries have died away and seem likely to be superseded by office or shopping projects offering very different types of employment opportunity, secures the services of Connolly, an economist who has worked in a central government department, where he has become disillusioned with the kind of large-scale econometric analysis on which he and his colleagues have been working. Lawson, a young lawyer who has specialized in planning inquiries, is appointed to the post at Lulsworth where there is rising concern over the contractual arrangements for the proposed town expansion scheme. Finally, the East Checkham selection panel appoints a social worker by the name of Fielding, who has been deeply involved in cross-cultural community relations. Since leaving local government service, she has worked extensively with voluntary neighbourhood groups, and shown much persistence in influencing the decisions of relevant government agencies.

Among the five representative groups, we shall suppose that there are some that are content to regard 'Community Reticulist' as the formal title of the post, but others that are not. Consequently, Lawson has to make do with the formal title of Assistant Town Clerk of Lulsworth, while Connolly takes up his post at Pitsdale as Community Development Officer. In the discussion that follows, however, we shall use the more explicit term of community reticulist in each case.

A network of interactive learning

At the outset of the experiment, it is agreed that the regional forum should meet monthly, with attendance invited from all the parish, district, and county councils involved in any way in the experiment, as well as from other relevant agencies. The forum meets at the University of Wenchester, where Webster has arranged for periodic presentations on relevant topics both from members of his own faculty and from other relevant centres of education and research. These include the Polytechnic at Adminster, which has a well-known department of urban and regional planning and where extensive use is made of participative teaching methods such as operational gaming, and also an independent research centre outside the region, which we shall call the Centre for Policy Analysis and Research.

Thus, an extensive network begins to evolve around the formal structure of the regional forum, where monthly attendances tend to vary between thirty and forty in all. For the five community reticulists, this provides a welcome source of external support. However, they soon find that they have to be somewhat guarded when talking at the full forum about the problems that have arisen in their various local situations, because of the many different interests represented. Accordingly, the five agree to meet among themselves once a week to talk more freely about the day-to-day difficulties they encounter and to compare notes on the working methods that they are attempting to apply to their respective problem situations.

Webster is invited to come to these meetings, and finds himself coming to be regarded as a pivotal figure so far as the methodology of the reticulist function is concerned. One of the first problems which confronts each of the five is how broadly the initial focus of their explorations should be defined, given an awareness of specific pressures for decision in the locality concerned yet also — in the first instance — a very incomplete understanding of the overall pattern of problems within the area, of the relationships between them, and of the organizational interests involved. Among the various approaches which are discussed is that of AIDA, which is received in a more positive way by some of those present than by others. However, two of the five feel encouraged to try to identify overlapping foci of planning concern by inviting other decision-makers to take part in a group exercise of the kind discussed in Chapter 6. In the case of the Greenward Valley, this exercise is taken further, towards an exploration of the various social impacts of a series of investment projects both in the area itself and in the adjoining Brawley New Town. This analysis is made considerably easier and more realistic by the direct collaboration of a planner and a finance officer from the New Town Corporation staff, even though the officers concerned are at first very cautious in their attitudes to the experiment.

Another analytical method which is introduced at one stage derives from the type of balance sheet presented in *Figure 41* in discussing the problems of Salwarpe Road. This is applied by Connolly to explore the local impacts of the large-scale and complex proposal for office and shop development which is currently under review at Pitsdale. Much time is spent by each of the five in attending meetings and holding individual discussions to pick up the flavour of ongoing decision processes, taking advantage of the formal under-standing that they should not be denied access, within reason, to relevant committee or departmental discussions of both the County and District Councils within the areas of which they are working.

Webster is especially concerned that the five community reticulists should develop comparative analyses of the organizational and political characteristics of the differing inter-agency situations in which they are attempting to operate. At one of the weekly meetings, he brings along a colleague of his in the Department of Politics at the University of Wenchester, who introduces a method of mapping relations between agencies and actors which has been the subject of a recent two-year research project. We shall suppose that this represents a significant advance on the methods we have used in this book for plotting the positions of actors on a standard institutional base map. The method is strongly criticized by Fielding and by Taplin, to whom it appears to exhibit a weakness they feel is characteristic of too much work in political science, a lack of sensitivity to the political dimensions of the phenomena being studied. However, it is eventually agreed that the method, with modifications, should be applied systematically to an analysis of the

Figure 88 Patterns of issues and organizational relations in the Outland regional experiment

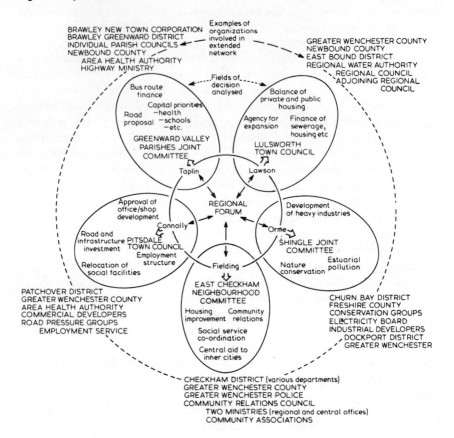

three or four major fields of decision which each of the five has diagnosed as important to his or her current local situation.

Progress and problems

The method does in fact yield some useful insights when some of the five find themselves faced with difficult problems of an ethical and quasi-political nature, and have to decide in what ways they should adapt their behaviour when faced with a variety of conflicting political pressures. We shall suppose that, twelve months after the beginning of the experiment, a pattern of network linkages has built up along the lines indicated in *Figure 88*. Each of the five has by now come to focus on a limited set of interconnected current issues which are of direct concern to the representative group to which he or she is accountable. These issues point towards a need to become engaged in exploratory processes, in so far as may be practicable, with a range of decision agencies of many different kinds, as indicated around the periphery of the diagram.

However, it is not always easy to secure and maintain a sufficient level of access. We shall suppose that two of the five have made disappointing progress, and are by now becoming quite frustrated. They have met with evasive responses from certain officers in such agencies as the Regional Water Authority, the Oil Company interested in estuarial development, and even one or two of the County or District Councils which are nominally committed to the experimental programme. In Pitsdale, Connolly has to decide how far to dissociate himself from local action groups which have mobilized themselves to fight the latest urban road proposals of the Metropolitan County and are adopting a highly combative stance; while in East Checkham, Fielding finds herself in a dilemma in deciding how far to cultivate contacts with individual families in order better to increase the level of awareness of their problems among responsible authorities. Also, she finds herself looked to by newly formed West Indian and Asian associations to help them in mobilizing resources to provide them with communal meeting places. However, her efforts in this direction soon arouse suspicion from some political sub-groups of the District Council, who see the leaders of these associations as adopting a more and more openly political role. Signs of political polarization are also appearing on the Greenward Parishes Joint Committee, because some of the villages are being increasingly taken over by commuters from Adminster, who are much less concerned than the original villagers — a high proportion of whom are of pensionable age — with such issues as the retention of rural bus services and the location of doctors' surgeries where they can be easily reached on foot or by public transport.

The group of five, advised by Webster, finds itself increasingly concerned with debating the ground rules that should be applied in such situations, especially in managing their relationships to their representative groups and other relevant agencies. It is agreed that there can be no easy solutions, and also that the problems faced are far from novel ones. Indeed, many of the specialist officers accountable to the larger District and County Councils themselves face similar dilemmas from time to time, although in some respects their position tends to be a less exposed one. It is suggested that the closest parallel might be with the position of the Community Development Project teams, and some experienced speakers from this field are invited to meet the group, to discover what might be learnt from their experience.

Despite some occasional problems of inter-personal relations among the five — exacerbated by communication problems arising from their differing professional backgrounds — they find themselves held together as a group by the similar external pressures to which they are subjected, and by their commitment, once a month, to discuss progress and problems in the wider context of the regional forum. This gives them an opportunity to air any problems which are proving difficult to handle without support from the wider network of those involved in the experimental process. However, they sometimes have to be careful in deciding which of the problems they have discussed within the group of five can safely and profitably be raised in the regional forum. Inevitably, the difficult position of Fielding in East Checkham comes up for anxious discussion from time to time, though discussion in the full regional forum tends to be inhibited by the presence of local politicians who are more concerned to prevent the experiment getting out of hand than to ensure its success. Also, at one point the controversy over industrial pollution in Churn Bay erupts in the regional press in a way that exposes Orme to accusations of misuse of confidential information. In the regional forum, he succeeds in justifying the stance he has taken, with the support of his representative group, to officers of the District and County Councils, but thereafter his position in the inter-agency networks he has helped to develop becomes marginally less secure.

Some changes of direction

Meanwhile, we may suppose, the programme has also begun to attract publicity of a more favourable kind. Most of the community reticulists, under pressure to demonstrate their worth to their local representative groups, have by now succeeded in giving the members of these groups new insights into the structures of the problems they face, and new opportunities for furthering their ends through more structured processes of exploration with other agencies. Also, several of the representative bodies taking part in the experiment have learnt how to make judicious use of public meetings, newspapers, and local radio stations in opening up a public discussion of issues at a formative stage, as opposed to waiting until formal proposals have been published and so leaving no means of participation open except through the politics of protest and objection. For Connolly in Pitsdale and for Lawson in Lulsworth, a topic of particular concern is the use to be made of the formal procedure for the 'examination in public' of County Structure Plans. This procedure opens up new kinds of opportunity for the systematic exploration of related policy issues. However, as Lawson argues, one of the key questions is that of how far the discussion can be allowed to range over issues that are interrelated in a very complex way, within the limits of a previously determined agenda. This, he feels, is a question very closely related to the responsibilities of the community reticulist role.

During the second year of the experiment, the local reticulists increasingly find themselves having to confront planning problems other than those upon which they focused in the earlier months. In the process, they also find themselves moving more and more into fields where they can obtain little practical help from their original professional disciplines. Orme, for instance, finds that his Committee's concern with estuarial pollution takes him more and more into a field of political confrontation with the Metropolitan County and the District of Dockport, lying up-river where many of the most noxious effluents originate. In this field, as in his earlier explorations into the implications of industrial development on the estuary itself, he finds himself drawn into a stance of challenging implicit values, in the form of locally unquestioned assumptions about the desirability for continued national economic growth. In drawing up rough-and-ready balance sheets of the impacts of policy options on different sectors of the community, he feels it is important not to exclude such considerations as incremental loss of non-renewable fossil fuels, or reduction of genetic variety in the natural environment. Orme still attempts to avoid imposing his own personal set of values on the information that he presents to his committee on the pattern of choices available. Inevitably, however, in his contacts with the Regional Water Authority and the neighbouring councils, he finds that he has to develop political skills in order to secure access to relevant actors, while using his basic discipline of operational research as a guide in framing relevant questions to ask once that access has been gained. In this process, his orientation changes perceptibly, so that he soon becomes impatient with those fellow-members of the Outland Operational Research Discussion Group who still talk confidently in terms of optimization, and believe that all problems can be solved within a corporate setting if only one can achieve a sufficient level of quantification.

In Lulsworth, Lawson had at first felt he could work well within his own field of professional competence in talking to the negotiating staff of the three principal councils directly associated with the proposed town expansion scheme — Greater Wenchester, Newbound County, and East Bound District — about the possible contractual arrangements for the financing and management of the development programme. However, he finds that the members of his non-executive Town Council are above all concerned that they should not lose influence within any management structure that might be set up. In particular, they bring to the process a sense of direct concern in the continuous evolution of the town — and especially its central area — to which they feel the majority of the East Bound Council members are not sufficiently sensitive. The overriding problem appears to the East Bound members to be in the field of housing — the balance between public and private housing, the financial contribution from Greater Wenchester, and questions of density and design standards. Lawson finds himself acting as a channel in bringing together these and other perceptions of the overall field of negotiation, and gradually becomes convinced that his basic lawyer's skill, which involves communicating primarily through the medium of the written and the spoken word, can usefully be supplemented by some of the less familiar forms of skill which he begins to absorb through contact with his fellow-reticulists in the weekly group meetings. Eventually, Lawson becomes almost as skilled as Taplin and the others in analysing the structure of related problems and uncertainties in graphical terms, which greatly surprises some of his former legal associates.

In East Checkham, Fielding has by now become increasingly involved with local residents' groups in decisions concerning prospective General Improvement Areas and Housing Action Areas. She has been trying to establish new channels of communication between departments of the Metropolitan District and other representative bodies in the wards that she covers, with the active support of some but not all of the ward councillors on her committee. She has also established a strong link with the local Community Relations Officer and members of his committee, and finds herself repeatedly offering suggestions as to how this officer might engage in constructive explorations with the Social Services, Housing, Education, and Planning departments of the District, and also with the Greater Wenchester Police Force, in order to further his aim of creating more understanding between local people of different cultures and national origins. This is a difficult task, because of the continuing tendency for conflicting ideologies to come to the surface. Meeting increasing frustration in operating at the grass-roots level, she turns to the question of how central or regional resources can best be channelled to help relieve the stresses of those inner city areas which are rapidly changing in their socio-economic structure. This offers the prospect of uniting her ward committee in her support, and she begins to spend much of her time in intensive discussions with regional and central officers of two of the ministries most directly concerned. Here, her experiences in field-work allow her to speak with some authority, but again — like Lawson — she finds that her own basic skills can be considerably reinforced by those other skills in the analysis of related policy options that she has absorbed through continuing contact with her other colleagues in the weekly group meetings.

The problems of concern in Pitsdale, in the meantime, are moving further and further from the focal issue of the proposed large-scale office and shopping complex, which remains a subject of deadlock between the two planning authorities concerned, Patchover District and Greater Wenchester County, as it has become locked into a continuing debate over the extent of the County's Structure Plan responsibilities. Connolly himself has contributed to a widening of the terms of this debate at informal meetings between representatives of Pitsdale Town Council and Patchover District, raising questions about the effects of the scheme on patterns of employment and commuting, and illuminating some of the uncertainties which have remained latent in the proposals for public investment in associated road works and other infrastructure. Connolly often finds he has to tread a very delicate path, especially where negotiations between public agencies and private developers are concerned. Being a cautious man, he finds that he can avoid some of the most sensitive areas in which his chances of survival in his job might be impaired, by concentrating mainly on issues of employment structure and of relocation of residents, clubs, and social services which are implicit in the office development proposal. This he finds a satisfying and worthwhile task, enabling him to maintain a sufficient level of support from the Town, District, and County Councils to keep discovering areas of consensus between them. However, like the others, he finds that his professional orientation undergoes some radical changes. Like his fellow-economist Webster, he soon becomes absorbed in new methods of analysing the changing patterns of political involvement in the decision-making process in terms that build upon Lindblom's concepts of partisan mutual adjustment.

In the Greenward Valley, with its newly found commuter affluence, Taplin's intuitive beliefs as a planner lead him to sympathize with the established rural population, whose options of life-style are much more limited than those of the incoming population. It is the new residents who are rapidly buying up and renovating many of the older houses, but they show little interest in pressing for the continuing support of rural bus services and the preservation of a dispersed pattern of schools, health centres, and entertainment facilities. Some of his nine parishes are dominated by the former interests, and some by the latter. However, one point that unites them is the sense that public investment in the Brawley Greenward District has for too long been dominated by the demands of Brawley New Town. The issue comes to a head over the question of a proposed highway, running the length of the Greenward Valley to link Brawley with Wenchester. Although this is seen locally as yet another threat originating from the New Town Development Corporation, Taplin finds that many of the Corporation's officers are themselves turning against the proposal, as they believe that too easy a link between Brawley and Wenchester could jeopardize the long-term aim of making the town self-sufficient. Taplin turns his attention increasingly towards the road proposal as a focal issue, and when it is publicly dropped from the Ministry's programme, he finds he has attracted much of the credit, while retaining the goodwill of both the Development Corporation and the majority of members on his local joint committee. At last, he feels able to shift his focus towards the issue that really concerns him, that of helping the ageing rural population to articulate to the relevant public authorities their demands for better bus services and continued ease of access to those social, shopping, and welfare facilities on which the survival of their traditional patterns of community life depends.

A gathering momentum?

While a variety of local experiences is building up in this way, some of them encouraging and others unsettling, the time approaches when decisions have to be faced as to whether or not the experiment should continue, and, if so, in what form. The setting within which a sense of success or failure can be most easily gauged will be that of the monthly regional forum, where the work of the five community reticulists is continuously evaluated by those representing a wide spectrum of interests. These include not only the local representative groups to which the five are most directly accountable, but also several prominent officers from the County and District Councils to which they are required to relate, together with a few representatives of health and water authorities and other relevant agencies. Among the scattering of elected members who find time to attend regularly — Conservative, Labour, Liberal, and Independent — there can be found a wide span of interest in different aspects of decision-making, because of the multiple roles some of them play in Regional, County, District, and Parish Councils, as well as in a variety of more specialized agencies.

As the time for taking stock of the situation approaches, we shall suppose that all the five community reticulists are still in post — some evidently enjoying the work, though one or two of them have run into increasingly rough weather, and talk of resignations has been heard from time to time. One hopeful sign is that none of the five representative groups has resorted to its right, under certain stipulated conditions, to withdraw from the experiment before the first stage has run its full course. However, recent changes among the ward representatives on the East Checkham neighbourhood committee suggest that Fielding's contract is unlikely to be renewed. In this instance, the situation is made more difficult by the need to rely for any continuation of local funds on the full District Council rather than any independently elected council or councils below the district level. Also, the continuation of Orme's contract has become uncertain because of a conflict of views between the two parish councils involved at Shingle, while the position of Lawson at Lulsworth has become difficult because of uneasy relations with some of the departmental officers on East Bound District Council.

However, we shall suppose that Webster and Nettlefold, as the two main initiators of the exercise, are by now able to point to two of the local situations, at Pitsdale and in the Greenward Valley, where the community reticulist has succeeded in attracting enough local appreciation of his efforts to become accepted as an integral aspect of the resources of the parish council or group of parish councils concerned. Indeed, the measure of public support which has developed is demonstrated when the elected members feel confident in facing their local parish elections with an explicit commitment to continue paying the costs of a reticulist service out of the discretionary local rate. Of course, they may prefer to use a term other than 'reticulist' when explaining to the public how such a service has helped the council to open up the exploration of important policy problems in such a way as to make other decision-making agencies more responsive to local interests. Also, they may not feel that a single full-time appointment necessarily reflects the requisite scale of activity to meet their own local needs. In the case of the Greenward Valley, we shall suppose that the possibility is discussed of widening the group of local parishes involved, while in Pitsdale a proposal is put forward to combine the reticulist function with the formal office of Clerk of the Town Council — a possibility about which Webster expresses some reservations, but, nevertheless, accepts as better than nothing. He is confronted with the argument that most good clerks or chief executives of local authorities are intuitive reticulists already; this he accepts, but he is doubtful whether the pressures on an officer through whom so many forms of statutory communication must flow will allow him the time and energy for the development of explicit techniques for exploring the structure of interrelated problems at a stage before extensive commitments have developed to particular lines of solution.

More or less simultaneously, however, we shall suppose that three events occur which give much encouragement to both Webster and Nettlefold. First, the Metropolitan District of Wenchester lets it be known that it would like to join the experiment; indeed, if — as is now publicly known — their neighbours in Checkham are no longer prepared to support the work of Fielding, they would be glad to offer her a contract to work in the adjoining South Wenchester neighbourhoods, paying, if necessary, entirely through their own local resources. As one of the more populous District Councils in the County, Wenchester had gone a long way towards decentralization of its various functions on an area basis, and would like to pursue the question of how the community reticulist concept might relate to its own initiatives in the field of internal devolution. Second, one or two of the County officers who take part in the regional forum begin to emerge as not only prepared to tolerate the idea of reticulist services at the sub-District scale, but to become advocates for its further extension. In particular, the County Planning Officer of Newbound — who has been building up a reputation as an innovator through presenting frequent papers at national professional conferences — seizes on the concept of the community reticulist and propounds the view that it can be a positive asset to those Counties that genuinely wish to confront the problems of urban and regional planning in a complex democratic society, and to reduce the incidence of those destructive forms of conflict between different public agencies which, he feels, have become increasingly pervasive in recent years. Finally, the leader of a regional study team, which has been working for the last year or so on the formulation of strategic options for Outland as a whole, suddenly discovers that the analyses of strategic options which have been made at a much more local level within the Outland Policy Network Development Programme can do much to illuminate the dilemmas of methodology that he and his team have been facing at regional level. Indeed, it seems possible that there can be as much useful transmission of experience from the local to the regional level as vice versa.

Some wider questions

Increasingly, the regional forum becomes a medium for the discussion of a variety of wider conjectures. One of the five reticulists, we shall now suppose, has become attracted to a long-term view of the reticulist as a distinctive public policy profession in its own right. If a community of ten to twenty thousand can support several local medical and legal practitioners, why should it not also be able to support at least one generalist practitioner in the field of public policy analysis, backed by appropriate forms of professional training to equip him with relevant techniques, and by a generally understood code of professional conduct? Indeed, one of the academics taking part in the forum intervenes to suggest that this kind of development might help to make a reality of the Redcliffe-Maud concept of the Local Council, and ultimately make the County District Council increasingly redundant in its intended role as a counterpoise to the remote County unit, at least outside the conurbations. If so, then perhaps the local government system might eventually revert back towards the simpler 'unitary' form proposed by Redcliffe-Maud, with more realistic assurances that adequate channels for local democratic influence could be maintained.

At this, the meeting almost breaks up in uproar. However, equilibrium is restored when the discussion turns back to the concept of the reticulist profession. One participant speculates that people combining relevant skills with a background in specialist techniques for linking the analysis of policy problems to the analysis of organizational relations could find themselves widely sought after at many levels of public affairs, including those of the County and District Councils, and could well come to qualify for leading management roles. This speculation is strongly resisted by some of the town planners and lawyers in the regional forum, each profession arguing that its own position is so central to the co-ordination of local decision processes that the answer is not to attempt to develop a new profession, so much as to modify the curricula of existing professions in such a way that a much fuller grounding in network managing skills can be included.

Other people, meanwhile, maintain that reticulist skills can only realistically be built up through long practical experience, under some form of informal apprenticeship to those already well steeped in the craft of managing inter-agency networks. But many of the most active participants in the forum, we shall suppose, have by now come to agree that the reticulist function can be more powerfully developed where there are opportunities to make at least some elements of reticulist skill more explicit through the introduction of clearly formulated analytical techniques, thus making it possible to disseminate these elements much more widely through carefully structured programmes of education and training, preferably with a strong element of interactive learning.

At this point, Webster goes on to argue that, in his own adopted discipline of political science, and also in related fields such as sociology and economics, large numbers of intelligent and restless students are being allowed to graduate with skills that equip them more to criticize the workings of governmental institutions from outside than to play a constructive though challenging role from within, thus helping to make those institutions more responsive to rapidly changing patterns of problem situations and social values. Further, he believes that the experience of the regional forum has opened up a whole range of exciting opportunities for research, which could help to overcome the evident deficiencies of the methods so far used for analysing the structures of policy problems on the one hand, and the structures of political and organizational relations on the other.

One idea which attracts Nettlefold is the possibility of developing an explicit role for the regional office as a reservoir of reticulist skill, from which qualified individuals could be detached or leased for limited periods to particular local councils that are confronted with urgent though transient planning problems; for example, that which faced Lulsworth in the negotiation of its arrangements for a town expansion programme. Such a reservoir of skills could not only be of benefit to local communities, but could also assist the regional office in keeping its own staff more closely in touch with grass-roots political issues. Accepting this point, Webster is inclined to see a reservoir of this kind as supplementing rather than replacing a dispersed reticulist service which is directly employed by local elected Councils. The latter arrangement, he believes, can provide more sustained opportunities for learning about the subtle and changing relationships of issues and organizational relations within a particular local context.

The question that Fielding sees as most important, and which is echoed by Connolly in Pitsdale, is that of how to ensure that local support for reticulist services does not tend to become concentrated in the more affluent areas, where resources of rateable value are most heavily concentrated and elected members and their constituents tend already to be more articulate in communicating with the various public agencies about decisions that may impinge on their affairs. She is emphatic that means must be found of redressing this imbalance, not only through an extension of the rate-support grant machinery but through carefully designed incentives to the growth of reticulist services in the more deprived urban areas. This, she argues, could be of direct national advantage in avoiding the dangers of widespread social disturbance and breakdown which she sees as looming increasingly large on the horizon in her own and similar inner city areas.

The responsibility for weighing up the lessons of the experiment from a national point of view falls particularly on Underwood, who has attended the regional forum as frequently as his other commitments allow. In reporting back to his Ministry, he is obliged to take a more detached view than his colleague Nettlefold at the regional office. He must evaluate the experiment against a variety of other recent experiences in different parts of the country, including national programmes supported by different Ministries, and it would be rash for us to speculate what may have happened by this time to the initiatives started, for instance, within the Home Office Community Development Programme or the Environment Ministry's Urban Guidelines Studies. There may also be developments to be surveyed in the widespread movement to encourage the formation of urban Neighbourhood Councils, supported by the Association for Neighbourhood Councils; in such initiatives as that of the Town and Country Planning Association in setting up a Planning Aid Service, or the Centre for Environmental Studies in setting up its pioneering Planning Exchange in Glasgow; and in numerous developments on the wider international scene. Also, some imaginative experiments may have been launched by some of the new local authorities themselves outside the Outland Region. Out of the corporate planning movement, new and more sensitive instruments of policy-making may have emerged which recognise more explicitly the essential plurality of the public planning process; while many new forms of collaborative arrangement between Counties and their constituent districts may be emerging in different parts of the country.

But there are limits to the extent to which it is profitable for us to speculate about the factors that may influence Underwood – or indeed any of the actors involved, from the Cabinet Minister to whom Underwood may be ultimately accountable, to the newest and most bemused voter in the Pitsdale local elections. At this stage, therefore, our crystal ball – such as it is – becomes more and more cloudy, and we must revert from a mood of conjecture to one of final reflection on the general messages of this book.

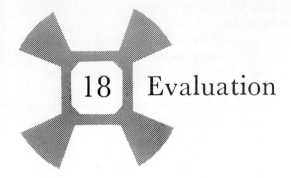

18   Evaluation

The four hypotheses reconsidered

By giving free rein to our imaginations in the preceding chapter, we have attempted to suggest one of many ways in which we believe a wide-ranging experimental process might be mobilized, and evidence might be gathered that would either support or cast doubt on the kinds of hypotheses that we formulated at the end of Chapter 16. We should, of course, be surprised if future initiatives towards innovation in planning followed at all closely the lines of our speculations in Chapter 17. Equally, however, we should be surprised if the future pattern of innovations were to develop in completely divergent directions. The pressures for effective mutual adjustment between different public agencies and different sets of constituency interests can, we believe, be expected to grow increasingly insistent, in England and indeed elsewhere. The result is likely to be a widespread search for innovative lines of response, even though such responses may in most cases take a more fragmented form than the 'Policy Network Development Programme' upon which we have just speculated.

If we accept the argument that the disposition of skills and opportunities relating to the selective activation of inter-agency decision networks is of considerable importance to the future of public planning, as suggested by the chain of propositions in *Figure*

69, and supported in our belief by most of our case material, then we are in a position to reflect further on the first of our four hypotheses, relating to the motivation towards external orientation. In our scenario, we pursued the possibility of concentrating experimental resources at the sub-district level of representative government where we believed the motivation towards outwardly connective styles of planning would be strongest. However, we have already argued that, in Britain, powerful motivations of this kind can also be expected to develop in the new County and District authorities, especially once their initial corporate structures have become well established, leaving difficult problems of adjustment both with each other and also with the new Health and Water Authorities. Therefore, we might expect many initiatives towards new styles of inter-agency exploration to emerge at the County and District levels, whether or not these are related in any way to a regional focus such as that which we introduced in Chapter 17.

However, our reason for selecting a regional scale for the devlopment of our scenario was to suggest what benefits might flow from a 'contextual reinforcement' of local experimentation, at a level where a diversity of experience could be matched by an input of relevant technical resources. In our belief, it is only through building a capacity to generalize on the basis of a variety of local experiences, and thus to move gradually from a reliance on purely personal skills towards a wider dissemination of techniques in which some at least of the elements of these skills can be encapsulated, that progress is likely to be sustained on a sufficiently wide front to generate its own momentum.

Our third hypothesis suggested that the more conscious development of outwardly connective capacities could ultimately be to the mutual advantage of those working in all representative agencies of government, whether or not actively committed to the search for innovation. This hypothesis will be by no means easy to sustain in practice, as we sought to indicate by building so many setbacks and conflicts into our scenario. However, our experience does offer some prospect that such a hypothesis may yet prove tenable, if a long-term perspective is taken, if only because of the discomfiture likely to be felt by actors and agencies who can be seen to take a repeatedly obstructive stance towards the evolution of new patterns of inter-agency planning activity.

Our final hypothesis, relating to the long-term influence of connective styles of planning on the processes of societal adaptation to change, is at the same time more difficult to refute and more difficult to support through limited experimental initiatives. Even if political processes do in future tend to channel an increasing proportion of a society's finite resources of human intelligence into exploratory activities that bring together different agencies of representative government, the extent and persistence of such a shift may be far from easy to gauge. However, in the long term, any movements in such a direction would probably be reflected in the increased status given to professions concerned with connective styles of planning, in an increasing ability of these professions to attract those with intelligence and imagination in competition with others, and probably in shifting views within the professions concerned about their own orientations and identities, such as have been seen lately within the town planning field in Britain (Cowan, 1973).

In so far as the scenario of Chapter 17 is purely speculative, it cannot of course be considered as in any sense a realistic test of these or any other hypotheses. However, the scenario does embody many facets of the personal experience of the authors, and to this extent we believe that the prospect of wide-ranging experimental initiatives of this kind is essentially a credible one, within any society where there can be found a comparable set of representative institutions to those of England. We have seen the capabilities for handling inter-agency decision networks that had been developed by different decision-makers in the many-sided local planning situation at Droitwich; we have seen the richness of connective activities that have been evolving around the new regional agencies and multi-organizational planning teams; and we have seen the variety of arrangements for inter-agency exploratory processes that have developed in situations of induced local change, including the inner city community projects. Whatever the local successes or failures of such innovations, we have witnessed a highly diffuse process of interactive learning which we believe to be essentially creative.

Further, we have ourselves been involved in the management of a complex experiment involving a pattern of participation that was similar in some respects to that postulated in *Figure 88*. This was the LOGIMP experiment of 1970 (CES, 1970), in which officers of ten English local authorities were actively involved, many of them working in inter-agency teams. In this experiment, the accent was on the testing of analytical techniques rather than on any innovations in inter-agency relations. Nevertheless, the exploratory processes which were generated frequently took the decision processes of the authorities concerned into directions that they might not otherwise have followed. In effect, the shapes of several local decision networks were modified by the commitment which was established to a

Figure 89　The evaluation of innovations in the management of local and regional change

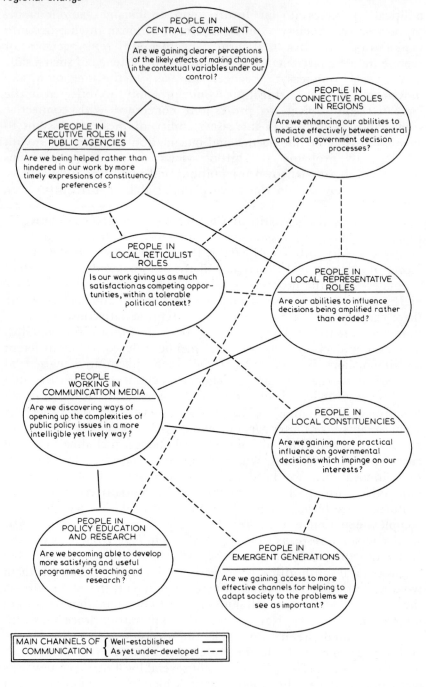

PEOPLE IN
CENTRAL GOVERNMENT

Are we gaining clearer perceptions
of the likely effects of making changes
in the contextual variables under our
control?

PEOPLE IN
CONNECTIVE ROLES
IN REGIONS

Are we enhancing our abilities to
mediate effectively between central
and local government decision
processes?

PEOPLE IN
EXECUTIVE ROLES IN
PUBLIC AGENCIES

Are we being helped rather than
hindered in our work by more
timely expressions of constituency
preferences?

PEOPLE IN
LOCAL RETICULIST
ROLES

Is our work giving us as much
satisfaction as competing opportunities, within a tolerable
political context?

PEOPLE IN
LOCAL REPRESENTATIVE
ROLES

Are our abilities to influence
decisions being amplified rather
than eroded?

PEOPLE
WORKING IN
COMMUNICATION MEDIA

Are we discovering ways of
opening up the complexities of
public policy issues in a more
intelligible yet lively way?

PEOPLE IN
LOCAL CONSTITUENCIES

Are we gaining more practical
influence on governmental
decisions which impinge on our
interests?

PEOPLE IN
POLICY EDUCATION
AND RESEARCH

Are we becoming able to develop
more satisfying and useful
programmes of teaching and
research?

PEOPLE IN
EMERGENT GENERATIONS

Are we gaining access to more
effective channels for helping to
adapt society to the problems we
see as important?

MAIN CHANNELS OF ⎰ Well-established ——————
COMMUNICATION ⎱ As yet under-developed ———

process of parallel experimentation. Implicitly, therefore, the analytical techniques used were shown to be of some relevance to the development of reticulist capabilities, at a local level of decision-making where, often, resources would have to be somewhat thinly deployed. The follow-up study by Bunker (1973), some two and a half years after the experiment, provides some encouraging envidence that the innovatory processes set in train in 1970 did not end with the formal conclusion of the exercise, and that several of the planners, economists, and others concerned have continued to test and modify the techniques through application to other planning problems, to compare them with other recent innovations in decision methodology, and to grapple with their wider organizational and political implications.

Perspectives of evaluation

The evaluation of any process of societal innovation is inevitably an elusive matter. Of course, merely by constructing sets of propositions and hypotheses on the basis of our own experience, we as authors have moved some way towards building an evaluative framework, which relates to our own research perspective. However, where the processes of innovation demand a wide span of involvement by actors with different allegiances and aspirations, there must be a corresponding variety in the perspectives from which those processes are evaluated. It would be contrary to all our arguments in this book to attempt to reduce the social process of evaluation to any kind of formal cost-benefit framework, through which some form of objective verdict on its success might be distilled. Rather, it is necessary to see the actors in the innovatory process – in much the same way as the actors in any planning process – responding to complexity through processes of bargaining within their shared 'opportunity space'. Therefore, we return to a reaffirmation of our second general proposition of *Figure 69* in the context of 'meta-policymaking', to adopt the terminology suggested by Dror (1968), that is, in relation to the planning of the planning process itself.

In *Figure 89*, we indicate some of the many possible perspectives of evaluation that could apply to any processes of innovation in the management of local and regional change. We recognise that the differentiation of roles as indicated does little justice to the richness of interconnection between these roles, either within the institutional structure or indeed at the level of the individual who may participate in a variety of different ways. However, it does suggest some of the kinds of question that we may expect different types of actor to ask in judging whether their future 'opportunity space' is being constrained or enlarged by any proposed incremental change in the evolution of those planning processes with which they are concerned. Any question of trade-offs between gains in one dimension and losses in another will then be a matter for value judgement, either through the political process or, in some instances, within the consciousness of the individual member of society.

In *Figure 89*, we have identified some of the main channels of communication through which such a system of social evaluation is connected, and have indicated some lines of connection that we believe can be strengthened in future. Although we have given explicit recognition in our diagram to those already playing reticulist roles at the local level, we believe that there is scope for innovation in developing channels of potential connection between these roles and others which are as yet inadequately developed. Also, we have introduced certain roles which we believe are important to the process of innovation in planning even though they have not figured very prominently in the decision networks of earlier chapters. These include people working in the fields of policy education and research – in universities, polytechnics, government departments, and independent research institutions – and also people working in the communication media through which any prospective innovations may become more widely debated and disseminated.

These two types of role are often closely connected. There is also a close connection between those working in the field of policy education and research, and the emergent generations of potential students, elected representatives, and public servants upon which the long-term adaptation of societies to changing problems and threats must ultimately depend. In many parts of the world, with widely differing systems of government, there is mounting concern over the tendency for the restlessness of emergent generations to turn into alienation, so that one of the most prominent axes of social polarization becomes that of conflict between the generations with their differing values, life-styles, and levels of commitment to established institutions. In this light, one of the most important issues of all may be that of how far the various public professions can in future succeed in providing recognised outlets for creative involvement in decision-making by those who have potentially most to contribute.

The long-term outlook

Looking ahead on the time horizon of the succession of generations, it must be expected that innovations in planning will jostle, merge, and become transformed in ways about which it would be fruitless to speculate in the style we adopted in Chapter 17. In contemplating the prospects for the progressive enrichment of planning processes against such a horizon, we are entering a field where the perspectives of our own professional disciplines, such as they are, become increasingly hard to distinguish. One of our own ambitions must remain to make operational research more political, and at the same time to make political science more operational. However, we remain conscious that the theoretical framework we have tried to articulate still remains inadequately developed to fulfil these and wider ambitions, and there is much scope for further exploration in relating it more clearly to the work of others.

In our concern to model the complex realities of the planning process — even from our modest local vantage point of Droitwich — we have found it far from easy at times to relate the richness of our experience to our chosen conceptual framework in an analytically satisfying way. However, we hope we have at least assembled a sufficient array of interlinked case material to provide some useful background for others who may in future seek to move further foward at the theoretical level. Indeed, at the time of writing one of us is already involved in further elaboration of the concept of the reticulist in relation to the published work of Lindblom and others in the field of political science (Power, 1974b). Meanwhile, for those of us in the Tavistock Institute, another fertile area for future exploration remains the field of overlap between our arguments about the relationship of social structure to problem structure, and the past work of other colleagues in the analysis of socio-technical systems (Emery and Trist, 1972; Trist, Higgin, Murray, Pollock, 1963).

In developing our conceptual framework and applying it to interpret our experiences, we have relied heavily on graphical forms of representation, as a glance back over our sequence of eighty-nine figures will show. Some of our diagrams have been directed towards representations of problem structure, others towards representation of the structure of relations between decision-makers, and others again towards relating these two frames of reference to each other and to more familiar dimensions such as those of space and time. Indeed, one of the underlying messages we have tried to project concerns the underexploited power of graphical as opposed to verbal or numerical languages, in seeking to understand the richness and complexity of public planning processes. With McLuhan (1964), we believe that the linearity of the textual form sets real constraints on some of the more significant forms of communication within society.

We have therefore sought to present our series of diagrams in such a way as to reinforce the main messages of the text, while at the same time facilitating rapid cross-reference at any stage to earlier arguments and illustrations.

Of course, the development of new languages of communication about the problems and processes of public planning cannot be a simple process. It is only to be expected, for instance, that some readers will have more difficulty than others in coming to grips with the graphical conventions and terminology to which we have resorted. If such languages are to be of practical value to decision-makers, then there must be a readiness to adapt them according to experience under different operational and political conditions, regarding intelligibility to lay people as an important test of usefulness. The creation of opportunities for testing and adjustment will be just as important in the case of techniques designed to give practical support to the craft of managing inter-agency networks, as it was in the case of the basic ideas about a 'Technology of Strategic Choice' which were put forward in *Local Government and Strategic Choice* (Friend and Jessop, 1969). We must, of course, recognise that the process of further development may become more difficult as we move towards areas where questions of political relations between actors and agencies may have to be confronted rather more directly. However, it is our belief that any search for enrichment in the processes of public planning can scarcely succeed if the emphasis remains a predominantly corporate one. In one way or another, the rich variety of political relations within society must ultimately be reflected within any future advances there may be towards more sensitive methodologies in the field of public policy choice.

As we seek to clarify our long-term perspective, our value position moves towards that of Faludi who, in his *Planning Theory* (1973), adopts a declared standpoint of belief in the potentialities of what he calls 'human growth', and concludes with a vision of the 'Planning Society' as the means through which he believes it may be possible to achieve a fuller realization of the human potential to master a changing environment. Like Faludi, we have found ourselves with the problem of creating, within such a society, a 'requisite variety' to master those factors in the human environment that lead towards greater interdependence and instability in the decision situations that are encountered. This is a problem which has concerned writers as diverse as: Lindblom in *The Intelligence of Democracy* (1965); Bray in *Decision in Government* (1970); Schon in *Beyond the Stable State*; and Emery and Trist in *Towards a Social Ecology* (1972). Implicit in all these works is a concern for a wide diffusion of problem solving and connective capacities, at the peripheral as well as the more central nodes of social organization, in order to achieve the requisite capabilities to adapt to a complex, disturbed, and in many ways increasingly turbulent environment.

Studies such as that of Meadows on the 'limits to growth' (1972), despite the controversy they have attracted, have succeeded in dramatizing the threat of environmental turbulence on a global scale. However, both the prophets of disaster and their critics agree that the problems of societal adaptation to such threats will impose severe strains on the political processes within nations, as well as at the international scale. If such strains are to be successfully absorbed, then, there must, in our belief, be a rich diffusion throughout the fabric of society of those forms of exploratory and connective skill on which the adaptation of representative institutions to unfamiliar problems must ultimately depend.

We do, however, see cause for encouragement in the evidence uncovered in the preceding chapters of a widespread, restless search for new modes of response to unfamiliar and complex problems of public planning, by decision-makers operating in widely different organizational contexts. Such a search was evident even within comparatively modest local decision networks such as those which evolved to manage different aspects of the Droitwich expansion scheme – or, for that matter, the rehabilitation of the Newtown neighbourhood. It was also evident in the wider processes of organizational change and institutional reform to which we turned in later chapters. However, it is important that such structural changes should be regarded not as setting new patterns of decision-making in themselves, but as presenting new opportunities for conscious experiment at the inter-agency level. We believe that these opportunities for experiment can only be fully exploited by building further on the capabilities for innovation which are to be found among people who are already skilled in the shaping of inter-agency decision networks. The question remains: how far can the lessons learnt from such experiences – at whatever scale – be generalized and diffused throughout the wider fabric of societal decision-making? This is a question which must be subjected to searching exploration and debate, if a belief in the progressive enrichment of public planning is to stand a realistic chance of surviving the test of time.

Bibliography

ABERCROMBIE, P. and JACKSON, H. (1948). *West Midlands Plan*. Draft report prepared for the Ministry of Town and Country Planning.

ADELSON, R.M. (1965). Criteria for Capital Investment: an Approach through Decision Theory. *Operational Research Quarterly* 16:19.

ALONSO, W. (1971). Beyond the Inter-disciplinary Approach to Planning. *American Institute of Planners Journal* 27:169.

ASHBY, W.R. (1956). *An Introduction to Cybernetics*. London: Chapman & Hall.

BARNES, J.A. (1954). Class and Committees in a Norwegian Island Parish. *Human Relations* 7:39.

BARNES, J.A. (1969). Networks and Political Processes. In J. Clyde Mitchell (ed.) *Social Networks in Urban Situations*. Manchester: Manchester University Press.

BENINGTON, J. (1972). Coventry CDP: Background and Progress. Occasional Paper No. 1. Coventry: Community Development Project.

BIRD, R.A. (1968). The Relationship of Economic and Physical Planning. Paper presented at Town and Country Planning Summer School, University of Manchester.

BOTT, E. (1957). *Family and Social Network*. London: Tavistock Publications. (Second edition 1971.)

BRAY, J. (1970). *Decision in Government*. London: Gollancz.

BUNKER, R. (1973). *Making Choices and Taking Decisions in Local Government*. In Proceedings of International Congress, Copenhagen, 9–14 September 1973. International Federation for Housing and Planning.

BURNS, T. and STALKER, G.M. (1961). *The Management of Innovation*. London: Tavistock Publications.

CADBURY, G.A.H. (1968). The Objectives and Manner of Working of the Regional Economic Planning Council. Paper presented at the conference of the West Midlands Branch of the Regional Studies Association, October. London: Regional Studies Association.

CARTER, K.R., FRIEND, J.K. and HICKLING, D.A. (1972). *Environmental Sciences and Regional Planning in Scotland: Report of a Pilot Project*. IOR Internal Report No.686R. London: Institute for Operational Research.

CARTER, K.R., FRIEND, J.K., LUCK, G.M., and YEWLETT, C.J.L. (1972). *Area Improvement Policies for the Inner City*. IOR Internal Report No.655. Occasional Paper No.6. Coventry: Coventry Community Development Project.

CENTRAL STATISTICAL OFFICE (1972). *Social Trends No.3*. London: HMSO.

CENTRE FOR ENVIRONMENTAL STUDIES (1970). *The LOGIMP Experiment: a Collaborative Exercise in the Application of a New Approach to Local Planning Problems*. Conference papers. London: CES Information Paper CES IP 25.

COVENTRY CITY COUNCIL, SOLIHULL COUNTY BOROUGH COUNCIL, and WARWICKSHIRE COUNTY COUNCIL (1971). *Coventry—Solihill—Warwickshire: a Strategy for the Sub-region: the Report on the Sub-Regional Planning Study*. Coventry.

COWAN, P. (1973). *The Future of Planning: a Study Sponsored by the Centre for Environmental Studies*. London: Heinemann.

COWLING, T.M. and STEELEY, G.C. (1973). *Sub-Regional Planning Studies: an Evaluation*. Oxford: Pergamon Press.

CROZIER, M. (1964). *The Bureaucratic Phenomenon*. Chicago: University of Chicago Press. London: Tavistock Publications.

CULLINGWORTH, J.B. (1970). *Town and Country Planning in England and Wales: the Changing Scene*. (3rd ed.). London: Allen & Unwin.

DALKEY, N.C. (1969). *The Delphi Method: an Experimental Study of Group Opinions*. Memorandum RM—5888—PR. Santa Monica, Calif: Rand Corporation.

DAVIES, A.F. (1972). The Concept of Administrative Style. In *Essays in Political Sociology*. Melbourne: Cheshire.

DAVIES, A.F. (1973). *Politics as Work*. Melbourne Politics Monograph.

DE BONO, E. (1967). *The Use of Lateral Thinking*. London: Jonathan Cape.

DEPARTMENT OF EDUCATION AND SCIENCE (1972). *Educational Priority. Vol. 1: Problems and Policies*. Edited by A.H. Halsey. London: HMSO.

DEPARTMENT OF ECONOMIC AFFAIRS (1965). *The West Midlands: a Regional Study*. London: HMSO.

DEPARTMENT OF THE ENVIRONMENT (1972). *New Local Authorities. Management and Structure*. Report of a study group. Chairman: M.A. Bains. London: HMSO.

DROITWICH DEVELOPMENT COMMITTEE (1964). *Interim Progress Report: 1st April 1964 to 31st October 1964*. Droitwich.

DROR, Y. (1968). *Public Policy Making Re-examined.* Scranton, Pa: Chandler.

ELTON, M.C.J., HILLS, P.M., HUNTER, J.M.H., MILLEN, D.W., and TUR-
NER, T.P. (1970). An approach to the Location of Government: a Joint
Study by the Civil Service Department and the Institute for Operational
Research. Paper presented at The Institute of Management Science
International Conference, London.

EMERY, F.E. and TRIST, E.L. (1972). *Towards a Social Ecology: Contextual
Appreciation of the Future in the Present.* London: Plenum.

ETZIONI, A. (1968). *The Active Society: a Theory of Societal and Political
Processes.* London: Collier-Macmillan.

FALUDI, A. (1973). *Planning Theory.* Oxford: Pergamon.

FRIEND, J.K. and HUNTER, J.M.H. (1970). Multi-organisational Decision
Processes in the Planned Expansion of Towns. *Environment and Planning*
2:33.

FRIEND, J.K. and JESSOP, W.M. (1969). *Local Government and Strategic
Choice: an Operational Research Approach to the Processes of Public
Planning.* London: Tavistock Publications.

FRIEND, J.K. and YEWLETT, C.J.L. (1971). Inter-agency Decision Processes:
Practice and Prospect. In *Beyond Local Government Reform: some Prospects
for Evolution in Public Policy Networks.* Institute for Operational Research
Conference Papers. Tavistock Institute of Human Relations: London.

GREEN, G. (1972). National, City, and Ward Components of Local Voting.
Policy and Politics 1:45.

GUPTA, S.K. and ROSENHEAD, J. (1968). Robustness in Sequential Investment Decisions. *Management Science* 15:B-18.

H.M. GOVERNMENT (1970). *Reform of Local Government in England.* Cmnd.
4276. London: HMSO.

H.M. GOVERNMENT (1972). *National Health Service Reorganisation: England.*
Cmnd. 5055. London: HMSO.

HEREFORD AND WORCESTER NEW COUNTY COMMITTEE (1972). *New
County of Hereford and Worcester: Report of Officers' Management
Structure Project Group.*

HERSON, J. (1972). The West Midlands — an Economic Appraisal. A discussion
paper produced for the West Midlands Branch of the Regional Studies
Association, January. London: Regional Studies Association.

HIGGIN, G. and JESSOP, N. (1965). *Communications in the Building Industry:
the Report of a Pilot Study.* London: Tavistock Publications.

KIDD, J.B. and MORGAN, J.R. (1968). A Predictive Information System for
Management. *Operational Research Quarterly* 20:149.

LEVIN, P.H. (1969). The Planning Inquiry Farce. *New Society* July 3rd: 17.

LICHFIELD, N. (1971). Cost-benefit Analysis in Planning: a Critique of the
Roskill Commission. *Regional Studies* 5:157

LINDBLOM, C.E. (1965). *The Intelligence of Democracy: Decision Making
through Mutual Adjustment.* New York: Free Press. London: Collier-
MacMillan.

LIVERPOOL SHELTER NEIGHBOURHOOD ACTION PROJECT (1972).
Another Chance for Cities. SNAP 69/72. London: Shelter.

518 Bibliography

LONG, J.R., (ed.) (1961). *The Wythall Inquiry: a Planning Test-case.* London: Estates Gazette.

LUCK, G.M., LUCKMAN, J., SMITH, B.W., and STRINGER, J. (1971). *Patients, Hospitals, and Operational Research.* London: Tavistock Publications.

LUCKMAN, J. (1967). An Approach to the Management of Design. *Operational Research Quarterly* 18:345.

MACKINTOSH, J.P. (1968). *The Devolution of Power: Local Democracy, Regionalism and Nationalism.* Harmondsworth: Penguin Books.

McLUHAN, M. (1964). *Understanding Media: the Extensions of Man.* London: Routledge & Kegan Paul.

MACK, R.P. (1971). *Planning on Uncertainty: Decision Making in Business and Government Administration.* New York: Wiley-Interscience.

MEADOWS, D.H. *et al.* (1972). *The Limits to Growth.* London: Earth Island.

MERRETT, A.J. and SYKES, A. (1966). *Capital Budgeting and Company Finance.* London: Longmans.

MILLER, E.J. and RICE, A.K. (1967). *Systems of Organization: the Control of Task and Sentient Boundaries.* London: Tavistock Publications..

MINISTRY OF HOUSING AND LOCAL GOVERNMENT (1965). *The First Hundred Families: a Guide to the Community Services and Facilities which should be Available for the First Families Arriving in an Expanding Town.* Prepared by a study group of four members of the Central Housing Advisory Committee. London: HMSO.

MINISTRY OF HOUSING and LOCAL GOVERNMENT and WELSH OFFICE (1966). *Our Older Homes: a Call for Action.* Report of the Sub-Committee on Standards of Housing Fitness. London: HMSO.

MINISTRY OF HOUSING and LOCAL GOVERNMENT and WELSH OFFICE (1967). *The Needs of New Communities: a Report of Social Provision in New and Expanding Communities.* Prepared by a Sub-Committee of the Central Housing Advisory Committee. London: HMSO.

MINISTRY OF HOUSING and LOCAL GOVERNMENT, SCOTTISH DEVELOPMENT DEPARTMENT, and WELSH OFFICE (1969). *People and Planning: Report of the Committee on Public Participation in Planning.* London: HMSO.

MINISTRY OF TRANSPORT (1963). *Traffic in Towns: a Study of the Long Term Problems of Traffic in Urban Areas.* London: HMSO.

MORGAN, J.R. (1971). *AIDA — a Technique for the Management of Design.* IOR Monograph No.2. London: Institute for Operational Research.

MORTON, J. (1970). *The Best Laid Schemes?: a Cool Look at Local Government Reform.* London: Charles Knight.

NEEDLEMAN, L. (1969). The Comparative Economics of Improvement and New Building. *Urban Studies* 6:196.

PAINTER, C. (1972). The Repercussions of Administrative Innovation: the West Midlands Economic Planning Council. *Public Administration* 50:467.

OZBEKHAN, H. (1971). Planning and Human Action. In P. Weiss (ed.) *Hierarchically Organised Systems in Theory and Practice.* New York: Hafner.

POPPER, K.R. (1968). *The Logic of Scientific Discovery.* (2nd ed.). London: Hutchinson.

POWER, J.M. (1971a). Organisational Technology and Public Planning. *Public Administration (Australia)* 30:83.

(1971b). Planning: Magic and Technique. In *Beyond Local Government Reform: some Prospects for Evolution in Public Networks*. Institute for Operational Research Conference Papers. Tavistock Institute of Human Relations: London.

(1974a). *The Pragmatics of Organizational Power*. Oxford: Pergamon.

(1974b). *The Changing Pattern of Regional Administration in New South Wales: a Study of Structural Reform in the Riveria*. (To be published in Australia.)

RIKER, T. (1962). *The Theory of Political Coalitions*. New Haven: Yale University Press.

ROYAL COMMISSION ON THE CONSTITUTION, (1969—73 (1973). *Report*. Vol. 1. Cmnd. 5460. *Memorandum of Dissent*. Vol. II. Cmnd. 5460—1. London: HMSO.

ROYAL COMMISSION ON LOCAL GOVERNMENT IN ENGLAND, 1966—1969 (1969). *Report*. Vol. I. Cmnd. 4040. London: HMSO.

ROYAL COMMISSION ON LOCAL GOVERNMENT IN SCOTLAND (1969). *Scotland: Local Government Reform*. Cmnd. 4150. Edinburgh: HMSO.

ROYAL TOWN PLANNING INSTITUTE (1972). *The Journal* 58:149—152.

RUDDY, S.A. (1969). Industrial Selection Schemes: an Administrative Study. Occasional Paper No. 5. Birmingham: Centre for Urban and Regional Studies.

SAMPSON, A. (1971). *The New Anatomy of Britain*. London: Hodder & Stoughton.

SCHARFP, F.W. (1972). Komplexität als Schranke der Politischen Planung. *Politische Innovation und Gesellschaftliche Wandel: Politische Vierteljahresschrift.*

SCHON, D.A. (1971). *Beyond the Stable State: Public and Private Learning in a Changing Society*. London: Temple Smith.

SCOTTISH DEVELOPMENT DEPARTMENT and DUNDEE UNIVERSITY (1970). *Tayside: Potential for Development*. Edinburgh: HMSO.

SHARP, E. (1969). *The Ministry of Housing and Local Government*. London: Allen & Unwin.

SMITH, B.C. (1969). *Advising Ministers*. London: Routledge & Kegan Paul.

SMITH, Barbara M.D. (1971). Industrial Development Certificate Control: an Institutional Influence on Industrial Mobility. *Journal of the Town Planning Institute* 57:65.

SMITH, B.M.D. (1972). Appraising the Appraisal: some Discursive Comments on reading the West Midlands Economic Planning Council's *The West Midlands: an Economic Appraisal*. A discussion paper for the Regional Studies Association, London.

SPENCER, P. (1971). *General Practice and Models of the Referral Process*. Health Report No. 6. London: Institute for Operational Research.

STEWART, J.D. (1971). *Management in Local Government: a Viewpoint*. London: Charles Knight.

STRINGER, J. (1967). Operational Research for 'Multi-Organisations'. *Operational Research Quarterly* 18:105.

THOMAS, R. (1969). *London's New Towns: a Study of Self-Contained and Balanced Communities*. Broadsheet 510. London: PEP.

TOWNROE, P.M. (1971). Industrial Location Decisions: a Study in Management Behaviour. Occasional Paper No. 15. Birmingham: Centre for Urban and Regional Studies.

TRIST, E.L., HIGGIN, G.W., MURRARY, H., and POLLOCK, A.B. (1963). *Organizational Choice: Capabilities of Groups at the Coal Face under Changing Technologies*. London: Tavistock Publications.

VICKERS, G. (1965). *The Art of Judgement: a Study of Policy Making*. London: Chapman & Hall.

WEST MIDLANDS ECONOMIC PLANNING COUNCIL (1967). *The West Midlands: Patterns of Growth*. Published for the Department of Economic Affairs. London: HMSO.

WEST MIDLANDS ECONOMIC PLANNING COUNCIL (1971). *The West Midlands: an Economic Appraisal*. Published for the Department of the Environment. London: HMSO.

WEST MIDLAND REGIONAL STUDY (1971). *A Developing Strategy for the West Midlands*. West Midlands Planning Authorities' Conference: Birmingham.

WRAITH, R.E. and LAMB, G.B. (1971). *Public Inquiries as an Instrument of Government*. Published for the Royal Institute of Public Administration. London: Allen & Unwin.

Name Index

Subject Index

confidence, increasing level of, 31, 35,
40, 175, 354, 449
connective planning, 39, 56, 408-9,
471, 472, 473, 475, 507
outwardly connective style, 471,
472, 473, 475, 507
conservation, 63, 303, 307, 315
Areas, 255
constituency(s), 29, 30, 31, 35, 37,
43, 57, 63,
interest(s), 46, 49, 63, 64, 82, 89,
105, 350, 354, 368, 373, 374,
382, 473, 505
contextual
control, 350-1, 352
enrichment, 474
reinforcement, 472, 484, 506
co-operation, 56, 104, 295, 473
co-ordination, 31, 33, 34, 39, 40, 46,
68, 81, 82, 103, 105, 109, 133,
330-1, 335-8, 360, 395, 413,
421, 424, 502
corporate
frame of reference, 349-52, 374-5,
496
planning, xxi, 374, 419, 465, 466,
472, 503, 512
costs, 34-5, 99, 120, 197, 263, 264,
277, 299, 307, 365, 483
see also finance
County, 450, 480
Boroughs, 13, 15, 61, 450, 453,
455, 477
Councils, xxv, 13, 66, 87, 161, 162,
163, 183, 424, 456, 460, 465,
472, 483, 486, 487, 490, 493,
494, 497, 499, 501
Districts, 13, 15, 66, 85, 162, 413,
424, 454, 455, 458, 477, 483
see also District Councils
County Councils Association, 449
Coventry, ix, x, xv, xvii, xix, xx, xxiv,
61, 79, 205, 261, 285, 347, 388,
397, 436-9, 441, 442, 457

Daventry, 227, 237, 380, 415, 416-18,
425
Dawley, 380, 384, 385, 387, 424
decision
area, 47, 49, 51, 53, 54, 55, 75, 175
field, 44, 55, 73, 75, 127, 231, 305,
373

makers, 22, 23, 24, 25, 27, 33, 40,
43, 46, 49, 53, 54, 55, 56, 154,
219, 220, 222, 233, 239, 247,
249, 281, 307, 362, 430, 491,
511, 512
takers, 27, 35, 43
decision-making, xi, xiii, xxi, xxiii,
xxvii, 3, 16, 19, 24, 25, 31, 33,
90, 105, 118, 184, 235, 275,
280, 352, 357, 361, 365, 372,
373, 375, 393, 405, 415, 419,
429, 442, 443, 483, 499, 500,
509
access to, 368, 493
community involvement in, 268,
280, 282, 283, 289, 291, 359
group processes, xvii, 23, 31, 157,
368
interactive, 34, 352
inter-agency, 54, 80, 301
process, xxv, xxvi, 25, 35, 40, 45,
46, 47, 55, 104, 127, 189, 202,
269, 271, 291, 293, 294-7, 341,
345, 349, 353, 356, 366, 457,
465, 470, 491
decision-network(s), xii, xiii, xvi,
xvii, xxiv, xxvii, 43-6, 49, 56,
106, 111, 277, 307, 309, 323,
356, 359, 361, 420, 513
activation (mobilization) of, 44, 80,
81, 181, 186, 356-60, 361, 362,
363, 364, 368, 373, 505
aformal, 45, 54
of Community Development
Officer, 334-5
of Estates Adviser, 239
of Group Engineer, 159, 181-4,
219, 362
of Group Housing Architect, 219
of Housing Manager, 219, 362
informal, 332, 479
inter-agency, 485, 507, 512
nodal positions in, 44, 199, 222, 305
regional, 398-401
decision problem(s), 22, 23, 24, 25,
27, 30, 35, 55, 56, 73, 177, 309
of the firm, 233-5
of the worker, 235-7
relationships between, 47, 55, 80,
367
Delphi method, of judging uncertainty,
141

for housing improvement 283, 285, 292-3
housing subsidy, 69, 91, 150, 196, 207, 210, 423
to industry, 223, 417, 418
for roads, 151, 162, 166, 169
for sewerage, 91, 94, 95, 413
for social facilities, 330-1, 436
firm(s), 222, 229, 231, 232, 239, 240-4, 247, 356
decision problems of, 233-5
international, 234, 242-4, 478
freedom of manoeuvre, 100, 104, 309, 353

gas, xi, 279, 313-19, 330, 337, 338, 341, 425, 465
General Improvement Area(s), 283, 287-300, 305, 309, 326, 339, 440
master plan, 297, 298, 299
working party, 289-99, 359
see also Newtown area
Glasgow, 7, 225
government, see central government; local government
Greater London, 13, 15, 66, 238, 406, 447, 470
Council, xv, xviii, 415, 418, 419
green-belt, xiii, 66, 67, 70, 72, 75, 96, 380, 387, 421, 457
guidelines, 347, 374-7, 378, 444, 470, 474
see also policy guidelines

health services, 16, 341, 419
community, 313, 322-6, 362
management, 445, 463-6, 506
Ministry, 11, 325
National Health Service, 322, 325, 339, 463
Herefordshire, County of, 85, 379, 458
Highway Ministry, 93, 148, 154, 157, 161, 163, 165, 166, 170, 183, 253, 271
historic buildings, 253, 255, 257, 258, 281, 424
Home Office, xviii, 279, 313, 440
Community Development Project(s), 411, 436, 441, 503

hospital
facilities, 322, 325
management, x, xi, xiii
housing, xxv, 11, 12, 59, 63, 72, 73, 77, 103, 127, 133, 140, 151, 154, 157, 181, 188-220, 235, 237, 265, 270, 310, 330, 361, 362, 382, 385, 413, 416, 421, 429, 435, 440, 455, 480
Act, 283, 286, 292, 440
balance of types, 93, 147
balance sheet, 73, 79, 199
building regulations, 192, 193
cost yardsticks, 192, 193, 203, 205, 207, 209, 219, 350
densities, 67, 202, 207, 430
development, 66, 68, 96, 99, 135, 139, 143, 150, 165, 169, 170, 193, 219, 225, 422
highrise buildings, 191, 199, 202, 203
improvement, 282-5
market, 155, 188, 220, 418, 478
Ministry, 153, 180, 188, 189, 192, 196, 201, 205, 207, 209, 211, 214, 219, 220, 283, 285, 287, 291, 293, 309, 332, 363
overspill, 70, 87, 90, 91, 431
Parker Morris standards, 192, 193, 203, 210
private, 9, 90, 153, 193, 195, 209, 216, 219, 220, 285, 292, 322, 387, 418, 480, 496
public rented, 9, 73, 90, 145, 188, 189, 190, 193, 195, 196-200, 202, 209, 213, 215, 216, 217, 241, 244, 246, 285, 318, 418, 429, 433, 480, 496
sponsored, 99, 135, 147, 148, 150, 153, 193, 195, 209, 211-19, 220, 307, 352
housing sites (Droitwich)
Boycott, 145, 147, 197, 216, 236, 327, 331, 332, 333-4
Briar Hill, 148
Chawson, 147, 150, 151, 155, 303, 327, 331, 332, 333, 335
Westacre, 145, 171, 173, 175, 180, 181, 202, 203-20, 229, 301, 303, 307, 333, 359, 366
hypotheses, 347, 445, 471-4, 475, 482, 484, 506, 509

Society, x
opportunity(s), 3, 4, 5, 411, 445, 471
  employment, 9, 63, 96, 221, 225,
    315, 489
  reticulist, 360-4, 420, 481, 482,
    502
  space, 54, 55, 157, 349, 352, 354,
    356, 367, 375, 509, 510
option(s), 47, 49-51, 90, 95-7, 103,
    104, 129, 195, 209, 211, 213,
    214, 237, 242, 253, 273, 275,
    292-3, 303, 306, 308, 309, 327,
    384, 395
  bars, 51
  graph, 51, 53, 54, 56
organizational relationships, xxvii, 23
  mapping, xxiv, 19-21, 81
'Outland' region, 477-504
overspill, 7, 17, 67, 69, 72, 75, 82, 91,
    92, 93, 99, 104, 121, 123, 213,
    215, 237, 380, 385, 415, 419,
    420, 442
  housing, 70, 87, 90, 91, 431
  planned, 9, 75, 225
  referendum, in Droitwich, 92, 93
  regional, 61, 95, 96, 97
  towns, 225, 226, 227, 232, 238,
    239, 321
  see also Birmingham

Parish, 453, 470
  Councils, 15, 85
  successor, 87, 456, 459, 471, 483,
    484, 486, 487
perceptions, 30-1, 35, 45, 149, 277,
    357
  of problem structure, 41, 42, 51,
    349, 365, 367, 376, 495
Peterborough, 427-9, 443
planning
  connective, 39, 56, 408-9, 471, 472,
    473, 475, 507
  corporate, xxi, 374, 419, 465, 466,
    472, 503, 512
  enrichment of, 471, 473, 511, 512
  innovation in, 82, 347, 374, 444,
    475, 505, 510
  inter-agency, 55, 56, 82, 188, 222,
    388
  inter-organization, xxiii, xxiv, 3, 20
  multi-organization, xii, xviii, xxiv

outwardly connective style, 471,
    472, 473, 475, 507
  public, xii, 47, 56-7, 345, 347, 349,
    350, 372-4, 376, 409, 445, 470,
    512
  transport, 163, 388
  see also economic planning;
    regional planning
policy guidelines, 24, 25, 30, 37, 39,
    40, 41, 42, 56, 65, 67, 118, 124,
    233, 244, 247, 259, 269, 351,
    479
policy system(s), xxiv, 23-41, 43, 46,
    49, 53, 54, 55, 56, 81, 118, 351,
    352, 364, 371, 449
  actors in, 27, 29, 30, 33, 35, 40,
    41, 42, 351, 364
  boundaries, 30, 37, 39, 43
  contiguous, 30, 31, 34, 35, 37, 39,
    40, 43, 44, 51, 53, 119, 294,
    357, 430, 449
  at Droitwich, 124-9, 186-7, 219-20,
    239, 244-7, 275-8
  multi-organizational, 42, 82, 127,
    372, 430
political
  authority, 43, 368, 369, 372, 403
  science, xv, xvi, 23, 491, 511
political parties
  Conservative, 11, 15, 63, 87, 190,
    211, 320, 423, 455, 463, 499
  Labour, 11, 15, 63, 86, 87, 125,
    189, 191, 320, 334, 381, 423,
    454, 455, 463, 499
  Liberal, 15, 423, 499
politicians, 30, 42, 45, 355
politics, 34, 40, 46, 53, 57, 189, 280,
    315, 349, 365, 376, 395, 405,
    435, 457, 480, 481, 484, 489,
    493, 495, 510, 512
population, 3, 4, 5, 7, 9, 64, 65, 80,
    410
  of Droitwich, 97, 107, 217, 247,
    255, 398
Post Office Corporation, 241, 279,
    311
pressure(s), 37, 41, 63, 70, 72, 80, 86,
    87, 89, 92-5, 125, 126, 155, 186,
    237, 241, 245, 257, 267, 268,
    274, 286, 318, 338, 350, 351,
    369, 374, 379, 392, 393, 461,
    471, 472, 473, 494, 500

constituency, 64, 353, 357, 372,
375, 480
groups, 71, 223, 232, 256, 371,
439
political, 22, 186, 226, 249, 355,
383, 447
private developers/development, 65,
97, 118, 135, 147, 215, 253,
255, 263, 427, 480
problem(s)
area(s), 49, 54, 55
decision, 22, 23, 24, 25, 27, 30, 35,
55, 73, 177, 233-7, 309
structure of, 51, 53-4, 365, 367,
376, 495, 496, 511
propositions, xiv, xxvi, 345, 347-8,
349-50, 352, 354, 356, 360,
364, 367, 372, 373, 374, 375,
376, 408, 410, 411, 444, 470,
505, 509
public
planning, xii, 47, 56-7, 345, 347,
349, 350, 372-4, 376, 409, 445,
470, 512
services, 310-41, 361, 382
transport, xii, 169, 313, 326-8, 389,
445, 458
public inquiry, 280, 422, 423
at Droitwich, 263, 265, 268-74,
277, 368
see also Wythall

railway (at Droitwich), 151, 165, 171,
174, 184, 203, 255, 285, 301
recreaction, xiii, 235, 313, 478, 480
facilities, 133, 303, 328-30
playing fields, 71, 75, 147, 148, 150,
329
Redditch, 68, 69, 70, 79, 91, 103, 125,
227, 317, 325, 380, 397, 423-5
reed warblers, 305, 306-7
regional
overspill, 61, 95, 96, 97
stocktaking, 384
Studies Association, 383, 391
see also management of local and
regional change
regional planning, xv, xxvii, 9, 77, 82,
187, 347, 373, 381, 397, 403
innovation in, 82, 374, 404-8
in the West Midlands, 383-93

relationships, 9, 44, 46, 55, 115, 366
between agencies, 87-90, 311, 351,
359, 367, 373
between decision problems, 47, 55,
80, 367
(inter-)organizational, xii, xxvii,
19-21, 23, 81, 181, 340, 425,
501
re-location
of industry, 70, 93, 173, 184, 226,
229, 231, 233, 236, 239, 244,
356
of trading interests, 257, 270, 277,
279, 337, 352
rents, 189, 190, 191, 192, 193, 197,
199, 203, 205, 220, 267, 270,
295, 421
resources, 64-6, 104, 106, 157, 175,
252, 273, 356, 366, 373, 382,
393, 435, 441, 443, 461, 471,
473, 480, 484, 497, 509
organizational, xxvii, 349, 367, 369,
371, 376
responsibility(s), 49, 77, 167, 311
see also roads
reticulist(s), 181, 365, 367-72, 485,
487, 500, 501, 510, 511
activity, 239, 372-4, 376, 434
community, xxviii, 483, 484, 486,
487, 490, 491, 495, 499, 500
judgement(s), xxiv, xxvii, 44, 45,
56, 360, 362, 363, 364, 365,
371, 399, 401, 425
opportunities, 360-4, 420, 481, 482,
502
skills, xxvii, 335, 338, 340, 349,
364-9, 376, 405, 408, 439, 442,
481-2, 485, 502
reticulation of knowledge, 356
risks, 40, 120, 267, 275
road(s), xxv, 133, 140, 150, 154, 157,
158, 159-87, 219, 235, 251, 281,
292, 310, 430
A38, 135, 137, 151, 163, 165, 166,
195
construction, 127, 179-81
distributor system, 148, 149, 165,
167, 169, 170, 171, 181, 184,
257, 361
inner ring road, 165, 166, 258, 262,
264, 265, 269, 270, 271, 273,
286, 325